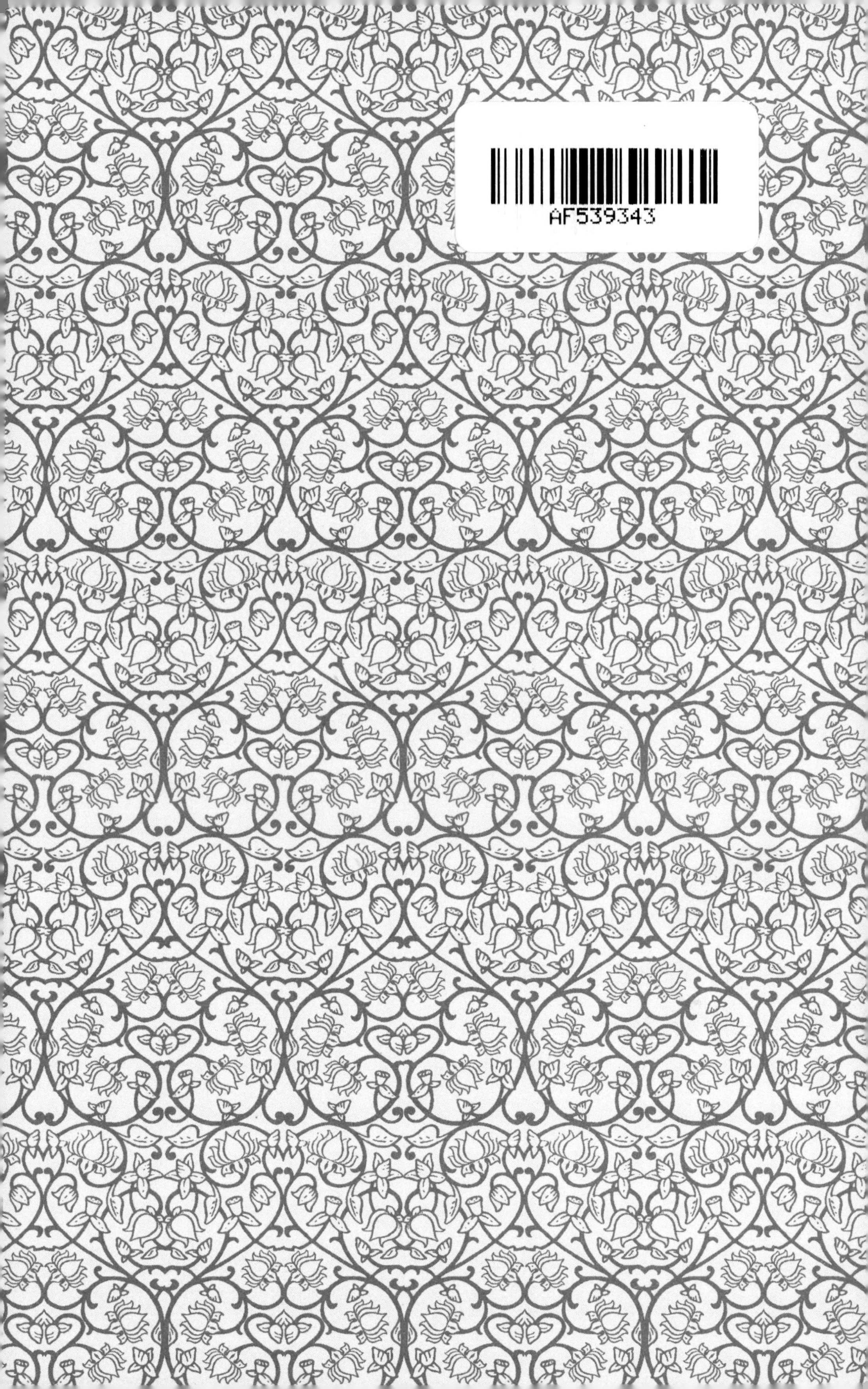

SRI SRI PARAMAHANSA YOGANANDA
(January 5, 1893 – March 7, 1952)

God Talks With Arjuna

THE BHAGAVAD GITA

Royal Science of God-Realization

The immortal dialogue between soul and Spirit
A new translation and commentary

Sri Sri Paramahansa Yogananda

Chapters 1-5

First Indian Hardcover Edition, 2002
Tenth Impression, 2023

An authorized publication of Yogoda Satsanga Society of India/Self-Realization Fellowship

The Yogoda Satsanga Society of India name and emblem shown above appear on all YSS books, recordings, and other publications, assuring the reader that a work originates with the society established by Sri Sri Paramahansa Yogananda and faithfully conveys his teachings.

Published in India by
YOGODA SATSANGA SOCIETY OF INDIA
Yogoda Satsanga Math
21, U. N. Mukherjee Road
Dakshineswar, Kolkata 700076

Printed in India by
Nutech Print Services
New Delhi 110020

ISBN 978-81-89535-00-1

Distributed by:

Manjul Publishing House

Also available from Yogoda Satsanga Society of India, Paramahansa Yogananda Path, Ranchi 834001, Jharkhand and at Yogoda Satsanga Ashrams and Dhyana Kendras throughout India.

Dedication

To the Arjuna-devotee
within every true seeker

THE SPIRITUAL LEGACY OF SRI SRI PARAMAHANSA YOGANANDA

His Complete Writings, Lectures, and Informal Talks

Paramahansa Yogananda founded Yogoda Satsanga Society of India (YSS) in 1917 and Self-Realization Fellowship (SRF) in 1920 to disseminate his teachings worldwide and to preserve their purity and integrity for generations to come. A prolific writer and lecturer from his earliest years in America, he created a renowned and voluminous body of works on the yoga science of meditation, the art of balanced living, and the underlying unity of all great religions. Today this unique and far-reaching spiritual legacy lives on, inspiring millions of truth seekers all over the world.

In accord with the express wishes of the great Guru, Yogoda Satsanga Society of India/Self-Realization Fellowship has continued the ongoing task of publishing and keeping permanently in print *The Complete Works of Paramahansa Yogananda*. These include not only the final editions of all the books he published during his lifetime, but also many new titles—works that had remained unpublished at the time of his passing in 1952, or which had been serialized over the years in incomplete form in Yogoda Satsanga Society of India/Self-Realization Fellowship's magazine, as well as hundreds of profoundly inspiring lectures and informal talks recorded but not printed before his passing.

Paramahansa Yogananda personally chose and trained those close disciples who formed the Yogoda Satsanga Society of India/Self-Realization Fellowship Publications Council, giving them specific guidelines for the preparation and publishing of his teachings. The members of the YSS/SRF Publications Council (monks and nuns who have taken lifelong vows of renunciation and selfless service) honour these guidelines as a sacred trust, in order that the universal message of this beloved world teacher will live on in its original power and authenticity.

The Yogoda Satsanga Society of India/Self-Realization Fellowship emblem (shown above) was designated by Paramahansa Yogananda to identify the nonprofit society he founded as the authorized source of his teachings. The YSS/SRF name and emblem appear on all YSS/SRF publications and recordings, assuring the reader that a work originates with the organization founded by Paramahansa Yogananda and conveys his teachings as he himself intended they be given.

—YOGODA SATSANGA SOCIETY OF INDIA/
SELF-REALIZATION FELLOWSHIP

CONTENTS

Volume I

Volume II

ILLUSTRATIONS

Volume I

Volume II

PUBLISHER'S NOTE

God Talks With Arjuna: The Bhagavad Gita was first published by Self-Realization Fellowship in 1995. Though only a few years have passed since the book's publication in the West, it is already being recognized as one of the twentieth century's most significant spiritual works. Reviewers and scholars as well as countless letters from individual readers around the world, have greeted the book with unqualified acclaim.

A review in *India Post called it* "a monumental work of translation and commentary .... a masterpiece of spiritual, literary, and philosophical work." *Publisher's Weekly* declared, "Yogananda's commentary penetrates to the heart of the Bhagavad Gita to reveal [its] deep spiritual and psychological truths."

One of the many scholars who praised the book, Quincy Howe, Ph.D., former professor of Comparative Religion and Sanskrit at the Claremont Colleges, stated: "Paramahansa Yogananda brings to his translation and commentary on the Bhagavad Gita a staggering sweep of psychology, spiritual instruction, linguistic discernment, esoteric physiology, cosmology, and yoga doctrine....The sheer breadth of the work makes it unique among Gita commentaries."

Another expert in the field, Dr. David Frawley, Director of the American Institute of Vedic Studies and author of many books on India's history and spiritual heritage, wrote: "Yogananda can be said to be the father of yoga in the West—not the mere physical yoga that has become popular, but the spiritual yoga, the science of Self-realization that is the real meaning of yoga....*God Talks With Arjuna* serves as a beacon to all who sincerely wish to approach the yogic path, regardless of their background....There is no important aspect of life and human existence that this book does not touch....This is a book that one can study and cherish for a lifetime. It will be remembered as one of the great commentaries on the Gita, along with those of Shankaracharya, Ramanuja, and Sri Aurobindo.... Yogananda appears as a sage of the highest order and a spiritual scientist, an avatar of yoga for the coming world civilization. The mark of his work will no doubt endure through the ages."

This Indian edition of the book has the Devanagari script of the slokas preceding Paramahansa Yoganandaji's English translation. The transliterated Sanskrit text appears in an Appendix at the back of each volume for readers who wish to refer to it.

Preface

By Sri Sri Daya Mata

Spiritual successor to Paramahansa Yogananda and president of Yogoda Satsanga Society of India/Self-Realization Fellowship from 1955 until her passing in 2010

"No *siddha* leaves this world without having given some truth to mankind. Every free soul has to shed on others his light of God-realization." How generously Paramahansa Yogananda fulfilled this obligation!—scriptural words voiced by him early in his world mission. Even if he had left to posterity nothing more than his lectures and writings, he would rightly be ranked as a munificent giver of divine light. And of the literary works that flowed so prolifically from his communion with God, the Bhagavad Gita translation and commentary may well be considered the Guru's most comprehensive offering—not merely in sheer volume but in its all-embracing thoughts.

My own first introduction to India's renowned scripture was as a youth of fifteen, when a copy of Sir Edwin Arnold's translation of the Gita was given to me. Its beautifully poetic lines filled my heart with a deep longing to know God. But where was someone who could show me the way to Him?

It was two years later, in 1931, that I met Paramahansa Yogananda. That he knew God was immediately, overwhelmingly apparent, in his countenance and in the joy and divine love that literally radiated from him. I soon entered his monastic ashram; and throughout the more than twenty years that followed I was blessed to live and seek God in his presence, with his guidance—as a disciple, and as his secretary in both ashram and organizational matters. The passing years only deepened my first awed recognition of his spiritual stature. I saw that in him the world had been given a true exemplar of the essence of the Gita—in his active life of service for the upliftment of humankind, and in his constant intimacy with God, a beloved God of unconditional love.

Paramahansaji manifested utter mastery of the yoga science of meditation cited by Lord Krishna in the Gita. I often observed how effortlessly he would enter the transcendent state of *samadhi;* each of us present would be bathed in the ineffable peace and bliss that emanated from his God-communion. By a touch, a word, or even a glance, he could awaken others to a greater awareness of God's presence, or bestow the experience of superconscious ecstasy on disciples who were in tune.

A passage in the *Upanishads* tells us: "That sage who has solely engaged himself in drinking the nectar which is no other than Brahman, the nectar which is the outcome of incessant meditation, that sage becomes the greatest of ascetics, *paramahansa,* and a philosopher free of worldly taint, *avadhuta.* By the sight of him the whole world becomes consecrated. Even an ignorant man who is devoted to his service becomes liberated."

Paramahansa Yogananda fit the description of a true guru, a God-realized master; he was a living scripture in wisdom, action, and love for God. As the Gita advocates, his spirit of renunciation and service was one of complete nonattachment to material things and to the acclaim heaped on him by thousands of followers. His indomitable inner strength and spiritual power resided in the sweetest natural humility, in which a self-centred ego found no place to dwell. Even when he made reference to himself and his work, it was without any sense of personal accomplishment. Having attained the ultimate realization of God as the true soul-essence of one's being, he knew no other identity apart from Him.

In the Gita, the zenith of Krishna's revelations to Arjuna comes in Chapter XI, the "vision of visions." The Lord reveals His cosmic form: universes upon universes, inconceivably vast, created and sustained by the infinite omnipotence of Spirit which is simultaneously aware of the tiniest particle of subatomic matter and the cosmic movement of the galactic immensities—of every thought, feeling, and action of every being on the material and heavenly planes of existence.

We witnessed the omnipresence of a guru's consciousness, and therefore his sphere of spiritual influence, when Paramahansa Yogananda was blessed with a similar universal vision. In June 1948, from late evening throughout the night until about ten o'clock the next morning, a few of us disciples were privileged to glimpse something of this unique experience through his ecstatic description of the cosmic revelation as it unfolded.

That awe-inspiring event foretold that his time on earth was drawing to a close. Soon after this, Paramahansaji began to remain more and more in seclusion in a small ashram in the Mojave Desert, devoting as much as possible of the time that was left to him to completing his writings. Those periods of concentration on the literary message he wished to leave to the world were a privileged time for those of us who could be in his presence. He was completely absorbed, completely at one with the truths he was perceiving within and expressing outwardly. "He came into the yard for a few minutes," recalled one of the monks working on the grounds around Paramahansaji's retreat. "There was a look of incalculable remoteness in his eyes, and he said to me: 'The three worlds are floating in me like bubbles.' The sheer power radiating from him actually moved me back several steps away from him."

Another monk, entering the room where Guruji was working, remembers: "The vibration in that room was unbelievable; it was like walking into God."

"I dictate scriptural interpretations and letters all day," Paramahansaji wrote to a student during this period, "with eyes closed to the world, but open always in heaven."

Paramahansaji's work on his Gita commentary had begun years earlier (a preliminary serialization had started in Self-Realization Fellowship's magazine in 1932) and was completed during this period in the desert, which included a review of the material that had been written over a period of so many years, clarification and amplification of many points, abbreviation of passages that contained duplication that had been necessary only in serialization for new readers, addition of new inspirations—including many details of yoga's deeper philosophical concepts that he had not attempted to convey in earlier years to a general audience not yet introduced to the unfolding discoveries in science that have since made the Gita's cosmology and view of man's physical, mental, and spiritual makeup much more understandable to the Western mind—all to be literarily prepared for publication in book form.

To help him with the editorial work, Gurudeva relied on Tara Mata (Laurie V. Pratt), a highly advanced disciple who had met him in 1924 and worked with him on his books and other writings at various times for a period of more than twenty-five years. I know without doubt that Paramahansaji would not have allowed this book to be published without due acknowledgement and commendation of the role played by this faithful disciple. "She was a great yogi," he told me, "who lived many lives hidden away from the world in India. She has come in this life to serve this work." On many public occasions he expressed his considered evaluation of her literary acumen and philosophical wisdom: "She is the best editor in the country; maybe anywhere. Excepting my great guru, Swami Sri Yukteswarji, there is no one with whom I have more enjoyed talking of Indian philosophy than Laurie."

In the latter years of his life, Paramahansaji also began to train another monastic disciple whom he had chosen to edit his writings: Mrinalini Mata. Gurudeva made clear to all of us the role for which he was preparing her, giving her personal instruction in every aspect of his teachings and in his wishes for the preparation and presentation of his writings and talks.

One day toward the end of his life on earth, he confided: "I am very worried about Laurie. Her health will not permit her to finish the work on my writings."

Knowing the Guru's great reliance on Tara Mata, Mrinalini Mata expressed concern: "But Master, who then can do that work?"

Gurudeva replied with quiet finality: "You will do it."

In the years after Paramahansaji's *mahasamadhi* in 1952, Tara Mata was able to continue uninterruptedly the serialization in the magazine of his commentaries on each Bhagavad Gita verse (despite her many time-consuming duties as a member and officer of the Board of Directors and editor-in-chief of all Yogoda Satsanga Society of India/Self-Realization Fellowship publications). However, as Paramahansaji had predicted, she passed away before she could complete the preparation of the Gita manuscript as he had intended. This task then fell on the shoulders of Mrinalini Mata. She is, as Guruji foresaw, the only person after Tara Mata's passing who could have accomplished it properly, because of her years of training from the Guru and her attunement with the Guru's thoughts.

The publication of Paramahansa Yogananda's Bhagavad Gita translation and commentary is the joyous fulfilment of many years of anticipation. Indeed, it is a milestone in the history of Self-Realization Fellowship, which celebrates this year its seventy-fifth anniversary.*

Paramahansa Yogananda had a dual role on this earth. His name and activities are uniquely identified with the worldwide organization he founded: Yogoda Satsanga Society of India/Self-Realization Fellowship; and for those thousands who embrace his YSS/SRF *Kriya Yoga* teachings, he is their personal guru. But he is also a *jagadguru,* a world teacher, whose life and universal message are a source of inspiration and upliftment for many followers of different paths and religions—his spiritual legacy a blessing offered to the entire world.

I recall his last day on earth, March 7, 1952. Gurudeva was very

* It was on September 19, 1920, that Paramahansa Yogananda arrived in America to found Self-Realization Fellowship for the dissemination worldwide of India's ancient science of yoga. *(Publisher's Note)*

quiet, his consciousness inwardly withdrawn to an even greater extent than usual. Often that day we disciples observed that his eyes were not focused on this finite world, but rather were gazing into the transcendent realm of God's presence. When he spoke at all, it was in terms of great affection, appreciation, and kindness. But what stands out most vividly in my memory was the influence, noticed by everyone who entered his room, of the vibrations of profound peace and intense divine love that emanated from him. The Divine Mother Herself—that aspect of the Infinite Spirit personified as the tender caring and compassion, the unconditional love, that is the salvation of the world—had taken complete possession of him, it seemed, and through him was sending out waves of love to embrace all of Her creation.

That evening, during a large reception in honour of the Ambassador of India, at which Paramahansaji was the principal speaker, the great Guru left his body for Omnipresence.

As with all those rare souls who have come on earth as saviours of humankind, Paramahansaji's influence lives on after him. His followers regard him as a *Premavatar,* incarnation of God's divine love. He came with God's love to awaken hearts sleeping in forgetfulness of their Creator, and to offer a path of enlightenment to those already seeking. In reviewing the Gita manuscript, I felt anew in Paramahansaji's commentaries the magnetism of divine love that ever calls to us to seek God, the Supreme Goal of every human soul, and that promises its sheltering presence all along the way.

I hear again and again, echoing in my own soul, Paramahansa Yogananda's consummate Universal Prayer—the one that perhaps most characterizes the force behind his world mission and his inspiration in giving to us this enlightening revelation of the holy Bhagavad Gita:

> *Heavenly Father, Mother, Friend, Beloved God,*
> *May Thy love shine forever on the sanctuary of my devotion,*
> *and may I be able to awaken Thy love in all hearts.*

Los Angeles
September 19, 1995

Introduction

The Bhagavad Gita is the most beloved scripture of India, a scripture of scriptures. It is the Hindu's Holy Testament, or Bible, the one book that all masters depend upon as a supreme source of scriptural authority. *Bhagavad Gita* means "Song of the Spirit," the divine communion of truth-realization between man and his Creator, the teachings of Spirit through the soul, that should be sung unceasingly.

The pantheistic doctrine of the Gita is that God is everything. Its verses celebrate the discovery of the Absolute, Spirit beyond creation, as being also the hidden Essence of all manifestation. Nature, with her infinite variety and inexorable laws, is an evolute of the Singular Reality through a cosmic delusion: *maya,* the "Magical Measurer" that makes the One appear as many embracing their own individuality—forms and intelligences existing in apparent separation from their Creator. Just as a dreamer differentiates his one consciousness into many dream beings in a dream world, so God, the Cosmic Dreamer, has separated His consciousness into all the cosmic manifestations, with souls individualized from His own One Being endowed with the egoity to dream their personalized existences within the Nature-ordained drama of the Universal Dream.

The main theme of the Bhagavad Gita

The main theme throughout the Gita is that one should be an adherent of *sannyasa,* a renouncer of this egoity ingrained through *avidya,* ignorance, within the physical self of man. By renunciation of all desires springing from the ego and its environments, which cause separateness between ego and Spirit; and by reunion with the Cosmic Dreamer through ecstatic yoga meditation, *samadhi,* man detaches himself from and ultimately dissolves the compellent forces of Nature that perpetuate the delusive dichotomy of the Self and Spirit. In *samadhi,* the cosmic dream delusion terminates and the ecstatic dream being awakens in oneness with the pure cosmic consciousness of the Supreme Being—ever-existing, ever-conscious, ever-new Bliss.

This God-realization cannot be attained merely by reading a book, but only by dwelling every day on the above truth that life is a variety entertainment of dream movies full of the hazards of duality—villains of evil and heroic adventures with goodness; and by deep yoga meditation, uniting human consciousness with God's cosmic consciousness. Thus does the Gita exhort the seeker to right action—physical, mental, and spiritual—toward this goal. We came from God and our ultimate destiny is to return to Him. The end and the means to the end is yoga, the timeless science of God-union.

So comprehensive as a spiritual guide is the Gita that it is declared to be the essence of the ponderous four Vedas, 108 Upanishads, and the six systems of Hindu philosophy. Only by intuitive study and understanding of these tomes, or else by contacting Cosmic Consciousness, can one fully comprehend the Bhagavad Gita. Indeed, the underlying essential truths of all great world scriptures can find common amity in the infinite wisdom of the Gita's mere 700 concise verses.

The entire knowledge of the cosmos is packed into the Gita. Supremely profound, yet couched in revelatory language of solacing beauty and simplicity, the Gita has been understood and applied on all levels of human endeavour and spiritual striving—sheltering a vast spectrum of human beings with their disparate natures and needs. Wherever one is on the way back to God, the Gita will shed its light on that segment of the journey.

HISTORICAL ORIGIN OF THE GITA

ART REVEALS THE MIND of a people—a crude arrow drawing suggests a crude mind—but the literature of a civilization is a much finer indication of a culture. Literature is the index of the mind of a nation. India has preserved in her literature her highly evolved civilization dating back to a glorious golden age. From the undated antiquity in which the Vedas first emerged, through a grand unfoldment of subsequent exalted verse and prose, the Hindus have left their civilization not in stone monoliths or crumbling edifices, but in architecture of ornamental writing sculpted in the euphonious language of Sanskrit. The very composition of the Bhagavad Gita—its rhetoric, alliteration, diction, style, and harmony—shows that India had long since passed through states of material and intellectual growth and had arrived at a lofty peak of spirituality.*

* The testament of the Hindu scriptures is that India's civilization goes back far earlier than contemporary Western historians acknowledge. Swami Sri Yukteswar, in *The Holy Science* (published by Yogoda Satsanga Society of India), calculates that the Golden Age, in which India's spiritual and material civilization reached its pinnacle, ended about 6700 B.C.—having flowered for many thousands of years before that. India's scriptural literature lists many generations of kings and sages who lived prior to the events that

The age and authorship of the Gita, as with so many of India's ancient writings and scriptures, remains an engaging subject of intellectual and scholarly research and dispute. Its verses are found in the sixth of eighteen books that constitute India's great epic poem, the *Mahabharata,* in the Bhishma Parva, sections 23–40. In 100,000 couplets this hoary epic—perhaps the longest poem in world literature—recounts the history of the descendants of King Bharata, the Pandavas and Kauravas, cousins whose dispute over a kingdom was the cause of the cataclysmic war of Kurukshetra. The Bhagavad Gita, a sacred dialogue on yoga between Bhagavan Krishna—who was at once an earthly king and a divine incarnation—and his chief disciple, the Pandava prince Arjuna, purportedly takes place on the eve of this fearsome war.

The authorship of the *Mahabharata,* including the Gita portion, is traditionally assigned to the illumined sage Vyasa, whose date is not definitely known.* It is said that the Vedic *rishis* manifested their immortality by appearing before mankind in different ages to play some role for man's spiritual upliftment. Thus they appeared and reappeared at various times throughout the extensive period of time encompassed by the revelation of the scriptures of India, a phenomenon confounding to any scholar who relies on facts rather than faith in an unenlightened age in which man has learned to use hardly ten percent of his brain capacity, and that quite awkwardly for the most part. Whether these immortals retain their physical forms like Mahavatar Babaji (as recounted in *Autobiography of a Yogi*), or remain immersed in Spirit, they emerge from time to time in some tangible expression to man.

So long as divine beings are in a state of absolute oneness with Spirit, as was Sage Vyasa, they cannot record in writing their inde-

---

are the main subject of the *Mahabharata*. In the Gita itself, Krishna describes the long descent of India's spiritual culture from a Golden Age to his own era, as the knowledge of yoga gradually was lost. "Most anthropologists, believing that 10,000 years ago humanity was living in a barbarous Stone Age, summarily dismiss as 'myths' the widespread traditions of very ancient civilizations in Lemuria, Atlantis, India, China, Japan, Egypt, Mexico, and many other lands," a passage in *Autobiography of a Yogi* reads. Recent scientific research, however, is beginning to suggest that the truth of ancient chronologies be reevaluated. *(Publisher's Note)*

* Of the Gita's author, the celebrated German philosopher A. W. Schlegel wrote in the foreword to his Latin translation of the Gita: "O thou sacred singer, thou inspired interpreter of divinity! Whatever may have been thy name among mortals, I bow before thee! Hail to thee, author of that mighty poem, whose oracles lift up the soul in joy ineffable, toward all that is sublime, eternal, and divine! Full of veneration, I salute thee above all singers, and I worship unceasingly by the trace of thy footsteps."

scribable spiritual perceptions. Such Self-realized souls have to come down from the state of Spirit-oneness, which is unalloyed by duality, to the state of human consciousness, which is governed by the law of relativity, in order to bring truth to mankind. When the little soul is blessed to merge with the vast ocean of blissful Spirit, it takes care not to lose its identity if it wants to come back and chronicle its experiences of the Infinite for the enlightenment of the world.

Tradition involves Vyasa in many literary works, primarily as an arranger of the four Vedas, for which he is referred to as Vedavyasa; compiler of *Puranas,* sacred books illustrating Vedic knowledge through historical and legendary tales of ancient India's avatars, saints and sages, kings and heroes; and author of the epic *Mahabharata,* which purportedly was accomplished nonstop in two and a half of his latter years spent in secluded retirement in the Himalayas. He not only authored the *Mahabharata* and its sacred Gita discourse, but showed himself throughout playing a significant role of involvement in the events and affairs of the Pandavas and Kauravas. Indeed, he is the paternal origin of these chief characters through the two sons he sired, Pandu and Dhritarashtra.

The Gita is generally conceded to predate the Christian era. The testimony of the *Mahabharata* itself is that the Kurukshetra war took place toward the end of Dwapara Yuga, when the world was on the verge of descending into the Dark Age or Kali Yuga. (The *yugas,* or world cycles, are explained in the commentary on IV:1.) Traditionally, many Hindus have fixed the beginning of the last descending Kali Yuga at 3102 B.C., thus placing the Kurukshetra war described in the *Mahabharata* a few decades prior to this.* Scholars of East and West have advanced various dates for the *Mahabharata* events—some basing

---

* Paramahansa Yogananda's guru, Swami Sri Yukteswar, who was a great authority on Vedic astrology as well as being a God-realized master, pointed out an error in the commonly accepted calculation of the *yugas'* dates: "The mistake crept into almanacs for the first time during the reign of Raja Parikshit, just after the completion of the last descending Dwapara Yuga. At that time Maharaja Yudhisthira, noticing the appearance of the dark Kali Yuga, made over his throne to his grandson, the said Raja Parikshit. Maharaja Yudhisthira, together with all the wise men of his court, retired to the Himalaya Mountains, the paradise of the world. Thus there was none in the court of Raja Parikshit who could understand the principle of correctly calculating the ages of the several *yugas.* Hence, after the completion of the 2,400 years of the then-current Dwapara Yuga, no one dared to make the introduction of the dark Kali Yuga more manifest by beginning to calculate from its first year and to put an end to the number of Dwapara years. According to this wrong method of calculation, therefore, the first year of Kali

their estimates on archaeological evidence and others on references in the poem to specific astronomical phenomena such as eclipses, solstices, positions of stars, and planetary conjunctions. By these means, the dates proposed for the Kurukshetra war range from as early as 6000 B.C. to as recently as 500 B.C.—hardly a definite consensus!*

There is no effort or presumption in this publication to add to the work of scholarly researchers and commentators who have laboured long and studiously to label and categorize such data dear to histori-

---

Yuga was numbered 2401 along with the age of Dwapara Yuga."

Thus, though it was known that the world was in Kali Yuga, year 1 of that *yuga* came to be figured as 2,400 years earlier than it actually was. (Even when it was pointed out, centuries later, that the scriptures specify the length of Kali Yuga as 1,200 years, the erroneous calculations persisted by scholars' assuming that these 1,200 years were "years of the gods," each lasting 360 ordinary years. Since that time, therefore, Kali Yuga has been held to endure for 432,000 years rather than 1,200. "A dark prospect!" Sri Yukteswarji wrote, "and fortunately one not true.")

Sri Yukteswar said that circa 3100 B.C. was actually the beginning of the descending Dwapara Yuga, not Kali; the latter, he stated, began in approximately 700 B.C. (3,100 minus 2,400). Since there is a 200-year transition period between the end of Dwapara proper and the beginning of Kali, the departure of Yudhisthira and the other Pandavas, described in the *Mahabharata* as occurring at the end of Dwapara Yuga and thirty-six years after the Kurukshetra war, may have been around 900 B.C. according to Sri Yukteswar's calculations—or earlier if one takes the *Mahabharata*'s account to mean merely that the Pandavas departed sometime near the end of Dwapara Yuga, not literally in the very last year of that age.

The end of the last descending Dwapara Yuga and the subsequent advent of the Dark Ages of spiritual ignorance also marked the beginning of the period when humanity at large lost sight of the true knowledge of the yoga science as taught by Bhagavan Krishna and mentioned in the Gita. Its reintroduction (as *Kriya Yoga*) by Mahavatar Babaji in modern times was only possible when the world had passed beyond the Dark Ages and had once more emerged into the gradual awakening of the present-day ascending Dwapara Yuga level of comprehension. (See commentary on IV:1, pages 424 ff.) *(Publisher's Note)*

* In *Astronomical Dating of the Mahabharata War* (Delhi: Agam Kala Prakashan, 1986) Dr. E. Vedavyas surveyed the researches done by 120 scholars over the past hundred years. Sixty-one of the scholars fixed the Kurukshetra war as having occurred between 3000 and 3200 B.C. The next favoured time period—subscribed to by forty of the scholars—was between 1000 and 1500 B.C.

In 1987 archaeologists discovered the ruins of a prosperous ancient city just off the west coast of India underwater in the Gulf of Kutch—the precise location where tradition places Dwarka, the city founded by Sri Krishna. The *Mahabharata* describes how at the end of Krishna's life the sea rose and engulfed Dwarka. According to the *MLBD Newsletter of Indological Bibliography* (September 1987 and January 1988), archaeologists believe that the newly discovered ruins may have been the site of Krishna's capital, and estimate that the ruins are approximately 3,500 years old. Whether or not this yields an accurate date for Krishna's lifetime is open to speculation, since it is known that Dwarka was built on the ruins of another, older city, according to Dr. S. R. Rao, leader of the undersea excavation. *(Publisher's Note)*

ans as authorship, time frames, and factuality of names, places, and events. These have their necessary place in the world library of knowledge, whether speculative or proven. My only purpose is to speak of the exoteric and esoteric—material and spiritual—message of the Bhagavad Gita based on the form and tradition in which it has been handed down to us from the archives of timeless truth by God-knowing sages. What may defy definitive scrutiny in one generation may prove to be quite commonplace in higher ages that mirror those more enlightened times in which such scriptures originated.

The ancient sacred writings do not clearly distinguish history from symbology; rather, they often intermix the two in the tradition of scriptural revelation. Prophets would pick up instances of the everyday life and events of their times and from them draw similes to express subtle spiritual truths. Divine profundities would not otherwise be conceivable by the ordinary man unless defined in common terms. When, as they often did, scriptural prophets wrote in more recondite metaphors and allegories, it was to conceal from ignorant, spiritually unprepared minds the deepest revelations of Spirit. Thus, in a language of simile, metaphor, and allegory, the Bhagavad Gita was very cleverly written by Sage Vyasa by interweaving historical facts with psychological and spiritual truths, presenting a word-painting of the tumultuous inner battles that must be waged by both the material and the spiritual man. In the hard shell of symbology, he hid the deepest spiritual meanings to protect them from the devastation of the ignorance of the Dark Ages toward which civilization was descending concurrent with the end of Sri Krishna's incarnation on earth.

Gita as history and as spiritual allegory

Historically, on the brink of such a horrendous war as that related in the *Mahabharata,* it is most unlikely that, as the Gita depicts, Krishna and Arjuna would draw their chariot into the open field between the two opposing armies at Kurukshetra and there engage in an extensive discourse on yoga. While many of the chief events and persons in the compendious *Mahabharata* indeed have their basis in historical fact, their poetic presentation in the epic has been arranged conveniently and meaningfully (and wonderfully condensed in the Bhagavad Gita portion) for the primary purpose of setting forth the essence of India's *Sanatana Dharma,* Eternal Religion.

In interpreting scripture, one must not, therefore, ignore the factual and historical elements in which the truth was couched. One must distinguish between an ordinary illustration of a moral doctrine or recounting of a spiritual phenomenon and that of a deeper esoteric intent. One has to know how to recognize the signs of the convergence of material illustrations with spiritual doctrines without trying to drag a hidden meaning out of everything. One must know how to intuit the cues and express declarations of the author and never fetch out meanings not intended, misled by enthusiasm and the imaginative habit of trying to squeeze spiritual significance from every word or statement.

The true way to understand scripture is through intuition, attuning oneself to the inner realization of truth.

A NEW REVELATION OF THE BHAGAVAD GITA FOR THE MODERN WORLD

MY GURU AND *PARAMGURUS*—Swami Sri Yukteswar, Lahiri Mahasaya, and Mahavatar Babaji—are *rishis* of this present age, masters who themselves are God-realized living scriptures. They have bequeathed to the world—along with the long-lost scientific technique of *Kriya Yoga*—a new revelation of the holy Bhagavad Gita, relevant primarily to the science of yoga and to *Kriya Yoga* in particular.*

Mahavatar Babaji, at one with Krishna in Spirit, through his grace intuitively transferred the true knowledge of the Bhagavad Gita to his disciple Lahiri Mahasaya—a *Yogavatar*, "Incarnation of Yoga"—through whom he revived for mankind the *Kriya Yoga* science as the technique of salvation for this age. Lahiri Mahasaya himself never wrote any books, but his divine expositions of the scriptures were expressed through the writings of various of his advanced disciples. Among his greatest disciples, Swami Sri Yukteswar, Swami Pranabananda, and Panchanon Bhattacharya recorded his Gita explanations. The earliest small edition of the Bhagavad Gita with Lahiri Mahasaya's interpretation was brought out by Panchanon Bhattacharya, founder of the Arya Mission Institution, Calcutta. Later, my guru Sri Yukteswarji—a *Jnanavatar*, "Incarnation of Wisdom"—in his elaborate unrivalled way, explained the most significant first nine chapters of the Gita according to Lahiri Mahasaya's interpretation.

After that, the great Swami Pranabananda, "the saint with two bodies" (about whom I have written in my *Autobiography of a Yogi*), brought forth an amazing interpretation of Lahiri Mahasaya's interpretation of the entire Gita. The eminent yogi, Bhupendra Nath

* The lives and missions of these illumined masters are recounted in *Autobiography of a Yogi* (available from Yogoda Satsanga Society of India; see page 1127).

Sanyal, whom I personally highly regard, also brought out a remarkable edition of Lahiri Mahasaya's interpretation of the Gita. I have had the blessing to be inspired in the greatest way about Lahiri Mahasaya's divine insight and perceptive method of explaining the Gita, which I learned first from my Master.

Through the help of a God-realized guru, one learns how to use the nutcracker of intuitive perception to crack open the hard shell of language and ambiguity to get at the kernels of truth in scriptural sayings. My guru, Swami Sri Yukteswar, never permitted me to read with mere theoretical interest any stanza of the Bhagavad Gita (or the aphorisms of Patanjali, India's greatest exponent of Yoga). Master made me meditate on the scriptural truths until I became one with them; then he would discuss them with me.* Once when in my enthusiasm I hurried Master to teach me faster, he sharply rebuked me: "Go and finish reading the Gita; why come to study it with me?" When I became calm, having stilled my intellectual eagerness, he told me to put myself in rapport with God as manifested in Krishna, Arjuna, and Vyasa when the message of the Gita was revealed through them.

In this way, during those precious years in the blessed company of Master, he gave to me the key to unlock the mystery of scripture. (It was from him I also learned how to put myself in tune with Christ to interpret his sayings as he wanted them to be understood.) Master's example was his guru, Lahiri Mahasaya. When disciples and students sought instruction from the *Yogavatar,* he used to close his eyes and read aloud from the book of his soul-realization. Sri Yukteswar did the same; and that method is what he taught to me. I am grateful to Master for this, for within the soul is a source of infinite realization, which I could not have gleaned in all my life from intellectual study. Now when I touch my pen, or look within and speak, it comes in boundless waves.

Master also taught me the specific symbology in just the first few verses of Chapter I of the Gita and a few related aphorisms of Patanjali. When he saw that I had mastered these through his instruction and my unfolding intuitive perception born of meditation, he declined to teach me further. Early on, he had foretold my work to interpret the Gita. Master said to me: "You don't want to understand and explain the Gita according to your own concepts or with the twistings of the

---

* "Wisdom is not assimilated with the eyes, but with the atoms," Sri Yukteswarji said. "When your conviction of a truth is not merely in your brain but in your being, you may diffidently vouch for its meaning."

intellect. You want to interpret to the world the actual dialogue between Krishna and Arjuna as perceived by Vyasa and revealed to you."

This Bhagavad Gita that I offer to the world, *God Talks With Arjuna,* is a spiritual commentary of the communion that takes place between the omnipresent Spirit (symbolized by Krishna) and the soul of the ideal devotee (represented by Arjuna). I arrived at the spiritual understanding expressed in these pages by attunement with Vyasa, and by perceiving the Spirit as God of creation relating wisdom to the awakened Arjuna within myself. I became Arjuna's soul and communed with Spirit; let the result speak for itself. I am not giving an interpretation, but am chronicling what I perceived as the Spirit pours Its wisdom into an attuned soul's devotional intuition in the various states of ecstasy.

Many truths buried in the Gita for generations are being expressed in English for the first time through me. And I again acknowledge that I owe much to my *paramgurus,* Mahavatar Babaji and Lahiri Mahasaya, and to my Gurudeva, for their revelations, which have inspired the birth of a new presentation of the Gita; and above all, to their grace in blessing my endeavour. This work is not mine; it belongs to them, and to God, Krishna, Arjuna, and Vyasa.

THE SPIRITUAL ALLEGORY HIDDEN IN THE GITA

ALL EVENTS AND ALL WISDOM are permanently recorded in the superether of omniscience, the akashic (etheric) record. They can be directly contacted by any advanced sage in any clime and age. Thus the whole span of history of the King Bharata dynasty could be perceived fully by Vyasa when later he conceived the *Mahabharata* and decided to write the epic as spiritual metaphor based on historical facts and persons.

That the instruction and revelations of the Bhagavad Gita are ascribed to Bhagavan Krishna, though probably not delivered by him as one discourse in the midst of a battlefield, is quite in keeping with the incarnate earth-mission of Krishna as Yogeshvara, "Lord of Yoga." In Chapter IV, Krishna proclaims his role in the dissemination of the eternal science of yoga. Vyasa's attunement with Krishna qualified him to compile from his own inner realization the holy revelations of Sri Krishna as a divine discourse, and to present it symbolically as a dialogue between God and an ideal devotee who enters the deep ecstatic state of inner communion.

Vyasa, being a liberated soul, knew how the consummate devotee,

Arjuna, found liberation through Krishna; how, by following the yoga science imparted to him by his sublime guru, Arjuna was liberated by God. As such, Vyasa could write this out as a dialogue between the soul and Spirit in the form of the Bhagavad Gita.

Thus, when we find in the Gita Bhagavan (God) speaking to Arjuna, we are to realize that God is revealing these truths through the intuition of the receptive devotee (Arjuna). Whenever Arjuna asks questions of God, it is to be understood that the meditating devotee by silent thoughts is communing with God. Any advanced devotee can translate into words of any language the silent intuitive communion between his soul and God; so Vyasa reproduced the inner experience between his soul and God as the Bhagavad Gita dialogue between the awakened soul of Arjuna and his omnipresent preceptor, the God-incarnate Krishna.

It will become evident to the reader after thoughtful perusal of the key to a few stanzas in the first chapter that the historical background of a battle and the contestants therein have been used for the purpose of illustrating the spiritual and psychological battle going on between the attributes of the pure discriminative intellect in attunement with the soul and the blind sense-infatuated mind under the delusive influence of the ego. In support of this analogy, there is shown an exact correspondence between the material and spiritual attributes of man as described by Patanjali in his *Yoga Sutras* and the warring contestants cited in the Gita: the clan of Pandu, representing Pure Intelligence; and that of the blind King Dhritarashtra, representing the Blind Mind with its offspring of wicked sense-tendencies.

Threefold meaning of the Gita: material, astral, spiritual

As with most scriptures—which are meant to be a source of inspiration to society, to materialists and moralists, and to people seeking God and spiritual enlightenment—the Bhagavad Gita has a threefold reading: material, astral, and spiritual, applicable to man on all levels of his being, his body, mind, and soul. Incarnate man is encased in a physical body of inert matter, which is animated by a subtle inner astral body of life energy and sensory powers; and both his astral and his physical body have evolved from a causal body of consciousness, which is the fine covering that gives individual existence and form to the soul. In this overview, the material interpretation of the Gita pertains to the physical and social duties and well-being of man. The astral is from the moral and psychological standpoint—man's character resulting from the astral Nature-born sensory and life-energy principles that influence the formation of habits, inclinations, and desires. And the spiritual interpretation is from the perspective of the divine nature and realization of the soul.

Hence, while I have emphasized the spiritual aspects of the Bhagavad Gita, the material and psychological import has also been interwoven to stress the need for practical application of the Gita wisdom in all phases of life. Truth is of all-round benefit to man; it is not for binding in an attractive cover to be reverently enshrined in a bookcase!

BHAGAVAN KRISHNA: THE CHRIST OF INDIA

THE KEY FIGURE OF the Bhagavad Gita is, of course, Bhagavan Krishna. The historical Krishna is enshrouded in the mystery of scriptural metaphor and mythology. Similarities in the titles "Krishna" and "Christ" and in the tales of the miraculous birth and early life of Krishna and Jesus led some analyzing minds to propose that they were indeed one and the same person. This idea can be wholly rejected, based on even scanty historical evidence in the countries of their origin.

Nevertheless, some similarities are there. Both were divinely conceived, and their births and God-ordained missions foretold. Jesus was born in a lowly manger; Krishna, in a prison (where his parents, Vasudeva and Devaki, were held captive by Devaki's wicked brother Kansa, who had usurped the throne of his father). Both Jesus and Krishna were successfully spirited away to safety from a death decree to all male infants meant to seek out and destroy them at birth. Jesus was referred to as the good shepherd; Krishna in his early years was a cowherd. Jesus was tempted and threatened by Satan; the evil force pursued Krishna in demonic forms seeking unsuccessfully to slay him.

"Christ" and "Krishna" are titles having the same spiritual connotation: Jesus the Christ and Yadava the Krishna (Yadava, a family name for Krishna, signifies his descent from Yadu, forerunner of the Vrishni dynasty). These titles identify the state of consciousness manifested by these two illumined beings, their incarnate oneness with the consciousness of God omnipresent in creation. The Universal Christ Consciousness or *Kutastha Chaitanya,* Universal Krishna Consciousness, is "the only begotten son" or sole undistorted reflection of God permeating every atom and point of space in the manifested cosmos. The full measure of God's consciousness is manifested in those who have full realization of the Christ or Krishna Consciousness. As their consciousness is universal, their light is shed on all the world.*

A *siddha* is a perfected being who has attained complete liberation in Spirit; he becomes a *paramukta,* "supremely free," and can then return to earth as an *avatara*—as did Krishna, Jesus, and many other saviours of mankind through the ages.† As often as virtue declines, a God-illumined soul comes on earth to draw virtue again to the fore (Gita IV:7–8). An avatar, or divine incarnation, has two purposes on earth: quantitative and qualitative. Quantitatively, he uplifts the general populace with his noble teachings of good against evil. But the main purpose of an avatar is qualitative—to create other God-realized souls, helping as many as possible to attain liberation. This latter is the very personal and private spiritual bond formed between guru and disciple, a union of loyal spiritual endeavour on the part of the disciple and divine blessings bestowed by the guru. Students are those who receive only a little light of truth. But disciples are those who follow completely and steadfastly, dedicated and devoted, until they have found their own freedom in God. In the Gita, Arjuna stands as the symbol of the ideal devotee, the perfect disciple.

When Sri Krishna incarnated on earth, Arjuna, a great sage in his previous life, took birth also to be his companion. Great ones always bring with them spiritual associates from past lives to assist them in their present mission. Krishna's father was the brother of Arjuna's mother; thus, Krishna and Arjuna were cousins—related by blood, but bound together in an even stronger spiritual unity.

SRI KRISHNA WAS RAISED IN A PASTORAL setting in Gokula and nearby Brindaban on the banks of the Yamuna River, having been secretly car-

---

* There are many derivations given to the word "Krishna," the most common of which is "dark," referring to the hue of Krishna's complexion. (He is often shown as dark blue to connote divinity. Blue is also the colour of the Christ Consciousness when epitomized in the spiritual eye as a circle of dark blue light surrounding the silvery white star of Cosmic Consciousness.) According to M. V. Sridatta Sarma ("On the Advent of Sri Krishna"), of the various other meanings given to the word "Krishna," several are found in the *Brahmavaivarta Purana.* He states that according to one of these derivations, "*Kṛṣṇa* means the Universal Spirit. *Kṛṣi* denotes a generic term, while *na* conveys the idea of the self, thus bringing forth the meaning 'Omniscient Spirit.'" In this we find a parallel to the Christ Consciousness as the Intelligence of God omnipresent in creation. It is of interest that a colloquial Bengali rendering of "Krishna" is *Krista* (cf. Greek *Christos* and Spanish *Cristo*). *(Publisher's Note)*

† The Sanskrit word *avatara* means "descent"; its roots are *ava,* "down," and *tri,* "to pass." In the Hindu scriptures, *avatara* signifies the descent of Divinity into flesh.

ried there by his father Vasudeva immediately after his birth to Devaki in the prison in Mathura. (Miraculously, the locked doors had opened and the guards had fallen into a deep stupor, allowing the infant to be carried safely to his foster home.) His foster parents were a kindly cowherd Nanda and his loving wife Yasoda. As a child in Brindaban, Krishna amazed all with his precocious wisdom and display of incredible powers. His inner joy frequently erupted in prankish outbursts—to the amusement and delight, and sometimes consternation, of those at whom his fun was directed.

❖ *The divine life of Lord Krishna* ❖

One such incident was the cause of revealing to Yasoda the divine nature of the child she was mothering. The infant Krishna loved to snatch away and consume the cheese made by the milkmaids. Once he had so stuffed his cheeks that Yasoda feared he would choke, so she rushed to pry open his gorged mouth. But instead of cheese (popular accounts say it was mud he had eaten), she beheld in his open mouth the whole universe—the infinite body (*vishvarupa*) of the Creator—including her own image. Awestricken, she turned away from the cosmic vision, happy to see and clasp to her bosom once again her beloved little boy.

Beautiful in form and feature, irresistible in charm and demeanour, an embodiment of divine love, giving joy to all, the young boy Krishna was beloved of everyone in the community, and an entrancing leader and friend to his childhood companions, the *gopas* and *gopis,* who with him tended the village herds of cows in the sylvan environs.

The world, addicted to the senses as the sole means of gratification, can little understand the purity of divine love and friendship that bears no taint of carnal expression or desire. It is absurd to take literally the supposed dalliances of Sri Krishna with the *gopis.* The symbolism is that of the unity of Spirit and Nature, which when dancing together in creation provides a divine *lila,* play, to entertain God's creatures. Sri Krishna, with the enchanting melodies of his heavenly flute, is calling all devotees to the bower of divine union in *samadhi* meditation, there to bask in the blissful love of God.

It would seem that Krishna was hardly more than a boy when it came time for him to leave Brindaban in fulfilment of the purpose of his incarnation: to assist the virtuous in restraining evil. His first feat—among many heroic and miraculous exploits—was the destruction of the wicked Kansa and the freeing of his parents Vasudeva and Devaki from prison. Thereafter, he and his brother Balarama were sent by

Vasudeva for their education to the ashram of the great sage Sandipani.

Of kingly birth, as an adult Sri Krishna fulfilled his kingly duties, engaging in many campaigns against the reigns of evil rulers. He established the capital of his own kingdom in Dwarka, on an offshore island in the western state of Gujarat. Much of his life is intertwined with that of the Pandavas and the Kauravas, whose capital was in north-central India near the present site of Delhi. He participated in many of their secular and spiritual affairs as ally and counsellor; and was particularly significant in the Kurukshetra war between the Pandus and Kurus.

When Sri Krishna had completed his divinely ordained mission on earth, he retired to the forest. There he relinquished his body as a result of an accidental wound inflicted by an arrow from the bow of a hunter who mistook him for a deer as he rested in a glade—an event that had been foretold as the cause of his earth exit.

Significance of Krishna's life for the modern world

IN THE BHAGAVAD GITA OUR ATTENTION is focused on the role of Sri Krishna as the guru and counsellor of Arjuna, and on the sublime yoga message he preached as preceptor to the world—the way of righteous activity and meditation for divine communion and salvation—the wisdom of which has enthroned him in the hearts and minds of devotees throughout the ages.

We hear of saintly ascetics, or prophets in the woods or secluded haunts, who were men of renunciation only; but Sri Krishna was one of the greatest exemplars of divinity, because he lived and manifested himself as a Christ and at the same time performed the duties of a noble king. His life demonstrates the ideal not of renunciation of action—which is a conflicting doctrine for man circumscribed by a world whose life breath is activity—but rather the renunciation of earth-binding desires for the fruits of action.

Without work human civilization would be a jungle of disease, famine, and confusion. If all the people in the world were to leave their material civilizations and live in the forests, the forests would then have to be transformed into cities, else the inhabitants would die because of lack of sanitation. On the other hand, material civilization is full of imperfections and misery. What possible remedy can be advocated?

Krishna's life demonstrates his philosophy that it is not necessary to flee the responsibilities of material life. The problem can be solved by bringing God here where He has placed us. No matter what our environment may be, into the mind where God-communion reigns, Heaven must come.

A grasping for ever more money, a plunging deeper into more prolonged work with attachment or blindness, will produce misery. Yet mere outward renunciation of material things, if one still harbours an inner attachment to them, leads only to hypocrisy and delusion. To avoid the pitfalls of the two extremes, renunciation of the world, or drowning in material life, man should so train his mind by constant meditation that he can perform the necessary dutiful actions of his daily life and still maintain the consciousness of God within. That is the example set by Krishna's life.

Sri Krishna's message in the Bhagavad Gita is the perfect answer for the modern age, and any age: Yoga of dutiful action, of nonattachment, and of meditation for God-realization. To work without the inner peace of God is Hades; and to work with His joy ever bubbling through the soul is to carry a portable paradise within, wherever one goes.

The path advocated by Sri Krishna in the Bhagavad Gita is the moderate, medium, golden path, both for the busy man of the world and for the highest spiritual aspirant. To follow the path advocated by the Bhagavad Gita would be their salvation, for it is a book of universal Self-realization, introducing man to his true Self, the soul—showing him how he has evolved from Spirit, how he may fulfil on earth his righteous duties, and how he may return to God. The Gita's wisdom is not for dry intellectualists to perform mental gymnastics with its sayings for the entertainment of dogmatists; but rather to show a man or woman living in the world, householder or renunciant, how to live a balanced life that includes the actual contact of God, by following the step-by-step methods of yoga.

The Epic Tale of the Kurus and Pandus

AS A BACKGROUND for this Gita exposition, the lengthy tale of the highly symbolic *Mahabharata,* in which the Krishna-Arjuna discourse is set, need not be recounted. But a brief summation touching upon some of the principal characters and events will provide a basis to show author Vyasa's allegorical intent.

The *Mahabharata* story begins three generations before the time of Krishna and Arjuna, at the time of King Shantanu. Shantanu's first queen was Ganga (personification of the holy river Ganges); she gave birth to eight sons, but the first seven were withdrawn by her, immersed in the sacred Ganges waters. The eighth son was Bhishma.

At the pleading of Shantanu, Bhishma was allowed to remain in the world; but in consequence, Ganga then immersed herself in the holy stream from which she had been personified. In time, Shantanu married his second queen Satyavati and through her begat two sons—Chitrangada and Vichitravirya; both of whom died without producing offspring: Chitrangada as a mere boy, and Vichitravirya leaving two widowed queens, Ambika and Ambalika.

Before her marriage to Shantanu, Satyavati had been raised as the daughter of a fisherman; she was cursed to smell so foully of fish that no one could come near her, let alone consider her a prospect for marriage. Taking pity on her for her plight, Sage Parasara blessed her not only with a son—who was none other than Vyasa—but also that thereafter she was radiant with beauty and the fragrance of lotuses. Therefore, Vyasa was half-brother to Vichitravirya. That the succession to the throne not be terminated because there was no successor to Vichitravirya, the law of the land was invoked whereby a brother could produce progeny on behalf of a childless brother. Vyasa was persuaded to fulfil this role: from Ambika, Dhritarashtra was born, blind at birth; and from Ambalika, Pandu was born. Dhritarashtra married Gandhari—who, out of respect for her blind husband, blindfolded her own eyes and thus shared his darkness throughout their life together. They had one hundred sons; Duryodhana, the eldest, in time became king-regent on behalf of his blind father. From his second wife, Vaishya, Dhritarashtra had another son.

Pandu had two wives, Kunti (sister of Vasudeva, Krishna's father) and Madri. For the accidental killing of a sage during a hunting expedition, Pandu had been cursed that if he embraced a woman he would die. It thus seemed that he and his two queens must remain childless. But Kunti then revealed that before her marriage to Pandu she had received the blessing of a miraculous power: Impressed by her piety and devotional service, a sage had granted her five *mantras* with which she could receive offspring from any god she chose to invoke. When Kunti told Pandu of her *mantras*, he entreated her to use them. She bore three sons for Pandu: Yudhisthira, Bhima, and Arjuna from invoking respectively the *devas* Dharma, Vayu, and Indra. As Pandu wished Madri also to have a child, he asked Kunti to give the remaining sacred *mantra* to her.* Having obtained the

Divine parentage of the Pandava brothers

* The fifth *mantra* had already been used by Kunti prior to her marriage to Pandu. To

Their thoughts fully on Me, their beings surrendered to Me, enlightening one another, proclaiming Me always, My devotees are contented and joyful.

—Bhagavad Gita X:9

❖

"As often as virtue declines, a God-illumined soul comes on earth to draw virtue again to the fore....

"As a child in Brindaban, Krishna amazed all with his precocious wisdom and display of incredible powers.... Beautiful in form and feature, irresistible in charm and demeanour, an embodiment of divine love, giving joy to all, the young boy Krishna was beloved of everyone in the community, and an entrancing leader and friend to his childhood companions, the gopas and gopis, who with him tended the village herds of cows in the sylvan environs.... Sri Krishna, with the enchanting melodies of his heavenly flute, is calling all devotees to the bower of divine union in samadhi meditation, there to bask in the blissful love of God."

—Paramahansa Yogananda

mantra, Madri invoked the twin *devas,* the Ashvins, and thereby received twin sons, Nakula and Sahadeva.

The five Pandava princes and the one hundred Kaurava offspring were raised and educated together, receiving the tutelage of their preceptor Drona. Arjuna excelled all of them in prowess; none could match him. Jealousy and enmity grew among the Kauravas against the Pandus. Duryodhana resented Yudhisthira's position as the rightful heir to the throne, so he conspired repeatedly but unsuccessfully to destroy the Pandus.

In an elaborate ceremony called *svayamvara,* held by King Drupada to choose a husband for his daughter Draupadi, Drupada made the condition that the hand of his daughter would be given only to the prince who could bend a gigantic bow provided for the occasion, and with it hit the eye of a cleverly concealed and suspended target. Princes from far and near tried and failed even to lift the bow. Arjuna succeeded easily. When the five Pandus returned home, their mother Kunti, hearing their approach from a distance and presuming they had won some wealth, called out to them that they must equally share their winnings. As the mother's word must be honoured, Draupadi became the wife of all five brothers. She bore one son by each.

Duryodhana filches the Pandavas' kingdom

In time, the dispute between the Kurus and Pandus over the rulership of the kingdom reached a climax. Duryodhana, consumed by jealous desire for supremacy, concocted a cunning scheme: a fraudulent game of dice. Through a clever plot hatched by Duryodhana and his wicked uncle Shakuni, who was an adept in trickery and deceit, Yudhisthira was defeated in throw after throw, finally losing his kingdom, then himself and his brothers, and then their wife Draupadi. Thus Duryodhana filched from the Pandus their kingdom and sent them into exile in the forest for twelve years, and to live a thirteenth year in disguise, unrecognized. Thereafter, if they survived, they could return and lay claim to their lost kingdom. At the allotted time, the good Pandus, having met all the conditions of their exile, returned and demanded their kingdom; but the Kurus refused to part with a piece of land even as long and as broad as a needle.

---

test her power, she invoked Surya, the sun *deva,* and Karna was born to her—yet she remained a virgin. Nevertheless, fearing rebuke that she had mothered an illegitimate child, she sealed him in a box and set it afloat on the river, where he was found and raised by an aged charioteer. Karna later played a major role in the *Mahabharata* story, as mentioned in the commentary on I:8.

When war became inevitable, Arjuna for the Pandus and Duryodhana for the Kurus sought Krishna's aid in their cause. Duryodhana arrived first at Krishna's palace and seated himself boldly at the head of the couch upon which Krishna was resting, feigning sleep. Arjuna arrived and stood humbly with folded hands at Krishna's feet. When the avatar opened his eyes, it was, therefore, Arjuna whom he saw first. Both requested Krishna to side with them in the war. Krishna stated that one party could have his massive army, and the other side could have himself as a personal counsellor—though he would not take up arms in the combat. Arjuna was given first choice. Without hesitation he wisely chose Krishna himself; the greedy Duryodhana rejoiced to be awarded the army.

Before the war, Krishna served as mediator to try to settle the dispute amicably, journeying from Dwarka to the Kuru capital city at Hastinapura to persuade Dhritarashtra, Duryodhana, and the other Kurus to restore to the Pandavas their rightful kingdom. But even he could not move the power-mad Duryodhana and his followers to accept a fair resolution, and war was declared; the field of conflict was Kurukshetra. The first verse of the Bhagavad Gita begins on the eve of this battle.

In the end it was a victory for the Pandus. The five brothers reigned nobly under the kingship of the eldest, Yudhisthira, until at the end of their lives they retired to the Himalayas and there entered the heavenly realm.

SPIRITUAL SYMBOLISM OF THE MAHABHARATA STORY

NOW FOR THE SYMBOLISM. As will be seen in the Gita commentary that follows, the genealogical descent of the Kurus and Pandus from Shantanu parallels in analogy the step-by-step descent of the universe and man from Spirit into matter. The Gita dialogue concerns itself with the process by which that descent may be reversed, enabling man to reascend from the limited consciousness of himself as a mortal being to the immortal consciousness of his true Self, the soul, one with the infinite Spirit.

The genealogy is diagrammed in the chart on page *xxxvii,* along with the spiritual significance of the various characters as was handed down from Lahiri Mahasaya. These esoteric meanings are not arbitrary. In explaining the inner meaning of words and names, the primary key is to hunt for it in the original Sanskrit root. Terrible mistakes are made in definitions of Sanskrit terms if there is no intuitive ability to arrive at the correct root, and then to decipher the correct meaning from that root according to its usage at the time of the origin of the word.* When the basis is correctly established, one may then also draw meaning from the various sources relative to the common meaning of words and the specific way they were used to form a cogent connective thought.

It is remarkable how the author of this great Bhagavad Gita has clothed every psychological tendency or faculty, as well as many metaphysical principles, with a suitable name. Each word, how beautiful! Each word growing from a Sanskrit root! A proliferation of pages would be required to delve fully into the Sanskrit underlying the metaphors—tedious to all but scholarly minds. But I have now and then given a

---

* The late Jagadguru Sri Shankaracharya of the ancient Govardhan Math in Puri, His Holiness Bharati Krishna Tirtha—a scholar of great repute and a revered spiritual leader of millions of Hindus—gives an intimation of the less-than-obvious meanings that can be drawn from Sanskrit literature. (See also page 280 for his unique discovery of the whole science of mathematics in sixteen seemingly unrelated verses in the Atharva Veda.)

"The very name we know India by, Bharata, gives us the necessary clue.…*Bha* means light and knowledge, and *rata* means devoted. *Bharata* means devoted to light as against darkness.…We have this unique feature with regard to our Sanskrit literature, that the language, the rules of grammar, the diction, etc., necessitates the use of words for denoting objects in such a manner that the philosophy, the science, and the theology behind the whole thing is clear.…The rules of the language dictate that every object is to be named with a significance of its own. Significance, not merely explaining its present condition, its present meaning, exigencies, requirements, etc., but how the name should be justified by actual action.…So Bharata is not the name of a mere geographical entity placed in some corner of the world and having its geographical, topographical, and other limitations. Bharata stands for every individual soul that has this idea of light, the dedication to the light, as against immersion in darkness. So we speak of the light that God's creation of the world began with, and we think of the Light that India claims to be its chief aspiration, its chief, its most important and most valued goal.…

"Sanskrit has a certain peculiarity about it that the same passage very often deals with a different subject and is capable of yielding different meanings relating to different subjects.…In some cases we have texts which bear not merely two meanings, but three or four and relate to different subjects altogether. In English we have the figure of speech called pun, when a word having two different meanings is used.…We have a very ordinary example in which a person poses a puzzle. He asks another, 'What's the difference between a schoolmaster and an engine driver?' And the answer is, 'The one minds the train, and the other trains the mind.'…Examples of this type are to be found infinitely in our Sanskrit texts.

"[Further] as a language develops and comes in contact with other languages, words change their meaning. Words get additional meaning, words get deteriorated in meaning.…In some case we have lost the clue to the changes. We're unable to say what historical background was responsible for such and such change of meaning, for such and such deterioration or exaltation of meaning and so forth.…'Knave' in modern English means rogue, scoundrel, a rascal, a man of bad character, a cheat. And in Chaucer's English, 'knave' simply meant 'male,' 'male child.'"—Extracts from *Vedic Metaphysics* (Varanasi: Motilal Banarsidas, 1970). *(Publisher's Note)*

few examples based in part on the explanations learned from my guru Sri Yukteswar.

The universe's creative principles and creation itself are deformations of the one Infinite Spirit become God the Father of Creation. Allegorically, Shantanu is Para-Brahman, God the Father of Creation, the transcendental unchanging Source and Essence of creation, the Sole Reality supporting the forces, forms, and beings that evolve from His cosmic consciousness. The first expression of this evolution is through the intelligence and the creative vibratory force that goes out of Him, represented by His two consorts, Ganga and Satyavati.

Ganga is the spiritual aspect, *Chaitanya* or Consciousness, Nature as Intelligence, Maha-Prakriti or Holy Ghost—God's consciousness which when differentiated becomes eight intelligences, or "eight sons": *Kutastha Chaitanya,* the Universal Unchangeable Spirit shining everywhere in the universe; six intelligences governing the three macrocosmic manifestations (en masse) and the three microcosmic manifestations (individual units) of the causal, astral, and physical universes; and *Abhasa Chaitanya,* the reflected Spirit. The latter is a reflection from the Universal Spirit (*Kutastha Chaitanya*) cast upon all individual material objects; by this, they are energized, spiritualized. Matter in this spiritualized state becomes conscious of a separate existence, endowed with mind, intellect, and consciousness. This self-consciousness is *ahamkara,* universal ego, the seeming dichotomy of Spirit and matter by individualization. This aspect of reflected Spirit Intelligence is represented as Bhishma, of whose role in the Gita Sri Yukteswar wrote: "He is called *Kuruvriddha,* ('the Aged Kuru'—I:12) as he is the veteran worldly man* and has existed ever since creation. But for him, our narrow worldly ideas and activities would not have any tendency to work. The whole created world is based on this individualistic force alone."

The eight intelligences of Spirit present in all creation

Spirit thus remains in creation in seven universal forms or intelli-

* The use of the masculine gender in this publication is rooted not in the narrowly exclusive sense of the word *man,* denoting only half of the human race, but in its broader original meaning; the word is derived from the same root as Sanskrit *manas,* mind—the uniquely human capacity for rational thought. The science of yoga deals with human consciousness from the point of view of the essentially androgynous Self (*atman*). As there is no other terminology in English that would convey these psychological and spiritual truths without excessive literary awkwardness, the use of *man* and related terms has been retained herein. *(Publisher's Note)*

Chronology of Creation, Symbolized in Genealogy of the Kurus and Pandus

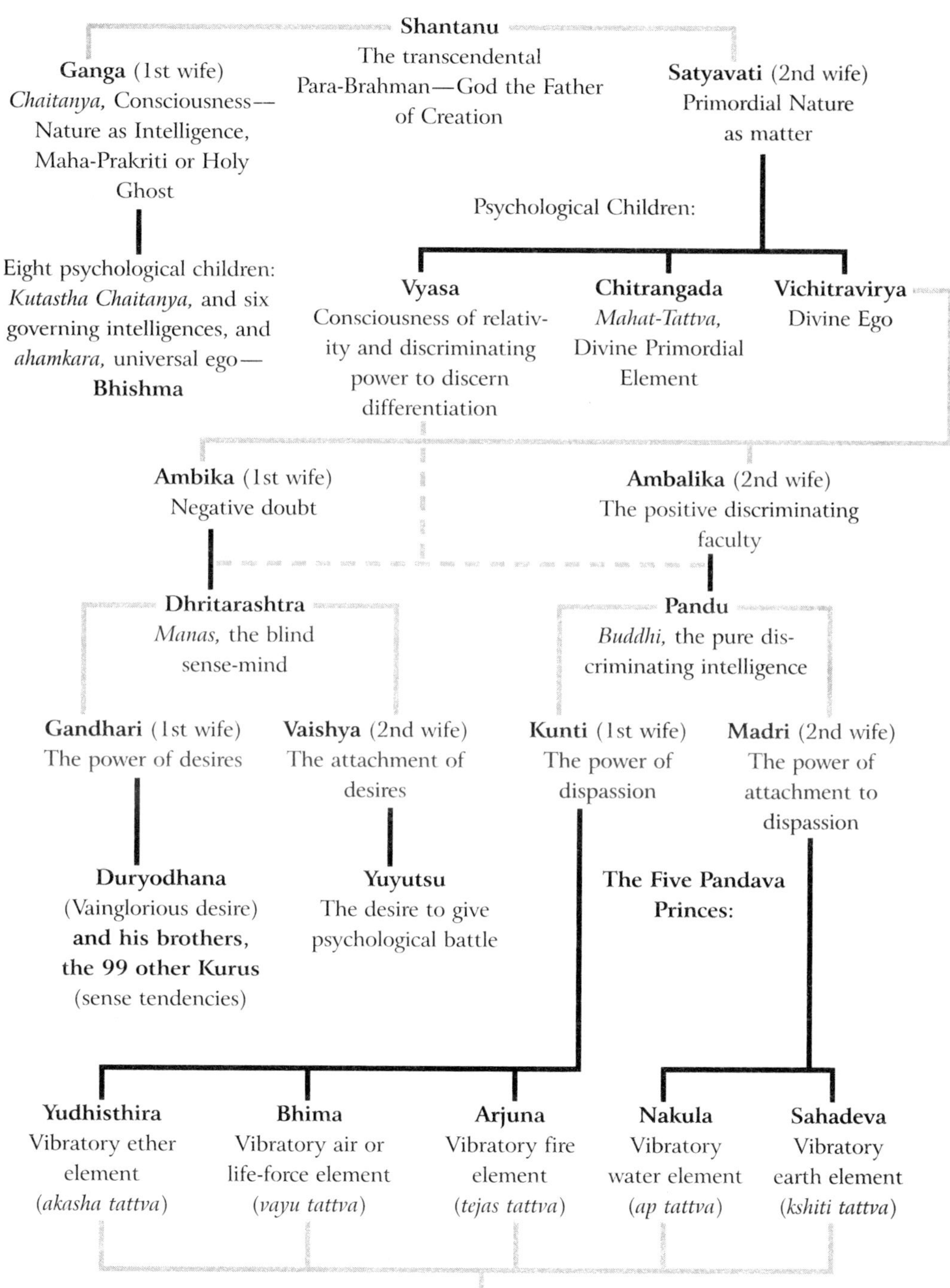

gences, but hidden from ordinary consciousness, "drowned" by Ganga in the universal stream. *Abhasa Chaitanya,* reflected Spirit, the eighth offspring, alone remains manifested in this world, working with and energizing the gross tendencies of the mind; yet it maintains an indifference as to the outcome of events. (Accordingly, Bhishma renounces his right to the throne of Shantanu and takes a vow never to marry. He loves, and in turn is revered by, both the Kurus and Pandus as their Grandsire.) Ego is noble or degraded only as it expresses its pure nature of divine individuality (soul consciousness expressing through the bodily instrument) or as it entangles itself with the gross inclinations of the sensory mind (see page 83).

As Ganga is the spiritual or consciousness aspect of Nature as Intelligence, Satyavati is the aspect of Primordial Nature as matter. From Satyavati evolve the forces that coalesce into a manifested universe and its sensory, thinking, active beings. Here the first expression, or offspring, is Vyasa: In order to conceive creation, God must cloak His consciousness in relativity, i.e., the Singular Reality must project the idea of duality and the discriminating power to perceive and discern differentiation; this is Vyasa, allegorically.

The other two sons of Satyavati are Chitrangada and Vichitravirya: Divine Primordial Element and Divine Ego, respectively. According to Sankhya philosophy (see II:39 and XIII:5–6), the first of twenty-four principles of creation is referred to as *mahat-tattva* (the primordial element), the basic inclusive mental consciousness, *chitta.* With this conscious awareness, or feeling, the primordial element precipitantly degenerates into constituent parts—symbolically, Chitrangada dies at an early age. The first transformation is the sense of "I" or ego as the experiencer—the pure or divine ego of the causal body of man, which individualizes the soul from Spirit.

❖

The evolution of manifested creation and its beings from Primordial Nature

❖

Vichitravirya, Divine Ego, had two wives, Ambika and Ambalika, the result of the differentiation of the forces: Ambika represents negative doubt (perception without clear discernment); and Ambalika, the positive discriminating faculty. When Vichitravirya dies, it means that the divine ego is obscured from subjective consciousness by its contact with these outward deformations of consciousness. Then Vyasa, relativity and discriminating power, sires through Ambika the blind Dhritarashtra—*manas,* the sense mind, blind because it lacks discriminating power. Through Ambalika, Vyasa also begets the pure offspring, Pandu, *buddhi,* the pure discriminating intelligence.

The blind Dhritarashtra, "the sense mind," gives birth through his first wife Gandhari, "the power of desires," to Duryodhana, "vain-glorious desire," and his ninety-nine brothers: the ten senses (five of perception and five of action) with their ten inclinations. From Vaishya, "the attachment of desires," the second wife of the sense mind, another son is born: Yuyutsu, "the desire to give psychological battle." In the war, Yuyutsu spurns his Kuru brothers and sides with the Pandavas.

Pandu, *buddhi,* the positive aspect of the mind, the pure discriminating intelligence, has five sons, the five *tattvas* or vibratory elements that inform all matter: earth, water, fire, air (*prana,* life force), and ether.* In the body of man they manifest in the five spinal *chakras,* subtle centres of life and consciousness, to create and sustain the body; and as awakened spiritual consciousness in the spinal centres, they bestow divine powers on the enlightened yogi. (See pages 65 ff.)

Spiritual symbolism of the five Pandava brothers

The first three sons are born of Kunti, "the power of dispassion" that invokes the cosmic principles governing creation: Yudhisthira, "divine calmness" and the "vibratory ether" in the *vishuddha* or cervical centre, born of Dharma, presiding deity of all righteousness; Bhima, "vibratory air" (*vayu* or life force) in the *anahata* or dorsal *chakra,* born of the strongest of the gods, Vayu or Pavana; and Arjuna, "divine self-control" and the "vibratory fire element" in the *manipura* or lumbar *chakra,* born of Indra, king of the gods.

Then from the second wife, Madri, "the power of attachment to dispassion," twin sons are born from the Ashvin *devas:* Nakula, the "divine power of adherence" and the "vibratory water element" in the *svadhisthana* or sacral *chakra;* and Sahadeva, the "divine power of resistance" and the "vibratory earth element" in the *muladhara* or coccygeal *chakra.*

Even the anatomy of the physical body hints at the symbology of the five Pandavas as coming from two mothers: Kunti, and then Madri through the instrumentality of Kunti. The spinal cord extends from the medulla to below the lumbar *chakra,* accommodating the location of the subtle centres of the first three brothers born of Kunti. From the lower end of the spinal cord extend the spinal nerves with

---

* The five elements, mentioned often in this Gita commentary, do not have the same connotation that the word "elements" did when it was believed that earth, water, fire, air, and ether were the elements or substance of creation. Nor are they actually "elements" as science interprets the term today, but rather five subtle vibratory forces into which the Creative Force differentiates itself.

their ganglia to the base of the spine, accommodating the location of the subtle centres of the twin sons of Madri. This, too, is metaphysically significant: though all five centres are operative in maintaining life and consciousness in the body and mind, the three upper spinal centres are especially auspicious and helpful to the aspiring devotee in his inner spiritual activities in meditation, while the two lower centres are a powerful support for the spiritualization of his external activities.

The common wife of the five Pandavas is Draupadi, the life force in the body that is coiled or centralized in the spine and referred to as *kula kundalini,* which awakens the spiritual powers in the spinal centres of the advanced devotee; i.e., produces a son for each of the Pandava princes in each of the five spinal *chakras.*

THE GITA DIALOGUE COMMENCES

SYMBOLICALLY, THEN, THIS is the scene as the Gita dialogue commences: Man's soul consciousness—the realization of his oneness with the eternal, all-blissful Spirit—has descended through various gradations into mortal body-consciousness. The senses and blind mind, and the power of pure discrimination, both reign in the bodily kingdom; there is constant conflict between the forces of the materialistic senses (engaging the consciousness in the pursuit of external pleasure) and the pure discriminative power that tries to return man's consciousness to its native state of soul-realization.

The "game of dice" is the game of delusion, through which man's consciousness devolves from Spirit to matter, from soul consciousness to bondage to the body. The game is very charming; and man stakes all his bodily kingdom, all his power of soul bliss, in gambling with the deceitful, matter-inclined senses, only to be overpowered by them—i.e., the pure discriminative intelligence of the soul is ousted from its reign over the bodily kingdom and sent into exile.

Originally, in childhood, man's senses and life force, and the development of his body, are governed more or less automatically by the soul's intelligent powers (pure discrimination and calmness). But with the onset of youth, strong sense desires are roused by temptations in this life and habit tendencies from past lives and begin to foment turmoil in the bodily kingdom to gain control. The kindred princely faculties of discrimination are enticed into a deceitful gamble with sense lures and are banished from the kingdom. After man goes through many years of evil experiences, and takes many painful "hard knocks" under the sense regime of greed, anger, sex, jealousy, and egotism, then discrimination and its noble offspring seek to regain their lost bodily kingdom.

Once bad sense habits are well established in the body, the free will of wisdom is banished for at least twelve years. Complete physiological and mental changes, as well as the creation and firm establishment of new good habits, often are possible only in twelve years. In twelve-year cycles man is slowly advanced in his spiritual evolution. (It requires twelve years of normal healthful living and observance of natural laws to effect even slight refinements in brain structure—and a million such transgression-free years to purify the brain sufficiently to express cosmic consciousness. By the technique of *Kriya Yoga,* however, this process of evolution is greatly hastened.)

The symbolic thirteenth year spent by the Pandus "in disguise" refers to *samadhi* yoga meditation, from which the devotee must draw the soul's discriminative qualities and make them ready for the battle to reclaim their bodily kingdom. Thus the Gita describes how—having roused and trained the psychological astral powers of Yudhisthira calmness, Bhima life-force control, Arjuna nonattachment of self-control, Nakula power to adhere to good rules, and Sahadeva power to resist evil—these offspring of discrimination along with their army and allies of good habits and spiritual inclinations try to return from banishment. But the crooked sense tendencies with their sense armies are loath to part with their reign over the bodily kingdom. So, with the help of Krishna (the guru, or awakened soul-consciousness, or meditation-born intuition), war must be fought—materially and mentally, and also spiritually in repeated experiences of *samadhi* meditation—to reclaim the kingdom from Ego and its army of evil mental tendencies. On the battlefield of man's body—Kurukshetra, "the field of action"—the offspring of the blind sense-mind and those of the pure discriminative intelligence now confront each other.

The negative aspects of the one hundred sense inclinations are formidable foes (whose variations can be innumerable). Some of the more recognizable offspring of the blind mind are as follows: material desire; anger; greed; avarice; hate; jealousy; wickedness; lust; sex attachment, abuse, and promiscuity; dishonesty; meanness; cruelty; ill will; desire to hurt others; destructive instinct; unkindness; harshness of speech and thought; impatience; covetousness; selfishness; arrogance; conceit; pride of caste or social birth; racial pride; false sense of delicacy; high-handedness; saucy

Characteristics of the one hundred sense inclinations (Kurus)

temper; impudence; ill feeling; quarrelsome attitude; inharmoniousness; revengefulness; sensitive feelings; physical laziness; lack of initiative; cowardice; absentmindedness and mental sloth; spiritual indifference; unwillingness to meditate; spiritual procrastination; impurity of body, mind, and soul; disloyalty to God; ungratefulness to God; stupidity; mental weakness; disease-consciousness; lack of vision; littleness of mind; lack of foresight; physical, mental, and spiritual ignorance; impulsiveness; fickle-mindedness; sense attachment; enjoyment in seeing evil, listening to evil, tasting evil, smelling evil, touching evil; thinking, willing, feeling, speaking, remembering, and doing evil; fear of disease and death; worry; superstition; swearing; immoderation; too much sleeping; too much eating; dissimulation; pretense of goodness; partiality; doubt; moroseness; pessimism; bitterness; dissatisfaction; shunning God; and postponing meditation.

These sense bolsheviks—offspring of the blind sense-mind—have brought only sickness, mental worries, and the pestilence of ignorance and spiritual famine, owing to the dearth of wisdom in the bodily kingdom. The awakened soul force and the meditation-evolved self-control must seize the kingdom and plant therein the banner of Spirit, establishing a reign resplendent with peace, wisdom, abundance, and health.

Each person has to fight his own battle of Kurukshetra. It is a war not only worth winning, but in the divine order of the universe and of the eternal relationship between the soul and God, a war that sooner or later must be won.

In the holy Bhagavad Gita, the quickest attainment of that victory is assured to the devotee who, through undiscourageable practice of the divine science of yoga meditation, learns like Arjuna to hearken to the inner wisdom-song of Spirit.

O Krishna, Lord of Yoga! surely there shall not fail
Blessing, and victory, and power, for Thy most mighty sake,
Where this song comes of Arjun, and how with God he spake.

—Chapter XVIII:76–78 (poetic rendering by Sir Edwin Arnold)

CHAPTER I

THE DESPONDENCY OF ARJUNA

❖

The Significance of Chapter I

❖

"What Did They?"—Survey of the Inner Psychological and Spiritual Battlefield

❖

The Opposing Armies of the Spiritual and Materialistic Forces

❖

The Conch Shells: Inner Vibratory Battle in Meditation

❖

The Devotee Observes the Enemies to Be Destroyed

❖

Arjuna's Refusal to Fight

"The timeless message of the Bhagavad Gita does not refer only to one historical battle, but to the cosmic conflict between good and evil: life as a series of battles between Spirit and matter, soul and body, life and death, knowledge and ignorance, health and disease, changelessness and transitoriness, self-control and temptations, discrimination and the blind sense-mind."

THE DESPONDENCY OF ARJUNA

THE SIGNIFICANCE OF CHAPTER I

AS A PRE-EMINENT TREATISE ON YOGA, the renowned Bhagavad Gita speaks both pragmatically and esoterically to embrace the broad spectrum of human seeking that has for generations sheltered itself in the counsel and solace found in the verses of this beloved scripture. It cites not only the practical application of spiritual principles required of the aspirant, but also the consummate expression of those principles as realized by the advanced yogi.

In modern books, the Introduction usually gives the reader a general idea of the contents; but the Hindu scriptural writers of ancient India often used the first chapter instead to indicate their purpose. Thus the opening chapter of the Bhagavad Gita serves as an introduction to the holy discourse that follows. But it does not merely set the scene and provide a backdrop, to be lightly perused as insubstantial. When read as the allegory intended by its author, the great sage Vyasa, it introduces the basic principles of the science of Yoga and describes the initial spiritual struggles of the yogi who sets out on the path to *kaivalya,* liberation, oneness with God: the goal of Yoga. To understand the implied truths in the first chapter is to begin the yoga journey with a clearly charted course.

My revered guru, Swami Sri Yukteswar—himself a *Jnanavatar,* incarnation of wisdom—taught me the hidden meaning in just a few significant verses from the first Gita chapter. "You now have the key," he said. "With calm inner perception, you will be able to open this scripture to any passage and understand both its substance and its essence." It is with his encouragement and by his grace that I offer this work.

"WHAT DID THEY?"—SURVEY OF THE INNER PSYCHOLOGICAL AND SPIRITUAL BATTLEFIELD

VERSE 1

धृतराष्ट्र उवाच
धर्मक्षेत्रे कुरुक्षेत्रे समवेता युयुत्सवः ।
मामकाः पाण्डवाश्चैव किमकुर्वत सञ्जय ॥

Dhritarashtra said:

"On the holy plain of Kurukshetra (dharmakshetra kurukshetra), when my offspring and the sons of Pandu had gathered together, eager for battle, what did they, O Sanjaya?"*

THE BLIND KING DHRITARASHTRA (the blind mind) enquired through the honest Sanjaya (impartial introspection): "When my offspring, the Kurus (the wicked impulsive mental and sense tendencies), and the sons of the virtuous Pandu (the pure discriminative tendencies) gathered together on the *dharmakshetra* (holy plain) of Kurukshetra (the bodily field of activity), eager to do battle for supremacy, what was the outcome?"

The earnest enquiry by the blind King Dhritarashtra, seeking an unbiased report from the impartial Sanjaya as to how fared the battle between the Kurus and the Pandavas (sons of Pandu) at Kurukshetra, is metaphorically the question to be asked by the spiritual aspirant as he reviews daily the events of his own righteous battle from which he seeks the victory of Self-realization. Through honest introspection he analyzes the deeds and assesses the strengths of the opposing armies of his good and bad tendencies: self-control versus sense indulgence, discriminative intelligence opposed by mental sense inclinations, spiritual resolve in meditation contested by mental resistance and physical restlessness, and divine soul-consciousness against the ignorance and magnetic attraction of the lower ego-nature.

Metaphorical significance of Dhritarashtra's question

The battlefield of these contending forces is Kurukshetra (*Kuru,* from the Sanskrit root *kṛi,* "work, material action"; and *kṣetra,* "field"). This "field of action" is the human body with its physical, mental, and soul faculties, the field on which all activities of one's life take place.

* The Sanskrit text of the Gita verses is transliterated in Roman script at the back of each volume.

It is referred to in this Gita stanza as Dharmakshetra (*dharma,* i.e., righteousness, virtue, holiness; thus, holy plain or field), for on this field the righteous battle is waged between the virtues of the soul's discriminative intelligence (sons of Pandu) and the ignoble, uncontrolled activities of the blind mind (the Kurus, or offspring of the blind King Dhritarashtra).

Dharmakshetra Kurukshetra refers also, respectively, to religious and spiritual duties and activities (those of the yogi in meditation) as contrasted with mundane responsibilities and activities. Thus, in this deeper metaphysical interpretation, Dharmakshetra Kurukshetra signifies the inner bodily field on which the spiritual action of yoga meditation takes place for the attainment of Self-realization: the plain of the cerebrospinal axis and its seven subtle centres of life and divine consciousness.

Two opposing forces: inclinations of the lower mind vs. soul discrimination

Competing on this field are two opposing forces or magnetic poles: discriminative intelligence (*buddhi*) and the sense-conscious mind (*manas*). *Buddhi,* the pure discriminating intellect, is allegorically represented as Pandu, husband of Kunti (the mother of Arjuna and the other Pandava princes who uphold the righteous principles of *nivritti,* renunciation of worldliness). The name Pandu derives from *pand,* "white"—a metaphorical implication of the clarity of a pure discriminating intellect. *Manas* is allegorically represented as the blind King Dhritarashtra, sire of the one hundred Kurus, or sensory impressions and inclinations, which are all bent toward *pravritti,* worldly enjoyment. *Buddhi* draws its right discernment from the superconsciousness of the soul manifesting in the causal seats of consciousness in the spiritual cerebrospinal centres. *Manas,* the sense mind, the subtle magnetic pole turned outward toward the world of matter, is in the pons Varolii, which physiologically is ever busy with sensory coordination.* Thus, *buddhi* intelligence draws the consciousness toward truth or the eternal realities, soul

* The pons Varolii is a part of the brain stem—situated above the medulla and centred below the two hemispheres of the cerebrum—connecting the cerebrum, cerebellum, and medulla. Small in size (1 x 1 x 1½ inches), it contains the ascending sensory and descending motor tracts that connect the brain to the rest of the body. These tracts travel through a dense network of nerve cells, called the reticular formation, whose function is to arouse to activity the rest of the brain and to regulate the twenty-four-hour cycle of sleep and waking. The pons Varolii contains a particular structure, the locus coeruleus ("blue place") — a small, concentrated cluster of cells containing norepinephrine, a chemical substance that stimulates the mobilization that prepares the body for action. This structure is involved in arousal, dreaming, sleep, and mood.

consciousness or Self-realization. *Manas* or sense mind repels the consciousness from truth and engages it in the external sensory activities of the body, and thus with the world of delusive relativities, *maya*.

The name Dhritarashtra derives from *dhṛta*, "held, supported, drawn tight (reins)," and *rāṣṭra*, "kingdom," from *rāj*, "to rule." By implication, we have the symbolic meaning, *dhṛtam rāṣṭraṁ yena*, "who upholds the kingdom (of the senses)," or "who rules by holding tightly the reins (of the senses)."

The mind (*manas*, or sense consciousness) gives coordination to the senses as the reins keep together the several horses of a chariot. The body is the chariot; the soul is the owner of the chariot; intelligence is the charioteer; the senses are the horses. The mind is said to be blind because it cannot see without the help of the senses and intelligence. The reins of a chariot receive and relay the impulses from the steeds and the guidance of the charioteer. Similarly, the blind mind on its own neither cognizes nor exerts guidance, but merely receives the impressions from the senses and relays the conclusions and instructions of the intelligence. If the intelligence is governed by *buddhi*, the pure discriminative power, the senses are controlled; if the intelligence is ruled by material desires, the senses are wild and unruly.

SANJAYA MEANS, LITERALLY, *completely victorious;* "one who has conquered himself." He alone who is not self-centred has the ability to see clearly and to be impartial. Thus, in the Gita, Sanjaya is divine insight; for the aspiring devotee, Sanjaya represents the power of impartial intuitive self-analysis, discerning introspection. It is the ability to stand aside, observe oneself without any prejudice, and judge accurately. Thoughts may be present without one's conscious awareness. Introspection is that power of intuition by which the consciousness can watch its thoughts. It does not reason, it feels—not with biased emotion, but with clear, calm intuition.

❖

Symbolism of Sanjaya: impartial intuitive self-analysis

❖

In the *Mahabharata*, of which the Bhagavad Gita is a part, the text of the Gita is introduced by the great *rishi* Vyasa bestowing on Sanjaya the spiritual power of being able to see from a distance everything taking place over the entire battlefield, so that he could give an account to the blind King Dhritarashtra as the events unfold. Therefore, one would expect the king's enquiry in the first verse to be in the present tense. Author Vyasa purposely had Sanjaya narrate the Gita dialogue retrospectively, and used a past tense of the verb ("What *did* they?"), as a clear hint to discerning students that the Gita is referring only incidentally to a historical battle on the plain of Kurukshetra in northern India. Primarily, Vyasa is describing a universal battle—the one that rages daily in man's life. Had Vyasa wished merely to report the progress of an actual battle that was taking place at the moment on the field of Kurukshetra, he would have had Dhritarashtra speak to the messenger Sanjaya in the present tense: "My children and the sons of Pandu—what *are* they doing now?"

This is an important point. The timeless message of the Bhagavad Gita does not refer only to one historical battle, but to the cosmic conflict between good and evil: life as a series of battles between Spirit and matter, soul and body, life and death, knowledge and ignorance, health and disease, changelessness and transitoriness, self-control and temptations, discrimination and the blind sense-mind. The past tense of the verb in the first stanza is therefore employed by Vyasa to indicate that the power of one's introspection is being invoked to review the conflicts of the day in one's mind in order to determine the favourable or unfavourable outcome.*

EXPANDED COMMENTARY: THE BATTLE OF LIFE

FROM THE MOMENT OF CONCEPTION to the surrender of the last breath, man has to fight in each incarnation innumerable battles—biological, hereditary, bacteriological, physiological, climatic, social, ethical, political, sociological, psychological, metaphysical—so many varieties of inner and outer conflicts. Competing for victory in every encounter are the forces of good and evil. The whole intent of the Gita is to align man's efforts on the side of *dharma,* or righteousness. The ultimate aim is Self-realization, the realization of man's true Self, the soul, as made in the image of God, one with the ever-existing, ever-conscious, ever-new bliss of Spirit.

The first contest of the soul in each incarnation is with other souls seeking rebirth. With the union of sperm and ovum to begin the formation of a new human body, a flash of light appears in the astral world, the heavenly home of souls between incarnations. That light

* This symbology explains why, even though Sanjaya had been given the power to perceive and describe the events at the same time they were happening, he did not narrate to Dhritarashtra the Gita discourse, which preceded the battle, until ten days of fighting had already taken place. *(Publisher's Note)*

transmits a pattern which attracts a soul according to that soul's karma—the self-created influences from actions of past lives. In each incarnation, karma works itself out partly through hereditary forces; the soul of a child is attracted into a family in which heredity is in conformance with the child's past karma. Many souls vie to enter this new cell of life; only one will be victorious. (In the case of a multiple conception, more than one primal cell is present.)

Within the mother's body, the unborn child struggles against disease, darkness, and periodic feelings of limitation and frustration as the soul consciousness in the unborn child remembers and then gradually forgets its greater freedom of expression during its astral sojourn. The soul within the embryo also has to contend with karma, which is influencing for good or ill the formation of the body in which it is now a resident. Additionally, it encounters the vibratory influences that reach it from outside—the environment and actions of the mother; external sounds and sensations; vibrations of love and hate, peace and anger.

After birth, the struggles of the infant are between its instincts to seek comfort and survival and the opposing relative helplessness of its immature bodily instrument.

A child begins his first conscious struggle when he has to choose between his desires to play aimlessly and his desire to learn, study, and pursue some course of systematic training. Gradually, more serious battles arise, forced upon him by karmic instincts from within or by bad company and environment from without.

The youth finds himself confronted suddenly with a host of problems that often he has been ill-prepared to meet: temptations of sex, greed, prevarication, money-making by easy but questionable means, pressure from the company he keeps, and social influences. The youth usually discovers he possesses no sword of wisdom with which to fight the invading armies of worldly experiences.

The adult who lives without cultivating and employing his innate powers of wisdom and spiritual discrimination finds inexorably that the kingdom of his body and mind is being overrun by the insurgents of misery-making wrong desires, destructive habits, failure, ignorance, disease, and unhappiness.

Few men are even aware that a state of constant warfare exists in their kingdom. Usually, it is only when the devastation is nearly complete that men helplessly realize the sad ruin of their lives. The psychological conflict for health, prosperity, self-control, and wisdom has to be started anew each day in order for man to advance toward victory, reclaiming inch by inch the territories of the soul occupied by the rebels of ignorance.

The yogi, the awakening man, is confronted not only with the external battles fought by all men, but also with the internal clash between the negative forces of restlessness (arising from *manas,* or sense consciousness) and the positive power of his desire and effort to meditate (supported by *buddhi* intelligence) when he tries to reestablish himself in the soul's inner spiritual kingdom: the subtle centres of life and divine consciousness in the spine and brain.*

THE GITA THEREFORE POINTS OUT in its very first stanza the prime necessity to man of nightly introspection, that he may clearly discern which force—the good or the evil†—has won the daily battle. To live in harmony with God's plan, man must ask himself each night the ever pertinent question: "Gathered together on the sacred bodily tract—the field of good and evil actions—what did my opposing tendencies do? Which side won today in the ceaseless struggle? The crooked, tempting, evil tendencies, and the opposing forces of self-discipline and discrimination—come now, tell me, what did they do?"

The necessity for nightly introspection

The yogi, after each practice of concentrated meditation, asks his power of introspection: "Assembled in the region of consciousness in the cerebrospinal axis and on the field of the body's sensory activity, eager for battle, the mental sense-faculties that try to pull the consciousness outward, and the children of the soul's discriminative tendencies that seek to reclaim the inner kingdom—what did they? who won this day?"

The ordinary individual, like a skirmish-scarred beleaguered warrior, is all too conversant with the battles. But often his haphazard training has been wanting in an understanding of the battlefield, and of the science behind the attacks of the opposing forces. That knowledge would increase his victories, and lessen the bewildering defeats.

In the historical telling of the cause of the war of Kurukshetra, the noble sons of Pandu reigned virtuously over their kingdom, until King Duryodhana, the wicked reigning son of the blind King Dhritarashtra,

---

* "Neither shall they say, Lo here! or, lo there! for, behold, the kingdom of God is within you" (Luke 17:21).

† "Good" being that which expresses truth and virtue and attracts the consciousness to God; and "evil" being ignorance and delusion, that which repels the consciousness from God.

cleverly took away from the Pandavas their kingdom, and banished them into exile.

Symbolically, the kingdom of body and mind rightfully belongs to King Soul and his noble subjects of virtuous tendencies. But King Ego* and his kinsmen of wicked, ignoble tendencies cunningly usurp the throne. When King Soul arises to reclaim his territory, the body and mind become the battleground.†

How King Soul rules over his bodily kingdom, loses and then regains it, is the essence of the Gita.

THE ORGANIZATION OF THE BODILY KINGDOM: DWELLING PLACE OF THE SOUL

THE ORGANIZATION OF MAN'S body and mind reveals, in its detailed perfection, the presence of a divine plan. "Know ye not that ye are the temple of God, and that the Spirit of God dwelleth in you?"‡ The Spirit of God, His reflection in man, is the soul.

The soul makes its entry into matter as a spark of omnipotent life and consciousness within the nucleus formed by the union of the sperm and ovum. As the body develops, this original "seat of life" remains in the medulla oblongata. The medulla is therefore referred to as the gateway of life through which King Soul makes his triumphal entrance into the bodily kingdom. In this "seat of life" is the first expression of the incarnate soul's fine perceptions, imprinted with the karmically designed pattern of the various phases of life to come. By the miraculous power of *prana,* or intelligent creative life force, guided by the faculties of the soul, the zygote develops through the embryonic and foetal stages into a human body.

The creative faculties or instruments of the soul are astral and causal in nature. When the soul enters the primal cell of life, it is wearing two subtle bodies: a causal form of thoughtrons, which in turn is encased in an astral form of lifetrons.§ The causal body, so named

* In the commentary on this stanza, the epithets King Soul and King Ego are used in this and succeeding metaphors in the broader sense of their meaning, and not necessarily referring to their specific usage in the Gita allegory wherein Krishna is the soul and Bhishma, the ego.

† See Introduction.

‡ I Corinthians 3:16.

§ To translate the Sanskrit word *prana* I have coined the word "lifetrons." The Hindu scriptures mention *anu,* "atom"; the *paramanu,* "beyond the atom"—finer electronic energies; and *prana,* "creative lifetronic force." Atoms and electrons are blind forces; *prana* is inherently intelligent. The *prana* or lifetrons in the spermatozoa and ova, for example, guide embryonic development according to a karmic design.

because it is the cause of the other two soul encasements, consists of thirty-five ideas or thought-forces (which I have termed "thoughtrons") from which is formed the astral body of nineteen elements and the physical body of sixteen gross chemical elements.

The nineteen elements of the astral body are intelligence (*buddhi*); ego (*ahamkara*); feeling (*chitta*); mind (*manas,* sense consciousness); five instruments of knowledge (the subtle counterparts of the senses of sight, hearing, smell, taste, touch); five instruments of action (the mental correspondence for the abilities to procreate, excrete, talk, walk, and exercise manual skill); and five instruments of *prana* (empowering the performance of the crystallizing, assimilating, eliminating, metabolizing, and circulatory functions of the physical body).

These nineteen powers in the astral body are what build, maintain, and enliven the gross physical form. The centres of life and consciousness from which these powers function are the astral brain (or "thousand-petalled lotus" of light), and the astral cerebrospinal axis (or *sushumna*) containing six subtle centres or *chakras*. These are located, in relation to the physical body, in the medulla and in five centres in the spine: cervical, opposite the throat; dorsal, opposite the heart; lumbar, opposite the navel; sacral, opposite the generative organs; and coccygeal, at the base of the spine.

Coarser forces of the mind manifest in grosser structures of the body, but the fine forces of the soul—consciousness, intelligence, will, feeling—require the medulla and delicate tissues of the brain in which to dwell and through which to manifest.

God-identified soul vs. body-identified ego

In simplistic terms, the inner chambers of the palace of King Soul are in the subtle centres of superconsciousness, Krishna or Christ Consciousness (*Kutastha Chaitanya,* or Universal Consciousness), and Cosmic Consciousness. These centres are, respectively, in the medulla, frontal part of the brain between the eyebrows (seat of the single or spiritual eye), and at the top of the cerebrum (the throne of the soul, in the "thousand-petalled lotus"). In these states of consciousness, King Soul reigns supreme—the pure image of God in man. But when the soul descends into body consciousness, it comes under the influence of *maya* (cosmic delusion) and *avidya* (individual delusion or ignorance, which creates ego consciousness). When deluded and tempted by cosmic delusion or psychological Satan, the soul becomes the limited ego, which identifies itself with the body and the body's relatives and possessions.

The soul, as the ego, ascribes to itself all the limitations and circumscriptions of the body. Once so identified, the soul can no longer express its omnipresence, omniscience, and omnipotence. It imagines itself to be limited—just as a rich prince, wandering in a state of amnesia in the slums, might imagine himself to be a pauper. In this state of delusion, King Ego takes command of the bodily kingdom.

The soul consciousness can say with the awakened Christ in Jesus, "I and my Father are one." The deluded ego consciousness says, "I am the body; this is my family and name; these are my possessions." Though ego thinks it rules, it is in reality a prisoner of the body and mind, which in turn are pawns of the subtle machinations of Cosmic Nature.

In the macrocosm of creation a great battle between Spirit and the imperfect expressions of Nature is continuously going on. Everywhere on earth we are the witnesses of the silent struggle between perfection and imperfection. The flawless patterns of Spirit strive ceaselessly against the ugly distortions manifested by the universal delusory force of *maya,* the deceiving attribute of the "devil."* One power is consciously expressing all good; the other force is secretly at work to manifest evil.

Similarly in the microcosm: the human body and mind are veritable battlegrounds for the war between wisdom and the conscious delusive force manifesting as *avidya,* ignorance. Every spiritual aspirant, aiming to establish within himself the rule of King Soul, must defeat the rebels, King Ego and his powerful allies. And this is the battle that takes place on the field of Dharmakshetra Kurukshetra.

❖

THE DIVISIONS OF DHARMAKSHETRA KURUKSHETRA

THIS BODILY FIELD of activity and consciousness is actually divided into three parts, according to the manifestation of the three *gunas* or influencing qualities inherent in Prakriti or Cosmic Nature. The three *gunas* are (1) *sattva,* (2) *rajas,* (3) *tamas. Sattva,* the positive attribute, influences toward good—truth, purity, spirituality. *Tamas,* the negative attribute,

---

* It should not be imagined that the truth about *maya* was understood only by the *rishis.* The Old Testament prophets called *maya* by the name of Satan (lit., in Hebrew, "the adversary"). The Greek Testament, as an equivalent for Satan, uses *diabolos* or devil. Satan or *Maya* is the Cosmic Magician who produces multiplicity of forms to hide the One Formless Verity. In God's plan and play (*lila*), the sole function of Satan or *Maya* is to attempt to divert man from Spirit to matter, from Reality to unreality.

Christ describes *maya* picturesquely as a devil, a murderer, and a liar. "The devil...was a murderer from the beginning, and abode not in the truth, because there is no truth in him. When he speaketh a lie, he speaketh of his own: for he is a liar, and

influences toward darkness or evil—untruth, inertia, ignorance. *Rajas,* the neutral attribute, is the activating quality: working on *sattva* to suppress *tamas* or on *tamas* to suppress *sattva,* it creates constant activity and motion.

The first portion of the three divisions of the bodily field consists of the periphery of the body and includes the five instruments of knowledge (ear, skin, eye, tongue, nose) and the five instruments of action (the mouth, which produces speech; the hands and feet; and the organs of excretion and procreation). This outer surface of the human body is the scene of continuous sensory and motor activities. Hence, it is fittingly called Kurukshetra, the field of external action where all activities of the outer world are accomplished.

First portion of the field: the surface of the body

This place is the abode of *rajas* and *tamas*—predominantly *rajas.* That is, the gross atomic matter of the physical body is created by the action of *tamas* on the cosmic creative elemental vibrations of earth, water, fire, air, and ether, causing matter to appear in its recognizable five different varieties: solid, liquid, fiery, gaseous, and ethereal. Being the negative or dark quality of Nature, *tamas* is thus responsible for concealing the true subtle essence of matter under the cover of grossness, and of creating ignorance in man, the perceiver. The predominance of *rajas,* the activating quality, in this field of Kurukshetra is evidenced in the restlessly active nature of man and in the ever-changing character of the world he strives so ineffectually to control.

The second portion of the bodily field of action is the cerebrospinal axis with its six subtle centres of life and consciousness (medulla, cervical, dorsal, lumbar, sacral, and coccygeal), and its two magnetic poles of mind (*manas*) and intelligence (*buddhi*). Pulled toward grossness by *manas,* the subtle faculties in these centres emerge outwardly, projecting like the rays of a full-flamed gas light, keeping the sensory and motor faculties active in the human body. Retiring inwardly, pulled by *buddhi,* the subtle faculties are absorbed in

Second portion: centres of life and consciousness in the spine and brain

---

the father of it" (John 8:44). "The devil sinneth from the beginning. For this purpose the Son of God was manifested, that he might destroy the works of the devil" (I John 3:8). That is, the manifestation of Christ Consciousness, within man's own being, effortlessly destroys the illusions or "works of the devil."

Maya is "from the beginning" because of its structural inherence in the phenomenal worlds. These are ever in transitional flux as antithesis to the Divine Immutability. (*Autobiography of a Yogi*)

the cerebral region and become merged into one soul consciousness, like the flames of a lowered gas light. This cerebrospinal axis with the six subtle centres is called Dharmakshetra Kurukshetra, field of subtle energies and supramental forces as well as of grosser action.

The dominant attributes of Nature here are *rajas* and *sattva. Rajas,* acting on the five subtle elemental vibrations mentioned before, produces the powers of the five organs of action: manual skill (hands), locomotion (feet), speech, procreation, and excretion; it also produces the five specialized currents of *prana* that sustain the vital bodily functions. *Sattva,* acting on the five subtle vibratory elements, creates the subtle organs of perception—the powers that enliven the five physical sense instruments. The true subtle nature of matter, and the calmness, self-control, and other spiritual powers (to be discussed) experienced in the cerebrospinal centres by the deeply meditating yogi are also the effects of *sattva* in this field of Dharmakshetra Kurukshetra.

Third portion: abode of divine consciousness in the brain

The third portion of the bodily field is in the brain. It extends the breadth of the extension of ten fingers from the point in the middle of the eyebrows to the circle or ring spot on top of the head (the frontal fontanelle, a little opening in the skull that gradually closes after the birth of the infant) to the medulla. This place is called Dharmakshetra, and consists of the medulla and the frontal and middle upper parts of the cerebrum, with their astral centres of the spiritual eye and thousand-petalled lotus, and corresponding states of divine consciousness.

The literal meaning of *dharma* applies here in this use of Dharmakshetra: "that which upholds," from the Sanskrit root *dhṛi,* "to hold or support." This Dharmakshetra portion of the bodily field upholds, or is the cause of, man's being. The expressions of life and consciousness here in their finest forms are the source of the forces that create and sustain man (and his physical, astral, and causal bodies) and through which forces the soul ultimately quits the three bodies and returns to Spirit. Thus *sattva,* the pure and enlightening quality of Nature, is the predominating attribute in the territory of Dharmakshetra.

This Dharmakshetra is the abode of the soul. From this realm, the pure soul consciousness in its individualized or incarnate state is the creator and ruler of the threefold bodily kingdom. But when the soul is concentrated within rather than manifesting outwardly, it is one with the absolute Spirit, ensconced on the throne of ever new bliss within the thousand-petalled lotus, in a region beyond circumscription by the three bodies and their subtle causes, and untouched by the creative attributes and activities of Nature.

From the thousand-petalled lotus and the sun of the spiritual eye in the cerebral region of Dharmakshetra, the subtle energies and vibratory forces that create life and sustain it flow down through the subtle and gross centres in the cerebrospinal axis to enliven the body and its senses of perception and action. But in addition to being channels for subtle and gross life energies, the brain and cerebrospinal axis are also spoken of as "the seat of consciousness."

From Dharmakshetra, soul consciousness follows the descent of life energy. Through the spiritual eye, the sun of the soul sends "electric rays" of consciousness down through the cerebrospinal axis into the six subtle centres. Behind the energetic forces in each centre is an expression of the divine consciousness of the soul. Descending further into the familiar subconscious and conscious states, the consciousness enters the physical spinal cord and flows out into the afferent and efferent nerve branches in the plexuses, and on to the periphery of the body. This is how, during the conscious state, the outer surface of the human body is kept responsive to the stimuli of the senses, identifying the externalized consciousness of the soul, as ego, with the body.

The battle of Kurukshetra described in the Gita is therefore the effort required to win the battles on all three portions of the bodily field:

(1) *The material and moral struggle* between good and evil, right and wrong action on the sensory plain of Kurukshetra.

(2) *The psychological war* waged in yoga meditation on the cerebrospinal plain of Dharmakshetra Kurukshetra between the mental tendencies and inclinations of *manas* pulling the life and consciousness outward toward matter, and the pure discriminative tendencies of *buddhi* intelligence drawing the life and consciousness inward toward the soul.

The three battles: moral, psychological, and spiritual

(3) *The spiritual battle,* fought in deeper yoga meditation on the cerebral plain of Dharmakshetra to overcome the lower states of consciousness and dissolve all egoity and sense of separation from God in *samadhi,* the victorious union of soul and Spirit in cosmic consciousness.

The advanced yogi may rejoice in this blissful achievement of *samadhi* many times, yet find that he cannot maintain this union permanently. He is drawn down again into ego and body consciousness by his karma—effects of past actions—and by remnants of desires and attachments. But through each triumphant contact with Spirit, the soul consciousness becomes strengthened and more firmly in control of the bodily kingdom. At last, karma is overcome, the lower nature of desires and attachments is subdued, and ego is slain—the yogi attains *kaivalya,* liberation: permanent union with God.

The liberated yogi may then discard his three bodily encasements and remain a free soul in the ever-existing, ever-conscious, ever-new bliss of Omnipresent Spirit. Or if he chooses to descend again from his *samadhi* into the consciousness and activities of his body, he does so in the sublime state of *nirvikalpa samadhi*. In this highest state of externalized soul consciousness, he remains in his pure soul nature, untouched and unchanged, with no loss of God-perception, while he outwardly performs whatever exacting duties may be his portion in the fulfilment of the Lord's cosmic plan. This supernal state of being is the uncontested reign of King Soul over the bodily kingdom.

The Bodily Kingdom Under the Reign of King Soul

By applying illustrative designations to specific areas of the body, and figurative personalities and names to the activities that take place therein, the bodily kingdom and how it is affected by its "rulers" and "inhabitants" can be vividly portrayed. Figure 1, the illustration on page 17, represents the bodily kingdom under the rule of King Soul.

From the Royal Palace—the centres of superconsciousness, Christ consciousness, and cosmic consciousness in the cerebrum and medulla—King Soul bestows his beneficence of bliss, wisdom, and vitality throughout all the kingdom.

The King is assisted by his loyal subjects—the lordly discriminative tendencies—in the Parliamentary "House of Lords," the "upper house" or higher seats of consciousness in the medulla, cervical, and dorsal centres. These are under the influence of Prime Minister Discrimination—*buddhi,* the intelligence that reveals truth and is attracted to Spirit.

In the Parliamentary "House of Commons"—in the "lower house," or lower seats of consciousness in lumbar, sacral, and coccygeal centres—the common sensory powers of *manas* (mind or sense consciousness) become obedient to the wise influence of Prime Minister Discrimination and the lordly discriminative tendencies. The ordinary man is primarily under the influence of the sense-conscious mind

Bodily Kingdom as Ruled by King Soul

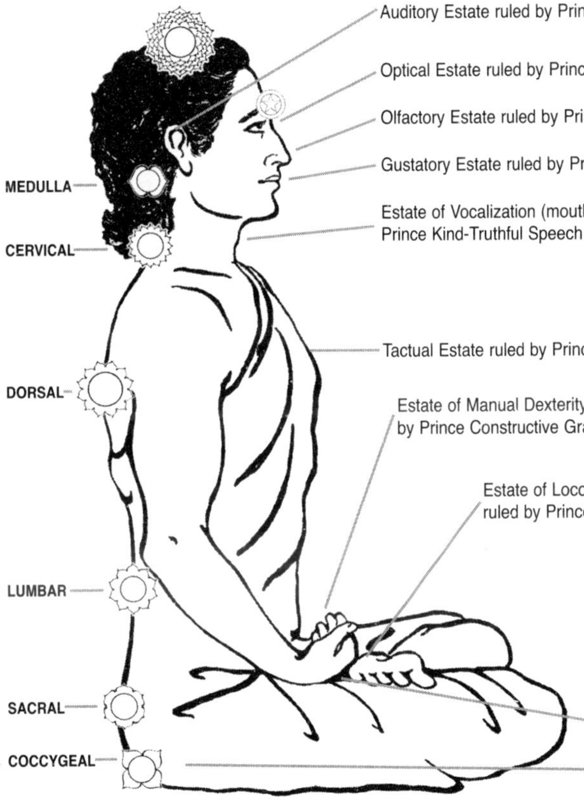

The Estates of the Ten Sense Princes: the five organs of knowledge and five organs of action with their princely powers:

Auditory Estate ruled by Prince Truth-Listener

Optical Estate ruled by Prince Noble Vision

Olfactory Estate ruled by Prince Pure Fragrance

Gustatory Estate ruled by Prince Right-Eating

Estate of Vocalization (mouth) ruled by Prince Kind-Truthful Speech

Tactual Estate ruled by Prince Peaceful Sensation

Estate of Manual Dexterity (hands) ruled by Prince Constructive Grasp

Estate of Locomotion (feet) ruled by Prince Virtuous Steps

Estate of Procreation (reproductive organs) ruled by Prince Controlled Creative Impulse

Estate of Elimination (anus) ruled by Prince Hygienic Purifier

The palace of King Soul: the centres of divine consciousness in the cerebrum and medulla

MEDULLA

CERVICAL

DORSAL

The Parliamentary "House of Lords" — lordly discriminative tendencies: in the "upper house" of consciousness in the medulla, cervical, and dorsal centres

LUMBAR

SACRAL

COCCYGEAL

The Parliamentary "House of Commons" — law-abiding common sensory powers: in the "lower house" of consciousness in the lumbar, sacral, and coccygeal centres

The tracts of the Bodily Kingdom: the coccygeal centre (with Nature's calm productive energy), and all the regions of flesh, including bones, marrow, organs, nerves, blood, veins, arteries, glands, muscles, skin

The freeborn Citizens of the Bodily Kingdom headed by Prime Minister Discrimination — the intelligent, vital, joyously contented citizenry of thoughts, will, feelings, trillions of cells, countless molecules, atoms, electrons, and units of creative life sparks — all live and work together in harmony, efficiency, and prosperity in the various regions of the body.

Figure 1

(*manas*), that power of repulsion from Spirit which obscures truth and links the consciousness to matter. Sense consciousness works through the three lower spinal centres. But when man's life comes under the guidance of the soul, the senses operating through the three lower centres become obedient to the discriminative tendencies in the upper cerebrospinal centres of consciousness. Thus it may be said that the worldly man lives in the lower centres of consciousness in the lumbar, sacral, and coccyx, with mind (*manas* or sense consciousness) predominating. The spiritual man lives in the upper centres of consciousness in the dorsal, cervical, and medulla, with discriminating intelligence (*buddhi,* or truth-revealing consciousness) predominating.

The physical tracts of the Bodily Kingdom are all kept vibrant under the rule of King Soul. These tracts include the coccygeal centre and all the regions of flesh: bones, marrow, organs, nerves, blood, arteries, veins, glands, muscles, skin. Of primary importance is the coccygeal centre. All the subtle powers of consciousness and life force at work in the higher centres come into physical manifestation through the channel of the coccygeal centre: Matter appears in five varieties (solid, liquid, gaseous, fiery, ethereal—from the action of the elemental vibrations of earth, water, fire, air, and ether in the coccygeal, sacral, lumbar, dorsal, and cervical centres) as the life force flows outward from the coccyx, creating and sustaining the tracts of flesh, bones, blood, and so forth. Under King Soul, the creative "Mother Nature" in the coccyx is calm and controlled, bringing health, beauty, and peace to the kingdom. At the command of the yogi in deep meditation, this creative force turns inward and flows back to its source in the thousand-petalled lotus, revealing the resplendent inner world of the divine forces and consciousness of the soul and Spirit. Yoga refers to this power flowing from the coccyx to Spirit as the awakened *kundalini*.

❖ *Health, beauty, and peace in the bodily kingdom* ❖

The physical tracts of the Bodily Kingdom all come under the influence of ten Sense Princes, sensory powers, which reside in their respective estates, or sensory organs. These are the five senses of *knowledge* (sight, sound, smell, taste, and touch) and five sensory powers of *execution* (the power of speech, the power of locomotion in the feet, the power of manual dexterity, the power of elimination in the anus and excretory muscles, and the power of reproduction in the genital organs).

The Sense Princes are all noble and good, in tune with the discriminative, harmonious powers of the soul. The senses thus serve their intended purpose of providing a means whereby the soul, incarnate as the pure consciousness in man, can experience and express itself in the world of matter as well as in the realm of Spirit.

The Citizens of the Bodily Kingdom are the beneficiaries of the blessings and wise guidance of King Soul, his Parliamentary Counsellors of discriminative and mental (sense) tendencies, the Prime Minister Discrimination, and the pure Sense Princes. The citizenry of thoughts, will, and feelings are wise, constructive, peaceful, and happy. The masses of conscious, intelligent labourers of cells, molecules, atoms, electrons, and units of creative life sparks (lifetrons, *prana*) are vital, harmonious, efficient.

During the rule of King Soul, all laws regarding the health, the mental efficiency, and the spiritual education of the thoughts, will, feelings, and intelligent cellular inhabitants of the bodily kingdom are carried on under the supreme guidance of wisdom. As a result, happiness, health, prosperity, peace, discrimination, efficiency, and intuitive guidance pervade the bodily kingdom—a pure realm of light and bliss!

THE BODILY KINGDOM UNDER THE REIGN OF KING EGO

FIGURE 2, THE ILLUSTRATION on page 20, represents man's nature when it is ruled by King Ego, the tool of the Cosmic Delusory Force that induces man to believe himself separate from God.

Figure 2 therefore represents a vastly different picture from that of Figure 1; the second figure illustrates the changes in the bodily kingdom when it has been usurped by King Ego and his rebels. The ego is called the pseudosoul, for it imitates the authority of King Soul and tries to dominate the entire bodily kingdom. But the Usurper can never gain entry to the palatial inner chambers of superconsciousness, Christ consciousness, and cosmic consciousness. Ego can rule only the conscious and subconscious states of man. The inwardly turned consciousness in the medullary centre is the soul's superconsciousness. Flowing outward into the subconscious and conscious states in the brain and spine, and becoming identified with the body instead of with Spirit, the consciousness as King Ego begins its desultory reign.

The lower chamber of consciousness and subconsciousness of the brain under King Ego is no longer ruled by the peaceful, all-knowing, all-powerful soul, but becomes the home of the ever-restless, proud, ignorant, body-limited weakling—the rebel Ego. The Prime Minister Ignorance, instead of Discrimination, wields its influential power.

Bodily Kingdom as Ruled by Rebel King Ego

The palace of dictatorial Rebel King Ego: centre of outward-turned consciousness in the medulla, and the conscious and subconscious body-identified states of being in the brain and spinal plexuses

The Ministry: ministers of desires, emotions, habits, and undisciplined sense inclinations under Prime Minister Ignorance. (The doors of the Parliamentary "House of Lords" are closed, and the lordly discriminative tendencies in the "upper house" of the medulla, cervical, and dorsal centres are rendered powerless. The common sensory powers in the "House of Commons," the "lower house" of the lumbar, sacral, and coccygeal centres, are influenced by Prime Minister Ignorance to support the base sense inclinations of King Ego.)

The tracts of the Bodily Kingdom: the coccygeal centre with Nature's restless sense-enslaved energy, and the various tracts of bones, marrow, organs, nerves, blood, veins, arteries, glands, muscles, skin

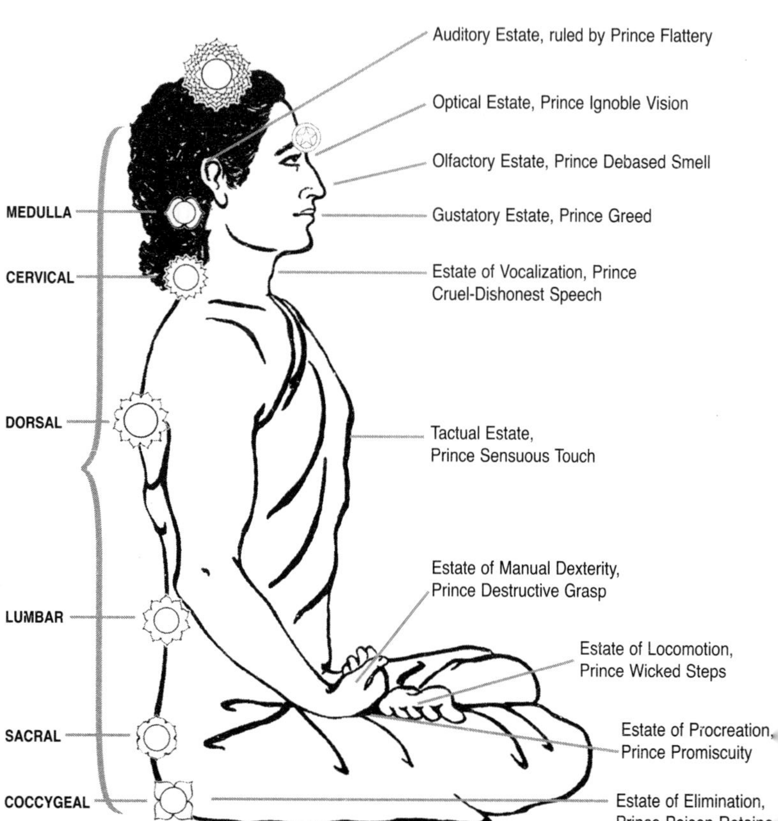

Enslaved citizens of the Bodily Kingdom: thoughts, will, feelings, cells, molecules, atoms, electrons, life sparks—all working in unnatural and inharmonious conditions to appease King Ego and his henchmen, and in consequence, suffering irritation, sickness, inefficiency.

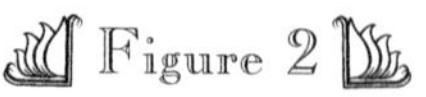
Figure 2

King Ego is a dictator; he only wants counsellors who are yes-men, and who will do his bidding to keep the bodily kingdom away from King Soul. Ego's ministers are material desires, emotions, habits, and undisciplined sense inclinations under Prime Minister Ignorance. These insurgents close the doors of the Parliamentary "House of Lords," and thereby render powerless the lordly discriminative tendencies in the "upper house" of the medulla, cervical, and dorsal centres. The common sensory powers in the "House of Commons," the "lower house" of the lumbar, sacral, and coccygeal centres, that were obedient and loyal to their former King Soul and Prime Minister Discrimination, are influenced by Prime Minister Ignorance to support instead the base sense inclinations of King Ego. That is, when the discriminative intelligence (*buddhi*) that reveals truth and is attracted to Spirit is overpowered by ego and the accompanying influence of ignorance (*maya* and *avidya*), then sense consciousness (mind, *manas*) predominates—*manas* being the power of repulsion from Spirit which obscures truth and links consciousness to matter.

The physical tracts of the bodily kingdom under King Ego are often fallow and unhealthy from epidemics of diseases and premature aging that spread over the realm. In the main tract—the coccygeal centre—creative "Mother Nature" is constantly agitated, her formative life energy abused and dissipated by the ungoverned demands of the senses.

The Sense Princes are body-identified pleasure-seekers, indulgent and self-centred. Influenced by ignorance, they fall into evil ways and self-destructive habits.

The citizenry of thoughts, will, feelings, become negative, limited, jaded, unhappy; the intelligent workers of cells and atomic and subatomic units of life become disorganized, inefficient, debilitated. Under the Ego regime, with Prime Minister Ignorance in charge, all laws are broken that would lead to the well-being of the mental and cellular citizens in man's kingdom. It is a realm of darkness fraught with many fears, uncertainties, and miseries to counteract every brief moment of pleasure.

COMPARISON OF THE SENSES AS RULED BY THE SOUL AND AS RULED BY THE EGO

The Optical Estate: When Prince Noble Vision is in charge of the optical estate, man sees only the good in everything. Good objects, nature's wonders, exquisite scenery, holy faces, spiritual expressions of art, saintly pictures, are photographed as sensations; their motion pictures are shown before the mental inhabitants in the brain (thoughts, will, and feelings) for their instruction, enjoyment, and peace.

The motion pictures of Ego's regime, promoted by Prince Ignoble Vision, give instruction in scenes of conflicts, and ugly places; luring, evil-awakening faces, and sense-rousing art; sensuous, materialistic suggestions are poured into the brain to degrade the natural good taste of all the intelligent cells and thoughts.

Ego's attraction to beautiful objects and faces leads to material attachments and sensual indulgences. The soul perceives in all beauty the expression of Divine Beauty and feels a blissful expansion of consciousness and love through that experience.

The Auditory Estate: During the Soul regime, the auditory estate is ruled by Prince Truth-Listener; the sense of hearing loves the voices of beneficial truth, which guide man's thoughts to the goal of wisdom.

Under the Ego regime, Prince Flattery prefers to hear nothing but artificially sweetened, poisonous untruths, leading the thoughts to a false consciousness of self-sufficiency and self-importance, and to a conviction that evil deeds carry no inherent punishment. Witness the big and little despots of this world!

Sweet words of sincere praise are desirable when they encourage a person to right action. Flattery, or false words, however, is pernicious—serving, as it often does, to hide psychological wounds, which then fester and poison man's whole nature. Flattery is like poisoned honey.

The voice of one's own thoughts, furthermore, tends often to insulate him from reality. He excuses his faults, and hides so far as possible the serious psychological tumors within him, instead of exposing them to the healing knife of analysis and self-discipline. Flattery from others and the comforting whispers of his own rationalizing thoughts strike sweetly on his sense of hearing.

Human wisdom is often carried a prisoner in the hands of poisonous flattering words. Many persons willingly sacrifice their time, money, health, reputation, and character just to receive constantly the honeyed praise of "parasitic" friends. In fact, most people prefer flattery to intelligent criticism. They indignantly deny a shred of truth to any analysis that reveals them in an unfavourable light. Often out of sheer egoistic spite against just criticism, persons readily dash themselves on the rocks of misbehaviour. Numerous are those who have perished by not listening to the stern words of right warning, and by embracing instead the easygoing philosophy of wicked associates. Better it is to live in hades with one harsh-speaking wise man than to dwell in heaven with ten sweet-mouthed liars! Fools turn a heaven into hades; a wise man transforms any hades into a heaven.

Many benefits accrue to those who listen quietly to kind criticism. Admirable the man who is able to receive harsh but true criticism, hearing it with a sincere smile and a sense of gratitude that someone is taking the trouble of trying to improve him. Few are already perfect! Without necessarily admitting one's faults to others, one should silently correct himself when justly criticized.

A saint I once knew had a sharp-tongued friend who employed most of his time in criticizing the master. One day a disciple of the saint arrived at the hermitage with momentous news.

"Master," he cried exultantly, "your enemy—the constant fault-finder—is dead!"

"Oh, I feel helpless!" the saint's eyes filled with tears. "I am heartbroken; my best spiritual critic is gone!"

One should ask himself, therefore, on many introspective nights: "How have I reacted today to mild or harsh criticism? Have I rejected the words of my associates without first considering the possibility that in them was much, or even a little, truth?"

It is not only sweet words of flattery that the ego loves to hear, but also praise for accomplishments and promises of devotion from loved ones. But the delusion here is that praise for name and fame in this world is fickle and evanescent, and promises of everlasting love come from the "must-die" lips of mortals; even the sweet voices of mothers at last become silent. All these will be buried in the grave of oblivion, unless in their echo one hears—as does the soul—the Divine Lover's voice, and recognizes therein His presence, His love, His approbation.

The Olfactory Estate: Under Soul's guidance, Prince Pure Fragrance loves to entertain with the natural scents of flowers and pure air; devotion-arousing temple incense; and the aroma of health-producing, savoury foods. Counselled by Prince Debased Smell, however, the thoughts and cells crave and indulge in heavy, sensuous perfumes; and their appetite is aroused by the smell of unhealthful, malnutritious, rich, or too-spicy foods. When the sense of smell is enslaved, it loses its natural attraction to simple foods that are good for the body, and develops a special attachment to the odours of meats, rich desserts, denatured preparations—foods that are injurious to the body.

Debased Smell may even find enjoyable the noxious odours of such evils as alcohol and cigarette smoke. When the thoughts and olfactory cells are coarsened and made less sensitive by Prince Debased Smell, the small olfactory protuberance in the middle of man's face can lead the body to greed and indulgences that result in ill health and lack of mental peace. Depending, therefore, on the pure or debased nature of the olfactory sense, one is either wise or ill-advised to adopt the old adage, "Follow your nose."

The Gustatory Estate: Under Soul's rule, Prince Right-Eating governs the gustatory estate. Guided by natural attraction, he supplies the right foods possessing all necessary elements, especially fresh raw fruits and vegetables with natural flavours and undestroyed vitamins. These natural foods nourish the body cells, helping to make them immune to disease, and aiding in preserving their youth and vitality.

Under the Ego regime, Prince Greed creates an unnatural craving for overcooked, devitalized, and injurious foods. The taste thoughts and body cells become vitiated, subject to indigestion and sickness.

Prince Greed also tempts man to eat more food than is necessary for health. Even as children, most human beings are tempted by taste-lures to come out of the protective entrenchment of right-eating habits. They find themselves shot by the bullets of indigestion; these "wounds," if chronically repeated, often develop into serious diseases later in life. Every pound of needless flesh puts an additional load on the heart, which must then pump its blood through needless territory. Obese men and women are not long-lived—a fact attested to by insurance companies.

Millions of people in each generation lose their daily battle with greed; they pass their lives as prisoners of disease, and die prematurely. In ordinary men, the sense of taste with its evil army of memories of uncontrolled eating, hasty swallowing, and other bad habits is daily victorious over the good inward soldiers whose counsel is ignored—the counsel of moderation, right selection of foods for a balanced diet, proper mastication, and so forth.

The man who allows the armies of greed to advance little by little over the territory of his proper dietary habits gradually finds himself surrounded by the enemy of disease. Morning, noon, and evening, when savory delicacies are spread before man's eyes, Prince Greed aims to lure him into trouble by sending psychological spies to delude his powers of self-control by whispering: "Eat a little more today; never mind what will happen to you one year hence." "Eat more today; you can quit overeating tomorrow." "Never mind yesterday's little warning of indigestion: just think how delicious tonight's dinner is!" "Eat today; never mind about tomorrow; who knows anything certain about tomorrow? Why then worry about it?"

Every time Prince Greed defeats a man, it leaves some slight mark of damage in the bodily kingdom, a damage that gradually becomes irreparable and ends in death.

Every day, before each meal, the aspirant to God-realization should say to himself: "Prince Greed and his taste-spies have been engaged in battle for a long time with Prince Right-Eating; which side has been winning?" If a man finds that Greed has been the victor, he should summon his armies of self-control, train them in spiritual resistance, and command them to show themselves worthy soldiers before the enemy, Greed, who relentlessly advances in hope of man's destruction. The sincere beginner in the spiritual path never eats without first reflecting that his action is reinforcing the power of one, or the other, inward army. One must weep, while the other rejoices! One is man's friend; the other, his enemy.

The Tactual Estate: Under the Soul regime, the bodily sense of touch as Prince Peaceful Sensation loves moderation in climate, food, and the real necessities of life. He loves the warmth of sun and the sensation of a cool breeze. Healthy and wholesome bodily habits—promptness, cleanliness, alertness, and activity—mathematically result in peace. Being consistently evenminded, Prince Peaceful Sensation is not affected or disturbed by extremes of heat and cold, hard and soft, that which is irritating and that which is soothing, that which is comfortable and that which is uncomfortable. He is constantly caressed by inner peace—an insulation against the friction of a rough world.

Under Ego's control, however, Prince Sensuous Touch makes the body attached to comforts and luxuries, and to sensuous feelings that rouse sexual desire. Anything not soothing causes great agitation in the thoughts and cells, and rouses fear of hurts and exertion. The body takes pleasure in idleness, lethargy, the oblivion of too much sleep. Prince Sensuous Touch makes the thoughts restless and the body cells nervous, lazy, sickly, and inert.

The Estate of Vocalization: Under Soul's rule, Prince Kind-Truthful Speech entertains the cells and thoughts with the magic of harmony and of euphonious words. Soul-awakening songs, peace-producing, heart-melting speech, vital words of truth, educate and inspire the thoughts and the cell-inhabitants of the body toward divine activities for the elevation of one's self and others.

Under the Ego regime, Prince Cruel-Dishonest Speech creates ugly vibrations by belching out fires of inharmonies, bombarding with cannons of cruel, angry, or vengeful words the castles of peace, friendship, and love—all those structures that might protect the happiness of the mental and cellular inhabitants in the bodily kingdom.

There is tremendous creative power behind the words of one who always speaks truth. But he must also be in attunement with the pure heart quality of feeling and the soul quality of wisdom to know in any given instance "What is truth?"—a question that even Jesus refused to answer, knowing that the one who questioned him would not understand. Facts, which can be hurtful, are not always truth, which brings only blessings. For example, the voicing of negative truths should usually be avoided. A man of broad sympathies does not refer needlessly to a cripple's infirmity or to a liar's unsavory reputation. Because there is indeed truth in such words is no excuse, in ordinary circumstances, for uttering them; only sadistic persons under the egoistic Prince Cruel-Dishonest Speech enjoy shooting arrows into the Achilles' heel or point of vulnerability that is present, in one form or another, in every human being.

It is also wrong to tell a man of his faults if he has not sought such criticism. And it is despicable to gossip and spread unkind rumours.

The voice is a valuable God-given power to be used to soothe, comfort, instruct, and convey wisdom and love—a veritable alchemist that removes taint by the magic of its vocalized potions.

The Estate of Manual Dexterity: Under Soul's rule, the instruments of manual action, the hands, guided by Prince Constructive Grasp, reach out for beneficial things, for constructive work and service, for doing good deeds and sharing with others, and for soothing and healing. Under Ego's rule, the hands are busy, almost automatically, in performing misdeeds—grasping for more possessions, taking more than one's share, thieving, murdering, striking out in anger or revenge—all actions that make for the inharmony and ruin of the inhabitants of the bodily kingdom. Prince Destructive Grasp would seem to need a hundred hands to satisfy his avarice, while Prince Constructive Grasp makes the world, as well as the bodily kingdom, a better place with only two.

The Estate of Locomotion: Under Soul's control, the instruments of motion, the human feet, seek places of inspiration—temples, spiritual services, good entertainments, nature's scenic acres, and the company of worthwhile friends and holy people. Prince Virtuous Steps also loves wholesome exercise to invigorate the cellular citizens of the body, and never shirks his responsibility to provide the necessary mobility for the other noble princes.

Under Ego's rule, the bodily footsteps are urged toward places of noxious amusements—gambling dens, bars, liquor shops, suggestive movies—and to evil, rowdy, distracting company. Prince Wicked Steps often becomes lazy and lethargic. When the power of motion refuses to move, the rest of the Princes and bodily inhabitants are also denied mobility.

The Estate of Elimination: Under Soul's rule, Prince Hygienic Purifier keeps all excretory muscles functioning properly to eliminate poisons from the system. Under Ego's rule, Prince Poison Retainer is sluggish and the muscular instruments of healthy action become weak and diseased, retaining poisons that infect the bodily kingdom.

The Estate of Procreation: Under Soul's rule, Prince Controlled Creative Impulse rightly guides the sex inclination, enabling parents to bring on earth, by the law of attraction, other noble spiritual human beings like themselves, who will by example guide matter-entangled souls, inspiring them to retrace their footsteps toward spiritual blessedness.

Under Soul's guidance, the sex impulse in man may also be transmuted into the creation—on a purely spiritual plane—of noble ideas, of artistic masterpieces, of soul-revolutionizing books.

Under the Ego regime, Prince Promiscuity lives in unbridled passion. The bodily kingdom is kept constantly excited and restless with morbid impulses of sex temptation. The insatiable lust imparted to the thought-citizens makes them sense slaves, subject to moodiness, depression, irritability; the cellular inhabitants suffer debility, ill health, and premature old age and death.

At the beginning of the cycle of manifested creation, God materialized all forms by direct, special, creative command: the "Word,"* or cosmic creative vibration of *Aum* (*Om*), with its manifest powers of creation, preservation, and dissolution. God endowed man, made in His omnipotent image, with this same creative power. But Adam and Eve (symbolic of the first pairs of human beings), yielding to touch-temptation, lost the power of "immaculate creation" by which they had been able to clothe all their mental pictures with energy and life, thus materializing children from the ether (bringing them into manifestation from the ideational world), even as gods.

Man and woman, instead of seeking emancipation in God through soul unity, sought satisfaction through the flesh. The seed of the original error of "Adam and Eve" remains in all human beings as the first temptation of the flesh against the immaculate laws of Spirit ("touch not the tree in the centre of the garden!"). Each individual since that dim era has had to engage his soul in battle with the cosmically present temptation of sex. The creator in man has become a dictatorial creature.

Uncontrolled sex instinct keeps man in body consciousness

The sex impulse is the single most physically magnetic power that pulls the life and consciousness down from Spirit in the higher centres in the brain, out through the coccygeal centre into matter and body consciousness. The beginner in yoga meditation experiences all too definitely how grounded he is by the stubborn attachment of his life and energy to the body, sometimes without realizing that it is his uncontrolled thoughts and acts of sex that are primarily responsible for his earthbound condition. The seeker after Self-realization is therefore urged by yoga to take command of this rebel force: married couples should practise moderation, with love and friendship predominating; the unmarried should abide by the pure laws of celibacy—in thought as well as in act.

They are blessed who are victorious over the sexual instinct. Because suppression may only increase one's difficulties, yoga teaches sublimation. The average person can be free of temptation by avoiding the company, environments, books, movies, that stimulate sex thoughts; and by training the armies of self-control, by seeking good company, by proper diet (eating little or no meat and taking more

* "In the beginning was the Word, and the Word was with God, and the Word was God.... All things were made by him; and without him was not any thing made that was made" (John 1:1, 3).

fresh fruits and vegetables), by exercising regularly, by engaging in creative activities such as art, invention, writing. Above all, by keeping the thoughts on the wonder, peace, and all-satisfying love of God, the insatiable desire for the pleasure of sex is transmuted by the divine love and ecstatic joy experienced in deep meditation.

The bravest of prophets dare to intrude their often unwelcome voices into the realm of this natural instinct to remind of the scriptural injunctions against promiscuity, adultery, aberrant behaviour—indulgences the modern world calls "free love." Slavery to sex is seldom based on love, and it is never "free." Condemnation by religious moralists, however, does little more than create feelings of guilt in the so-called "sinner"; or cause him either to turn against religion or, more commonly, to justify his behaviour by associating with those of comparable standards—the availability of whom is never lacking.

Morality, like a chameleon, tends to take on the colour of the circumambient society; but the inscrutable laws of Nature, through which God upholds His creation, are ever unaltered by man's determinations. The simple fact is, man enslaves himself in bonds of karmic fetters whenever he transgresses any sacred code of nature; and then when suffering results, he woefully cries, "Why me, Lord?" Understanding is the art of untying the Gordian knots bound by ignorance. Thus yoga teaches why man, Nature's highest achievement, should have respect for her sacred mode of procreation, and, correspondingly, why it should not be abused.

Harmonizing the masculine and feminine natures

Consider, as a start, that every being is in essence a soul, made in the image of God—neither man nor woman, but in the embodied state possessing both a masculine and a feminine nature. The masculine tendency manifests in the powers of discrimination, self-control, exacting judgement—all the qualities of reason or intellect. The emotional element in every being, consisting of the tenderness of love, sympathy, kindness, mercy—all the qualities of feeling—constitute the feminine nature. Unless these two phases are properly united and harmonized, spiritual procreation, whose offspring is permanent peace, is impossible. Spiritual procreation requires the proper "mating"—within oneself—of the sterner masculine qualities with the softer feminine nature; it results in, and manifests in, the birth and expression of true knowledge and total Self-contentment. In one who has attained Self-realization, this perfect union has been achieved. In the ordinary man, the imbalance makes him dissatisfied and restless. The attraction between man and woman, when based on true love and not sensual obsession, is the effort of the soul to regain its normal harmony. This gives birth to the oft abused argument proclaiming the necessity to seek and find one's soul mate. But all too frequently attraction for the wrong reasons results instead in cell mates!

Karmic patterns created by a person's past actions—mental and physical—determine the birth of that person's soul in either a male or female body. The sexless soul has experienced both forms throughout its many incarnations—one good reason to respect the equality and virtues of both these expressions of God. Marriage between man and woman is for the purpose of each partner helping to uplift the other in a commitment of divine friendship, love, and loyalty that will move both souls closer to their true nature in the incarnation they share. And it further provides the medium and right environment to invite other souls seeking rebirth on earth to come into the circle of their expanding love.

Whether one seeks soul harmony through right marriage or a celibate life, the culmination will be finally achieved by union with God: that is, the reunion of a man or a woman—both of which are the products of Nature, the negative or feminine aspect—with the Positive Force, the one true Beloved of all lovelorn souls, Spirit.

MANY PSYCHOLOGICAL SKIRMISHES occur before King Soul reigns supreme, or before King Ego gains total control of the bodily kingdom.

No matter how many times in one life or in many incarnations King Ego appears to be in complete domination of the bodily kingdom, he cannot rule for eternity. But if King Soul once gets firm control of man's kingdom, he rules forever. This is owing to the blessed truth that sin and ignorance are only temporary veils of the soul; wisdom and bliss are its essential nature. Although a man may be a sinner for a time, it is impossible for him to be a sinner forever or to suffer everlasting perdition. Made as man is in the image of God, he may seemingly deface that image, through the human misuse of free choice, but the soot of ignorance cannot destroy the immortal stamp of God in man.

Ego cannot rule forever

Because the divine image in man can never be fully hidden, even the darkest kingdom has some illuminating rays of virtue. By introspecting on the infallible criteria suggested by the comparison of the two analogous illustrations under discussion, the devotee should analyze his daily mental and physical actions to determine just how much of his life is ruled by the ego's ignorance (delusion) and body consciousness, and how much he is able to express of the soul's wisdom and divine nature.

HABIT VERSUS DISCRIMINATIVE FREE CHOICE

WHETHER AN ACTION is in tune with the discriminating soul or with the deluded ego depends on the decision a man makes, consciously or unconsciously, when that action is initiated.

Actions of each human being are determined in several ways. A man may be guided by free choice, or by the influence of prenatal karmic tendencies (the habits and effects of actions carried over from past lives), or by the suggestions of postnatal habits, or by environmental vibrations.

The great paradoxes and anomalies of life observed as deep contrasts between rich unhealthy persons, for instance, and poor healthy persons; some living a long life, some dying at an early age; some who succeed at everything, some who fail repeatedly; persons who are naturally peaceful, and those who are chronically choleric—all are the results of their own prenatal and postnatal actions. A wicked man, an artist, a businessman, a dogmatist, an intellectual, a talkative do-nothing, a man of Self-realization, are all self-made. Very few human beings, however, use exclusively their God-given power of free choice in making themselves the persons they want to be. The majority allow their characteristics to change passively and desultorily in various, undirected ways, according to the patterns of passing moods engendered by specific environments, or according to the helpful or sinister influences of prenatal and postnatal habits.

Prenatal habits establish themselves in the trenches of the subconscious mind and try to influence the discriminative power of the conscious mind. I believe that any man may become an ideal person if his prenatal habits, under the guise of heredity, are not permitted to influence his divine power of free choice.

Every person should be able to act freely, guided only by the highest wisdom, uninfluenced by any undesirable prenatal habit. The influence of prenatal good habits is not harmful, of course, but it is best to perform good actions chiefly through the inspiration of the present free choice of the soul.

Similarly, one should not allow his good judgement to be enslaved by bad habits acquired in this life. Most people do not know the consequences of acting under the influence of bad habits until they suffer excruciating bodily pain or undergo heartbreaking sorrow. It is pain and sorrow that impel man—all too late—to inquire into the cause of his present condition.

Very seldom does man realize that his health, success, and wisdom depend in great part on the issue of the battle between his good and bad habits. He who would establish within himself the rule of the soul must not allow the bodily kingdom to be occupied by bad habits. All such evils must be banished by training diverse good habits in the art of victorious psychological warfare.

The soldiers of bad habits, ill health, and negativeness become invigorated by any actual performance by man of a bad action; whereas the soldiers of good habits are happily stimulated by any performance of a good action. Bad habits must not, therefore, be fed with bad actions. They should be starved out by self-control; and good habits strengthened with the nourishing food of good actions.

No action, inner or outer, is possible without the energizing power of will. Will power is that which changes thought into energy.* Man is endowed with free will and should not abdicate his freedom of choice and action. To ensure right action, the challenge to the seeker after Self-realization is to overcome prenatal and postnatal bad habits with good habits, and to increase actions that are initiated solely by wisdom-guided free choice, emancipated from all karmic, habitual, and environmental influences.

---

* Among modern scientists, Nobel laureate Sir John Eccles has confirmed the relationship of will to action in human beings. A 1983 article in the *Dallas Times-Herald* reported: "Sir John Eccles knows from his research that when you move a finger, that apparently simple motion is the culmination of millions of unutterably complex chemical and electrical interactions, occurring within milliseconds in neatly ordered sequence in your brain. That is what won him a Nobel prize in 1963: his pioneering exploration of the chemical ways that nerve cells transmit instructions from one to another.

"Recent research has shown that the entire process of moving that finger, what Eccles called 'the firing mechanism,' starts in a region at the top of the brain, called the supplementary motor area, he said. 'But that still doesn't answer the primary question: How is the firing mechanism initiated?'

"Further research offered a clue. If the subject of an experiment did not actually move his finger at all, but merely thought about moving it, detectors indicated that his supplementary motor area was firing, although the motor cortex of the brain, which controls the movement of the muscles themselves, was not....'So,' Eccles said triumphantly, 'the supplementary motor area is fired by intention. The mind is working on the brain. Thought does cause brain cells to fire.'

"The physiology of movement proves to Eccles that we have freedom of will, that something outside of a purely mechanical process is involved in our actions. 'You have the mental ability to decide to act,' he said. 'If you can do it on an elementary level—moving a finger—it follows that you can do it on more complex levels of human action and interaction.'" *(Publisher's Note)*

TRANSMUTING DESIRES

INEXTRICABLY LINKED to the senses and habits is desire. The saints call this foe "man's greatest enemy," because it is desire that ties the soul to endless rounds of rebirths in the realm of delusion.

So another important battle the soul must win consists in rising above all personal desires—whether for money, mental power, physical health, possessions, name, fame—whatever binds the soul to matter and makes the consciousness forgetful of God.

Desirelessness does not mean an ambitionless existence. It means to work for the highest and noblest goals without attachment. The desire to destroy poverty and ill-health, for example, is a laudable one, and to be encouraged. But, after winning riches and health, one must still rise above all material conditions of the body to ultimately reach Spirit.

The modern trend is to use religion and God as "baits" for mere health, prosperity, and material happiness. One should seek God first, last, and all the time, not for His gifts, but as one's ultimate Aim. Then he will find, in the abundance of God's love, all else for which he longs. "But seek ye first the kingdom of God, and His righteousness; and all these things shall be added unto you."* In oneness with God, man finds the satisfaction of the heart's every desire.

As an awakened "son of God," man may rightfully demand of his loving Father health, prosperity, or anything else needful. Before discovering God, people usually want the toys of material things; after finding Him, however, even the greatest material desires become insipid—not through indifference, but through comparison with the all-satisfying, all desire-quenching God-Bliss. Many people unsuccessfully strive for a material goal all their lives, failing to realize that if they had put forth one-tenth of the concentration used in seeking worldly things into an effort to find God first, they could then have had fulfilments of not only *some,* but *all* of their hearts' desires.

Seeking God wholeheartedly does not imply nor excuse neglect of the various physical and worldly battles of life. As a casket of even the most brilliant jewels cannot be seen in the dark, so the presence of God cannot be felt in the darkness of spiritual ignorance, mental inharmony, or overpowering disease. The spiritual aspirant therefore learns to conquer in *all* battles in order to make the kingdom of life free from every cause of darkness, so that God's perfect presence therein may be perceived.

---

* Matthew 6:33.

Maintaining Health in the Bodily Kingdom

THEREFORE, THE NEXT BATTLE to be mentioned is one's duty to maintain the guardian forces of health in the bodily kingdom. Material success, mental efficiency, the practise of meditation for attaining Self-realization—all are made easier if the body is not a hindrance because of debility or illness.

To possess health, man should live in such a hygienic way as to make his body immune to disease. An ideal diet should generally consist chiefly of fruits, vegetables, grains, milk and milk products. He should exercise and have plenty of fresh air and sunshine; practice self-control of the senses; and employ techniques to relax body and mind. Overindulgence in the senses (especially sex), overeating, wrong eating, lack of exercise, lack of fresh air, lack of sunshine, lack of cleanliness, habitual worry, nervousness and stress, ungoverned emotions—all help to destroy the body's natural immunity to disease.

Sluggish circulation often culminates in poisonous deposits in the system. By exercise and fresh air, the tissues, cells, and red and white corpuscles become charged with fresh *prana*-laden oxygen. The system of Energization Exercises, which I discovered and developed in 1916, is a most beneficial, simple, and nonstrenuous method for recharging the body consciously with life-giving *prana*. This stimulation and electrification of the tissues, cells, and blood helps to immunize them against disease.

When vitality is low—that is, when the life force in the body is insufficient or not functioning properly—the body becomes susceptible to invasion of all kinds of diseases and disorders. The life force will perform efficiently when kept replenished and nourished with right health habits as mentioned above, and also with the necessary reinforcement of good character, positive thoughts, right living, and right meditation.

Raising the Level of Consciousness

A MAN IS NOT YET a master if he is still engaged in the ordinary life-battles—those of sensory temptations, desires, habits; identification with the physiology and limitations of the body; restlessness of mental doubts and complexes; and soul ignorance. His perceptions are limited, and include consciousness of bodily weight and other physiological conditions; of internal sensations, arising from activities of the inner organs and of the breath within the body; of sensations of touch, smell, taste, hearing, and sight; of hunger, thirst, pain, passion, attachment, sleepiness, fatigue, wakefulness; and of his mental powers of reasoning, feeling, and willing. The consciousness of this ordinary man is subject to fears about death, poverty, disease, and innumerable other ills. He is bound by attachments to name, social standing, family, race, and possessions.

Spiritually, the ordinary man cannot feel his presence beyond the body except in his imagination. In subconsciousness he sleeps, dreams, and can move in an unreal world of fanciful imaginings. By flights of fancy he can move through the stars and vast spaces, but only in mind; such thoughts do not belong to the domain of outer reality.

In short, the average human being is conscious only of his body and mind and of their outer connections. He remains hypnotized by the world delusions (expressed in many ways in ancient and present-day literature) which reinforce his tacit assumption that he is a finite and limited creature.

Having descended from omnipresent Spirit to the little body, and having become identified with physical imperfections, the soul appears to lose its omnipresent, perfect status; it must battle to overcome all the limitations of the physical world. The soul must dissolve all sense of identification with duality—both the good and the bad conditions that limit the body and all material life. For instance, disease is a state of sailing the boat of life over stormy seas. Health is a state of skimming over a gently stirred Sea of Being. Wisdom is the state of realizing one's native soul-independence of all matter; no longer clinging to the fleshly boat of a *maya*-tossed surface existence, the liberated consciousness of man plunges boldly into the Sea of Spirit.

So long as man concentrates wholly on the changing waves of the alternates of this world of relativity, so long will he forget to reidentify himself with the underlying changeless sea of all-protecting Spirit. Only in soul-realization does he get away from the superficial flux and attain the changeless state: one in which health and disease, life and death, pleasure and pain, and all pairs of opposites appear merely as waves of change, rising and falling on the ocean-bosom of Changelessness.

Identification of the consciousness with the alternating waves of change is known as *restlessness;* identity with Changelessness is *calmness.* The conquest of the soul's calmness over the ego's restlessness advances in four stages: (1) Always restless, never calm. (2) Part of the time restless, part of the time calm. (3) Most of the time calm, occasionally restless. (4) Always calm, never restless. These states are elaborated as follows:

(1) Under the control of Ego, the characteristic state of the bodily kingdom is restlessness. With restlessness comes the eclipse of discrimination (*buddhi*). The sense mind (*manas*), under complete control of ego and desire, makes no effort to fight evil and to bring back the noble General Calmness as the protector of the fortress of life. The mind therefore suffers from continuous restlessness, inefficiency, and ignorance (as illustrated in Figure 2, page 20).

(2) In the second stage of psychological battle, King Soul occasionally attains a temporary victory in the enemy kingdom of restlessness and ignorance. This stage is reached when Calmness makes long, strenuous efforts to bombard the ramparts of restlessness. His guns are the regularly repeated, continuous sieges of months of deep meditation.

In this state the bodily kingdom is still infested with restlessness, broken occasionally by calmness.

(3) In the third stage of psychological battle General Calmness and his soldiers, by repeated invasions with the big guns of deep and continuously higher meditation, are able to advance significantly farther into the territory occupied by restlessness. The glorious result of this battle is made known by a state of prolonged peace; the bodily kingdom experiences only occasional outbreaks from the rebels of restlessness.

(4) In the fourth stage of the psychological battle, King Ego and all his soldiers are completely routed; the peaceful kingdom of King Soul is forever established as the Empire of Life. This state is the one illustrated in Figure 1 (on page 17).

In a body and mind ruled by King Soul and his discriminative faculties, all rebels have met their just fate: decapitation! The enemies—ego, fear, anger, greed, attachment, pride, desires, habits, temptations—no longer lurk in the secret subconscious cellars to plot against the rightful king. The peaceful realm manifests nothing but abundance, harmony, and wisdom. No disease, failure, or consciousness of death dwell in the bodily realm under the reign of King Soul.

THE METHOD OF ATTAINING VICTORY

THE PRACTICAL METAPHYSICIAN, in the course of his attempts to free his soul from material bondage, learns the exact methods for victory.

By consistently right thoughts and actions, in harmony with divine law, the soul of man ascends slowly in the course of natural evolution. The yogi, however, chooses the quicker evolution-hastening method: scientific meditation, by which the flow of consciousness is reversed from matter to Spirit through the same cerebrospinal centres of life and divine consciousness that channelled the soul's descent into the body. Even the novitiate meditator quickly finds that he is able to draw upon the spiritual power and consciousness of the inner world of soul and Spirit to enlighten his bodily kingdom and activities—physical, mental, and spiritual. The more adept he becomes, the greater the divine influence.

As the yogi's consciousness moves ever upward from body consciousness to cosmic consciousness, he experiences the following:

Stages of progress toward superconsciousness

First: By the practice of guru-given meditation, the aspiring yogi is strengthened in his resolve to find God through Self-realization.* He no longer wishes to remain identified with worldliness, subject to the limitations of the body and the delusions of nature's opposites of life-death, joy-sorrow, health-disease. With newly awakened discrimination, the yogi is able to free his consciousness from egoistic attachment to his earthly possessions and his little circle of friends. His motive is not a limited and negative one of denial, but a natural expansion toward all-inclusiveness. He severs limiting mental attachments, that they stand not in the way of his perception of the Omnipresent. After achieving his Goal, the love of the perfect yogi includes not only his own family and friends, but all mankind. The ordinary human being is the loser by attachment to a few persons and things, all of which he must forsake at death. The wise yogi

* Guru: spiritual teacher. The *Guru Gita* (verse 17) aptly describes the guru as "dispeller of darkness" (from *gu,* "darkness," and *ru,* "that which dispels"). Though today the word *guru* is commonly used to refer simply to a teacher or instructor, a true guru is one who is God-illumined. In his attainment of self-mastery, he has realized his identity with the omnipresent Spirit. Such a one is uniquely qualified to lead the seeker on his or her spiritual journey toward enlightenment and liberation.

"To keep company with the guru," wrote Swami Sri Yukteswar in *The Holy Science,* "is not only to be in his physical presence (as this is sometimes impossible), but mainly means to keep him in our hearts and to be one with him in principle and to attune ourselves with him."

therefore first reclaims his divine birthright; then he finds flowing to him all needful experiences and possessions.

Second: Though the yogi finds his consciousness free of all external attachments, it still clings tenaciously within to body consciousness when he tries to meditate on God. Experiences of peace and intuitive flashes of the bliss to come encourage him to persevere against the resistance of restlessness and of the ensuing doubts as to whether his efforts are truly worthwhile.

Third: By deep concentration on yoga techniques, the yogi next tries to silence the internal and external body-sensations, so that his thoughts may focus solely on God.

Fourth: By the right technique of life-force control (*pranayama*), the yogi learns to quiet his breath and his heart; he withdraws his attention and his life energy into the spinal centres.

Fifth: When the yogi can quiet his heart at will, he enters superconsciousness.

The ego experiences joy and relaxation when it feels in peaceful sleep the subconscious mind. In the sleep state, the heart still works, pumping blood through the blood vessels while the senses are asleep. When in meditation the yogi consciously withdraws his attention and energy from his heart, muscles, and senses, these all remain as though asleep, but he has passed beyond the subconscious sleep-state of mental awareness into superconsciousness. Such *conscious* sensory-motor sleep bestows on the yogi a joy greater than that of a million ordinary dreamless sleeps; greater than that of any sleep a man might experience after many days of enforced sleeplessness!

IN THE STATE OF SUPERCONSCIOUSNESS, man's perceptions are internalized rather than externalized. An analogy will explain this:

The yogi's experiences in the state of superconsciousness

Man may be said to possess two bundles of searchlights, one inner and one outer: The ego, or body-identified consciousness, holds five outer sensory searchlights of sight, smell, sound, taste, and touch; and the soul holds five inner searchlights that reveal God and the true nature of creation. A searchlight reveals only objects in front of it, not those behind. The outer searchlights of the senses, turned toward matter, reveal to the ego only the various forms of transient and external material objects, not the vast kingdom within. The ego, with its attention identified with the five outer senses, thus becomes attached to the world of matter and its gross limitations.

When in superconscious meditation the heart is calmed, and the yogi can stimulate at will the spiritual centre of the medulla or point between the eyebrows, he can control the inner and outer searchlights of perception. When he switches off the lights of the gross senses, all material distractions vanish. Then the ego automatically turns to behold, through the reinforced inner searchlights held by the soul, the forgotten beauty of the inner astral kingdom.

The heart-quieted yogi in superconsciousness becomes able to see visions and great lights; to hear astral sounds; and to become identified with a vast dimly lighted space—alive with glimpses of beauties hitherto unknown.

In the external conscious state, man does not see God's active manifestation as the beautiful Cosmic Energy that is present in every point of space, and that constitutes the luminous building blocks of every object; he perceives only the gross dimensional forms of human faces, of flowers, and of other beauties of nature. The soul coaxes man to turn his attention-searchlights inward to behold, through its astral vision, the ever-burning, ever-changing, multicoloured lights of the fountain of Cosmic Energy playing through the pores of all atoms.

The physical beauty of a face, or of nature, is fleeting; its perception depends on the power of the physical eyes. The beauty of Cosmic Energy is everlasting, and can be seen with or without the physical eyes. God makes a grand display of Cosmic Energy in the astral realm of vibratory light. The astral loveliness of roses, scenery, heavenly faces, all play their infinitely fascinating roles of ever-changing colours on the stage of the astral cosmos. Beholding this panorama, the yogi can never again be foolishly attached to the changeable objects of bedimmed beauty in nature, nor expect any everlasting beauty from earth. The most exquisite face wrinkles and droops with age. Roses too must wither, mocking man's desire for any eternal beauty in materiality. Death will destroy the buds of youth; cataclysms will demolish the grandeurs of this earth, but nothing can destroy the splendour of the astral cosmos (and of the still finer ideational world from which emanates all cosmic artistry). The astral atoms assume wonderful forms of light at the mere command of the imagination of one in this subtle realm, and disappear when he so wishes. They wake again, in an ever new garb of beauty, at his call.

In superconsciousness, the physical body, which once seemed so solid and vulnerable, takes on a new dimension composed of energy, light, and thought—a marvellous combination of currents emanating from the elemental creative vibrations of earth, water, fire, air, and ether in the subtle cerebrospinal centres.

The yogi who moves his consciousness to the coccyx or earth centre feels all solid matter to be composed of the atomic and subatomic energy of life force, *prana*.

When the yogi draws his consciousness and energy to the sacral or water centre, he experiences all liquid forms to be composed of rivers of electrons of the subtle life force.

When the yogi retires to the lumbar or fire centre, he sees all forms of light as made of the cosmic "fire" of *prana*.

When the yogi retires his consciousness to the dorsal or air centre, he sees all gaseous forms and air as made of pure *prana*.

When the yogi is able to place his consciousness within the cervical or ether centre, he perceives that the subtle etheric background on which grosser forces are imprinted is made of sparks of cosmic intelligent life force, or *prana*.*

---

* The Sanskrit word *akasha,* translated as both "ether" and "space," refers specifically to the vibratory element that is the subtlest in the material world, the "screen on which the image of the body and all nature is projected."

"Ether-permeated space is the boundary line between heaven, or the astral world, and earth," Paramahansaji said. "All the finer forces God has created are composed of light, or thought-forms, and are merely hidden behind a particular vibration that manifests as ether. Were this etheric vibration removed, you would see the astral cosmos behind this physical universe. But our sensory perceptions of sight, hearing, smell, taste, and touch are limited to this finite world....

"Space is another dimension: the 'gates' of heaven. Through the spiritual eye, which exists within at the point between the eyebrows, you can enter these gates. Your consciousness must pass through the astral star in the spiritual eye to behold that higher realm, the astral world."

Modern physics has discarded the hypothetical "ether" postulated by nineteenth-century scientists as the medium through which light is transmitted through the emptiness of outer space. "Still," writes Professor Arthur Zajonc in *Catching the Light: The Entwined History of Light and Mind* (New York: Bantam Books, 1993), "although innumerable experiments deny the ether, an equal number seem to affirm the wavelike character of light. If we take both seriously and suppose light to be, in some sense, a wave, then what is it that is waving? In the cases of water waves, sound waves, vibrating strings, some*thing* is always waving. The figure of sound is borne by air. What bears the fleeting figure we call light? One thing has become certain, whatever it is, it is not material!"

The problem has convinced some scientists that what is "waving" is space itself—and that the very definition of "space" has to be enlarged. Michio Kaku, in *Hyperspace* (New York: Oxford University Press, 1994), writes of "a scientific revolution created by the theory of hyperspace, which states that dimensions exist beyond the commonly accepted four of space and time. There is a growing acknowledgement among physicists worldwide, including several Nobel laureates, that the universe may actually exist in higher dimensional space....Light, in fact, can be explained as vibrations in the fifth dimension....Higher dimensional space, instead of being an empty, passive backdrop

When the yogi retires into the medulla centre, and into the point between the eyebrows, he knows all matter, energy, and intelligent *prana* to be composed of thought force. These two centres in the brain are electrical switches of life force and consciousness that are responsible for the creation of the supervitaphone picture of the body through the action of earth, water, fire, air, and ether—the five elements that compose all matter.* (The profound cosmological branch of the yoga science—dealing with the true nature of the macrocosm of the universe and the microcosm of man's body—is treated extensively in various Hindu scriptures, and will be discussed further in the interpretation of other related Gita verses.)

Persons whose knowledge comes through books and not through intuition may often speak of matter as thought, yet still remain grossly attached to the body and material limitations. Only the yogi whose knowledge is based on experience, not on imagination—the yogi who can withdraw his consciousness as well as his life force from the body by quieting the heart, taking them through the cerebrospinal centres to the point between the eyebrows—is developed enough to say: "All matter is thought." Unless consciousness and energy reach the medullary plane, all matter will be experienced as solid, real—quite different from thought no matter how fervently one intellectualizes otherwise. Only upon

---

against which quarks play out their eternal roles, actually becomes the central actor in the drama of nature."

Sensory consciousness perceives the world as existing in four physical dimensions. Yoga science describes ether-permeated space as the barrier between these and higher dimensions of existence. Beyond the subtlest physical vibration (*akasha*, ether), Paramahansa Yogananda explained, is the superether, "a finer manifestation and therefore not classified as one of the physical vibratory elements (*tattvas*), of which there are only five—earth, water, fire, air, ether. Some yoga treatises define this *tattva* as mind, or 'non-matter,' as opposed to matter or gross vibration."

Is "mind" a "higher dimension" needed to account for the scientifically observed nature of physical reality? Many physicists do not consider this question as falling within their domain; certainly no conclusive consensus has yet been reached among them. However, in *Elemental Mind: Human Consciousness and the New Physics* (New York: Penguin Books, 1993), physicist Nick Herbert, Ph.D., writes: "Far from being a rare occurrence in complex biological or computational systems, mind is a fundamental process in its own right, as widespread and deeply embedded in nature as light or electricity. Along with the more familiar elementary particles and forces that science has identified as building blocks of the physical world, mind (in this view) must be considered an equally basic constituent of the natural world. Mind is, in a word, elemental, and it interacts with matter at an equally elemental level, at the level of the emergence into actuality of individual quantum events." See also VII:4, page 669. *(Publisher's Note)*

* Vitaphone: an early term for motion-picture films with sound. *(Publisher's Note)*

reaching the medullary plane (through Self-realization acquired by years of yoga practice with the aid of the guru) is one enabled truly to proclaim that all matter is merely the condensed thoughts or visualized dreams of God. And only when one goes beyond superconsciousness to cosmic consciousness can one *demonstrate* the dream-thought nature of matter.

A legendary story here will illustrate the "matter is thought" point. A great master in India used to travel by foot from village to village with many disciples. At the devotional plea one day of their host, the saint ate meat; he told his disciples, however, to take only fruit. The whole group then undertook a long march through the woods to another village. A disgruntled disciple began to spread discontent by saying: "The master, who preaches the nonexistence of matter, himself eats meat! He gives us only watery, unsubstantial food! Certainly he can march without fatigue; hasn't he good meat in his stomach? We are tired; the fruits we ate were all digested long ago!"

The master sensed this criticism, but said nothing until the group arrived at a cottage where a blacksmith was making nails from molten iron.

"Can you eat and digest everything I can?" the master inquired of the troublemaking student.

Thinking the master was going to offer him meat, which he saw roasting on a fire nearby, the student answered: "Yes, sir!"

The master bent over the fire of the blacksmith. Pulling out, with his bare fingers, some of the red-hot nails—still pliably soft from the intense heat—the master began to eat them.

"Come, son," he remarked encouragingly, "eat and digest! To me all foods—meat or molten nails—are identically the same; they are Spirit!"*

---

* This story, with some variation in details, is a part of the lore (particularly in South India) woven around the life of Swami Shankara: India's greatest philosopher; a rare combination of saint, scholar, and man of action. Often referred to as Adi ("the first") Shankaracharya, he spent most of his brief thirty-two years of life journeying to every part of India, spreading his *advaita* (nondualistic) doctrine. Millions gathered eagerly to hear the solacing flow of wisdom from the lips of the barefooted young monk.

A few records indicate that the peerless monist lived in the sixth century B.C.; the sage Anandagiri gives the dates 44–12 B.C.; Western historians assign Shankara to the eighth or early ninth century A.D.

Shankara's reforming zeal included the reorganization of the ancient monastic Swami Order. He also founded *maths* (monastic educational centres) in four localities—Sringeri in the south, Puri in the east, Dwarka in the west, and Badrinath in the Himalayan north. His object in locating his *maths* in the four corners of India was the promotion of religious and national unity throughout the vast land. *(Publisher's Note)*

A necessary warning to students is this: "Do not think you are spiritually advanced just because you have heard a lecture or read a book on cosmic consciousness, or because you fancy yourself to have attained it, or even because you have experienced astral visions (entertaining and enlightening, but still in the domain of matter)." You can *know* all matter to be thought only when you are able to withdraw life force and consciousness to the medullary plane, and can enter the spiritual eye—doorway to the highest states of consciousness.

THE SOUL HAS WON BACK ITS KINGDOM

THIS, THEN, IS THE BATTLE of consciousness that every man must fight—the war between the human consciousness that beholds the alternately pleasurable and suffering lives of mortals in delusive, changeable matter, and the cosmic consciousness of the soul, beholding the kingdom of all-powerful, ever-blissful Omnipresence!

The deeper the yogi's meditations, and the more he is able to hold on to the aftereffects of awakened soul-virtues and perceptions and express them in his daily life, the more spiritualized his bodily kingdom becomes. His unfolding Self-realization is the triumphal reestablishing of the reign of King Soul. Amazing changes take place within an ordinary man when King Soul and his noble courtiers of intuition, peace, bliss, calmness, self-control, life-force control, will power, concentration, discrimination, omniscience, rule the bodily kingdom!

Spiritualized perceptions of the illumined yogi

The yogi who has won the battle of consciousness has overcome the misguided ego's attachment to human titles, such as, "I am a man, an American, with so many pounds of flesh, a millionaire of this city," and so on, and has released the prisoner of his attention from all limiting delusion. His freed attention, which beheld creation only through the restrictive outer searchlights of the senses, withdraws into an infinite kingdom seen only through the searchlights of inner perception.

In the ordinary man, the ego, the pseudosoul, floats down the current of sense pleasure, finally wrecking itself in the torrents of satiety and ignorance. In the superman, the entire current of life force, attention, and wisdom moves floodlike toward the soul; the consciousness swims in a sea of God's omnipresent peace and bliss.

In the ordinary man, the senses (searchlights turned on matter) reveal only the pseudopleasurable, the superficially attractive presence of gross matter. In the superman, the inwardly reversed searchlights of perception reveal to the yogi the hiding place of the ever beautiful, ever joyous Spirit in all creation.

Entering the door of the spiritual eye, he ascends to Christ consciousness (union with God's omnipresence in all creation) and cosmic consciousness (union with God's omnipresence in *and beyond* all creation).*

The man of cosmic consciousness, never feeling himself as limited to a body or as reaching only to the brain, or only to the cerebral-lotus light of a thousand rays, instead feels by true intuitive power the ever-bubbling Bliss that dances in every particle of his little body, and in his big Cosmic Body of the universe, and in his absolute nature as one with the Eternal Spirit beyond manifested forms.

The man into whose pure hand his divine bodily kingdom has been wholly delivered is no longer a human being with limited ego consciousness. In reality, he is the soul, individualized ever-existent, ever-conscious, ever-new Bliss, the pure reflection of Spirit, endowed with cosmic consciousness. Never a victim of imaginary perceptions, fanciful inspirations, or "wisdom" hallucinations, the superman is always intensely conscious of the Unmanifested Spirit and also of the entire cosmos in all its bewildering variety.

With his consciousness extended and awakened in every particle in the circumambience of infinite space, the exalted yogi feels his little physical body and all its perceptions not as an ordinary human being, but in oneness with omniscient Spirit.

Freed from the intoxications of delusion and delusive mortal limitations, the superman knows his earthly name and possessions, but is never possessed or limited by them. Living *in* the world, he is not *of* the world. He is aware of hunger, thirst, and other conditions of the body, but his inner consciousness identifies itself, not with the body, but with Spirit. The advanced yogi may own many possessions, but will never

---

* The spiritual eye is the single eye of intuition and omnipresent perception at the Christ (*Kutastha*) centre (*ajna chakra*) between the eyebrows, which is directly connected by polarity with the medulla centre.

The deeply meditating devotee beholds the spiritual eye as a ring of golden light encircling a sphere of opalescent blue, and at the centre, a pentagonal white star. Microcosmically, these forms and colours epitomize, respectively, the vibratory realm of creation (Prakriti, Cosmic Nature); the universal intelligence of God in creation (*Kutastha Chaitanya;* Krishna or Christ Consciousness); and the vibrationless Spirit beyond all creation (Brahman).

In deep meditation the devotee's consciousness penetrates the spiritual eye into the three realms epitomized therein.

sorrow if all things are taken away. If he happens to be materially poor, he knows that, in Spirit, he is rich beyond all dreams of avarice.

The spiritual man performs all right actions of seeing, touching, smelling, tasting, and hearing without feeling any mental attachment. His soul floats on the foul waters of dark earthly experiences—of man's sad indifference to God—like an unsoiled lotus arising from the muddy waters of a lake.

The superman experiences sensations, not in the sensory organs but as perceptions in the brain. The ordinary man feels cold or heat on the body surface; he sees lovely flowers externally, in a garden; he hears sounds in the ears; he tastes with the palate; and smells through olfactory nerves; but the superman experiences all such sensations in the *brain*. He can distinguish between pure sensation and the reaction on it of thought. He perceives sensations, feelings, will, body, perception—everything—in thought, as mere suggestions of God as He dreams through man's consciousness.

The superman beholds the body, not as flesh, but as a bundle of condensed electrons and life force, ready to be dematerialized or materialized at the yogi's will. He feels no weight of the body, but perceives the flesh merely as electric energy. He sees the motion picture of the cosmos going backward and forward on the screen of his consciousness: he knows in this way that time and space are dimensional forms of thought, displaying cosmic motion pictures, dreams that are constantly new, infinitely varied—and true-to-touch, true-to-sound, true-to-smell, true-to-taste, and true-to-sight.

The superman sees that the birth of his body was merely the beginning of certain changes; he knows death to be the change that naturally follows earthly life. He is ready and able, at the moment of his choosing, to part consciously with his bodily dwelling.

Being one with God, he dreams within his cosmic consciousness all the divine dreams of cosmic creation.

The superman's body is the universe, and all things that happen in the universe are his sensations.

He who has become one with the omnipresent, omniscient, and omnipotent God is aware of the coursing of a planet trillions of light-years distant, and, at the same moment, of the flight of a nearby sparrow. A superman does not see Spirit as apart from the body; he becomes one with Spirit, and beholds, as existing within himself, his own body as well as the bodies of all other creatures. He feels his body, a tiny atom, within his vast luminous cosmic body.

Withdrawing his attention, during deep meditation, from the outward sensory world, the superman perceives by the power of the inner eye. Through the searchlights of the astral powers of vision, sound, smell, taste, and touch, and through the even finer causal perception of pure intuition, he beholds the territory of omnipresent Cosmic Consciousness.

In this state, the superman knows the twinkling atoms of cosmic energy to be his own eyes, through which he peers into every pore of space and into Infinity.

He enjoys in all creation the fragrance of Bliss; and inhales the sweetness of astral atom-blossoms, blooming in the cosmic garden.

He tastes the astral nectar of liquid cosmic energy, and sips the fluid honey of a tangible joy, existing in the honeycomb of electronic space. No longer is he lured by material food, but lives by his own divine energy.

He feels his voice vibrate, not in a human body, but in the throat of all vibrations, and in his body of all finite matter. He listens to his voice of creative cosmic *Aum,* conjoined with the song of Spirit, singing through the flute of atoms, and through the shimmering waves of all creation; and he desires to hear naught else.

He feels his blood of perception run through the veins in the body of all finite vibratory creation. Having conquered the touch-sense of material-comfort desires of the body, the divine man feels the sensations of all matter as expressions of God's creative cosmic energy playing upon his cosmic body, in a bliss unmatched by any physical pleasure of touch. He feels the smooth glide of the river over the breast of the earth. He feels the home of his Being in the ocean of space, and perceives the swimming waves of island universes on his own sea bosom. He knows the softness of the petals of blossoms, and the tenderness of the love in all hearts, the aliveness of youth in all bodies. His own youthfulness, as the ageless soul, is everlasting.

The superman knows births and deaths only as changes dancing on the Sea of Life—even as waves of the ocean rise, fall, and rise again. He cognizes all past and future, but lives in the eternal present. For him, the conundrum of the why of being is resolved in the singular realization: "From Joy we have come. In Joy we live and move and have our being. And in that sacred perennial Joy we melt again."

This is Self-realization, man's native state as the soul, the pure reflection of Spirit. Dreams of incarnations play on the delusive screen of individuality; but in reality, never for a moment is man separate from God. We are His thought; He is our being. From Him we have come. In Him we are to live as expressions of His wisdom, His love, His joy. In Him our egoity must melt again, in the ever-wakeful dreamlessness of eternal Bliss.

❖

EVERY HUMAN BEING MUST FIGHT THE BATTLE OF KURUKSHETRA

THUS HAS BEEN DESCRIBED the metaphorical significance of the battle of Kurukshetra, and the victorious goal to be won. Every man is confronted with the same challenge. The timeless popularity of the Gita lies in its universality as a divine textbook for living, applicable to all men. It enlightens every plane of existence.

The material man will know inner peace and happiness only if he sides with goodness and wins the battle between the good and evil inclinations that guide his actions on the external bodily field of action, or Kurukshetra.

The spiritual aspirant of any true religious path must in addition win the victory on the inner field of Dharmakshetra Kurukshetra, the subtle cerebrospinal centres where the interiorization of God-communion takes place (in deep prayer, in meditation, and in practicing the presence of God during daily activities), defeating the opposition of mental restlessness and sense attractions.

The yogi, he who seeks the ultimate goal of Self-realization and *kaivalya* (liberation), leads in battle his righteous warriors of self-control and moral behaviour on the Kurukshetra plain of material action; he fights for the victory of interiorized God-communion on the inner spiritual plain of Dharmakshetra Kurukshetra; and further, on the field of Dharmakshetra, or spiritualized consciousness, he strives to maintain, against the pull of the lower ego nature of body consciousness, the superconsciousness, Christ consciousness, and cosmic consciousness attained by successful yoga meditation.

The vastness of the import of the first stanza of the Bhagavad Gita is glimpsed when we thus see how it is to be applied in practical experience.

God, through Krishna, or the soul, talks to Arjuna, the devotee: "O Arjuna, each night ask your impartial introspection (Sanjaya) to reveal to your blind mind (Dhritarashtra): 'The impulsive mental and sense tendencies, and the self-disciplined offspring of the soul's discrimination, assembled on the bodily field of sensory activities and spiritual activities, eager for psychological battle, what did they do?' Tell all My future devotees to keep each night, like you, a mental vigil-diary in order to assess their daily inner battles, and thereby to better resist the forces of their blind mental impulses and to support the soldiers of discerning wisdom."

Each worldly person, moralist, spiritual aspirant, and yogi—like a devotee—should every night before retiring ask his intuition whether his spiritual faculties or his physical inclinations of temptation won the day's battles between good and bad habits; between temperance and greed; between self-control and lust; between honest desire for necessary money and inordinate craving for gold; between forgiveness and anger; between joy and grief; between moroseness and pleasantness; between kindness and cruelty; between selfishness and unselfishness; between understanding and jealousy; between bravery and cowardice; between confidence and fear; between faith and doubt; between humbleness and pride; between desire to commune with God in meditation and the restless urge for worldly activities; between spiritual and material desires; between divine ecstasy and sensory perceptions; between soul consciousness and egoity.

THE OPPOSING ARMIES OF THE SPIRITUAL AND MATERIALISTIC FORCES

VERSE 2

सञ्जय उवाच
दृष्ट्वा तु पाण्डवानीकं व्यूढं दुर्योधनस्तदा।
आचार्यमुपसङ्गम्य राजा वचनमब्रवीत्॥

Sanjaya said:

Then King Duryodhana, after having seen the armies of the Pandavas in battle array, retired to his preceptor (Drona), and spoke as follows:

"SANJAYA (THE IMPARTIAL INTROSPECTION of Arjuna, the devotee) revealed:

" 'After beholding the armies of the Pandavas (the discriminative qualities) in array for psychological battle (ready to fight the sense tendencies), King Duryodhana (material desire, royal offspring of the blind sense-mind) conferred solicitously with his preceptor Drona (*samskara,* the impressions left by past thoughts and actions, which create a strong inner urge for repetition).'"

The blind King Dhritarashtra had one hundred sons, Duryodhana being the first, or eldest. Because his father was blind, Duryodhana ruled in his stead, and was thus recognized as *raja,* or king. The metaphorical analysis is that the one hundred offspring of the blind sense-mind (King Dhritarashtra) consist of the five sense instruments of perception (sight, hearing, smell, taste, and touch) and the five sense instruments of action (speech, manual ability, locomotion, procreation, and excretion), each of which has ten propensities. All together, these make one hundred offspring born of the sense mind. The eldest, Duryodhana, represents Material Desire—the firstborn, that which wields power over all the other sense inclinations of the bodily kingdom. He is one who is well-known for evil wars or causes. The metaphorical derivation of Duryodhana is *duḥ-yudhaṁ yaḥ saḥ*—"one who is hard to be countered in any way." His very name comes from the Sanskrit *dur,* "difficult" and *yudh,* "to fight." Material desire is extremely powerful, for it is the king and leader of all worldly enjoyments, and is the cause and perpetrator of the battle against the soul's rightful claim to the bodily kingdom.

Duryodhana: symbolic of material desire

The second stanza of the Gita points out that as soon as the spiritual aspirant introspects to rouse and train by meditation his soldiers of discrimination, immediate opposition is manifested by the king of all sense tendencies, Material Desire. Fearful of losing the mental and bodily kingdom, Material Desire seeks to reinforce himself by consulting his preceptor Drona, representing *samskara,* the impressions made on the conscious and subconscious mind by past thoughts and actions.

The name Drona comes from the Sanskrit root *dru,* "to melt."* Therefore, Drona implies "that which remains in a melted state." A thought or physical act once performed does not cease to be, but remains in the consciousness in a more subtle or "melted" form as an impression of that gross expression of thought or action. These impressions are called *samskaras.* They create strong inner urges, tendencies, or propensities that influence the intelligence to repeat those thoughts and

Drona: powerful force of habitual tendencies

* Traditionally, scholars assign to the root *dru* in Drona another meaning, "wood or any wooden implement," corresponding to the metaphorical account that Drona was conceived in a wooden vessel from the seed of a great sage.

actions. Oft-repeated, such impulses become compelling habits. Thus, we may simplify the translation of *samskara* in this context as inner tendency or urge, or habit. The preceptor Drona symbolizes *samskara,* broadly defined as inner tendency, or habit.

According to the historical story in the *Mahabharata,* Drona was the masterly preceptor who had taught archery to both the Kurus and the Pandavas. During the battle between the two parties, however, Drona sided with the Kurus.

The good discriminative tendencies of the soul's pure intelligence (*buddhi*) and the wicked mental tendencies of the sense mind (*manas*) had both learned from Inner Tendency, Drona, the battle arts of wielding, respectively, the weapons of soul-revealing wisdom, and of truth-obscuring sense consciousness.

The subconscious urges of one's *samskaras,* if good, help to create present good thoughts, actions, and habits. When these innate urges are evil, they rouse wicked thoughts that turn into evil actions and habits. Just as a bird turns its head to focus one eye at a time on a given object, so Drona, the *samskara-* or habit-guided intelligence, uses one-sided vision and supports the dominant tendencies. This Drona, inner urge, joins the wicked mental tendencies (Kurus) when they are predominant in a man. Therefore, unless *samskara,* or the sense-habit inclination, is purified by wisdom, it will be found to be a follower of Duryodhana, or King Material Desire. This is why, in the devotee who has yet to win the victory in the battle of Kurukshetra, Drona or the bad-habit-influenced intelligence joins the side of the Kurus or the wicked mental tendencies, helping them to direct their arrows of piercing evil against the discriminative powers.

Battle strategy of material desire and habit

MATERIAL DESIRE IS THE SUPREME RULER in the person who does not meditate. It is Desire's power that lures man to follow the path of sense pleasure rather than the path of soul happiness. The ordinary person, knowing nothing of the intoxicating Joy flowing from meditational practices, unwittingly reconciles himself to sense pleasures. But as soon as meditation awakens discriminative qualities, so that the devotee tastes the true joys of the inner world of Spirit, King Material Desire becomes alarmed and begins to reinforce his position by summoning Drona—recalling to man's mind the pleasures of past sense indulgences.

King Material Desire, acting alone in the shape of a series of new desires, is easily overcome by an act of judgement, but Material Desire that is supported by Habit is hard to eject merely by discrimination. Therefore, the battle strategy of King Material Desire is to try to overcome discriminative tendencies by presenting alluring memories of the joys of past bad habits.

Devotee, beware! As soon as the spiritual aspirant tries to meditate and to rouse the powers of self-control and discrimination, he will find King Material Desire tempting him in several ways. New desires will invade his thoughts to distract him from meditation: "There is an excellent movie at the neighbourhood theatre....Your favourite television show is on....Remember you wanted to call your friend about next week's party....Now is a good time to do those neglected extra chores....You have worked hard, take a little sleep first....Go ahead, get these things off your mind, *then* you can meditate." Too often, the time for "then" never comes. Even the resolute devotee who resists these lures and sits to meditate will be invaded by pernicious inner urges of past habits of restlessness, mental lethargy and sleepiness, and spiritual indifference.

The aspiring devotee should be aware of these dangers, which are merely tests easily mastered if one is forewarned by wisdom. By deep spiritual introspective intuition, he will discover these invariable ruses of King Material Desire.

The restless man who does not cultivate spiritual discrimination and self-control becomes the victim of Duryodhana–Material Desire's temptations and of Drona-Samskara's inner urges of past habits of spiritual indifference and sense pleasures. The worldly man foolishly resists any suggestions to explore the deeper, unending joys and wisdom-whispers of those inner perceptions which are to be felt in yoga meditation by concentrating on the subtle centres of divine life and consciousness in the spine and in the spiritual eye between the two eyebrows.

By constant self-indulgence, the ordinary person remains sense-ensnared. He finds himself limited to enjoyments connected only with the surface of the flesh. This sense pleasure yields a fleeting happiness, but shuts off the manifestation of the subtle, more pure and lasting enjoyments—the taste of silent blessedness and the innumerable blissful perceptions that appear whenever the meditating yogi's consciousness is turned from the outer sensory world to the inner cosmos of Spirit. The transient, misleading physical sense emotions are a poor substitute for heaven!

The life of an ordinary man is monotonous, at best. He wakes, bathes his body, enjoys the after-bath sensation, eats breakfast, hurries to work, begins to get weary, is refreshed by lunch, again pursues his work, and finally goes home, bored and listless. The hour of his too-heavy dinner is punctuated by various noises from radio or television and often ill-humoured remarks from wife or children. This typical man may then attend the movies or a party for a brief diversionary respite; he comes home late, is very tired and sleeps heavily. What a life! But he repeats this performance, with unimaginative variations, throughout the best years of his life.

By habits man becomes a human automaton

By such habits man becomes like a machine, a human automaton, fuelled with food, automatically performing tasks sluggishly and unwillingly, without joy or inspiration, and partially shutting down its activities by sleep—only to repeat, on the following day, the same routine.

The Bhagavad Gita commands man to avoid this mere "existence." Its verses proclaim that the practice of contacting God in the ever new joy of yoga meditation will enable man to keep the state of blissful consciousness ever present with him, even during the performance of those mechanical actions that must enter into all human lives. Discontent, boredom, and unhappiness are the harvest of a mechanical life; whereas the infinite spiritual perceptions gained in meditation whisper joyously to man countless thrilling inspirations of wisdom that enlighten and enliven every aspect of his life.

The Gita does not teach that it is a sin to use the senses with discrimination and self-control, nor that living an upright, honest family life necessarily makes one worldly; but a spiritual aspirant is warned not to allow these to crowd out his supreme duty to seek God and Self-realization. Settling into ruts of material habits and sense pleasures causes forgetfulness of God and loss of desire to seek the unending ever-increasing happiness of the true nature of the soul felt in meditation. Mental peace and happiness are forfeited when sensory passions displace soul perceptions. Can they be considered as other than fools who drown their souls' inimitable happiness in mires of sensory enslavement, indulged in against the warnings of reason and conscience? That entrapment by delusion is what is at issue in the Gita. Pure enjoyments of the senses, experienced with spiritual discrimination and self-control, are not enslaving to a man of Self-realization. Pure sense pleasures are known to the yogi *after* he has won by meditation the true contact of God.

Thus we find the second stanza of the Bhagavad Gita forewarning the spiritual aspirant that King Duryodhana–Material Desire will try to arouse man's Drona sense-habit tendencies to fight against the soul's forces of discrimination.

When the sense faculties (the Kurus) have been allowed to take command of the bodily kingdom, man's powers of introspection and discrimination are held incommunicado, in silent exile, by the sense armies. The dictates of Duryodhana–Material Desire, supported by Drona-Habit, are all-powerful. But when the devotee is ready to support the soul's discriminative tendencies (the Pandavas) to help them become victorious, Material Desire and the evil protégés of Drona-urge will be driven out pell-mell.

VERSE 3

पश्यैतां पाण्डुपुत्राणामाचार्य महतीं चमूम्।
व्यूढां द्रुपदपुत्रेण तव शिष्येण धीमता॥

O Teacher, behold this great army of the sons of Pandu, arranged in battle order by thy talented disciple, the son of Drupada.

(KING MATERIAL DESIRE, during the devotee's introspection, addresses his preceptor Drona, Habit:)

"Behold the mighty army of the Pandavas (the discriminative forces entrenched in the spinal centres) all poised for battle under the direction of thy disciple (the calm inner light of intuitive awakening, disciple of the 'Drona' past habit of meditation). This son of Drupada (born of the 'Drupada' dispassion for material enjoyment resulting from deep spiritual ardour and divine devotion) was trained by thee to be skillful in psychological wars. He now stands against us! a powerful general of the Pandava army (a leader of the occult soldiers of discrimination)."

Symbolic power of calm inner light of divine perception

Duryodhana–Material Desire is both astonished and displeased to find that the formidable general who is preparing the pure discriminative faculties for psychological battle is a brother disciple, the son of King Drupada, a skilled pupil of Duryodhana's own teacher and chief supporter, Past Habit, Drona. The son of Drupada, Dhrishtadyumna, metaphorically represents the calm inner light of divine perception, the awakening intuition of the devotee. A brief reference to the *Mahabharata* allegory will explain the significance:

In their youth, Drona and Drupada were close friends. In later years when Drupada ascended to the throne as King of Panchala, he scorned Drona, who presuming on their former friendship came seeking favours from the king. The angered Drona, with the aid of the Pandavas, took revenge on Drupada by causing him to suffer a humiliating military defeat in which he lost his kingdom and was taken prisoner by Drona. Out of kindness, Drona released Drupada and allowed him to retain the southern half of his former kingdom. Drupada, however, vowed vengeance against Drona. Through sacrificial rite he prayed for, and was granted, a son who would have the courage and ability to destroy Drona. This son, Dhrishtadyumna, rose out of the sacrificial fire as a celestial warrior, shining with a great brilliance and endowed with confident courage. During the war of Kurukshetra, it was at the hand of Dhrishtadyumna that Drona was finally slain.

It has already been established that Drona represents *samskara* or past habit-tendency. Drupada, as will be explained more fully in the next verse, represents dispassion, a distaste for material enjoyment because of deep spiritual ardour and divine devotion. In the beginning, the devotee finds that his fervent spiritual desire and his inner inclinations, or *samskaras,* seem to be friends. But when *samskara* manifests its material sense tendencies, spiritual desire spurns that company. Then habit retaliates and seeks to take revenge on the devotee's spiritual ardour by making it a prisoner of past habits and latent tendencies roused to thwart him. Until the devotee is strongly established in his spiritual life, he will first be confronted with his bad habits. Shunning these, he will suddenly find that his cherished sovereign freedom is still not wholly free, but imprisoned by heretofore latent *samskaras* that bind his discriminative free will. The devotee sees that his spiritual ardour can rule effectively that half of the bodily kingdom connected with the materially inclined senses—the southern portion, or lower spinal centres, which govern the sensory activities of the physical bodily kingdom. But habit, with its compelling tendencies and impulses, still holds in thralldom the realm of pure discrimination. The determined devotee then rouses his spiritual ardour with the resolution to liberate the soul from all bondage. His persistent, deep devotion gives him an offspring, a son, which is the truth-revealing light and power of awakening intuition, Dhrishtadyumna. This inner conviction, trained by the habit of meditation, becomes the general of the devotee's spiritual forces, determining the requisite battle array and strategy that controls his restless mind in meditation and leads the discriminative forces to victory.

Dhritarashtra said: "On the holy plain of Kurukshetra (dharmakshetra kurukshetra), when my offspring and the sons of Pandu had gathered together, eager for battle, what did they, O Sanjaya?"

—Bhagavad Gita I:1

❖

"The blind King Dhritarashtra symbolically represents the sense-mind. The mind is said to be blind because it cannot see without the help of the senses and intelligence; it merely receives the impressions from the senses and relays the conclusions and instructions of the intelligence....

"For the aspiring devotee, Sanjaya represents the power of impartial intuitive self-analysis, discerning introspection. It is the ability to stand aside, observe oneself without any prejudice, and judge accurately....The Gita is referring only incidentally to a historical battle on the plain of Kurukshetra in northern India. Primarily, Vyasa is describing a universal battle—the one that rages daily in man's life....

"The earnest enquiry by the blind King Dhritarashtra, seeking an unbiased report from the impartial Sanjaya as to how fared the battle between the Kurus and the Pandavas (sons of Pandu) at Kurukshetra, is metaphorically the question to be asked by the spiritual aspirant as he reviews daily the events of his own righteous battle from which he seeks the victory of Self-realization. Through honest introspection he analyzes the deeds and assesses the strengths of the opposing armies of his good and bad tendencies: self-control versus sense indulgence, discriminative intelligence opposed by mental sense inclinations, spiritual resolve in meditation contested by mental resistance and physical restlessness, and divine soul-consciousness against the ignorance and magnetic attraction of the lower ego-nature."

—Paramahansa Yogananda

Good powers, trained by habit, are able to destroy their brother disciples, material desires and their evil powers, which, too, are habit-trained. But ultimately the yogi rises above the influence of all habits and relies solely on the soul's pure discriminative faculty, intuition, to guide all actions. It is the pure discriminative light of intuition alone, divine realization, that has the power to slay Drona, or habit. In the name Dhrishtadyumna we find this implied. *Dṛṣṭa* means bold, daring, confident; *dyumna* means splendour, glory, strength. From this we get, "bold or confident splendour," which can be defined as Calm Inner Light, truth-revealing intuition, which is bold and confident because it is unerring; it is the only power that can destroy habit. It is the inner light of increasing realization in meditation, evolving ultimately into *samadhi,* that destroys all bondage of *samskaras.*

Dhrishtadyumna is spoken of as the skilled disciple of Drona (*samskara* in its good or spiritual aspect) because the power of habit repeatedly applied to the practice of meditation is what develops the Calm Inner Light of intuitive divine perception. In time of need, this Calm Inner Light is seen or felt by the meditating devotee, guiding, supporting, and encouraging his meditative efforts.

Habit is the "preceptor" of good as well as evil tendencies

It is a psychological truth that habit is the "preceptor" of both good and evil tendencies in man. When evil Material Desire tries to exercise the influence of habit to destroy the powers of discrimination, the King of Evil is amazed to find that there are good protégés of habit, which are prepared to resist. It is a consoling thought for man that, no matter how strong the powers of evil habit and material desire are at any given moment, soldiers of good habits of this life and of past incarnations exist, ever ready to give battle. These good *samskaras,* the good impressions of divine perceptions left by past habit actions, are the occult soldiers, the rear guard, of King Soul. These warriors remain hidden behind the psychological armies of discrimination, eager to rush forward and display their prowess if the battle seems about to be won by the evil sense-soldiers of Material Desire. That is, when the devotee has a strong army of good *samskara* tendencies from past habits and actions, they will timely come to his aid to support present good habits and discriminative actions.

Most people, however, voluntarily allow their kingdom of consciousness to be ruled by the evil tendencies born of past habits. Thus the discriminative tendencies become ostracized; and the discriminative occult soldiers of past habits, the metaphysical rear guards hidden behind the armies of discrimination, must also remain without action.

The man who is always restless and who never meditates believes that he is "all right" because he has become accustomed to being a sense slave. He realizes his true plight as soon as spiritual desire awakens in him and he tries to meditate and be calm; he then naturally meets fierce resistance from the bad habits of mental fickleness.

The yogi-beginner finds his soldiers of discrimination guided by a desire to be good, yet suffering many discouraging defeats. As he meditates longer and prays ardently for inner help, he sees that the calm conviction of intuitive perception, the veteran occult general of awakening Inner Light, emerges from the superconsciousness to be the active guide for the forces of discrimination. No matter how many times he suffers from powerful attacks of sense habits, the meditation-born occult soldiers of this life and past lives still come to his aid. When the habits of restlessness try to usurp the throne of his consciousness, these occult soldiers offer effective resistance.

The occult soldiers appear at the scene of a psychological battle on two occasions only: first, when the advance soldiers of discrimination have been routed by the soldiers of sense lures; secondly, when the discriminative soldiers, through the trumpet call of meditation, have asked the aid of the occult forces. Together, the occult soldiers of past realizations and the soldiers of discrimination can easily rout the forces of restlessness if the battle takes place *before* the throne of consciousness has been completely usurped by King Material Desire. It is much more difficult for the occult soldiers to help in reclaiming the kingdom of peace once it has fallen into the hands of Material Desire. One, therefore, must make the most of his spiritual inclination while the forces of his willingness-to-meditate are strong. It is good to start meditation at an early age; or, failing that, to start meditation on a regular daily schedule as soon as the mental discriminative inclination develops.

Habits of meditation, whether acquired recently or in the distant past, have the power to bring forth the General of Inner Light. Persons who become discouraged in meditation because of restlessness are yet unaware of the evil-resisting power of their discriminative tendencies and the rear guard of occult soldiers of past good habits of meditation. But even though they are prisoners in the hands of restlessness, if they persist in struggling to calm themselves, they will become aware that hidden occult soldiers—the redoubtable, sturdy, intuitional powers—

are trying to emerge from the superconsciousness to offer spiritual aid.

Thus it is explained in this verse of the Bhagavad Gita that when Material Desire and his army of sense tendencies and their restless thoughts try to reinforce themselves by Past Material Habit in order to dissuade the spiritual aspirant from the practice of meditation, they find that the Calm Inner Light of awakening intuition, well trained in meditation by Past Spiritual Habit, has effectively arrayed the discriminative faculties to give metaphysical resistance.

VERSES 4–6

अत्र शूरा महेष्वासा भीमार्जुनसमा युधि।
युयुधानो विराटश्च द्रुपदश्च महारथः॥ (4)

धृष्टकेतुश्चेकितानः काशिराजश्च वीर्यवान्।
पुरुजित्कुन्तिभोजश्च शैब्यश्च नरपुङ्गवः॥ (5)

युधामन्युश्च विक्रान्त उत्तमौजाश्च वीर्यवान्।
सौभद्रो द्रौपदेयाश्च सर्व एव महारथाः॥ (6)

(4) Here present are mighty heroes, extraordinary bowmen as skillful in battle as Bhima and Arjuna—the veteran warriors, Yuyudhana, Virata, and Drupada;
(5) The powerful Dhrishtaketu, Chekitana, and Kashiraja; eminent among men, Purujit; and Kuntibhoja, and Shaibya;
(6) The strong Yudhamanyu, the valiant Uttamaujas, the son of Subhadra, and the sons of Draupadi—all lords of great chariots.*

THE DIVINELY GUIDED INTROSPECTION of Arjuna reveals King Duryodhana–Material Desire pointing out to Drona-Samskara, the preceptor of evil and good tendencies:

"Archers of discrimination, like unto the masterful Arjuna (Self-Control) and Bhima (Life Control), mighty swayers of the bodily chariot, are all arrayed to destroy my soldiers of sense activities. They are Yuyudhana (Divine Devotion), Virata (Samadhi), Drupada (Extreme

---

* *Mahāratha,* "great chariot-warrior" (*mahā,* from *mahat,* "great, lordly, kingly"; *ratha,* "chariot, warrior") denotes one who is highly skilled in the science of battle, commanding thousands of men, and able singlehandedly to fight ten thousand archers at one time.

Dispassion); Dhrishtaketu (Power of Mental Resistance), Chekitana (Spiritual Memory), Kashiraja* (Discriminative Intelligence), Purujit (Mental Interiorization), Kuntibhoja (Right Posture), Shaibya (Power of Mental Adherence); Yudhamanyu (Life-Force Control), Uttamaujas (Vital Celibacy); son of Subhadra, i.e., Abhimanyu (Self-Mastery); and the sons of Draupadi (the manifestations characteristic of each of the five awakened spinal centres)."

The above fourth, fifth, and sixth stanzas shall be taken together because of their interrelated meaning. These describe the metaphysical soldiers of the soul that are aroused by meditation in preparation for the inner spiritual battle by these forces of Self-realization against those of the innate sense-habits of body-identification—a contest that must be won by the spiritual forces before the soul, enthroned in its cerebral palace, can reign with its divine courtiers of intuitional qualities.

The soul enters this highest metaphysical battle after winning the moral fight between good and evil thoughts and actions, and the initial inner psychological war that takes place in the early stages of spiritual endeavour between the pull of the sense mind toward body-conscious physical and mental restlessness and the pull of the inner discriminative forces of the soul toward calmness and concentration on God. The moral and psychological battles between sense-mind inclinations and the discriminative soul qualities are fought with the aid of habits and the occult soldiers of the inner tendencies (*samskaras*) that result from past actions, good or bad. The metaphysical battle is concerned with the still deeper conflict of inner forces, when the yogi has begun to experience in meditation the fruits of his *sadhana* or spiritual practices.

EXPANDED COMMENTARY: THE SYMBOLIC FORCES OF SOUL QUALITIES

A POPULAR MISCONCEPTION is that the practice of yoga is for adept mystics only, and that this science is beyond even the ken of ordinary man. Yet yoga is the science of the whole creation. Man, as also every atom in the universe, is an externalized result of this divine science at work. The practice of yoga is a set of disciplines through which an

* King of Kashi. Here a title has been used, rather than a proper name.

understanding of this science unfolds through direct personal experience of God, the Supreme Cause.

The material scientist starts with the observable effect of matter and attempts to work backward toward a cause. Yoga, on the other hand, describes the Cause and how it evolved outward into the phenomena of matter, and shows how to follow that process in *reverse* to experience the true Spirit-nature of the universe and man.

To understand the significance of the Gita verses 4, 5, and 6, which describe the metaphysical soldiers of the soul (and the following verses that describe the opposing soldiers of body consciousness), certain basics of the yoga science must be kept in mind.

YOGA PHYSIOLOGY OF THE ASTRAL AND CAUSAL BODIES

THE PHYSICAL WORLD is in reality nothing more than inert matter. The inherent life and animation in all forms, from atoms to man, come from the subtle forces of the astral world. These, in turn, have evolved from the still finer forces of the causal or ideational creation, the creative vibratory thoughts emanating from the consciousness of God. Man, the microcosm, is in all respects an epitome of the macrocosm. His physical body is gross matter; his life and his ability to perceive through the senses and cognize through the consciousness are dependent on the subtle powers and forces of his astral and causal bodies—instruments of the indwelling soul, or individualized consciousness of God.*

The physical body is directly created and sustained by the forces

* The role of the subtle astral and causal forces of consciousness in the operation of man's sensory awareness has not yet been identified by material science. "As fundamental as our senses are, many of their secrets have not yielded to scientific inquiry," stated a report in *Discover* magazine (June 1993) that summarized the latest research on sense perception. For example, "The sense of touch, and the physical world it ushers into existence, has much more to do with what is going on in our heads than at our fingertips."

In *The Brain Revolution* (New York: Bantam Books, 1973), Marilyn Ferguson writes: "Through myriad transactions in the brain, we perceive; our senses select from the stimuli, cerebral structures in the brain interpret the data, but there is no ultimate model of reality out there against which our perceptions can be measured as true or false.... A rose is only a rose because man sees it as such; without him it would be only a pattern of energy vortices."

"The senses routinely perform two miracles," says Robert Ornstein, Ph.D., in *The Psychology of Consciousness* (New York: Penguin Books, 1986). The first, he explains, is the brain's transformation of the various forms of physical energy from the external world—light, sound, vibrations of chemical molecules—into electrical signals in the

of the astral body. The astral body and powers are principally life current or *prana*. Life current is a mixture of consciousness and electrons, to which I have given the terminology "lifetrons." The difference between lifetrons and electrons is that the former is intelligent and the latter is mechanical. The electricity shining in a bulb does not grow a bulb. There is only a mechanical relation between the bulb and the electricity burning in it. But life current present in the united sperm and ovum cell develops that primal cell into an embryo and ultimately into a full-grown human being. The creative life energy of the astral body descends into the physical body through seven subtle centres in the spine and brain, and remains concentrated in and expresses outwardly through these centres. Within only days after conception, a "neural groove" may be distinguished in the embryo. From this first developmental phase is formed the spine, brain, and nervous system, and from these developing parts, the rest of the human organism evolves—all the work of the forces of the astral body.

As the physical body has a brain, spinal cord with nerve pairs forming plexuses at the cervical, dorsal, lumbar, sacral, and coccygeal regions, and a many-branched peripheral nervous system, so the astral body has an astral brain of a thousand rays (the thousand-petalled lotus), an astral spine with subtle centres of light and energy, and an astral nervous system whose myriad luminous channels are called *nadis*. The physiology of the astral body animates the physiology of the physical body. The astral body is the source of the powers and instruments of the five senses of perception and five of action. The astral nervous system channels the flow of life or *prana* in its five differentiated forms that in the physical body manifest as crystallisation, circulation, assimilation, metabolism, and elimination. The main astral spine of light, the *sushumna,* has within it two other luminous spines. The

---

brain. "This process is called *transduction*," he writes. "The eye transduces light, the ear transduces sound waves, the nose transduces gaseous molecules." The second "miracle" is even more remarkable: "The billions of electrical explosions and chemical secretions of 'neural firing' become trees and cakes, silverfish and laughter—the conscious world of human experience.

"These two miracles occur every moment of our lives, and are so continuous and routine that we are naturally unaware of them. We are on our way to understanding how the first miracle works, but everyone in science remains completely mystified by the second."

Australian physicist Raynor Johnson put it this way: "Cathedrals and primroses, works of art and works of steel—what a world the mind has constructed from the electrical storms in a few cubic centimetres of grey matter!' " *(Publisher's Note)*

sushumna, or outer covering of light, controls the gross function of the astral lifetrons (those associated with all the functions carried on by the seven astral spinal centres with their five vibratory creative elements—earth, water, fire, air, and ether) that create and sustain the physical body.* The *sushumna* extends from the *muladhara chakra,* or coccygeal centre, to the brain. Auxiliary to the *sushumna* are two astral *nadis* on either side of it —on the left, *ida;* on the right, *pingala.* These two, pre-eminent among 72,000 *nadis,* constitute the primary channels of the astral sympathetic nervous system—which, in turn, controls the corresponding sympathetic nervous system of the gross physical body.†

Within the *sushumna* is the second astral spine called *vajra,* which provides the powers of expansion, contraction, and all activities of motion of the astral body. The *vajra* extends upward from the *svadhishthana chakra,* or sacral centre. Within the *vajra* is hidden the *chitra* astral spine,

---

* See XIII:1 for details of how the physical body is created and enlivened by the action of the three *gunas—tamas, rajas, sattva*—on the five elements.

† The anatomy of the gross physical body, being an externalization of the finer astral forces, is patterned in a general way after the lifetronic astral form. The physical spinal cord and the chains of ganglia of the sympathetic nervous system that run alongside the spine coincide, respectively, with the astral *sushumna* and the *nadis* of the *ida* and *pingala* on the left and right of the *sushumna.* As the *sushumna* is the outermost sheath of the two subtler astral spinal channels (*vajra* and *chitra*), and of the causal "spine" of consciousness (*brahmanadi*)—described in the commentary on this verse—the physical spinal cord likewise consists of four concentric layers protected by the vertebrae:

(1) Outermost is a narrow lymph-filled capillary space bounded on the outside by a sturdy membrane, the *dura mater;* (2) a layer of spongy tissue filled with cerebrospinal fluid, covered by the delicate arachnoid membrane; (3) the white and grey matter, which is surrounded by a vascular membrane called the *pia mater,* and which contains afferent and efferent nerve tracts connecting the brain to the muscles, senses, and vital organs via the peripheral nerves; and (4) an extremely thin central canal in the middle of the grey matter.

The two eyes of the physical body, through which the world of duality is perceived, are patterned after the three phases of the astral spiritual eye: the golden halo of the astral eye encircling a sphere of blue light, in the centre of which is a bright starry light of five rays, is simulated in the physical eyes—in the white, the iris, and the pupil, respectively.

The physical body as a whole, when positioned with the arms outstretched to the sides and feet apart, resembles a five-pointed star, symbolizing the five starry rays seen in the spiritual eye that send forth the five vibratory elements which create the physical body: earth, water, fire, air, and ether (the head representing the finest element, ether; the two arms, air and fire; and the two feet, the grosser elements of water and earth).

The entire physical creation, so awe-inspiring to human mentality and intriguing to the inquisitive probings of science, provides only tantalizing hints to the underlying wonders of being—ideograms of the Cosmic Author to be deciphered by enlightened minds.

which controls the spiritual activities (those related to consciousness). The activities of these three astral spines are controlled primarily by the astral brain or *sahasrara* of a thousand rays. Specific rays of life and intelligence from the thousand-petalled lotus of light are directly reflected in the different astral spinal centres, giving each its characteristic activities and consciousness, just as portions of the physical brain are connected to specific nerves and nerve centres in the physical spinal plexuses.

As the physical body is made principally of flesh, and the astral body of *prana,* intelligent light or lifetrons, so the causal body is made specifically of consciousness, ideas, which I have termed "thoughtrons." It is the presence of the forces of the causal body behind the astral and physical bodies that causes and sustains their very existence and makes man a conscious, sentient being. The causal body has a spiritual brain of wisdom, and a spiritual spine called the *brahmanadi*. The *brahmanadi* has no covering of light as does the threefold astral spine; it is made of a strong current of consciousness. The *brahmanadi* is commonly described as inside, or *the* inside, of the *chitra* astral spine. This is at once both a fact and a misnomer. The *brahmanadi,* being the "spine" of the causal body, which is thought vibrations or consciousness, can only be described in relative terms as being "inside" or covered by the three astral spines, which in turn are covered by the spine of the physical body. The "forms" of the three bodies and their "spines" are a matter of degree of grossness superimposed on one another, with the finer obscured by the grosser, though not obstructed by it. The physical, astral, and causal instruments of the soul exist and function as an integrated whole through interaction between the various gross and finer forces.

❖
Structure of the astral and causal spines
❖

Within the causal cerebrospinal "channel," or *brahmanadi,* are seven spiritual centres of consciousness, corresponding to the subtle centres of light and power in the astral body. The physical, astral, and causal bodies are knitted together at these centres, uniting the three bodies to work together: a physical vehicle, empowered by astral life, with causal consciousness providing the power to cognize, think, will, and feel.

The causal brain is a reservoir of cosmic consciousness, the ever-existing, ever-conscious, ever-new bliss of Spirit, and of Its individualized expression, the soul. As this consciousness descends through the causal cerebrospinal centres, it manifests as wisdom in the causal cerebrum, intuition in the causal medulla, calmness in the causal cervical centre, the consciousness behind the power of life force in the causal dorsal centre, the consciousness or power of self-control in the causal lumbar centre, the power of adherence in the causal sacral centre, and the power of restraint in the causal coccygeal centre. These manifestations of the cosmic consciousness of the soul descending through the causal cerebrospinal centres, send wisdom, through the action of will, to the "cells" of endless thoughts which constitute the causal body.

As this consciousness flows outward from the causal body into the astral body, and then into the physical body, drawn by the magnetism of sense attachment to matter, the fine expression of original cosmic consciousness becomes increasingly deluded and gross, losing its true Spirit nature. Pure blissful intelligence, or wisdom, becomes discrimination. Discrimination distorted by the limitations of sense impressions becomes the blind whim-led mind. Expressing even more grossly, mind becomes life without cognizing power. Life becomes inert matter.

The koshas, stages of evolution in creation and man

These stages of expression are referred to in yoga as sheaths or *koshas*. All creation is encased in one or more of five *koshas*. These are screens of delusion, each of which, in descending order, obscures to a greater degree the real Cause and Essence of all creation, God. The five *koshas* are *anandamaya kosha,* or bliss sheath; *jnanamaya kosha,* the intellect or discriminative sheath; *manomaya kosha,* the sheath of the mind, *manas; pranamaya kosha,* the life sheath or *prana;* and *annamaya kosha,* gross matter. The bliss sheath is that which covers and causes the causal world and body of man. The three sheaths of intellect, mind, and life are the coverings of the astral universe and body of man. The matter sheath manifests as the physical universe and body of man.

In ascending order, from matter to Spirit, the five natural evolutionary stages of life are results of these five sheaths. When one by one the sheaths are unfolded, there is a corresponding manifestation of a progressively higher expression of life.

Inert minerals are enlocked in all five sheaths. With the unfolding of the *annamaya kosha* or matter sheath, *pranamaya kosha* or the life sheath is revealed, and the resulting manifestation is the life in plants. When *pranamaya kosha* is unfolded and *manomaya kosha* or the mind sheath becomes manifested, the animal kingdom is expressed. (Animals have perceptions and consciousness, but not the intellect to discriminate between right and wrong.) When *manomaya kosha* is unfolded, and *jnanamaya kosha* or the discriminative sheath is revealed, we have the manifestation of intellect, or man, with the ability to think, reason, and guide his actions by discrimination and free choice. When man rightly uses this discriminative power, *jnanamaya kosha* is ultimately rolled back and *anandamaya kosha* or the bliss sheath is revealed. This is the state of the divine man, with just a thin veil of individuality between himself and God.*

Man, being a microcosm of the universe, has within him all five sheaths—matter, life, mind, intellect, and bliss. He alone, of all forms of creation, has the ability to unfold all of these sheaths and free his soul to become one with God. Yoga, as described in the Bhagavad

---

* "In the ultimate analysis," declared the noted British geneticist J. B. S. Haldane, "the universe can be nothing less than the progressive manifestation of God."

Recent discoveries in many branches of research are gradually dispelling the long-held scientific opinion that the upward evolution of life and intelligence that produced human beings was an accidental process. The very existence of living matter is leading many scientists to acknowledge an inherent design in creation. "Careful analysis suggests that even a mildly impressive living molecule is quite unlikely to form randomly," *Time* magazine, December 28, 1992, reported. And an article in *Newsweek,* July 19, 1993, asked: "How did wisps of gas and specks of clay come to life?...Wherever the ingredients of life first evolved, combining them into something fully alive still seems madly improbable. Fred Hoyle, the British astronomer [founder of the Institute for Theoretical Astronomy at Cambridge University], once said the event is about as likely as assembling a Boeing 747 by sending a whirling tornado into a junkyard."

"One intriguing observation that has bubbled up from physics," the article in *Time* stated, "is that the universe seems calibrated for life's existence. If the force of gravity were pushed upward a bit, stars would burn out faster, leaving little time for life to evolve on the planets circling them. If the relative masses of protons and neutrons were changed by a hair, stars might never be born, since the hydrogen they eat wouldn't exist. If, at the Big Bang, some basic numbers—the 'initial conditions'—had been jiggled, matter and energy would never have coagulated into galaxies, stars, planets or any other platforms stable enough for life as we know it.

"One little-publicized fact is that many, perhaps most, evolutionary biologists now believe that evolution was very likely, given enough time, to create a species with our essential property: an intelligence so great that it becomes aware of itself and starts figuring out how things work. In fact, many biologists have long believed that [given the fundamental structure of the universe] the coming of highly intelligent life was close to inevitable."

In *The Immense Journey* (New York: Random House, 1957), biologist Loren Eiseley commented on the supposedly blind evolutionary processes of "natural selection" and "survival of the fittest" that fashioned complex living creatures from the earth's raw materials: "Men talk much of matter and energy, of the struggle for existence which moulds life. These things exist, it is true; but more delicate, elusive, quicker than fins in water, is that mysterious principle known as *organization,* which leaves all other mysteries concerned with life stale and insignificant by comparison. For that without organization life does not persist is obvious. Yet, this organization itself is not strictly the product of life, nor of selection. Like some dark and passing shadow within matter, it cups out the eyes' small windows or spaces the notes of a meadowlark's song....If 'dead' matter has reared up this curious landscape of fiddling crickets, song sparrows, and wondering men, it must be plain to even the most devoted materialist that the matter of which he speaks contains amazing, if not dreadful powers, and may not impossibly be, as Hardy has suggested, 'but one mask of many worn by the Great Face behind.'" *(Publisher's Note)*

Gita and elucidated in these present stanzas, is the method through which this liberation can be attained. By the correct practice of meditation, the accomplished yogi, through *pranayama,* or life-force control, "unfolds" the life-energy sheath (*pranamaya kosha*). He finds that this life energy is the link between matter and Spirit. With mastery of the life force he realizes the true nature of matter (the *annamaya kosha*) as a delusive objectification of Spirit. And as the inwardly flowing life energy disconnects the consciousness from identification with the limited sense-mind (*manomaya kosha*), that sheath unfolds so that the discriminative qualities of the intellect sheath or *buddhi* (*jnanamaya kosha*) can predominate in his life and in his meditation. The cultivation of the discriminative qualities by right spiritual action and yoga meditation gives him ultimately the ability to roll back the intellect sheath to reveal the fine bliss sheath (*anandamaya kosha*), which is the causal-body covering of his soul with its faculty of pure all-knowing intuition and wisdom. Unfolding the bliss sheath in deepest meditation, the yogi merges his soul in blissful oneness with God.

❖

The Principal Discriminative Powers of the Soul

As explained in the discussion of the first verse, the devotee may attain enlightening experiences in meditation, and even the bliss of *samadhi,* but still find that he is unable to maintain that consciousness permanently—as he is drawn back again into body consciousness by *samskaras,* or imprints, remaining on his consciousness from past habits and desires. This, then, is the state of the yogi as he prepares for the metaphysical battle. The pure discriminative powers—the principal ones being symbolically represented as the five divine sons of Pandu—have been roused within the yogi, ready to reclaim the bodily kingdom of the soul.

The five Pandavas are the central heroic figures of the Gita analogy, controlling the armies of consciousness and energy (*prana*) in the five subtle centres of the spine. They represent the qualities and powers acquired by the devotee whose deep meditation is attuned to the astral and causal centres of life and divine consciousness.

In ascending order, the significance of the five Pandavas is as follows:

Sahadeva: Restraint, Power to Stay Away From Evil (*Dama,* the active power of resistance, tenacity, by which restless outer sense organs can be controlled); and the vibratory earth element in the coccyx centre, or *muladhara chakra.*

NAKULA: Adherence, Power to Obey Good Rules (*Sama,* the positive or absorbing power, attention, by which mental tendencies can be controlled); and the vibrating water element in the sacral centre, or *svadhishthana chakra.*

ARJUNA: Self-Control; and the vibratory fire element in the lumbar centre. This centre, the *manipura chakra,* bestows the fire-force of mental and bodily strength to fight against the vast onslaught of the sense soldiers. It is the reinforcer of good habits and actions; the habit trainer. It holds the body upright, and causes purification of the body and mind, and makes deep meditation possible.

We see further why this centre allegorically represents Arjuna, the most skilled of all the Pandava army, when we consider its dual function. It is the pivotal or turning point of the devotee's life from gross materialism to finer spiritual qualities. From the lumbar to the sacral and coccygeal centres life and consciousness flow downward and outward to materialistic, sense-bound body consciousness. But in meditation, when the devotee assists the life and consciousness to be attracted to the magnetic pull in the higher or dorsal centre,* the power of this fiery lumbar centre dissociates itself from material concerns and upholds the spiritual work of the devotee through the powers in the higher centres.

When the devotee's consciousness has gone very deep in meditation, traversing the physical consciousness and the primary states of the astral soul-encasement, he finds in the inmost astral spine (the *chitra*) at the lumbar centre or *manipura chakra,* the opening from the astral body to the finer soul covering of the causal body. This is the common opening of the *brahmanadi,* or causal spine with its centres of divine consciousness, leading through the *chitra, vajra,* and *sushumna.* When the life and consciousness have been reversed inward in deep meditation, here is where the devotee merges in the stream of *brahmanadi* and enters the finer causal realm of the soul, the last encasement through which the yogi must pass before he can, by still deeper meditation, ultimately ascend through *brahmanadi* to Spirit.

When Arjuna, the power of self-control in the lumbar centre, rouses the fire of meditation and spiritual patience and determination, he draws upward the life and consciousness that was flowing downward and outward through the lumbar, sacral, and coccygeal centres, and thereby gives the meditating yogi the necessary mental and bodily strength to pursue

---

* See I:21–22 for reference to the magnetism between the coccygeal, dorsal, and spiritual-eye centres.

the course of deep meditation leading to Self-realization. Without this fire and self-control, no spiritual progress is possible. Thus Arjuna, more literally, also represents the devotee of self-control, patience, and determination within whom the battle of Kurukshetra is taking place. He is the chief devotee and disciple of the Lord, Bhagavan Krishna, who in the Gita dialogue is being shown by Krishna the way to victory.

The remaining two Pandavas are:

BHIMA: Power of Vitality, soul-controlled life force (*prana*); and the vibratory creative air (or *prana*) element in the dorsal centre, or *anahata chakra.* The power of this centre aids the devotee in the practice of the right techniques of *pranayama* to calm the breath and control the mind and sensory onslaughts. It is the power to still the internal and external organs and thus destroy the invasion of any passion (as of sex, greed, or anger). It is the destroyer of disease and doubt. It is the centre of divine love and spiritual creativity.

YUDHISTHIRA: Divine Calmness; and the creative vibratory ether element in the cervical centre, or *vishuddha chakra.* Yudhisthira, the eldest of the five offspring of Pandu (*buddhi,* or pure intellect) is fittingly portrayed as the king of all discriminative faculties, for calmness is the principal factor necessary for any expression of right discernment. Anything that ripples the consciousness, sensual or emotional, distorts whatever is perceived. But calmness is clarity of perception, intuition itself. As the ubiquitous ether remains unchanged, notwithstanding the violent roil of Nature's forces that play upon it, so the Yudhisthira discriminative faculty is the immutable calmness that discerns all things without distortion. It is the power of being able to plan the overthrow of an enemy passion. It is the power of attention, continued attention on the right object. It governs the span of attention, and the penetration of attention. It is the power of inference of the effects of wrong actions, and the power of assimilation of goodness through calmness. It is the power of comparison between good and evil; and common sense in perceiving the virtue of reinforcing a friend and destroying an enemy (as of the senses and habits, for example). It is the power of intuitive imagination, the ability to image or visualize a truth until it manifests.*

* Recent scientific research into the mind's materializing power of visualization has confirmed that people can learn how to harness their ability to create and work with vivid mental imagery for physical, mental, emotional and spiritual well-being. In one seven-year study, Dr. S. Rappaport analyzed twenty-five individuals who had accomplished

The Pandavas' chief counsellor and support is the Lord Himself, who, in the form of Krishna, represents variously the Spirit, the soul, or intuition as manifested in the states of superconsciousness, *Kutastha Chaitanya* or Christ consciousness, and cosmic consciousness in the medulla, *Kutastha* or Christ centre, and thousand-petalled lotus; or as the guru instructing his disciple, the devotee Arjuna. Within the devotee, Lord Krishna is thus the guiding Divine Intelligence speaking to the lower self that has gone astray in the entanglements of sensory consciousness. This Higher Intelligence is the master and teacher, and the lower mental intellect is the disciple; the Higher Intelligence advises the lower vitiated self on how to uplift itself in accord with the eternal verities, and in fulfilment of its inherent God-given duty.

CORRELATION OF PATANJALI'S YOGA WITH GITA'S ALLEGORICAL BATTLE

A DESCRIPTION OF THE SUBTLE cerebrospinal centres and their intricate functions of life and consciousness has challenged the minds of scholars for generations. Ponderous volumes have been produced, in which even the keenest intellects have become lost in labyrinths of their own making. The untold thousands of *nadis* (astral nerve-conductors of *prana*), the electromagnetic forces of the astral and causal bodies, their interaction on consciousness, all serve to operate the atomic, cellular, and chemical activities, and the states of consciousness, of the gross physical body and mind. But being of another dimension, they strain the resources of the language of man and fit uncomfortably in the limited confines of a three-dimensional sphere. Yet even without an intellectual understanding, there have been in every clime and age those who, practising the basics of true religion, have arrived at an intuitive perception of the real nature of man and the universe in which he lives, and the Divine Cause from which both have come. The ponderous *Mahabharata* of the divine seer Vyasa is not only a history but a comprehensive allegory of this science of creation and the nature of the Creator. The Gita, a small portion of the *Mahabharata* epic, is the essence of that yoga science. It sets forth the essentials of true religion by the practice of which Self-realization is attained.

---

extraordinary physical transformations—overcoming birth defects, recovering from "incurable" illnesses, regaining function after severely crippling accidents, and so on. "All these people told me the same thing," she reported. "They all had an image in their minds of who and what they wanted to be, and they literally grew their physical bodies into that imagined form." *(Publisher's Note)*

India's great sage Patanjali, whose date is a matter of conjecture by the scholars,* understood that the Bhagavad Gita was the "Song Celestial" by which the Lord wanted to unite the soul of His ignorant and wandering children with His own Spirit. This was to be accomplished scientifically through physical, mental, and spiritual law. Patanjali explained this spiritual science in definite metaphysical terms in his renowned *Yoga Sutras*. His purpose was to get at the very core of yoga, the application of which provides the means for the devotee to realize God and from that vantage point to know, through intuitive Self-realization, the intricate phenomena of manifested creation. While the Gita describes in allegory the process of realizing God, Patanjali speaks of the scientific method of uniting the soul with the undifferentiated Spirit in such a beautiful, clear, and concise way that generations of scholars have acknowledged him as the foremost exponent of yoga.

Intent of the Gita made clear when correlated with yoga

The intent of the Gita is brought immediately into focus when we see how each of the warriors mentioned in verses 4 through 8 relate to the practice of yoga as described by Patanjali in his *Yoga Sutras*. The correlation is found in the metaphorical significance of the various metaphysical warriors, implied in the meaning derived from their names, or from a Sanskrit root within their names, or from their significance in the *Mahabharata* epic.

In verses 4, 5, and 6, King Desire (Duryodhana) informs his preceptor Past Habit (Drona) about the spiritual soldiers in the cerebrospinal centres that have lined up in battle array. These metaphysical soldiers, which have gathered to support the cause of the five Pandavas, are the spiritual effects engendered by the devotee's practice of yoga. They, along with the five principal Pandavas, come to the aid of the yogi to help him battle the evil soldiers of the sense mind.

Duryodhana identifies them as Yuyudhana, Virata, Drupada, Dhrishtaketu, Chekitana, King of Kashi (Kashiraja), Purujit, Kuntibhoja, Shaibya, Yudhamanyu, Uttamaujas, the son of Subhadra (Abhimanyu),

* "Patanjali's date is unknown, though many scholars assign him to the second century B.C. The *rishis* wrote treatises on a vast number of subjects with such insight that the ages have been powerless to outmode them; yet, to the subsequent consternation of historians, the sages made no effort to attach their own dates and stamp of personality to their literary works. They knew that their brief spans were only temporarily important as flashes of the great infinite Life; and that truth is timeless, impossible to trademark, and no private possession of their own."—*Autobiography of a Yogi*

and the five sons of Draupadi. Their metaphorical significance will be explained in the categorical order adopted by Patanjali.

Patanjali begins his *Yoga Sutras* with the definition of yoga as "the neutralization of the alternating waves in consciousness" (*chitta vritti nirodha*—I:2). This may also be translated as "cessation of the modifications of the mind-stuff." I have explained in *Autobiography of a Yogi,* "*Chitta* is a comprehensive term for the thinking principle, which includes the pranic life forces, *manas* (mind or sense consciousness), *ahamkara* (egoity), and *buddhi* (intuitive intelligence). *Vritti* (literally 'whirlpool') refers to the waves of thought and emotion that ceaselessly arise and subside in man's consciousness. *Nirodha* means neutralization, cessation, control."

Patanjali continues: "Then the seer abides in his own nature or self" (I:3). This refers to his true Self, or soul. That is, he attains Self-realization, oneness of his soul with God. Patanjali explains in *sutras* I:20–21: "[The attainment of this goal of yoga] is preceded by *shraddha* (devotion), *virya* (vital celibacy), *smriti* (memory), *samadhi* (the experience of God-union during meditation), *prajna* (discriminative intelligence). Its attainment is nearest to those possessing *tivra-samvega,* divine ardour (fervent devotion and striving for God, and extreme dispassion toward the world of the senses)."

From these *sutras* we have the first six metaphysical soldiers, which stand in readiness to aid the yogi's battle for Self-realization:

1. YUYUDHANA—DIVINE DEVOTION (SHRADDHA)

From the Sanskrit root *yudh,* "to fight," Yuyudhana means literally "he who has been fighting for his own benefit." The metaphorical derivation: *Yudhaṁ caitanya-prakāśayitum eṣaṇaḥ abhilaṣamāna iti*—"One who has an ardent desire to fight to express spiritual consciousness." It represents the attracting principle of love whose "duty" it is to draw creation back to God. Felt by the devotee as *shraddha,* or devotion for God, it is an inherent pull of the heart in longing to know Him. It stirs the devotee to spiritual action and supports his *sadhana* (spiritual practices). *Shraddha* is frequently translated as faith; but it is more accurately defined as the natural inclination, or devotion, of the heart quality to turn toward its Source, and faith is an integral part of surrendering to this pull. Creation is a result of repulsion, a going away from God—an externalization of Spirit. But inherent in matter is the force of attraction. This is the love of God, a magnet that ultimately pulls creation back to Him. The more the devotee is attuned to it, the stronger the pull becomes, and the sweeter the purifying effects of the yogi's divine devotion.

Yuyudhana, Divine Devotion, fights the forces of irreverent satanic disbelief or doubt, which try to dissuade and discourage the aspirant.

2. UTTAMAUJAS—VITAL CELIBACY (VIRYA)

The literal meaning of Uttamaujas, the *Mahabharata* warrior, is "of excellent valour." The common interpretation given to Patanjali's *virya* is heroism or courage. But in yoga philosophy, *virya* also refers to the creative semen, which, if instead of being sensually dissipated is transmuted into its pure vital essence, gives great bodily strength, vitality, and moral courage.* Thus we find that Uttamaujas from the Sanskrit *uttama,* "chief, principal" and *ojas,* "energy, power, bodily strength," may also be translated as "the principal power, the chief bodily strength." Thus, the metaphorical derivation: *Uttamam ojo yasya sa iti*—"One whose power is supreme (of highest or superlative quality)." The vital essence, when mastered by the yogi, is a principal source of his spiritual strength and moral fortitude.

The vital essence, the sense mind, the breath, and *prana* (the life force or vitality) are closely interrelated. Mastery of even one gives control over the other three also. The devotee who employs scientific yoga techniques to control simultaneously all four forces quickly reaches a higher state of consciousness.

Uttamaujas, Vital Celibacy, lends its power to the devotee to defeat the forces of temptations and habits of debauchery, and thus to free the life force to be lifted up from gross pleasure to divine bliss.

3. CHEKITANA—SPIRITUAL MEMORY (SMRITI)

Chekitana means "intelligent." From its Sanskrit root *chit* come the derivative meanings, "to appear, to shine, to remember." The metaphorical derivation: *Ciketi jānāti iti*—"He remembers, realizes, true knowledge whose perception is clear, concentrated." Patanjali's *smriti* means memory, divine and human. It is that faculty by which the yogi recalls his true nature as made in the image of God. As this memory appears or shines on his consciousness, it gives him that intelligence or clear perception which helps to light his path.

* The female equivalent of semen is in the reproductive elements that produce the ovum and develop it into a vital being. Yoga teaches that in sexual intercourse, both men and women dissipate the reservoir of subtle life force inherent in the reproductive organs.

Chekitana, Spiritual Memory, stands in readiness to oppose the material delusion that makes man forget God and consider himself a body-bound mortal being.

4. VIRATA—ECSTASY (SAMADHI)

When the five Pandavas were exiled from their kingdom by Duryodhana, the conditions were that they must spend twelve years in the forest and that in the thirteenth year they must live undiscovered by the spies of Duryodhana. Thus it was that the Pandavas spent the thirteenth year in disguise in the court of King Virata. The metaphorical significance is that once material desires as habits take complete control, it requires a cycle of twelve years to rid the bodily kingdom of the usurpers. Before the rightful discriminative qualities can regain their kingdom, the devotee must draw those qualities from his experiences in *samadhi* meditation, and then be able to hold on to them while expressing through the physical body and senses. When the discriminative qualities have thus proven their power, they are ready for the metaphysical battle to reclaim their bodily kingdom. Thus, Virata represents Patanjali's *samadhi,* the temporary states of divine union in meditation from which the yogi draws spiritual strength. Virata comes from the Sanskrit *vi-rāj,* "to rule, to shine forth." *Vi* expresses distinction, opposition, implying the difference between ruling in an ordinary way and ruling or reigning from the divine consciousness experienced in *samadhi*. The metaphorical derivation: *Viśeṣeṇa ātmani rājate iti*—"One who is wholly immersed in his inner Self." Under the influence or rule of *samadhi,* the devotee himself is illuminated and governs his actions by divine wisdom.

Virata, Samadhi, the state of oneness with God attained during deep meditation, routs the delusion that has made the soul behold, through its ego nature, not the One True Spirit, but the diverse forms of matter and the pairs of opposites.

5. KASHIRAJA—DISCRIMINATIVE INTELLIGENCE (PRAJNA)

The word Kashiraja derives from *kāśi,* "shining, splendid, brilliant," and *rāj,* "to reign, to rule, to shine." It means to reign with light, or in a splendid or brilliant way; the light that reveals the substance behind the seeming. The metaphorical derivation: *Padārthān kāśyan prakāśayan rājate vibhāti iti*—"One whose shining causes other things to shine (to be accurately revealed)." This ally of the Pandavas represents Patanjali's *prajna,* discriminative intelligence—insight or wisdom—which is the principal enlightening faculty in the devotee. *Prajna* is not the mere intellect of the scholar, bound by logic, reason, and memory, but an expression of the divine faculty of the Supreme Knower.

Kashiraja, Discriminative Intelligence, protects the devotee from entrapment by the cunning troops of false reasoning.

6. DRUPADA—EXTREME DISPASSION (TIVRA-SAMVEGA)

The literal translation of the Sanskrit roots in Drupada are *dru,* "to run, hasten," and *pada,* "pace or step." The metaphorical derivation: *Drutam padam yasya sa iti*—"One whose steps are quick, or swift." The implied meaning is one who advances swiftly. This correlates with Patanjali's *tivra-samvega;* literally, *tīvra,* "extreme," and *samvega,* from *sam,* "together," and *vij,* "to move quickly, to speed." The word *samvega* also means dispassion toward the things of the world arising from an ardent longing for emancipation. This dispassionate detachment from worldly objects and concerns is referred to elsewhere in the Gita as *vairagya.** Patanjali says, as cited earlier, that the goal of yoga is nearest (that is, is reached most quickly by) those who possess *tivra-samvega.* This intense dispassion is not a negative disinterest or deprived state of renunciation. The meaning of the word rather encompasses such an ardent devotion for attaining the spiritual goal—a feeling that stirs the devotee into positive action and mental intensity—that longing for the world is transmuted naturally into a fulfilling desire for God.

Drupada, Extreme Dispassion, supports the devotee's fight against the strong army of material attachment that seeks to turn him from his spiritual goal.

THE EIGHT ESSENTIAL STEPS OF RAJA YOGA

THE NEXT PANDAVA ALLIES represent the essentials of yoga. These *yogangas,* or limbs of yoga, have come to be known as Patanjali's Eightfold Path of Yoga. They are enumerated in his *Yoga Sutras,* II:29: *Yama* (moral conduct, the avoidance of immoral actions); *niyama* (religious observances); *asana* (right posture for bodily and mental control); *pranayama* (control of *prana* or life force); *pratyahara* (interiorization of the mind); *dharana* (concentration); *dhyana* (meditation); and *samadhi* (divine union).

Continuing, then, to describe the metaphysical soldiers:

* See, for example, VI:35 and XVIII:52.

7. Dhrishtaketu—Power of Mental Resistance (Yama)

In the Sanskrit root *dhriṣ* are the meanings, "to be bold and courageous; to dare to attack." *Ketu* means "chief or leader"; also "brightness, clearness; intellect, judgement." The metaphorical derivation: *Yena ketavaḥ āpadaḥ dhṛṣyate anena iti*—"One by whose discriminative intellect difficulties are overpowered." The object against which Dhrishtaketu directs his power is found also within his name. In addition to meaning bold and daring, *dhrishta* means "licentious." Dhrishtaketu represents that power within the devotee which has the right judgement to attack with courage—that is, the mental power to resist—evil inclinations toward immoral behaviour. It thus represents Patanjali's *yama,* moral conduct. This first step of the Eightfold Path is fulfilled by observing the "thou shalt nots"—abstaining from injury to others, falsehood, stealing, incontinence, and covetousness. Understood in the full sense of their meaning, these proscripts embrace the whole of moral conduct. By their observance, the yogi avoids the primary or fundamental difficulties that could block his progress toward Self-realization. Breaking the rules of moral conduct creates not only present misery, but long-lasting karmic effects that bind the devotee to suffering and mortal limitation.

Dhrishtaketu, Power of Mental Resistance, battles the desires to indulge in behaviour that is contrary to spiritual law, and helps to neutralise the karmic effects of past mistakes.

8. Shaibya—Power of Mental Adherence (Niyama)

Shaibya, often written *Shaivya,* relates to Shiva, which word in turn derives from the Sanskrit root *śī,* "in whom all things lie." Shiva also means "auspicious, benevolent, happy; welfare." The metaphorical derivation of Shaibya: *Śivaṁ maṅgalaṁ tat-sambandhī-yam iti maṅgala-dāyakaṁ*—"One who adheres to what is good or auspicious—to what is conducive to one's welfare." Shaibya corresponds to Patanjali's *niyama,* religious observances. It represents the devotee's power to adhere to the spiritual prescriptions of *niyama,* the "thou shalts": purity of body and mind, contentment in all circumstances, self-discipline, self-study (contemplation), and devotion to God.

Shaibya, Power of Mental Adherence, provides the yogi with an army of positive spiritual self-discipline to defeat the battalions of evil misery-producing ways and the effects of past bad karma.

Yama-niyama are the foundation on which the yogi begins to build his spiritual life. They harmonize body and mind with the divine laws of nature, or creation, producing an inner and outer well-being, happiness, and strength that attract the devotee to deeper spiritual practices and make him receptive to the blessings of his guru-given *sadhana* (spiritual path).

9. KUNTIBHOJA—RIGHT POSTURE (ASANA)

Bhoja, in Kuntibhoja, derives from *bhuj,* "to take possession of, to rule or govern." Kuntibhoja is the adoptive father of Kunti. The metaphorical derivation: *Yena kuntiṁ kunā āmantraṇā daiva-vibhūtī ākarṣikā śaktiṁ bhunakti pālayate yaḥ saḥ*—"He who takes possession of and supports the spiritual force—Kunti—by which divine powers are invoked and drawn to oneself." Kunti is the wife of Pandu and mother of the three elder Pandava brothers—Yudhisthira, Bhima, and Arjuna—and stepmother to the two younger brothers, twins—Nakula and Sahadeva. She had the power to invoke the gods (cosmic creative forces), and through this means these five sons were born.* Metaphorically, Kunti (from *ku,* to call) is the ardent devotee's spiritual power to invoke the aid of the creative life force in his *sadhana*. Kunti (as does Drupada) represents the devotee's dispassion for the world and longing for God which, during meditation, reverses the outward flowing life force to concentrate within. When the life force and consciousness are united to Pandu, *buddhi* (discrimination), the *tattvas* or elements in the subtle spinal centres (conceived in the microcosmic womb or centres of the body by the macrocosmic or universal creative forces) become manifested to the yogi (that is, are given birth to by Kunti).

Kuntibhoja represents Patanjali's *asana,* the faculty derived from the poise or control of the body, for the correct posture is essential to the yogi's practice of life-force control. As Kuntibhoja "adopted and reared" Kunti, so does *asana* "support" the ability to invoke divine life energy in preparation for the practice of *pranayama,* or life-force control (the step following *asana* on the Eightfold Path).

Asana prescribes the necessary correct posture for yoga meditation. Though many variations have evolved, the essential basics are a steady body with straight, erect spine; chin parallel to the ground; shoulders back, chest out, abdomen in; and eyes focused at the *Kutastha* centre between the eyebrows. The body must be still and unmoving, without strain or tension. When mastered, the correct posture or *asana* becomes as expressed by Patanjali, "steady and pleasant."† It bestows

* See Introduction, page *xxvii.*

† *Yoga Sutras* II:46.

bodily control and mental and physical calmness, enabling the yogi to meditate for hours, if so desired, without fatigue or restlessness.

It is evident, then, why *asana* is essential to life-force control: It supports the inner dispassion toward the demands of the body and the ardent power necessary to invoke the aid of the life energies in turning the consciousness inward to the world of Spirit.

Kuntibhoja, Right Posture, provides the physical and mental pacification necessary to fight the body-bound tendencies toward laziness, restlessness, and flesh attachment.

10. Yudhamanyu—Life-force Control (Pranayama)

From *yudh,* "to fight," and *manyu,* "high spirit or ardour," Yudhamanyu means "he who fights with great zeal and determination." The metaphorical derivation: *Yudhaṁ caitanya-prakāśayitum eva manyu-kriyā yasya saḥ*—"One whose chief action is to fight to manifest divine consciousness." The life force is the link between matter and Spirit. Flowing outward it reveals the spuriously alluring world of the senses; reversed inward it pulls the consciousness to the eternally satisfying bliss of God. The meditating devotee sits between these two worlds, striving to enter the kingdom of God, but kept engaged in battling the senses. With the aid of a scientific technique of *pranayama,* the yogi is at last victorious in reversing the outward-flowing life energy that externalized his consciousness in the action of breath, heart, and sense-ensnared life currents. He enters the natural inner calm realm of the soul and Spirit.

Yudhamanyu, Life-Force Control, is the invaluable warrior in the Pandava army that disarms and renders powerless the sense army of the blind mind.

11. Purujit—Interiorization (Pratyahara)

Purujit, translated literally, means "conquering many," from *puru* (root *pṝ*), "many," and *jit* (root *ji*), "conquering; removing (in meditation)." The metaphorical derivation: *Paurān indriya-adhiṣṭhātṛ-devān jayati iti*—"One who has conquered the fortresses of the astral powers ruling the senses." The Sanskrit word *pur* (root *pṝ*) means "fortress" and here refers to the sensory strongholds of the mind (*manas*) and its sensory organs, the functions of which are governed by the astral powers in the subtle cerebrospinal centres. In the Sanskrit root *ji* is the meaning "subdue, master." Purujit, as referred to in the Gita context, implies the one by which the many (the sense soldiers) of the sensory fortresses of the body are mastered or subdued. That is, Purujit represents Patanjali's *pratyahara,* the withdrawal of consciousness from the senses, the result of successful practice of *pranayama* or control of the life force (the astral powers) that enlivens the senses and bears their messages to the brain. When the devotee has attained *pratyahara,* the life is switched off from the senses, and the mind and consciousness are still and interiorized.

Purujit, Interiorization, provides the yogi with that steadiness of mental calm that prevents the prenatal habits of the sense army from causing sudden scattering of the mind on the material world.

12. Saubhadra, i.e., Son of Subhadra (Abhimanyu)—Self-mastery (Samyama)

Subhadra is the wife of Arjuna. Their son's name is Abhimanyu, from *abhi,* "with intensity; toward, into," and *manyu,* "spirit, mood, mind; ardour." Abhimanyu represents the intense mental state (one's spiritual mood, or *bhava*) in which the consciousness is drawn "toward" or "into" union with the object of its concentration or ardour, giving perfect self-control or self-mastery. It is referred to by Patanjali in his *Yoga Sutras,* III:1–4, as *samyama,* a collective term under which the last three steps of the Eightfold Path are grouped together.

The first five steps are the preliminaries of yoga. *Samyama,* from *sam,* "together," and *yama,* "holding," consists of the occult trio, *dharana* (concentration), *dhyana* (meditation), and *samadhi* (divine union), and is yoga proper. When the mind has been withdrawn from sensory disturbances (*pratyahara*), then *dharana* and *dhyana* in conjunction produce the varying stages of *samadhi:* ecstatic realization and, finally, divine union. *Dhyana,* or meditation, is the focusing of the freed attention on Spirit. It involves the meditator, the process or technique of meditation, and the object of meditation. *Dharana* is concentration or fixity on that inner conception or object of meditation. Thus arises from this contemplation the perception of the Divine Presence, first within oneself, and then evolving into cosmic conception—conceiving of the vastness of Spirit, omnipresent within and beyond all creation. The culmination of *samyama* self-mastery is when the meditator, the process of meditating, and the object of meditation become one—the full realization of oneness with Spirit.

By reference in the Gita text to Abhimanyu's metronymic, Saubhadra, we are directed to the meaning of Subhadra, "glorious, splendid." Thus Abhimanyu is that self-mastery which bestows light or illumination. The metaphorical derivation: *Abhi sarvatra manute prakāśate iti*—"One whose intensely concentrating mind shines everywhere," i.e., lights or reveals everything; makes manifest the illumined state of Self-realization.

Abhimanyu, Self-Mastery, is that great Pandava warrior whose victories enable the yogi to hold back the onslaught of the restless, delusive consciousness of ego, senses, and habits and thus to remain longer and longer in the state of divine soul consciousness—both during and after meditation.

13. SONS OF DRAUPADI—FIVE SPINAL CENTRES AWAKENED BY KUNDALINI

Draupadi is the daughter of Drupada (Extreme Dispassion). She represents the spiritual power or feeling of *kundalini,** which is roused, or born of, the Drupada divine ardour and dispassion. When *kundalini* is lifted upward, it is "wedded" to the five Pandavas (the creative vibratory elements and consciousness in the five spinal centres), and thereby gives birth to five sons.

The sons of Draupadi are the manifestations of the five opened or awakened spinal centres—such as the specific forms, lights, or sounds characteristic of each centre—upon which the yogi concentrates to draw divine discriminative power to fight the sense mind and its offspring.

VERSE 7

अस्माकं तु विशिष्टा ये तान्निबोध द्विजोत्तम।
नायका मम सैन्यस्य सञ्ज्ञार्थं तान्ब्रवीमि ते॥

Listen, too, O Flower of the twice-born (best of the Brahmins), about the generals of my army who are prominent amongst ourselves: these I speak about now for thine information.

THE DIVINELY GUIDED INTROSPECTION of Arjuna, the devotee, continues: "O Learned One (Drona—Habit—common preceptor of both good and evil tendencies), having reviewed the commanding generals of the soldiers of wisdom, I, Duryodhana, King Material Desire, relate now for your information the names of the most distinguished and powerful defenders of my sense army, poised to annihilate the wisdom forces."

* See page 18.

VERSE 8

भवान्भीष्मश्च कर्णश्च कृपश्च समितिञ्जयः ।
अश्वत्थामा विकर्णश्च सौमदत्तिर्जयद्रथः ॥

These warriors are thyself (Drona), Bhishma, Karna, and Kripa —victors in battles; Ashvatthaman, Vikarna, the son of Somadatta, and Jayadratha.*

"THE LEADERS OF MY SENSE ARMY are thyself (Drona, Habit or Inner Tendency), Bhishma (Inner-seeing Ego), Karna (Attachment), Kripa (Individual Delusion), Ashvatthaman (Latent Desire), Vikarna (Repulsion), Somadatti (son of Somadatta, i.e., Bhurishravas, representing Karma or Material Action) and Jayadratha (Body Attachment)."

King Duryodhana–Material Desire, having reviewed in fear the awesome power of the rival forces of discrimination, now tries to console his alarmed mind and that of his preceptor Drona-Habit by describing the strength of his own army—the sense soldiers and generals arrayed to defend him.

Man's inclination toward material desire, when confronted by the host of resistance of discriminative reason, newly aroused to assert its lost right, becomes internally nervous, conscious of its own weakness and impending defeat. Frailties and weaknesses that have become one's comfortable second nature are always troubled by the awakening of sleeping conscience and inherent discernment. Desire generally has undisputed sway over the bodily kingdom of the sense-inclined mind. As long as desire satisfactorily and uninterruptedly gratifies all its propensities and fulfils its ends, it doesn't bother anyone. But desire becomes alarmed as soon as the sense-identified animal-man (bound mostly by *manomaya kosha*) awakens through introspection his higher discriminative faculties (unfolds more fully the *jnanamaya kosha*) with its clearer consciousness of duty and right action. Then no more has desire its free sway, for these new discriminative warriors begin to interrupt desire's wayward ungodly activities.

---

* Among the more than seventy Sanskrit Gita commentaries produced by highly regarded scholars—the first available one having been written by Adi Shankaracharya—an occasional variation occurs in the Gita Sanskrit *slokas.* The word Jayadratha, for example, appears in some versions after "the son of Somadatta," but not in others. When the allegory of the Gita is correlated to Patanjali's *Yoga Sutras,* as in this commentary by Paramahansaji, the necessity for the inclusion of Jayadratha becomes evident. *(Publisher's Note)*

King Material Desire wishes Past Habit-Tendency, which has sided with the prevailing evil sense inclinations, to be in possession of the full facts about the strength of the opposing metaphysical army, so that the necessary means might be devised to overcome it.

EXPANDED COMMENTARY: SYMBOLIC FORCES THAT OPPOSE SOUL QUALITIES

AS THE PANDAVAS ENUMERATED in verses 4–6 represent the principles necessary for the yogi to attain realization or oneness with God, the Kauravas named by Duryodhana in verse 8 are metaphorically representative of specific principles that oppose spiritual progress.

In the *Yoga Sutras,* I:24, Patanjali says: "The Lord (Ishvara) is untouched by *klesha* (troubles), *karma* (action), *vipaka* (habit), and *ashaya* (desire)." In the *Yoga Sutras,* II:3, *klesha,* or troubles, is defined as fivefold: *avidya* (ignorance), *asmita* (ego), *raga* (attachment), *dvesha* (aversion), *abhinivesha* (body attachment). Since the Lord is free from these eight imperfections inherent in creation, the yogi who seeks union with God must likewise first rid his consciousness of these obstacles to spiritual victory. Correlating these principles, in the order given by Patanjali, with the Gita warriors named by Duryodhana, we have the following:

1. KRIPA—INDIVIDUAL DELUSION (AVIDYA)

Traditionally, the name Kripa is said to derive from the Sanskrit root *kṛip,* "to pity." But phonetically, which is the basis of pure Sanskrit, in transliteration the root corresponds to *klṛip*.* From this root is the meaning "to imagine," the intent of author Vyasa in symbolizing Kripa as *avidya,* individual delusion—ignorance, illusion. The metaphorical derivation: *Vastunyanyatvam kalpayati iti*—"One who imagines matter to be other than what it is." *Avidya* is the first of the five *kleshas*. This individual delusion is the ignorance in man that clouds his perception and gives him a false concept of reality. Patanjali describes *avidya*

---

* The renowned Sanskritist, W. D. Whitney, in his noted work *The Roots, Verb-forms, and Primary Derivatives of the Sanskrit Language,* lists the roots *kṛp* [*kṛip*] and *klp* (the latter of which is rendered as *klṛip* by Monier-Williams). In his analysis of *kḷp,* Whitney notes: "With this root are apparently related *kṛp* [*kṛip*] (from the time of the Vedas and Brahmanas), *kṛpa* [*kṛipa*] (from the Vedas onwards)." *(Publisher's Note)*

in these words: "Ignorance is perceiving the non-eternal, impure, evil, and what is not soul, to be eternal, pure, good, and the soul."*

Maya, cosmic delusion, is the universal substance of forms in the Infinite Formless. *Avidya* is the individual cosmic hypnosis or illusion imposed on the forms that makes them express, perceive, and interact with one another as though each has its own separate reality. God's omnipresent undifferentiated cosmic consciousness underlies its mayic separations into parts through which the Creator expresses His manifoldness. By the visualization of His thoughts, through the power of *maya*, "the magical measurer," God creates, sustains, and dissolves dream worlds and beings.

Maya and avidya: delusion and ignorance

Similarly, man's unmodified divine consciousness, as the individualized soul, is the basis of all his expressions. God's mayic power of visualization has been inherited by man in the form of *avidya*. Through this personalized "measurer," man's one soul-consciousness becomes differentiated. By delusive imagination, the power of visualization or imaging the ego's concepts, man creates his own illusions of reality and "materializes" or brings them into being or expression through the instruments of his differentiated consciousness (mind, intelligence, feeling, and sensory organs of perception and action).† Thus is he a miniature creator, fashioning good or ill for himself and the phenomenal world of which he is an operative part. It is this creative force inherent in man's thoughts that makes them so formidable. The truth in the adage "Thoughts are things" should be duly respected!

---

* *Yoga Sutras* II:5.

† "Vision requires far more than a functioning physical organ; without an inner light, without a formative visual imagination, we are blind," writes Professor Arthur Zajonc in *Catching the Light: The Entwined History of Light and Mind* (New York: Bantam Books, 1993). He quotes the French eye surgeon Moreau: "It would be an error to suppose that a patient whose sight has been restored to him by surgical intervention can thereafter see the external world." Removal of cataracts in people blind from birth leaves them able to perceive little more than varying intensities of blurry light; they cannot distinguish objects or people. "To give back sight to a congenitally blind person is more the work of an educator than of a surgeon," said Dr. Moreau.

"The lights of nature and of mind entwine within the eye and call forth vision," Professor Zajonc explains. "Two lights brighten our world. One is provided by the sun, but another answers to it—the light of the eye. Only through their entwining do we see; lacking either, we are blind.... Besides an outer light and eye, sight requires an 'inner light,' one whose luminance complements the familiar outer light and transforms raw sensation into meaningful perception. The light of the mind must flow into and marry with the light of nature to bring forth a world." *(Publisher's Note)*

The influence of the force of *avidya* is such that no matter how irksome the illusion, deluded man is loath to part with it. Anyone who has tried to change the view of an opinionated person—or even to alter his own strong opinion, for that matter—knows how compelling the "reality" of *avidya*-fashioned concepts can be to the one who cherishes them. And therein lies the ignorance. The confirmed materialist, captive in his own realm of "reality," is ignorant of his deluded state and therefore has no wish nor will to exchange it for the sole Reality, Spirit. He perceives the temporal world as reality, eternal substance—insofar as he is able to grasp the concept of eternity. He imagines the grossness of sensory experience to be the pure essence of feeling and perception. He fabricates his own standards of morality and behaviour and calls them good, irrespective of their inharmony with eternal Divine Law. And he thinks that his ego, his mortal sense of being—with its inflated self-importance as the almighty doer—is the image of his soul as created by God.

Characteristics of spiritual ignorance

Avidya is a mighty archenemy of divine realization when under the negative influence of worldly sense inclinations. Yet in the *Mahabharata* epic, we see that Kripa, the Kuru warrior-general representing *avidya,* is one of the few survivors of the war of Kurukshetra; and that after the battle he makes peace with the Pandavas and is appointed a tutor to Parikshit, grandson of Arjuna—sole heir and progenitor of the Pandavas. The meaning is that in the creative sphere of relativity, naught can exist without this principle of individuality. If *avidya* is completely withdrawn, the form that it maintains would resolve again into formless Spirit.

Ordinary man is dumbfounded by the enticing propositions of illusory sense experiences, and clings to delusive material forms as though they were the reality and the cause and security of his existence. The yogi, on the other hand, is ever conscious inwardly of the sole Reality, Spirit, and sees *maya* and *avidya*—universal and individual delusion—as merely a tenuous web holding together the atomic, magnetic, and spiritual forces that give him a body and mind with which to play a part in the cosmic drama of the Lord's creation.

2. BHISHMA—EGO (ASMITA)

Yasmāt pañcatattvani vibheti saḥ—"One who 'frightens,' rouses or causes the manifestation of, the five *tattvas* (elements)." The metaphorical significance of Bhishma as Ego has already been explained (see Introduction, page *xxxvi*). He is the grandsire of individual existence, the cause for which form and the perception of form come into being through the creative elements (*tattvas*) that produce the body of man and its instruments of sense perception and action.

The name Bhishma derives from the Sanskrit root *bhī* or *bhīṣ,* "to frighten." By the power of this awesome force—which is reflected Spirit (*abhasa chaitanya*) whose individuality identifies not with Spirit but with the world of seeming—the forces of nature through the *tattvas* are roused from quiescence to produce and enliven a bodily instrument for expression. In the psychological-metaphysical battle being described, Bhishma-Ego is the most powerful opponent of the Pandavas, thus igniting the greatest fear in the hearts of the spiritual forces in the spinal centres that are striving to turn toward Spirit to reestablish the kingdom of divine soul consciousness.

Patanjali's *asmita,* the second of the *kleshas,* derives from the Sanskrit *asmi,* "I am," (from *as,* to be). It is thus egoism, the same as the allegorical Bhishma in the Gita.

The consciousness of a man in a dream becomes many images—beings, creatures, objects. In his dream, he gives his own existence to all forms and sensory objects. To each human character he lends his own ego consciousness so that they all behave, think, walk, talk to the dreamer as individualized beings, with separate "soul" identities, even though all are created by the one spirit and mind of the dreamer. Similarly, God in His cosmic dream becomes earth, stars, minerals, trees, animals, and manifold human souls. God lends His own consciousness of existence to all things in His cosmic dream, and sentient creatures feel it as though it were their own separate identities.

Patanjali describes the *klesha* of the individualized sense of being thus: "*Asmita* (egoism) is the identifying of the seer with the instruments of seeing."* Ego is when the soul, or seer, the image of God in man, forgets its true divine Self and becomes identified with the powers of perception and action in the instruments of the body and mind. *Asmita* is therefore the consciousness in which the seer (the soul or its pseudonature, the ego) and its discriminating powers are present as though indivisibly one and the same.

The degree of ignorance or enlightenment inherent in this identification depends on the nature of the respective instruments through which the "I-ness" or individuality is manifesting. When identified with the gross senses and their objects (the physical body and material

* *Yoga Sutras* II:6.

world), the "I-ness" becomes the wisdom-destroying physical ego. When identified with the subtle instruments of perception and knowledge in the astral body, the "I-ness" becomes a clearer sense of being, the astral ego, whose true nature may be adversely affected by the delusive influence of the physical nature; or, conversely, be in tune with the instrumentality of the wisdom consciousness of the causal body and thus become the discriminating ego.

Physical ego versus divine ego

When the "I-ness" expresses solely through pure intuitive wisdom, the instrument of the causal body, it becomes the pure discriminating ego (the divine ego), or its highest expression, the soul, the individualized reflection of Spirit. The soul, the purest individualized sense of being, knows its Spirit-identity of omniscience and omnipresence, and merely uses the instruments of the body and mind as a means of communication and interaction with objectified creation. Thus the Hindu scriptures say: "When this 'I' shall die, then will I know who am I."

In the context of this present verse, in which the inner metaphysical forces of the Kaurava army are described, the implication of Bhishma–Ego Consciousness is in the form of the astral, or inner-seeing ego: the consciousness identified with the subtle form of the instruments of sense mind (*manas*), intelligence (*buddhi*), and feeling (*chitta*). At this stage of the devotee's advancement, this astral or inner-seeing ego is strongly affected by the outward pull of the sense mind; that is, it has sided with the Kurus. In the victory of *samadhi,* this "I-ness" (*asmita*), inner-seeing ego, becomes more transcendent as the discriminating ego of the astral and causal bodily instruments, and ultimately as the pure individualized sense of being, the soul.*

3. KARNA—ATTACHMENT (RAGA)

The name Karna derives from the Sanskrit root *kṛi,* "to do, to work."† The metaphorical derivation: *Karaṇaśīla iti*—"One who be-

---

* See also "Expanded Commentary: The Nature of the Ego," I:11; *sasmita samprajnata* and *asamprajnata samadhi,* I:15–18; and discriminating ego and soul, VII:5–6.

† Scholars, taking the literal approach to definitions, usually link the derivation of the name of this Gita warrior to the word *karṇa,* ("ear"), from the similar root *kṛī,* instead of *kṛi,* "to do, to work." In the allegorical telling, Karna is said to have been born adorned with marvellous earrings and armour, giving him invincibility. These ornaments he ultimately gave to the god Indra, who in disguise as a Brahmin coveted them in order to protect Arjuna whom Karna had vowed to kill. The relinquishment of these was followed by Karna's downfall.

haves according to his natural habitual tendency in performing actions (that give pleasure)."

Karna signifies the propensity for pursuing material action, toward which there is natural attachment because of enjoyment or pleasure derived from it. Thus Karna represents Patanjali's *raga,* the third *klesha,* which is described in *Yoga Sutras* II:7: "*Raga* is that inclination (attachment) which dwells on pleasure."

Karna is a half-brother to the five Pandavas. Their common mother Kunti, before her marriage to Pandu, used her divinely given power to invoke the god Surya, the sun, through whom she was given a son, Karna. Because she was unmarried at the time, she abandoned the child, who was found and raised by a charioteer and his wife. Karna became a close friend of Duryodhana and thus sided with him in the battle of Kurukshetra, even though he had learned of his true relationship with the Pandavas. Out of spite he became the avowed enemy of the Pandavas, especially Arjuna. The significance is that Kunti, the power of invoking spiritual energy, begets an offspring from the sun, the light of the spiritual eye, which is the light from which the whole body of man, the devotee, evolves. "The light of the body is the eye: if therefore thine eye be single, thy whole body shall be full of light."* Because this power of invoking spiritual energy, Kunti, is not yet united to the divine discriminative power, or Pandu, the offspring Karna (attachment to pleasure) comes under the influence of the material sense inclinations and thus sides with them in opposition to the righteous Pandava qualities.† Karna feels it is his duty to be loyal to the friendship he has given to Duryodhana, Material Desire. *Raga,* or Karna, then is the principle in the deluded man that causes him to seek that work or action to which he is attached because of the pleasure it gives him.

---

* Matthew 6:22.

† Though Karna is born of the light of the consciousness of the spiritual eye ("the sun"), he is "reared" in the metaphysical centre in the pons Varolii, the seat of *manas,* the sense mind symbolized by Dhritarashtra (see I:1, page 5). Here also one may turn inward into the spiritual world. My guru, Sri Yukteswar, noted the significance of the name Karna in a play of words, common in the Hindu scriptures, in which the word *karna* means also "the helm of a ship." Thus, this consciousness represented as Karna may at this pivotal point be "steered" either inward through the door of the spiritual eye into the astral spine with its centres of divine awareness, or outward into the sensory nerves and material consciousness. Having chosen to side with the forces of the sense mind, the Karna attachment to material pleasure (along with his brother-in-arms, Vikarna; see Kuru number 4 on page 86) carries on its materialistic propensities in the subtle lumbar *chakra* of the spine in opposition there to its archenemy the Arjuna divine power of self-control (see I:11, page 106).

And he justifies that action by proclaiming it to be his duty. Thus whatever he wants to do, because of his attachment to it, he can rationalize as necessary and right.

4. VIKARNA—REPULSION (DVESHA)

As Karna represents attachment, so *Vi*-karna implies the opposite. The metaphorical derivation: *Akaraṇaśīla iti*—"One who behaves according to his natural habitual tendency in avoiding actions (that do not give pleasure—that are disagreeable)." Vikarna is symbolic of Patanjali's fourth *klesha, dvesha,* or aversion. *Yoga Sutras* II:8 says: "*Dvesha* is aversion toward that which brings suffering." Ordinarily the avoidance of suffering is a noble goal; but as applied in this context, suffering has a baser implication: that which is disagreeable. Man's ignorance (*avidya*) distorts his sense of right and wrong, good and evil, and creates in him the dual opposites of likes and dislikes (*raga* and *dvesha*). He is attached to what he likes and avoids what he dislikes, rather than exercising discriminative free choice and following what is truly right and best for him.

5. JAYADRATHA—BODY-BOUND INCLINATION (ABHINIVESHA)

The metaphorical derivation: *Ramitvā anurakto bhūtvā jayati utkṛṣṭa-rūpeṇa tiṣṭhati iti*—"One who conquers by deep attachment to life—deep attachment to the continuation of one's embodied state of existence." *Jayad* (from *jayat*) means "conquering," and *ratha* means "chariot," i.e., the body. Jayadratha represents an inherent tenacity of body attachment that seeks to conquer the devotee's aspirations toward Self-realization by making him cling to mortal consciousness. This tenacity is a finer or more subtle grade of attachment than the possessiveness man feels for objects or persons. Even when these latter attachments are burned in the fire of wisdom, the strong body-attachment persists as the last remaining dying embers. My gurudeva, Swami Sri Yukteswarji, often illustrated in these words the obstinate affection man feels for his mortal bodily residence: "Just as the long-caged bird, when offered freedom, is afraid of it and is reluctant to leave its enclosure, so even great men whose wisdom is constant are nevertheless subject to infatuation about the body at the time of death." Western psychologists have labelled this inherent compelling force "the desire for self-preservation," and noted that it is the strongest natural urge in man. It not only expresses itself as fear of death, but also gives rise in man to a host of mortal characteristics and actions contrary to the immortal nature of the true Self, the soul—selfishness,

Bhagavan Krishna with the five Pandava brothers—Yudhisthira (greeting Krishna with the worshipful salutation of *pranam*), Bhima (with mace), Arjuna, and the twins Nakula and Sahadeva. To the left of Sri Krishna are Kunti (far left) and Draupadi.

❖

"The five Pandavas are the central heroic figures of the Gita analogy, controlling the armies of consciousness and energy (prana) in the five subtle centres of the spine. They represent the qualities and powers acquired by the devotee whose deep meditation is attuned to the astral and causal centres of life and divine consciousness."

❖

"The Gita describes how—having roused and trained the psychological astral powers of Yudhisthira calmness, Bhima life-force control, Arjuna nonattachment of self-control, Nakula power to adhere to good rules, and Sahadeva power to resist evil—these offspring of discrimination along with their army and allies of good habits and spiritual inclinations try to return from banishment. But the crooked sense tendencies with their sense armies are loath to part with their reign over the bodily kingdom. So, with the help of Krishna (the guru, or awakened soul-consciousness, or meditation-born intuition), war must be fought—materially and mentally, and also spiritually in repeated experiences of samadhi meditation—to reclaim the kingdom from Ego and its army of evil mental tendencies."

—Paramahansa Yogananda

greed, possessiveness, the storing-up of treasures on earth as though this will be his permanent home.

Jayadratha, then, represents this subtle tenacity to body attachment, and is the correlate to Patanjali's fifth *klesha, abhinivesha,* in *Yoga Sutras* II:9: "The tenacity that clings to life as a result of body attachment, even in the wise, and that propagates itself (from the subtle memory of repeated experiences of death in previous incarnations) is *abhinivesha.*"

6. SON OF SOMADATTA, I.E., BHURISHRAVAS—MATERIAL ACTION (KARMA)

In the name Bhurishravas is the meaning "frequent or repeated" (*bhūri*), and "stream, flow" (*śravas*). The metaphorical derivation: *Bhūrī bahulam śravaḥ kṣaraṇaṁ yaḥ saḥ iti*—"That flow which frequently, repeatedly disappears (wanes, vanishes)." That which disappears frequently and repeatedly is obviously replaced in order to maintain this continuity. It can be likened to water in a stream, which flows by, yet the flow remains continuous because of the water following that which passes. This is akin to man's actions and the results accruing from them. Bhurishravas thus represents karma, the sixth obstacle listed by Patanjali in *Yoga Sutras* I:24, cited previously.

Here karma means material action, that which is instigated by egoistic desire. It sets into motion the law of cause and effect. The action produces a result that binds itself to the doer until the cause is compensated by the appropriate effect, whether forthcoming immediately or carried over from one lifetime to another. Though not always as literal, it is as exacting as the Old Testament law "an eye for an eye." One's present condition and circumstances are a composite of current free-will-initiated action and the bondage of the accumulated effects of past actions, the causes of which have often been long-since forgotten or disassociated from the results. Thus man laments his present misfortunes as bad luck, fate, injustice. By enduring, learning from, and constructively and spiritually working his way out of these effects, past karma is destroyed. But unless present actions are guided by wisdom, and thereby carry no binding impressions, new karmic effects will replace those that have been justly compensated. So long as karmic effects from past and present actions do not fade away by being worked out or dissolved by wisdom, it is impossible to attain final emancipation.

Karma or action is of four kinds according to Patanjali, *Yoga Sutras* IV:7. "The actions of a yogi are neither pure nor dark; in others, they are of three kinds [pure, dark, or a mixture of pure and dark]." The actions of an evil man are dark, binding him to disastrous effects.

The works of the ordinary worldly man are a mixture of both good and evil, binding him to the corresponding results of same. The actions of a spiritual man are pure. They produce good effects that lead toward freedom; but even good karmic effects are binding. The works of a yogi who is established in Self-realization, the ultimate wisdom, leave no impressions, either good or evil, to bind him. Bhurishravas—material action that produces binding effects because it is instigated by egoistic desire—is thus to be conquered by the aspiring yogi.

7. DRONA (ADDRESSED IN THIS VERSE AS BHAVAN, "THOU")—HABIT OR SAMSKARA, INNER TENDENCY (VIPAKA)

The metaphorical derivation: *Karmaṇāṁ dravībhāvanām vipākaḥ iti*—"The fruition of actions (karma) that are dormant (i.e., in the subtle or 'melted' state)."

The allegorical significance of Drona was established in the second verse. He represents habit, or more precisely, *samskara,* the impressions made on the consciousness by past thoughts and actions, which create strong tendencies to repeat themselves. It was seen that the name Drona comes from the Sanskrit root *dru,* implying that which remains in the melted state. That is, past actions remain in a subtle or "melted" form as these impressions, or *samskaras.* We therefore find the concomitance between Drona and Patanjali's *vipaka*. The word *vipaka* derives from *vi-pac,* from which come the derivative meanings "to bear fruit, develop consequences" and "to melt, liquefy." The *samskaras* or impressions of past actions in their subtle or "melted" state will ultimately, under the right conditions, come to fruition as the consequences of those actions. *Yoga Sutras* II:12–13 says: "Impressions of action have their root (cause) in the *kleshas* [the five obstacles just described], and are experienced in the seen (manifested in the present life) or the unseen (lying partially dormant awaiting the right conditions; often carried over into the next or a future life). From these roots the specifics of one's rebirths are determined—what type of man, his health and vitality, his joys and sorrows."

8. ASHVATTHAMAN—LATENT DESIRE (ASHAYA)

The metaphorical derivation: *Aśnuvan sañcayan tiṣṭhati iti*—"That which remains stored up or preserved." The allegorical meaning of Ashvatthaman is found in the key Sanskrit roots from which the name derives. *Ās-va* means "preserved or stored up"; and *tthāman* (from the root *sthā*), "to remain, to continue in a particular condition" and "to continue to be or exist (as opposed to 'perish')." That which accumulates and remains unchanged, and does not perish with death is desire—Patanjali's *ashaya* (from *ā-śā*). More specifically, it is latent desire or desire-seed—*vasana,* or the impressions of desire on the consciousness. The *Yoga Sutras* IV:10 states: "This desire is the eternal root of Nature's creation." It is the universal cause of all that exists since the beginning of time.

The Hindu scriptures say that it is the desireless desire of Spirit to enjoy Its singular nature in many forms that spawns this drama of the universal cosmic dream. This impression of the wish to exist and to enjoy the experience of existing is part of the nucleus of individuality in these multiple forms of Spirit. Desire is thus a fundamental law that assures the continuity of creation. Men dream their individual desires within the ever awake somnolence of the Cosmic Dreamer. *Avidya,* ignorance, produces egoism; from ego arises feeling or desire and concomitant identification with the senses and sense objects as a means of enjoyment. This leads to desire-motivated good and bad actions and their results or impressions, which in turn produce new causes and effects from one lifetime to another in a self-perpetuating cycle. So long as there is no end to desire, there is no end to rebirth.

In man, this desire-seed or latent desire (Ashvatthaman) should be distinguished from active desire (Duryodhana). There is a vast difference between the two. Active desire is an impulse of the mind that produces an independent wish. This act of the mind has no roots in the subconscious. When this impulse arises fresh in the mind of the agent, it is not powerful enough that it cannot be easily checked or suppressed by a quick act of will. Every desire, however, whether acted on or not, is soon followed by another. Such desires for the gratification of ego do not cease even when they are supposedly satisfied; in every worldly accomplishment or every attainment of a material possession, something always remains unfulfilled. Desire-seeds are born of these ego-instigated active desires. Every unfulfilled active desire, unless roasted by wisdom, plants a new desire-seed in the mind. These desire-seeds are more compelling than impulsive fresh desires, deeply rooting themselves in the subconscious, ready to spring up suddenly with demands that are most often unreasonable, frustrating, and sorrow-producing. As desire begets desires, the only way to end the cycle is to destroy the causes.

At the end of the Mahabharata war, after the Pandava defeat of the Kurus, we find that Ashvatthaman has survived but is rendered powerless, and is destined to roam the world forever, alone and friendless.

When the yogi attains liberation, becoming irrevocably established in divine soul consciousness, his "desires" are like the desireless desire of Spirit, having no conquering power or ability to bind the soul.

The destruction of the causes of bondage—material desire, ego, habit, attachment, and so forth—is thus the aim of the yogi-devotee as he battles the evil Kuru forces with the divine Pandava army of discrimination and soul power.

VERSE 9

अन्ये च बहवः शूरा मदर्थे त्यक्तजीविताः ।
नानाशस्त्रप्रहरणाः सर्वे युद्धविशारदाः ॥

And numerous other warriors, all well-trained for battle and armed with various weapons, are here present, ready for my sake to lay down their lives.

"DIVERSE WARRIORS OF TEMPTATION and prowess, well-skilled in psychological and spiritual warfare against good, and armed with the various sense lures, are abiding in the kingdom of the body, all prepared to expend their entire vitality in fighting for me (King Material Desire)."

The massive Kuru army has been rallied from the one hundred offspring of Dhritarashtra (the ten materialistic propensities of each of the ten senses—five instruments of knowledge and five of action—of the blind sense-mind); the loyal forces built up by them (illimitable sense temptations); and the well-skilled Kaurava allies, with their powers to obstruct and destroy (the principal ones of which have just been enumerated by Duryodhana in verse 8).

Here, then, is introduced a specialized grouping of the Kaurava forces. Lest the reader feel perplexed at yet another "list," he should rather let his thought processes merge with those of the *rishis,* ancient and modern, who realized that yoga is a science demanding exactitude in definition. Like the scientist who correlates interacting and related forces and principles in the attempt to define them, the *rishis* compartmentalized those principles that interrelate to produce a specific effect. As each is a part of the whole, there are inevitable overlappings and shades of difference in meanings according to the specific concept under consideration.

❖

The Six Faults of the Materially Identified Ego

When the ego or "I" consciousness has sided with the materialistic forces of creation, it is said to have six faults (*doshas*): 1. *kama* (lust); 2. *krodha* (anger); 3. *lobha* (greed); 4. *moha* (delusion); 5. *mada* (pride); and 6. *matsarya* (envy). Only when man has conquered these does he acquire knowledge of his true soul nature.

These enemies give further insight as to the nature of some of the Kurus already mentioned, and also introduce other of the warriors who play significant roles in the battle of Kurukshetra as analogized in the *Mahabharata,* warriors not specifically mentioned in the Gita but alluded to in discussion of the qualities they represent. For example, in XVI:7–24, in the definition of the demonic or wholly egotistical being, we find a general correspondence with the six faults of the ego.*

Within man's weakness, therefore, there hides the stamp of ego. Since ego loves matter and narrow form, all the different phases of consciousness that are trained by it receive its narrow formal selfish quality. As a result, the following troubles (*doshas*) visit the human mind:

1. Kama (Lust)

In the name and guise of fulfilling one's needs, ego lures man to continuous seeking of self-satisfaction, resulting in suffering and vexation. What would content the soul is forgotten, and the ego goes on endlessly trying to satisfy its insatiable desires. *Kama* (lust) is therefore the compelling desire to indulge in sensory temptations. Coercive materialistic desire is the instigator of man's wrong thoughts and actions. Interacting with the other forces that obstruct man's divine nature—influencing as well as being influenced by them—lustful desire is the consummate enemy. The perfect exemplar is Duryodhana, whose unwillingness to part with even an inch of sensory territory or pleasure was the cause of the war of Kurukshetra. Only little by little, with fierce determination in battle, could the Pandavas win back their kingdom.

Kama, or lustful desire, supported by the other Kaurava forces, can corrupt the sensory instruments of man to expression of their basest instincts. It is taught in the Hindu scriptures that under the strong influence of *kama,* sane learned men act like asses, monkeys, goats, and swine.

---

* See pages 973 ff.

Lust applies to the abuse of any or all of the senses in the pursuit of pleasure or gratification. Through the sense of sight man may lust after material objects; through the sense of hearing, he craves the sweet, slow poison of flattery, and vibratory sounds as of voices and music that rouse his material nature; through the lustful pleasure of smell he is enticed toward wrong environments and actions; lust for food and drink causes him to please his taste at the expense of health; through the sense of touch he lusts after inordinate physical comfort and abuses the creative sex impulse. Lust also seeks gratification in wealth, status, power, domination—all that satisfies the "I, me, mine" in the egotistical man. Lustful desire is egotism, the lowest rung of the ladder of human character evolution. By the force of its insatiable passion, *kama* loves to destroy one's happiness, health, brain power, clarity of thought, memory, and discriminative judgement.

2. KRODHA (ANGER)

Desire that is frustrated results in anger. Thus the first son of the blind sense-mind King Dhritarashtra is Duryodhana–Material Desire, and his second son (closest brother to Duryodhana) is Duhshasana, symbolizing anger. The name means, "hard to restrain or control," from the Sanskrit *duḥ*, "difficult"; and *śās*, "to restrain or control." In the *Mahabharata*, the altogether despicable Duhshasana well characterizes the evil of anger. In the second chapter of the Gita,* Krishna explains to Arjuna that anger causes the wrongdoer to be enveloped in delusion, which then obscures memory of the correct behaviour of the Self, causing decay of the discriminative faculty. From this confusion of intelligence, annihilation of right behaviour follows.

Anger demonstrates its peace-destroying, reason-blinding, health-impairing behaviour in many forms: impatience, violence, irritation, inner seething, jealousy, resentment; malicious anger, passionate anger, childish and superficial anger; Lucifer-anger, satanic in violence and meanness; paroxysms of anger, arising from little or no external stimulation, caused by a chronic habit of anger; and deep-rooted anger from past-life bad karma. Even if anger is supposedly justified, so-called "righteous anger," it must never take the place of calm, discriminative judgement and action.

* II:63.

3. Lobha (Greed)

Ego makes one enslaved to his whims, so that he fails to scrutinize and judge the errors that might be ingrained in his conceptions and ideas of things. Under this influence, he acts not for the sake of duty, or rightness, but to fulfil undisciplined whims. From childhood, most persons are conditioned to be governed by their ego, and hence led by their feelings and guided by scheduled likes and dislikes. This enslavement to whim, likes and dislikes, is *lobha,* greed. It is covetousness, avarice, acquisitiveness, a confusion of the mind between necessary necessities and unnecessary "necessities."

It has already been shown that the Kaurava warriors, Karna and Vikarna, attachment to material action and repulsion to what is disagreeable, are the root of likes and dislikes. Therefore, of the faults of the ego, Karna and Vikarna represent *lobha* or greed.

The most common form of greed is man's ungoverned appetite for food. But the following principles apply equally to any expression of the ego's gluttony. Depending on the power of its influence, greed may be insatiable gluttony; mental attachment that dwells on the thought and desire for food, even when the body has been well-fed; powerful greed that is unquenchable until health is ruined (as in overeating and wrong eating, fully knowing the consequences of doing so); medium greed, possible to be checked momentarily, usually when it has produced suffering; mild greed, often labelled "harmless indulgence," but which is never so.

In its most covetous and avaricious display, greed leads to stealing, dishonesty, cheating, self-surfeit at the expense of the well-being of others. If man allows himself to be conquered by greed, his life and spirit will be ruined and shattered by suffering.

Krishna warns the devotee Arjuna that the threefold gate to hell is lust, anger, and greed; therefore, these must be abandoned.*

4. Moha (Delusion)

This fault of the ego suppresses the evolution and manifestation of the soul. Ego is the pseudosoul, or the consciousness under the influence of delusion. The soul and ego are like light and darkness, respectively, unable to live together. Ego and soul both are subjectively conscious entities. But ego is born and conditioned; the soul is immortal

* XVI:21.

and unconditional. The ego is circumscribed by age, nationality, likes and dislikes, form, possession, wish for fame, personality, pride, attachment—everything that serves to circumscribe and limit. It is the consciousness within man that connects him with his body and environment through the instruments of feeling, will, and cognition. As it is true that the material man cannot be self-conscious if ego is subtracted, so it is true that ego cannot for long remain disassociated from its binding inner and outer environment. It loses itself if there is no attachment.

Moha is the basic attachment of the ego, its indivisible cohesion to delusion. *Avidya,* individual delusion, represented by the Kuru ally Kripa, was explained in verse 8. This illusion of individuality produces the ego or "I" consciousness as that which perceives and experiences through this individuality. *Moha* is the ego's attachment to this delusion, causing the mind to become darkened, unable to perceive what is truth and reality. The word *moha* means "delusion, illusion, ignorance, bewilderment, infatuation (attachment)." But in addition, it means a magical art employed to bewilder an enemy.

In the *Mahabharata* allegory, *moha* is represented by the Kuru Shakuni, brother of the first wife of the blind King Dhritarashtra, Gandhari. Shakuni was noted for his mastery of illusion, winning battles through deceptive bewilderment of his opponents. It was Shakuni's counsel that urged Duryodhana to challenge the five Pandavas to a game of dice in which they were forced to stake their kingdom. Shakuni threw the dice, and by clever deceit won all from the Pandavas for Duryodhana.* When the symbology of the characters is understood, the meaning of the allegory cannot be missed. Through the "dice-play" of delusive sense temptations and material lures, the soul and its divine discriminative qualities are banished from the bodily kingdom. The consciousness of man is thereafter ruled over by the ego with its six faults.

Through this attachment to delusion, the proscriptions of human limitations are made firm. The ego not only gives human beings the consciousness of certain positive things that they can do, but it negatively influences with the consciousness of limitations of what mortals think they are unable to do. This is the most dangerous aspect of being under the subjection of the ego regime, for it obstructs the potentially omniscient and omnipotent power of the true Self, the soul. To break this attachment to delusion is to allow the soul to express its supremacy, establish its influence, and enlarge the manifestation of its infinite possibilities.

---

* See Introduction, page *xxviii.*

5. MADA (PRIDE)

This fault of the ego makes the mind narrow and limited. Pride chokes and suppresses the illimitable soul qualities by its constricted consciousness. Pride here means that love for the "I" or ego-self that is constantly on the defensive (or offensive) to support and promote the interests of that self. Because of *mada,* within the ego there arises arrogance, conceit, haughtiness, presumptuous behaviour, and passionate or wanton lust after the desires, interests, or demands of the "I, me, and mine." "My good name, my rights, my status, my race, my religion, my feelings. I am justified, I am as good or better than anyone else, I want, I have, I am." Among the meanings encompassed by the word *mada,* in addition to "pride," are "intoxication, insanity." It could aptly be said that *mada* is such an intoxication with the ego "I" consciousness that man takes leave of his sane or true Self, the soul.

In the *Mahabharata* allegory, *mada* as pride is represented by Shalya. He is the maternal uncle of the two younger Pandavas, Sahadeva and Nakula. Shalya set out to join forces with them against the Kurus, but Duryodhana bribed him with flattery and gifts, so that he sided with the Kurus instead. Thus does egoistic pride often turn man's head—and feet—in the wrong direction. The word *shalya* means "fault or defect," implying in this context the nearsightedness of ego's pride, the narrow perspective of which confuses man's reason and judgement.

Shalya also means "abuse, defamation." *Mada* creates in the ego-man a hostile power that expresses its self-centred haughtiness toward others as intolerance, prejudice, bigotry, unforgiving attitude, and the prejudiced or fearful hostility of hatred. Pride makes the egotistical man, consciously or unconsciously, try to cut off the heads of others to make himself appear taller. It likes to belittle or humiliate others, to gloat on their mistakes and discomfiture, and to gossip and criticize. But woe unto any person, even well-meaning, who intrudes into ego pride's own sanctum sanctorum. He is met with instant wrath, vengefulness, or at the very best, a "you should feel ashamed for hurting my feelings."

Ego pride in a man repulses others, producing in them vexation and dislike toward him; whereas good qualities of humbleness, calmness, thoughtfulness, cheerful sincere smiles, patient understanding, always engender in others joy and peace and comfort. Thus the man of discriminative qualities has an attractive personality; through sympathy he truly rules the hearts of others. The proud only deceive themselves that their overbearing attitude makes them leaders among men.

Even a very spiritual man may fall from a great height because of pride in his attainments. Such is the nature of *mada* that the ego esteems itself not only for the good it has in actuality attained, but also for qualities that it falsely imagines it possesses. The greater the good in man, the more there is to be proud about, increasing the chance of succumbing to egotistic pride. Cunning, indeed, are the traps of delusion!

6. MATSARYA (ENVY, MATERIAL ATTACHMENT)

The marvel of the Sanskrit language is its ability to convey an entire concept in one word, understood by those already versed in the concept being defined. Sanskrit evolved as "the language of the gods," through which scripture was conveyed to mortals. Each word may have many meanings, the context determining the correct application. The difficulty of translation into English is the cumbersome definition required to convey that which is implied by a single term. To avoid repetitious verbiage, a relevant English phrase or word is thus chosen to represent the meaning, which is then to be understood in its full philosophical sense. *Matsarya,* commonly translated as "envy," in the broader sense signifies material attachment. The word derives from *matsara,* meaning "envy, jealousy, selfishness, hostility; passion for; exhilarating; intoxicating or addictive." The meaning of *matsarya,* then, is that the wealth of possible possessions and attainments in the world of matter creates in the ego dissatisfaction, and a passion (envy) for obtaining those material enjoyments. This rouses an exhilaration, a power or force, directed toward fulfilment and resulting in intoxication with and addiction to the objects gained, i.e., material attachment. Sometimes hostile in nature, this material attachment can be jealous, malicious, and selfish.

The Kaurava warrior representing this fault of the ego is Kritavarma. He was the only Yadava (the clan of Sri Krishna) who supported Duryodhana in the war of Kurukshetra. He became maliciously envious when the bride he coveted was denied to him, and taken instead to Krishna's kingdom.

Matsarya, or ego envy, in its full implication, incites the lust of desire, and makes it practically impossible for one to reach straightway to one's goal and ideal of life. It is a dreamer. It makes man dream of a world of fulfilled desires, causing him to run after them through endless corridors of births and rebirths. It makes one forget his true duty, those actions that are correct for his own soul evolution, and creates in him longings to imitate the position of others—that he might be or have what has roused envy in him. To destroy this consciousness, one should disassociate himself from his own personality and in his imagination identify himself with others. He will find out that the resultant state of mind is the same in everyone—momentary pleasure followed by dissatisfaction and more desires. Ceasing to desire, he will discover that what he really wants is not ego-satisfaction, or whim-satisfaction, but satisfaction of the Self or soul.

The soul, being unlimited, does not allow itself to be circumscribed by the ego's narrowness. The destruction of ego consciousness does not mean that we should live aimless lives, but that we should not limit ourselves by being identified with ego's attachments. We are not to throw away our possessions, or not take care of the things we have, or cease trying to possess what we really need; but in the course of performing our duties, we should eliminate the bondage of attachment. Those who free themselves from ego's narrowness and the consciousness of ego's possessions hold dominion over earth and heaven. A child of Spirit who is free from ego's material attachment may surely have everything that is in the universe as his rightful divine inheritance. All his desires are satisfied.

In sum, the principal practical evil that comes along with ego consciousness and its six faults is the increasing compulsion to forget one's Self—the soul—and its expression, manifestation, and requirements; and to become stubbornly inclined to engage oneself in pursuing the insatiable "necessities" of the ego.

Ego consciousness is a false personality

Psychologically, ego consciousness is a transference and grafting of a false personality. It is necessary to understand and uproot the picketing of ego consciousness and its various tendencies, which preclude familiarity with the true Self. The aspiring yogi should always bear in mind, when he feels angry, "That is not me!" When his self-possession is being overpowered by lust or greed, he should say to himself, "That is not me!" When hatred tries to obscure his real nature with a mask of ugly emotion, he should forcefully dissociate himself from it: "That is not me!" He learns to shut the doors of his consciousness against all undesirable visitors seeking lodging within. And whenever that devotee has been used or abused by others, and yet he feels within a stirring of the holy spirit of forgiveness and love, he can then affirm with conviction, "*That* is me! That is my real nature."

Yoga meditation is the process of cultivating and stabilizing the awareness of one's real nature, through definite spiritual and psychophysical methods and laws by which the narrow ego, the flawed hereditary human consciousness, is displaced by the consciousness of the soul.

VERSE 10

अपर्याप्तं तदस्माकं बलं भीष्माभिरक्षितम् ।
पर्याप्तं त्विदमेतेषां बलं भीमाभिरक्षितम् ॥

These our forces protected by Bhishma are unlimited (but may be insufficient); whereas their army, defended by Bhima, is limited (but quite adequate).*

Ego's function: maintaining delusions of body and material world

"OUR FORCES OF DESIRES and sensory temptations, though unlimited in number and protected by the vehement power of the ego nature, may yet be inadequate because our strength is relative to the body-identified state; whereas the Pandava army, though it may be limited in number, consists of absolute principles of unchanging truth and is defended by the power of soul-guided life force; together these are capable of destroying body identification and thereby defeating our cause."

Bhishma (*asmita* or delusion-born ego consciousness) is the supreme commander over all units of the sense army. The purpose of Bhishma, the ego or pseudosoul, is to keep the consciousness continually busy with sensory reports and activities by focusing the searchlight of attention outwardly on the body and the world of matter, instead of inwardly on God and the true soul nature. This deluded flesh-bound consciousness is responsible for awakening all the countless soldiers of temptations and attachments couched within the human body.

Without ego consciousness the entire army of evil and temptation vanishes like a forgotten dream. If the soul dwelt in the body without being identified with it, as do the souls of saints, no temptations or attachments could keep it tied to the body. The troubles of an ordinary

* The Sanskrit words *aparyāptaṁ* and *paryāptaṁ* mean not only unlimited and limited respectively, but also the opposite implication of insufficient or inadequate, and sufficient or adequate. Either translation is tenable if the intent is understood. One principle of truth—being unconditioned and eternal—if rightly applied, is capable of routing a horde of evil tendencies whose relative existence depends on the temporal nature of delusion.

man arise from the fact that when the soul descends into the body, it projects its individualized, ever-conscious, ever-new-bliss nature into the flesh and thereafter identifies itself with the limitations of a physical form. The soul then thinks of itself as the miserable ego of many temptations. The identification of the soul with the body, however, is only imaginary, not real. Essentially the soul is ever pure. Ordinary mortals allow their souls to live as flesh-entangled egos, not as Spirit's reflection or true soul.

A wealthy young prince, held captive in the slums, lived there so long that he thought he was poor and miserable. He accepted as his own all the troubles that go with poverty. When he was at last returned to his palace and had lived there again for some time, he realized that, except in his imagination created by his temporary experiences, he had never really been poor.

It is hard, however, for mortal man to realize that he is not a fleshly being, that in reality he is neither an Indian nor an American nor any of the other limited things he appears to be. In sleep, in an unconscious way, the soul makes one forget the flesh consciousness. Sleep is a temporary healing salve to relieve one's hallucinations about matter. Meditation is the real panacea by which man can permanently cure himself of the daydream of matter and all its evils, and realize himself as pure Spirit.

Pranayama, key to the yogi's victory

Duryodhana–Material Desire knows that his kingdom is seriously threatened when the aspiring devotee begins to rouse the inner spiritual army by the practice of meditation. Bhima, the soul-guided vital force, is the primary general of this army, for life force is the link between matter and Spirit; no realization is possible until this energy is brought under control and turned toward Spirit. As the meditating devotee becomes adept in the proper *pranayama* techniques, Bhima, the inwardly turned life force and resultant life and breath control, leads that victorious yogi to divine consciousness.

By the proper breathing exercises of *pranayama,* the venous blood is purified and man's body is directly supplied with cosmic energy. Decay in the body is arrested, and the heart receives a welcome rest from the usually unceasing task of oxygenating and nourishing the body through blood circulation, and of directing the life force to the five sense telephones of touch, smell, taste, sound, and sight. When life force is shut off from the sensory organs, material sensations cannot reach the brain to snatch away the meditator's attention from God. This is why

Bhima, or the power of life-force control, and a few other strong soldiers—concentration, intuition, inner perception, calmness, self-control, and so on (as described in verses 4–6)—must be awakened to fight the forces of the pseudosoul or ego. Bhima, or soul-guided life force, heads the spiritual army and is the principal enemy of ego or Bhishma, because when the invasion of the five senses is halted by life-force control, the soul is automatically freed from the captivity of the body-identified ego-consciousness. The soul, having regained supreme command of the consciousness, says: "I was never anything but joyous Spirit; I only imagined for a time that I was mortal man being imprisoned by delusive limitations and sensory temptations."

This "awakening" of the soul, or Self-realization, occurs first as a temporary awareness during the experience of *samadhi* in deep meditation, after successful practice of *pranayama* has produced life-force control and reversed the life and consciousness from the senses to the divine inner states of soul- and God-awareness. As the yogi's *samadhi* experiences deepen and expand, this realization becomes a permanent state of consciousness.

Attaining *samadhi* or oneness with God is the only method by which the ego consciousness can be completely defeated.

Stages of samadhi, oneness with God

There are varying degrees of realization or oneness with God. First there is the realization of the oneness of the ego and the soul in superconsciousness. Then there is the realization of the oneness of the soul and Spirit in the states of Christ consciousness (*Kutastha Chaitanya*) and cosmic consciousness.

As there are progressively expansive states of realization, so are there different states of *samadhi* in which these experiences occur. Broadly classified, there are three kinds of *samadhi: jada* or unconscious trance; *savikalpa* or perception of Spirit, without the waves of creation; and *nirvikalpa,* the highest state—that of simultaneous perception of the ocean of Spirit and all its waves of creation.

Jada samadhi, or the unconscious cataleptic state, is spiritually useless because it only temporarily suspends the consciousness and actions of the ego; it cannot transform material consciousness into spiritual consciousness. *Jada samadhi,* or unconscious trance, is produced by methods of physical control, or by the mental anaesthetic of keeping the mind blank, or by pressing on certain glands. In this state a sense-bound man can do no more than temporarily refrain from increasing his desires, attachments, and karmic indebtedness—he can never acquire wisdom nor eliminate the seeds of prenatal or postnatal karma and bad habits.

A story from the ancient religious lore of India relates that a wicked snake charmer put himself into a trance, and in doing so fell into a well. In time, the well dried up and became filled with dirt. The man remained buried there, his body perfectly preserved in a state of suspended animation. A hundred years later, a group of villagers who were digging out the old well found the man and revived him by the application of hot water. As soon as he regained consciousness he began to scold everyone within earshot, accusing the group of having stolen the musical instruments with which he charmed his snakes. The hundred years of unconscious trance had no salutary effect on the snake charmer's behaviour, nor did it destroy the seeds of evil habits lodged in his brain. *Jada samadhi* had in no way improved the man's wicked nature.

In the state of *savikalpa samadhi,* the attention and the life force are switched off from the senses and are consciously kept identified with the ever joyous Spirit. In this state the soul is released from the ego consciousness and becomes aware of Spirit beyond creation. The soul is then able to absorb the fire of Spirit-Wisdom that "roasts" or destroys the seeds of body-bound inclinations. The soul as the meditator, its state of meditation, and the Spirit as the object of meditation—all become one. The separate wave of the soul meditating in the ocean of Spirit becomes merged with the Spirit. The soul does not lose its identity, but only expands into Spirit. In *savikalpa samadhi* the mind is conscious only of the Spirit within; it is not conscious of creation without (the exterior world). The body is in a trancelike state, but the consciousness is fully perceptive of its blissful experience within.

In the most advanced state, *nirvikalpa samadhi,* the soul realizes itself and Spirit as one. The ego consciousness, the soul consciousness, and the ocean of Spirit are seen all existing together. It is the state of simultaneously watching the ocean of Spirit and the waves of creation. The individual no longer sees himself as a "John Smith" related to a particular environment; he realizes that the ocean of Spirit has become not only the wave of John Smith but also the waves of all other lives. In *nirvikalpa* the soul is simultaneously conscious of Spirit within and of creation without. The divine man in the *nirvikalpa* state may even engage in performance of his material duties with no loss of inner God-union.

The *savikalpa* and *nirvikalpa* states of *samadhi* are described in the following ancient Hindu song:

In savikalpa samadhi yoga
You will drown yourself (ego) in Yourself (Spirit);
In nirvikalpa samadhi yoga
*You will find yourself (ego) in Yourself (Spirit).**

The ego consciousness in man keeps the soul attached to matter by presenting a series of mortal desires, and by emphasizing the "individuality" or peculiarities of each man, reminding him of the limited physical relations of country, race, nation, family, possessions, individual characteristics, and so forth. The soul, a reflection of Spirit, should manifest its omnipresent, all-knowing character. *Samadhi* reminds the soul of its omnipresence. Struggling for the state of *samadhi* through meditation is thus the way to overcome the ego consciousness.

VERSE 11

अयनेषु च सर्वेषु यथाभागमवस्थिताः ।
भीष्ममेवाभिरक्षन्तु भवन्तः सर्व एव हि ॥

All of you, properly stationed in your places in the divisions of the army, do protect Bhishma.

"ALL OF YOU (DRONA-SAMSKARA, and the rest of our Kaurava army of sense inclinations and supportive allies) stand firm in your respective places on the bodily field of Kurukshetra and on the inner plains of the cerebrospinal centres, and concentrate your forces on protecting Bhishma-Ego."

King Duryodhana–Material Desire is fearful by nature; he is never quite sure of his kingdom. He knows that his very existence is precarious, based as it is on the support of the false or illusory ego consciousness. The ego, or the consciousness of being identified with a body, is carried through many incarnations in the heart of the soul. It is this persistence of body identification that has made King Material Desire strong and rouses him to strive by all means to perpetuate

* Paramahansa Yogananda set this song to music and included it in his *Words of Cosmic Chants* (see page 1129).

the body consciousness—for it is that consciousness along with its army of limitations that can and does keep the soul a prisoner of matter. Material Desire knows that if the ego consciousness once meets complete defeat at the hands of the soldiers of meditation, the soul will remember its perfect state and will then totally annihilate the armies of desire and delusion.

The ego is even more powerful in exercising delusive influence and in defeating the soldiers of the soul than Material Desire's preceptor, Past Habit-Tendency. Thus Duryodhana presumes to order even his respected teacher Drona to place himself in defense of the ego. Even if past evil tendencies are destroyed, other evil tendencies, or even egotistical good tendencies, can easily be created to keep the soul in bondage. Since the ego consciousness is the primary power to delude the soul and to entangle it in the meshes of flesh and matter, King Material Desire stresses the importance of defending Bhishma-Ego at all costs. He knows it will be very hard to kill the basic ego consciousness if it is staunchly protected by Drona-Samskara and the rest of the sense army.

Summary of the Forces Gathered to Do Spiritual Battle

A review of the principal warriors and generals in the Kuru and Pandu armies, who have been described in verses 4–9, will show that the strength of both sides is nearly equal. For every evil inclination, desire, or bad habit there is a corresponding divine discriminative quality that the determined yogi can employ to defeat or rout the enemy. Or, conversely, it can be said that, in the negligent or slothful devotee, for every good quality there is an evil counterpart well-prepared to deter the army of Self-realization.

The spiritual battle array is as follows:

The soldiers of the soul, present in man's seven cerebrospinal centres, are: (1) Sahadeva, the power to observe the negative rules of morality (the "thou-shalt-nots"), in the coccygeal or earth centre; (2) Nakula, the power to follow the prescribed positive spiritual rules (the "thou-shalts"), in the sacral or water centre; (3) Arjuna, or divine fire-force, and the power of patience and self-control, in the lumbar or fire centre; (4) Bhima, soul-controlled vital breath and life force, in the dorsal or air centre; (5) Yudhisthira, or King Calmness as divine discrimination, in the cervical or ether centre; (6) the Soul or superconscious *samadhi,* intuitional oneness with God, in the medulla; and Krishna or the Spirit as Christ Consciousness, in the point between the two eyebrows, directly connected and interrelated with the medulla centre; (7) Pure Spirit, in the *sahasrara* or "thousand-petalled lotus" in the brain.

Supporting them are the metaphysical warriors described in verses 4–6: Yuyudhana–Divine Devotion (*shraddha*), Uttamaujas–Vital Celibacy (*virya*), Chekitana–Spiritual Memory (*smriti*), Virata-Ecstasy (*samadhi*), Kashiraja–Discriminative Intelligence (*prajna*), Drupada–Extreme Dispassion (*tivra-samvega*), Dhrishtaketu–Power of Mental Resistance (*yama*), Shaibya–Power of Mental Adherence (*niyama*), Kuntibhoja–Right Posture (*asana*), Yudhamanyu–Life-Force Control (*pranayama*), Purujit-Interiorization (*pratyahara*), Abhimanyu–Self-Mastery (*samyama—dharana, dhyana,* and *samadhi*), and Draupadeya or the manifested spiritual vibrations, lights, and sounds of the five spinal centres, which are focal points of meditation.

The *Mahabharata* describes the divisions of the Pandava army as facing east. East means wisdom. In the body, or field of Kurukshetra, the east is inward, in the all-seeing spiritual eye.

The battle array on the evil or Kaurava side is facing west, outward toward the senses. Together with the forces of the three Pandavas that are in the lower spinal centres, the soldiers of King Material Desire occupy the coccygeal, sacral, and lumbar centres—which govern body-identified sense activity—plus the entire skin surface and the stronghold encampments of the ego-controlled sense organs and their nerve forces in the physical brain and spinal plexuses.

Metaphysical conflict in each cerebrospinal centre

IN A DEEPER METAPHYSICAL interpretation, it may be said that the Pandava forces in the medulla and five spinal centres are directly confronted by the evil Kaurava forces in the same six centres. Each centre has a spiritual and a gross function, as was cited by the example of Arjuna in the lumbar centre. All creation and creative forces emanate from Spirit. In the microcosm of the human body, the Divine and Its reflection, the soul, are enthroned in the highest spiritual centres in the brain, with subdynamos of life and consciousness in the medulla and spinal centres. The interaction of the creative principles produces the physical body and human consciousness. When ego and its supporters of delusion, ignorance, attachments, desires, habits, senses, persistently pull outward on the Spirit-attuned creative forces and consciousness, man becomes identified with grossness as the normal, desirable "reality." A duality or polarity has been established: the negative pull of the sense mind and ego, turning the currents and perceptions outward toward identification with matter; and the positive pull of the soul, through the pure discriminative intelligence that reveals truth, by which the consciousness and life currents are kept in attunement with the soul and Spirit.

When the awakening yogi, by the application of right action and meditation,* tries to regain his natural state of divine consciousness, he finds at each point of advancement the negative opposition of the Kuru forces. Having won the moral battle by his power to resist wrong actions and adhere to spiritual duties, and the inner psychological battle of restlessness by control of the body, mind, and life force, he now confronts the metaphysical battle in the cerebrospinal centres. As he tries to lift his consciousness upward through the centres to Spirit, he is fiercely resisted by the strong habitual body-bound powers and attachments.

Material desire and the forces of delusory ego consciousness

The instigator of the war against the divine Pandava qualities in the centres is Duryodhana–Material Desire (*kama*) in the coccygeal centre—the main channel of strong outflowing life force and consciousness—that feeds lustful sense desires and produces gross egotism and materialism. Duryodhana's existence depends on the support of Bhishma–Ego (*asmita*), Drona–Habit Tendencies (*samskara*), and Kripa–Individual Delusion (*avidya*) located in the medulla centre. The spiritual consciousness in this centre, turned inward, is the superconsciousness of the soul. Turned outward it becomes the pseudosoul and its inclinations. This is why Duryodhana in this present verse exhorts all the Kuru forces to protect Ego with all their might. The consciousness must not be allowed to reach this centre and turn inward to the soul and Spirit.† To this end, the rest of the Kuru army is roused

---

* Patanjali's Eightfold Path of Yoga.

† The pivotal role played in man's consciousness by the medulla oblongata and associated structures in the brain stem—known for centuries to yoga science—is now being articulated by neurophysiologists as well. Connecting the medulla oblongata (the seat, according to yoga, of man's self-consciousness, whether as soul or ego) and the pons Varolii (seat of *manas*, the lower sensory mind), is the reticular formation—a complex pathway of neurons in the centre of the brain stem, of which physicist Nick Herbert, Ph.D., writes in *Elemental Mind: Human Consciousness and the New Physics* (New York: Penguin Books, 1993):

"All major sensory and motor pathways must pass through this diffuse neuronal thicket on their way to and from the brain....Kilmer and his colleagues at MIT have described the function of the reticular formation as 'the nervous centre which integrates the complex of sensory-motor and autonomic-nervous relations so as to permit an organism to function as a unit instead of a mere collection of organs. Its primary job is to commit the organism to one or another of about sixteen gross modes of behaviour—

into action in their various positions of combat in the spinal centres to oppose the spiritual progress of the Pandava forces therein:

Duhshasana, as anger, hard to control (*krodha*); and Jayadratha, as fear of death (*abhinivesha*), in the sacral centre. Karna, as attachment to material actions (*raga*), and Vikarna as repulsion to unpleasantness (*dvesha*)—together, Karna and Vikarna produce likes and dislikes, or greed (*lobha*)—active in the lumbar centre. Shakuni, as attachment to delusion (*moha*), in the dorsal centre. Shalya, as pride (*mada*) in the cervical centre.

Supporting these Kaurava forces in the six subtle cerebrospinal centres—from Bhishma, Drona, and Kripa in the medulla to Duryodhana in the coccygeal centre—are the remaining aforementioned, firmly entrenched, Kritavarma, envy, material attachment (*matsarya*); Bhurishravas, the binding effects of material action (*karma*); Ashvatthaman, latent desire (*ashaya* or *vasana*), the son of Drona; and, additionally, all of the other principals and subordinates of the sense army.*

The two opposing armies are equally powerful, as alternately they rule the kingdom of the body. But the yogi draws courage and perseverance from knowledge that the inevitable final victory will be on the side of virtue. He holds to the truth that it is unnatural to be evil or allow unhappy disturbing conditions born of delusion and wrong action to rule one's mind, whereas it is quite natural to be virtuous and blessed. Man is created by God in His own image. It is because of this spiritual inheritance that he can rightfully claim to possess the all-conquering qualities of Omnipotent Spirit.

---

i.e., run, fight, sleep, speak—as a function of the nerve impulses that have played in upon it during the last fraction of a second.' Thus the reticular formation seems to make the moment-to-moment decisions about what the whole body should do with itself.

"Here is where the central executive dwells who selects, chooses, and above all experiences some of the activities carried out by the other brain structures. Here is where our search for the secret of human consciousness rightly begins.... Most evidence points to the conclusion that I, as a person, reside in my brain stem, in and around the reticular formation.... Human spirit enters matter in some unknown way through just this mysterious neural thicket.... We fit this dreamy organ as a hand fits a glove." (See also pages 5 and 10.) *(Publisher's Note)*

* Of necessity, this commentary on the warriors of Kurukshetra is simplified, as has been done in the Gita itself, concentrating on the principal allegorical characters that represent the yoga ascendency to Spirit and the forces that oppose. The unwritten volumes of detail are known by the devotee through the instancy of realization when he enters the *samadhi* of deep guru-given yoga meditation.

EXPANDED COMMENTARY: THE NATURE OF THE EGO

BHISHMA, OR EGO, is *chidabhasa,* reflected consciousness; not the true Self or light, but reflected light.* Ego is the sensualization of superconsciousness or subjective soul—the identifying of the superconscious soul with the sense-bound consciousness of the body. Ego is the pseudosoul, described also as the shadow of the soul. It is the reflected, subjective consciousness within man that makes him conscious of his feelings, will, cognition (sensation, perception, conception), and his environment. It is the conscious nucleus of "I-ness" around which all human thoughts, feelings, and experiences revolve. All of these may be subtracted from the ego, but still the ego itself would remain—aloof, always beyond reach, like the will-o'-the-wisp; seemingly beyond the power to define it, except to explain what it is not. Hence negatively defined, the ego or "I"—the subject—is that which cannot be eliminated from myself as can everything else with which the "I" thinks that it is identified.

The aloofness of the ego is only superficial, however, and is different from the soul's aloofness and power of transcendental indifference. The ego cannot maintain its self-conscious expression without its titles; indeed, the ego defines itself by these identifying marks. The ego's titles are amassed from its accumulation of experiences and traits, and are thus constantly changing, even as its bodily instrumentation undergoes metamorphosis: The child changes into a youth, the youth grows and passes through adolescence into adulthood, and the adult progresses into old age.

Positively defined, "I" or ego is the changeless consciousness of sameness during the processes of ever-changing thoughts and sensory-motor experiences. Everything that clusters around the ego, all the accoutrements of the "I," are in a state of constant flux, but the "I-ness" as the individual who is undergoing these remains the same. Hence this nucleus is the central life of the little self and its experiences. It is the author of them, the subject who lords over these changes: "I think, I see, I hear, I will, I love, I hate, I have pain, I have joy."

The subject lording over experiences is distinctly different from

---

* See also reference to Bhishma as "reflected consciousness," universal ego, in Introduction, page *xxvi.*

the thoughts and the objects of the thinking process. When a person says that he is blind, that is a misnomer. The eyes are blind. If my eyes are gone, am I gone also? No. If I lost my hand, I would not say that I am gone. The delusion of the ego is such that in spite of man's best rationalization, he cannot help but identify the "I," the experiencer, with the experiencing. It is because of this identification that the ego impresses human consciousness with the idea of change and impermanency. Yet, if everything is removed—thoughts, sensations, emotions, the body itself—the "I" would still remain. By what power does the "I" know it exists, bereft of all else? By the intuitive power of the true eternal Self, the soul.

Nature of the soul's power of intuition

Intuition is like a light, a flame of knowledge, that comes from the soul. It possesses all-sided power to know all there is to be known. Every man inherently possesses something of this power; but in most it is undeveloped. This undeveloped intuition is a crystal placed before the soul, producing a double image. The soul itself is the real image; the reflection is unreal—the ego or pseudosoul. The more undeveloped the intuition is, the more distorted the ego image will be. When human life is guided by this false identity, which is brought about by the presence of undeveloped intuition, it is subject to all the limitations and false notions of delusion. A chaotic existence of error and its consequences is therefore inevitable.

Without ego, with its vestige of intuition, undeveloped though it may be, man would be relegated to the domain of animal consciousness—sensation plus instinct. Man is ego plus sensations, plus some discriminative intellect, plus latent intuition. Man's ego, with its superior faculties, is considered as some kind of a master and central principal. If there were thousands of persons working in a factory without any guide or principal, there would be no coordination. But if they all accept the leadership of one principal, then they will act in harmony. In man, ego is that principal. It is that quality of "I-ness" in man without which the different phases of consciousness—thinking, feeling, and willing—cannot cooperate to work toward a consciously intended end. Without the ego, the ordinary man could not relate to his thoughts, feelings, experiences; he would not know what he was doing. For example, in insanity, the ego is affected and forgets to understand its relations with thoughts and experiences, producing uncoordinated, irresponsible behaviour.

While animals are guided primarily by instinct, and ordinary man is guided by his ego, the yogi who is united to the Self is guided by the soul. Animals, bound by instinct, have very limited intelligence. Man as super-animal, guided by ego, has more power and intelligence than beasts, but is still very limited by thoughts and sensations. The yogi alone is free from limitations, guided by the limitless Self.

THE EGO IN THE ORDINARY MAN is not the pure ego, but ego entangled in all the ramifications that have grown out of it—that is, from its identification with the intellect, mind, and senses. When man becomes conscious of the pure ego, untrammelled by any of its evolutionary products, he is very near to soul-realization. The pure ego is nothing but the soul, the *jivatman* or incarnate individualized Self. (See commentary on I:8.) The intent of yoga is to provide measures by which the purity of the ego can be established outwardly as well as inwardly. The fault-infested ego of the ordinary man is the mind-ego, the ego that has the potential of being perverted by intellect waves, mental vibrations, and sense impressions. When the possibility of the ego's being influenced by these has been removed, then and only then is man safe from the disturbances and sufferings inevitable in forgetfulness of the soul.

Pure and impure ego

In sleep, man gets a glimpse of the soul. When the ego sleeps, it takes with it into the subconscious, in a latent way, its experiences. Indirectly in sleep, the ego has to forsake its titles, possessions, name, and form. The senses are absorbed into the mind, the mind into the intellect, and the intellect into the ego. But the possibility of disturbances has not been removed. These faculties have merely become inactive and shrunken, but are yet ready to express themselves again in dreaming or in waking. In the deepest dreamless sleep, man contacts the blissful pure ego or soul; but because he enters this state unconsciously he loses the spiritual benefit of it. If he can go into this state consciously, in *samadhi* meditation, spiritual growth is at his command. The pure conscious feeling of "I exist" is then ready to be absorbed into the highest realization of soul consciousness.

Each day in sleep, man glimpses the soul

Daily in sleep, every man becomes a renunciant, sloughing off all his sham titles; and once in a while he even becomes a saint. But because of sense habits during the conscious state, he cannot preserve that nonattachment while actively engaged in duties.

If man can for a sufficient length of time remain unidentified with his thoughts and sensations, without being in a blank or unconscious state, he will know his true Self through undistorted pure intuition. Thus the absolute calmness of deep meditation is the only way the ego consciousness can be eliminated. Having removed the crystal of undeveloped intuition that was reflecting the soul in a distorted way, there is no longer any conflict in the yogi as to his true identity.

In the *Mahabharata,* we find that from the beginning of Duryodhana's determination to fight the Pandavas, Bhishma counselled him against war and encouraged an amicable settlement; for Bhishma-Ego is the grandsire of both the Kauravas and Pandavas, and regards them equally. That is, the ego serves its purpose of keeping the consciousness sense-bound to the body whether a man's desires and actions are basically good or evil. When the Kauravas or offspring of the sense mind are stronger, Bhishma sides with them. However, as the divine discriminative qualities become more victorious, Bhishma-Ego wearies of supporting evil. It begins to feel more tenderness toward the discriminative qualities. But their victory of Self-realization or Soul rule cannot be complete so long as Ego lives. Bhishma is invincible, however, for the "I" can never be destroyed without its consent and cooperation. So Bhishma himself finally reveals to the Pandavas the sole way he can be killed in battle by the skill of Arjuna, the devotee in deep meditation. After this most fierce of all battles, Bhishma's body is mortally wounded by Arjuna's countless arrows. Even so, Bhishma says he will remain thus on this bed of arrows and not give up his body until the sun moves north in the heavens. Literally, this is taken to refer to an astronomical calculation of the seasonal placement of the sun. But symbolically, it means that even though the ego is rendered powerless and benign by the *samadhi* meditation of the devotee, it will not fully die (the pure sense of "I-ness" or individuality remains) until the sun of divine consciousness in the spiritual eye during *savikalpa samadhi* moves to the north—upward to the place of the finer forces in the brain; that is, in the innermost divine region in the *sahasrara* (the highest spiritual centre in the body), in union with Spirit in *nirvikalpa samadhi.*

❖ *The defeat of Bhishma-Ego by Arjuna–Self-Control* ❖

At this point in the Gita, however, Ego still stands as the most formidable force confronting the Pandavas in their quest to regain their rightful kingdom.

THE CONCH SHELLS: INNER VIBRATORY BATTLE IN MEDITATION

VERSE 12

तस्य सञ्जनयन्हर्षं कुरुवृद्धः पितामहः ।
सिंहनादं विनद्योच्चैः शङ्खं दध्मौ प्रतापवान् ॥

Grandsire Bhishma, oldest and most powerful of the Kurus, with the purpose of cheering Duryodhana, blew his conch shell with a resounding lion's roar.

DURYODHANA–MATERIAL DESIRE did not find immediate response from his preceptor Drona-Habit, even though (in stanza 11) he had said to him: "Let all the soldiers of the restless mind (the Kurus) get together and protect the ego consciousness (Bhishma)." Seeing that lack of response from Drona, and with the purpose of cheering King Material Desire and preventing him from getting discouraged, the all-knower Bhishma-Ego sent forth a strong vibration of pride and determination, and "blew his conch shell" of restless breath that causes body identification and disrupts the stillness of deep meditation.*

Drona is depicted as not altogether enthusiastic about fighting the Pandavas. This is because, as stated before, he is not only the preceptor of the wicked Kurus but of the good Pandus as well. Until the yogi is firmly established in Self-realization, the Drona–Habit Tendency in him is a miscellany of both good and evil *samskaras*, or habit tendencies brought over from past incarnations, most of which have manifested themselves as fixed habits in the present life. However, since Drona–Habit Tendency has presently sided with the evil Kurus, or body-bound sense habits and wicked mental tendencies, his concentration is on protecting those Kaurava forces against the threat posed by the invasion of good habits and habit-destroying discriminative tendencies.

Alliance of habit, ego, and material desire

* Paramahansa Yogananda wrote: "The influx of innumerable cosmic currents into man by way of the breath induces restlessness in his mind. Thus the breath links him with the fleeting phenomenal worlds. To escape from the sorrows of transitoriness and to enter the blissful realm of Reality, the yogi learns to quiet the breath by scientific meditation." (*Whispers from Eternity,* published by Yogoda Satsanga Society of India.)

The very nature of habit is automatic compulsion to do what one has become accustomed to do. Habits go on repeating their same old pattern, often ignoring a desire's new command. When bad habits are challenged, their self-preserving instinct makes them behave as though they were sufficient unto themselves to crush opposing good habits and intentions, and have no time to pay attention to urgings to cooperate with a long-range and broader view of action. Bad habits are therefore ultimately self-defeating—circumscribed by their narrow fixity and shortsightedness, dependent for their very existence on the important parts played by Material Desire and Ego. For example, in a psychological battle between the habit of yielding to a temptation and the habit of self-control, if self-control is stronger it may easily subdue temptation. But good habits find it very hard to overcome the persistence of a constantly replenished army engaged in evolving endless new material desires, and in reinforcing the body-bound inclinations of the ego. Without Ego's attachment to the body, there would be no Material Desire; and without Desire there would be no Samskara, or Habit. Conversely, Ego can be slain if not protected by Habit and Material Desire.

Thus Ego, in his own defense, initiates the call to arms. In the context of this Gita verse, this means that during deep meditation, when the breath has become calm, producing a very enjoyable state of peace wherein the mind is withdrawn from the senses, the worried ego rouses in the devotee the thought of body identification, reviving the restless breath, which is like a lion's roar compared to the absolute stillness of the interiorized meditative state. As soon as the devotee resumes his "natural" practice of dependency on fast breathing (the "blowing of the conch shell" that produces the consciousness of material sounds through the vibration of the gross *akasha* or ether), the Material Desire of the body is aroused and cheered on to rally the senses against the powers of meditation.

❖ *The restless breath keeps consciousness body-bound* ❖

The devotee should not be discouraged at this, which is due to a lack of long-continued practice of meditation. The truth is, in the earlier stages of meditation all devotees find their limited body-consciousness resisting expansion into Omnipresence. The Ego, through Material Desire and his sense army, uses all kinds of tactics to drive away the blissful consciousness of Omnipresent Spirit that manifests only in meditative stillness. Any vibration sent forth by Ego during meditation helps to awaken Material Desire to revive the consciousness of the body and dispel the consciousness of Spirit. By deeper and longer concentration, the meditating yogi must learn to hold on to the hard-won territory of calmness of breath and senses, in spite of the efforts of Ego and the army of sense distractions of Material Desire.

VERSE 13

ततः शङ्खाश्च भेर्यश्च पणवानकगोमुखाः ।
सहसैवाभ्यहन्यन्त स शब्दस्तुमुलोऽभवत् ॥

Then suddenly (after Bhishma's first note), a great chorus from conch shells, kettledrums, cymbals, tabors, and cowhorn-trumpets sounded (from the side of the Kurus); the noise was terrific.

AFTER THE EGO CREATES A MATERIAL vibration, reawakening the thought of body consciousness and rousing the restless breath, the senses also begin to send out their various distracting vibratory sounds in order to disrupt the devotee's meditation. The vibrations of the senses (Kurus), which keep the devotee's attention upon the internal sounds of the physical body, are shrill and disturbing—comparable to shattering a quiet atmosphere with the clamour of drums, horns, and cymbals.

Stanzas 12–18 describe the inner psychological battle that is carried on in meditation through the vibratory sounds emanating from the sense tendencies on the one side and the discriminative tendencies on the other. It is a battle in which both the physical and the astral vibratory sounds of the senses pull the consciousness toward the body; and the vibrations of a wondrous astral music, emitted by the inner discriminative powers and vital activities in the spinal centres, draws the consciousness toward the soul and Spirit.

Vibratory sounds experienced as the consciousness passes from the material world to the spiritual realm through the intermediate astral plane

In meditation, the return of the consciousness to the kingdom of the soul requires the yogi to pass from awareness of flesh to awareness of astral existence. That is, the way from body consciousness to superconsciousness lies through an intermediate world—man's astral or vital-electrical system. The 12th and 13th stanzas describe not only the gross physical vibrations emanating from the senses, but also the ugly agitated and agitating vibratory noises of the aroused astral *nadis* (subtle astral "nerve" currents) that incite sensory and other bodily activities. Stanzas 14–18, in contrast, describe the spiritual experiences and divine uplifting vibrations emanating from the soul and the astral kingdom. The gross vibrations are heard when man is still on the plane of body consciousness. The astral vibrations are not heard until the yogi's consciousness reaches the inner astral plane.

Aspiring yogis know all too well from experience that during the first state of meditation the concentration may become deep enough to shut off the sounds of the external world, but the resultant inner peace is short-lived. When ego consciousness is still awake and blows the conch shell of breath, the sense organs of heart, circulation, and lungs make many peculiar thumping, throbbing, and purring sounds; behind these is a cacophony of their body-bound astral counterparts. But no fine astral music is heard. The mind becomes discouraged and unsteady, a prisoner of its own sense-enslaved nature. The body begins to complain and wants to break its meditation pose.

Great determination of will is required to win this first inner psychological battle to keep the concentration steady and interiorized.

Four factors in meditation: mind, breath, vital essence, life force

The devotee will be aided in this if he recognizes the intimate interrelation of the four factors of mind, breath, vital essence, and bodily life energy. When any one of the four factors is disturbed, the other three are also automatically disturbed, as is the case when the ego consciousness revives the senses by disrupting the calmness of breathlessness.

The devotee, therefore, who aspires to develop steadily in spirituality must calm the mind by the practice of the right techniques of concentration; must keep the breath quiet by *pranayama* and proper breathing exercises; must preserve the vital essence (generally the most abused of the senses) by self-control and by seeking only the company of good people; and must free the body from restlessness and aimless motions by conscious control of the life force, and by keeping the body in good health and training it by patient discipline to sit absolutely still in meditation.

VERSE 14

ततः श्वेतैर्हयैर्युक्ते महति स्यन्दने स्थितौ।
माधवः पाण्डवश्चैव दिव्यौ शङ्खौ प्रदध्मतुः॥

Then also, Madhava (Krishna) and Pandava (Arjuna), seated in their grand chariot with its yoke of white horses, splendidly blew their celestial conch shells.

WHEN THE EGO DISTURBS THE BREATH during deep meditation, the soul again tries to revive the intuitive consciousness in the persevering devotee by sounding a series of astral vibrations, and illumining the inner gaze with divine light.

Pandava, or the devotee Arjuna, seated in the chariot of meditative intuition, with his attention focused on the Spirit as Krishna or divine Christ Consciousness at the *Kutastha* centre between the eyebrows, beholds the light of the spiritual eye and hears the sacred sound of *Pranava,* the creative *Aum* vibration with its different cosmic sounds vibrating from the spinal centres in the astral body.

The devotee, first listening within, hears only the gross sounds of the breath, heart, circulation, and so on—and perhaps the astral vibratory sounds behind these—ready to bring him back to matter. As his attention deepens, he hears the astral music of divine consciousness within. If his concentration is steady he may also see the light of the spiritual eye, the intuitive all-seeing eye of the soul.

Behold the chariot of intuition drawn by stallions of white lights racing in all directions from a dark blue centre (soul's abode)!

Krishna in this verse is referred to as Madhava (*Ma,* Prakriti,* or Primordial Nature; *Dhava,* husband—the blue radiance of the telescopic spiritual eye—the sole "door" through which a devotee is able to enter the state of Krishna or *Kutastha Chaitanya,* Universal Christ Consciousness).

Surrounding this blue light is the brilliant white or golden light—the telescopic astral eye through which all Nature is perceived. In the centre of the blue light is a white starlike light, doorway to the Infinite Spirit, or Cosmic Consciousness.

VERSES 15–18

पाञ्चजन्यं हृषीकेशो देवदत्तं धनञ्जयः ।
पौण्ड्रं दध्मौ महाशङ्खं भीमकर्मा वृकोदरः ॥ *(15)*

---

* Prakriti or Nature, the "consort" of Spirit, has been given many names according to the various aspects She represents, such as Lakshmi, Sarasvati, Kali; or the Holy Ghost of the Christian scripture. Spirit is the unmanifested Absolute. To evolve creation God sends forth a creative vibration, Holy Ghost or Maha-Prakriti, in which He Himself is present in an unchanged, unaffected reflection, the Universal Spirit in creation: *Kutastha Chaitanya,* Krishna or Christ Consciousness. In the womb of Mother Nature, Spirit gives birth to creation. The light of the spiritual eye seen in meditation is a microcosm of the light of Nature, Christ or Krishna Consciousness, and Spirit or Cosmic Consciousness. The triune light of the spiritual eye leads to union with these three macrocosmic states of consciousness.

अनन्तविजयं राजा कुन्तीपुत्रो युधिष्ठिरः।
नकुलः सहदेवश्च सुघोषमणिपुष्पकौ॥ *(16)*

काश्यश्च परमेष्वासः शिखण्डी च महारथः।
धृष्टद्युम्नो विराटश्च सात्यकिश्चापराजितः॥ *(17)*

द्रुपदो द्रौपदेयाश्च सर्वशः पृथिवीपते।
सौभद्रश्च महाबाहुः शङ्खान्दध्मुः पृथक् पृथक्॥ *(18)*

(15) Hrishikesha (Krishna) blew his Panchajanya; Dhananjaya (Arjuna), his Devadatta; and Vrikodara (Bhima), of terrible deeds, blew his great conch Paundra.

(16) King Yudhisthira, the son of Kunti, blew his Anantavijaya; Nakula and Sahadeva blew, respectively, their Sughosha and Manipushpaka.

(17) The King of Kashi, excellent archer; Sikhandi, the great warrior; Dhrishtadyumna, Virata, the invincible Satyaki,

(18) Drupada, the sons of Draupadi, and the mighty-armed son of Subhadra, all blew their own conches, O Lord of Earth.

IN THESE VERSES REFERENCE IS MADE to the specific vibratory sounds (the conch shells of the various Pandavas) the meditating devotee hears emanating from the astral centres in the spine and medulla. *Pranava,* the sound of the creative *Aum* vibration, is the mother of all sounds. The intelligent cosmic energy of *Aum* that issues forth from God, and is the manifestation of God, is the creator and substance of all matter. This holy vibration is the link between matter and Spirit. Meditation on *Aum* is the way to realize the true Spirit-essence of all creation. By inwardly following the sound of *Pranava* to its source, the yogi's consciousness is carried aloft to God.

In the microcosmic universe of the body of man, the *Aum* vibration works through the vital activities in the astral spinal centres of life with their creative vibratory elements (*tattvas*) of earth, water, fire, air, and ether. Through these, man's body is created, enlivened, and sustained. These vibrations emit characteristic variations of *Pranava* as they operate.* The devotee whose consciousness becomes attuned to

* "I was in the Spirit (spiritual consciousness) on the Lord's day (the day of contacting the divine realms of truth), and heard behind me (in the medulla, 'behind' or in the

these inner astral sounds finds himself gradually ascending to higher states of realization.

STAGES OF INTERIORIZED MEDITATION

PATANJALI DEFINES these states in his classification of the various stages of interiorized meditation. In *Yoga Sutras* I:17–18, he refers to two basic categories of *samadhi:* (1) *samprajnata* and (2) *asamprajnata.* As applied to advanced stages of realization, *samprajnata* refers to *savikalpa* ("with difference") *samadhi,* or divine union in which there remains some distinction between the knower and the known, as in the realization "Thou and I are One." In greater or lesser degree, some modifications of nature remain. But in *asamprajnata samadhi,* all differentiations of nature are resolved into the one Spirit. The consciousness of "Thou and I are One" becomes "I am He, who has become this little form of 'I' and all forms." This is not the egotist's proclamation, "I am God!"—the brass crown of megalomania—but rather the full realization of the absolute truth: God is the only Reality. Thus *asamprajnata,* in its absolute definition, is *nirvikalpa* ("without difference") *samadhi,* the highest yoga or union manifested by fully liberated masters or those on the threshold of soul freedom.

Distinguishing initial supersensory experiences in meditation from true samadhi or union

However, when used to define the preliminary stages of realization rather than its advanced states of fulfilment, then *samprajnata* and *asamprajnata* are relative terms used to distinguish initial supersensory experiences in meditation (*samprajnata*) from true *samadhi* or union with the object of meditation (*asamprajnata*). *Samprajnata* then refers to those primary states wherein the object of meditation is "known accurately or thoroughly" through intuition that is still somewhat mixed with, or interpreted by, nature's subtle instruments of perception—an interaction of the knower, the knowing, and the known. It is therefore sometimes called "conscious" *samadhi* because those faculties of nature that operate outwardly in ordinary consciousness—such as mind (*manas*), intellect (*buddhi*), feeling (*chitta*), ego (*asmita*)—are active inwardly in their pure or subtle form.

---

back of the head) a great voice, as of a trumpet (the great blissful sound of *Aum*)....And I turned to see the voice that spake with me. And being turned, I saw seven golden candlesticks (the seven astral centres); and in the midst of the seven candlesticks one (the astral body) like unto the son of man (similar in appearance to the physical body)...and his voice as the sound of many waters (the sound of the elements, *tattvas,* emanating from the astral centres)" (Revelation 1:10, 12, 13, 15).

By contrast, *asamprajnata* then means those superconscious experiences that are perceived through pure intuition or realization—the direct perception of the soul by being one with the object of meditation—transcendent of any intervening instrument or principle of nature. Intuition is the "face-to-face" knowledge of reality, without any intermediary.*

Patanjali says that *asamprajnata* is the result of the *samskara* (impression) left by *samprajnata samadhi.* In other words, by repeated efforts at deeper and deeper *samprajnata* meditation, the end result is the transcendent state of *asamprajnata samadhi.* But it is a misnomer to refer to this latter state as "unconscious *samadhi*" in keeping with the previous state's being called "conscious." Rather, as *samprajnata* means "known accurately or thoroughly," that idea does not arise in the opposite, *asamprajnata,* because in the unity of the knower and known there is nothing to be known; the devotee becomes the object of his meditation. Far from unconsciousness, it is a state of supreme heightened awareness and enlightenment.

Samprajnata and asamprajnata samadhi

Patanjali divides *samprajnata samadhi* into four stages:† (1) *savitarka* ("with doubt or conjecture"): intuitive experience mixed with argumentative or doubt-ridden mind; (2) *savichara* ("with reasoning or pondering"): intuitive experience mixed with discrimination-guided intellect; (3) *sananda* ("with joy"): interiorized intuitive experience interpreted by *chitta* or joy-permeated feeling; and (4) *sasmita* ("with 'I-ness'" or individuality): intuitive experience mixed with a pure sense of being. These four states, which come after interiorization (*pratyahara*), are the result of deep concentration (*dharana*), or superconscious perception as limited to the body.

When these four stages of *samprajnata* have been resolved one by one into the next higher state, the yogi goes beyond them and attains *asamprajnata samadhi.* This comes in deep meditation (*dhyana*) in which concentration (*dharana*) is continuous, with no flicker of interruption; then the object of meditation (i.e., a particular concept or manifestation of God) is experienced as manifested not only in the body but in omnipresence. Beyond these states, in the advanced stages of realiza-

* "But when that which is perfect is come, then that which is in part shall be done away....For now we see through a glass, darkly; but then face-to-face: now I know in part; but then shall I know even as also I am known" (I Corinthians 13:10, 12).

† *Yoga Sutras* I:17.

tion, *samprajnata* and *asamprajnata* are understood to mean, respectively, *savikalpa* and *nirvikalpa samadhi.*

Patanjali says that attainment of the highest *samadhi* is possible "by profound, devoted meditation on (the Lord) Ishvara (I:23)....His symbol is *Aum* (I:27)."

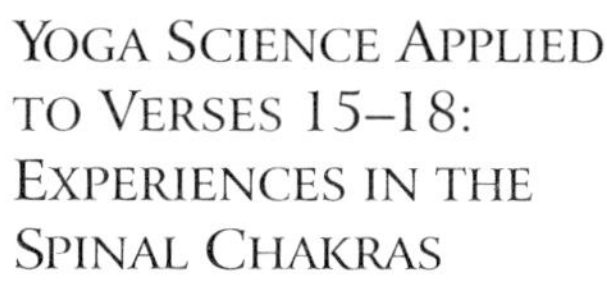

YOGA SCIENCE APPLIED TO VERSES 15–18: EXPERIENCES IN THE SPINAL CHAKRAS

THE APPLICATION OF ALL the foregoing to Gita verses 15–18 is as follows: (The significance of the conches of the five sons of Pandu, mentioned in verses 15 and 16, is given first, explained according to the spiritual progression of realization rather than in the sequence in which they are referred to in the verses).

Sahadeva, with his conch called Manipushpaka ("that which becomes manifest by its sound"),* represents the earth element in the coccygeal centre (*muladhara chakra*) in the spine. The devotee concentrating upon this centre hears the *Aum* or cosmic vibration in a peculiar sound like the drone of a honey-mad bee. The devotee then wonders doubtfully whether this sound is a bodily vibration or an astral sound. This state of concentration is therefore called *savitarka samprajnata samadhi,* "the doubt-ridden state of inner absorption." This centre is the abode of the interiorized meditational mind in its very first stage.

Nakula, with his conch named Sughosha ("that which sounds clearly and sweetly"), represents the water element manifested in the sacral centre (*svadhishthana chakra*). The devotee concentrating upon this centre is lifted beyond the doubting state of mind to a surer, more discriminating state; he listens to a higher astral sound, which is similar to the beautiful tones of a flute. The doubting ceases, and his intellect begins to fathom the nature of this sound. This state is called *savichara samprajnata samadhi,* or the "intellectual, reason-guided state of inner absorption."

---

* The allegorical significance is found not in the literal translation of the words *mani* (jewel) and *pushpa* (flower) but in the Sanskrit roots *man,* "to sound"; and *puṣ,* "unfold or display."

The reason and conjecture of scholarly minds may arrive at the literal or traditional interpretation of the terminology used by Rishi Vyasa in the Gita; but the deeper meanings are often hidden in clues within the words—even as Jesus hid truth in parables, and the apostle John concealed the meaning of his realization in the metaphors of *The Revelation of St. John.* The obvious interpretation is for the inspiration of the ordinary man; the hidden metaphor is for the serious practitioner of the yoga science.

Arjuna (here referred to as Dhananjaya, "Winner of Wealth"), with his conch named Devadatta ("that which gives joy"),* represents the fire element in the lumbar centre (*manipura chakra*). The devotee concentrating upon this centre hears an astral sound that is like a harp or vina. Owing to the dissolution of the doubting mental state and of the discriminating intellectual state, he now attains the state of perceptive Self-realization in which the clear perception of the sound and its true nature produces a joy-permeated feeling of inner absorption or *sananda samprajnata samadhi*.

Bhima, with his conch named Paundra ("that which disintegrates" the lower states),† represents the air or life-force (*prana*) element in the dorsal centre (*anahata chakra*). The devotee concentrating on this centre hears the *Aum* "symbol of God" as a deep, long-drawn-out astral bell. The mental, intellectual, and perceptive states having all been dissolved, the devotee arrives at an intuitive inner-bliss absorption that is mixed with ego consciousness, not as body consciousness but as a pure sense of individualized being or "I am." This state is *sasmita samprajnata samadhi*.

Yudhisthira, with his conch named Anantavijaya ("that which conquers infinity"), represents the ether element in the cervical centre of the spine (*vishuddha chakra*). The devotee concentrating at this centre hears the eternity-controlling, infinity-spreading cosmic sound of the all-pervasive etheric vibration of *Aum* whose sound is like thunder, or the roar of a distant mighty ocean. In this state, the four preceding phases of interiorization—mental (*manas*), intellectual (*buddhi*), perceptive (*chitta*), and egoistic (*asmita*)—have been dissolved, giving rise to a deeper state of pure intuitive perception of limitless bliss, the state called *asamprajnata samadhi*.

Although the cognitive instruments of human consciousness are now extinct, *asamprajnata samadhi* is not unconsciousness, but a direct knowing through Self-realization, the pure intuition of the soul. As the devotee's "I-ness" or sense of individual existence has been transcended, his consciousness identifies with the etheric vibration of *Aum* in all space: expanding from the little body to infinity, his blissful consciousness embraces omnipresence.

---

* Devadatta means literally, "gift of God." In this allegorical context, its significance is found in one of the many meanings of the Sanskrit root of *deva*, which is *div*, and means "to rejoice or have delight in."

† From the inherent Sanskrit root *pund*, lit., "to reduce to powder," i.e., disintegrate.

Sri Krishna (who is here referred to as Hrishikesha, "Lord of the Senses") then blows his conch called Panchajanya, "that which generates the five *tattvas* or elements." The sound is a mingling of the various sounds of the five lower centres. This is the true or undifferentiated cosmic *Aum* vibration. This "symphony" of the five sounds of *Pranava* is heard in the united medullary and Christ-consciousness centre (*ajna chakra*). Here the devotee enjoys a greater *savikalpa samadhi.* He attains full realization of God in His creative aspect, manifested as the *Aum* vibration. "In the beginning was the Word (the creative vibration—the Holy Ghost, Amen, or *Aum*), and the Word was with God, and the Word was God."* Attunement with God as *Aum* lifts the consciousness to the immanent Christ Consciousness. Through Christ Consciousness the advanced yogi ascends to Cosmic Consciousness in the highest cerebral centre. "No man cometh unto the Father (Cosmic Consciousness), but by me (through the Son, or Christ Consciousness)."† These states of the "Holy Trinity" are symbolized in Hindu scriptures as *Aum, Tat, Sat*—Holy Ghost vibration, *Kutastha* or Christ Consciousness, and God or Cosmic Consciousness.

When the devotee attains cosmic consciousness in the highest cerebral centre (the *sahasrara*) and can enter that state at will and remain in it as long as he wishes, he will in time be blessed to experience that ecstasy in the supreme or final undifferentiated state—*nirvikalpa samadhi.*

When the yogi's union with God is experienced in these elevated states wherein the consciousness has been lifted to the centres in the medulla (pure superconsciousness of the soul), the point between the eyebrows (*Kutastha* or Christ consciousness), and the cerebrum (cosmic consciousness), he realizes the higher significance of *samprajnata* and *asamprajnata* as, respectively, *savikalpa samadhi* and *nirvikalpa samadhi.*

In *samprajnata savikalpa samadhi,* the *savitarka* experience of God is not "doubt-ridden" in a negative sense, but a questioning with reverence and wonderment: "Is this really the Lord, He who has been so silent and invisible in the universe? Is it true that He has come at last to me?" The *savichara* experience is a keen discernment of the nature of God in one of His many aspects or qualities—Cosmic Love, Bliss, Wisdom, and so forth. The *sananda* experience tastes the indefinable bliss that accompanies communion with God in His eternal nature of ever-existing, ever-conscious, ever-new Bliss. In the state of *sasmita,* the devotee feels his expanded self in every atom of space as though all creation were his

---

* John 1:1. † John 14:6.

own body—it is a state of perfect calmness in which the devotee is like a mirror reflecting all things. When the devotee becomes anchored in cosmic consciousness and retains his state of God-perception and omnipresence even when he returns to body consciousness and material activities, he has then attained *asamprajnata nirvikalpa samadhi.*

Now, in Gita verses 17 and 18, are mentioned the other key Pandava warriors whose significance has been elaborated on in the interpretation of earlier verses. These divine Pandavas, following the lead of Krishna and the five Pandus, sound their respective conches. These are the supportive *nadis,* or astral nerve currents, conductors of life energy, whose vibratory activities also produce characteristic sounds. All these vibrations during meditation are turned Godward to spiritualize the whole body and mind and draw the consciousness inward toward Self-realization.

The layman, reading these explanations, may wonder what it is all about! But those conscientious seekers after truth who have practised right methods of *Raja Yoga* meditation, as do those devotees who follow Lahiri Mahasaya's *Kriya Yoga* path through the *Yogoda Satsanga Lessons,* know from their own experience that these astral sounds may be distinctly heard. This truth can be proved by anyone who practises the yoga techniques. In a book available to the general public I cannot give the techniques themselves; for they are sacred, and certain ancient spiritual injunctions must first be followed to insure that they are received with reverence and confidentiality, and thereafter practised correctly. I have, however, throughout this manuscript, endeavoured to give sufficient theoretical explanation to satisfy any intelligent layman that yoga is indeed a science, perfectly organized by the sages of ancient India. In preparing the interpretation of the holy Bhagavad Gita, my intent and prayer is to awaken new hearts and minds to the physical, mental, and spiritual blessings available through right knowledge and application of the yoga science, and to encourage and hasten the progress of those devotees who are already steadfast on the yoga path.

❖

ANALOGY OF CREATION AS A COSMIC MOTION PICTURE

AN ILLUSTRATION MAY help to explain the deep subject in these present Gita verses:

A primitive tribesman who has had no contact with modern civilization, and who sees a talking motion picture for the first time, might easily believe the motions to be those of living men and women. One way to convince him that the talking picture is nothing but a play of film and electric vibrations is to take him near the screen and there let him touch the shadowy images to discover their deceptive nature. Another way to educate him that the talking pictures are a play of lights and shadows is to show him the film and movie equipment, and how the torrent of electric light emanating from the opening in the operating booth is carrying within its beam the power to project on a screen a series of realistic forms.

To a materialist, the whole world—its complications of solids, liquids, fire, gases, and so forth—seems to be composed of real material substances: "This is the way I perceive it; therefore, it must be fact." But the advanced yogi, whose Self-realization has penetrated to the inner source of external matter, is able to say: "This world, this cosmos, are only shadows of life thrown on the screen of space, and reflected in our conscious and subconscious mental chambers."

Just as the etheric flood of light going out of the movie booth is seen to be like a transparent searchlight free from any inherent pictures, yet images mysteriously appear on the screen; so God, from His booth in the centre of eternity, is emanating a spherical bundle of rays, invisible searchlights, which—passing through the film of delusion's interacting principles of nature—produce within their core on the screen of space an endless variety of apparently real pictures. But the images are shadowy illusions; the only reality is God and His individualized consciousness in the forms that behold and interact in the play of cosmic delusion.

The world and cosmos are shadows of life thrown on the screen of space

The yogi, peering with closed eyes into the dark invisibility within, finally finds there six subtle astral booths—the coccygeal, sacral, lumbar, dorsal, cervical, and the combined medullary and Christ centres, situated in the spinal column, and at the base of the brain and the point between the eyebrows. He sees that the true-to-life picture of his body is produced by an earth current in the coccyx, a water vibration in the sacral, a fire vibration in the lumbar, an air vibration in the dorsal, an ether vibration in the cervical, and a consciousness-and-life-force vibration in the medulla and Christ centres.

Just as the beam of electric light thrown on a screen makes a peculiar noise at its source, which is caused by electrical vibration, so the astral spinal centres emanate different "musical" sounds as they send out their various pranic, life-force, currents that produce the technicolour picture of the physical body, with its true-to-sight, true-to-touch, true-to-hearing, true-to-smell, true-to-taste perceptions. By concentrating on the six centres, the meditating devotee hears successively the music of the bumblebee, the flute, the harp, the gong bell, the sea roar, and then the symphony of all the astral sounds. These emanations from the six centres are the vibrations of the five elements or *tattvas* in nature, macrocosmically present in the universe, and microcosmically operative in the body of man.

The earth life-current in the coccyx is the force responsible for the solidifying of the primal life force into atoms of flesh, and for producing the sense of smell; as it operates, this centre emanates the sound of a buzzing bee.

The five elemental vibrations create and sustain the body

The water element in the sacral centre sustains the atoms of all the watery substances in the body, and is responsible for the sense of taste; its work makes the musical sound of a flute.

The fire element in the lumbar centre maintains the astral life-glow and electrical heat of the body, and produces the sense of sight —activities that are accompanied by beautiful harplike sounds.

The air element in the dorsal centre enables the oxygen and life energy, or *prana,* in the body to combine with the physical cells and is also responsible for the sense of touch; its work gives forth a bell-like or gong sound.

The ether element in the cervical plexus maintains the etheric background in the body, timing it to all spatial vibrations. The subtle etheric vibration is the screen on which the image of the body and all nature is projected. The cervical centre produces the sense of hearing, and reverberates with the cosmic vibration of ocean rumblings.

The united medulla and Christ centre is the dynamo of consciousness, of life force, and of the vibratory-element matrixes. This high centre continuously recharges with life and consciousness all the subdynamos of the elemental vibrations of earth, water, fire, air, and ether that maintain the body's flesh, blood and all watery substances, heat, oxygen and life force, and etheric activities.*

In other words, the body is not at all what it appears to be! It is a complicated result of the combination of six currents that emanate from six astral centres. And these currents are, in turn, emanations of the spherical cosmic energy of the creative *Aum* vibration, which produces in its core the macrocosmic dream pictures of the universe.

The spiritual aspirant, eager to solve the mystery of the body, only

---

* An elaboration of these subtle elemental activities in the spinal centres is given in XIII:1.

understands it when his attention is withdrawn from the body to the six inner booths, which, throwing out six currents, are responsible for producing the picture of the body. By knowledge of those six currents, and by years of meditation, the yogi learns to know the body, not as a solid mass, but as a manifestation of vibratory light. The yogi then rightly understands that the basis of the physical cells is atomic energy, which comes from lifetrons or astral energy, which comes from thoughtrons or causal (mental) energy; and that all these are different rates of vibration of cosmic consciousness, or different dreams of God's mind. When that perception becomes a part of the yogi's own Self-realization, he will be able to control consciously all functions of the bodily instruments and even to materialize or dematerialize his body at will.*

TO SUMMARIZE THE IMPORTANT significance of the sounding of conch shells by the Pandavas in these Gita verses:

The worldly man whose attention is matter-bound hears only the noises of the external world. But in the psychological and metaphysical battle between the sense mind and the soul-bound discrimination, both the warring senses and the soul forces give rise to various vibrations in an effort to win the consciousness of the meditating devotee.

❖
Summary: vibrations of the senses and soul forces
❖

During meditation, the devotee's attention first leaves the realm of physical sounds in the material world. Then the attention is caught by the various sounds resulting from the inner activities of the physical body—such as the circulation of the blood, the pumping of the heart, the restlessness of the breath. These vibrations become very audible and disturbing when man's attention is fully con-

---

* Australian physicist Paul Davies, Ph.D., winner of the 1995 Templeton Prize for Progress in Religion, wrote in *Superforce* (New York: Simon and Schuster, 1984): "To the naive realist the universe is a collection of objects. To the quantum physicist it is an inseparable web of vibrating energy patterns in which no one component has reality independent of the entirety; and included in that entirety is the observer."

Professor Brian D. Josephson of Cambridge University, winner of the Nobel Prize in physics in 1973, commended the ancient Hindu systems of philosophy: "Vedanta and Sankhya hold the key to the laws of mind and thought process, which are correlated to the quantum field, i.e., the operation and distribution of particles at atomic and molecular levels."

Many examples of the powers of advanced yogis—those who have mastered the science of Yoga, the practical application of the Vedanta and Sankhya wisdom—have been recounted in *Autobiography of a Yogi,* including a chapter on "The Law of Miracles." *(Publisher's Note)*

centrated within. By deeper meditation, the devotee goes beyond the inner physical sounds; and when he passes through the astral kingdom, he begins to hear the various vibratory sounds of the astral vital forces (sounds like the blowing of conch shells: or round, full, rolling vibrations of musical quality): the bumblebee, flute, harp, gong bell, sea roar, and astral symphony. Following those sounds, he learns to locate the centres of life and consciousness. Locating the centres, he in time actually sees them. This achievement ordinarily requires years of meditation under the guidance and blessing of an advanced guru. Finally, viewing the centres, and ascending his consciousness through them in the various stages of *samadhi,* the yogi has solved the mystery of the body; he knows it as a manipulatable form of light vibrations.

VERSE 19

स घोषो धार्तराष्ट्राणां हृदयानि व्यदारयत्।
नभश्च पृथिवीं चैव तुमुलो व्यनुनादयन्॥

That tremendous sound reverberating throughout heaven and earth pierced the heart of the Dhritarashtra clan.

"THE VIBRATORY SOUNDS (the conch shells of the Pandavas' army) emanating from the activity of the astral centres, as heard by the devotee in meditation—resounding in the astral body (heaven) and the physical body (earth)—discouraged the body-bound mental and material desires and senses (Dhritarashtra's clan)."

The soldiers of King Material Desire become much worried at seeing the devotee fast escaping from the snares of the sense plane.

Just as materially minded children delight in the primitive rhythms of jazz and take no interest in the great symphonies, so the senses love the noisy world of gross pleasures and are insensible to the soothing music of the astral world. When a devotee develops sufficiently to be able to hear the astral harmonies, he feels distaste for materialistic sense pleasures and carefully avoids the noisy surroundings of sense-ensnared people.

Stanza 12 stated that the ego creates many material vibrations to cheer the mind and its restless clan. In stanza 19 we find an opposite development; the astral sounds exert a stupefying effect on the undisciplined mental tendencies.

The Devotee Observes the Enemies to Be Destroyed

Verses 20–23

अथ व्यवस्थितान्दृष्ट्वा धार्तराष्ट्रान् कपिध्वजः ।
प्रवृत्ते शस्त्रसम्पाते धनुरुद्यम्य पाण्डवः ॥ *(20)*

हृषीकेशं तदा वाक्यमिदमाह महीपते ।
सेनयोरुभयोर्मध्ये रथं स्थापय मेऽच्युत ॥ *(21)*

यावदेतान्निरीक्षेऽहं योद्धुकामानवस्थितान् ।
कैर्मया सह योद्धव्यमस्मिन्रणसमुद्यमे ॥ *(22)*

योत्स्यमानानवेक्षेऽहं य एतेऽत्र समागताः ।
धार्तराष्ट्रस्य दुर्बुद्धेर्युद्धे प्रियचिकीर्षवः ॥ *(23)*

(20) Beholding the dynasty of Dhritarashtra ready to begin battle, Pandava (Arjuna), he whose flag bears the monkey emblem, lifted his bow and addressed Hrishikesha (Krishna).

(21–22) Arjuna said: O Changeless Krishna, please place my chariot between the two armies, that I may regard those who stand ready in battle array. On the eve of this war, let me comprehend with whom I must fight.

(23) Here in this field (of Kurukshetra) I wish to observe all those who have gathered with desire to fight on the side of Dhritarashtra's wicked son (Duryodhana).

During meditation, Pandava (the soulful powers of discrimination) beholds the mind's resentment at the devotee's enjoyment of the music of the astral plane. The devotee then triumphantly hoists his flag of self-control with the monkey emblem, signifying man's control over restlessness. He straightens his spine: by holding his neck straight, pulling his shoulders back and pushing his chest forward, and drawing his abdomen in. This position of the spine, curved in the front and not in the back, is called "the bow of meditation," well strung and ready for the battle with the senses!

In all physical activities, man sends thought and energy down from the brain to the bodily surfaces, thus keeping the ego engaged in material things.

In every process of meditation, man sends thought and life energy away from the sense centres toward the brain.

For the spiritual adept, the "monkey emblem" signifies the control of restless thoughts by certain guru-given spiritual exercises of reversing the life force from the external senses to the medulla, aided by the practice of *Khechari Mudra:* touching the tip of the "little tongue," or uvula (the negative pole), with the tip of the regular tongue (the positive pole). When this exercise is practised under the guru's guidance by an advanced yogi—such as one who has first made significant spiritual progress in *Kriya Yoga*—it turns the sense-bound life current Godward.

Right posture: essential to successful meditation

AN ESSENTIAL ADJUNCT to successful meditation is right posture. A bent spine throws the spinal vertebrae out of their proper order, thus squeezing the nerves of the principal plexuses of the nervous system. These maladjustments prevent clear sensory perceptions of material objects, and also retard the flow of life force into the brain to reveal the Spirit. Just as a rubber tube, squeezed in the middle, stops the flow of water forward or backward, so the pinched spinal nerves, due to misplaced vertebrae, do not conduct to the senses the amount of outgoing energy necessary to obtain clear sense perceptions; and during meditation, the squeezed spinal nerve plexuses obstruct the retirement of energy from the senses to the brain.

Thus the devotee who meditates with a bent spine gets little spiritual result. His bent spine is a broken bow, unable to protect him against the forces of restlessness. When he tries to concentrate and fix his attention at the point between the eyebrows, he finds his consciousness tied with the outgoing nerve current flowing toward the senses. Owing to the pinched nerves, the flow of life force cannot reverse itself through the spinal centres.

Devotees who unscientifically try to "enter the silence" are unable to do so as long as the currents of life energy flow downward to the senses. The scientifically trained yogi knows how to withdraw the life energy as well as the mind from the senses. When the life energy retires into the spine, the five sense telephones of smell, taste, sight, sound, and touch are automatically switched off, preventing mental disturbance by sensations.

After making the spine straight, and hoisting the flag of self-control, the devotee directs the nerve-force flow inwardly through the spine into the abode of Spirit in the cerebrum. This is the state in which Pandava (the discriminating soul faculty) addresses Krishna, the Spirit (here referred to as Hrishikesha, "Lord of the Senses")—a state in which the devotee's discrimination stands ready to discharge its missiles of unshaken concentration at any outbreak of rebellion from restless thoughts.

In this perfectly recollected state, the devotee prays: "O Spirit, station the chariot of my intuition in the spinal centres, that I may behold therein the forces ready to oppose each other and thereby understand the enemy I must fight."

The *Mahabharata* tells us that in the battle between the good Pandus and the wicked Kurus, Krishna became the charioteer of the noble Pandu brother, Arjuna. The interpretation of this allegory is that when man's fiery self-control (Arjuna) is ready to battle all the forces of the senses, then the Spirit (Krishna) becomes the devotee's charioteer, or guiding power. The Spirit expresses Itself through the instrumentality of the intuition of the soul, Spirit's individualized reflection in man.

In the first stage of meditation, the devotee's mind is inextricably bound up with sense consciousness. His mind is concentrated upon material sounds and restless thoughts. He is aghast to behold all the forces of restlessness and mental opposition arrayed against him. Millions of superficial devotees never pass beyond this state of a deadlocked psychological struggle between the senses and the soul forces of calmness and intuition.

Two phases of the inner battle of meditation

The devotee who is victorious in the initial psychological battle enters the second state of meditation, the metaphysical battle wherein his consciousness and life energy become centralized in the spinal centres. He sees himself as a warrior on the battlefield of the spine—the common field of spiritual forces and of the opposing mental or sense tendencies in their subtle form. When this battle is about to begin, the devotee feels a simultaneous pull toward the outgoing sense tendencies in the spinal centres and toward the inwardly turned spiritual forces of the soul. It is then that the devotee contacts the calm Spirit within and prayerfully asks that Divine Power to place the chariot of intuition between the subtle divine perceptions and the gross sense perceptions. The devotee expects, with the aid of the Spirit, to rally his forces of meditation to fight the forces of restlessness.

If the senses win, the devotee falls prisoner to the flesh, and that particular meditative battle is lost. If the spiritual intuitive forces win, the devotee is taken deeper into the kingdom of pure Spirit. This is the third state of meditation—deep, blissful *samadhi,* in which there is little danger that the consciousness could be caught by any sensory invasion.

In stanzas 21–22, it is the second state of meditation that is being described; that is, before the devotee has secured his consciousness in blissful *samadhi.* These verses hold a further, deeper meaning, which I shall explain briefly.

The placement of the chariot of intuitive perception between the opposing forces refers in general to the spinal centres, but also specifically to the coccyx, dorsal, and medullary-Christ centres. These are three important places, intuitional caravanserai, vantage points in which the devotee's consciousness becomes ensconced while moving Godward through the centres to the brain. There is a special polarity between these centres that helps the attuned consciousness to be lifted upward. First there is the magnetism between the negative pole of the coccyx centre (*muladhara*) and the higher or positive dorsal centre (*anahata*). Then by deep meditation, when the consciousness is raised to the dorsal centre, that centre becomes a negative pole and the medullary-Christ (*Kutastha*) centre becomes the positive pole, pulling the consciousness upward to the centres of highest realization in the brain. From the intuitive perceptions received during his sojourn in these three centres, the devotee gains full understanding of the principles of his lower (material) nature, by experiencing them at their source in their subtle form.

Polarity between coccyx, dorsal, and medullary-Christ centres

It has already been noted that the thousand-petalled lotus (*sahasrara*) in the cerebrum is the matrix of all forces in the body, operative through the subdynamos of the spinal centres. The ancient seers correlated the vibrations of the cerebral forces and their respective centres in the spine. From the seed sounds emitted by the action of these vibrations, the *rishis* evolved the phonetically perfect Sanskrit alphabet.* In a footnote in *Autobiography of a Yogi,* I wrote regarding Sanskrit: "*Sanskrita,* 'polished, complete.' Sanskrit is the older sister of all Indo-European tongues. Its alphabetical script is called *Devanagari;* literally, 'divine abode.' 'Who knows my grammar knows God!' Panini, great philologist of ancient India, paid that tribute to the mathemati-

* In his *Sanskrit Grammar,* the renowned scholar Sir M. Monier-Williams wrote: "The Devanagari character, in which the Sanskrit language is written, is adapted to the expression of almost every known gradation of sound; and every letter has a fixed and invariable pronunciation." *(Publisher's Note)*

cal and psychological perfection of Sanskrit. He who would track language to its lair must indeed end as omniscient."

In a highly simplified description, it may be said that the fifty letters or sounds of the Sanskrit alphabet are on the petals of the *sahasrara,** and that each alphabetical vibration in turn is connected with a specific petal on the lotuses in the spinal centres (which have a total of fifty corresponding petals: coccygeal, 4; sacral, 6; lumbar, 10; dorsal, 12; cervical, 16; and medullary-Christ centre, 2). "Petals" mean rays or vibrations. These vibrations, singularly and in combinations, and in conjunction with the five elements (*tattvas*) and other principles of nature, are responsible for various psychological and physiological activities in the physical and astral bodies of man. I include with this commentary (on page 1121) a chart authored by my *paramguru,* Yogavatar Lahiri Mahasaya, diagramming this concept as he perceived it. The illustration is a basic outline, for the total number of *nadis* in the body are variously numbered by the scriptures to be as many as 72,000. During my visit to India in 1935, a copy of Lahiri Mahasaya's chart was given to me by Ananda Mohan Lahiri, grandson of my *paramguru,* for inclusion in the Gita commentary he knew I had undertaken to write.†

From the realization of the potencies of these vibratory *bija* or "seed" sounds, the *rishis* devised *mantras* that, when properly intoned, activate these creative forces to produce the desired result. *Mantras,* therefore, are one means of tuning in with subtle or divine forces. Too often, however, the inquiring seeker focuses on the forces of nature, and the resulting effects are thus in the realm of phenomena and powers, an entrapment to be avoided by the sincere devotee who seeks union with God. Those sacred *mantras* that are a part of the *Kriya Yoga* science, including meditation on *Aum* as mentioned in I:15–18‡ (and

---

* Actually, the sounds are synonymous with the petals, i.e., vibratory powers. The fifty letters or sounds, in multiples of twenty, equal the one thousand petals of the *sahasrara.*

† Ananda Mohan Lahiri, who had himself attained a very high degree of divine realization, was a close friend and a great benefactor of my school and work in India from its inception. He was especially helpful during my visit to India in 1935 when I was striving to place the school and Yogoda work on a firm foundation. What was to be his final expression of loving support came in his last letter to me, written shortly before his passing in 1951, encouraging me in my endeavours to complete this new commentary on the Gita: "Write your Gita in your own way, straight from Krishna and Arjuna, and imitate no ancient abstruse interpreter," and signed it, "Yours in eternity."

‡ *Aum* is the supreme *mantra,* the primordial manifestation of Spirit (Para-Brahman) as cosmic creative vibration, known as Shabda-Brahman, or Spirit in its manifested aspect as sound. It is therefore the source and container of all other vibratory sounds.

other techniques and instructions of the *Kriya* path), take the devotee's consciousness straightway to God.

I have mentioned in this commentary the various vibratory seed sounds and their derivations because they are a part of the details of the yoga science. They need not be concentrated on, however; their effects will be automatically realized by the advanced devotee, as follows:

When the devotee's mind is concentrated at the coccygeal centre, he hears the vibratory sound between the coccyx and the sacral centres; he then understands the domain of desires. This centre is the first stopping place.

When the devotee understands the vibration of the seed sounds in the dorsal centre, he is enabled to feel his coccygeal, sacral, lumbar, and dorsal centres simultaneously, and comprehends the mysteries of their subtle powers. This stage constitutes the second stopping place.

When the advancing devotee understands the vibration of the seed sound between the cervical and the medulla-Christ centres, he understands the six centres (the elements of earth, water, fire, air, ether, and superether) in their subtle, separated state; and understands, further, the combinations of the elements that take place in order to produce man's illusion of the solid, physical body.

VERSES 24–25

सञ्जय उवाच
एवमुक्तो हृषीकेशो गुडाकेशेन भारत।
सेनयोरुभयोर्मध्ये स्थापयित्वा रथोत्तमम्॥ *(24)*

भीष्मद्रोणप्रमुखतः सर्वेषां च महीक्षिताम्।
उवाच पार्थ पश्यैतान् समवेतान्कुरूनिति॥ *(25)*

Sanjaya said (to Dhritarashtra):

O descendant of Bharata, requested thus by Gudakesha (Arjuna), Hrishikesha (Krishna) drove that best of chariots to a point between the two armies, in front of Bhishma, Drona, and all the rulers of the earth, and then said: "See, Partha (Arjuna), this gathering of all the Kurus!"

INTROSPECTION (SANJAYA) REVEALED to the blind mind (Dhritarashtra, here referred to as the descendant of King Bharata: common ancestor of the Kurus and Pandus; symbolically, Cosmic Consciousness*):

"Ordered thus by the devotee (Gudakesha, 'ever-ready, sleepless, delusion-defeating'), the Soul (Hrishikesha, 'King of the Senses') drove the best of chariots (spiritual perception) between the Pandava army of Discrimination and the Kaurava army of Material Desire, confronting the mental generals, Ego and Latent Tendency, and all the other rulers of body consciousness (earth)—the powerful ruling material tendencies—and intuitively commanded the devotee to face (acknowledge) his inner enemies."

Now is the moment of decision. When the good and evil in the spiritual aspirant are poised to fight, each side facing a "do-or-die" struggle for victory, the uncertain devotee begins to rationalize what such a battle really means. So his charioteer-soul—at one with Spirit—places him face-to-face with the enemies he must destroy.

THE SPIRITUAL ASPIRANT—who is worthy to be called Gudakesha when he conquers sleep, or sloth, in order to meditate long and deeply—can command his soul-identified consciousness to centralize, or focus clearly and impartially, his spiritual perception. This perception is the grand chariot with which a devotee moves from the wilderness of the misery-inflaming senses through the oasis of the spinal centres to the plane of omnipresent consciousness in the divine cerebral centres. When the devotee is spiritually advanced, he can centralize his car of spiritual perception on any plane. The "ever-awake" devotee in his blissful soul-centred state beholds his chariot of spiritual perception properly situated for right observation between the crooked sense tendencies of the mind and the discriminative tendencies of the soul.

The chariot of spiritual perception

The state of man on the material plane is marked by the complete identification of consciousness with worldly struggles and goals. This is the perception of the ordinary businessman, for instance, who never tries to understand the Intelligence behind his brain—the Power without which no business can be carried on.

By sporadic attempts at deep meditation, the awakening devotee reaches the second plane of perception in which once in a while he gets away from the senses and feels the deep peace and joy of his soul.

On the third plane of perception, the self-controlled yogi has ar-

* Bharata, from *bhā,* "light," and *rata,* "attached or devoted to"; reference to one who is illumined, i.e., who has attained cosmic consciousness, realization of the Absolute.

rived at the middle point wherein he finds glimpses of Bliss and divine realization as his consciousness becomes centralized in the spinal centres. Here he sees the soul qualities and sense tendencies evenly matched. This point is reached as a result of steady meditation and proper schooling in the right habits of yoga.

On the fourth plane of perception, when the consciousness becomes completely one with the only good, or God, the devotee goes beyond the opposites of good and evil. Man, awake in God, is not subject to the dualities of Nature—joyous and sorrowful experiences, health and disease, life and death. These phantoms of "good" and "evil" vanish, like the dreams they are.

All relativities are expressions of one Absolute

The yogi is ever mindful that all consciousness of good and evil and of material and intuitive tendencies in man are relatives of the same Absolute Consciousness (referred to symbolically in this stanza as Bharata, common ancestor of both the Kurus and the Pandus). Absence of light is darkness; absence of darkness is light. Similarly, lack of self-control is weakness; lack of weakness is self-control. In this sense we can understand how duality, or good and evil, are the contrasted (positive and negative) expressions of the Sole Unity—God.

Each man's individual characteristics of behaviour are in large measure the sum total of all his habits. These habits, both good and bad, are formed by man's own consciousness—through repetition of a thought, and by thought-produced actions. If the consciousness can think and dream itself into bad habits, it has only to think and dream differently in order to form good habits. Good and bad ideas are different forms or different dreams of consciousness. It is better to dream beautiful phases of consciousness than to have nightmares. Consciousness is imaginative, sensitive, and pliable; it can think and dream itself into any state.

The devotee's consciousness, when degraded, is spoken of as the "mind racing blindly with uncontrolled sense steeds." When man's consciousness is moving toward the soul, it has reached the disciplined "state of discrimination."

Consciousness, when identified with the soul, is called "Krishna, the King of the Senses," or "the Saviour, the *Kutastha* or Christ Consciousness in man," the pure reflection of Spirit, the charioteer that leads the discriminating tendencies victoriously toward the kingdom of the Infinite.

Man's consciousness, when identified with egoism, is called the

"Bhishma" state. When the consciousness is one with the past tendencies, that stage is called the "Drona-Samskara" or latent tendency state. When the mind impartially weighs all the faculties of the soul against sense pleasures, it is called "Sanjaya" or the introspective state. When the consciousness of the devotee is ever ready to meditate, scorning sleep, it has reached the "Arjuna-Gudakesha" state of fiery spiritual determination and self-control. The "Arjuna-Partha" state is that consciousness in which the devotee feels sympathetic toward the mental sense tendencies (his Kuru relatives) and needs to be reminded that he is the son of Pritha* (another name for Kunti) who represents the power of dispassion, or renunciation; and that he should therefore act accordingly and not give in to instincts born of nature.

The duality of consciousness, the progenitor of all states of both good and evil, with their common ancestor of the Absolute, or Cosmic Consciousness, will now be the cause of a painful quandary in the devotee. The Bhagavad Gita—a comprehensive metaphysical and psychological treatise—describes all experiences that will come to the spiritual traveller on the path of emancipation. Thus far, concentration has been primarily on the positive states the devotee is striving toward. In the verses that follow—to the end of Chapter I and the first part of Chapter II—warning is given as to the negative states that try to intimidate the devotee and turn him from his goal. "Forewarned is forearmed!" The devotee who understands the route he must travel will never feel unsure or dismayed at inevitable opposition.

The true devotee gives not only trust to God; he worships Him through understanding and wisdom. Blind piety is not unacceptable to the Supreme Being, but it is a low form of spiritual-mindedness. Man, blessed with the divine gift of intelligence, of reason and free choice, should worship his Creator in truth and in understanding. It pleases the Lord to see His human children, made in His own image, employ in their quest of Him the highest gift He has given to them: their divine birthright of intelligence. The devotee who uses this intelligence to study sincerely the message of the Gita will find it a faithful travel companion that will not only guide and encourage, but also caution and protect.

---

* Partha means "son of Pritha." See also explanation of symbolic meaning of Pritha in commentary on II:3.

VERSE 26

तत्रापश्यत्स्थितान् पार्थः पितॄनथ पितामहान्।
आचार्यान्मातुलान्भ्रातॄन्पुत्रान्पौत्रान्सखींस्तथा॥ *(26)*
श्वशुरान् सुहृदश्चैव सेनयोरुभयोरपि।* *(27)*

Partha (Arjuna) beheld positioned there—as members of both armies—grandfathers, fathers, fathers-in-law, uncles, brothers and cousins, sons, and grandsons, and also comrades, friends, and teachers.

THROUGH INTUITIVE SELF-CONTROL born of meditation, the devotee beholds his good and bad psychological† relatives in the warring armies of divine discrimination and of the wicked senses. There are the psychological grandfathers, the good or evil deep-seated ego-consciousness; mental fathers and fathers-in-law, such as the paternal tendency of keen dispassion with its negative inner feminine-tendency (or daughter) of coiled life force; psychological uncles, such as pride and other delusion-intoxicating tendencies; brothers and cousins of discriminative powers and of sense tendencies; psychological children-tendencies, evolved from self-control and from other discriminative powers, and also from the sensory mind; grandsons, or interrelated offshoots of good and evil desires; friendly good and bad habits; and action-inspiring past tendencies, teachers of the soul qualities and the sensory inclinations.

When the devotee passes through the initial state of meditation and arrives at the middle state, as described in the previous stanza, he obtains this keen vision of his dear psychological relatives of good and bad tendencies gathered together on the battlefield of consciousness, ready to destroy one another.‡

---

* This last line is the first half of verse 27, but is included with verse 26 to provide a complete thought in English translation. For the same reason, Paramahansa Yogananda's rendering of verses 27–31 consists of the second line from one verse followed by the first line of the next. *(Publisher's Note)*

† "Psychological" means the inner nature of the Kuru and Pandu forces as materialistic and spiritual expressions of the devotee's consciousness, which he perceives during introspective meditation, in contradistinction to the outer or physical responses and actions they engender.

‡ "It is illusory to think that a person has one mind, good or bad. There is no single mind but many; we are a coalition, not a single person." This conclusion was reached after many years of research into brain functions and evolutionary biology by Robert Ornstein, Ph.D., a psychologist who teaches at University of California Medical Centre

SYMBOLIC MEANING OF RELATIVES AND FRIENDS IN THE WARRING CLANS

TO NAME A FEW, the devotee can find the good and bad grandfathers, or good and bad egos. The good ego draws the devotee toward meditation and good action; the bad ego attracts one to evil. A person is born with either a spiritual or a material ego predominating, according to his actions in past lives. This chief ego or "individuality" of any particular life is called the "grandfather tendency" because it rules all other tendencies. Psychological "grandfathers" can be dual or triple in a complex personality. Many persons are Jekylls-and-Hydes—those whose good and bad egos in one life are equally powerful.

The father-in-law psychological tendency (Drupada) is keen dispassion, which "fathers" or rouses the coiled life force (Draupadi) at the base of the spine. When the devotee causes the coiled force at the coccyx centre to reverse its flow from the senses to the brain through the inner insulation of the spinal cord, it awakens the spinal centres; and when this Spiritward life force unites with the five Pandus (*tattvas*) in

---

in San Francisco and at Stanford University. In *Multimind: A New Way of Looking at Human Behavior* (New York: Bantam Doubleday Dell, 1986), Dr. Ornstein continues:

"Instead of a single, intellectual entity that can judge many different kinds of events equably, the mind is diverse and complex. It contains a changeable conglomeration of different kinds of 'small minds'—fixed reactions, talents, flexible thinking—and these different entities are temporarily employed—'wheeled into consciousness'—and then usually discarded, returned to their place, after use....

"Some of the small minds that get wheeled in are the result of many diverse centres of control in the brain. These centres have developed over millions of years to regulate the body, to guard against danger, and generally to organize and plan effort. The separate mental components have different priorities and are often at cross purposes, with each other and with our life today, but they do exist and, more soberly, 'they' are us. It would be a good idea, I think, if we could come to see the primitive bases of many of our judgements and decisions so that we might try to do something about them.

"Our problem as individuals is that most often we act unconsciously and automatically, thus we do not often know which one of the multiple 'small minds' is operating at any time. And often we do not select the appropriate 'small minds' at the right time."

"People can consciously redirect their minds, but, like learning to read or to do math, this ability doesn't come naturally," Dr. Ornstein wrote in *The Evolution of Consciousness* (New York: Simon and Schuster, 1991). "It has to be nurtured. We have to know who is in there to order around....

"For millennia individuals have been attracted to the idea of 'higher selves' or 'mystical experiences.' We now need to be aware that these experiences are important for our future and recognize that they are within the range of all. We can remake our minds by shifting the 'mind in place.' The traditional term for controlling ourselves...is *will,* an unfashionable term nowadays. If there is a will, it will reside in the selection of the differing minds that we call into play....Conscious control is a small and weak force in most minds, a force that we can develop by self-observation." *(Publisher's Note)*

these centres, it gives birth to offspring of divine qualities that arouse a longing for God and a bitter distaste for material things. These qualities are called "Draupadeya" (sons of Draupadi). When the devotee in meditation controls the coiled life force and reverses its flow, his consciousness in the spinal centres becomes the "husband" of Draupadi and he meets his "father-in-law" Drupada, or keen dispassion.

The psychological uncles are the intoxicating delusion-creating tendencies of attachment to the senses, to material objects, and so forth; and false pride, with its narrow-mindedness that tries to dissuade the devotee from giving up social position, and from bearing criticism from others for "foolishly" following the path to God. Such "uncles" are almost fatherly in their power because they wield vast control over the human consciousness.

Among the psychological brothers and cousins are the five divine Pandu brothers born of discrimination, and their one hundred cousins born of the blind sense-mind. The cousin sense-tendencies at first seem friendly, like well-meaning but wrongly informed brothers who try to convince the devotee of the justness of their cause.

The psychological sons consist of the devotee's spiritual qualities, born of self-control and the other offspring of Draupadi (as mentioned above); and also the offspring of the evil sense tendencies. The psychological grandsons are the good and bad desires that evolve out of the practice, feeling, and perception of good and evil.

"Friends and comrades" —good and bad habits

The psychological friends and comrades are good and bad habits; good habits are helpful and friendly to one in his performance of good actions, just as evil habits are friendly and helpful when one is performing evil actions. The psychological teachers are the strong tendencies of good and evil from past good and bad habits that serve as the stimulating motive power of present good and evil actions and habits.

Until one is wholly under the influence of the independent wisdom of the soul, almost all that he is and does is a result of habit, or conditioning. If one is bound by a bad ego, subject to desires and likes and dislikes, conditioned to respond in a materialistic way to his senses; if his thoughts and actions are under the compulsion of delusion, his will bound by karma—then, because of the way these influences control and condition his mental makeup and manner of behaviour, all of them may be said to be "bad habits," the army of the Kurus.

Conversely, "good habits" are the spiritual opposites, the army of the Pandus, the friends and supporters of the cause of the soul that are necessary to oust the evil or materialistic nature. The aspiring devotee reconditions his consciousness with the cultivation of spiritual qualities until these predominate as his natural habits, the aggregate of his nature. The good habits, having then fulfilled their purpose, willingly surrender their rights to the wisdom reign of the soul.

Meditation is the inner war-drum that rouses these good and bad habits from a long slumber of indifference and makes each side willing to increase its forces in order to obtain full victory over man's consciousness. When one is passively under the influence of bad habits—his materialistic nature—he does not find any noticeable resistance from his innate good habits—his soul qualities or spiritual nature. It is only when the devotee actively tries to cultivate good habits—concentration, calmness, peace—and marches them as soldiers toward the kingdom of the soul, that fierce resistance is stirred up from bad habits—fickleness, restlessness, disquietude.

The enthusiastic spiritual beginner, in the heat of his zeal, does not realize the power of resistance possessed by bad habits. Nor do the bad habits notice, at first, the silent invasion of good habits. It is only when the devotee "means business" and makes repeated struggles to establish the generals of good habits in the kingdom of consciousness that the generals of bad habits become alarmed and make furious attempts to oust the "intruders."

Thus it was with Arjuna (self-control of the devotee). After he had been placed by Krishna (soul perception) between the two armies of good discrimination and bad sense-tendencies, Arjuna looks at the array with awe, for the members of both armies are his own dear relatives, his self-created good and bad habits. In spite of a growing power of discrimination behind the army of good habits, self-control will find it hard, and often distressing, to destroy the dear old familial bad habits.

Arjuna's Refusal to Fight

Verse 27

तान्समीक्ष्य स कौन्तेयः सर्वान्बन्धूनवस्थितान्॥ *(27)*
कृपया परयाविष्टो विषीदन्निदमब्रवीत्। *(28)*

Beholding all those relatives arrayed before him, the son of Kunti (Arjuna) became filled with deep sympathy and spoke dolefully:

WHEN THE DEVOTEE ARJUNA, son of Kunti, beheld his favoured bad habits about to be slain by the accumulated wisdom of meditation, his positive masculine nature of fiery self-control became influenced by the inner negative feminine nature of feeling. With foolish emotional sympathy, the devotee dolefully introspects.

In every being there exists a masculine and a feminine nature. The masculine or positive side reveals itself as the powers of discrimination, self-control, exacting judgement—qualities that express or respond to reason. The negative or feminine nature consists of feeling—love, sympathy, kindness, mercy, joy. In the ideal being, these two aspects are perfectly balanced. But if reason lacks feeling, it becomes calculating, harsh, judgemental; and if feeling lacks reason it becomes blind emotion.*

---

* Neurophysiologists have delineated these and other differences between men and women based on the distinctive functions of the left and right hemispheres of the brain. Researchers have noted that, generally speaking, the left side of the brain—which specializes in analytical, logical, and verbal tasks—is more active in men; while the right side—which activates the artistic and creative functions, working more with metaphor, emotions, and feelings—is more active in women.

"Steadily, from about two or three million years ago, man's organ of thought became increasingly bifurcated," writes David Darling, Ph.D., in *Equations of Eternity* (Hyperion Press: New York, 1993). "This is particularly true of the human male, because the polarization of the right and left hemispheres seems to be more pronounced in men than in women....

"Many religious world models display an intuitive knowledge of left- and right-brain functioning. In Taoism, for instance, there is a male principle, known as *yang*.... At the other extreme is *yin*, the female force...."

In *The Tao of Physics*, Fritjof Capra describes the ancient Chinese view of *yang* as "the strong, male, creative power" and *yin* as "the receptive, female, and maternal element....In the realm of thought, *yin* is the complex, female, intuitive mind, *yang* the clear and rational male intellect. *Yin* is the quiet contemplative stillness of the sage, *yang* the strong, creative action of the king."

Especially pertinent to this Gita stanza is the work of University of Alberta psychiatrist Pierre Flor-Henry, who has done extensive research on the different characteristics of the brain's two hemispheres. Flor-Henry believes that one of the qualities locatable in the left hemisphere is "fighting power." Feelings such as wariness, depression, and anxiety, he says, are more characteristic of the right side of the brain.

"Half our mistakes in life arise from feeling where we ought to think and thinking where we ought to feel," observed the British writer J. C. Collins. Both left and right hemispheres—and both the masculine and feminine natures—have characteristic strengths as well as characteristic weaknesses; the evidence from brain-hemisphere research does not exalt one over the other. "In Western culture the left side of the brain is the more active and the male principle dominates, which may explain why the West is so technically advanced and yet in some ways is so spiritually impoverished," Dr. Darling writes. "Our brains have evolved so as to see the world in two different, complementary but also mutually exclusive ways. Each of us, figuratively speaking, has the East and the West, the male and the female principle, in his or her head. But usually one or the other has ascendency. Either we are too concerned with rationality and so, from the [Eastern] point

Arjuna, the devotee, is here referred to as the son of Kunti, signifying his mental state as one who is subject to nature; that is, he is behaving not as the soul, but as an ordinary man born of woman. Furthermore, because his masculine good judgement and self-control have given way to feminine emotionalism of unwise sympathy toward the enemy forces, this epithet also means he needs to be reminded that he should behave more like a true son of the noble Kunti (who represents the ardent devotee's power to invoke the aid of spiritual energy in his *sadhana*).

The devotee's reluctance to slay his worldly tendencies

The devotee, following the path of meditation in hope of complete emancipation, realizes that he has to destroy his material tendencies because they militate against the pursuance of the superior soul pleasures. But because of his long familial relationship with these tendencies, he becomes dejected at the prospect and is spoken of as feeling sympathetic toward these dear psychological relatives. What mortal does not feel this tender compassion for self? After all, "That's me; that's the way I am." But the Gita is addressing the true Self, the soul, cautioning the aspiring devotee against sympathy for that part of the nature that opposes the soul. It is good to feel good about the good in one's self; but it is bad to feel bad for the bad that should be destroyed.

The reason few people seek God in earnest as do the saints is that millions believe they cannot do without evil, misery-producing pleasures. They are addicted, as is the alcoholic toward health-killing drink. But these very persons, if they were to form good habits, would say: "We cannot do without the pleasure and peace of meditation. We become miserable now if we have to mingle in our old environments."

Those who cling to their materialistic nature fail to understand why the pleasure-producing senses are inimical to the joy of the Spirit. "Why," they ask, "were the senses given to man if he is not to enjoy them?" (This query is supposed to completely "floor" the ascetic!)

The metaphysical reason for self-control is nothing but a spiritual business proposition calculated to bring the greatest happiness to man. Just as one must invest a certain sum of money in order to reap a greater gain, so the devotee forgoes indulgence in materialistic pleasures for the sake of gaining the pure joy of Spirit found in meditation.

---

of view, fall out of harmony with nature, or we are too introspective and fail to achieve materialistic growth. Both mental modes are apparently essential to human consciousness and so ought to be brought more into balance." *(Publisher's Note)*

Man is the image of God; within himself, as the tree is hidden in the seed, is the latent unmanifested bliss of the Spirit. As roasted seeds do not germinate, so when the seed of consciousness is scorched by flames of material desires, the innate tree of Divine Happiness never has a chance to sprout.

Therefore, self-control is not self-torture, but leads instead to soul happiness. By withdrawing the mind from indulgence in lower kinds of paltry pleasures of the senses, man enters a vast kingdom of unending joy. It is the arrant chicanery of the malevolent ego that tells man otherwise.

VERSES 28–30

दृष्ट्वेमं स्वजनं कृष्ण युयुत्सुं समुपस्थितम्॥ *(28)*

सीदन्ति मम गात्राणि मुखं च परिशुष्यति।
वेपथुश्च शरीरे मे रोमहर्षश्च जायते॥ *(29)*

गाण्डीवं स्रंसते हस्तात्त्वक्चैव परिदह्यते।
न च शक्नोम्यवस्थातुं भ्रमतीव च मे मनः॥ *(30)*

निमित्तानि च पश्यामि विपरीतानि केशव। *(31)*

O Krishna, seeing these, my relatives, met together desirous of battle, my limbs are failing and my mouth is parched. My body trembles; my hair stands on end. The sacred bow Gandiva slips away from my grip, and my skin is afire. Neither can I remain standing upright. My mind is rambling; and, O Keshava (Krishna),* I behold evil omens.

THE DEVOTEE SAYS to his inner soul-guide:

"Because of love for my indwelling, clashing, good and bad habits, I am reluctant to kill my kinsmen of the senses who have dwelt so long in my bodily kingdom! My limbs of will-power-to-exercise-self-control are failing me, and my mouth of spiritual intuition is dry. I am quivering with mental nervousness. My energies and thoughts shoot toward the senses. The sacred bow of self-control and of spinal perceptions is slipping away, and my mental skin (covering my consciousness) is

---

* Keshava is an epithet for Krishna as a destroyer of evil; i.e., referring to the slayer of the demon Keshi.

burning with restlessness. O Soul, destroyer of evil, I cannot keep my mental balance. My mind wanders as I face the enemy-senses in meditation. I feel a premonition of impending disaster."

This is a true description of the state experienced by devotees after they have travelled some distance on the spiritual path. The beginner yogi, in the initial stages of soul contact, is eager, happy, satisfied. With further progress, he finds that the sense desires are diehard inmates of his life; he begins to wonder, even in the midst of divine realizations, if he has been wise in his decision to kill material joys for the sake of gaining spiritual happiness. In such confusion, the devotee tries to split his allegiance—giving half his attention to the body and its sense enjoyments and half to the inner assembly of soul joys. The result of these half-measures is that the devotee's limbs of will power become paralysed by the disease of latent sense attachment. He feels a dying-away of the finer intuitive spiritual perceptions; the taste for material habits, like a fire, dries up the taste for the subtle spiritual perceptions.

Counsel for the period when initial spiritual enthusiasm dies away

Just as physical fear causes the hair to stand on end, so mental nervousness at the prospect of losing sense enjoyment causes the devotee's thoughts and his hairlike nerve energies to flow like streams away from soul happiness toward the region of the senses. During this period of dubiousness, the devotee finds that the astral perceptions of the spine begin to fade away. As described in previous stanzas, when one walks, or works in any way with the body, he is cognizant of sensory perceptions; but in meditation bodily sensations gradually vanish, the sense of physical weight is forgotten, and a strong perception of astral spinal power and of blissful calmness takes possession of the consciousness. But because the devotee is not yet advanced enough to hold on to this state and deepen it, his materialistic tendencies—his karma or the effects of all his past bad sensory actions—rise up in the consciousness. When the devotee then begins to be restless, the spiritual bow of spinal energy and perception (which kills sense attachments with arrows of soul happiness) slips away from the grasp of self-control. All thoughts lose their power of concentration and start to burn with restlessness, even as skin is scorched by an overexposure to the sun's rays. The mind wanders again and again into subconscious experiences—led by the *samskaras* or strong impressions of past wrong actions—and is unable to remain concentrated upon the object of meditation. It feels instead a dreary loneliness, and beholds a mental desert created by the renunciation of material joys.

When tilling the ground for cultivating crops, the lush growth of useless weeds must first be destroyed. Their disappearance causes the ground to look barren, until the time arrives for the invisible potential within the seeds to sprout up into plants and yield a goodly harvest! The field of consciousness is similarly overgrown with weeds of meaningless sense pleasures—habits which, in the beginning, are very difficult to forsake.

People would rather do anything to while away their time except meditate. Witness the hours lost in movies, card-playing, aimless chattering, reading cheap novels or sensational newspapers, watching television. When the guru and the self-control of the aspiring devotee ask him to destroy his mental weeds and to plant the spiritual seeds of meditation, his habits suddenly make him see his life as a desolate desert if it lacks the customary weedy abundance of useless activities.

In this pitiable state of momentary bleakness, the devotee must cast away all feelings of doubt and despair and have faith that after the field of consciousness has been well sown with the seeds of deep meditation, they will produce the mystic trees of Omnipresence, bearing fruits of undying happiness.

It is not to the long-established sense "upstarts" in the bodily kingdom that the devotee owes his loyalty, but to the long-banished soul perceptions.

VERSE 31

न च श्रेयोऽनुपश्यामि हत्वा स्वजनमाहवे ॥ *(31)*
न काङ्क्षे विजयं कृष्ण न च राज्यं सुखानि च । *(32)*

O Krishna, neither do I perceive any worthwhile effect in slaying my own kinsmen in the battle. I crave neither triumph, nor kingdom, nor pleasures!

"O SOUL, I DO NOT PERCEIVE any beneficial result to be gained by slaying my intimate sense habits. My mind loathes the idea of destruction of sense pleasures. I crave nothing—neither mental victory, nor the kingdom of soul happiness, nor sense pleasures!"

In this despondent state of mental vacillation the devotee suddenly makes a negative decision. "I don't see any use in destroying all sense comforts," he reflects. "I do not crave an empty mental victory. I don't want the kingdom of cosmic consciousness. I don't want sense happiness either!"

The devotee thus turns from a torturing state of bewilderment to the state of negative definiteness. The devotee says to himself: "Down with both spiritual and sense happiness! I want nothing! I can forgo the possession of cosmic consciousness, if, to obtain it, I have to destroy the dear sense habits with whom I have long dwelt in the cozy home of life."

This is one of man's favourite ploys, mastered early in childhood: "If I have to eat my carrots before I can have ice cream, then I don't want ice cream either!" The plan is that this will be applauded as a great sacrifice worthy, at least, of pity; and better still, of favourable compromise. The wise parent doesn't give in to the wilful child; the wise cosmic law is passively unmoved by the devotee's "heroic" display of negative renunciation.

This state of negative renunciation may occur not only in meditation, as in this context, but also *after* deep meditation. The devotee who has for some time made concerted spiritual effort—practising self-denial and regular meditation—may find his complacency shattered when after a quiet meditation he suddenly is thrown into restlessness by the memory or *samskaras* of sense joys. He feels distressed and bewildered, realizing he has neither passing pleasures nor inner joys. Since he *has* neither, he pacifies his discouragement by proclaiming he *wants* neither. If he doesn't pull himself out of this indifference, he becomes a slothful devotee whose spiritual life will stagnate and die. But if he continues to persevere, he finds that this state is only a momentary vacuum in his *sadhana.*

❖
Renunciation is a shifting of tastes from inferior pleasures to everlasting joy
❖

Renunciation is not an end in itself. Parting with a small sum of money in order to invest it may place a poor man temporarily in a very awkward financial position, but that small sacrifice may later yield him an immense fortune. The wise devotee similarly knows that renunciation of paltry materialistic passions is necessary to attain the never-ending happiness of Spirit. He knows that he is not denying himself anything, but is only shifting his tastes from inferior, impermanent sense pleasures to superior, lasting soul happiness. As one should be glad to renounce a hundred dollars in order to gain five thousand dollars, so the devotee is happy to renounce a sensory pittance for the everlasting joy found in God-realization. The divine state of final emancipation is not a state of blank nothingness or a condition of inner extinction; it is, rather, the demesne of a positive conscious sense of eternal blessed expansion.

Nevertheless, worldly people are seldom impressed by stories of the saints who have worn sackcloth and lived in seclusion. "What lives of foolish self-denial and misery!" With this airy summing-up, the average man turns his entire attention on the world. To him it appears that happiness must be sought in family life, with its dinner parties, dances, and general stimulation of the senses. The unthinking man does not notice that mankind, busily engaged like himself in chasing the rainbow of lasting happiness, never finds it. Materially minded people suffer from conflicting desires and remain in a mire of suffering. Saints, on the other hand, are well aware that true and undying happiness can be found only in the inner perceptions of the Blissful Source of unalloyed eternal joy.

Many spiritually sincere persons reason that renunciation of material involvement, as exemplified by ascetics, is almost an impossibility in the modern world. No saint, however, advises that man has to seek solitude in Himalayan caves in order to find God. The ideal is to be *in* the world and yet not *of* it. Superconsciously awakened men—those who have meditated long, deeply, and persistently, no matter what their responsibilities or environment—become nonattached to material objects, but are not indifferent! The true devotee is not like a hobo, too lazy to make any decent effort to enjoy either material or spiritual prosperity! The yogi who has tasted the extra-fine perceptions of soul bliss remains unmoved and without cravings for material pleasures even though he may move among them. He has reached the true, secure spiritual state.

Perseverance produces positive fruits of renunciation

Spiritually weak devotees often do not persevere long enough to know the positive fruits of renunciation, and so give up meditation after a few trials, or even after a few years of halfhearted effort. Plunging again into the eddies of ordinary habits of living, they finally drown in ignorance. The sincere devotee is not misled when the crafty sense-attached mind says to him: "Why give up the pleasures indulged in by most people? Why sit in the dark in fruitless meditation? Go out every day to the movies or social gatherings, and have a good time!"

The devotee must fortify his good resolutions by remembering the example of Jesus and the great masters who attained immortality and everlasting happiness by renouncing the false pleasures offered man by the Satan of Cosmic Delusion.* Whenever the mind feels a longing for

* "Again, the devil taketh him up into an exceeding high mountain, and sheweth him all the kingdoms of the world, and the glory of them; And saith unto him, All these

the forsaken sense pleasures, the devotee should instantly picture to himself the end of his pleasure-loving body—its eventual entry into the earth or the crematory flames. A realization of this inexorable destiny for the body arouses in man a powerful anxiety to get acquainted with his indestructible Self, the Scorner of Death—the soul. The meditating devotee who has felt, even once, the inexhaustible charm of the soul and its eternal relationship with God can never forget the joy of it. He may pass through dreary tests in which he comes down from that state for a while, as typified in the despondency of Arjuna; but as long as the devotee continues to make the effort, the haunting memory of that pure joy will call again and again to urge him forward on the divine path.

VERSES 32–34

किं नो राज्येन गोविन्द किं भोगैर्जीवितेन वा ॥ *(32)*

येषामर्थे काङ्क्षितं नो राज्यं भोगाः सुखानि च।
त इमेऽवस्थिता युद्धे प्राणांस्त्यक्त्वा धनानि च ॥ *(33)*

आचार्याः पितरः पुत्रास्तथैव च पितामहाः।
मातुलाः श्वशुराः पौत्राः श्यालाः सम्बन्धिनस्तथा ॥ *(34)*

Of what use to us is dominion; of what avail happiness or even the continuance of life, O Govinda (Krishna)?* The very ones for whose sake we desire empire, enjoyment, pleasure, remain poised here for battle, ready to relinquish wealth and life—preceptors, fathers, sons, grandfathers, uncles, fathers-in-law, grandsons, brothers-in-law, and other kinsmen.

"IF BY KILLING THE EGO FORCES I attain dominion over the bodily empire, and establish therein the kingdom of God† with the soul as monarch, I fear the victory would be meaningless. If all my desires—

---

things will I give thee, if thou wilt fall down and worship me. Then saith Jesus unto him, Get thee hence, Satan: for it is written, Thou shalt worship the Lord thy God, and Him only shalt thou serve" (Matthew 4:8–10).

* Govinda, "chief herdsman." Krishna was known by this name in childhood when he tended the cattle of his foster parents in the fields of Brindaban; allegorically, he who presides over and is in control of the "cows" of the senses.

† "Thy kingdom come...on earth as it is in heaven" (Matthew 6:10).

the relatives and supporters of King Material Desire—are killed by spiritual discipline, how can I be happy? Even with the kingdom of God in my possession, can I possibly enjoy it if I am bereft of all desire?"

The Hindu scriptures describe the body as a product of Nature, with six defects of delusion: "It is born; it exists; it grows; it changes; it decays; it is annihilated." Most human beings nevertheless expect permanent happiness from this impermanent body. Because of the precedence of the experience of material pleasures, the ego is unwilling and unable to conceive of any higher state of happiness. Even heaven is often pictured as containing beautiful things that please the senses of vision, hearing, smell, taste, and touch—a place of glorified earthly enjoyments.

The devotee who is still bound by the habit of sensory experience clings subconsciously to the notion that divine attainment consists in forever enjoying the kingdom of God—with the senses. In the light of intuitional awakening, when he discovers that the soul forces are ready to destroy his material desires, his sensory-conditioned logic begins to mislead him. He reasons that if he annihilates the ego-consciousness and all its gross sensory pleasures, desires, habits, in order to gain spiritual dominion over the bodily empire, the victory will be meaningless without these channels of enjoyment. He thinks: "If I destroy all desires—all these forces of King Material Desire—then no energy or ambition or interest will be left in me with which to enjoy the newly acquired soul-governed kingdom."

VERSE 35

एतान्न हन्तुमिच्छामि घ्नतोऽपि मधुसूदन।
अपि त्रैलोक्यराज्यस्य हेतोः किं नु महीकृते ॥

Even though these relatives should try to destroy me, O Madhusudana (Krishna),* still I could not want to destroy them, not even if thereby I attained mastery over the three worlds; how much less, then, for the sake of this mundane territory of earth!

"O MY DIVINE SOUL, DESTROYER OF ALL DIFFICULTIES, though these sense desires may try to destroy my spiritual life with their temptations, still

* Slayer of the demon Madhu; i.e., slayer of the demon of ignorance or spiritual difficulties.

I do not wish to slay them, even if by doing so I would attain dominion over the three worlds—physical, astral, and causal. How much less willing am I to kill these my relatives for the sake of spiritual mastery over the little territory of the physical body (earth)!"

Thwarted in his efforts to delve deep into soul happiness, the devotee loses confidence in his spiritual future. He has already determined that all the golden hopes of eternal happiness pictured by inner wisdom would be empty and useless if desire is slain. Now his subconscious habitual love for sense pleasure leads his power of reason into deeper doubt. He is momentarily not even sure there is a greater happiness beyond the senses. His irrationality asserts itself to the limit as he weighs the tangible against the Intangible:

"O Soul, I should not destroy my favourite present sense pleasures, even if they destroy my unknown future spiritual happiness. I cannot live in hopes of a perhaps nonexistent blessedness and thus lose tangible pleasures that are entertaining me now."

It is difficult to forsake any earthly happiness that is present and active in the consciousness and that sways the mind with the influence of habit. It is hard to give up the known sense pleasures of the present for unknown pleasures that may arrive in the future. This is the reason why millions of people would rather eat, drink, and try to be merry today than take the trouble to meditate and make an investment for a future of lasting happiness.

Irrationality of not seeking cosmic consciousness

To be an emperor of the whole earth is not the highest goal man can aim for, because he has to leave it all at death; but to possess cosmic consciousness, oneness with God—the Creator who is able to materialize worlds out of ideas—is an everlasting power given to all supremely advanced souls in the spiritual path. The beginner devotee, nevertheless, may be so much attached to immediate material passions that he passes through these periods of irrational doubt in which he does not crave the bliss and security of cosmic consciousness, with its mastery over the three worlds.

When this mental state arises in the devotee—when he thinks that he would rather die in sense indulgence than look for an unknown happiness in the bleakness of self-control—he should reason in the following way: "I lack spiritual imagination and spiritual experience; that is why I think that the present sense happiness is the only happiness worth possessing. Let me rather believe in the truthful words of the scriptures and of my guru. Let me meditate deeply and attain cosmic consciousness; then I shall see the difference between everlasting divine happiness and the temporary enjoyment of sensory entertainment. I shall then reverse my present judgement and say that I would rather die for spiritual happiness than yield to the false promises of the senses."

VERSE 36

निहत्य धार्तराष्ट्रान्नः का प्रीतिः स्याज्जनार्दन।
पापमेवाश्रयेदस्मान्हत्वैतानाततायिनः ॥

What happiness could we gain, O Janardana (Krishna),* from destroying the clan of Dhritarashtra? The slaying of these felons would only put us in the clutches of sin.

"WHAT STRANGE HAPPINESS COULD be expected by destroying Material Desire and the other offspring of the blind sense-mind, King Dhritarashtra? The slaying of these friendly enemies, even though they have committed painful felonies against me, would leave my life dismally empty; and would be sinful according to the highest scriptures—which teach that we should live in harmony with cosmic law, and which also advocate love rather than violence in confronting one's enemies."

False rationalizations of the devotee's sense-enslaved reason

Through divine intervention, a glimmer of an edifying thought springs up in the mind of the rationalizing, dubious devotee: "The senses are indeed felons (*atatayin*), deserving extinction, because they have already given me physical, mental, and spiritual suffering." Through intuition, the Divine Presence thus reminds the devotee of the many ills that have come to him through sense indulgence—disease, disillusionment, heartaches, bereavements, and ignorance. Yet the devotee may still argue: "O Spirit, Deliverer of Devotees! although it seems right to slay these inimical senses that have already hurt me, nevertheless, according to the scriptures, we incur sin when we go against cosmic law; and after all, the sense properties are a result of the divinely created forces of Nature through which man and the universe exist. Surely it is sinful to interfere with what is only nat-

* Vishnu or Krishna, who grants men's prayers for salvation; Janardana is that aspect to whom men pray for fulfilment—from *jana,* "men," and *ardana* (Sanskrit root *ard*), "to request or implore."

ural to the embodied soul endowed with these sensory instruments. Also, the scriptures say we must love our enemies. Is it not better, O Lord, gradually to win the senses, by loving example, to the spiritual mode of living—rather than destroy them?" A brilliant remonstrance! What better support for false reasoning than quoting scripture.

"Have a little compassion and understanding for your weaknesses, which are a natural inheritance of all mortals." This is one of the strongest arguments advanced by the wily sense habits in order to keep the would-be fleeing devotee in their clutches. The scriptures and masters do instruct the devotee not to destroy the actual senses, but to slay their bad habits. The devotee is not asked to blind his eyes, deafen his ears, nor to paralyse his senses of smell, taste, and touch. He is directed only to dislodge the enemies of optical, auditory, olfactory, gustatory, and tactual attachments, which keep the soul imprisoned, forgetful of its omnipresent kingdom.

When all sensory attachments—unwholesome lure of physical beauty, love of flattery and of words of temptation, bondage of greed, attraction of sex—are dislodged from the matrixes of the senses, it is then that the senses relinquish their material prejudices, inclinations, instincts, and obsessions; they become ready to be attached only to divine bliss.

When false argument invades the mind of the devotee, he should suggest to himself: "By the repetition of my ignorance-born evil actions and bad habits initiated by me, I have been compelled to love sense pleasures. Now I will undo all the evils by substituting good actions through the exercise of self-control, until good habits are firmly formed. I will substitute for the evil habit of sensory restlessness the good habit of calmness in meditation. My good habits will so convert my senses that I may truly say that I see, smell, taste, touch, hear, think, and feel only that which is good."

This is the challenge for the strong-minded, self-controlled devotee. Halfheartedness will not suffice. Lackadaisical measures to substitute good habits for bad habits is a veritable fortress that will continue to protect the evil forces behind parapets of false reasoning and procrastination.

VERSE 37

तस्मान्नार्हा वयं हन्तुं धार्तराष्ट्रान् स्वबान्धवान्।
स्वजनं हि कथं हत्वा सुखिनः स्याम माधव॥

Therefore, we are not justified in annihilating our very own relatives, the progeny of Dhritarashtra. O Madhava (Krishna),* how indeed could we attain happiness by killing our own kindred?

"O SOUL, WE ARE NOT JUSTIFIED in slaughtering our sense habits, the offspring of our own mind. How could we benefit by destroying the senses, through which alone the mind expresses itself?"

When false reasoning reaches a wrong conclusion and becomes attached to it, the intelligence loses more and more of its discriminative and intuitive powers, and instead relies on rationalization to justify its conviction. This is what has happened to Arjuna, the devotee.

I have diagnosed many psychological "patients," and have witnessed many curious traits in people when they feel called upon to support their own favourite habits. One student, an inveterate smoker and a coffee-drinker, but a rabid vegetarian, was arguing one day with another student who occasionally ate chicken, lamb, and fish, but who strictly abstained from smoking and from drinking coffee.

Worldly man reasons not according to truth, but according to his habits

"How terrible of you to eat a decaying carcass!" the vegetarian exclaimed. "I can't see how anyone can eat meat! Think of the poor animal that is killed to satisfy your appetite; and besides, meat is harmful to man's body."

"It is impossible to eat anything that is not killed," the other man retorted. "You chop off the head of the cauliflower and eat its boiled carcass! No matter what you eat you are destroying some form of life and transmuting it into a different form as a part of your own living body. Anyway, the big fish eat the little fish; why should man not assert his superiority and eat the big fish? Meat is nourishing—but how dreadful of you deliberately to inhale nicotine and to swallow caffeine when science tells you they are injurious!"

Here both students were arguing according to the influence of their favoured habits.

Man, at the behest of Director Habit, performs, like an obedient actor, various psychological roles on the stage of consciousness. When he is identified with his good habits and moods, he feels sympathetic toward the performance of good actions and apathetic toward evil actions; but when he is under the influence of unwholesome moods and

* God of Fortune; referring to Krishna as an incarnation of Vishnu whose consort, or *shakti*, "divine power," is Lakshmi, goddess of wealth and fortune. (See also I:14, page 115.)

habits, he leans toward evil. This is the way, by being an actor of good roles, the devotee acts as his own friend, and by being an actor of evil roles, he unknowingly acts as his own enemy.

This stanza of the Gita carries a great ethical warning for devotees, even for those travelling fast on the metaphysical path. Most devotees who sincerely take up the spiritual path do so because they are already imbued with good habits, and so are fully inclined toward good. Nevertheless, if hidden inner seeds (*samskaras*) of bad prenatal or postnatal actions germinate under suitable psychological circumstances, the "good" devotee becomes strongly inclined to do evil. For instance, if a man has formed habits of moderate eating, of regularity in work, in recreation, in meditation, and in mixing in good company, he will feel that is the only possible life for him. If, however, latent bad tendencies suddenly surface as a result of temptation, environment, or other such conducive circumstances, the man may alter his habits—suddenly feeling desires for immoderate eating, for irregular habits (overwork or idleness), for disregard of meditation, and for the unholy pleasures of mixing with bad company.

So the warning to be inferred from this stanza is that the devotee who suddenly becomes identified with the enemy (bad habits and moods) will find himself sympathizing with and justifying unwholesome actions. By a little psychological analysis of himself, he can discover how apt he is to support equally his good or bad actions when he is under their specific influence. Man is in a dangerous state when he responds to his evil habits as easily, as pleasantly, and as willingly as he responds, in a better frame of mind, to his good habits.

Verses 38–39

यद्यप्येते न पश्यन्ति लोभोपहतचेतसः ।
कुलक्षयकृतं दोषं मित्रद्रोहे च पातकम् ॥ *(38)*

कथं न ज्ञेयमस्माभिः पापादस्मान्निवर्तितुम् ।
कुलक्षयकृतं दोषं प्रपश्यद्भिर्जनार्दन ॥ *(39)*

Even if these others (the Kurus), whose understanding is eclipsed by greed, behold no calamity in the ruin of families, and no evil in enmity to friends, should we not know to avoid this sin, O Janardana (Krishna)—we who do distinctly perceive the evil in the disintegration of the family?

"THE CLAN OF THE BLIND SENSE-MIND (*manas*), its understanding eclipsed by greed (passionate attachment to likes and dislikes), follows its outward wanton inclinations in seeking gratification. Because this is the habitual or natural mode of expression of the blind senses when they are not guided by discrimination (*buddhi*), they behold no calamity in the decay of the human personality, and no wrong in their hostility to their true friends, the discriminative faculties. But we, the discriminative forces, do distinctly perceive what evil can befall the consciousness if all its faculties do not perform their functions as a united, harmonious family—so should we not turn away from the sin of this battle, which will surely destroy many members of this family?"

The devotee reasons that the sense inclinations are necessary for the expression and experience of the incarnate soul, just as much as wisdom inclinations are, and thus he sees no reason why the one set of sense members of the family of consciousness should be destroyed and the other set of discriminating inclinations should be allowed to live on. It seems unreasonable to destroy the family clan of sense inclinations, since they have their specific functions to perform in the drama of life.

So the devotee in introspection says to the Inner Self:

"O Soul, since you are Creator and Lord of the senses as well as of discrimination, why counsel me to destroy the pleasure-giving senses by the wisdom-bringing forces of discrimination? They are both members of my consciousness! How could I live with only the dry wisdom-bringing inclinations, deprived of the company of my merrymaking senses?"

THE DEVOTEE IS CAUTIONED about the overwhelming influence of bad habits. From past experience, bad habits seem to have little fear—they behold no evil consequences—that they will not be able to destroy their psychological kinsmen, the good inclinations. They are strengthened in this conviction as the devotee continues to think in the same strain of sympathy towards these sense habits: "What a pity my favourite bad habits do not see how foolish they are to fight my favourite good habits and thus take the risk of being destroyed!"

Danger of wanting to preserve both good and bad habits

In this state, the devotee wants to carry on with both good and bad habits; apparently they both satisfy him. How quickly he forgets that his sweet-mouthed bad habits, though they belong to his own family of consciousness, stealthily carry with them the weapons that slay his peace.

The devotee at this stage believes that the evil or animal-like (devoid of discrimination) sense-indulging habits could exist side by side with the good habits and thus make the kingdom of life complete. But it is impossible to have harmony and peace as long as contradictory forces work in one's life. The good habits and the bad habits, though they are the offspring of the same consciousness, manifest different results.

When the devotee asks himself, "Why can't I enjoy material and spiritual pleasures together?" such reasoning is tantamount to arguing the reasonableness of using devitalizing "dope" while at the same time taking an invigorating tonic; the effect of the dope will counteract the effect of the tonic! If, however, one is faithful in taking the strengthening tonic and has the will power simultaneously to ingest less and less dope, that is one way to freedom from the drug habit.

Similarly, those who equally enjoy sensory indulgences and meditational pleasures will not get anywhere for a long time. "A double minded man is unstable in all his ways."* However, even if one cannot immediately conquer the flesh, he should meditate just the same, for then he will have at least some standard of comparison between the material gratification of the senses and the inner fulfilments of the soul. Those who fail to conquer sensory passions and who also give up meditation fall into an almost hopeless condition of spiritual decay.

One who meditates daily and cultivates the taste for peace and contentment, gradually forsaking indulgence in sense pleasures, has a chance for spiritual emancipation. A very good habit to cultivate is the one of meditating immediately upon awakening from sleep. After that period of meditation, filled with the offerings of the soul, one may enjoy, with no feeling of compulsion or sensory attachment, the self-controlled use of the senses in such pleasures as eating, association with friends, and so forth. In this way man finds that he is spiritualizing or changing the quality of all material enjoyments. In other words, if a man caters to his bad habits of greed and eats himself to ill health and death—that is bad; but if he harnesses the pleasure of eating to the power of self-control and moderation—that is good.

Recognizing temptations lurking in subconscious mind

The difficulty is that the spiritual beginner—and even the advancing devotee when he temporarily falls into a negative state—can scarcely distinguish between his reason-governed use of the senses and his greed-governed sense appetites. His bad sense habits, even if they appear to be under control and friendly, may be merely waiting for the right moment to destroy him with their temptations.

* James 1:8.

A story will illustrate this point. John, a drunkard, met a saint and made an abstainer's vow. He asked his servants to keep the key to the wine cellar and not to serve him, even at his command, with any liquor. Everything went along satisfactorily for some time because of John's elation over his new resolution. For a while he did not feel the unseen gripping lure of the liquor-tempting habit.

As time went on, John asked his servants to leave the key to the wine cellar with him so that he himself could serve his friends. Then he decided it was too much bother to go to the cellar; he placed some wine bottles in a cabinet in the parlour. After a few days, John thought: "Since I am proof against liquor, let me look at the sparkling red wine in a bottle on the table."

Every day he looked at the bottle. Then he thought: "Since I no longer care for liquor, I will take a mouthful of wine, taste it, and then spit it out." After he had done this, he had a further inspiration. "Since I am fully free from liquor temptation, there will be no harm if I have a little swallow." After that he thought: "Since I have conquered the liquor habit, why should I not take wine again at meal times? My will is quite unenslaved." From that day on, John was again a drunkard, in spite of his protesting will.

A bad habit may be temporarily subdued by a good resolution and self-control; but not necessarily conquered. John failed to realize that his resolution had not had enough time to ripen into a good habit. It may take from eight to twelve years to substitute a good habit for a strong bad habit. Before the strong good habit is fully formed, a man must not put himself in the way of temptation. John disregarded this psychological law; he brought near him the wine bottle, reviving memories of the drinking habit. To starve out bad habits, one must get away from evil surroundings; and above all, one must never dwell mentally on evil thoughts. The latter reinforces the influence of the former and is more dangerous. One must fortify himself with the right outer environment and the right inner environment.

John not only forgot that he should not have brought liquor so near him, but he also failed to recognize the psychological weapons of flattery and false reasoning by which his bad habit defeated his good resolution. The liquor habit remained hidden in his subconscious mind, secretly sending out armed spies of desire and pleasing thoughts of taste; thus the way was prepared for the reinvasion of the alcoholic habit.

Man is plagued by such soul-humiliating defeats at the hands of his own particular habits until his consciousness is securely anchored in his true divine nature. The sensory functions have their rightful place in man's life only after he has subordinated them by realizing himself as the soul, one with Spirit, not a body subject to sense domination.

VERSES 40–41

कुलक्षये प्रणश्यन्ति कुलधर्माः सनातनाः ।
धर्मे नष्टे कुलं कृत्स्नमधर्मोऽभिभवत्युत ॥ *(40)*

अधर्माभिभवात्कृष्ण प्रदुष्यन्ति कुलस्त्रियः ।
स्त्रीषु दुष्टासु वार्ष्णेय जायते वर्णसङ्करः ॥ *(41)*

(40) With the decimation of the family, the age-old religious rites of the family fade away. When the upholding religion is annihilated, then sin overpowers the whole family.

(41) O Krishna, from lack of religion the women of the family become bad. O Varshneya (Krishna),* women being thus contaminated, adultery is engendered among castes.

"BY DESTROYING THE FAMILY MEMBERS of sense inclinations, the age-old sense rituals, *'dharmas,'* of the family of consciousness will fade away—because the senses, having thus lost their power to produce sense enjoyment, will cease to perform the rites of their specific duties. With the annihilation of these rites of the senses—which have been the upholding principle of conscious existence—sin (sorrow and corruption) will overtake all of the family members of human consciousness.

"If we, the wisdom forces, suspend in ecstasy the sense capabilities, then from *'adharma'* (lack of the performance of the sense rituals) the sense perceptions (the feminine force or 'feeling' for material things) will become corrupted. From neglect and disuse, they will forget, and stray from, their individual functions or caste and become mixed with indifference, indolence, and confusion. All of the sense clan, and the rest of the members of the family of consciousness, following the adulterous feminine force of feeling, will similarly lose their distinctive 'caste' characteristics (their individualized powers and functions)."

---

* Lit., "scion of the Vrishni clan." The word *vrishni* means "masterfully strong, powerful."

The "family" refers to the inner and outer forces of cognition and expression through which the ego (or the soul, in the enlightened man) is provided with a means of experiencing and interacting with its environment. The members of this family consist of the powers of sight, smell, taste, touch, hearing; the powers of speech, and of activity involved in the motions of the hands and feet, and in the genital (reproduction) and rectal (elimination) muscles; the mind (*manas*), which, like chariot reins, holds together the stallions of the senses; the five life forces (the metabolizing, circulatory, assimilating, eliminating, and crystallizing functions of the One Life present in the body); and the head of the family, intelligence (*buddhi*). All are expressions of the one cosmic consciousness of Spirit through Its individualized Self, the soul.

Constituents of the psychological "family": individualized functions through which the soul interacts with the world

Each member of the family of consciousness, with both its inner and outer nature, manifests a characteristic behaviour, or "performs the ritual" of a specific function. For example, the duty of the sense of sight is to see, the duty of the mind is to coordinate the senses, and the duty of the life force is to keep the senses, body, and mind together in a psychophysical unity. The duty of intelligence is to harmonize the inner and outer forces, inspiring them to live according to the supreme plan of wisdom, as behooves the followers of the will of God.

Dharma, referred to in these two Gita verses, is often translated as "religion" or "duty." It is a comprehensive term for the natural laws governing the universe and man, inherent in which are prescribed duties applicable to given circumstances. Broadly speaking, man's *dharma* is to adhere to that natural righteousness that will save him from suffering and lead him to salvation. The *dharma* or natural law of a seed is to produce a plant. The *dharma* or natural order of the senses is to provide a means of exchange between the perceiving ego or soul and the objects perceived. The rationalizing devotee in his negative doubting state descends further into misunderstanding as he argues in concern about destroying the natural "rites" of the senses, which are an integral part of the *dharma,* or natural order, of the family of consciousness.

To be destroyed: not the senses themselves, but desires for objects of the senses

The family members to be destroyed by the devotee are not the senses themselves, but their offspring, or inclinations—desires for objects of the senses. There are two kinds of objects. The first kind consists of material objects, perceptible to man's outer senses. The second kind consists of subtle objects in the astral world, which are perceived by the God-ward-moving inner consciousness. The outward objects of the senses breed material attachment; the inner objects of the senses destroy this physical attachment. However, long-continued association with even the inner objects of sense may divert the mind of the devotee from higher soul perceptions and ultimate realization of God—a caution to devotees who become preoccupied with phenomena and powers.

These material and astral objects are perceived and acted upon by the ten senses, by the five life forces, and by the mind and intelligence. The action and interaction of these seventeen inner and outer forces of perception, and their ego-guided or soul-governed reaction to the objects of perception, arouse in the devotee accordingly either good or evil inclinations: desire or self-control, attachment or dispassion, and so forth.

The meditating devotee is shown as having arrived at a state in which he feels that, in the battle for Self-realization, with the growing perception of the Inner Self, all the inclinations of the inner and outer members of the family of consciousness will be annihilated; and that without these inclinations with their desires for inner and outer objects, the specific functions of the senses, mind, vital forces, and intelligence will be lost.

The novitiate devotee who has yet to experience the deeper states of meditation, and even the advancing yogi who has reached the early stages of *samadhi* (as described by Patanjali and explained in I:15–18), feels some apprehension about the new states of consciousness he is moving toward. Age-old attachment to his familiar family members of inner and outer faculties does not let go easily in favour of an as-yet-unknown ecstatic state of consciousness beyond the functioning of these powers.

God-contact destroys harmful sense-attachments, but revitalizes the senses themselves

In an ecstatic contact with God, though the soul consciousness is awake and keenly alert, the senses, mind, vital forces, and intelligence remain in a suspended state. The devotee wonders if all these inner and outer functions, remaining long in a suspended state, will ultimately be annihilated, or rendered impotent or confused. Will the senses, with their natural inclinations destroyed, lose their power to enjoy the outer objects of the beauties of Nature and the exquisite inner astral objects perceived during visions; or being suppressed, become confused and misled by fanciful imaginings or hallucinations? Will the mind lose its power of coordination, and the intelligence its power of determination and discrimination?

Such concerns are born of untrue surmises—foolish fears. In the conscious contact of God, the inner and outer members of consciousness, though suspended, do not lose their individual powers or become distorted. Instead, they are doubly recharged in perceptive power from the cosmic battery—the spring of all life. The senses become rejuvenated and develop more subtle powers in expressing their individual characteristics. With enhanced perceptions rooted in a knowledge of the unending joy of God, the advanced yogi, far more than a worldly man, is able to enjoy the sensory world—its people, its roses, its skies!

Even in sleep the inner and outer powers are partially suspended, as the vital functions slow down and the senses turn inward. They do not die as a result, but are recharged by the accumulated cosmic current in the brain. In conscious ecstasy (*samadhi*) the truant inner and outer forces of consciousness turn away from their malevolent, devitalizing wanderings over the land of matter, and return to the presence of all-rejuvenating God. As these inner and outer sensibilities move in the deepest tracts of Spirit and become wholly engrossed in God, they are invisible and imperceptible in the body. In Revelation 1:17, Saint John described this state of ecstasy, saying: "And when I saw Him, I fell at His feet as dead." When John perceived the Spirit, he did not become unconscious, but his expanded soul consciousness kept vibrating in his astral body above the physical body and was hovering over the latter as it remained in a trance state of suspended animation. So he speaks of perceiving his physical body as dead, or in a deathlike, restful, deep trance; but not "dead" as human beings understand the term. One can revive his bodily consciousness at will from the trance state; but not from the mysterious bourne of death.

The state of ecstasy (attained by consciously passing beyond dreamless sleep to the superconsciousness, and ultimately to cosmic consciousness) not only rests, but reinforces, the inner powers with limitless keenness, vitality, and divine wisdom.

The man of realization develops extraordinary powers of clairaudience and clairvoyance; the mind comprehends everything intuitively; the intelligence is no longer guided by fallible human reason but by unerring divine wisdom. It is as ridiculous for a person to fear that his various powers will be annihilated by entering the superior ecstatic state of God-union, as it would be for him to fear the extinction of any of his powers by their nightly state of suspended animation in sleep.

VERSES 42–43

सङ्करो नरकायैव कुलघ्नानां कुलस्य च।
पतन्ति पितरो ह्येषां लुप्तपिण्डोदकक्रियाः ॥ (42)

दोषैरेतैः कुलघ्नानां वर्णसङ्करकारकैः।
उत्साद्यन्ते जातिधर्माः कुलधर्माश्च शाश्वताः ॥ (43)

(42) The adulteration of family blood consigns to hell the clan-destroyers, along with the family itself. Their ancestors, by being denied the oblations of rice-ball and water, are degraded.

(43) By these misdeeds of the family-destroyers, producing admixture of castes, the time-old rites (dharmas) of the caste and clan are annihilated.

"IF THE SELF-DENIAL activities of the wisdom forces destroy the clan of masculine sense inclinations, then the feminine sense perceptions will become a mixture of castes—precipitated by the intermixing of the distinctive powers and functions, or caste characteristics, of the senses with discrimination and of their outer with their inner forces. The clan-destroying wisdom forces, as well as the other remaining members of the family of consciousness, will find themselves fallen into a living hades of inner loneliness and meaninglessness. Without the stimulation of the senses, the discriminating faculties will become weak from lack of use and will not make the proper offerings to inspire the family ancestors (ego, soul, intuition) to bless their offspring (the family of consciousness).

"By this disruption of the natural external activities of the faculties of consciousness, and by their ultimate suspension in *samadhi,* surely all the rites (activities) of the family of consciousness will be annihilated."

THE DEVOTEE CONTINUES to add new arguments to his same trend of rationalization. As he tries to make up his mind to engage in a battle to destroy the senses—that is, to withdraw in meditation his wisdom and life force which enliven the senses—he now expresses apprehension lest his discriminative faculties suffer disintegration owing to their lack of interaction with the senses. If the wisdom faculties are not utilized in the normal enjoyment of the senses, but are made to reside in the inner sanctum of the soul, will not the wisdom faculties along with the sense fac-

❖
Devotee's fear that subjecting sense faculties to soul discrimination will create psychological problems
❖

ulties then be thrown into a hades of loneliness and meaninglessness?

His assertion, furthermore, is that in ecstasy the family rites (*dharmas*)—the accustomed functions of the sense and wisdom faculties—will be annihilated if these faculties lose their "caste" or distinctive characteristics by a mixing of family blood (the mixing of the external faculties of consciousness with their inner proclivities, and the intermixing of the sense and wisdom propensities). The absurdity of such a conclusion—that the family of consciousness suffers disintegration in ecstasy—was exposed in the commentary on the two previous verses.

The truth of the matter is quite to the contrary. The negative feminine sense pleasures (the feeling or experiences of the senses) are guided by the positive masculine sense capabilities. If the masculine sense faculties—desire, material achievement, creative ability, initiative for material enjoyment—are destroyed in their battle with the discriminative faculties, then the feminine or "feeling" sense faculties—material pleasure, attachment, delusion, sense slavery—lose their "caste" consciousness of materiality and submit to the inner proclivities of the discriminative faculties. That is, when the springs of sense activities, sense desires, are destroyed, the feminine sense perceptions lose their material edge and guiding spirit, owing to the powerful influence of the discriminative tendencies. The whole clan of sense faculties thereby becomes not extinguished, but enlightened, by this domination of the wisdom faculties.

But the devotee in his state of confusion falsely reasons (as described in the two preceding verses) that after the wisdom faculties have destroyed the masculine sense inclinations, the feminine sense pleasures will merely become adulterous with indifference, indolence, and confusion, leading all the family of consciousness into caste admixture, or loss of their distinctive functions. The devotee's irrational imaginings warn that not only will the senses lose their inherent faculties (*dharmas* or rites) to enjoy pleasure, but their vanquishment will cause the discriminative faculties also to lose their distinctive external function from lack of interaction with the senses. And then both the sense clan and the discriminative clan of the family of consciousness will find themselves in a hades of meaningless existence.

This error of reasoning is born of the attachment of the devotee's mind to the world of sense pleasures. When he withdraws his wisdom faculties from the enslavement of sense pleasures, he at first feels an emptiness; but when he goes deeper into meditation, his discriminative faculties consciously enjoy a new world of superconscious bliss, found only in soul contact with the Infinite.

THE "ANCESTORS" OF THE FAMILY of human consciousness are the soul and its faculties of the inner-seeing ego,* intuition, and so forth. These ancestors are degraded into ordinary human sense consciousness unless they receive from the wisdom faculties a flow of inspiration and inwardly turned life force (water) and regular offerings of vital spiritual enthusiasm (rice-balls). When the vitality of concentration and wisdom is developed, it inspires the soul and the intuitional powers; the inspired soul in turn reinforces the wisdom and intuition with all-seeing powers.

The yogi, inwardly performing the true "ancestral oblation," elevates the entire psychological clan

But the devotee persists in his erroneous conjecturing: "If I destroy the sense inclinations, the discriminative faculties will be starved from lack of action; the emaciated wisdom will fail to inspire the soul; the uninspired soul will cease to illumine man. Thus human wisdom will degenerate."

The baseless fears of the devotee are suggested to his mind by the forces of King Material Desire. Their skill in argument is equalled only by their duplicity!

The advancing yogi, firm in meditative self-control, performs the true ancestral ceremony. He astrally disconnects the life force from the sensory nerves; it begins to flow inward and, becoming focused at the point between the eyebrows, forms into an opalescent light. The inward astral flow and the inner light are the oblations of the human wisdom to its ancestors of soul, divine ego, and intuition.† Human wisdom must offer these vitalities to the soul faculties. Without the oblations of inwardly flowing life force and spiritual perceptions, and of the light of the spiritual eye, the soul faculties remain dormant, degradingly undeveloped.

Instead of being doubtful or despondent, the seeker of God should be glad to consign all sense pleasures to limbo in exchange for the lavish treasures of the soul. And with purest devotion and mastery of *pranayama,* he should perform the true ancestral rite of offering oblations to the enlightenment-bestowing soul.

---

* See I:8, page 84.

† The inward flow of the life force is the "oblation of water," *udaka,* lit., "that which flows or issues forth." The divine light that appears in the forehead from the life energy focused there is the offering symbolized by the "rice-ball," *pinda,* from the Sanskrit root *pind,* "to gather; to form into a 'ball' or sphere"—the light of the spherical spiritual eye.

VERSES 44–46

उत्सन्नकुलधर्माणां मनुष्याणां जनार्दन।
नरकेऽनियतं वासो भवतीत्यनुशुश्रुम॥ *(44)*

अहो बत महत्पापं कर्तुं व्यवसिता वयम्।
यद्राज्यसुखलोभेन हन्तुं स्वजनमुद्यताः॥ *(45)*

यदि मामप्रतीकारमशस्त्रं शस्त्रपाणयः।
धार्तराष्ट्रा रणे हन्युस्तन्मे क्षेमतरं भवेत्॥ *(46)*

(44) O Janardana (Krishna), often have we heard that men devoid of family religious rites are most certainly committed to reside indefinitely in hell.*

(45) Alas! actuated by greed for the comfort of possessing a kingdom, we are prepared to kill our own kinsmen—an act surely entangling us in great iniquity.

(46) If, weapons in hand, the sons of Dhritarashtra kill me, wholly resigned and weaponless in the battle, that solution will be more welcome and beneficial to me!

"THOSE MEN IN WHOM THE SENSE and wisdom faculties no longer perform their accustomed rites of habitual body-bound behaviour are surely consigned thereafter to a hellish life of corroding inner boredom and torturing emptiness. Yet out of greed to acquire sole possession of the kingdom of consciousness, in the uncertain hope of some future better gratification, we the discriminative forces are willing to incur the sin (unhappy existence) of killing our sense kinsmen. It would be better for me if the armed children of King Dhritarashtra (the sense inclinations of the blind sense-mind) were instead to slay me in battle, unresisting and unarmed."

The beginner yogi, forced to be quiet in meditation to peer behind the screen of darkness, often wonders if he is not being foolish to relinquish the tangible pleasures of the senses for a possible glimpse of

---

* *Narake* (in hell) *'niyataṁ* (*aniyataṁ*, "indefinitely") *vāso bhavatī* (to be or reside in a place or dwelling). An alternate Sanskrit reading supplies the word *niyataṁ* (certainly, inevitably) instead of *aniyataṁ*. Both possibilities have been combined in this translation.

the presently intangible pleasures of the Spirit. While he is held captive in this negative state of mind by past bad habits and karmic influences, he feels disinclined to arm himself with the austere laws of self-control. "Soul pleasures are a matter of future speculation," he finds himself believing. "I would be foolish to give up present tangible joys. My life will be sunk in constant misery by the destruction of my God-given sense pleasures, so easily available to me right now! Later on I may be more ready to meditate deeply and to seek God more one-pointedly."

Surrendering to the demands of the senses does not satisfy them, but rather creates insatiable desires for further sense experiences. Sense pleasure is like a drink of hemlock, which, instead of quenching thirst, only increases it! Soul pleasure, though hard to attain, when once gained is never diminished; it knows no satiety, and yields ever new joys.

The despondent devotee thinks: "It would be a better fate for me to meet disillusionment and death from the senses—like all other worldly people who travel through life unarmed by any weapon of self-control—rather than to be involved in a devastating battle between the discriminative forces and the sense proclivities."

He thus concludes: "I will refrain from further practice of meditation. I will not use the weapon of life-control (*pranayama*) to destroy the magnetic attraction of the senses. It does not matter if I am overpowered by the material instincts and suffer at their hands! I simply will not become a semiparalytic, a half-dead individual, deprived of all desires for material things!"

In this state of mind the devotee is dissatisfied both because of his lack of spiritual progress and because of his long separation from his accustomed sense habits. These ready arguments of self-pity show why self-discipline demands not only the forswearing of indulgence in wrong pleasures, but also, with the sword of wisdom, the destruction of the thoughts of them from the sense-sympathetic mind. At this unpropitious moment, however, when the Inner Self is urging the devotee to destroy even the mental or imaginary gratification of a sense pleasure, he reacts childishly by rebelling against all modes of self-discipline. The devotee should now relax and not be too strict in disciplining the unruly child, his unconvinced mind. This state is finally overcome by concentrating upon the peace born of even partial renunciation and reasonable effort in meditation, enjoying moderate appeasement in wholesome sense pleasures.

In addition, the devotee should use a little spiritual imagination to visualize the lasting joys of spiritual attainment. When he finds himself bothered with doubts, picturing a hollow victory with his mind a deserted battlefield full of the corpses of wisdom-slain material desires (dear friends and relatives), he should rather think of the habitual material desires as enemies in disguise. They promised him happiness, yet planned to give him only worries, insatiable longings, broken hopes, disillusionments, and death! Although it is hard in the beginning for him to give up the kinds of material pleasures that obstruct the expression of the soul, renouncing such evil is his only hope of gaining lasting spiritual blessedness. And while self-control, in itself, in the negative state, produces momentary unhappiness because of separation from pleasure-yielding bad habits, after self-control achieves its end the devotee experiences finer perceptions and joys of the soul—far superior to those he knew when he lived identified with the ego and its gross pleasures. The devotee is amply compensated for any sacrifice made when he at last attains the peerless ever new bliss of the soul's awakening in Spirit.

VERSE 47

सञ्जय उवाच
एवमुक्त्वार्जुनः सङ्ख्ये रथोपस्थ उपाविशत्।
विसृज्य सशरं चापं शोकसंविग्नमानसः ॥

Sanjaya said to Dhritarashtra:
Arjuna, having spoken thus on the battlefield, his mind disturbed by grief, flinging away his bow and arrows, sat down on the seat of his chariot.

ARJUNA, OR SELF-CONTROL, casting away his bow of meditation and the ignorance-piercing arrows of inner powers, remains at a standstill in the middle of the psychological-metaphysical battlefield—though not actually leaving the chariot of intuition.

It often happens that, unless the devotee has sufficient spiritual power to quiet his doubts, he feels himself to be a weakling, unfit for battle. Full of grief, and casting away his divine weapons, he indifferently settles on a piece of intuitive experience (seats himself in the chariot). The chariot represents intuitive perception, the vehicle in which the devotee's discriminative forces engage in psychological and metaphysical battle with the sense hordes. The seat of the chariot on which the devotee settles himself in withdrawal from battle signifies the particular powerful sense perception which at that moment has been strong enough to cause his spiritual dejection and refusal to fight.

If devotees do not progress, it is because they discard their weapons of self-control; a discouraged devotee often gives up all self-discipline when he does not attain spectacular achievements in the spiritual path. He refuses to meditate, avoids his spiritual instructor (teacher or lessons), and drifts into a mental dimness of spiritual indifference in which there is only an occasional glimmer of intuitive perception. This lackadaisical state of mind should be remedied by regular meditation and constant discrimination against the sense mind's false arguments. All is far from lost so long as the devotee thus strives to attune himself to the guidance and grace of the Divine Charioteer who, in the next chapter of the Gita, comes to the aid of the devotee.

ॐतत्सदिति श्रीमद्भगवद्गीतासूपनिषत्सु ब्रह्मविद्यायां योगशास्त्रे
श्रीकृष्णार्जुनसंवादेऽर्जुनविषादयोगो नाम प्रथमोऽध्यायः ॥

Aum, Tat, Sat.
In the Upanishad of the holy Bhagavad Gita—the discourse of Lord Krishna to Arjuna, which is the scripture of yoga and the science of God-realization—this is the first chapter, called "The Despondency of Arjuna on the Path of Yoga."

CHAPTER II

SANKHYA AND YOGA: COSMIC WISDOM AND THE METHOD OF ITS ATTAINMENT

❖

The Lord's Exhortation to the Devotee, and the Devotee's Plea for Guidance

❖

The Eternal, Transcendental Nature of the Soul

❖

The Righteous Battle Is Man's Religious Duty

❖

Yoga: Remedy for Doubt, Confusion, and Intellectual Dissatisfaction

❖

The Yoga Art of Right Action That Leads to Infinite Wisdom

❖

Qualities of the Self-realized

"With Arjuna basking in the illumining smile of Spirit and attuned to the inner Divine Voice, the sublime spiritual discourse of Bhagavan Krishna to Arjuna (the Lord to the devotee) begins fully to unfold—'The Song of Spirit' that in the 700 verses of the Gita encompasses the essence of the ponderous four Vedas, the 108 Upanishads, and the six systems of Hindu philosophy—a universal message for the solace and emancipation of all mankind."

SANKHYA AND YOGA: COSMIC WISDOM AND THE METHOD OF ITS ATTAINMENT

THE LORD'S EXHORTATION TO THE DEVOTEE, AND THE DEVOTEE'S PLEA FOR GUIDANCE

VERSE 1

सञ्जय उवाच
तं तथा कृपयाविष्टमश्रुपूर्णाकुलेक्षणम्।
विषीदन्तमिदं वाक्यमुवाच मधुसूदनः ॥

Sanjaya said to Dhritarashtra:
Madhusudana (Krishna) then addressed him whose eyes were bedimmed with tears, and who was overcome with pity and discouragement.

THE LORD, WHO IS THE DESTROYER of ignorance, now comes to the aid of the distraught devotee, Arjuna, whose tear-bedimmed eyes plead for consolation. These tears are not only from memories of sense enjoyments lost through intense spiritual discipline—and to be forever renounced—but are also the devotee's expression of grief for not having advanced far enough on the spiritual path to be showered with ecstatic bliss.

In this state, having gained happiness neither from the senses nor from meditation, the devotee weeps, "I gave up tangibles for intangibles; now I have nothing!" Of its very nature, the despondency is a longing for spiritual progress. If there were no such desire, there would be no regret over lost sense enjoyments, for they could be returned to instantly—their ready availability being indigenous to life itself. Therefore the first chapter of the Gita is referred to as

"Arjuna Vishada Yoga," or the sorrow involved in the devotee's initial effort to attain scientific union (yoga) with God.

The second chapter opens with a better outlook for the devotee. After the dismal state of being thrown into doubt and the inability to gain happiness either in the forsaken senses or in the state of meditation, the devotee suddenly feels a great inner sympathetic response. This development comes about as a result of one's past and present hard, steady work in meditation. Spirituality is generated slowly, sometimes imperceptibly. Even though the meditating devotee feels that his attempts at controlling the mind are fruitless, yet if he continues with zeal, believing in the words of his preceptor, he suddenly finds response from God, intimated through his long-silent meditation. A thrill passes through his entire being from this sudden ecstatic contact with the Divine (symbolized in this stanza as the response of Krishna).

God talks through the devotee's awakened intuition

SPIRIT DOES NOT NECESSARILY talk through the lips of a form in a vision, or a materialized human body, but may intimate words of wisdom through the medium of the devotee's awakened intuition. God may counsel a devotee by assuming the form of a saint, but usually He adopts the simple method of speaking through the devotee's own intuitive perception.

Mind and intelligence perceive and enjoy the five different kinds of material sense pleasures; when the sixth sense, intuition—the God-attuned all-knowing faculty of the soul—is suddenly awakened as a result of the spiritual meditating habit, the devotee feels a blissful exhilaration throughout his entire nervous system. His tears of despondency turn into tears of joy that shut out the vision of the external world and rivet the devotee's mind on an indescribable internal happiness of divine communion.

Thus far, the devotee's sense-enslaved mental faculties have been wandering in rationalization. Now, a calmness of spiritual surrender and receptive devotion settles over the distressed consciousness. Truth-revealing intuition—beyond thoughts, perceptions, and inference—expresses the inexpressible Spirit and soul and Their nature of supernal bliss. It silences the ego's strong mental assertions: false conviction under the influence of erroneous judgement; self-sufficiency; imagination; false hope; attachment to desires in expectation of fulfilment; conviction invaded by doubts—fallacy upon which the ego has built its existence and its obstinacy in persisting in these delusions. Intuition, the voice of Spirit and of Its immanent manifestation as the soul, begins an unfoldment of revelations that ultimately will quell all doubts and establish the consciousness in its true Self.

VERSE 2

श्रीभगवानुवाच
कुतस्त्वा कश्मलमिदं विषमे समुपस्थितम्।
अनार्यजुष्टमस्वर्ग्यमकीर्तिकरमर्जुन॥

The Blessed Lord said:
In such a critical moment, whence comes upon thee, O Arjuna, this despondency—behaviour improper for an Aryan, disgraceful, detrimental to the attainment of heaven?

HAVING FELT GOD'S RESPONSE, the devotee's consciousness soars to the transcendent *Kutastha* state, attunement to the *Kutastha Chaitanya* (the universal Krishna or Christ Consciousness), the presence of Spirit immanent in all creation and individually manifested in each being as the soul whose voice is intuition. Spirit speaks to the devotee through that intelligible intuitive voice:

"O devotee Arjuna, prince of self-control, why are you overcome by dejection? These relatives are your fierce enemies and have but one purpose—to destroy your soul's peace. To feel pity for them is un-Aryan* (not befitting a noble saint), a disgraceful treachery to the soul, a weakness that will tie you to the nether spheres of bodily limitation and deny you the heaven of blissful omnipresence."

Any sincere, persistent devotee can feel within in meditation the urgings of Spirit. But it is evident that the devotee must be far advanced in the path of meditation before he can prevail on the Infinite to vibrate Its presence through an intelligible voice of counsel. Such a devotee has already gone through a great many battles with the senses

---

* The Sanskrit root of the word *Aryan* is *ārya,* "worthy, holy, noble." The ancient name for India is Aryavarta, literally, "abode of the Aryans—the noble, holy, excellent ones." The later ethnological misuse of *Aryan* to signify not spiritual, but physical, characteristics, brought forth this remonstrance from the renowned Orientalist Max Müller: "To me an ethnologist who speaks of an Aryan race, Aryan blood, Aryan eyes and hair, is as great a sinner as a linguist would be if he spoke of a dolichocephalic dictionary or brachycephalic grammar."

and has attained a high spiritual state before being blessed to hear the voice of God made manifest through etheric vibration.

A devotee who has once reached that exalted state of consciousness might be supposed to be completely free from all attachment to his lower nature. However, owing to past incarnations of ignorant identification with the body, even an advanced devotee may temporarily lose sight of the divine state and consequently feel a miserable longing for the fulfilments he has renounced.

At this time, Spirit—ever conscious of the aspirant—comes to the rescue of the devotee, who then hears the Voice of God, pleading with him from within. Thus it is that this stanza describes Spirit, or Lord Krishna, talking to Arjuna, the true devotee—he who through self-control has procured God-communion.

God comes to the rescue of the faltering devotee

Speaking through the power of intuition, the Lord rebukes Arjuna for despondency. The Spirit points out to the aspiring yogi that the senses, through proximity, have established themselves as his relatives. But, as enemies can pose as friends and thus gain entry to one's home, so material desires, the great enemies of man, can reside, apparently harmlessly, within his consciousness along with his true friends, the spiritual faculties. The senses appear friendly because they promise a temporary intoxicating pleasure in the flesh, but in the end invariably bring misery.

The first effort of Spirit is to strike at the root of the devotee's momentary lapse. The pity Arjuna feels for his relatives—the devotee's sympathetic rationalization in favour of the senses—is the channel of exchange between the material and spiritual forces. The Spirit warns the devotee not to sorrow over the senses. To lower a drawbridge of pity over the moat that separates the wisdom-castled soul and the segregated inimical senses is to permit psychical enemies to break through the ramparts of self-control and overrun the fair inner kingdom. Instead of feeling pity, the devotee should rouse the ardour of psychological battle until every inordinate desire of the senses has been completely annihilated! To sympathize with evil is ultimately to hand over to it the throne of one's consciousness.

Do no evil, do not let evil be done through others by your command, and do not tolerate evil by silence. Noncooperation with evil is the best way—without making a pretentious display of your own goodness. A true devotee will not foolishly attract evil states unto himself through sympathy with them. He who feels sorrow for lost sense happiness, and who dares to sympathize with it, allots to a lower place the superior, lasting happiness he has known in meditation. Such an ignorant reversal of values is a disgraceful thought for a devotee.

Krishna thus refers to this weakness as "un-Aryan," an attitude unbecoming one of spiritual nobility. A wise man feels pity for the banished good qualities, not for the ostracized evil qualities.

MAN'S LIFE IS A PARADOX. He is the soul, made in the image of Spirit, which can be satisfied only with divine pleasures; yet bodily incarnate, he is familiar only with sensory experiences. Placed as he is between the material and the spiritual, he must use his endowment of discrimination to distinguish between the real soul pleasures and the illusory pleasures of the senses. Krishna says: "If you want to know the joy of heavenly consciousness vibrating in every cell of the ether, do away with sense attachment!"

"Heaven," in this stanza, consists of the limitless spheres of divine consciousness, as contrasted with the nether region of bodily limitation. Every soul that is imprisoned by the senses is an omnipresent child of heaven serving out a jail sentence of bodily existence.

When the soul is identified with Spirit, it feels itself as one with the Joy of limitless space; when the soul, as ego, limits itself to a particular body, it is pitiably "cabin'd, cribb'd, confin'd." The soul, identified with the body, loses its consciousness of omnipresence and becomes identified with the trials and misfortunes of a small ego.

As the ordinary man's consciousness dwells in the brain and heart, so God's consciousness dwells in the universe; as human consciousness is felt in every cell of the body, so God's intelligence dwells in every cell-unit of space. The devotee who is constantly responsive to bodily sense gratifications is unable to spread his consciousness into the space cells and thus share the vaster joys of the Space-Dweller, or Spirit. Dulled by material pleasures, man loses all fine sensitiveness to the rarefied joys of Spirit. Thirsting for physical enjoyment, circumscribed within the walls of the body, such a one fails to visualize the attainment of omnipresent heaven. If one loves the bodily prison, how can he attract the divine experience of living in the joy of God resplendent in every atom of space?

VERSE 3

क्लैब्यं मा स्म गमः पार्थ नैतत्त्वय्युपपद्यते ।
क्षुद्रं हृदयदौर्बल्यं त्यक्त्वोत्तिष्ठ परन्तप ॥

O Partha ("Son of Pritha," Arjuna), surrender not to unmanliness; it is unbecoming to thee. O Scorcher of Foes, forsake this small weakheartedness! Arise!

"O DEVOTEE, SON OF RENUNCIATION, surrender not to behaviour that is unbecoming to the positive nature of your true Self, the soul. O Scorcher of Foes, use your fiery will of self-control to overcome this frail weakheartedness resulting from your attachment to sense habits. Arise! Lift yourself from the sense strongholds to the higher spinal centres of divine consciousness."

By the devotee's continued meditation, divine guidance becomes more and more tangible; God manifests His presence to the devotee through a profound peace, joy, or wisdom felt in the thousands of sensory channels in the inner lining of the body and its encompassing cuticle. In this state, the advancing devotee is intuitively instructed by the Spirit as he hears, within, the voice of the Infinite.

In referring to Arjuna as Partha ("son of Pritha"), the Inner Voice is reminding the devotee-prince of his inherent power of renunciation that can save him from his present weakness if he but exerts his will.

Pritha was the beautiful, virtuous daughter of the great King Shura (grandfather of Krishna; Pritha's elder brother Vasudeva was Krishna's father). When she was a very young girl, Pritha was given in adoption to Kuntibhoja, Shura's childless cousin and close friend. Because of her willingness to leave her own father to fill the emptiness of the home of her foster father, Pritha metaphorically signifies the power of renunciative will of the devotee. When she became the child of Kuntibhoja, Pritha was thereafter called Kunti, the excellent heroine of the *Mahabharata,* mother of the noble Pandu princes Yudhisthira, Bhima, and Arjuna, and stepmother of Nakula and Sahadeva—all sired as a result of Kunti's power to invoke the gods. Thus, spiritually interpreted, Pritha-become-Kunti signifies the devotee's power to invoke divinity gained through dispassion, or renunciative will.

❖
"Partha": the power of renouncing all that is contrary to the nature of the soul
❖

Every man has the power to resist the influence of his sense-identified, habit-bound existence. This power of renunciation does not involve any loss to the devotee, but gives him opportunity to remove and forsake all those things that retard his spiritual progress. As Pritha renounced a noble father in response to fulfilling a higher duty, so the devotee does not hesitate to reject the guidance of his dearest bad habits that display a fatherly interest in subjugating his will.

The Inner Voice says: "Forsake attachment to the senses! Use the power of renunciation to relinquish all unmanly qualities! Do nothing that goes against the grain of the soul!"

"Unmanliness" signifies that which is unbecoming to the positive aspect of the soul. To be unmanly is to be either negative or indifferent.* The devotee in a negative state of mind has lost sight of his manly, positive will factor. Without the positive action of will, the devotee succumbs to unmanly neutrality, the condition that has overtaken Arjuna. The Spirit therefore warns him not to be neutral; that state is worse than negativeness! In the negative state the devotee is afraid to forsake sense attachment; in the neutral state he has attachment neither to God nor to the senses—his entire powers of activity are paralysed.

It requires some mental activity even to entertain negative thoughts, but in neutrality of mind the devotee becomes incapable of any activity, good or bad. The Spirit warns him about falling into such a state of inertia, wherein the desire for good or evil uniformly vanishes.

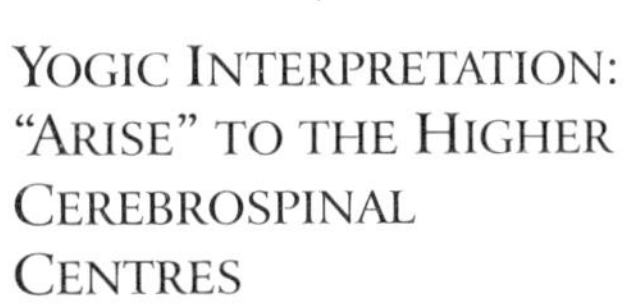

Yogic Interpretation: "Arise" to the Higher Cerebrospinal Centres

The encouraging Inner Voice intuitionally urges the devotee: "O thou scorcher of sense foes, with thy fiery will, arise—lift thyself from the lower planes where sense attachments dwell, up to the higher seats of consciousness in the spine."

The word *arise* is well chosen. With this command, taken literally, Krishna seeks to rouse Arjuna to positive dutiful action befitting his true soul nature. The key to the deeper spiritual implication is in the epithet *scorcher of foes,* reference to Arjuna as symbolizing the power of the fire element in the lumbar centre, or *manipura chakra*.† Life energy and consciousness flowing downward and outward from this *chakra* energize the two lower centres; these three centres then become associated with all sentient body consciousness. When instead, by the power of Arjuna or self-control in the lumbar centre, the fire energy is turned upward, concentrating life and consciousness in the higher centres, the whole being becomes spiritualized.

Though all sensations are felt in the brain, they appear to be localized in certain points on or within the skin-covering of the body. The entire skin surface possesses various kinds of sensitiveness; taste

---

* See also commentary and note on I:27, page 140. *(Publisher's Note)*

† See I:4–6, page 66.

is perceived by the mouth, sound through the eardrums, touch with the skin, sight through the eyes, and smell by the nostrils.

The materialistic man identifies his consciousness with these outer sensibilities. The devotee does away with "living on the skin surface"; he is tired of gambling with sense pleasures! He withdraws his consciousness from the coccygeal, sacral, and lumbar plexuses, which control the lower sense inclinations, into the dorsal and cervical centres, or roams even further, into the high Christ centre.

The dorsal is the divine-love and life-energy-control centre; the cervical is the oceanic vibratory and divine-calmness centre; the Krishna, or Christ, Centre (the *Kutastha,* at the point between the eyebrows) is a focus for the *Kutastha Chaitanya* or Christ Consciousness, which is the Intelligence—the reflection of Spirit—within every atom of creation and circumambient space.

A man who is mentally negative, or neutral, or identified with sex thoughts or other sensory preoccupations, finds his consciousness operating outwardly through the three lower centres of the spine. He is said to be "living on the skin surface" because his consciousness is bounded by the periphery of his own small body.

Whenever anyone feels divine love or spiritual vitality, his consciousness has reached the dorsal centre. During the contact of the cosmic vibratory energy and cosmic calmness, the devotee roams in the cervical region. An experience of the ever new bliss felt in meditation means that the devotee is functioning in the *Kutastha*-Christ Centre.

The mind of Arjuna had been wandering in the delusion-localized sense centres on the skin surface; Spirit, felt as the ever new bliss of meditation, is therefore sending him an intuitive call: "O devotee, do not wander lost in the garden of the sense sirens! They promise a little honey of pleasure in the beginning, but are poisoned with unending sorrow! Come back to the Castle of Inner Perception in the higher spiritual centres, where joys are pure and inexhaustible!"

❖

Without yoga meditation, there is little hope of overcoming the lower nature

❖

Without deep yoga meditation, in which the devotee trains the mind and life force to remain concentrated in the higher spiritual centres of expression, there is little hope of the sensory self-control necessary to overcome the bad habits that constitute one's lower nature.*

* "We know that man is usually helpless against evil passions; but these are rendered powerless and man finds no motive for indulging in them when there dawns on him a

Habits, according to psychologists, are both mental and physiological. To conquer temptation, the devotee must not only drive evil from the mind, but should also withdraw his mind—by training it through self-control in meditation—from those sense centres on the outer surface of the body which give rise to mental temptations.

Physiological sense habits, with mental cooperation, become mental habits. Mental habits solidify into physiological habits; bad habits must therefore be driven from the senses as well as from the mind. Think no evil, and come in contact with nothing that can give rise to thoughts of evil.

VERSE 4

अर्जुन उवाच
कथं भीष्ममहं सङ्ख्ये द्रोणं च मधुसूदन।
इषुभिः प्रतियोत्स्यामि पूजार्हावरिसूदन॥

Arjuna said:

O Slayer of Madhu, O Destroyer of Foes (Krishna)! how can I, in this war, direct arrows against Bhishma and Drona—beings who should be worshipped!

THE RATIONALIZING THOUGHTS of Self-Control responded to the inner voice of Intuition: "O Slayer of the Demon of Ignorance and of Inner Temptations! how can I, in this psychological war, loose the arrows of my determination against my psychological grandparent Bhishma–Ego and my preceptor Drona–Past Habits? These are venerable mentor-tendencies, originators of my present mental states! How frightful to destroy them by spiritual renunciation and by the arrows of yoga meditation!"

As previously cited, the various characters mentioned in the Bhagavad Gita symbolize the different psychological states with which a devotee is identified. When the devotee is identified with the restless mind, he is spoken of as being in the desireful "Duryodhana state,"

---

consciousness of superior and lasting bliss through *Kriya Yoga*. Here the give-up, the negation of the lower nature, synchronizes with a take-up, the experience of beatitude. Without such a course, moral maxims that embody mere negatives are useless to us." —Sri Ananda Mohan Lahiri, grandson of Lahiri Mahasaya, in *Autobiography of a Yogi*

very difficult to control. The state in which the devotee is concentrated on the human instincts and the prenatal tendencies (*samskaras*) born of past-life habits is said to be the "Drona state." When the devotee forgets his true soul nature and is identified with all the circumscriptions of the mortal body, then he is in the ego or "Bhishma state."

The devotee's reluctance to destroy habits and ego

During meditation, when the life force and the mind are withdrawn internally, this partially interiorized state of Self-realization is spoken of as the "Arjuna state," or state of self-control.

As the yogi withdraws his mind within, and his sixth sense, intuition, begins to develop, he finds himself pulled toward the vastness of his soul. He gradually loses sight of all mental and physical boundaries. At this time, the devotee feels a certain fear, like a person on his first airplane flight, when he has left behind customary landmarks and is soaring into a wall-less ether.

When he has only half-climbed the spinal centres of inner perception (the Arjuna state of self-control being in the third or lumbar centre), he is afraid to look at the roofless Infinity toward which he appears to be headed. He loses sight of his physical ego-consciousness. This does not signify the loss of consciousness, but only the forgetting of the confinements of the human ego. Discovering this illimitability, the devotee begins to be fearful of losing all human traits. This state signifies the killing of Bhishma, the venerable psychological relative, the Ego, or grandfather of all mental tendencies.

In this inner meditative state, the devotee also finds himself rising above all habitual instincts and tendencies, no longer seeking mundane happiness. This state signifies the killing of "Drona."

In this stanza the meditating devotee is described as being filled with the memory of the vanishing ego and of those habits and instincts that have become so "natural" to him. He is reluctant to use the darts of his inwardly retiring life force (through *pranayama*) and of his controlled mind (through *pratyahara*) to destroy his association with his ego and his so-called pleasurable sense habits and inner tendencies in order to gain the native but deeply profound pleasures of soul expansion.

To take the mind from the senses by meditation means the devotee must involve his self-control in a psychological war in which the retiring life force and concentration act as arrows to destroy the venerable, ignorantly worshipped physical ego and the inner habitual tendencies that keep man in a state of delusion.

Verse 5

गुरूनहत्वा हि महानुभावान् श्रेयो भोक्तुं भैक्ष्यमपीह लोके।
हत्वार्थकामांस्तु गुरूनिहैव भुञ्जीय भोगान् रुधिरप्रदिग्धान्॥

Even a life of beggary would be more salutary for me than a life marred by slaying my high-souled preceptors! If I do destroy these mentors who are intent on wealth and possessions (the objects of the senses), then surely here on earth all my would-be enjoyment of material happiness will be dreadfully bloodstained!

"I WOULD FEEL BETTER as a conscience-free beggar than as a king who has destroyed his preceptors, Ego and Prenatal Habit-instincts! If I annihilate these chief inmates of my mental kingdom, then for the remainder of my life whatever wealth of glory, sense comforts, and fulfilled desires I have will be 'blood-stained'—I shall see them as permeated with evil vibrations that will repulse me from any enjoyment of my hard-won psychological and spiritual victory. It would therefore be better to live by begging pleasure from the senses than for the sake of an otherworldly spiritual kingdom to destroy my lifelong masters—Ego and Past Habits, who have guided and shaped my destiny throughout incarnations."

In ordinary consciousness, the ego is the guiding principle of thoughts, feelings, and aspirations; it moulds desires and ambitions according to the influence of habits. The ego and the bodily habits are thus the preceptors of all human activities.

Why egoistic habits are so tenacious

THIS STANZA POINTS OUT the persistent power of the ego-habit delusion that assails the advancing devotee. At this stage he is still reiterating, as in previous stanzas, his fear that a spiritual victory will mean a desolate existence. Without ego and habit-inclinations—the guardian stimulators, preceptors, and counsellors of his mental tendencies—will he then, for the remainder of his life, look upon all material things and sensory experiences as being permeated with evil vibrations ("bloodstained") in contradistinction to his victorious soul-state?

The answer, of course, is *no*. Evil lies only in the misuse of the powers and products of nature. The senses touched by the bliss of the soul will spiritualize their perceptions; the enjoyments of the "wealth" of possessions will be unsullied by attachments; the inclinations, habit-free, will seek fulfilment in the noblest achievements. But even though the devotee knows this as a promise in the scriptures and from the lips of God-knowing souls, his attachment to the influences of the Ego-Habit stubbornly persists, woven as it is into the very fibre of human nature.

All bad habits, and their enjoyer, the ego, are very tenacious and monopolizing in their claims on human beings. No matter how pernicious in its effect a habit is, it is hard to remove because of the ego's attachment to it. When a person sincerely tries repeatedly to get rid of a bad habit and does not succeed, he becomes despondent and cannot summon up courageous thoughts. Bad habits almost paralyse the will. The victim helplessly thinks: "What is the use of trying?"

Mental slavery to a sense habit is the result of continued repetition of the specific act that gives birth to a particular habit. By attentively thinking about a certain thing every day, an individual makes that thing a part of his consciousness. When a habit becomes an integral facet of one's thought, it becomes "second nature." This "second nature" is so powerful it convinces one that he can never get rid of his own "nature," even if in exchange he were to receive a whole world of superior satisfaction.

How many people are convinced that they cannot sacrifice even a little sleep to attain the high bliss of meditation. Some think that they could never give up living on the sex plane, even if they received in exchange the ever new joy of Eternal God. Others are sure they could never give up one iota of attachment to family, friends, fame, or any portion of material success in order to acquire divine bliss. Because most people have no true basis of comparison, they cannot separate sense pleasures from their conception of soul pleasures. Continuously catering to sense demands, they thus involve themselves in ever-growing dissatisfactions, disillusionments, and suffocating inner afflictions.

Only when one pleasure after another fails him does man finally begin to wonder if, after all, happiness is possible through the senses. This thought has a liberating effect: man tries to find joy in meditation, in silence, in wisdom, in service, in contentment, and in self-control. He forsakes the old restless pursuit of desires, with their concomitant noisy actions, ignorant behaviour, and sense slavery. When a man discovers that sense joys are not a synonym for human happiness, he then sincerely wishes to get rid of his parasitical senses, his so-called "relatives," who apparently offer him solace and sympathy and yet continually practise deception.

Then also, Madhava (Krishna) and Pandava (Arjuna), seated in their grand chariot with its yoke of white horses, splendidly blew their celestial conch shells.

—Bhagavad Gita I:14

❖

"Arjuna, seated in the chariot of meditative intuition, with his attention focused on the Spirit as Krishna or divine Christ Consciousness at the Kutastha centre between the eyebrows, beholds the light of the spiritual eye and hears the sacred sound of Pranava, the creative Aum vibration with its different cosmic sounds ["conch shells"] vibrating from the spinal centres in the astral body....

"Behold the chariot of intuition drawn by stallions of white lights racing in all directions from a dark blue centre (soul's abode)!...

"Surrounding this blue light is the brilliant white or golden light—the telescopic astral eye through which all Nature is perceived. In the centre of the blue light is a white starlike light, doorway to the Infinite Spirit, or Cosmic Consciousness."

"Pranava, the sound of the creative Aum vibration, is the mother of all sounds. The intelligent cosmic energy of Aum that issues forth from God, and is the manifestation of God, is the creator and substance of all matter. This holy vibration is the link between matter and Spirit. Meditation on Aum is the way to realize the true Spirit-essence of all creation. By inwardly following the sound of Pranava to its source, the yogi's consciousness is carried aloft to God."

—Paramahansa Yogananda

THE DETERMINED YOGI, imploring the aid of divine guidance, begins to disentangle himself from the ego-habit cords of his "second nature" by learning to differentiate clearly between body and soul, which is Self and not Self; and why, metaphysically, sense pleasures are not considered pleasures at all, since they produce only the illusion of happiness and ultimately end in sorrow.

Understanding the true nature of sensory pleasures

Sense delights, in reality, are felt as pleasurable only through an act of imagination by the soul, created by the interaction of the sense mind with the objects of the senses. Man can be truly happy only within his soul nature of bliss, omniscience, and wisdom. He can never be contented by imagining himself to be happy because the senses are happy.

A mother, for example, might be able to resist the sensation of hunger during a food shortage in a besieged city by saying: "I am happy if my starving child eats." If, however, she continues to go without food, she finds that her hunger is being satisfied only in fancy and not in reality. Sense identification, similarly, is very delusive; it makes man believe, only in mind and imagination, that he is contented with sense indulgences.

Therefore it is important to understand why sense pleasures are not true pleasures, and why soul pleasures are real happiness.

First of all, the sensations of beauty, melody, fragrance, taste, and touch are not experienced on the skin surface, but in the brain. The sensation of the taste of a strawberry is felt in the brain as a mental reaction, evolving from the contact of the fruit with the surface of the tongue. When the mind identifies favourably with the sensation of strawberry flavour, it likes it. However, the taste of strawberries was at first very unpleasant to me; I had to acquire a taste for them, and now I like them—my mind was influenced by seeing how much Americans enjoy them. Therefore, no one can say generally that strawberry flavour is pleasing. Everyone agrees, though, that sensations produced by burning or physical blows cause uncomfortable feelings and thoughts in the body and brain, and therefore are called painful sensations. Other sensations that are not necessarily painful are not necessarily pleasurable either. By mental training, the so-called most pleasurable sensations can be made very repulsive to the mind; and, conversely, the most unpleasant, or even painful, sensations can be made pleasurable. Thus the need for soul discrimination, rather than ego-habit, in guiding the blind mind in its contact with objects of sense.

Much of man's suffering in this world is caused by his inability to discriminate between good sensations and bad ones. Any sensation of the body whose ultimate effect on the consciousness is suffering, remote or immediate, must be termed bad. Any sensation that impresses on the consciousness lasting peace is good. A sensation may cause initial displeasure, but may carry with it an ensuing consciousness of peace; or a sensation may produce momentary satisfaction, and thus wrongly be thought to be good, while the lasting effect will be suffering. Whether a sensation is good or bad cannot be judged solely from the thoughts and feelings that flow immediately from its contact. Only by careful and patient discrimination and watchfulness can the true nature of a sensation be clearly detected. Therefore it is prudent to follow the guidance of the spiritually wise, or to wait and find out through one's own deeper powers, as to whether the first impression of a sensation is lasting or temporary, sincere or hypocritical, in its behaviour. It is very difficult to distinguish between good and bad, friendly and unfriendly, sensations, because both use disguises. Out of ignorance, people accept the first impressions that a good or bad sensation presents to them. Thus they welcome and desire to repeat "pleasant" sensations and try to reject "unpleasant" ones, regardless of the immediate or long-term end result. Once repetition of an action or mental concept allows the law of habit to take hold, the mind becomes greatly prejudiced in its judgement as to what is good or bad.

The need for soul discrimination in guiding the blind mind in its contact with objects of sense

All sensations that are harmonious to our sense organs and are favourably interpreted by the mind as soothing or pleasurable are given ready shelter by their mental host. But no sensation of sight, sound, touch, smell, or taste should be luring or enthralling enough to enslave the mind. It is when the mind becomes attached to a sensation that it develops a correspondingly pleasing idea in the brain. This pleasant idea about a sensation causes an individual to repeat his experiences with that sensation. When a sensation is constantly repeated, it causes a repetition of its corresponding pleasing idea. This liking-idea becomes "grooved" in the brain and fixed in the mind as a mental habit. This mental habit—formed by repeating a pleasing idea that evolved from a sensation—is what causes the attractiveness of sensations. Just as everybody is more or less in love with his own ideas about things, whether they are right or not, so also, the mind likes its own personal collection of mental sense habits.

The mind can contact sensations only through thoughts. In the ultimate analysis, sensations are nothing but relatively different thoughts about God-thought things. The dream state is the best analogy. The enjoyment of encountering the sensation of ice cream in a dream is nothing but an idea that is pleasurably enjoyed by another idea: The idea taste of ice cream is reacted upon by another idea of pleasurably enjoying it. The consumer of ice cream, the mental reaction, the sensations accruing from the consciousness of a dream mouth and palate tasting the ice cream, and the resulting pleasure are all made of nothing but relative ideas. Hence, it cannot be assumed that the sensation of ice cream in dreamland is pleasurable, except that it is an idea that is liked by another idea.

One lesson that God tries to teach us through the experience of dreams is that we should recognize the dream nature of this seemingly real world. All sensation-producing objects are materialized ideas of God, which create the ideas of pleasure or pain in our minds. We should stop being fooled into thinking that the sensations of touch, smell, taste, sound, and sight have pleasure in themselves. There is no enjoyment in sensations except as we react favourably and pleasurably toward them.

The soul, the individualized image of Spirit, is not imposed upon by these ideas or sensations, as is the mind. The soul is self-born, with inherent bliss-producing qualities. Contentment, ever new joy, omniscience, omnipotence, and omnipresence are not acquired qualities, but are an integral part of the soul. Hence, the devotee who is engrossed in these soul qualities is enjoying real lasting happiness belonging to his own true Self.

As there is a difference between the self-born contentment of one's mind and the happiness issuing from the external stimulus of beholding a long-lost dear friend, so also, the bliss of meditation is self-born, whereas the ego's enjoyment of a sensation is due to identification with the bodily senses.

To take the mind from the senses by meditation is to destroy the physical ego and habit tendencies, the venerated patriarchs of the state of delusive ignorance, in order to regain the true joy self-born in the soul.*

---

* "Through meditation,...you can set the stage for important mind- and habit-altering brain change." Herbert Benson, M.D., Professor of Medicine at Harvard Medical School, thus summarizes the results of his extensive research reported in *Your Maximum Mind* (New York: Random House, 1987).

"Over the years," he writes, "you develop 'circuits' and 'channels' of thought in your brain. These are physical pathways which control the way you think, the way you act, and often, the way you feel. Many times, these pathways or habits become so fixed

VERSE 6

न चैतद्विद्मः कतरन्नो गरीयो यद्वा जयेम यदि वा नो जयेयुः ।
यानेव हत्वा न जिजीविषामस्तेऽवस्थिताः प्रमुखे धार्तराष्ट्राः ॥

I can hardly decide which end would be better—that they should conquer us? or that we should conquer them? Confronting us are Dhritarashtra's children—the very ones whose death would make our life undesirable!

THE DEVOTEE THINKS: "I do not know the right standard for decision—is it better for the sake of my happiness to surrender to the senses? or to conquer them by soul discrimination? Destroying the desire-children of the mind will leave nothing to live for."

Worldly people decry sense renunciation as a method of torture—

---

that they turn into what I call 'wiring.' In other words, the circuits or channels become so deeply ingrained that it seems almost impossible to transform them."

There are approximately 100 billion nerve cells in the brain; and each of these communicates with the others through connections called synapses. The total number of possible connections is 25,000,000,000,000,000,000,000,000,000,000, Dr. Benson estimates. Put another way, if you made a stack of sheets of standard typing paper, with one sheet for each neuron connection, the resulting pile of paper would be approximately 16 billion light years high—stretching beyond the limits of the known universe. And according to another renowned brain researcher, Robert Ornstein, M.D., of the University of California, San Francisco, the number of possible connections in the brain is greater than the number of atoms in the universe. Therefore, Dr. Benson believes, the brain's potential for forming new pathways—and thus new habits of thought and behaviour—seems to be practically unlimited.

"It's largely the established circuits of the left side of our brain that are telling us, 'You can't change your way of living....Your bad habits are forever....You're just made in a certain way, and you have to live with that fact.' That simply is not true."

"Scientific research has shown that electrical activity between the left and right sides of the brain becomes coordinated during certain kinds of meditation or prayer," he explains. "Through these processes, the mind definitely becomes more capable of being altered and having its capacities maximized....When you are in this state of enhanced left-right hemispheric communication...'plasticity of cognition' occurs, in which you actually change the way you view the world....If you focus or concentrate on some sort of written passage which represents the direction in which you wish your life to be heading, [this] more directed thought process will help you to rewire the circuits in your brain in more positive directions....When we change our patterns of thinking and acting, the brain cells begin to establish additional connections, or new 'wirings.' These new connections then communicate in fresh ways with other cells, and before long, the pathways or wirings that kept the phobia or other habit alive are replaced or altered....Changed actions and a changed life will follow. The implications are exciting and even staggering." *(Publisher's Note)*

not realizing that their sense slavery is excruciating to the soul qualities! Even the resolute devotee questing for soul joy wearies now and then of the requisite constant self-discipline. But disciplining the senses is essential for well-being in every stratum of life. As servants of the soul, the senses should be trained always to please it. When the wisdom of the soul is overpowered by the vagaries of the impulse-directed, habit-blinded senses, the result of this anarchy is misery.

Though the senses in unison cry: "Please us, and never mind the soul!" man nevertheless finds himself unable to satisfy their ever-increasing demands. The sense consciousness, active from birth in human beings, early establishes its dominion. Even to the advancing devotee, soul happiness seems exotic, while sense joys appear familiar, indigenous. But behind the clamour of the senses lie the silent calls of the bliss-demanding soul. The law is: The greater the false sense happiness, the weaker the soul happiness.

The life energy that flows outwardly in the nerves to the five senses makes sensory experiences attractive to man. When he is asked by his guru to reverse that flow of life energy and to withdraw his mind and energy from the senses, that instruction appears to be bizarre, impractical—and perhaps even irrational! Man moans: "Oh, what is the use of living at all, if I have to deny myself the tangible joys of sense indulgences?"

Only a sense slave finds it torture to eat moderately, to control the sex urges, to abstain from intoxicants. Even a well-balanced worldly man, not to mention a saint, knows from practical experience how necessary for well-being is a discipline of the senses. The sense slave eats to satisfy his palate and ultimately finds himself the victim of disease. The soul urges man to discipline the palate; after a short period of demonstrations of outraged dignity, the palate gives no further trouble! Like a good servant, the sense of taste learns to be satisfied with the wholesome decisions of its master, the soul.

The senses disregard the bliss of the soul and try to be happy by making the soul miserable. The soul, on the other hand, does not seek to torture the senses, but to relegate them to their true station of man's servant, not master.

VERSE 7

कार्पण्यदोषोपहतस्वभावः पृच्छामि त्वां धर्मसम्मूढचेताः ।
यच्छ्रेयः स्यान्निश्चितं ब्रूहि तन्मे शिष्यस्तेऽहं शाधि मां त्वां प्रपन्नम् ॥

With my inner nature overshadowed by weak sympathy and pity, with a mind in bewilderment about duty, I implore Thee to advise me what is the best path for me to follow. I am Thy disciple. Teach me, whose refuge is in Thee.

"WEAK THOUGHTS OF COMMISERATION with the senses have so overpowered my real nature that I do not know whether my duty lies in leading a self-controlled existence by destroying my sense kinsmen, or in making the senses happy. I implore the Spirit within me to tell me decisively, a duty-confused individual, what is for my highest good. O Lord! I am Thy *shishya* (disciple), taking refuge in Thee!"

The devotee, after egotistically pleading the cause of the senses, at last is filled with remorse and acknowledges his ineptitude. He prostrates himself in humble surrender before his inner Self (or before his guru-preceptor, if he has one), thus demonstrating both his need and his sincere desire for divine guidance. The devotee feels that although he is naturally drawn to his sense relatives, still he is intuitively devoted to the glimpses of soul peace he has felt during deep meditation.

Sometimes clinging to the memories of sense comforts and sometimes inclining toward the soul's bliss, he reaches the supreme act of renouncing faulty self-determination in favour of impeccable wisdom. In this state the devotee becomes open or receptive to his Inner Self and to his spiritual guide on earth, the first stage of obedience to higher principles. By tuning in to the instruction of the Invisible Spirit within (through the intuition of the soul) and by following faithfully the advice of his guru, the devotee can get out of his mental entanglements.

The purpose and value of a true guru

IN THE PRIMARY STATE OF MEDITATION, the voice of Inner Silence lacks clarity; hence the advice of a spiritual guru is highly desirable. He gives the disciple a *sadhana,* those guideposts and practices by which the devotee is led unerringly. The devotee should listen eagerly to the guru, learning from him the deep truths of soul development. It is easy to misinterpret the Inner Voice or to act against it, but no such excuse exists for not heeding the definite counsel and warnings of a true guru.

Even in hermitage life many spiritual novices are tormented with inner weakness and mental doubts. They undergo a sort of psychological tug-of-war between good and evil. Evil may seem alluring, and good dryly unattractive. At this time, the doubt-inflicted student throws himself at the feet of his preceptor and says: "Master, I don't know the way. You, who know, must instruct me, your disciple."

The advanced devotee who has a penitent, all-surrendering attitude toward God, and who meditates deeply and persistently, will gradually, intuitively feel response from the Inner Silence.

So long as egoism puffs up the devotee, he may cultivate a false pride in his own strength. "I myself will gain heaven!" he may think. "I will enslave God Himself by my meditation!"

To the proud the highest spiritual realization does not accrue. Only in the valley of inner humbleness do the floods of divine mercy come and remain.

In India the masters teach only extremely willing, self-surrendering disciples. There is no coddling or coaxing of "church members"—no lack of administering discipline when discipline is necessary! The true master does not have an eye on his disciples' wealth; therefore he talks freely for their good, and is not afraid of their "leaving" if admonished.

So this stanza of the Gita illustrates how the bewildered, doubt-drenched devotee must humbly take refuge in the uncompromising advice of the Inner Self and of his guru-preceptor.

VERSE 8

न हि प्रपश्यामि ममापनुद्याद् यच्छोकमुच्छोषणमिन्द्रियाणाम्।
अवाप्य भूमावसपत्नमृद्धंराज्यं सुराणामपि चाधिपत्यम्॥

I behold nothing that will do away with this inner affliction that pounds my senses—nothing! not even my possession of an unrivalled and prosperous kingship over this earth and lordship over the deities of heaven!

"I AM UNABLE TO SEE ANYTHING in my spiritual vision by which I can become free of this haunting mental affliction of attachment to sense pleasure; it pounds away at the sense organs and stimulates them to incessant activity. I feel that even if I gained a prosperous and adversary-free kingship over this earth (the body) and mastery of the inherent subtle forces of life (the 'deities,' or heavenly astral powers that enliven the body), still I would not get rid of attachment to the senses, and could not without devastating sorrow even think of relinquishing their pleasures."

In the previous stanza, the devotee expressed his desire and need for divine guidance. He continues by emphasizing his feeling of being hopelessly bound by attachment to the senses, seeing no way to be free of them. He is saying, in effect, "It cannot be done! Even if I possess a bodily kingdom that has no enemies and is prosperous with health and well-being, I will still be attached to the senses; for without them, such a 'perfect' kingdom would be virtually inanimate, devoid of both perception and expression. As long as I dwell in the body, I would have to communicate and experience through the senses. I would thereby continue to be dependent on them, and thus to enjoy the pleasure they give. Why, then, do I have to engage in a battle against these, my dear supportive relations and friends?"

THE "EARTH" STANDS for the perishable body; its "prosperity" is health, well-being, and happiness as a result of freedom from its basic threefold troubles. These three evils or inner rivals of the welfare of the bodily kingdom are as follows:

(1) Impaired inner subtle life-forces, causing bodily ravages and disturbances in the form of colds and disorders of body heat, respiration, and pancreatic action (digestion).

(2) Bad karma, or the influences of past wrong actions. Unless these seeds of action lodged in the brain are roasted by the fire of wisdom, it is difficult to reap the desired fruits of newly initiated action. For example, if one has a karmic tendency toward physical weakness, carried over from a past life in which he disobeyed health laws, and he strives for health in this life, he may not get enough results from his present actions to bring about a healthy condition, unless he also destroys the prenatal karmic seeds of ill-health tendencies.

Threefold deliverance from bodily adversities

(3) *Samskaras* of bodily identification and sense attachment—compelling inclinations of past habits of the delusion of bodily limitation, and of evil tendencies of sense attachment that create insa-

tiable desires which burn out the bodily instruments, destroy peace, and give untold misery to the soul.

Threefold deliverance from these bodily adversaries means freeing the body from disease, from susceptibility to the irritations of the universal opposites—heat and cold and so forth—and from the devastation of old age; conditioning the mind to hold to the consciousness of health and other perfect attributes of the soul, thus making the body feel an all-accomplishing, ever-growing vigour of mental youthfulness; and liberating the body from slavery to the *samskaras* of bodily limitations and sense attachments, and from the consciousness of death by beholding the corporeal form as a dream of God, a shadow of the indwelling immortal Self, the soul.

When the body is purged of the threefold disturbances, it is spoken of as "free from rivals," or enemies. This desirable state is attained only by practising the eightfold yoga (embodying the prescriptions and proscriptions of self-discipline; posture; mastery of the life energy or *pranayama;* mental interiorization; concentration and meditation; and ecstasy).

Through yoga, the body becomes ripe with wisdom and spiritual power, and invulnerable to physical maladies through the yogi's control over atomic vibrations, acquired by contacting in meditation the cosmic vibration of *Aum,* the source of all powers of life. This state is known as "gaining spiritual prosperity on earth."

This stanza depicts the depth of material attachment in which the devotee is sunk, even to the extent of being ready to abandon the efforts that would assure him a wisdom-permeated, disease-free body. Preferring sense-instigated actions in seeking health and well-being, he ignores the wisdom of acquiring the power to control the bodily atoms and life itself, a power by which man may understand the body to be a dream shadow of the ever-perfect deathless soul.

In the mentally depraved state, the devotee inclines toward his love for sense pleasures to such a degree that he is willing to forgo even the idea of attainment of divine bliss. When a good thing is abhorred and an evil thing is craved, the man possessing such thoughts is in a dangerous state; he is quite likely to plunge into material indulgences, oblivious to all liberating aspirations. Unless this state is quickly removed by deeper meditation, the devotee is sure to fall from grace and to lose himself in delusion.

VERSE 9

सञ्जय उवाच
एवमुक्त्वा हृषीकेशं गुडाकेशः परन्तपः।
न योत्स्य इति गोविन्दमुक्त्वा तूष्णीं बभूव ह॥

Sanjaya said to Dhritarashtra:
Having thus addressed Hrishikesha (Krishna), Gudakesha-Parantapa (Arjuna) declared to Govinda (Krishna): "I will not fight!"; then remained silent.*

THIS STANZA REVEALS a peculiar psychological state in which the devotee is sufficiently developed to behold Spirit as the Lord of the Senses, and is far enough advanced to be spoken of as the "Conqueror of Ignorance" and "the Tormentor of the Sense Enemies through the Fire of Self-Control"—yet has not attained an unshakeable determination to subdue the senses. He remains mentally inactive, neither advancing spiritually nor going backward.

All these experiences are revealed by introspection (Sanjaya) to the sense-inclined, wisdom-blind mind (Dhritarashtra). When the devotee becomes spiritually blind, the sense-bent mind is delighted, expecting an easy recapture of the devotee from the soldiers of self-control. But introspection also reveals to the prematurely rejoicing blind mind that the fall of the devotee may be only temporary. Introspective discrimination reminds the blind mind that, though the devotee remains inactive at present, undecided as to whether or not he will meditate, yet he has already proven himself to be a potential "conqueror of ignorance" and a habitual "scorcher of the senses by the fire of self-control."

In this stage the devotee beholds the glory of the Spirit as the Sustainer of the body, the senses, and the cosmos; yet, owing to the subconscious pull of bad habits, he is not fully awakened for action. The devotee realizes that he is a conqueror of ignorance and has the ability to destroy with self-control† his sense inclinations—yet he feels pity for his once-dear habits, which turned into enemies when he became spiritually inclined. Unable to decide, and finding the pull between virtue and vice of equal strength, he remains without further

* Hrishikesha: "Lord of the Senses"; Gudakesha-Parantapa: "the Conqueror of Sleep and the Scorcher of Enemies."

† See also reference to *samyama,* self-mastery in meditation, I:4–6 page 77.

efforts at meditating, inwardly saying: "O God of the Universe! I will not go through the pitiable task of this slaughter!"

VERSE 10

तमुवाच हृषीकेशः प्रहसन्निव भारत।
सेनयोरुभयोर्मध्ये विषीदन्तमिदं वचः ॥

O Bharata (Dhritarashtra), to him who was lamenting between the two armies, the Lord of the Senses (Krishna), as if smiling, spoke in the following way:

THE ADVANCED DEVOTEE—who has found himself in an uncompromisable position between the sense soldiers of the ego and the discriminative warriors of the soul, who is lamenting the necessity for renouncing sense habits, and who has therefore become indecisively inactive, surrendering himself passively to the Infinite—beholds the Spirit, come to dispel the gloom of doubt with the gentle light of His smile and His voice of wisdom heard through intuition.

Those devotees who, during the invasion of doubt, completely give themselves up to Spirit in inner silence and submission are able to perceive the indescribable, all-purifying Light of God playing across the firmament of their inner perception. When the mind remains neutral while beholding the two opposing armies of self-control and sense temptation, it feels sad and discouraged; but that devotee who offers absolute resignation to the Divine Will hears the voice of Spirit speak to him through the wondrously strange whispers of his intuition.

Only devotees who have led a clean spiritual life (proper eating, right behaviour, and deep meditation), and have thus attained advancement, are fortunate enough to behold the "smile" of Spirit and to hear His voice of wisdom. Even though such a devotee is temporarily not advancing, if he surrenders completely to God, and lifts his consciousness from the senses and focuses it at the *Kutastha* (Krishna or Christ centre), he will hear the instructive etheric vibrations of Spirit—the secret sounds of emancipating vibrations. In the elevated state of Krishna or Christ consciousness, the devotee actually hears the voice of Spirit vibrating into intelligible, instructive words in the etheric expanse of his mind. As one's conscience whispers silent words of advice, so the Spirit vibrates words of counsel to the yogi's mind. (This is why the Vedas, the Wisdom Scriptures, are spoken of as *shruti*—"that which has been heard.")

The whispers of mind are different from the whispers of conscience; and different from both is the Voice of Spirit. The mental voice is nothing but the vibrations of an undecided sense mind. The voice of conscience is that of discrimination and inner wisdom. But the Voice of God, from which prophecies come forth, is the Presence of an Infallible Intuition.

With Arjuna thus basking in the illumining smile of Spirit and attuned to the inner Divine Voice, the sublime spiritual discourse of Bhagavan Krishna to Arjuna (the Lord to the devotee) begins fully to unfold—"The Song of Spirit" that in the 700 verses of the Gita encompasses the essence of the ponderous four Vedas, the 108 *Upanishads,* and the six systems of Hindu philosophy—a universal message for the solace and emancipation of all mankind.

THE ETERNAL, TRANSCENDENTAL NATURE OF THE SOUL

VERSE 11

श्रीभगवानुवाच
अशोच्यानन्वशोचस्त्वं प्रज्ञावादांश्च भाषसे।
गतासूनगतासूंश्च नानुशोचन्ति पण्डिताः ॥

The Blessed Lord said:

Thou hast been lamenting for those not worth thy lamentations! Yet thou dost utter words of lore. The truly wise mourn neither for those who are living nor for those who have passed away.

"YOUR HEART IS SHEDDING TEARS of blood for those whose death merits no grief! You justify your sorrow with arguments from the lore of ages. But the truly wise, endowed with celestial knowledge, do not allow their discernment to become besmirched with the foul delusion of viewing as reality the restlessness called life, and the seemingly endless sleep in the gloom of the grave, called death."

To speak like the wise and to behave like the ignorant: is it not contradictory? The devotee under the influence of delusion experiences the state in which he can utter words of wisdom even while he is acting like a simpleton! Yogi-novices may speak as if they were calm with wisdom, while in reality they are motivated by restlessness. Between the words of such a person and what he is, there is an unbridged gulf. One ought not to be a hypocrite in anything. There should be a connection of equality between one's life and the expression of one's thoughts.

A devotee, who is willing to relinquish the high joys of the soul kingdom rather than destroy the beloved sense enemies, may assume an affectation of a man of wisdom and renunciation. His state is one, rather, of dejection and "cold feet"! Mental weakness is never wisdom, but a sign of deep subconscious attachment to the ego and its delusive pleasures. He who cannot stand firm in righteous behaviour before a test of the Almighty loses the right to speak as a wise man.

And what of the many people in the world who, while speaking words of wisdom, are sunk in unbecoming misery and worries of their own making? For the merest trifle—if they so much as miss breakfast, lunch, or dinner—their calmness is stressed. The test of man's wisdom is his equanimity. Little stones that are pelted into the lake of consciousness should not throw the whole lake into commotion.

The moral here is that one must relinquish the mental state of playing the roles of Jekyll-and-Hyde, of talking like the wise and acting like the ignorant. This duality must be avoided by acting wisely as well as speaking like the wise. The illumined devotee synchronizes his actions with his utterances, and follows the good advice he may often give to others!

Be anchored in the Changeless

TO FORSAKE THE IGNORANT double-life, the devotee should not be stirred by the restless changes of life nor fearful of the momentary calmness of so-called death (suspension of physical activity). This is what is meant by the wise mourning neither for the living nor the dead. The wise do not indulge in grief for things that are inevitably changeable and evanescent. Those who always weep and complain that life is filled with bitter things reveal the narrowness of their minds. In God's consciousness, all worldly things are trifles, because they are not eternal. The distressful changes in life and death seem real because of man's sense of possession—"my body, my family, my acquirements." This is God's world; death reminds us that nothing belongs to us, except what we are as souls. To be identified with the body and its surroundings is to meet time and again with the unexpected—the frightful changes that bend one down in unwilling submission.

The dance of life and the *danse macabre* must be unchangingly, immovably, unswervingly perceived from the safe anchorage of soul consciousness. The unsettled devotee only talks like one immovably anchored in Spirit. But those resolute devotees who deeply practise the technique of yoga concentration become riveted to the supreme unchangeable state in Spirit. They master the restlessness that is synonymous with mortal life, and experience consciously the complete calmness, or silence, accompanying freedom from identification with the body.* When such a devotee reaches this immutable state of perfection, he witnesses all the changes of life and death without being moved by them. Identification with the waves of changes leads to misery, for to live and find pleasure in the changeable is to be separated from the Eternal. The wise, therefore, are not tossed with the ups and downs of the waves of happiness and misery. They dive deep into the Spirit-Ocean of Bliss, avoiding the storms of delusion, the waves of change that rage on the surface of human consciousness.

The state of constant calmness (neutralization of restless thoughts) is attained by the continuous practice of meditation and by keeping the attention fixed at the point between the eyebrows. In this state of calmness, man witnesses the thoughts and emotions and their workings without being disturbed at all, reflecting in his consciousness only the unchangeable image of Spirit.

Those who look at the surface of the sea must behold the birth and death of the waves, but those who seek the depths of the ocean behold one indivisible mass of water. Similarly, those who acknowledge "life" and "death" are tossed by sorrow, while those who live in the illimitable superconsciousness behold and feel the One Ineffable Bliss.

The contrasting experiences of dreamland are tricks of one consciousness. During the state of a sense-conscious dream, a man

---

* In this Gita verse, the Sanskrit *gatāsūn,* "dead," (from *gata,* "gone away, departed," and *asu,* "breath, or life") means literally "one whose breath has gone." *Agātāsūn,* "living" means "one whose breath has not gone." Breath is synonymous with mortal life, and is the first cause of identification with body consciousness. It is the stimulator of the restlessness or motion associated with life. Yogis who by *pranayama* enter the breathless state of *samadhi* (referred to by Saint Paul: "I protest by your rejoicing which I have in Christ Jesus our Lord, I die daily"—I Corinthians 15:31) are able to subdue every ripple of restlessness, and experience the absolute calmness of Reality, and from that consciousness to understand the delusive nature of matter and its motions of constant change.

beholds its sorrowful and delightful changes with one part of his subconscious mind; with another part he beholds himself as the dreamer witnessing the dream. Similarly, the wise man, in his inner Self, perceives the One Undiluted Spirit as the Dreamer of this cosmic dream, apart from the excitement of the dream cosmos; in his outer consciousness he learns to witness the awesomeness of death and all the sad and joyous experiences of life as nothing but contrary events in God's cosmic dreamland. Attainment of oneness with God in cosmic consciousness bestows the ultimate perception in which all the differences of dream life melt into one Everlasting Joy.

Forget the past, for it is gone from your domain! Forget the future, for it is beyond your reach! Control the present! Live supremely well now! It will whitewash the dark past, and compel the future to be bright! This is the way of the wise.

VERSE 12

न त्वेवाहं जातु नासं न त्वं नेमे जनाधिपाः ।
न चैव न भविष्यामः सर्वे वयमतः परम् ॥

It is not that I have never before been incarnated; nor thou, nor these other royal ones! And never in all futurity shall any one of us not exist!

I have bloomed before in the garden of life,
Even as now!
You, and all these royal ones—here once more!—
Blossomed fragrantly in lives long gone.
All barren trees of future lives
We may choose to adorn anew
With buds of our reincarnated souls!
Erstwhile did we abide in formless form
In Spirit's everlastingness,
And thither do we wend again!

IN THE TRANSIENT REALM OF TIME and space, there is constant change, or cessation, in form and expression; but the essence within these changes endures. Everlasting is the soul of man (the true Self) and the soul of the universe (*Kutastha Chaitanya,* the Krishna or Christ Consciousness)—

the "thou and I" expressions of Spirit. Permanent also are the principles of Nature, the Spirit-essentials of being or manifestation—"these other royal ones." In some form or another all that is and has been shall ever be. (This concept is developed further in II:16.)

A mortal has the consciousness of duality, which seemingly separates the "present" from both the "past" and the "future." Through the operation of the law of relativity or duality that is structurally inherent in phenomenal creation, a mortal man, in a particular body, is convinced that he is living only "now"—as essentially distinguished from a life either in the past or in the future. He is circumscribed by his experience that he, and all his contemporaries, are living only "now."

Past, future, and the Eternal Now

The truth is that man lives in an "Eternal Now." The emancipated devotee rightly realizes the Eternal Now through his omnipresent God-consciousness; the mortal man experiences the Eternal Now through a punctuated series of lives, whose settings, alternately, are the physical world and the astral world.

Not only has man existed in some form from an indeterminate past, but, so long as he is ignorantly identified with his body (either the gross physical body or the subtle astral body), he will continue, throughout an indefinite future, to reinhabit fresh bodies.

"Reincarnation" signifies not only a change of residence by the soul from one body to another body, but also a change in the composite expression of the ego from one state of consciousness to another state of consciousness within one lifetime. A man of fifty years, for instance, might introspect and say to himself and to his present consciousness (i.e., "you and I") and to other noble thoughts (the "royal ones") that he had existed before in the states of childhood, young manhood, maturity, and so forth; and that, if his body lives for a few more decades, he will continue to exist in other states in the future. In this sense, one can live many lives in one life span—simultaneously conscious of all the different lives (or habits of life) encompassed by that one incarnation, with no imposition of the forgetfulness of intervening death.

The soul (or Krishna, the preceptor of Arjuna), possessing cosmic consciousness (the ever awake consciousness uninterrupted by death), could perceive all the stars of its series of reincarnations as they twinkled in the firmament of the "Eternal Now" consciousness.

Krishna therefore points out to Arjuna that all mortals who appear "now" to be separate individuals (one's self and one's contemporaries) are mere cause-and-effect expressions, in bodily form, of desires carried over by the ego from the past (previous lives); and that all new desires engendered "now" by the ego would be required to find expression through new bodies in the future. Krishna, the Spirit, asks the devotee to rise above the law of causation and mortal desires, which chain man to a series of inherently painful incarnations, and to become established instead in the eternal freedom of his immortal soul.

VERSE 13

देहिनोऽस्मिन्यथा देहे कौमारं यौवनं जरा।
तथा देहान्तरप्राप्तिर्धीरस्तत्र न मुह्यति॥

As in the body the embodied Self passes through childhood, youth, and old age, so is its passage into another body; the wise thereat are not disturbed.

THE EGO IS CONTINUOUSLY CONSCIOUS of itself in childhood, youth, and old age; the embodied soul is uninterruptedly conscious, not only in infancy, adolescence, and old age, but also of its series of "lives" and "deaths"—the ego's alternations between the physical and the astral worlds. The soul perceives all the bubbles of states of consciousness floating in the past-present-future river of time.

The ordinary man, without severing his sense of "I-ness" or ego consciousness, gradually perceives the states of infancy, youth, and old age; a sage perceives the series of lives and deaths to be different experiences in an uninterrupted consciousness of soul perception.

A mortal does not experience a prenatal and postmortem continuity of consciousness; he therefore sees the past as dark, and the future as unknown. But a meditating devotee shifts his consciousness from the changes of birth and death to the Changeless Being in whose bosom all changes dance. He beholds all prenatal, postnatal, and postmortem changes without being emotionally affected by them. This unattachment insures the devotee of an everlasting, changeless happiness. Those who are engrossed in change delusively expect permanent happiness from the changeable sense world.

The wise do not expect to reap everlasting happiness from friends, beloved family, or dear possessions! The forms of loved ones are snatched away by death. Material objects turn out to be meaningless when one becomes used to them; or when, in old age, the senses grow unappreciative, powerless. Concentrate on the immortal Spirit through meditation and find there a harvest of eternal, ever new peace!

VERSE 14

मात्रास्पर्शास्तु कौन्तेय शीतोष्णसुखदुःखदाः ।
आगमापायिनोऽनित्यास्तांस्तितिक्षस्व भारत ॥

O Son of Kunti (Arjuna), the ideas of heat and cold, pleasure and pain, are produced by the contacts of the senses with their objects. Such ideas are limited by a beginning and an end. They are transitory, O Descendant of Bharata (Arjuna); bear them with patience!

"WHEN THE FRAIL SENSES WANTONLY consort with sensory objects, a motley throng of pain and pleasure, of warmth and chill, dances wildly through the temple of life. The individual dualities in these troublesome crowds revel or sigh for a while, then finally die, leaving traces of confusion in the sanctum of the soul. Fear them not, however strong and perdurable they may seem; they come and go, like bubbles on the sea of time. Ignore them, or bear them with a brave, cheerful heart and an even mind!

"O devotee, as you are the son of Kunti, born of nature, striving to call forth the power of renunciation and divine ardour, the feminine quality of feeling still grips your consciousness, making it susceptible to dualities. But within you, awaiting divine arousal, is the positive masculine power of cosmic consciousness, your ancestral inheritance as a descendant of Bharata (Spirit)—your true manliness of unconquerable equipoise and transcendence."

How man's feelings and reactions arise from sensations

THE SENSE ORGANS ARE REACTIVELY sensitive; their nature is to respond pleasurably or painfully to stimuli. They have been conditioned to have strong likes and dislikes; thus, liking produces enjoyment, and disliking causes repulsion, or pain. The sense impressions flow through the tunnel of fine nerve-points, using the life force and mind as the rivers to carry them along. When good and bad, or hot and cold, material objects contact the sensitive sense organs, the result is pleasure and pain, or heat and cold. These resultant sensations are transitory, fickle, evanescent. They come and go; man should bear them with patience, with mental evenness (*titiksha*).

An environment-enslaved body is a constant trouble to the mind, holding in bondage the potentially all-powerful mental faculties. In the Western world, the general tendency is to concentrate on removing external causes of discomfort. Buy a cozy warm coat if you are cold! Install a heating system—even if you have to borrow the money! If the climate is a hot one, install an air-conditioning machine! And so on.

The Eastern masters admire the Western ingenuity and inventive genius. They teach, however, that while man should adopt reasonable measures to overcome external discomfort, he should also develop a state of inner "aboveness." He should not permit his mind to be adversely affected by sensations.

Man experiences sensations as the feelings produced by the contact of the senses with matter. A sensation or first-flowing feeling produced in the mind is elaborated initially as a perception. It is then expanded into conception by the action of the intelligence. And lastly, the conception changes into feeling, the faculty that passes judgement on the experience in terms of pain or pleasure of the body, sorrow or happiness of the mind, according to habitual attitudes of likes and dislikes. Therefore, the masters teach, if feeling can be neutralised—made impervious to transitory dualities of heat and cold, pleasure and pain—then all experiences will be merely intellectually cognized, ideas to be properly acted upon.

A stone contacting a block of ice becomes cold. A man holding a piece of ice feels cold. In both cases the stone and the human hand become cold, but the reactions are different. There is no doubt that there are hot and cold objects, and that they produce hot and cold sensations in a body equipped with sensitivity; it is obvious, however, that the stone, unlike the human hand, possesses no inner organs of response to external stimuli.

The ice on a man's hand is reported to the brain, through the sensory nerves and life force, as a sensation. The mind reacts through perception and recognizes the sensation as "cold." The preconditioned feeling then interprets the sensation as pleasurable or disagreeable, and the body responds accordingly. The coldness of the flesh is material, the cold sensation or perception is purely mental. All experiences of cold and heat, in order to be cognized as such, must first be converted into mental perceptions. A chloroformed man feels no sensations of cold when a piece of ice is placed on his hand. In short, the mind is the sole power for recognition of any bodily sensation.

Sensations are powerful or powerless according to whether the mind is, or is not, impressed by them. Continuous impressions of cold or hot sensations gradually make the mind accustomed to them, with the result that less and less sensation of cold or heat is perceived. This is the reason why man's mind becomes acclimatized to extremes of frigid or torrid weather. A strong, controlled mind can ignore external stimuli, for no sensory sensations can be perceived by man without the acceptance and response of his mind.

So the Eastern savants say that the influences of cold and heat, or pleasurable and painful sensations, produced in the body through the contact of objects with the sense organs, can be neutralised if man can meet them with an unresponsive state of mind. This mental victory over, or "aboveness" to, the invasion of temporary sensations leads to self-mastery, to the ultimate knowledge that material objects or sensory stimuli possess no inherent power over man. This is what Krishna is stressing in this stanza by the use of the word *titiksha*, "endurance with firmness of mind."

Yoga discipline of rising above sense slavery

THE YOGA SYSTEM OF BODILY DISCIPLINE and endurance is not intended to be a method of self-torture, but a necessary mental conditioning for lessening the disturbing effects of sensations by developing the resisting power of the mind. *Titiksha* does not mean rashness. If the body is sense-enslaved and unspiritualized, it should be reasonably protected from harmful extremes while mentally and gradually disciplining it to rise above its slavery. Continued catering to sensitiveness weakens the mind, thus nurturing pain and constant mental irritation.

The conditioned responses of the mind—through perception, cognition, and feeling—are largely hereditary, having been bequeathed to mankind from his early ancestors who fell from their godly nature into matter-bound consciousness. But the degree of sensitivity in each person, which determines how much he is bound by this inheritance, is of his own making.

Through ignorance, the mind of the ordinary man chooses to be sensitive and to imagine itself hurt through the senses. The devotee, therefore, should lay great stress upon a mental "rising above" cold and heat, pain and temporary pleasures. When a cold or a hot sensation invades the body, when a pleasure visits or a pain attacks, it tries to overwhelm man's mind with the idea that the sensation has an inherent power of permanence. Aware of this "trick," man should try to adopt a transcendental, indifferent attitude in his response to the inroads of all sensations.

When a man adopts a nonexcitable state toward sorrows, a nonattached state toward temporary happiness, a stoicism toward irritants that rouse fear and anger and pain, his mind attains an unruffled state of poise.*

VERSE 15

यं हि न व्यथयन्त्येते पुरुषं पुरुषर्षभ।
समदुःखसुखं धीरं सोऽमृतत्वाय कल्पते॥

O Flower among Men (Arjuna)! he who cannot be ruffled by these (contacts of the senses with their objects), who is calm and evenminded during pain and pleasure, he alone is fit to attain everlastingness!

"THAT BLESSED BEING WHO IS unchanged like the anvil under the hammer stroke of trials, the one who is evenminded during both cloudy winter days of pain and sunny springtime days of pleasures, the one

---

* "It has been said that man pays with greater misery for his more advanced central nervous structure," writes Steven F. Brena, M.D., professor at Emory University School of Medicine and head of the Pain Control Institute of Georgia. "Medical evidence is now showing, to the contrary, that man suffers more pain because he refuses to use properly his refined nervous system, keeping it unbalanced and out of control.

"In human beings, response to the pain experience is never merely a nervous reflex, as in animals; but always, even in the most acute emergencies, the ultimate expression of an intricate, integrated brain process involving both cognitive and emotional factors....It has been found that no technique of external physiological treatment may be expected to provide a cure for *chronic* pain unless the patient commits himself or herself to systematic inner changes in thoughts and behaviour. As a result of this discovery, pain specialists are beginning to recognize the great practical utility of the science of yoga in dealing with the physical and mental causes of chronic pain.

"In scientific terms, 'endurance' can be thought of as *the extent to which we can control our response to sensory input, so that the performance of body and mind can remain unimpaired despite pain.* Endurance and optimal performance are rooted in self-control. Without self-control no athlete can win an Olympic medal, no mystic can reach an elevated state of consciousness—nor can any human being learn to cease being a victim of pain. My clinical experience with thousands of chronic-pain patients has shown that to learn self-control requires will power and training in right thinking, right attitudes, right activity—the very things one learns from following the disciplines of yoga. The combined practice of all these principles in an integrated pain-control therapy has enabled us to see clinical results that medicine would call miraculous." *(Publisher's Note)*

who calmly absorbs trials into himself as the sea quietly swallows rivers, he is ordained by the gods to attain the eternal kingdom!"

The basic principle of creation is duality. If one knows pleasure he must know pain. One who cognizes heat must cognize cold also. If creation had manifested only heat or only cold, only sorrow or only pleasure, human beings would not be the irritated victims of the pranks of duality. But then, what would life be like in a monotone existence? Some contrast is necessary; it is man's response to dualities that causes his trouble. So long as one is slavishly influenced by the dualities, he lives under the domination of the changeful phenomenal world.

Man's egoistic feelings, expressing as likes and dislikes, are entirely responsible for the bondage of the soul to the body and earthly environment. His cognizing intelligence is a mere registrar of experiences, in a disinterested, academic way; it records the events of a dear one's death or the birth of one's child alike in the same honest, prosaic manner. Whereas intelligence simply informs human consciousness about its loss of a dear friend, feeling marks and classifies this experience as distinctly painful. Likewise, the birth of a baby, cognized by an interested human consciousness, is classified by feeling as a distinctly pleasurable experience.

Likes and dislikes are responsible for the bondage of the soul

These psychological twins, man's feelings of pleasure and sorrow, have a common father: they spring from desire. Fulfilled desire is pleasure and contradicted desire is pain or sorrow. They are inseparable: Just as night inevitably follows day as the earth revolves on its axis, so pleasure and pain revolve on the axis of desire—the one ever alternating with the other.

Desire is produced by indiscriminate contact with the objects of the senses. Expressing as the likes and dislikes of the ego, desire creeps into the consciousness of one who is not watchful enough in governing the reaction of his feelings to his various experiences in the world. It is a condition the ego imposes on itself, and is therefore detrimental to man's evenmindedness. Whatever has its origin in desire is a disturbing element, for desires are like stones pelted into the calm lake of consciousness. Attachment to pleasure or aversion to pain both destroy the equilibrium of the inner nature.

Recognizing the inseparability of the opposites, the masters of India deem that even pleasures, being temporary, are harbingers of pain. Pleasure that comes like a brief straw-fire to illumine a dark heart with a message of joy and then suddenly dies down only deepens the original sorrow. This is why the Gita teaches that the excitation of pleasures should be avoided as avidly as one seeks to avoid the unpleasantness of pain. Only when feeling is neutralised toward both opposites does one rise above all suffering. It is very difficult, indeed, to hurt an ever-smiling wise man.

In order to attain mental aboveness, man must *practise* a neutral attitude to all earthly changes. Many people reason: "Ah, well! if I cultivate a neutral attitude, how could I enjoy life?" The answer is a matter of logic. Even though we enjoy pleasure after pain, still it seems hardly reasonable that, in order to appreciate health, we should first undergo accidents and disease! or that, in order to enjoy peace, we should first experience excruciating mental suffering! Friendship may surely exist between two persons without their first indulging in enmity! The mortal way, therefore, of taking life "as it is," of accepting as inevitable the periodical incursions of pain and pleasure, is *not* the right way of carrying on this mundane existence.

Evenmindedness: key to happiness and peace

The saints have found that happiness lies in a constant mental state of unruffled peace during all the experiences of earthly dualities. A changeable mind perceives a changeable creation, and is easily disturbed; the unchangeable soul and the unruffled mind, on the other hand, behold, behind the masks of change, the Eternal Spirit. The man whose mind is like an oscillating mirror beholds all creation as distorted into waves of change; but the man who holds his mental mirror steady beholds there naught but the reflections of the Sole Unity—God. Through realization, not mere imagination, he sees that his body and all things are the condensed consciousness of Spirit. The mind, free of artificial excitation, remains centred in its native state of inner peace and soul joy.

When the mind by deep spiritual development manifests its aboveness to the suggestions born of the external activity of the senses, the advancing yogi, like Arjuna, finds that before he can attain the promised state of everlastingness he must also neutralise, by meditation, the effects of the *inner action* of the sensory powers.

When by guru-given techniques the yogi withdraws his attention and life force from the muscles and heart, and plies his boat of meditation over the river of spinal electricity, he finds (like Ulysses of old) that the sirens of sound, touch, smell, taste, and sight take many forms and try to lure him toward dangerous waters. If the mind is impressed by these subtle sense promises, the soul-boat of meditation enters a whirlpool of ignorance. The sincere devotee, however, finds that this lure of the senses does not last long; it soon wears off. These "sense sirens" are only the last vestiges of prenatal tendencies, long ingrained in the brain.

The devotee should ignore all astral and mental impediments and keep his mind riveted to the pinpoint of luminous light in the centre of the spiritual eye, perceived between the two eyebrows during deep meditation. The devotee thus reaches the celestial land of permanency; never again is he thrown back into a whirlpool of reincarnations and misery!

VERSE 16

नासतो विद्यते भावो नाभावो विद्यते सतः ।
उभयोरपि दृष्टोऽन्तस्त्वनयोस्तत्त्वदर्शिभिः ॥

Of the unreal, there is no existence. Of the real, there is no nonexistence. The final truth of both of these is known by men of wisdom.

THE SENSES SAY THAT THE FLOWER that was never born has shed no fragrance; things that were never real have ever been nonexistent. But the garden rose, by its fragrance, and the stars, by their twinkle in the sky, proclaim their reality. The seers of truth, however, know them all to be equally unreal; for the rose will fade away, and many a distant star whose glimmer dots the heavens has long since ceased to be. Could something become nothing? Possessors of wisdom perceive as real only That which changes not—the Essence that became the star and the idea of the flower in the poet's mind. The wise alone know the mystery of the real and the unreal.

The ocean can exist without the waves, but the waves cannot manifest without the ocean. The ocean is the real substance; the waves are only temporary changes on the ocean, and therefore "unreal" (in themselves they have no independent existence). The ocean, in essence, does not change whether it is calm or restless with waves; but the waves change their forms—they come and they go. Their essence is change, and therefore unreality.*

---

* "All objects...are fictions: chimeras of the mind. It is our left [brain] hemispheres...that trick us into seeing sheep, trees, human beings, and all the rest of our neatly compartmentalized world. We seek out stability with our reasoning consciousness, and ignore

THE ETERNAL SUBSTANCE is said to be divided into two—the *Sat* or Changeless Spirit, and the *Asat,* the unreal or the ever-changing Nature, the Cosmic Mother of twenty-four attributes.*

Sat and Asat, Spirit and Nature

There are two ways of perceiving Substance: as the changeless Spirit, and as the ever-changing creation. These modes of perception are called *anuloma* (in the correct direction) and *viloma* (turned in the wrong way). To behold Nature (Spirit as matter) is the *viloma* (delusive) way, in which the vision, being directed outward through the senses toward the "end products," perceives only the waves of delusive creation. To turn the perception inward, and thus to see from the outward peripheries of matter into the inner point of Spirit, is the *anuloma* or wisdom mode of vision. Through inward-turned perception, one can trace the cause of all activities of creation. When the mind is fixed on the Primal Root Principle of all manifestation, one realizes that gross matter is the result of the mixture of the five subtle astral elements of earth, water, fire, air, and ether; and that all elements successively melt into the Ultimate Cause, or Spirit.

Those, therefore, who do not look into matter through the senses but who look through matter into Spirit, really know the mystery of the unreal and the Real. The Real, unchanged through eternity, is existent; the unreal, changeable, is only relatively existent. Substance

---

flux....Through this classifying and simplifying approach we make sections through the stream of change, and we call these sections 'things.' And yet a sheep is not a sheep. It is a temporary aggregation of subatomic particles in constant motion—particles which were once scattered across an interstellar cloud, and each of which remains within the process that is the sheep for only a brief period of time. That is the actual, irrefutable case....

"We slip so easily into the habit of assuming that what we see and feel in our minds is what is actually going on outside ourselves, beyond the portal of the senses. After all, we are only inches away from the borders of this seemingly familiar land. But there are no colours *out there,* no hot or cold, no pleasure or pain. Although we experience the world as a series of sensory objects, what actually comes to our senses is energy in the form of vibrations of different frequencies: very low frequencies for hearing and touch, higher frequencies for warmth, and higher still for vision....The radiations we pick up trigger neural codes that are made by the brain into a model of the external world. Then this model is given subjective value and, by a trick of the brain, projected outward to form the subjective world. That inner experience is what we habitually equate with external objectivity....But it is *not* objective....All of perceived reality is a fiction."—*Equations of Eternity: Speculations on Consciousness, Meaning, and the Mathematical Rules that Orchestrate the Cosmos,* by David Darling, Ph.D. (New York: Hyperion, 1993). *(Publisher's Note)*

* See XIII:5–6.

exists; phenomena, which cannot exist without the existence of Substance, have no separate existence.

The ordinary individual considers matter as real (because manifest); he ignores the Spirit as unreal (because hidden). This delusion enshrouds him in ignorance and suffering. The wise man tears aside the appearance of delusive creation and, perceiving the Everlasting Reality, is permanently happy.

Sages behold the way in which the waves of unreality crop up from Reality and cover Its oneness—just as many waves hide the inseverable unity of the ocean. By this view, the wise ones become fixed in the unchangeable Spirit and ignore the changes of the so-called matter-of-fact world. Knowledge of Reality does not make one vague or visionary, shirking his duties! The knower of Reality may be said to be a sane person in the midst of lunacy!

VERSE 17

अविनाशि तु तद्विद्धि येन सर्वमिदं ततम्।
विनाशमव्ययस्यास्य न कश्चित्कर्तुमर्हति॥

Know as imperishable the One by whom everything has been manifested and pervaded. No one has power to bring about the annihilation of this Unchangeable Spirit.

THE ONE LIFE THAT BREATHES into existence all temporal things, forming them out of His own one Being, is indestructible, everlasting. Though all changeable objects of creation melt away, nothing affects the immutability of God.

When an adobe house is shattered by an earthquake, the clay does not change its nature. Similarly, when this cosmic clay-house of change is touched by dissolution, its essence remains unchanged.

Just as electrons, or atoms of hydrogen and oxygen that compose steam, water, and ice, are manifestations of different rates of vibration of one primal energy, so man, beasts, worlds, and all projections of creation are changeable forms of the One Spirit. Even if planets were hurled from their orbits, even if all matter were to melt into nothingness, there could be no iota of vacant space—space empty of Spirit. Forms of creation and the Great Void—both are equally pervaded by Spirit. Kingdoms may topple, oceans evaporate, and the earth turn into vapour—still Spirit remains untouched, hidden and indestructible.

When, through meditation, man chooses to be identified with the unchangeable Spirit, he will no longer be deluded and tortured by the pandemonium of change.

VERSE 18

अन्तवन्त इमे देहा नित्यस्योक्ताः शरीरिणः ।
अनाशिनोऽप्रमेयस्य तस्माद्युध्यस्व भारत ॥

Regarded as having a termination of existence are these fleshly garments; immutable, imperishable, and limitless is the Indwelling Self. With this wisdom, O Descendant of Bharata (Arjuna), battle thou!

"THE DIVINE INDWELLER, the Ever Youthful One whom the fingers of decay dare not touch, the One whose home is the region without boundaries, the One who can never be invaded by destruction—he it is who wears many costumes of flesh. Though his bodily garments decay, he himself is imperishable! Equipped with this armour of wisdom, O Arjuna, descendant of brave Bharata! boldly enter the arena of inner battle!"

The devotee, while still contending with the strong inner persuasion of delusion—attached to the body, afraid to relinquish the senses and identification with mortal consciousness—is a bird of eternity locked in a little cage. Man, as an eagle of immortality, at home in eternal space, should not be fearful to rise above the body from which, in any case, he will be ousted at the call of Death.

Krishna therefore tells Arjuna: "Concentrate on your Inner Self, the image of the Eternal Spirit, which, like It, is immortal! Fear not to fight the senses and to destroy the attachment to the body! This, sooner or later, you will be compelled to do!"

The dread of losing the body often invades even an advanced devotee when the delusive cohesion between body and soul makes him temporarily forget that, as he is immortal Spirit, his body is no part of him.

The yogi aims at such complete mastery over the body that its very atoms will obey his command, even as Jesus and Kabir*—and many

* "Kabir was a great 16th-century saint whose large following included Hindus and Moslems. At the time of Kabir's death the disciples quarrelled over the manner of con-

other illumined masters—were able not only to give up the body at will, but also to demonstrate its illusory nature by resurrecting it after death or dematerializing it into Spirit.

Even in a material war of righteousness, where the protection of the weak is necessary, a soldier should not be afraid to give up his perishable body. Virtue acquired by sacrifice is never lost. Better a death of righteousness than the ordinary ignoble death! It is more laudable to die for the general welfare than to expire on the comfortable bed of selfishness!

VERSE 19

य एनं वेत्ति हन्तारं यश्चैनं मन्यते हतम्।
उभौ तौ न विजानीतो नायं हन्ति न हन्यते॥

He who considers the Self as the slayer; he who deems that it can be slain: neither of these knows the truth. The Self does not kill, nor is it killed.

HE DREAMS WHO DEEMS the Self a dark slayer. Error-drunk is he who thinks death can touch the Self. Neither view is truth. The Self could never soil its hands of justice with the blood of slaughter; nor is there any power by which the soul may be slain!

Just as the dying hero on a motion picture screen has not really been slain, so the soul of man, playing a role in the cosmic motion picture of life, is ever living. The victim and the killer in the screen drama are only two forms of electric shadows. The villain of the screen, and the villain of Death, alike kill no one!

The immortal Self remains untouched when its body-cloak is destroyed, just as a man does not die when his house crumbles away. One soul cannot kill another soul—both are reflections of the immortal Spirit.

---

ducting the funeral ceremonies. The exasperated master rose from his final sleep, and gave his instructions. 'Half of my remains should be buried with Moslem rites,' he said. 'Let the other half be cremated with a Hindu sacrament.' He then vanished. When the disciples removed the shroud that had covered his body, nothing was found but a beautiful array of flowers. Half of these were obediently buried, in Maghar, by the Moslems, who revere his shrine to this day. The other half was cremated with Hindu ceremonies in Banaras."—*Autobiography of a Yogi.*

This deep philosophy should not be misused by those who may erroneously think: "Let us murder our enemies! Their souls are immortal anyway. We cannot be called killers even if we do kill." This kind of reasoning impresses neither God nor the mundane police!

The quantity of water contained in ocean waves remains the same whether the waves play on the sea breast or lie hidden beneath it. Similarly, the soul-waves of life remain constant whether they play on the surface of the sea of life or rest deep within its bosom.

This stanza expresses the profound truth of the immortal nature not only of the soul but of matter. As a reflection of Spirit, even matter is indestructible. The essence of matter is never destroyed; the human body, made of patterns of condensed electrons that are superficially changed by death, is in reality never annihilated.

Every form, thought, motion that has been exhibited on the screen of time and space is recorded permanently. These cosmic motion pictures—and they were never more than that, portrayed by immortal souls—are preserved in the Infinite Archives. Those God-realized souls who earn entrance into the secret vaults of Spirit know the wonder of this mystery of immortality.

VERSE 20

न जायते म्रियते वा कदाचिन्नायं भूत्वा भविता वा न भूयः।
अजो नित्यः शाश्वतोऽयं पुराणो न हन्यते हन्यमाने शरीरे॥

This Self is never born nor does it ever perish; nor having come into existence will it again cease to be. It is birthless, eternal, changeless, ever-same (unaffected by the usual processes associated with time). It is not slain when the body is killed.

THE SOUL, IN ESSENCE the reflection of Spirit, never undergoes the pangs of birth nor the throes of death. Nor having once been projected from the womb of immortal Spirit will Prince Soul, on return to Spirit, lose its individuality; having entered the portals of nativity, its existence will never cease. In all its bodily births, the Spirit-soul never felt birth; it exists everlastingly, untouched by the *maya*-magic fingers of change. It is ever the same—now, past, future—as it has always been; ageless, unchanged, since its immemorial beginnings. The deathless soul dwelling in the destructible body is ever constant through all cycles of bodily disintegrations; it does not taste death even when the body quaffs that fatal cup of hemlock.

The body, as a part of matter, is spoken of as undergoing the following six transformations of impermanent Nature: birth, existence, development, change, decay, and annihilation. The man dwelling in a perishable body forgets the imperishable soul within it. His body-identified consciousness is aware only of its six conditions. The wise man learns by meditation to differentiate between the indwelling immortal soul and its perishable bodily encasement. People who believe that the Absolute Spirit (ever-existing, ever-conscious, ever-new Bliss) is immortal must also accept the truth that Its reflection, the soul, even though encased in a mortal body, is immortal too. Bhagavan Krishna's words in these lines particularly emphasize this truth. As God is immortal, every man's soul, made in the image of God, must also be immortal.

THE DIFFERENCE BETWEEN SOUL and Spirit is this: The Spirit is ever-existing, ever-conscious, ever-new *omnipresent* Joy; the soul is the *individualized* reflection of ever-existing, ever-conscious, ever-new Joy, confined within the body of each and every being.

Souls: radiating rays of Spirit

Souls are the radiating rays of Spirit, individualized as formless, vibrationless "atoms" and "tissues" of Spirit. Hence, they are coexistent with Spirit and of the same essence, as the sun and its rays are one. Though incarnate, the soul belongs to the noumenal region, which changes not. All material forms belong to the regions of phenomena; their very nature being alienated from Spirit, they change constantly. Phenomena arise from and are inseparably linked with noumena; but the latter, being of Spirit, are immutable and transcendent. The outer surface of the soul's consciousness that is cloaked with the instrumentalities of the ego, mind, and senses undergoes the permutations of Nature, but the soul's essence remains inviolable.

Worldly men do not know what the soul is, or how it comes into the physical body, and then, after a short sojourn, to what destiny it slips away. Trillions of men have mysteriously come on earth and just as mysteriously departed. That is why people in general cannot but wonder if the soul undergoes extinction along with the destruction of the body.

The following analogy gives an illustration of the nature and immortality of the soul. (No analogies are perfect in expressing absolute verities, but they do help the mind to image abstract concepts.) The moon is reflected in a cup containing water; the cup is broken and the water runs out; where does the reflection of the moon go? The reflection of the moon may be said to have returned to its inseverable identity in the moon itself. If another cup of water is placed under the moon, another reflection of the moon would be reincarnated!

The soul is similarly reflected in the bodily cup filled with the water of the mind; within it we see the moon-soul, circumscribed by the bodily limitations, as the reflection of the omnipresent moon of Spirit. With the destruction of the body-cup, the moon reflection may for a time disappear in the Spirit; but, by use of the power of the free choice bestowed on it as the image of the Spirit, it created desires and karma while on earth that cause it to choose to be reflected again as the moon-soul within another bodily cup. Thus, though the bodies of man be mortal and changeable, immortal is the soul within them.

The reflected moon, circumscribed by a little cup, becomes, at the destruction of the cup, the one moon whose rays spread over the sky. Similarly, the soul, when fully liberated from imprisoning desires, becomes omnipresent like the Spirit.

However, man has three bodies from which he must free his consciousness before he can achieve final emancipation. These soul confinements are the physical body of sixteen elements; the astral body of nineteen elements; and the causal body of thirty-five elemental ideas. The physical body is made of blood and flesh; the astral body is composed of life force and mind; and the causal or ideational body is woven together with wisdom and ever new bliss.

Liberation from the three bodies

God originated, in the form of the causal body, thirty-five *ideas* as the matrix of human creation. These ideas are the basic or thought forces required to create the astral and physical body. Nineteen of these ideas were manifested as the subtle astral body, which contains the ten senses; the five life forces; and the ego, feeling, mind, and intelligence. The remaining sixteen ideas were converted into the gross physical body of sixteen basic elements. In other words, before God created the physical body consisting of iron, phosphorous, calcium, and so forth, and the subtle astral body of lifetronic composition, He had first to project them as ideas, the constituents of the causal body. Each of the three bodies has its distinguishing qualities. The dense physical body is the result of solidified vibrations, the astral body of energy and mind vibrations, and the causal body of nearly pure vibrations of Cosmic Consciousness.

The physical body may be said to be dependent on food; the astral body is dependent on energy, will, and evolution of thought; the causal body is dependent on the ambrosia of wisdom and bliss. The soul is encased in these three bodies. At death the physical body is destroyed. The other two bodies, astral and causal, are still held together by desires and by unworked-out karma. The soul, wearing these two bodies, repeatedly reincarnates in new physical forms. When all desires are conquered by meditation, the three body-prisons are dissolved; the soul becomes Spirit.

Again, an analogy may help to illustrate the reabsorption of the soul into Spirit:

The perfected man's consciousness is apparently dissolved in the Ocean of God. Those soul-waves which are not driven by any postmortem storms of desires become Absolute Oceanic Spirit. In becoming Spirit, they possess omnipresent memory, even of the individual consciousness of their own past soul-wave. The fully dissolved wave merges into the Ocean of Spirit but still remembers that, from the original Ocean of Spirit, it became a soul-wave, and again changed from a soul-wave into the One Spirit.

For example: God is the soul of a particular man, John, a mortal through delusory body identification. By meditation, John again united himself with God, finding that it was God in the first place who became John; by developing wisdom, John again became God. In the deluded mortal state, John found himself to be the soul-wave apart from the Ocean of Spirit. Then, by spreading his consciousness and realizing the Spirit as his Foundation, he discovered it was the Spirit-Ocean that had become his soul-wave, now merged again in the One Spirit. The liberated soul of John, even though one with Spirit, would retain its individuality in the sense that it would always remember and know that it had once been John, the soul-wave that, without knowing it, had floated on the surface of the Ocean of Spirit. When John the mortal became John the immortal, he did not lose his identity, but realized that he was John the soul-wave (mortal man), as well as John the Ocean of Spirit (immortal man). John, the wise man, lost the consciousness of his separation from God only as the awakened soul-wave loses the consciousness of its separation from the Ocean of Spirit.

Man's individuality can never be erased from him

Man's individuality as an existent entity can never be erased from him. In the ordinary death-in-bondage, the soul of man merely

This Self is never born nor does it ever perish; nor having come into existence will it again cease to be. It is birthless, eternal, changeless, ever-same (unaffected by the usual processes associated with time). It is not slain when the body is killed....

Just as an individual forsaking dilapidated raiment dons new clothes, so the body-encased soul, relinquishing decayed bodily habitations, enters others that are new.

No weapon can pierce the soul; no fire can burn it; no water can moisten it; nor can any wind wither it. The soul is uncleavable; it cannot be burnt or wetted or dried. The soul is immutable, all-permeating, ever calm, and immovable—eternally the same.

—Bhagavad Gita II:20, 22–24

❖

"From joy people are born; for joy they live; in joy they melt at death. Death is an ecstasy, for it removes the burden of the body and frees the soul of all pain springing from body identification. It is the cessation of pain and sorrow....Ordinary persons enjoy the rest of a peaceful death-sleep in the astral heaven. Virtuous souls alternate sleep with wakefulness in this land of blissful freedom and beauty. Devoid of the harsh, often destructive clashes of gross matter, these virtuous astral beings move freely and at will in bodies of light through endless tracts of rainbow-hued densities of luminosity that inform multivaried lifetronic landscapes, scenes, and beings. Their very breath and sustenance are rays of subtle lifetrons."

—Paramahansa Yogananda

changes its residence; and in the final death-in-freedom, the soul expands into the Spirit, at home in Infinity!

The deep truths of the Gita should not be looked upon as metaphysical abstractions, but should be applied in daily life. Particularly during those times when cosmic delusion presents sickness, physical torture, the experience of ordinary death, and morbid thoughts of the impermanency of the body, one should strongly counteract these negative suggestions by remembering the truth that the Self is reflected Spirit-Immortality, ever itself and free from the whims of change.

Thus does the Bhagavad Gita emphasize the following qualities of the Self: It is unborn, though born in a body; it is eternal, though its bodily dwelling is impermanent; it is changeless, though it may experience change; it is ever the same, though in the long pathway of reincarnation which ultimately leads to God, the soul appears in countless forms; the soul is not slain when the body dies; and even when the soul returns to Spirit, it does not lose its identity, but will exist unto everlastingness.

VERSE 21

वेदाविनाशिनं नित्यं य एनमजमव्ययम्।
कथं स पुरुषः पार्थ कं घातयति हन्ति कम्॥

How can he who knows the Self to be imperishable, everlastingly permanent, birthless and changeless, possibly think that this Self can cause the destruction of another? O Partha (Arjuna), whom does it slay?

THAT PERSON WHOSE VISION is in his spiritual eye beholds the true nature of the soul; and thus, through direct perception, is absolutely certain that the Self is immutable—above birth and death, change and annihilation. Such a yogi sees the indestructible Beam of Spirit as the Cause of the formal life and death in the cosmic dream pictures of being, and thus cannot consider himself as the extinguisher of life or even as the indirect cause of extinction of life in another.

The moral interpretation is that in a material struggle wherein virtuous people, without provocation, are attacked by vicious people, it is not unrighteous for the good people to defend themselves. If the latter, in the course of protecting their innocent women and children, should slay some of the invaders, such action is not incompatible with the laws of virtue. Krishna points out that, although the physical bodies of the wicked people are slain, their souls cannot be destroyed. Of course, this should not be used as an argument to kill wicked people; but a soldier, for instance, who is defending his country and righteously protecting helpless persons, may console his conscience about killing the enemy by realizing that he is the instrument and not the real author of the destruction of wicked beings.* Even on the battlefield he should feel he is not the doer, but that all things have been ordained by Nature and God. He must not think that he slays or that God slays, but that the karmic forces of evolution have evicted the invaders from their bodily fortresses to reinhabit other residences in which they will have a new opportunity to learn necessary lessons.

When killing is morally justified

Above all, the soldier should realize that all living is a mock battle between life and death, and that those who are killed in a battle are not really dead, and that those surviving are not really living (since man in his ordinary state is separated from God, the Only Life).

In a dream one may behold a battle between the righteous and the wicked, and may witness the killing of the evil by the good. On waking from the dream, the dreamer will realize that the killing of the vicious people and the surviving of the righteous were both an outcome of his interior imagination; there was no actual destruction. Similarly, Krishna told Arjuna that the battle between his righteous relatives and his wicked ones was nothing but a struggle witnessed by Arjuna in a state of cosmic delusion in which he was spiritually asleep or not yet awake in wisdom. Krishna reminded Arjuna that the cosmic consciousness of all-pervading Spirit should be retained within himself under all circumstances, whether during a physical or an inner battle or any other experience.

THIS STANZA CONVEYS ALSO a deep metaphysical lesson. The soul, Krishna, says to the ego, Arjuna: "O my lower self, you must lift yourself to my plane of higher soul consciousness! Even if you destroy the wicked attachments of the senses, you are foolish to think that the senses themselves will be destroyed! Your higher Self only purifies the lower self; It does not destroy it."

Metaphysical import of verse 21

* See also II:32 concerning righteous wars.

The preceptor is telling the student that even if the devotee slays sense pleasures by self-restraint and renunciation, or causes them to be slain by soul force in deep meditation, he can nevertheless lift his consciousness to the plane of wisdom and perceive that nothing has been destroyed; all things are immortal. Thus, not even the senses of human beings can be killed or annihilated permanently; they only pass through a process of change.

When sense pleasures are routed by self-control, their forces are at first inhibited, suppressed within. The devotee's continued spiritual actions then cause the Self to transmute them to a finer state for the sensing of higher bliss. For example, if a person is greedy and eats too much, he may suffer from indigestion; if by self-control he abstains from overeating, he is initially only suppressing greed. But if he transmutes his greed for physical food into greed for continuous communion with God, he does not destroy his excessive appetite but changes it from an evil agent into a medium for good.

When a man begins to slay his temptations and desires for material comfort, he should not condemn himself as a cruel tyrant, a joy-killer! Nor should he label the Divinity within him as the Devourer of sense pleasures! As the devotee gradually destroys his evil inclinations and feels desolate without those pleasures, he should console himself with the thought that his pleasure-loving experiences have not been destroyed; they are in the process of transformation, to be lifted through meditation from the plane of misery to the joyful plane of God-attachment.

The devotee is therefore justified in transmuting his evil desires. He does not suppress or kill them, for that would make him a mental fossil. On the contrary, it is through the thirsty mouth of transmuted desires that he drinks the immortal nectar of God-Bliss!

VERSE 22

वासांसि जीर्णानि यथा विहाय नवानि गृह्णाति नरोऽपराणि।
तथा शरीराणि विहाय जीर्णान्यन्यानि संयाति नवानि देही॥

Just as an individual forsaking dilapidated raiment dons new clothes, so the body-encased soul, relinquishing decayed bodily habitations, enters others that are new.

AS IT IS COMMON PRACTICE for a human being during a lifetime to change his attire many times, so it is a habit of the eternal soul, during its wanderings on the path of delusion and mortal desires, to cast off karma-worn bodies for new ones. As a person is glad to throw away worn-out, useless clothes for new garments, so should an individual rejoice and feel it just as natural to change a disease-torn or karmically outdated body for a new one.

This stanza refers to the doctrine of reincarnation. Its lines remove the gruesome conception of a *danse macabre* in which a motley crowd of human beings is led to a chasm of destruction; death is here described as nothing more than the discarding of a worn-out garment for a new one. When the body becomes diseased, old, or karmically useless, the undying soul forsakes it for a fresh disguise.

The doctrine of reincarnation

A stage director sends his players in new costumes to play various characters on the stage at different times; similarly, the Immortal Cosmic Director sends soul-actors, made in His image, to play the parts of numerous incarnations on this stage of life. The actors, costumed variously, look different in each new role, yet remain themselves unchanged.

Costumes and makeup disguise an actor and identify him with a particular role; the actor can even be changed from man to woman, or vice versa. Similarly, when a soul changes its fleshly costume, it is no longer recognizable to those who were familiar with its identity in a previous-life role. Only masters who can peer behind the stage and watch the changing parts and disguises recognize individual souls from one lifetime to another, no matter their different raiment. The eyes, facial features, and bodily characteristics reveal a certain similarity to the soul's costume in a former existence—to the master who knows how to read those signs. He sees truly that death is but a change of attire in an uninterrupted continuity of immortality.

The life span or durability of a physical body in any one incarnation is ordained by the law of karma (the law of cause and effect governing human actions). According to the natural order of evolution, the body should mature gradually over a period of many years; and then, like ripened fruit, fall voluntarily and without resistance from the tree of life. Transgressions against God and Nature—in the present or in past lives—may, however, cut short that normal span by disease or accident. Or virtue, also, may win the soul an early release. In every case, the bodily dwelling is fashioned and destined to best serve, for each lifetime, the self-created karmic pattern of the indwelling ego-identified soul.

A DELUSION-STEEPED INDIVIDUAL considers (in practice if not in theory) his body, family, and position as invulnerable; therefore, at the sudden advent of death in the family he is shocked and bewildered. Not understanding the difference between the immortal soul and the changeable mortal body, he is stricken with grief and horror when he witnesses death or sees himself nearing it. He finds it very difficult to maintain mental balance when confronted by seemingly cruel Death, arriving like a tyrant to mar the harmony and peace of life!

Spiritual understanding of death

Usually, it is not difficult for an individual to give up an old garment when he has the prospect of a new one, but some persons are so deeply attached to their possessions that they are loath to discard even worn-out but highly prized clothing! Similarly, ordinary mortals—no matter what wisdom is offered them—grieve when they have to give up their much-loved bodies.

Because the ordinary body-bound individual is lacking in divine inner assurance of the continuity of life, and has no recollection of the countless times he, the soul, has walked in and out of the portals of birth and death, he is full of fear, as well as grief, at the approach of death. As children fear the possibility of meeting ghosts in the dark, so some people are afraid of the unknown awaiting them beyond the door of death. As frightening ghost stories are told by people with strong imaginations, so death is depicted by ignorant men as a gruesome and terrible experience!

In sleep every night an individual discards the consciousness of the tired body and mind and so finds peace; in the greater sleep of death, a man forsakes the disease-torn body and the attachment-corroded mind for a restful state of joy.

From joy people are born; for joy they live; in joy they melt at death. Death is an ecstasy, for it removes the burden of the body and frees the soul of all pain springing from body identification. It is the cessation of pain and sorrow. Though death is often erroneously associated with a state of suffering, the physical tortures of disease are far worse than the liberating experience of death. Often, the consciousness passing out of the old body at death feels a wonderful sense of release and peace: "So this is death. Oh, how

Death is an ecstasy, for it removes the burden of body identification

nice! It is not at all as I thought. I am life apart from the sensitive, troublesome body. God's anaesthetic of death has removed from me all physical pain."

For a time, there may linger a sense of mental suffering of losing the physical body and of parting with loved ones: "How can I leave those whom I had thought were mine?" There is then a gradual diminishment of the memories of earthly existence. Ordinary persons enjoy the rest of a peaceful death-sleep in the astral heaven. Virtuous souls alternate sleep with wakefulness in this land of blissful freedom and beauty. Devoid of the harsh, often destructive clashes of gross matter, these virtuous astral beings move freely and at will in bodies of light through endless tracts of rainbow-hued densities of luminosity that inform multivaried lifetronic landscapes, scenes, and beings. Their very breath and sustenance are rays of subtle lifetrons. In time, again determined by their karma, their mortal inclinations, transgressions, and latent material desires draw them back into new physical embodiments.

As desire for life brings the sleeping man to the state of wakefulness, so subconscious desires for a lost physical body and for the earth environment act as vibratory attractive forces that reembody the soul again within a mother's womb.

Meditation frees man from attachment to the body

A BIRD LONG CONFINED in a cage may return to it even when set free; so also, a man much attached to bodily existence desires to return to a physical form even after being released by death. Long imprisonment in a cage makes the bird forget its free home in the skies; similarly, the soul consciousness of man, confined in the bodily prison through many incarnations, forgets its free blessed home in vast space.

It takes a long time—many incarnations of right action, good company, help of the guru, self-awakening, wisdom, and meditation—for man to regain his soul consciousness of immortality. To reach this state of Self-realization, each man must practise meditation to transfer his consciousness from the limited body to the unlimited sphere of joy felt in meditation. By continuous unity with Spirit in *samadhi,* and by nonattachment to the body, the devotee realizes the body as a temporary place of confinement; he looks forward eagerly to return to his home of everlasting blessedness in Spirit. Devotees who are not rudely hurled out of the flesh by Death, but who depart in conscious dignity through meditation-acquired power, find their way back to oneness with Omnipresent Bliss.

Swami Pranabananda,* an exalted disciple of Lahiri Mahasaya, who was about to transfer his soul from the limitations of the physical body to the omnipresent kingdom of Spirit, found his disciples crying. "Beloved ones," he said consolingly, "I have been long with you, serving you with joy of divine wisdom. Please don't be selfish about your loss in me, but rejoice that I am discarding the prison house of my body by having worked out my term of karmic obligation. I go now to reclaim my kingdom of omnipresence, to meet my Cosmic Beloved!" So saying, he blessed the devotees; and, practising the advanced technique of *Kriya Yoga,* consciously left his body.

VERSE 23

नैनं छिन्दन्ति शस्त्राणि नैनं दहति पावकः ।
न चैनं क्लेदयन्त्यापो न शोषयति मारुतः ॥

No weapon can pierce the soul; no fire can burn it; no water can moisten it; nor can any wind wither it.

IMMUTABLE EVER, OF THE FINEST VIBRATION of Spirit-Bliss, this soul cannot be touched or harmed by anything of grosser vibratory quality—neither by cruel thrusts of weapons nor hungry all-consuming flames; nor can liquids drench or drown it, nor defile its lips, which quaff only immortal drink; nor can the stoutest wind render it dry unto dust, nor withholding, take away its breath of life.

The Spirit differentiates Its manifestations in creation into two sets of distinctly different attributes: the invisible soul and its powers of life, mind, and wisdom; and the visible forms of vibratory body and matter.

By the use of fine vibrations, the Spirit created the soul, intellect, mind, life; and, by grosser vibrations, body, kinetic energy, and atomic matter. The "weapons" of earth or solids, of fire or energy, of water or liquids, of air or wind—all these constitute gross vibrations.

---

* See *Autobiography of a Yogi,* chapter entitled "The Saint With Two Bodies," and reference to Swami Pranabananda's dramatic earth-exit in the chapter "Founding a Yoga School in Ranchi." *(Publisher's Note)*

The soul, the individualized reflection of Spirit, is made of a "vibrationless" or reactionless vibration of joy—the immortal, omniscient, omnipresent, ever new Bliss of Spirit—it cannot be disturbed by the gross vibrations of solids, liquids, air, or energy. Ice collides with ice, water dashes against water, energy is matched against energy; but stones cannot impinge upon the finer vibratory elements of air or fire. Similarly, gross vibrations of matter or "atomic stones" cannot in any way impose their crudity on soul consciousness.

Gross and fine vibratory manifestations are both naught but one dreaming consciousness of Spirit, expressing through Its individualized dreaming consciousness, the soul. Even as God creates on a cosmic scale, the consciousness of man in the dream state can create individualized personalities, or "souls," will, thought, and feeling, and also the appearances of bodies, solids, liquids, gases, and energy. The man's dream might depict a battle with terrible weapons, or show the devastation of floods, fires, or storms, but none of these affect the inner ego-consciousness of the dreamer. He is not hurt or destroyed by any dream object or weapon, water, fire, or energy. Neither is the soul affected by its cosmic-dream-created objects of solids, liquids, wind, and fire. Just as the dreamer is untouched by his dream, so the soul—one with Spirit—is unaffected by the objects evolved and vibrated out of the divine dream-consciousness of the Dreamer-Spirit.

The awakened soul becomes conscious of its oneness with Spirit. When the physical consciousness of man changes by meditation from delusive dreams to the divine wakefulness of soul consciousness, he beholds all solids, liquids, energies as a play of forces—as dream images floating in the mind of the Cosmic Dreamer. Then he knows that in reality the dream sword cannot slay the dream body nor is anything able to harm or destroy him!

No matter how devastating the happenings in his dream, the dreamer is never hurt by them; he finds himself safe after the dream is over. Similarly, the human soul-dreamer may be frightened temporarily by his experiences during this dream of life, but when he awakes in God, lo! he is safe and sound.

VERSE 24

अच्छेद्योऽयमदाह्योऽयमक्लेद्योऽशोष्य एव च।
नित्यः सर्वगतः स्थाणुरचलोऽयं सनातनः॥

The soul is uncleavable; it cannot be burnt or wetted or dried. The soul is immutable, all-permeating, ever calm, and immovable—eternally the same.

THE MYSTERIOUS SOUL abides forever, changing never, even when the bubble of cosmos melts in the spatial Ocean of Infinity.* The subtle soul secretly sleeps in every blade of grass, in every nook of creation. The soul hides in the honeycomb of atoms. Thoughts cannot ruffle it. It loves to live in the grottos of change, ever steadfast and immovable. It never dreams aught but eternity.

In the previous stanza, the Gita proclaims that no outside objects, whether weapons, fire, water, or wind, can affect the soul. It now further explains that the soul itself possesses those mysterious qualities of self-conscious existence that are not vulnerable to any phenomena. Every man is a soul and has a body. Through delusion, he constantly finds his soul identified with the body; thus he ascribes to himself all the bodily limitations. It is the body that can be cut, burned, wetted, dried, hurt, made restless; moved from one place to another, yet able to occupy only one place at a time because it is circumscribed by a small space; and it is short-lasting. So the individual identified with the body thinks that it is he who is thus afflicted and then subjected to the final indignity of death!

The man of Self-realization, on the other hand, knows himself to be the soul—omnipresent, eternal, ever undisturbed in the largest and the tiniest caves of vibrations.

The paradox of delusion is possible because man, as mortal, is a mixture of the changeless soul and the changeable body. If he wants to avoid permanently all forms of misery, he must learn soul identification. By body identification, man has to suffer incarnations of soul-oblivion, undergoing numerous rebirths and their attendant miseries.

No matter how much one has been meditating, if he still becomes overwhelmed with bodily suffering or is afraid of disease or death, he has advanced little and has realized little. The aspirant must meditate deeper and deeper until he can attain ecstatic communion with God and thus forget the limitations of the body. During meditation he must not only think, but realize, that he is formless,

---

* Having once come into existence, the soul never ceases to be (II:20), even at the time of cosmic dissolution when all matter is resolved into Spirit in the universal cycles of comings and goings.

omnipresent, omniscient, far above all bodily changes!

Every advanced devotee during ecstasy realizes omnipresence, omniscience, and ever new joy of Spirit. After coming out of ecstasy, he should try to retain in the conscious mind those experiences of Spirit. Human consciousness thus becomes expanded into Cosmic Consciousness.

VERSE 25

अव्यक्तोऽयमचिन्त्योऽयमविकार्योऽयमुच्यते ।
तस्मादेवं विदित्वैनं नानुशोचितुमर्हसि ॥

The soul is said to be imponderable, unmanifested, and unchangeable. Therefore, knowing it to be such, thou shouldst not lament!

BEFORE THE SPARKS OF CREATION blinked their luminous eyes, before the cosmic dream took form, the soul resided ever awake and unmanifested in Spirit. Before the Spirit spumed Its thought waves, the soul remained in Its bosom unthinkable by thought, undisturbed by change. And when Spirit cast forth Its dreams of universes, and the soul dreamed dreams of body-covered forms, still the soul remained the same. Anyone who—espousing this truth—knows the soul to be the image of immortal Spirit should not behave in a contradictory manner and foolishly lament, thinking the Self to be vulnerable and destructible with the afflicted and perishable body.

The soul dreams the existence of the body

A METAPHYSICAL CONTROVERSY arises when the Bhagavad Gita speaks of the soul as unmanifested while it is apparently manifested in the body of every individual. This paradox can be explained by analyzing the dream state. If John dreams that he has become a fabulous giant catching wild elephants and holding them captive in the palm of his hand, his dream consciousness undergoes a temporary change; but when he wakes up, he finds that his essential ego or "John" consciousness has remained unchanged by the absurd dream experience. The essence of his consciousness was aloof or unmanifested in the dream; and the dream thoughts were not aware or conscious of the true "John" consciousness. The soul similarly dreams the body, and ascribes to the dream ego inherent in it all the dream body states. When man enters deep dreamless sleep, however, the soul temporarily forgets all its dreams about the body and the world and remains locked up in its true nature of bliss. Thus, even during the period of delusion throughout which the soul has daydreams about the body, the soul itself remains unchanged, unborn with the dream. The dream comes and goes; the soul is changeless. The flowers of many lives successively come and go; the soul soil of the garden remains the same.

The body emanating from the soul is not conscious of the soul, but the soul is aware of the body. Just as a person can watch through a screen a crowd of people in front of him, without himself being seen by them, so the soul through the screen of intuition watches all its thoughts, but the unenlightened thoughts cannot know the soul. That is why the Gita speaks of the soul as imponderable—beyond thought.

The "I," or ego—the dream projection of the soul, and the subject of the objective dream—is what thinks and uses its powers of sensation to know and relate to the dream of material creation. Thus, thought and sensation are not a part of the soul, but are the experience of the ego consciousness in the dream. "Thinking" is inseparable in concept from the one who is doing the thinking and the object about which he is thinking. It thus involves the subjective and objective consciousness as well as the thinking process itself. One knows he exists because of the confirmation of his thoughts and feelings that it is so. But what of a person in deep sleep or absolute calmness in which—even if for just an instant—there is neither thought nor feeling, nor is he unconscious (that is, without any consciousness)? He is not nonexistent at that time; but his existence is without the consciousness of ego and without the support of thinking "I exist." This fragmentary "moment of truth" is intuition, fleeting because undeveloped. It reveals momentarily the presence of the soul, which exists above ego and its instruments of thought and feeling.

Thoughts and sensations are like searchlights: they throw their rays in front on material objects; they do not reveal the soul behind them. Intuition is like a spherical light, with rays on all sides, revealing the soul and also its outward projections of thoughts and sensations connected with the ego. Intuition is the bridge between the soul and the ego's thoughts and sensations. If one can for a sufficient length of time remain unidentified with thoughts and sensations, and without being unconscious, he will know through the development of intuition the nature of the soul. When one is thus perfectly calm, neither thinking or sentient, nor unconscious, yet *knowing* he exists—a keenness of joyful being in which the thinking, thought, and thinker have become one (unity of the knower, knowing, and known)—therein is the soul's consciousness.

From this unmanifested aboveness, the soul, the individualization of the Creator, projects those forces that create the bodily form and the ability to experience through that image.

Just as the light falling on the movie screen produces many motion pictures, so the "ray" of the soul coming from Spirit produces a picture of the body on the screen of human consciousness and of space. A person watching motion pictures on a theatre screen may take his attention away from them and look up; he will see over his head a transparent beam of light in which there are no visible pictures whatever. It may therefore be said that the electric ray that produces pictures on the screen is unchanged or unborn, even though the pictures emanating from it change, and are born from it.

When a man is identified with his body, he feels nothing more than the sensations of sight, smell, taste, touch, sound, weight, and movement. If by meditation he withdraws his consciousness within, he finds a silent light, finer and subtler than X-rays—the ray of the soul coming from the Spirit—projecting the picture of the body on the screen of human consciousness and of space. Through his eye of intuition the devotee perceives this soul-ray; in it is no body with its various complexities, yet it is producing on the screen of human consciousness the changeable picture of the body. The body is not "matter," but is composed of several forces, emanating from the soul's ray. As the movie beam creates pictures on the screen by passing through a film that differentiates its light into forms, so the ray of the soul passing through the film of *maya* (delusion) is differentiated into the various creative forces that become the body and its inherent powers of consciousness and life (ego, mind, life force, and so forth) that enable it to act in and react to its environment. Modern science is moving closer to truth in acknowledging the body to be an expression of electromagnetic waves.*

---

* In recent years, this understanding has had far-reaching effects on the practice of medicine and the healing arts—contributing to an emerging focus on healing through life energy. Based on years of research into the electromagnetic nature of the body, Robert Becker, M.D., professor of medicine at the State University of New York, wrote in *The Body Electric: Electromagnetism and the Foundation of Life* (New York: Morrow and Company, 1978): "There is only one health, but diseases are many. Likewise, there appears to be one fundamental force that heals, although the myriad schools of medicine all

God sent man to earth to be entertained by the bodily dreams, not to obscure his consciousness of immortality by being identified with the body. It is therefore foolish for one to grieve about the bodily changes of which the soul, the Self, is the changeless witness.

The advanced student should meditate deeply until his thoughts

---

have their favourite ways of cajoling it into action. Our prevailing mythology denies the existence of any such generalized force in favour of thousands of little ones sitting on pharmacists' shelves, each one potent against only a few ailments or even a part of one. This system often works fairly well, especially for treatment of bacterial diseases, but...the inner force can be tapped in many ways, [including] faith healing, magic healing, psychic healing, and spontaneous [self] healing....By whatever means, if the energy is successfully focused, it results in a marvellous transformation. What seemed like an inexorable decline suddenly reverses itself....

"The means may be direct—the psychic methods mentioned above—or indirect: Herbs can be used to stimulate recovery; this tradition extends from prehistoric wise-women...to the prevailing drug therapies of the present. Fasting, controlled nutrition, and regulation of living habits to avoid stress can be used to coax the latent healing force from the sick body; we can trace this approach back from today's naturopaths to Galen and Hippocrates....All worthwhile medical research and every medicine man's intuition is part of the same quest for knowledge of the same elusive healing energy."

The Saturday Review of July 8, 1978, reported that Dr. Becker made medical history when, working on frogs and rats who had lost a leg, he used electrical stimulation to grow a new limb—"with cartilage and bone, muscle, nerves, and veins, all in awesome anatomical precision." (Unlike other animals such as crabs and salamanders, frogs and rats do not naturally regenerate body parts.) In addition, *Saturday Review* stated, Dr. Becker "applied the newly found healing mechanism to broken human bones, successfully knitting fractures that had failed to heal even after extensive surgical procedures. He and his colleagues have now reached the point where they can confidently predict that regeneration of human parts can and will be achieved, possibly in the next few decades."

Other researchers studying the subtle energies underlying the physical body have focused on mental and spiritual techniques of awakening the life force for healing. Positive thinking, visualization, prayer, and affirmation (see also XV:14 and XVII:14–17), as well as physical therapies based on life-energy stimulation, such as acupuncture, massage, etc., are among those whose effectiveness has been demonstrated by various scientific studies.

In light of yoga's teaching that the body is a materialization of thought through the instrumentality of *prana* (life energy), the following report from *The Brain Revolution* by Marilyn Ferguson (New York: Bantam, 1973) is of particular interest: "Scientists in the Soviet Union have been researching the electromagnetic radiation (called 'bioplasma') given off by the human body. They have charted the effects of different stimuli on that radiation. They found that chemicals, such as adrenaline, had the weakest effect. Massage of acupuncture points had the next strongest effect, followed by electrical stimulation and exposure to mild laser light. Most powerful of all, as observed by changes in the bioplasma, is human volition. If the subject quietly directs his thought toward a specific part of the body, the bioplasma shows corresponding changes."

"Will power is that which changes thought into energy," Paramahansa Yogananda stated. In *Man's Eternal Quest, The Divine Romance,* and especially in the *Yogoda Satsanga Lessons* (see page 1131), he presents yoga principles and techniques for applying this principle to the healing of the body. *(Publisher's Note)*

become dissolved into intuition. In the lake of intuition, free from the waves of thought, the yogi can see the unruffled reflection of the moon of the soul. Forgetting his dreams of the body, he knows that the soul exists behind the screen of thoughts and is therefore unknown to them. When the yogi perceives the soul as made in the image of Spirit, he knows himself to be unchangeable, unmanifested, ever calm, like the Spirit. All devotees should meditate and interiorize their consciousness until they realize the true nature of the soul.

VERSES 26–27

अथ चैनं नित्यजातं नित्यं वा मन्यसे मृतम्।
तथापि त्वं महाबाहो नैवं शोचितुमर्हसि॥ *(26)*

जातस्य हि ध्रुवो मृत्युर्ध्रुवं जन्म मृतस्य च।
तस्मादपरिहार्येऽर्थे न त्वं शोचितुमर्हसि॥ *(27)*

But if thou dost imagine this soul incessantly to be born and to die, even in that case, O Mighty-armed (Arjuna), thou shouldst not grieve for it. For that which is born must die, and that which is dead must be born again. Why then shouldst thou grieve about the unavoidable?

"BUT IF DELUSION'S DREAM makes you think of the Self as constantly modifying itself with its change of mortal residences, even then, O devotee Arjuna, you should not allow yourself to sorrow! You who are mighty-armed with mental power and self-control should perceive the uselessness in lamenting what is unavoidable—a fate of one's own making. For the deluded Self that is enamoured of its cosmic-dream bodily residence must be prepared to undergo, through the magic potion of karma, the nightmares of bodily births inevitably pursued by bodily deaths, and dreams of physical dissolutions followed by physical manifestations!"

The greatest dread of ordinary man is death, with its rude imposition interrupting fortuitous plans and fondest attachments with an unknown and unwelcome change. The yogi is a conqueror of the grief associated with death. By control of mind and life force and the development of wisdom, he makes friends with the change of consciousness called death—he becomes familiar with the state of inner calmness and aloofness from identification with the mortal body. However, when the aspiring devotee persistently but only absentmindedly meditates, seemingly without making progress, he cannot always maintain that mental neutrality. Then, like the ordinary man, he is sometimes haunted with the desire to avoid his inevitable death—severing him from familiar moorings and memories—and its corollary of rebirth in which he has to start all over again in a slowly developing new form, among new faces, new surroundings, and new circumstances.

Overcoming fear of death

If, through delusion, the devotee still feels himself, the soul, somehow inextricably linked with a perishable body, it is nevertheless foolish for him to grieve. So long as the soul is compelled by karma to be imprisoned in the chambers of births and deaths, nothing is gained by succumbing to grief. It is more profitable and in keeping with his true nature for the devotee to concentrate in a positive way on destroying the subconsciously stored prenatal and postnatal reincarnation-making impulses by exercising his will force and determination, and by identification of his mind with the blissful soul.

It is senseless to bemoan the operation of universal laws. According to the law of cause and effect, the soul is destined to change its mortal residences. Once the soul has been caught by *maya,* or delusion, it must occupy a series of prison houses of births and deaths to fulfil its desires and pay to the Justice of Cause and Effect the debts incurred by its own actions. There is no use in lamenting!* Rather, man should take practical steps to try in every way to extricate himself from all earthly attachments and bodily identification by tuning in with Spirit in meditation and thus parole himself from the mortal prison into the free world of immortality.

The average person, suffering from ignorance and material attachment, lives a narrow life—he is born, he marries, and he dies! He must unavoidably repeat the same experiences until by meditation and identification with Spirit, he gains eternal freedom. Once the immortal soul loses its body identification, it is free! The true pragmatist, eager for

---

* The Moving Finger writes; and, having writ,
Moves on: nor all thy Piety nor Wit
Shall lure it back to cancel half a Line,6
Nor all thy Tears wash out a Word of it.

—*The Rubaiyat of Omar Khayyam* (Translated by Edward FitzGerald). Paramahansa Yogananda's spiritual interpretation of this poetic classic, *Wine of the Mystic,* is available from Yogoda Satsanga Society of India.

"results," will therefore spend time in deep meditation rather than waste his life occupied in nothing more than trivial material pursuits and vague speculations about the wheel of births and deaths.

There are two kinds of births and deaths: the breath way and the astral way. Human birth is accompanied by the presence of breath (inhalation and exhalation of the airborne cosmic currents). Earthly death is marked by the absence of bodily breath. The breath-marked births and deaths are peculiar to the earthly plane of existence.

Two kinds of birth and death: earthly and astral

The astral way of birth and death has a deeper meaning. In the physical world the soul is encased in a fleshly body made of sixteen gross elements. After death the soul is rid of its heavy overcoat of flesh but remains encased in its two other subtle garments—the astral body of nineteen subtle principles and the causal body of thirty-five ideas or thought forces. ("Body" signifies any encasement, whether gross or subtle, which surrounds the soul.)*

When a devotee by divine ecstasy completely identifies himself with omnipresent Spirit, he goes out of the three bodies and attains Omnipresence. But when a man leaves the physical body in ignorance, he awakens in an astral world, encased in his astral body. In accordance with karmic law, he lives and develops in the astral for some time, working out some of his past tendencies. At the timing of cosmic law, man again experiences the death-disintegration of the astral body and is reborn once more in the physical world.

At physical death man loses his consciousness of the flesh and becomes conscious of his astral body in the astral world. Thus physical death is astral birth. Later, he passes from the consciousness of luminous astral birth to the consciousness of dark astral death and awakens in a new physical body. Thus astral death is physical birth. These recurrent cycles of physical and astral encasements are the ineluctable destiny of all unenlightened men.

A truth-seeker realizes by introspection and self-analysis and by study under a God-realized guru that the universal laws which govern the phenomenal world ordain that the karma-pursued man must undergo this series of births and deaths. The wise devotee does not grieve over his dire fate and difficult future experiences; rather he concen-

* See II:20, page 213.

trates his utmost powers to destroy those evil karmas by identifying himself with the omniscient Spirit!

Births and deaths are inevitable for man only during the state of ignorance in which he thinks he is the body and cannot exist without it. Only the man who will not seek the awakening of wisdom must suffer the nightmares and delusive dreams of births and deaths and the fanciful miseries and limitations attending them. A man through persistent wrong living may suffer from continual nightmares that he is being suffocated and murdered. Only by right living may he disgorge his subconscious mind of those evil impulses which are the sole cause of his nightly hallucinations.

Ending the cycle of births and deaths

A man with an extreme fear of the cycle of births and deaths may dream every night that he is being born as a baby and then that he dies after he becomes an adult. These dreams may continue indefinitely, until by wisdom the man becomes free from the harrowing fears that are motivating his dreams.

The same truth may be applied to the soul: if a man through delusion experiences births followed by deaths, he must inexorably continue to do so until by wisdom, meditation, discrimination, and ecstatic communion with God he identifies his soul with Spirit. A man awake in omnipresent Spirit loses all delusive nightmares.

VERSE 28

अव्यक्तादीनि भूतानि व्यक्तमध्यानि भारत।
अव्यक्तनिधनान्येव तत्र का परिदेवना॥

The beginning of all creatures is veiled, the middle is manifested, and the end again is imperceptible, O Bharata (Arjuna). Why, then, lament this truth?

THE SOURCE OF THE DANCING STREAM of lives is secretly hidden behind mists of delusive ignorance; the end of the same silvery stream is also shrouded in mystery. Only the middle part is visible to humanity's myopic vision. Why, then, grieve over a matter no mortal can solve?

Every man wonders from what mystery chamber came original man, birds, amphibians, crustaceans, stones, flowers, rivers, light, magnetism, electricity, worlds, stars, and universes. From what source do they appear on the screen of human consciousness? And—engrossing puzzle!—what happens to the two billion population of the globe* which, every century, vanishes without a trace?

Through history, biology, and other sciences, man learns only about the manifested period of human existence on earth. No physical science sheds light on either the beginning or the end of that existence.

Solving the mystery of life

When we see a tray of watches displayed in a shop window, we may note their shapes, sizes, and styles, and hear them tick; but we do not see their factory of origin. Nor do we know what fate will befall the watches after they have been bought and used by various people. We are concerned casually only about the middle or present existence of those timepieces. We should look with like equanimity upon the mysteries of life, which seem understandable and comprehensible in the middle, but inscrutable in their source and end.

Negative and grief-inducing philosophies inquire mainly about the prenatal and postmortem conditions of man—rejoicing in birth and lamenting the advent of death. Pessimistic philosophers concede the insolubility of the beginning and end of life, and surrender either to conjecture or to blind belief in some dogma about the unknown. The wise, instead, use the precious moments of the present in practising the laws of concentration, meditation, and self-discipline by which they can contact the Absolute and know from Him, if He would condescend to explain, the secrets of His eternal kingdom!

Human beings endowed with a questioning intelligence are sent to this partly understandable world to do their best to struggle and succeed according to the light of their intelligence; no clear outward revelation is vouchsafed them regarding the purpose of life or its source or final end. This fact is a clue to the entire mystery; it silently suggests that the search for truth must be not an outer but an inner one.

The stage of the earth is well set with food, air, water, and fire; man has to study Nature to his best advantage and to act out his part according to the innate guidance of his intuition, and by imitation of his fellow beings. The great Dramatist-Director of this mystery play of lives on the stage of the earth remains hidden somewhere! everywhere! directing the play of His children-actors only through the suggestions of conscience and innate understanding.

The drama, though puzzling, is not inexplicable. Even ordinary

* I.e., in 1950. *(Publisher's Note)*

men tend to reform their lives in some degree when they discover, by the warnings of self-created suffering, that they have not been acting according to the wishes of the Infinite Director!

Devotees who are trying to contact God through the study of philosophy and the practice of self-discipline, yoga, and meditation should not divert their attention, like worldly men, in lamenting about fate, destiny, and the ineffectiveness of human reason as a tool in discovering the solution of life's enigmas.

I remember occasions in the past when, finding great joy in contacting God by meditation, my mind would suddenly be very curious. "Why not ask God for further information about Jesus, Krishna, Shakespeare—or about my own relatives now departed from the earth?" When the Lord would not immediately respond to these irrelevant if not irreverent inquiries, I would become a doubting Thomas and cast myself into a dungeon of grief. Knowledge of the complete history of the series of incarnations of every man on earth and in heaven (I would later feel remorsefully) would not be worth the temporary loss of the blissful God-contact!

The devotee must beware of the dangers involved in wandering into the byways of curiosity, forgetful of the direct highway to God. Many, many devotees would have found God and heard from His infinite lips the solution to all puzzles had they not strayed into blind alleys of unsatisfied spiritual or intellectual curiosity.

Man should not desire knowledge of the mysteries of God's creation in preference to knowledge of God Himself. The true devotee loves God so ardently that He is compelled to manifest Himself in the devotional consciousness; the devotee leaves unto God the right to reveal, or not reveal, the secrets of His kingdom. Even with the best human friends, one does not betray a vulgar curiosity! Eventually those friends, without one's rude probing, confide fully and naturally all secrets of their lives.

UNTIL A DEVOTEE'S INTELLIGENCE becomes cosmic consciousness, God cannot convey to man the meaning of creation. How to explain to the highest human faculty—reason, which reduces all concepts to cause-effect relationships—the motives of the uncaused God?*

* "For My thoughts are not your thoughts, neither are your ways My ways, saith the Lord. For as the heavens are higher than the earth, so are My ways higher than your ways, and My thoughts than your thoughts" (Isaiah 55:8–9).

All created things seem to be explainable in the middle, as we have seen, but are infinite and invisible in beginning and end. This mystery should spur man to trace the visible effect to the Invisible Cause, the Spirit. Nothing can be gained by grief about an unknown fate or the unanswered "whys," or by negative thought about the limitations of reason—the prevalent philosophies of our era discourage man from seeking in meditation to go beyond reason. The only way to know the beginning and the end of all things is to contact God.

Human reason cannot grasp the meaning of creation

This wonderful drama of life, this mystery play, this visible effect of Universal Existence, could never have come into being without a Cause; having existed, it could not be annihilated into nonexistence! Something cannot spring from nothing; neither can something end in nothing. All enigmas can be solved by the development of intuition, the divine medium of communication between God and man.

VERSE 29

आश्चर्यवत्पश्यति कश्चिदेनमाश्चर्यवद्वदति तथैव चान्यः ।
आश्चर्यवच्चैनमन्यः शृणोति श्रुत्वाप्येनं वेद न चैव कश्चित् ॥

Some behold the soul in amazement. Similarly, others describe it as marvellous. Still others listen about the soul as wondrous. And there are others who, even after hearing all about the soul, do not comprehend it at all.

THROUGH THE INSTRUCTION of a true guru, the deep-delving devotee with beatific vision beholds the soul as an amazing luminous wonder. Others, diving into the ocean of ecstasy, describe it unceasingly as a marvellous vibratory entity of wisdom. Others who listen to the wondrous Cosmic Vibration of *Aum,* the Amen, feel the soul as an exquisite dream-song of ever new joy. There are others who have not experienced the soul; their ears of spiritual perception are deaf, unable to grasp its philosophy even when they repeatedly hear about it.

THE THREE MODES of perceiving the soul mentioned in this stanza—beholding, describing or speaking of, and listening about—imply three of the manifestations by which the soul reveals itself: *Light* (beholding); *Wisdom* (describing its wonder); and *Cosmic Sound* (hearing; communion with the bliss-imparting cosmic sound of *Aum*).

The Spirit in the unmanifested state is ever-existing, ever-conscious, ever-new Bliss; the soul is a ray of the Spirit. The Spirit manifests Itself as bliss-imparting Cosmic Light, Cosmic Wisdom, and Cosmic Sound; the soul, therefore, is also perceived as blissful Cosmic Light, Cosmic Wisdom, and Cosmic Sound. Through various techniques, learned through a true guru, the devotee finds his intuition absorbed in these manifestations of the soul. When yogis develop deep intuition, they may experience the soul as an amazing mystical Light. When devotees feel the soul as a ray of Cosmic Intelligence, they speak of it in terms of marvellous Wisdom. Others perceive the soul as an exquisite audible vibration of the wondrous Cosmic Sound, or blissful *Aum.*

Spirit and soul manifest as light, wisdom, and sound

Superficial truth-seekers remain so engrossed in restlessness that no matter how many times they listen to a wise man's discourse about the soul, they understand him no better than if listening to one speaking a foreign language! It can be safely said that only an advanced devotee perceives the soul as Cosmic Light or Cosmic Wisdom or Cosmic Sound.

ORDINARY HUMAN BEINGS, studying and working with material life, are circumscribed in their understanding by their sense perceptions and rationalizing intelligence. With undeveloped intuition, their limited power of intellectuality cannot truly comprehend matters of the spirit even when such truth is expounded to them. Though colossal intellects and famous theologians may be well read about the soul, they may nevertheless understand little about it! On the other hand, even illiterates given to deep meditation will be able clearly to describe the nature of the soul from their own direct experience. Intuition bridges the chasm between intellectual knowledge of the soul and actual realization of the divine Self.

Intuition bridges the chasm between intellectual knowledge and realization

Soul and Spirit and all inner truths can be apprehended only by developing the power of intuition by regular deep meditation. Intelligence and sense perceptions can perceive only phenomena or *qualities* of the Eternal Substance; intuition alone can perceive the *essence* of that Substance. Therefore, it is evident that the culture of intuition by meditation must precede true perception.

In the life of every person, two forces of knowledge are operative from birth: (1) the power of human reason, along with its satellites of sensation, perception, conception, and so forth; (2) the power of intuition. The former is developed through social institutions and interactions. The latter usually remains uncultured, undeveloped, because of want of proper guidance and methods of training.

In almost everyone, lower forms of intuition now and again express themselves in otherwise inexplicable experiences of "knowing"—those that come of themselves independent of the testimony of the senses and reason. These intuitive glimpses are so-called hunches, strong inner feelings, premonitions, "prophetic" dreams. These are sometimes the crystallised experiences of former births (for example, certain knowledge about persons or events carried over from the past that have a predictable future), and have no great spiritual value. Other such experiences indicate a little capacity for being calm and intuitively receptive; others indicate just an unusually keen but passive rationality.

All power of knowing borrows its ability from intuition. The highest expression of intuition is that by which the soul knows Itself: The knower, knowing, and known exist as one. When intuition comes in touch with matter, it passes through various stages of evolution. As the soul evolves in expression through five stages, or *koshas**—as the various qualities of inert matter in minerals, as life without cognizing power in plants, as consciousness and sense perception in animals, as intellect and ego consciousness in man, and as divinity in enlightened man—so also the knowing powers of the soul undergo evolutional progress and refinement through these various stages of soul evolution: as unconscious response in minerals, as feeling in plant life, as instinctive knowledge in animals, as intellect, reason, and undeveloped introspective intuition in man, and as pure intuition in the superman.

In man, the conscious awakening of intuition expresses itself in five forms, as determined by the effects of the five *koshas* inherent in his consciousness. They are as follows:

❖ *Five forms of intuition* ❖

The first form of intuition, the crudest form, is the basic feeling that "I exist with a body and a mind." This feeling every human being has. This is called the intuition of the *annamaya kosha*—the consciousness of existence in the gross

---

* See I:4–6, page 63.

or matter plane. When one is limited to sense knowledge or inferential knowledge, he is on this crude plane of intuition. Why is this called intuition at all? Because in every thinking or sensing process, there is the immediate feeling of "my-ness." This feeling is a direct awareness; it cannot be given by any mediary in the world. Every being knows that he exists. It is a feeling that is with him even in sleep and dreams. This knowing comes from the knowledge or intuition of the ever conscious soul.

The second form of intuition is of the pranic energy, the vital or life current that courses through every cell of the body. It is the intuition, or immediate knowledge, of the *pranamaya kosha,* the plane of the life forces that create and sustain the body. In the primary form of this intuition, one hears subtle sounds, sees subtle lights, feels subtle sensations, smells subtle fragrances, and tastes subtle flavours. These are not outward sensations; they have nothing to do with the physical sense organs. In the higher form of this intuition, one feels the pranic force in the subtlest way in every part of the body. Intensified forms of the intuition of *prana*—for example when the yogi perceives the soul as Cosmic Sound, as noted in this Gita stanza—depend upon the succeeding stages of intuition. When one is in this second form of intuitive knowledge, or *prana,* he has partially or wholly withdrawn his consciousness from the matter plane of *annamaya kosha.*

The third form of intuition is the direct knowledge of *manas* or mind—its effects and its combinations with other principles of perception and cognition—along with the separate knowledge of the subtle organs of sense. When one has attained this stage of intuition, the attention is not on the matter plane—that is, the body—nor much on the pranic plane; though some action of *prana* may be involved in the experiences of this state. This is called the intuition of the *manomaya kosha,* or mind plane. The consciousness in this plane may be worked on by *prana,* or life energy, and visions are then seen. In this form of intuition, one is not conscious of the outside world at all, or very little, depending on the depth of meditation. In the undeveloped stage of this form of intuition, one may see visions of all sorts, either fitfully generated, or voluntarily willed. For some people, it is not under control and so visions are fitfully generated. For the adept, such phenomena are voluntary and under control of the will. Visions are astral in substance, projections of *prana* and consciousness as lifetronic images. Visions experienced by those whose intuition is still in undeveloped stages may be little more than entertaining phenomena—

glimpses into the subtle astral realms (distractions eschewed by the serious God-seeker). Meaningful visions, having true spiritual value, are engendered by the soul and Spirit through pure intuition working on *prana* and the God-attuned consciousness of the devotee for the purpose of elevating him to ever higher spiritual states—as for example, beholding the soul as Cosmic Light.

The fourth form of intuition is the direct knowledge of the operation of *buddhi,* or discriminative intellect along with knowledge of the ego. One in this stage does not feel the whirl of mind, the race of *prana,* or the weight and confinement of the body. He feels existent above them, an existence without any other adjunct or condition; though there may remain a doubt in him whether he is knowing his true Self or not. This is the intuition of the *jnanamaya kosha,* or intellect plane. When this stage is high, fully developed, it is called cognitive meditation. It begets keen discernment of truth, manifesting as Wisdom.

The fifth form of intuition is the direct knowledge of bliss as depending upon no object, mediary, or condition. This is intuition of *anandamaya kosha.* It bestows all-fulfilling joy, crowning divine experiences with ultimate satisfaction. In this, as in the previous states, the consciousness has been wholly withdrawn from the body plane, or at least nearly so.

Remember that the first form of intuition is possessed by everyone; the other four forms must be developed. These latter four forms of intuition are not wholly separate. As they develop, one form may manifest when others are present also in some measure. In meditation, when the devotee sees subtle light or hears subtle sound, for example, he may have the intuition of bliss mixed with it to some degree. Or when he intuitively feels himself consciously existent without consciousness of the body (as in the intuition of *jnanamaya kosha*) he may have simultaneously the intuition of unending bliss flowing throughout his being. The highly advanced devotee has this intuitive experience: He feels the soul reflected in the purified, adjunctless intellect and ego; and that *ananda,* divine bliss, is flowing therefrom. Even during the performance of worldly duties, the higher intuition of that spiritual man remains with him in greater or lesser extent according to his spiritual development.

Only the highest of spiritual beings—very few in this world—have pure soul intuition

Pure intuition is soul intuition—knowing the soul by the soul;

seeing the soul with the eyes of the soul, so to speak. Here there are no modifications of intuition—as the intuition of intellect, or *prana,* or mind, or matter. The yogi in this state is above them all—knower, knowing, and known having become one. He is fully conscious of his true Self. This is the real soul-consciousness; and, in fact, it is God-consciousness, for the soul is realized as nothing other than the reflection of Spirit.

Only the highest of spiritual beings—very few in this world—have this pure soul intuition. Some have it at times, as when in deep meditation. Some are often fixed in it for longer periods, even after meditation. The more one is anchored in this consciousness, the more one feels the whole world to be akin. Stars, earth, plants, animals, man—he feels all to be pervaded by the same soul, which he feels to be himself. When soul intuition intensifies, and the yogi remains unbrokenly in that consciousness for a long time, with no desire or effort to hold on to the accoutrements of delusion, then even his body-cage cannot last. He is one with God.

Thus is it declared in this Gita stanza, the wonder of the soul; and that it cannot be known by the ordinary or even keen intellect, but only by those who actually perceive it through intuition. Progressively unfolding by the practice of the right techniques of meditation, intuition makes possible the experience of the various manifestations of the soul, and ultimately the realization of oneself as soul, one with Spirit.

VERSE 30

देही नित्यमवध्योऽयं देहे सर्वस्य भारत।
तस्मात्सर्वाणि भूतानि न त्वं शोचितुमर्हसि॥

O Bharata (Arjuna), the One who dwells in the bodies of all is eternally inviolable. Grieve not, therefore, for any created being.

AS THE DREAMER REMAINS unchanged even though he nightly witnesses himself participating in different dream fantasies, so the invisible soul, dreaming the bodies of many incarnations, itself remains unchanged. Knowing that the bodies of all creatures are spumescent bubbles on God's cosmic dream-ocean of creation, there is no cause to lament when any cosmic-dream-manifested body is withdrawn into the Infinite Dreamless Dreamer.

IT IS NATURAL FOR HUMAN beings to moan the loss of loved ones. But the Bhagavad Gita points out the proper attitude of mind that will free one from inordinate grief.

Life and death, pleasure and pain, and all opposites of this world of relativity, produce in man distinct states, depending on his specific sensitivity. Bereavement over the loss of one's mother may be thus differently experienced by two individuals. The sensitive person, unprotected by a balance of reason, is overwhelmed by his loss; and like one who has taken leave of his senses, he becomes emotionally incapable of even carrying on with his worldly duties. The less sensitive person is only normally affected by his sorrow; he grieves, but life goes on for him. The sensitive man on the battlefield of life has no armour to protect him when he fights the invading hordes of sentiments. He is therefore likely to be overpowered, or slain. The average man finds protection, to some degree, behind his armour of reason.

❖ *The proper attitude that will free one from inordinate grief* ❖

The yogi, the man of perfect equilibrium, is neither hypersensitive nor stoically heartless. During bereavement caused by the death of a loved one, he understands, and thus feels and appreciates, the nature of the loss he has sustained. But inwardly he remains neutral and unmoved, because he perceives that the nature of all material things is impermanent, and that it is thus foolishness to expect permanent happiness by clinging to material forms and objects. Knowledge is light; it illumines and reveals the nature of reality. Hence, the yogi, enlightened by wisdom, is prepared beforehand to meet such changes. Understanding also gives him great sympathy and compassion for those who incur devastating losses without the buffer of wisdom.

In India, those possessing spiritual understanding never speak of an individual's death. They would not say, "Rama is dead." Instead, they say, "Rama has left his body." The ordinary expression, "John is dead," is misleading and a very saddening thought. It presumes the annihilation of the owner of the body along with the death of the body. The wise do not grieve for a soul who has gone from one bodily residence into another, just as an understanding person does not grieve for someone who leaves one residence to move into another house.

Grief is born of ignorance, attachment, and selfish love, because the ordinary man sees only the present frame of existence. The universal nature of his true Self and of all souls is incomprehensible to him—if indeed not untenable—in his time-space capsule of what and who is "mine" in the known now. When those whom he calls his own are snatched away by death, he rails at his loss, little knowing that in truth there is no loss at all in the limitless scope of the soul's eternal existence.

Even while dreaming different forms and experiences, the dreamer's basic consciousness remains the same, unchanged. Upon awakening, it absorbs into itself all the dream manifestations; the dreamer's imagination retains within it all the elements of his dream. Similarly, God dreams many beings through the dreams of countless immutable souls made in His image. In each dream incarnation, unchanging souls wear new bodily forms to play different roles in God's dream. The new dream image forgets its previous roles, but the soul remembers them all. And God's consciousness forever retains the dream images of all human beings. Instead of helplessly grieving for the loss of human relatives or friends, one should get in touch with God, who, to satisfy the desires of a devotee, can project into instant visibility any vanished loved one.

Once, while beholding a motion picture about the life of Abraham Lincoln, I became interested in the wonderful acting and noble deeds of this historical hero; I became his ardent friend! Later in the picture he was slain; I felt very sad. As I got up to leave the theatre, the thought struck me that if I waited for the rerun, I could again see his noble living presence! At the start of the second showing I was as pleased to behold him, moving and laughing, as if he had indeed been resurrected! I kept on watching the show until it was nearly time for him again to be slain. Then I left the theatre precipitantly! In my memory he is still living!

True devotees may successfully pray to God to show them the cosmic-motion-picture manifestation of their "dead" loved ones. All persons, being the materialized thoughts of God, are at last again dissolved into His consciousness but can never be annihilated. God can manifest those beings at will. That is how Elijah and Moses appeared to Jesus Christ,* and how Lahiri Mahasaya† appeared and appears before many of his devotees on earth.

Some waves are on the surface of the ocean and some waves retire into its bosom; but in either case, the wave and the ocean are one. Similarly, human beings who are floating in "life" on the Cosmic

---

* Matthew 17:3.

† See *Autobiography of a Yogi,* especially chapters 1, 35, 36.

Bosom or who are hidden within it through "death," are equally at home in the Eternal Sea.

Realizing that the nature of the soul is immortality, human beings will not unwisely grieve about others' deaths. When a being is gone from earth, it is almost impossible to get in touch with that form unless one is spiritually far advanced. It is therefore futile to moan helplessly. But if one has spiritual perseverance and patience, he can again see his departed loved ones, by first contacting God. In attunement with Him, one can surely see, or know about, his missing dear ones.

The Gita does not teach us to be heartless, to forget friends or obliterate their memory, but merely to avoid unreasonable feelings of bereavement and useless lamentations. It is not good to mourn ignorantly for loved ones whom death has taken away, and thus send them sad vibrations, or to try to keep them earth-bound or to disturb them in the astral world.

The mother, for example, should not lament long or unduly over the loss by death of her child. A child may be required to leave the earth for the purpose of a higher education in the astral world, or for a definite release from physical torture due to an incurable disease, or for certain imperative karmic duties elsewhere. It is God who gives us children and friends; we should be grateful so long as we have them, and grateful for our memories of them when it suits the Divine Planner to remove them to another plane of existence.

A widower might do well never to remarry if in his departed wife he had found satisfaction in his heart for the demands of an ideal divine love. He should always remember her gratefully as one who gave him release, through fulfilment, from the earthly duties of matrimony. If a man found some happiness with his first wife and married again after her death, he should not forget all the good vibrations he received from his first wife, but should occasionally send messages of goodwill to her in the astral world.

Advanced devotees on earth can consciously broadcast vibratory communications to persons who are spiritually evolved in the astral world. Such conscious communication is possible only between advanced souls. But even the ordinary man has power to waft his weightless thoughts in love toward departed dear ones; the vibrations of good thoughts are never lost, but are a quiet stimulus of joy and well-being to those beloved ones who have gone on to the astral world.

The grief of most human beings over the deaths of those close to them is due to selfishness, because of a personal loss of some form of service or comfort. Very few people love others without a tinge of selfish interest—that is the nature of human love. Most people grieve, not for the beloved, but for their personal deprivement!

Divine love recognizes all good persons who enter our lives as expressions of God's love for us. Every friend—in the guise of relatives, friends, beloved, spouse—who is with us now or who has left this earth is a medium through which God Himself symbolizes His friendship. To ignore or abuse friendship, therefore, is an affront to God. In all our harmonious relations we must remember that it is God who is playing hide-and-seek from behind the living hearts. We should never ignore or forget any kindness or service extended to us by a friend. Ingratitude and indifference wither even the stoutest oak of friendship.

Man should not, however, limit the manifestation of God through friendship to only one or a few relatives and friends. All mankind are not only our friends, but our Self! Friends are God in disguise. God the Friend behind all friends! God the only faithful Lover!

God gives us friends and beloved relatives that we may have the opportunity through these relationships to culture elementary love, the first stage of expansion beyond self-love toward divine love. But because man becomes attached to dear ones in a limiting way, the divine law takes them away, not as a punishment, but to teach the law of universal love. It is God who appears for a time as a loving son or daughter—or mother, father, friend, or beloved—and it is He who disappears again from view. If karmic bonds are strong, especially spiritual ties, He may come again in relationships with the same souls in different incarnations.

❖

Loved ones are taken away not as a punishment, but to teach the law of universal love

❖

It is God, and God alone, who has encased Himself as the soul in the many human beings He has created. And when one human being loves another with pure divine love, he sees the spirit of God manifesting in that person. In order to demonstrate His Spirit-nature as soul, distinct from the body, the one God who exists in all bodies appears in one form, takes leave of another; reappears in new forms, then again disappears. It follows, therefore, that it is not the body we should love, but the immortal Spirit within. Those who love the body as the self, rather than as the tabernacle of the true Self, are unduly grieved in the end because the body must perish. Those who love the indwelling Spirit hold on to a lasting joy, because they know the soul is immortal—death cannot touch it at all. The lover of the body has his eyes fixed on the body and cannot see the immortal

Spirit within; so when the body is taken from view his eyes grow dim with tears. Those who learn how to keep their gaze fixed on the souls of their loved ones, do not lose "sight" of them, even when their bodies perish; hence, that relationship is not marred by selfish grief.

Metaphysical interpretation of verse 30

ON THE METAPHYSICAL PLANE of interpretation, as relates to the inner spiritual battle of the devotee-Arjuna, an important point is made in this and preceding verses about the inviolability of the soul. The Lord reminds the aspirant of his innate soul-power to become victorious over his lower ego-nature. Devotees who are addicted to the weakness of their senses and bad habits are not only reluctant to destroy these friendly enemies, but also feel that the overwhelming power of these forces shall surely succeed in the genocide of the soul's divine qualities and aspirations. But though ego, habit, senses, desires, may enshroud man's consciousness for a while, they cannot destroy nor change the soul, nor suppress it forever. Every soul, no matter how "dead" it seems, nor how deeply buried beneath bad habits of ego consciousness, is able to resurrect itself from the sepulchre of wickedness and prenatal and postnatal weaknesses. The soul is indestructible, and untouched and unchanged by its would-be enemies; it only awaits the rallying call of the determined divine warrior.

THE RIGHTEOUS BATTLE IS MAN'S RELIGIOUS DUTY

VERSE 31

स्वधर्ममपि चावेक्ष्य न विकम्पितुमर्हसि ।
धर्म्याद्धि युद्धाच्छ्रेयोऽन्यत्क्षत्रियस्य न विद्यते ॥

Even from the point of view of thine own dharma (one's rightful duty) thou shouldst not inwardly oscillate! There is nothing more propitious for a Kshatriya than a righteous battle.

BEHOLDING THE "GODDESS of righteous duty" as she stands on the sacred altar of life, the spiritual warrior should not hesitate to accept his supreme duty to strive to rout her enemy invaders of ignorance by fighting to acquire wisdom.

Nor should a strong soldier, nurtured on the lap of his mother country, ever waver in protecting her and safeguarding her worthy interests and ideals.

LIFE IN MAN'S BODILY KINGDOM is cooperatively served and protected in general by the head, skin surface, hands, and feet. The feet provide basic labour and service in the form of support and locomotion of the whole body. The surface of the body (including the sense organs) carries on all the "business" transactions through communication with the outer world; and it is also a "field" tilled and reaped of experiences connected with material life. The hands act as shields to protect the body from harm, and govern the body by providing for its needs, care, and welfare. The head with its mental faculties provides the intelligence and the spiritual and moral counsel necessary for maintaining a wise and harmonious kingdom of trillions of cells, and countless sensations, perceptions, and activities. Man instinctively imitated the archetype of the bodily government when organizing his society. Each nation has its intellectual and spiritual people or Brahmins, its soldiers and rulers or Kshatriyas, its businessmen or Vaishyas ("tillers of the soil"), and its labourers or Sudras.

What is man's rightful duty?

By scientists' discoveries of seals, potteries, coins, statues, from ancient cities unearthed in Mohenjo-Daro and Harappa in the Indus Valley, northern India, India's civilization has been established as far older than that of Egypt—"taking us back to an age that can only be dimly surmised."* As the most ancient civilization on earth, India is the cradle of all forms of culture.† Her *rishis* found that every nation

* Sir John Marshall, *Mohenjo-Daro and the Indus Civilization,* 1931.

† "India's tradition had reached a certain point of maturity even at the time of the Indus Valley civilization that flourished five thousand years ago," said Lakhan L. Mehrotra in an article published in *Self-Realization* magazine. "The two most prominent artifacts of that ancient civilization are those representing the Mother Goddess—Shakti, personifying the intelligent creative life force, and the Maha Yogi—Shiva, sitting cross-legged with the symbol of the spiritual eye of wisdom in his forehead. Now, if that spiritual tradition of yoga and meditation could find expression five thousand years ago in an art form, then it must have originated several thousand years before that....

"Looking at the great major centres of civilization that flourished in those ancient times, we find four: (1) along the Nile in Egypt, (2) along the Tigris and the Euphrates in the Middle East—Mesopotamia, (3) along the Yangtze (Ch'ang) and the Yellow River

evolves through physical, emotional, intellectual, and spiritual states—even as a man passes through the state of physical growth in childhood (bodily activity governed by restless energy), the emotional state of youth (activities and desires spurred by heightened sense awareness), and the intellectual and spiritual states of maturity (reason-guided action to meet needs and responsibilities; and ultimately a deepening of consciousness in understanding, wisdom, and spiritual values).

The sages of India were the first to pattern their civilization after the bodily government. That is why they emphasized the recognition of four natural castes, according to man's natural qualifications and actions.* The *rishis* maintained that four castes are necessary in the

---

(Huang Ho) in China, and (4) along the Indus in India. What has happened to all these civilizations?...And yet, in the land of the Indus and the Ganges, that perennial, ancient stream of wisdom still flows with the same vigour.

"In each century India has given birth to lofty spiritual personages. Though she has reached great heights in every field of culture, when that tradition declined somewhat in material terms, its spiritual lustre was nevertheless upheld by these luminaries who appeared, one after another, upon the Indian scene."

At the time India was conquered by Western colonial powers, according to historian Dr. J. T. Sunderland, she was the wealthiest nation on the globe: "This [material] wealth was created by the Hindus' vast and varied industries. Nearly every kind of manufacture or product known to the civilized world—nearly every kind of creation of man's hand and brain, existing anywhere and prized either for its utility or beauty—had long, long been produced in India. India was a far greater industrial and manufacturing nation than any in Europe or any other in Asia" (*India in Bondage,* New York: Simon and Schuster, 1929).

"Let us remember," wrote the eminent historian and philosopher Will Durant (in *The Case for India,* New York: Simon and Schuster, 1930), "that India was the motherland of our race, and Sanskrit the mother of Europe's languages; that she was the mother of our philosophy, mother, through the Arabs, of much of our mathematics, mother...of the ideals embodied in Christianity, mother, through the village community, of self-government and democracy. Mother India is in many ways the mother of us all."

World religions authority Huston Smith recalls that in the 1950s the eminent British historian Arnold Toynbee predicted that in the 21st century "India the conquered would conquer her conquerors."

"He didn't mean by that that we would become Hindus," said Smith in an interview in the *San Diego Union-Tribune,* April 7, 1990. "What he meant was that basic Indian insights would find their way into our Western culture, and, because of their metaphysical and psychological profundity, our way of thinking in the West would be influenced by Indian thought just as Indian technology has been influenced by ours." *(Publisher's Note)*

* The four natural classes of mankind are described allegorically in the Vedas as issuing from the body of Purusha, the Supreme Being: "From his mouth was born the Brahmin; from his two arms, the Rajanya (royal rulers and warriors); from his two thighs, the Vaishya; and from his feet, the Sudra." This earliest scriptural reference is traditionally accepted as the original basis of the caste system that was later elaborated by the lawgiver Manu.

proper government of a country. The intellectual and spiritual Brahmins, the Kshatriya soldiers and rulers, the Vaishya businessmen, and the Sudra labourers should cooperate in a successful government of a country—even as the brain, the hands, the tissues, and the feet all cooperate for the successful maintenance and progress of the bodily kingdom.

In India the four castes were originally based on the innate qualities and the outward actions of the people. All had a respected and necessary place in society. Later, through ignorance, the caste rules became a hereditary halter. Confusion crept in; unworthy children of intellectual and spiritual Brahmins claimed to be Brahmins by sheer virtue of birth, without a corresponding spiritual stature. Children of Kshatriyas became soldiers and rulers even if they had no aptitude or skill in arms or capability to govern. The children of the Vaishyas, even without understanding management of agriculture or trade, laid claim to their inheritance as farmers or businessmen. Sudras were confined to menial labour and servitude, regardless of their superior qualifications. This rigid hereditary caste system is defended only by the orthodox minority in India.

A "caste" system is pernicious also in the West, where divisions have been created according to money, colour, and race. The breeder of hatred and wars! The Bible says all nations have been made of one blood;* that all men—irrespective of colour and race—have been made in the image of God; that all men are the children of common parents, symbolically called Adam and Eve. The grouping of races according to an Aryan and Nordic superiority over other races is a fiction fostered by races suffering from a "superiority complex." The Hindus originally considered themselves, as Aryans or "nobles," to be superior to other nations; in those days India possessed both spiritual and material power. The Western nations, now materially more prosperous than the Eastern nations, consider themselves as superior. Westerners who profess to follow Christ should follow the doctrine of the brotherhood of man and the fatherhood of God, thus banishing hatred-making, war-inciting distinctions. Wise men like Lincoln try to destroy divisions in the West, as the sages of India are trying to destroy the superficial divisions of caste, and class, and creed.

---

* "God that made the world and all things therein...hath made of one blood all nations of men for to dwell on all the face of the earth" (Acts 17:24, 26).

APART FROM DIVISIONS OF CASTE and class, there is a spiritual interpretation of the caste system that applies to the natural classes of humanity. Every human being belongs to one of the four *natural* castes, according to his predominant quality. A slave of the senses is in the Sudra, or Kayastha,* state (*kaya,* body; *stha,* attached to), the body-identified state; often he is a materialist who doubts the existence of Spirit, owing to his sense enslavement. Anyone who is cultivating wisdom and weeding out ignorance is in the Vaishya state, "cultivating" the discriminative spiritual states of mind. One who is fighting in meditation the invasion of sense proclivities, instincts, moods, and evils in the bodily kingdom is considered to be going through the Kshatriya or fighting state of mind; ruling with the power of self-control. He who possesses the knowledge of Spirit through communion with God in meditation has attained the Brahmin or Spirit-identified state.

Spiritual meaning of the caste system

According to the spiritual interpretation of the bodily kingdom, man in the sense-identified or Sudra state of mind should struggle to recognize his senses as his servants, not his masters. The duty of the devotee who is in the "cultivation" or Vaishya state of spirituality is to weed out ignorance and to sow wisdom-seeds within the field of consciousness. In the Kshatriya state the spiritual warrior must do his utmost to protect his mental kingdom from the invasion of the meditation-disrupting inner forces of ego, habit, and senses. He thus passes naturally into the Brahmin state of invulnerability—God-realization.

This stanza of the Gita has special reference to the duty of a spiri-

* In the roil of caste demarcation that has plagued India for centuries, the origin and status of Kayasthas as a caste remain controversial. In modern times, Kayastha in Bengal and Northern India is generally held to designate a respected upper division of the Kshatriya caste. In other classifications, however, it is equated with the Sudra caste. Professor P. V. Kane—oft quoted on the subject—has shown that from a review of early literature and historical records, dating from the era of the eminent sage Yajnavalkya, Kayastha referred not to a caste at all but to scribes and accountants in the service of the king or other public office. Professor Kane concludes: "It would be more in accordance with the evidence to say that a Kayastha was originally an official entrusted with state or public writing work...that the office was held sometimes at least even by Brahmanas, and that in some territories it might have been held by a separate caste" (*New Indian Antiquary,* "A Note on the Kayasthas," March 1939). Therefore, since there is neither a historical basis for Kayastha as a caste division, nor does the formation of the word itself—*kaya-stha* "staying in the body"—have any link with its traditional association with the profession of writing, it may be understood to be a descriptive word apropos of the original intent to identify the natural caste, or state (not a social birth caste), of one whose nature is predominantly body-identified. (See also reference to Kayastha in III:24, page 385). *(Publisher's Note)*

tual man who has attained the Kshatriya state. Krishna, the soul, says to the devotee: "O Arjuna, you are in the warrior state of spirituality! Your duty lies in fighting the momentarily pleasurable sense attachments of body consciousness! Do not waver! Awake! Rouse the soldiers of discrimination and meditative calmness! Assemble them on the battlefield of introspection! Rout the invading forces of sense attachments!"

The same spiritual instruction can be applied in everyday life. In a righteous material battle, for instance, one should fight nobly and fearlessly to defend his homeland from evil invading forces, safeguarding the well-being and interests of his countrymen and upholding the ideals of virtuous human existence.

VERSE 32

यदृच्छया चोपपन्नं स्वर्गद्वारमपावृतम् ।
सुखिनः क्षत्रियाः पार्थ लभन्ते युद्धमीदृशम् ॥

O Son of Pritha (Arjuna), fortunate are the Kshatriyas when such a righteous battle has, unprovoked, fallen to their lot; they find therein an open door to heaven.

"O PRITHA'S WAVERING SON, a noble-minded warrior should eagerly seize any opportunity of fighting for an exalted cause! Those who respond to the call of a righteous battle, one that comes without aggressive seeking and demands fulfilment of the karmic law of justice, will surely behold in that duty a secret door to heavenly happiness!"

There are two kinds of noble warriors—the soldier of any land who engages himself in a righteous war for the protection of his country, and the spiritual warrior who is ready to use self-control and undaunted endeavour to protect the inner kingdom of peace. No warriors of the Spirit should hesitate because of the delusive stratagem of the inner enemy; no dutiful soldier should waver because of the danger to his life or because of the necessary bloodshed.

In Krishna's exhortation to Arjuna that he must perform his righteous duty as a Kshatriya (warrior), the Gita warns man against the temptation to use a metaphysical doctrine of nonviolence as a subterfuge for tolerating the slaughter of innocent people by conscienceless marauders. The doctrine of nonviolence as taught by Leo Tolstoy and by Mahatma Gandhi includes resistance to evil. A nonviolent person should resist evil, however, not with physical force but with spiritual force. Gandhi was a warrior without armour, save the invulnerable breastplate of Truth. Nonviolence is passive resistance to evil by love and by spiritual force and reason, without a use of physical force. The nonviolent man maintains that if it is necessary to shed blood in the protection of innocence, then let that blood be his own! If a person spiritually resists a program of wrong, to the point of inviting his own death at the hands of his infuriated foes, there will ultimately be less blood shed in the world. The point has been proven a practical truth in recent Indian history—India's victory of independence from foreign rule through Gandhi's principles of passive resistance.

Thousands of Gandhi's followers martyred themselves in adhering to the doctrine of nonviolence. On numerous occasions Gandhi's unarmed followers resisted by noncooperation a law that they considered unjust; they were attacked and beaten by political enemies. Many of Gandhi's disciples, mercilessly cudgelled, rose again to their feet and, calmly pointing to their broken skulls and limbs, urged their enemies to beat them again! Witnesses have testified that this display of nonviolent courage caused many political enemies to throw down their weapons, remorseful at having attacked brave men who, for the sake of their convictions, were not afraid either of maiming or death.

Right application of doctrine of nonviolence

The doctrine of nonviolence maintains that the sacrifice of one's self teaches one's enemies, through the awakening of conscience and the inner urgings of repentance, to eschew violence. This premise presupposes that the enemy's conscience is capable of being touched. If you walk into a tiger's cage and start preaching nonviolence to him, his bestial nature, which is unprincipled in the moral standards of man, will cause him to devour you—utterly ruining your fine dissertation! The tiger learns nothing from the experience unless it be that a fool is an easy meal. The smart crack of a trainer's whip might have engendered a more meaningful conversation between man and beast.

Parallelisms can be drawn from accounts of atrocities in the history of man. Though force in itself is an evil, when employed against a greater evil, the lesser of the two evils becomes in this world of relativity an act of righteousness. But this is not a free license to resort to force or retaliation. For example, there is a great difference between a righteous and an unrighteous war. A country may be purposely aggressive and foment wars to satisfy its greed; a war so motivated is unrighteous action by the aggressors and no soldier should cooperate with it. To defend one's country against the aggression of another, however—protecting innocent, helpless people and preserving their noble ideals and freedom—is righteous duty.

It is best to consult true men of God whenever there is doubt as to whether or not a war is righteous.

To condone defensive force in certain circumstances is not to demean the superiority of spiritual power over brute force. Even a tiger in the company of a yogi filled with the love of God becomes a pussycat. Patanjali says: "In the presence of a man perfected in *ahimsa* (nonviolence), enmity [in any creature] does not arise."*

"Love your enemies"† is a central part of the teachings of Christ. This is not a sentimental dictum nor a gesture merely to ennoble the giver, but expresses an important divine law. Good and evil are relative opposites in this world of duality. Good draws its power from the pure creative vibrations of Spirit; evil derives its force from delusion. The effect of delusion is to divide, agitate, and cause inharmony. Love is the attracting power of Spirit that unites and harmonizes. When man tunes in with God's love and consciously directs its vibratory force against evil, it neutralises the power of evil and reinforces the vibrations of good. Hate, vengeance, anger, on the other hand, are of the same ilk as the evil being resisted, and so only inflame the evil vibration. Love smothers that fire by denying it fuel! God has shown me many times the power of His love in conquering evil.

The resistance of evil by good, not by evil, is thus the ideal method for eradicating the plague of war. The use of force down the millenniums has certainly not banished that plague!

Jesus said, "All they that take the sword shall perish with the sword."‡ Yet how many so-called "righteous wars" have been fought in the name of that beloved Christ! If one brandishes his sword against his enemy, that act excites his foe to use any weapon he can get to defend himself. War breeds war. War can be outmoded by practising a doctrine of peace in international life. Aggressive wars should be effectively outlawed. Wars of defense are not wrong, but a far greater achievement is to be able to conquer one's would-be conquerors by nonviolent resistance. Jesus could have borrowed twelve legions of di-

* *Yoga Sutras* II:35.

† "Love your enemies, bless them that curse you, do good to them that hate you, and pray for them which despitefully use you, and persecute you" (Matthew 5:44).

‡ Matthew 26:52.

vinely armed angels to destroy his enemies*—but he chose the way of nonviolence. He conquered not only the Roman Empire, but mankind, by his love and by saying: "Father, forgive them; for they know not what they do."† The nonviolent Jesus, allowing his blood to be shed and his body to be destroyed, immortalized himself in the eyes of God and man. A nation that can maintain its independence by peaceful methods will be the greatest example and saviour to the arming and warring nations of the earth.

Gandhi maintained, however, that it is better to resist with physical force than to be a coward. If a man and his family, for example, are attacked by a criminal who levels his gun at them, and the man (being actuated by inward fear) says: "Gunman, I forgive you for whatever you may do," and then flies away, leaving his helpless family—these actions cannot be called a display of nonviolence but of cowardice. According to Gandhi, a man in such a situation should resort even to force rather than hide his act of cowardice under a mask of nonviolence.‡

To return a slap for a slap is easy, but more difficult it is to resist a slap by love! Any warrior who uses physical force or spiritual power to defend a righteous cause always derives in his soul a heavenly satisfaction.

According to the law of karma a man who dies courageously on a battlefield with a clear conscience attains a blissful state after death and is reborn on earth with a valiant mind in a noble family. A storm creates changeful waves on the bosom of the ocean; when the storm vanishes, it is seen that the waves, far from having been destroyed, had merely disappeared by slipping back into the bosom of the sea. A soldier in a righteous war confronted with the grim spectre of death has to keep this reality foremost in his mind: There is no death, only a return of the soul-wave to the Sea. And when righteous people, even indirectly, are the cause of slaying evildoers in a battle, they should not flatter themselves by thinking that they personally have any power of destruction! Evil, by the judgement of cosmic law, writes its own death

---

* Matthew 26:53.

† Luke 23:34.

‡ "I accept the interpretation of *ahimsa,* namely, that it is not merely a negative state of harmlessness but it is a positive state of love, of doing good even to the evildoer. But it does not mean helping the evildoer to continue the wrong or tolerating it by passive acquiescence. On the contrary, love, the active state of *ahimsa,* requires you to resist the wrongdoer by dissociating yourself from him even though it may offend him or injure him physically."—*Mahatma Gandhi*

sentence. The hero and the villain are karmically in the right place at the right time (according to God's view, not man's) for the judgement to be carried out.*

Applying these principles to the spiritual warrior, when he finds himself in a scene of inner psychological war in which peace and spiritual victory are threatened by sense temptations, he should not waver, but should see in his inner battle an opportunity to conquer his enemy-habits and, further, to establish within himself the heaven of permanent happiness.

A devotee who tries to conquer his psychological tests and the trials of delusion by the Christ-command of his self-control, as Jesus stilled the storm on the sea,† will gradually find within himself a per-

---

* Excerpts from a letter written by Paramahansa Yogananda to help a young man garner courage and right attitude as he faced the prospect of going to war:

"As much as possible, try not to think about your loneliness, but put your heart and soul into the duty that lies before you, placing your faith in God. I do not know if you are a student of Self-Realization Fellowship teachings; but if so, practise your techniques of meditation and look to the Divine Father for comfort and guidance. Remember, you are not alone. God, whose son you are, is waiting, just behind your heart's throb, just behind your thoughts, for you to look within and recognize Him. Wherever you are and wherever you may be called to go, remember you are with God. Though for a time you may feel you are forsaken, separated from those you love, God has not forsaken you—nor have I, nor your true friends. Within the heart of each one, you are remembered, and our prayers are with you.

"Life is a series of tests which, if squarely faced, give us greater mental strength and peace of mind. Learn to rely more on your Heavenly Father for guidance and understanding. Fill your empty moments with love for Him, and you will *know* that you are not alone, nor can you be lonely.

"During the time of the recent war in Spain [the Civil War, 1936–1939] when women and children were among the hundreds of thousands bombed, I prayed to God in great sadness to show me what happened to them after death. This was the answer I received: 'Realize that life is a cosmic dream. Birth and death are experiences of the dream. Those who were killed I woke from their nightmare to make them realize they were awake in Me and safe from harm—alive in Me evermore. I freed them from the terrors of their existence.'

"Fear nothing if you have to go to war. God is with you no matter where you are. Go bravely, thinking that what you are doing is for God and your country.

"Besides, those who die for a noble cause are honoured in heaven—the astral world.

"Astral beings develop from receiving the goodwill of others, especially if they were spiritual during their incarnation on earth. If you meditate deeply now, then no matter where you are, when you go to the astral world you will through the force of habit remember to practise God-communion and will thereby develop on that plane faster than others who didn't know meditation during their earth life.

"God bless you; and may you feel His protection and guidance with you constantly, bringing you safely home to your loved ones."

† Mark 4:37–39; Luke 8:23–24.

manent state of heavenly peace. According to the spiritual law, the devotee who holds on to the aftereffects of meditation and who maintains, against any trial, his inward peace and joy in this life will pass after death to the Eternal Blissful Peace of God.

VERSE 33

अथ चेत्त्वमिमं धर्म्यं सङ्ग्रामं न करिष्यसि।
ततः स्वधर्मं कीर्तिं च हित्वा पापमवाप्स्यसि॥

But if thou declinest to undertake this righteous combat, then, having relinquished thine own dharma and glory, thou wilt reap sin.

"IF YOU REFUSE THE OPPORTUNITY to fight and conquer the enemies that are threatening your welfare and inner kingdom of true happiness, you will have shirked your righteous duty and sullied the honour of your true Self—a sin against the Divine Image in which you are made."

The beauty of the Gita is the universality of its teachings, applicable to all phases of life.

The path of the warrior in daily life

This stanza instructs the businessman, for instance, that when he enters the spiritual path he must not become indolent, unpractical, or foolish in his ordinary worldly affairs—forgetting to protect righteously his interests against unscrupulous competitors. He can practise unselfishness without neglecting his own necessary interests. A businessman who through foolhardiness and false spirituality declines to fight a righteous business battle will surely lose the glory and the success befitting his position. By his neglect of business laws, he invites the state or "sin" of uncalled-for losses and failures. Nor should a businessman rob Peter to pay Paul—that is, make money dishonestly in order to use it for philanthropic purposes! One should earn his living honestly, and should fight all crafty business competition that tries to paralyse him! It is possible to be unselfish and nonattached to possessions, without supinely permitting others to trample on one's rights. A spiritual businessman who allows unethical persons to crowd him out of existence is guilty of tolerating injustice and thus of permitting evil practices to spread in the business world. In short, nearly every good businessman must be, in modern competitive life, an embattled warrior!

The moral man, one who tries to subjugate the seemingly uncontrollable proclivities of the senses, so trains them that they rejoice in his true happiness and not rebel against it. The self-controlled moral individual does not give quarter to any temptation that militates against the pure nature and true happiness of the soul.

"Sense-controlled" is applied to a man who is the slave of his senses. The "self-controlled" devotee is one who is governed and disciplined by the wisdom of the Self. The more an individual becomes sense-controlled, the less is he self-controlled. He who has tasted the happiness of a self-controlled life automatically resists the inordinate temptations of the senses.

He is a deserter who does not want to battle the wicked cravings of the conscious or subconscious mind. He loses honour and virtue and the joy of self-control; ultimately he falls into the "sinful" or sorrow-making pit of an uncontrolled existence. Just as an automobile with a broken steering rod becomes a runaway from its proper path and falls into a ditch by the roadside, so a man with broken self-control falls into the pit of inner disquietude. To avoid the miserable state of a moral derelict, everyone should protect himself against the invaders of false temptations, those that promise happiness but impart misery.

Many a moralist encounters an inner psychological battle when companions tempt him to digress from the straight and narrow path of morality. Confronted by unscrupulous individuals with blunt consciences and poor spiritual judgement, the true moralist should redouble his mental determination to travel in the path of contentment, continuously fighting any temptation that waylays him to prevent his reaching the destination of happiness.

Similarly, any husband or wife who forgets to protect the happiness of a moral life together will certainly plunge that relationship into the pit of disharmony and complex sufferings. One's self-controlled happiness must be staunchly guarded against attacks of the wandering hordes of visual, auditory, olfactory, gustatory, and tactual sensations. Even though entrenched by self-control, one must constantly be on the watch for the sudden guerrilla-warfare tactics of sense temptations.

The mental and moral strength of man become successively stronger by valiantly battling every trial and temptation. The law of life offers man the power of resistance in his God-given will and immortal soul qualities. It is his duty to bring out this hidden strength, this divine heritage, and prove himself a worthy "son of God." And it is a sin against soul progress for a man to lay down his arms of will and self-control and acknowledge defeat when challenged by any kind of trial.

EVERY SPIRITUAL DEVOTEE who regularly and deeply meditates realizes that he is the emperor of a kingdom of peace which he himself has won by battling the forces of restlessness. But before the empire has been fully secured, even a veteran warrior will find that he is subject to manifold outer and inner influences that strive to usurp the glorious realm. On such occasions the spiritual conqueror must advance boldly. Any devotee who refuses to engage himself in a righteous conflict with the suddenly invading soldiers of disquietude and unmeditative moods will lose the strenuously gained, honourable, enviable, and unending joy of the soul.

The yogi who strives scientifically to unite his soul with Spirit through guru-given techniques of meditation realizes that the greatest *dharma* or protective virtue of the soul is ever new joy. The religion of the soul consists in the manifestation of this true spiritual happiness, gained by constant efforts of deep meditation. After having earned this soul joy by waging many wars with restlessness, the devotee should be perpetually vigilant, never jeopardizing his joyful kingdom by becoming careless and negative during the invasion of cosmic delusion through the channels of sense disturbances.

Adepts who have become extremely elated by a metaphysical victory over the senses and by the first overwhelming perception of the joy of the soul may forget that the soldiers of restlessness can again rise up and usurp the newly conquered kingdom of peace. Instead of relaxing carelessly on his laurels, the devotee should concentrate on permanently identifying the mind with the soul's intuition and ineffable peace, that no invasion of sensations or subconscious thoughts ever again gain victory!

Once ego consciousness has been metamorphosed into soul consciousness, no sense invasion has power

Once the ego consciousness of the body has been metamorphosed by meditation into soul consciousness, no sense invasion has any further power. Until that finality is securely gained, however, the devotee must protect the vulnerable perceptions of the soul's ever new joy (the firstborn of meditative ecstasy) by manifesting a vigilant willingness to wage a righteous war with restlessness and body consciousness. If at any time he forsakes this duty and surrenders instead to the consciousness of the flesh, he sins against the image of God in which his true Self is made.

Ignorance (born of cosmic delusion) is the greatest sin because it eclipses that divine Self and produces the limitation of ego or body consciousness, the root cause of the threefold sorrow of man—physical, mental, and spiritual. "The wages of sin is death."* The unspiritual man living in the sin of ignorance experiences a living death—denied the life breath of truth-realization, he is a dream puppet dancing on strings of illusion. The yogi, too, reaps the wages of the sin of delusion in the death of his spiritual perceptions—if only momentarily—whenever he neglects his righteous duty to battle in meditation the onslaughts of body consciousness. The devotee must rather demonstrate to the glory and honour of his true Self—the "son of God," the image of God dwelling in the flesh—his immortal kinship with the beloved Father-God.

VERSE 34

अकीर्तिं चापि भूतानि कथयिष्यन्ति तेऽव्ययाम्।
सम्भावितस्य चाकीर्तिर्मरणादतिरिच्यते ॥

Men will ever speak of thine ignominy. To the man of repute, dishonour is veritably worse than death.

THE PERDURABLE DARK MONUMENT of a dishonourable action draws criticism from men of the world even for centuries to come! Beware, that the valiant spiritual hero betrothed to virtue be not disloyal to her! He who falls into disrepute in the eyes of honourable virtue suffers pangs in life worse than physical death. A life stripped of honour is a living death.

A deserter brings disrepute upon himself for failing his country; he is an object of wide derision. Stigmatized with cowardice, his unhappy lot is to go through the experience of a living death of world censure and self-recrimination. Death obliterates physical suffering; but a dishonourable act infects the living mind and body. A deserter finds no peace within himself or in society.

He also is a coward who permits sense temptations to devastate his bodily kingdom. It requires definite mental resistance and will power to fight the battalions of strong sensual cravings. A moral deserter finds himself constantly criticized by his own conscience, not to mention the hordes of "holier-than-thou" worldly people!

* Romans 6:23.

The moral hero who once reigned as the master of his respectful thoughts undergoes severe mental disquietude when he permits those thoughts to become lax and disobedient. Physical death obliterates from man's consciousness any memory of dishonour; so a life of moral turpitude, fraught with painful memories of a forfeited honourable past, is worse than death. A backsliding devotee finds all his refined happiness dead within him; he must live with gibing memories of his lost moral wealth.

Therefore, he who dishonourably relinquishes the fight against temptations experiences a living death. So long as life lasts, the moral hero must never submit to defeat nor fly away from a difficult battle with temptation. No matter how many times the soldiers of evil tendencies invade the castle of self-control, the emperor of peace—he who is at peace with himself and the spiritual laws of his Creator—must again and again launch his battles of inner resistance, never courting the perpetual disgrace of moral desertion.

"Let the dead bury their dead"

Jesus said: "Follow me; and let the dead bury their dead."* Jesus meant that the man who was bent on burying the dead was himself spiritually dead, without having noticed it! All persons who live a temporarily enjoyable life without ever perceiving in communion with God the everlasting joy of Spirit are the dead-while-living. The physical life without spirituality can be spoken of as a "variant" of death! The physical life, temporary and subject to death, is not true life. Spiritual consciousness, eternal and devoid of the change of death, is the true state of life.

Devotees who have enjoyed the really living state through the meditative contact of God, and who then fall from grace through the influence of body consciousness and materialistic habits, are the living dead. Such formerly spiritually living but subsequently spiritually dead men experience the mental torture of loss of God-consciousness. But even though they have lost their divine wealth out of spiritual negligence, they can never fully lose the memory of their spiritual happiness; it is never completely forgotten no matter how sunk in materialism such persons become. Though one be spiritually dead, he will not be free from suffering an acute, ever present sense of loss urging him to reclaim his relinquished blessedness. A devotee, even in earlier stages of spiritual progress, who has attained calmness in meditation but later succumbs to habits

---

* Matthew 8:22.

of restlessness constantly feels the painful contrast—a contrast he also endures between the formerly experienced deep happiness of the meditative state and the subsequently experienced evanescent mundane pleasures if he returns to his "old ways" of materialistic habits after a deep meditation. The lustre of earthly pleasure is pale before the splendour of God-joy! From communion with the bliss of God the devotee breathes true life and happiness—once quaffed, never forgotten!

A devotee who has experienced divine bliss should not permit any obstacle to stop his accelerated progress in God. No matter how many times he is dislodged from the divine state, the devotee should make renewed efforts at concentration to counteract the adverse sense victories. Spurning the deserter's badge of dishonour, let him conquer the inner enemies of restlessness, delusion, and temptation by the all-powerful soldiers of spiritual resistance.

VERSE 35

भयाद्रणादुपरतं मंस्यन्ते त्वां महारथाः ।
येषां च त्वं बहुमतो भूत्वा यास्यसि लाघवम् ॥

The mighty chariot warriors will assume that thou hast shunned this war through fear. Thus wilt thou be lightly regarded by those who had thought highly of thee.

"O DEVOTEE, THE ALL-POWERFUL chariot-warriors of spiritual faculties—which have so long fought with you against the materialistic ego-forces, and rejoiced with you in many victories—will assume that out of fear (weakness) you have forsaken the righteous cause. They who looked to you for leadership will begin to regard you doubtfully, seeing you as a conqueror of the senses who has given in to inner weakness."

When a devotee, swayed by attachment to material habits, shrinks from waging the psychological battle, he falls into disrepute in the eyes of his own powerful faculties of spiritual resistance. These faculties born of soul wisdom are allegorically spoken of as chariot warriors, for they help the devotee to control the vehicle of consciousness that is drawn by the stallions of the ten senses. Warrior-devotees of prowess and bravery who successfully use their mind-chariots to fight the destructive forces are spoken of as *maharathas,* "lords of great chariots"—great chariot warriors. (See I:6, page 57.)

When a mighty devotee falls from a victorious psychological-warrior state, he is considered by his inner forces of wisdom as one who shrinks from battle. His faculties of self-control and will power revile him as a psychological coward, a spiritual deserter. In the light of introspection the oscillating devotee beholds himself as an object of pity. His inner faculties ridicule him: "What is the matter with you? You whom we always esteemed as invincible; you, conqueror of many inner wars! now yielded to cowardice and mental lethargy!"

Those who are wont to conquer thoughts of strong temptations find themselves thus inwardly criticized when they shrink from fighting the smaller temptations that beset their daily life and harass meditative efforts.

Many devotees who by powerful acts of daily concentration have driven away the forces of restlessness may suddenly be stricken with love of bodily happiness and of easygoing ways of life and thus refrain from combatting, by fresh acts of deep meditations, mental inertia and distractions.

Every devotee who at will can command his attention to retire from the territory of the senses and to enthrone itself within is an object of admiration in the eyes of his own thoughts.

It is not salutary, not spiritually wholesome, to discourage the usually triumphant habits of deep meditation by sudden fitful abandonment. The will-disciplined devotee must not allow himself to lose his composure and resolution in unexpected trials.

VERSE 36

अवाच्यवादांश्च बहून्वदिष्यन्ति तवाहिताः ।
निन्दन्तस्तव सामर्थ्यं ततो दुःखतरं नु किम् ॥

Thy foes will speak contemptuously (words improper to utter), maligning thy powers. What could be more painful than this?

WHEN A VETERAN SELF-DISCIPLINARIAN suddenly succumbs to some subconscious temptation, the hitherto-restrained inimical senses rejoice and ridicule the erstwhile supremacy of their master. What else could so painfully destroy inner tranquillity than such derision hurled at a defeated self-control?

Both good and bad habits people the kingdom of consciousness.

When the devotee plays the searchlight of his introspection on his inner kingdom and beholds the invading hordes of evil tendencies advancing to obtain the wealth of his peace and to defeat the protecting soldiers of good tendencies, he should act then as a spiritual general to reinforce his good qualities. If, instead, the devotee—through misjudgement, mental inertia, or fear of resistance—fails to fight his base instincts, he will find himself jeered and mocked at by his own evil habits.

When a man is afraid to fight the inner battle, his evil tendencies appear, as though in the shapes of distinct mental personalities, to taunt him from all sides like spectres darting out from gloomy shadows. Their mockery riddles the fallen devotee with a gnawing remorse. Physical pain invades only the body, but uncontrolled moods and lack of spiritual government produce disorganization within the entire inner being.

The backsliding devotee is thus doubly criticized by his good and his evil habits. When the good tendencies find themselves deserted by their Kshatriya-warrior leader, they silently rebuke him. And the evil tendencies silently throw invectives and shoot psychological darts: "You cowardly one! you dare not raise your head to resist our onslaughts!" The devotee of self-respect does not tolerate an audacious invasion by the evil tendencies of his own past and present.

VERSE 37

हतो वा प्राप्स्यसि स्वर्गं जित्वा वा भोक्ष्यसे महीम्।
तस्मादुत्तिष्ठ कौन्तेय युद्धाय कृतनिश्चयः ॥

If thou shouldst die (battling thine enemies), thou wilt gain heaven; if thou conquerest, thou wilt enjoy the earth. Therefore, O son of Kunti (Arjuna), lift thyself up! Be determined to fight!

THOSE WHO ENTER THE PORTALS of death while engaged in righteous battle to banish any kind of evil fall asleep on the soft down of meritorious inner soul-satisfaction and are lifted in glory to the astral heaven. Those who on earth attain valiant victory over darkness will bask in the light and glory of a tangible peace and inner happiness. A victor in the battle with the senses enjoys the ineffable peace of self-control on earth. A devotee who dies fighting the inimical senses, even without being able completely to subjugate them, attains heavenly peace in the hereafter and great merit in his next life for his resistance to evil. Therefore, "O son of Kunti, endowed with her spiritual ardour to invoke divine power," forsake negative psychological weakness; arise and be determined to wage an overpowering battle with your opponents.

THIS STANZA CAN BE INTERPRETED in three ways.

(1) Life is a battle; each man has to struggle for his physical existence, and is more or less subject to his own peculiar difficulties. Everyone who conscientiously fights will either be victorious in solving his problems or fail in the attempt. The Gita points out, however, that a man who puts up a great fight against a particular problem and fails to solve it, has gained rather than lost, for he has acquired strength in the struggle. So valiant a loser has not been an idle coward.

Those who resist failure to the end are reborn in the next life as individuals ready for success. Anyone who dies with the thought of having been completely vanquished will be reborn, through the cosmic law of cause and effect, with a tendency toward failure. So no individual should remain in a state of inertia; when confronted with failures and difficult problems he should, if necessary, die struggling. On the other hand, he who continuously battles to conquer his problems may succeed, thus enjoying satisfaction even in this life. Struggle! and keep struggling! no matter how difficult the problem.

This applies also to those called to bear arms in a war of defense against unholy aggression. The soldier should not shrink from a righteous battle; the noble-minded and valiant will but gain in the end. If he dies in fulfilling his duty of protecting the innocent, the warrior's good karma will follow him into the afterlife, bestowing on him an ineffable inner contentment in the astral world. Or if he be victorious, he will enjoy on earth the happiness and satisfaction of heroism.

(2) The man who is a victim of sensuality, greed, anger, or egotism must in no wise become neutral and give up the battle just because many times he has failed. To remain in a state of inertia is to be a prisoner of evil in this life and hereafter. The indolent man who dies in the consciousness of his inability or unwillingness to fight his evil habits is reborn with a negative weak will lorded over by formidable inner tendencies that dictate the policies, moods, and habits of his life. But he who struggles against evil tendencies every day in his existence, never

realizing complete success, will nevertheless accumulate sufficient merit to come back in his next life as a man of self-control with a strong tendency to resist temptations and fight bad habits. It is far better to be reborn with a serious weakness plus a determination to fight it, than to be reborn with a serious weakness plus a sense of helplessness!

The sense slave who continually fights his temptations ultimately conquers them. No evil tendency, no matter how strong, is as powerful as the mighty soul—which every individual has inherited from God. Even a supreme "sinner" who never gives up trying to conquer his moral difficulties draws on this invincible power. He who attains a well-earned victory over his senses by continuous exercise of the soul power of self-control will find himself enjoying a tangible mental and physical happiness in this world.

(3) Spiritually, the devotee should strive continuously to win back his lost soul kingdom of bliss and immortality, no matter how many incarnations of accumulated ignorance he has to fight. Those who acquire scant progress after years of regular but mechanical and absent-minded meditation may become discouraged at not having gained a footing in the kingdom of Cosmic Consciousness. They fail to perceive that the accumulation of incarnations of delusion cannot be removed with the indifferent spiritual efforts of a few years of one lifetime.

Only the yogi who can delve into the region of superconsciousness can know precisely the karmic ratio between his virtuous and evil tendencies. But everyone knows generally whether his good or his evil traits outweigh the other. If an individual has acquired a preponderance of evil traits in previous lives, he might wrongly conclude that his lesser good tendencies have no chance. But just below the crude coverings of evil and the fine covering of spirituality is the omnipotent, transcendent soul. By meditation, the devotee steadily increases the strength and number of his virtuous tendencies by attuning his consciousness to the consummate goodness of the soul.

Every man, no matter what his predominant tendencies, should strive to rouse his spiritual powers with scientific techniques of meditation. If the spiritual aspirant finds himself habitually wandering into the hands of restless thoughts during meditation, he should not discontinue his efforts. If he dies in a state of discouragement he will be reborn with the same weak tendencies; again he will be confronted with similar temptations. Until all inner evils have been overpowered by a devotee, they pursue him through many lives, causing unending woes. No matter how restless a devotee's mind is, he should continuously try to achieve deeper concentration in meditation.

The devotee whose physical death takes place amidst the continuum of his spiritual efforts and constant practice of meditation experiences a state of high spirituality in the after-death state. According to the cosmic law of cause and effect, he attracts to himself, after death and during his next incarnation, a high spiritual consciousness. He is reborn with stronger mental equipment and valiant spiritual resolve.

No matter how much restlessness—born of habits of delusion—a man may harbour in his subconscious mind, he can always successfully fight it through an indomitable determination. Any devotee who continuously tries to meditate regularly and deeply will ultimately find himself a master of the kingdom of happiness. That devotee who is able to conquer all evil tendencies by continuous ever-increasing depths of meditation will become established in the everlasting bliss of cosmic consciousness. He will enjoy transcendent happiness and freedom forever in the Eternal Now.

VERSE 38

सुखदु:खे समे कृत्वा लाभालाभौ जयाजयौ।
ततो युद्धाय युज्यस्व नैवं पापमवाप्स्यसि ॥

Equalizing (by evenmindedness) happiness and sorrow, profit and loss, triumph and failure—so encounter thou the battle! Thus thou wilt not acquire sin.

THE DEVOTEE OF DIVINE FORTITUDE remains unchanged like a stainless steel—alike whether under the sunshine of happiness, gain, or victory, or under a corroding vapour from a sea of melancholy, loss, and failure! The brilliancy of his being thus does not become encrusted by the sin of wrong judgement and action and their corrosive karmic effects. By calmly acting in the divinely imposed dream drama of life he will be free from the anguishes and afflictions caused by contrary emotions.

A basic principle of yoga is that practising mental equilibrium neutralises the effects of delusion. Without the involvement of the emotions of the dreamer reacting to the sensations and incidents of a dream, the dream loses its significance—and especially its hurtful effects. Similarly, the cosmic dream of life loses its delusive power to affect the yogi who with unruffled inner calmness and evenmindedness views the dream of life without emotional involvement. This advice of the Gita enables the yogi to keep himself aloof from the agitation and sting caused by the clash of the opposites sporting on the mental screen of his consciousness, even while he perceives and enacts his part in the dream drama.

This does not mean that a yogi goes through life as an automaton; but he remains in control of contrary emotions, attachment and repulsion, longing and unwillingness. Discriminative and self-controlled, devoted to God and ambitious only to please Him by playing well his unique part in the dream drama, the calm yogi remains free of the sin of ignorance and its devastating karmic effects, and finds his way to liberation in the ever-wakeful blessedness of Spirit.

THE WORLDLY MAN MAY INTERPRET this Gita stanza in the following way:

Applied to business success

Anyone who seeks material fulfilment should keep his mind unruffled during success or failure. A businessman who is not overelated by achievements finds that his concentration is ready for the path of greater successes. A man overjoyed at temporary success seldom attains permanent prosperity; in false self-confidence he may spend his money unwisely and thus court failure. On the other hand, a man who becomes depressed by business reverses loses the focusing power of his concentration, thus impairing his ability to renew his efforts.

A general who is overelated at temporary success in a battle loses concentration on preventing any further invasion by the enemy. And one who grieves too much for a temporary loss in battle is psychologically unfitted to win future battles.

Every worldly man seeking success in the financial arena or in any other kind of competition needs to keep his mind calm to meet the constantly changing circumstances of his life. He must be able like a tractor to move easily over ups and downs in the field of life.

An evenminded individual is like a mirror of discretion that reflects the true nature and appearances of favourable and unfavourable events; thus he holds himself in readiness to act wisely and properly without being misled by emotional distortions.

THE MORAL MAN can derive inspiration from this stanza in the following way:

A fairly successful moral man should not become unduly overjoyed at his victory over his senses, for then he might relax his efforts and try to run over the thin ice of deficient self-control and consequently fall into deep waters of temptation. Until the final victory is gained, no moral man should be overconfident. Nor should he be despondent during temporary lack of self-control and thus acknowledge defeat.

Moral success

The resolute evenminded moral man steadily marches on to the goal of complete self-mastery. The premature joy of temporary success or the depression of temporary failure should not be allowed to obstruct the way of moral progress.

THE PRACTICAL ADVICE in this stanza for the spiritual man is as follows:

The devotee who knows the art of systematically destroying delusion practises evenmindedness even in regard to his spiritual endeavours. A few years of deep meditation gives the devotee wonderful glimpses of divine joy, but this should not make him presumptuous—he has not yet reached the final beatitude! Many devotees become self-satisfied with the superconscious joy of the soul and with beholding a few astral lights and make no further deep efforts at meditation; thus they fail to project their consciousness on the omnipresent joy and light of the Spirit.

Spiritual success

Neither should a devotee who meditates regularly but who finds himself battered by a sudden storm of subconscious restlessness become discouraged nor stop making renewed efforts at deeper meditation and God-contact. Until one is anchored in the Infinite, he must valiantly and evenly race his mental ship of concentration on the calm or rough seas of inner experiences. A yogi whose mind is free from the waves of temporary mental elation, sadness, or emotional disturbances finds within himself the clear reflection of Spirit.

The inner calmness of the meditating yogi penetrates like X-rays through all outer material obstructions; it photographs the hidden Spirit. A constant unruffled tranquillity can be gained by ever deeper meditation, ultimately becoming an all-penetrating light that runs through the coverings of matter into the heart of the omnipresent Spirit. The yogi intent on the attainment of cosmic consciousness, union with God, must keep his mind steadily fixed on the inner perception acquired by meditation, not overly involving his mind with the excitation of the initial stages of superconscious joy or the explosion of temporary subconscious restlessness. Such a yogi finds his unchangeable altar of calmness the resting-place of Spirit.

YOGA: REMEDY FOR DOUBT, CONFUSION, AND INTELLECTUAL DISSATISFACTION

VERSE 39

एषा तेऽभिहिता साङ्ख्ये बुद्धिर्योगे त्विमां शृणु।
बुद्ध्या युक्तो यया पार्थ कर्मबन्धं प्रहास्यसि॥

The ultimate wisdom of Sankhya I have explained to thee. But now thou must hear about the wisdom of Yoga, equipped with which, O Partha (Arjuna), thou shalt shatter the bonds of karma.

HAVING RECEIVED INSTRUCTION about the sublime wisdom of Self-realization (Sankhya),* the devotee must then learn about the secret celestial route of Yoga, by which Self-realization can be attained—the way that leads out of the prison of karma. When by yoga the ego is united to the soul, and the soul to the Spirit, the ego loses its delusion of being a mortal whose actions are governed by the law of karma.

The wisdom of the cosmos is knowledge of twenty-four principles of Nature in interplay with Spirit. All inference, perception, and understanding about creation are explained in Sankhya philosophy. Yoga is the science or techniques for practical realization of the philosophical truths of Sankhya.

The word *yoga* signifies "union," mergence. When the soul of man unites with the Spirit, the union is described as yoga. This yoga is the goal of every truth-seeker. Anyone who practices an effective technique to attain this supreme union is a yogi.

Realizing the theoretical Sankhya by practical Yoga has a definite meaning. The yogi "involves" creation (reverses the twenty-four evolutionary processes of Nature, as expounded in Sankhya), starting with matter (the grossest form of creation) and proceeding through the linked chain of the twenty-four primordial qualities, whose origin is Spirit.†

---

* From Sanskrit *saṁ*, "union; completeness," and *khyā*, "to be known; knowledge"—i.e., to have complete knowledge; to attain the ultimate wisdom, or Self-realization and God-union.

† According to Sankhya, the twenty-four principles of the evolutionary process of Nature, from Spirit into matter, are as follows: (1) *Prakriti* (the basic creative power bringing forth all phenomena); (2) *Mahat-tattva* (Cosmic Intelligence; referred to in Yoga as

By ascent of the consciousness through the subtle centres of life and spiritual awakening in the spine, the yogi learns the inner science of changing the consciousness of gross matter into the consciousness of its primordial principles. He resolves the five vibratory elements along with their manifestation of the five senses, five organs of action, and five life forces from grosser to finer principles: changing the consciousness of vibratory earth into the consciousness of vibratory water; the consciousness of water into that of vibratory fire; the consciousness of fire into that of vibratory air; the consciousness of air into that of vibratory ether; the consciousness of ether into that of mind (sense consciousness or *manas*); the consciousness of mind into that of discrimination (*buddhi*); the consciousness of discrimination into that of ego (*ahamkara*); the consciousness of ego into that of feeling (*chitta*). By thus dissolving the twenty-four principles successively into one another, the yogi then merges the con-

The "involution" of the twenty-four principles of creation

---

chitta) from which comes *buddhi* (individual discriminative intelligence); (3) *ahamkara* (egoism); (4) *manas* (mind); (5–14) *jnanendriyas* and *karmendriyas* (ten senses—five of perception and five of action); (15–19) *tanmatras* (five supersensible or abstract qualities of matter); (20–24) *mahabhutas* (five subtle elements or vibratory motions, the conglomeration of which appear as gross matter in solid, liquid, fiery, gaseous, and etheric form).

In Yoga, which is concerned with the practical application of the principles by which Spirit becomes matter and by which matter can be resolved again into Spirit, Sankhya's *tanmatras* (abstract qualities of matter) and the *mahabhutas* (subtle elements of gross matter that arise from the *tanmatras*) are implicitly included as one. The five *pranas*, or life forces, are enumerated instead of the *tanmatras*. Elaborated on, the Sankhya-Yoga cosmology is as follows:

Prakriti is the creative power of God, the aspect of Spirit as creative Mother Nature—Pure Nature or Holy Ghost. As such it is imbued with the seed of twenty-four attributes, the workings of which give birth to all manifestation. From Prakriti evolve (1) *chitta* (intelligent consciousness, the power of feeling—the basic mental consciousness—Sankhya's *Mahat-tattva*), inherent in which are (2) *ahamkara* (ego); (3) *buddhi* (discriminative intelligence); and (4) *manas* (sense mind). From *chitta,* polarized by *manas* and *buddhi,* arise five causal creative principles (*panchatattvas*) that are the quintessence and root causes of the remaining twenty evolutes of creation. These causal principles are acted upon by the three *gunas,* or qualities, of Nature (*sattva, rajas,* and *tamas*) and become manifested as (5–9) the *jnanendriyas* (five instruments of sense perception); (10–14) the *karmendriyas* (five instruments of action); (15–19) the *mahabhutas* (or *mahatattvas*: earth, water, fire, air, and ether—the five subtle vibratory "elements" or individualized forces [motions] of the Cosmic Creative Vibration); (20–24) the *five pranas* (five instruments of life force empowering circulation, crystallisation, assimilation, metabolism, and elimination). The *pranas,* together with the five subtle vibratory elements, inform all matter in solid, liquid, fiery, gaseous, and etheric form. (See also XIII:1 and XIII:5–6.)

sciousness of feeling into that of the primordial cosmic vibratory force (*Aum*), and the consciousness of *Aum* into Spirit. He thereby reaches the Ultimate Unity—the One from whom has sprung the many.

By gradual steps the yogi in this way converts all consciousness of matter into the consciousness of Spirit. This realization is not attainable through either reason or imagination, but solely through intuitive experience. Such experience is, in nearly all cases, the result of practising meditation and yoga techniques as taught by the great sages of ancient and modern India.

A poet or philosopher may imagine this cosmos to be only mind. But that imagination cannot help him overcome death and attain immortality. The yogi, on the other hand, wins an unshakeable knowledge that all matter is Spirit by daily employing a technique that uproots from his mind all the delusions implanted in it by *maya,* the cosmic delusive force. He thus beholds the universe as a dream of God—a dream from which one awakens only when he is conscious of the omnipresent Spirit.

Anyone who uses the yoga techniques is a yogi-practitioner, but he who attains the final union with Spirit is a perfected yogi. Self-realization consists in experiencing the different states of intuitive consciousness attained by meditation that lead to this ultimate union.

Sankhya-Yoga philosophy, therefore, is not only analytical and discriminative knowledge of the cosmos but includes definite methods for Self-realization. By Sankhya-Yoga the yogi perceives the exact nature of his body, mind, and soul, as well as of the cosmos in its entirety. Through scientific techniques he attains by gradual steps the knowledge of the Ultimate Substance of creation. Without yoga no devotee can know the true character of all forces in nature, in cosmic vibration, and in Spirit.

By the moral discipline of yoga (right action and renouncing desires—that is, *Karma Yoga*) and the use of a technique of meditation (*Raja Yoga*), the devotee gradually frees himself from experiencing, over and over again, the fruits of his past actions and stored-up tendencies. He learns to destroy the stored-up seeds of this life and of all previous existences. The devotee who knows the art of yoga, experiencing the pure joy of meditation, does not further involve himself in new desires and new karma. And by yoga techniques the cosmic energy "cauterizes" the brain-cell grooves in which past tendencies are hidden. Yoga practice therefore

Yoga "cauterizes" the brain-cell grooves in which past tendencies are hidden

not only prevents the formation of new karma-making desires, but also scientifically frees the devotee from impending karma (nearly ripe fruits of past actions).

Every individual acts partly with free choice and partly under influences from past tendencies. The latter appear as psychological biases that modify and prejudice man's power of free will. The predominating tendencies of good or evil in a child have their roots in his past life. Every truth-seeker should analyze himself to discover the extent to which his free will is guided by the dictators of his past tendencies, which appear now as octopus-like habits. The daily events of one's life tend to resurrect in man's subconscious mind his ancient habits of response, good or bad, to external stimuli.

Different individuals have different "fates." The sense-enslaved man is guided largely by his habits of the past; his free will is meagre. He is permeated with desires (whether able or not to fulfil them). A spiritual man, on the other hand, has freed himself from all worldly desires springing from past-life seeds, and has thus redeemed from bondage his free will. The ordinary man eclipses his free will with dark shadows of the past. The spiritual man, ever watchful for freedom, safeguards it by meditation. When the will is free, it vibrates in harmony with the Infinite. Man's will is then God's will.

Blind renunciation of material objects does not insure freedom; it is by enjoying the bliss of Spirit in meditation and by comparing it with the lesser joy of the senses that the devotee becomes eager to follow the spiritual path.

VERSE 40

नेहाभिक्रमनाशोऽस्ति प्रत्यवायो न विद्यते ।
स्वल्पमप्यस्य धर्मस्य त्रायते महतो भयात् ॥

In this path (of yoga action) there is no loss of the unfinished effort for realization, nor is there creation of contrary effects. Even a tiny bit of this real religion protects one from great fear (the colossal sufferings inherent in the repeated cycles of birth and death).

YOGA IS THE PATH OF SPIRITUAL ACTION, the infallible means by which concept is transmuted into realization. For those who embrace this "real religion," there is no waste of any holy effort! The least attempt will be to their lasting benefit. Mathematically certain, right spiritual endeavour to reach God produces only salutary results; whereas material pursuits are like wandering in blind alleys, risking encounters with their unseen hazards.

Poignant reminders abound that it is a surer protection to live under the canopy of truth than to expose oneself on the open fields of error! Even a little practice of the divine method of yoga will bring relief from the dire disease of ignorance and its sufferings. This last sentence of this Gita verse was often quoted by Mahavatar Babaji in referring to *Kriya Yoga.**

Herein is a message of encouragement to devotees who, having entered the spiritual path, have not yet achieved any noticeable progress. In the material world, all successes are known by their tangible, though often short-lasting, results. But in the spiritual path all results, being primarily psychological, are intangible. They are real, nonetheless, and everlastingly beneficial.

Spiritual results begin as subtle transformations in the consciousness of the inner being. They are to be measured according to their peace-giving qualities. When a devotee meditates deeply, he is bound to feel an ever-increasing peace, which, after all, is more precious than any worldly possession! To maintain the peace within, in spite of the ever-changing circumstances of life, is to be happier than a king, who, amid outwardly favourable circumstances, may be inwardly miserable.

When a devotee advances very far, this inner peace becomes the consciousness of omnipresence, omniscience, and omnipotence. The devotee then controls the switch that runs the factory of cosmic creation.

ANOTHER INTERPRETATION of this stanza is that the correct practice of true yoga can never produce harmful effects; whereas certain formal religious rites calculated to give specific powers, as described in various scriptural texts, may produce no results or wrong results if performed with even the slightest inaccuracy.

Right methods of meditation never produce harmful results

This point is illustrated in a story in the *Puranas*. An inept practitioner of *Mantra Yoga* (incantations) was trying out the efficacy of certain vibratory seed-words in order to destroy his enemy; but because he pronounced them wrongly he turned that power

* See *Autobiography of a Yogi*, Chapter 34.

against himself instead. (The word *peace,* for instance, normally produces a peaceful effect, but if one says the same word loudly and angrily, the result is not peace but disturbance. Certain vibratory sounds, known by occultists, produce by proper pronunciation a specific good or malefic result; the slightest mistake, however, may give rise to results opposite to those expected.)

The incantator of our story was an avowed enemy of the god Indra. Planning to destroy Indra by psychic means, he was performing a prescribed ritual, but was unwittingly intoning "Indra's enemy!" instead of "Indra, the enemy!"—thus changing, by mispronunciation, the entire direction of the vibratory power set in motion. By uttering "Indra's enemy," he was unknowingly designating himself as the victim. The incantation operated in accordance with his words, not his intention; at the end of the ceremony, it was not Indra but "Indra's enemy" who lay dead!

The devotee should understand that at the worst it is dangerous, and at best it is spiritually worthless, to meddle with psychic phenomena and powers, or with ceremonial rituals of uncertain or limited results. In following the spiritual path of right action and of right methods of meditation for the purpose of realizing God, there is no waste of any spiritual toil, and all efforts are divinely rewarded.

Right methods of meditation can never produce untoward results. Wrong methods, of course, are not beneficial—whether in meditation or in anything else! Charlatans occasionally devise strange methods, which they prudently fail to practise themselves, but which they recommend to their followers to impress and mystify them! Some misled or unbalanced people, following wrong techniques, such as violent breathing exercises or other deviations from the pure science of meditation, have found themselves in trouble. Citing these aberrants as examples, uninformed people then look with suspicion even on true, salvation-giving yoga techniques.

Great masters who have realized God have taught the spiritual methods and techniques that lead to God-realization and liberation. As pure sugar can never taste bitter, so divine techniques of meditation—such as *Kriya Yoga*—can produce nothing but the sweetness of peace and infinite blessings—and ultimately, God-contact.

Saints have declared that if a person, even once, really desires salvation, that desire is firmly planted in the superconscious mind; no matter how long ignored, it will germinate when favourable opportunity arises, whether in this life or in a later incarnation. So the devotee should remember that even a momentary entry into the kingdom of meditation may ultimately mean his freedom from the karmic prison of births and deaths. Some day, some life, each man must take that first divine step.

The power of sincere desire for God

This stanza does not mean, of course, that a little meditation will ensure freedom from cosmic delusion. The Gita simply points out that it is far better to *start* on the path of eternal safety by meditation than to remain on the death-ending material plane of thought.

If even the mere desire for liberation ultimately leads one to liberation, as the sages promise, it is obvious that determined, steady efforts at meditation must immensely quicken one's spiritual evolution.

Until the desire for liberation is first awakened in the heart, and fulfilled by meditation, salvation is impossible even though one passes through innumerable incarnations.

VERSE 41

व्यवसायात्मिका बुद्धिरेकेह कुरुनन्दन।
बहुशाखा ह्यनन्ताश्च बुद्धयोऽव्यवसायिनाम्॥

In this Yoga, O Scion of Kuru* (Arjuna), the inner determination is single, one-pointed; whereas the reasonings of the undecided mind are unending and variously ramified.

THE YOGI FOCUSES HIS MIND on God, and on naught else. Undecided dreamers dissipate their mental powers in the confusion of endless, many-branched pathways of interests and desires. The yogi reaches the great Goal of his life. The restless person wanders incessantly in the labyrinths of successive births and deaths, unable to find fulfilment.

The Gita points out the difference between the meditating devotee who is intent on finding God, and the restless individual who is content with theoretical teachings.

A curiosity seeker pursues haphazardly numerous paths of philosophy and religion, but in his newfound views and beliefs he stumbles constantly over doubts and dissatisfactions. The yogi, on the other

* Kuru was an ancestor of both the Pandavas and the Kauravas, thus Arjuna is here referred to as Kurunandana, descendant of Kuru; *nandana* also has the connotation of something that causes rejoicing—thus Krishna encourages Arjuna by addressing him as "the pride or choice son of the Kuru dynasty."

hand, having fixed his discrimination and concentration on a single goal—God-Bliss—begins quickly to prove through his own inner awakening the Divine Reality.

The Self-realized devotee, having reached God, finds that the thirst of his desires of many incarnations becomes quenched at once; he is released from all reincarnation-making desires. But the curiosity seeker, ever indecisive and uncommitted, remains tangled in his fancies and complex of desires; fettered by karma, he is forced to incarnate again and again.

The spiritual aspirant needs to forsake indecision. Following one true guru-preceptor and one definite path, he will save himself from endless roamings.

Many persons do not take religion seriously; they consider it a matter of intellectual speculation or emotional stimulation. New philosophical theories engage their immediate interest; they ignore any practice of the ancient, the time-proven, truths! He who considers a spiritual path of discipline to be outmoded and useless because it lacks the appeal of emotional and intellectual novelty will always be travelling in new lanes and strange bypaths, never arriving at the final destination of divine blessedness.

The real spiritual aspirant, single-pointed on God alone, quickly recognizes a true guru and a true path of Self-realization; he occupies his time with the guru-given technique of meditation that leads to God. Thus, without difficulty, steadfast in his aim, he reaches the pinnacle of spiritual emancipation.

A chronic wanderer in the path of theologies seldom tastes even a sip of the pure divine waters of truth. He craves only newly flavoured ideational concoctions! This desire for untried novelties merely leads one into a desert tract of intellectual doubts. The God-thirsty individual is busy drinking the nectar of joy in God.

VERSES 42–44

यामिमां पुष्पितां वाचं प्रवदन्त्यविपश्चितः ।
वेदवादरताः पार्थ नान्यदस्तीति वादिनः ॥ *(42)*

कामात्मानः स्वर्गपरा जन्मकर्मफलप्रदाम् ।
क्रियाविशेषबहुलां भोगैश्वर्यगतिं प्रति ॥ *(43)*

भोगैश्वर्यप्रसक्तानां तयापहृतचेतसाम्।
व्यवसायात्मिका बुद्धिः समाधौ न विधीयते॥ *(44)*

O Partha (Arjuna), no single-pointed resolution (no fixity of mind) in the meditative state of samadhi grows in those who cling tenaciously to power and sense delights, and whose discriminative intelligence is led astray by the flowery declamations of the spiritually ignorant. Contending that there is naught else than to rejoice in the laudatory aphorisms of the Vedas, their true nature being afflicted with earthly inclinations, having heaven (the pleasurable phenomena of the astral world) as their highest goal, performing the numerous specific sacrificial rites for the purpose of obtaining enjoyment and power—such persons embrace instead the cause of new births, the consequences of these (desire-instigated) actions.

THOSE WHO ARE ATTACHED to sense pleasures and powers, whether of the material world or astral in nature, cannot gain the mental equilibrium of meditation; they fail to receive union with God through ecstasy (*samadhi*). Misled by specious words of the unenlightened, desire-infected and paradise-loving, eagerly scanning the scriptures about a "profitable" heaven, rejoicing in the rhetoric of Holy Writ and exuberant in performing outer ceremonies that promise gifts of pleasure and power, here and in the hereafter, such men lose all of their spiritual discrimination and seek no higher aspiration. Their actions, filled with desire, sow inexorable seeds of births and deaths.

These inner delusions prevent men from tuning in with cosmic consciousness, ecstatic union with God. As a radio may register the static of various atmospheric conditions and thus be prevented from clearly receiving a broadcasting program, so the man who is filled with the static of material desires—including those masquerading as spiritual aspirations—cannot fine-tune his inner radio to the one-pointed *samadhi* state of God-consciousness. These delusions or psychological static of desires arise from attachment to power and sense pleasures.

The devotee should avoid undiscriminating belief in the superficially convincing words of the unwise. He is advised to guard his spiritual discrimination, lest it be stolen by the sophistry of those who espouse the philosophy of sensory aggrandizement—those who are pleasure-mongers or seekers of psychic and astral powers. The devotee should concentrate not on astral phenomena or miraculous powers, but only on the attainment of joy in God.

The Gita also warns the devotee against desires for the pleasures and engrossing phenomena of the astral heaven as the highest goal. Nor should he desire a heaven after death that is nothing more than a glorified place for sense pleasures. Heaven is not a "happy hunting ground"—a land where, without satiety, earthly sense pleasures will continue to be enjoyed! He who desires any other heaven than oneness with God—the very Source of Bliss!—is in delusion.

A man is also caught in delusion if he concentrates on the employment of scriptural rites and sacrificial rituals for material rewards—the evanescent pleasures and supernatural abilities that may be attained by the literal performance of the deeply symbolic Vedic or other scriptural rites.

These delusions based on desires for enhanced forms of pleasure and grandiose powers fragment the singularity of desire for God. Being of matter, not Spirit, the karmic fruits of these desires are planted not in liberation but in the soil of compulsory rebirth—a dire consequence the true yogi longs to avoid.

An individual might reason thus: "Since I do not bear any burden of knowing what I was before this life nor what I shall be afterward, why should I fear various births and deaths?" It is true that man's ego is embodied only once under one personality and form. But although the ego successively relinquishes the individualities of its incarnations, it yet carries, within subconscious chambers, the pleasures and terrors of the experiences of all past lives. Each man feels within himself many subterranean fears that are rooted in dark experiences of lives long forgotten.

Those who spend their earthly sojourns in emotionally reacting to the endless dream pictures of life continue to behold turbulent dream pictures of death and new incarnations. Until such men abandon their search for a paradise of pleasures in the emotional dream-drama—lured by the specious promises of the flowery enticements of the senses—they cannot merge in the changeless Everlasting Blessedness behind the fanciful tumult of change. By deep *samadhi* meditation, the haunting spectres of man's inexplicable fears are eradicated, along with mandatory rebirths.

VERSE 45

त्रैगुण्यविषया वेदा निस्त्रैगुण्यो भवार्जुन।
निर्द्वन्द्वो नित्यसत्त्वस्थो निर्योगक्षेम आत्मवान्॥

The Vedas are concerned with the three universal qualities or gunas. O Arjuna, free thyself from the triple qualities and from the pairs of opposites! Ever calm, harbouring no thoughts of receiving and keeping, become thou settled in the Self.

"THE VEDAS PRAISE AND WORSHIP the activating forces of Nature that spume her many forms from the roil of the trifold qualities. But, O devotee, concentrate your attention not on matter but on Spirit, and thus free yourself from emotional involvement in Nature's dream pictures of good, active, and evil existence. Ever adherent to your true nature (*nityasattvastha*)—quiescent, undisturbed by the triadic qualities and their light-and-shadow pairs of opposites—free from the delusion-woven nets of desires and attachments, become permanently established in your transcendent Self."

This stanza points out the spiritual inefficacy of the practice, however perfect and austere, of the merely external rites mentioned in the scriptures. Nothing but the cleansing of man's inward being has the power to free him from the trifold reincarnation-making qualities of human nature—the sattvic (elevating), the rajasic (activating), and the tamasic (degrading).

External rites may bestow powers, but not liberation

Many Vedic scriptures, profoundly symbolic and carrying hidden meanings not apparent to the superficial scholar, also possess external significance as rites and rituals for merely worldly purposes. Some Vedic stanzas, on the surface, are concerned with methods for developing the rajasic or activating qualities of man for definite results, such as victory in battle over one's enemies, or making mundane life healthful or profitable or progressive. Other Vedic verses tell of the development of tamasic qualities, powers and acquisitions that feed man's vanity and base nature. Still others deal with the culture of sattvic qualities, those that sweeten and ennoble a man.

The ordinary devotee who understands only the surface import of the Vedas and who blindly follows the literal instruction is unaware of the truth that any man who concerns himself primarily with the phenomenal world of the three qualities is thereby subject to reincarnation through the strength of associated desires. If, for instance, a man employs certain Vedic chants in order to triumph over an enemy, his success in that aim will establish in his consciousness a desire for the power of future victories. This subconscious desire leads to the development of the activating (rajasic) quality in the devotee, and is the direct cause of another rebirth in which he must work out the unfulfilled desire. Any desire develops in man one or more of the three qualities—elevating, activating, or degrading—and ties him to the wheel of reincarnation.

The word *Veda* signifies knowledge. The Vedas, the "divinely revealed," most highly revered Hindu scriptures, are books of wisdom both material and spiritual. A scripture is meant primarily for the liberation of the soul from the bondage of rebirth and secondarily for teaching the art of success in material life. Certain classes of people blindly worship the Vedas and consider all of their injunctions—to be observed literally—as divine prescriptions essential to liberation. The authors of these ancient treatises were wise enough to stimulate interest in the scriptures by showing the general populace ways of material success, and then to try to lead them on to follow those self-disciplinary rules that end in spiritual liberation.

THE GITA, THE QUINTESSENCE of the path to liberation, advises the devotee to free himself from any activities that rouse the reincarnation-making threefold human qualities, and to develop, instead, the desireless intuitive state by right meditation. He who receives the freely given all-sufficient blessings and guidance of God in divine inner communion need not propitiate the lesser "gods" of natural forces, who extract a karmic fee for favours.

Gita advises calm desirelessness to free man from bondage

By remaining ever calm, a natural sequel to deep meditation, the sincere devotee frees himself from the sway of the pairs of opposite qualities coexistent with the triad of *gunas:* good and bad, virtue and vice, happiness and sorrow, heat and cold, like and dislike, and so forth. When man develops one quality, he is automatically required to experience its opposite. One who has pain looks for happiness, and one who has happiness is afraid of losing it!

The tranquil, evenly balanced state of mind that cannot be disturbed by pain or happiness leads the devotee to the unchangeable ever new joy hidden in the soul. Materially minded people shun this philosophy because they are afraid of a tasteless, colourless existence. They are so used to clinging to the buffeted raft of delusive mundane hopes, they do not know that real unending joy lies in attuning the consciousness to its true, ever calm soul nature by meditation, and in thus preventing the mind from riding on the crests of sorrow and happiness or from sinking into the depths of indifference.

The gain of temporary happiness is followed by its loss, thus increasing one's misery. Therefore the devotee is advised to liberate himself from all exciting qualities and to concentrate on the bliss nature of the soul.

Further, the soul's superconsciousness should become anchored on the immutable rock of cosmic consciousness where no waves of change make any impression. The devotee should remove all forms of conditioned existence that stimulate desires and attachments—the frantic consciousness of getting and holding on to objects; his goal should be unconditioned Existence in God.

Esoteric interpretation of Vedas, according to yoga

GREAT YOGIS GIVE A SPIRITUAL interpretation of the Vedas and their injunctions. The exoteric division of the Vedas is that which deals with rituals; and the esoteric, with knowledge. The outer surface of the body and the nerve centres that stimulate sensory-motor activity are compared to the exoteric ceremonial rites of the Vedas. The inner subtle astral centres and higher states of consciousness correspond to the esoteric principles of the Vedas. The yogis say that the meditating devotee on his way to the perception of the Self rises above the consciousness of the world, the senses, and the body (the Vedic rituals) and becomes concentrated on the spinal region and its subtle spiritual centres of consciousness and vital energy (the Vedic esoteric principles). The devotee is then counselled to rise above the perceptions of the coccygeal, sacral, and lumbar regions (corresponding to the three lower Vedas that deal with the material side of life) and to concentrate on the regions of the dorsal, cervical, medullary, and cerebral centres (corresponding to the Rig Veda, the highest and most spiritual of the Vedas).*

* Of the four Vedas, the Rig Veda is the oldest, or original text. Its philosophy and prescriptions show an evolution from worship of the forces of Nature to the recognition of one Supreme Spirit—Brahman—and, correspondingly, evolution from dependence on the favours of the "gods" to Self-mastery. The Yajur Veda and Sama Veda are considered generally to be derived from the Rig Veda. The Yajur is a special arrangement of rituals—a handbook for priests who conduct the ceremonial rites. The Sama Veda contains selected chants and defines their proper melodic intonation as applicable to the Vedic rituals. The Atharva Veda is of later origin, and is primarily incantations and magical formulas designed to appease negative forces and gain mundane favours. Among its practical prescriptions are those that have been called the beginning of Indian medical science.

Sages who are able with divine intuition to read not the surface meanings, but the

VERSE 46

यावानर्थ उदपाने सर्वतः सम्प्लुतोदके ।
तावान्सर्वेषु वेदेषु ब्राह्मणस्य विजानतः ॥

To the knower of Brahman (Spirit), all the Vedas (scriptures) are of no more utility than is a reservoir when there is a flood from all directions.

THE BRAHMIN, HE WHO POSSESSES the supreme sacred knowledge, realization of Spirit, finds needless any study of the descriptions of God that appear in the scriptures. Even as a reservoir is useless when a flood spreads everywhere, so formal scriptures are superfluous to one who is merged in the Infinite Sea. At one with the Supreme Wisdom of Spirit, the yogi finds all other forms of knowledge of little consequence.

The world's scriptures are superseded by the fullness of direct experience when the devotee has commingled his consciousness in the Ocean of God.

Jesus said: "But seek ye first the kingdom of God, and His righteousness; and all these things shall be added unto you."* Expansion of human consciousness into cosmic consciousness by the art of concentration brings to the devotee a joyous wisdom far greater than the satisfaction of theoretical knowledge—however profound—resulting from the study of books. That devotee is like a man who has been trying all his life to get one thousand dollars, and who suddenly finds himself a billionaire!

The yogi who goes into the depths of silence, the kingdom of God

---

true essence of Vedic thought, declare these scriptures a timeless source of knowledge touching on all secular as well as religious arts and sciences.

(*Publisher's Note:*) For example, the renowned Shankaracharya of Puri, His Holiness Jagadguru Swami Sri Bharati Krishna Tirtha, found in sixteen *slokas* of the Atharva Veda, the "Ganita Sutras"—which have been dismissed by many Western scholars as "unintelligible nonsense"—unique formulas applicable to mathematics in all its branches from simple arithmetic to calculus and physics and all forms of applied mathematics. (See *Vedic Mathematics* written by His Holiness, published by Motilal Banarsidas, Varanasi, 1965. In 1958, His Holiness—head of the Gowardhan Math in Puri, and a direct spiritual successor of the eighth-century Adi Shankara—toured the United States under the auspices of Self-Realization Fellowship. During his three-month tour, he spoke on Vedic metaphysics and mathematics in major universities across the country. It was an historic event—the first time any Shankaracharya had travelled to the West.)

* Matthew 6:33.

within, finds that as his consciousness and life force begin to withdraw from body consciousness, he soars through the aesthetic tunnel of the spine into the God-contact perceptible in the subtle cerebral centres as ever new Bliss. Enthroned in this palace of joy, the yogi never yearns again for the suffocating slums of sense pleasures!

The true devotee may be said to lose desire for "Vedic rites" (sensory knowledge) when he becomes an omniscient knower of Brahman (Spirit).

THE YOGA ART OF RIGHT ACTION THAT LEADS TO INFINITE WISDOM

VERSE 47

कर्मण्येवाधिकारस्ते मा फलेषु कदाचन।
मा कर्मफलहेतुर्भूर्मा ते सङ्गोऽस्त्वकर्मणि॥

Thy human right is for activity only, never for the resultant fruit of actions. Do not consider thyself the creator of the fruits of thy activities; neither allow thyself attachment to inactivity.

THE DEVOTEE IS A DIVINE LARK, immersed in the spirit of his song; he has no thought about personal gain or impressing others with his singing. The actions of the devotee are for the Infinite alone, not to please mankind nor to satisfy his own material desires. Hence, he does not concentrate on expected rewards but is devoted to right activity for its own sake, to please his Divine Beloved. Knowing that it is God who has made him an incarnate being with faculties of animation for the purpose of enacting a part in the cosmic drama, the devotee ever recognizes God's image and power within him as the initiator and doer of all actions. As such, he has no claim on, nor can he be held accountable for, the effects of his God-identified activities. But in surrendering to God the fruits of action, the devotee takes care lest his mind, being denied its accustomed reward, steer him toward apathetic inaction.

Thus the Gita expresses the art of wise action by which true happiness and freedom can be attained.

MEN WITH THEIR DIFFERING MOTIVES and the results of those motives can be classified in the following way:

(1) The first group consists of those who live for their own selfish happiness and for no other reason. The self-centred man may acquire wealth by his works and, for that reason, the respect of his family and others who benefit thereby; but with the approach of death he is forced to relinquish everything he has treasured. Such people, when it is too late, may discover by many types of worldly disillusionment that happiness does not follow a life of egotistical interest. The intelligent man perceives by reflection that he is not the ultimate creator of actions or duties; thus the work assigned to him by God should never be performed merely for self. Those who act for themselves must bear the binding karmic burden of responsibility for their actions. Human beings should therefore play their designated roles, not for the satisfaction of their own egos, but for the working-out of the divine plan.

How selfish action, withdrawal from action, and spiritually liberating action differ

This teaching does not mean that human life is mathematically predestined in every way; it simply points out that human beings endowed with free choice and intuition must properly use these faculties to discover and fulfil the duties assigned to them by God. Even though it is difficult for a man to find out what his life's duties are, still, if he seeks God in meditation, the voice of his inner conscience guides him aright. Whether one's work is that of a corporate executive or managing a household and bringing up a family, such duties fulfil a necessary and noble part in the cosmic scenario.

Many people falsely think it is impossible to carry out material endeavours without possessing a motivating personal desire for the fruit of action in the form of success. The truth is that when a person works for his own material gain he is not so alert, wise, and happy as when he executes his small or large plans just to please God.

A rich man who accomplishes his business ends only for selfish gain, and who considers himself to be the sole creator and owner of his success, dreads the thought that he will be dispossessed of everything by death. But if a successful magnate employs his abilities with the consciousness that his accomplishments are for God, and uses his good fortune for worthy causes and to help those less fortunate, he will find the newly roused attributes of his soul bestowing on him an even greater enthusiasm for success and a joyous inner fulfilment in being able to do more for God's children. Far better this is than hoarding wealth for personal satisfactions, only to have to part with it at the edge of the grave, leaving it, generally, to unworthy relatives to fight over and squander.

(2) There is a second class of persons, who, through misunderstanding of the scriptural injunctions, think of all human activities and ambitions as the outcome of egotism; hence in sanctimonious retreat from duty they espouse inactivity. The Gita warns against such a view; even egotistical activity is better than nonactivity!

The egotistical performer of his life's duties, giving no credit to God as the Originator of all actions, nevertheless does perform his duties; therefore he receives divine grace in the form of some good karma and material happiness. But the inactive man who bluntly refuses to work either for egotistical or divine satisfaction is deprived, with a grim justice, of both material and spiritual reward!

This is also a warning to all "half-baked" spiritual aspirants who, in the name of being unattached to the fruits of actions, become mentally and physically slothful and idle. Spiritual growth is impossible in the stagnant soil of indolence.

(3) The third class of beings consists of those who are wise and perform all mundane, moral, and spiritual duties only with the thought of pleasing God.*

When the Gita says not to desire the fruits of action it does not mean that one should work like an automaton, without thought for the probable results of one's activities! The teaching of the Gita is to work intelligently, ambitiously, keenly! trying to create the right fruits of actions, not for oneself, but for God and all His children.

The devotee who performs all good actions just for God lives on earth with divine approval and great inner satisfaction, without being hurt by failures or overjoyed by successes. When a true devotee meets with some failure, in spite of his mathematically laid plans, he is not discouraged, but continuously tries harder for a successful outcome to offer to God. When his efforts are crowned with success, he is not unduly elated or self-congratulatory, but divinely content with

---

* It is the bounden duty of every soul as a child of God to win the approbation of the Father, spoken of Jesus: "This is My beloved son, in whom I am well pleased" (Matthew 3:17). To work toward liberation is to please God; to please God is to become liberated.

the thought that he may have pleased God and served others by his accomplishment.

The ordinary man does not know why he "happened" to be born in a certain family, nor why he "happened" to have certain specific duties (rather than other duties) assigned to him. Realizing his ignorance, the devotee-aspirant lays all responsibility on God ("renounces the personal fruits of actions"). He denies all satisfaction to his human ego that falsely considers itself as the doer, quite crowding God out of the picture!

A righteous man who performs his duties to the body, such as eating, bathing, and exercising, and who performs his duties to the mind by educating it and teaching it concentration, and who performs his duties to his soul by meditation, realizes that these activities are aimless and futile except for one purpose—that of attaining God-consciousness.

Man should think of the body as a divine animal that God has given into his charge; therefore, he takes proper care of it.* He should harbour beautiful thoughts just because the mind is a temple of the Lord; man is merely a custodian of that mental temple. He should honour his soul and contact its superconsciousness by meditation just because the soul is an image of the Heavenly Father.

The actions of the body, mind, and soul, when performed with egotism, induce one to concentrate on the fruits of actions; these lead to complex karmic reactions and desires, which, in turn, give rise to rebirths. But he who lives in and cares for a body, mind, and soul just for God and not for his ego, is devoid of all reincarnation-making desires; at death he is liberated in Omnipresence.

Therefore, each devotee should perform all duties to the body, mind, and soul by hygienic, thoughtful, and meditative living, avoiding selfishly ambitious activity by being divinely ambitious, and avoiding nonactivity which satisfies neither the human ego nor God.

---

* The God-loving Saint Francis of Assisi referred to his body as "Brother Donkey" because of its usefulness but frequent stubbornness. In *Saints That Moved the World* (Thomas Y. Crowell Co., 1945), René Fülöp-Miller relates that when Saint Francis was building the church at San Damian, he "designated his own body to serve him as beast of burden. He lifted the heavy stones, one at a time, and said: 'Now, Brother Donkey, carry it to San Damian.' And when Donkey Body broke down at times under the great burden, driver Francis would encourage and calm him and sternly he would add: 'Brother Donkey, the Father wills it, we must hurry.' Then Donkey Body would obey.... Francis' soul was used to sing when it felt happy.... Donkey Body chimed in as best he could. And then a very strange thing happened. Donkey Body and the soul which heard the voice of God became one."

ACTORS ON THE STAGE of life who remain inactive or become rebellious, throw the divine drama into confusion. In a theatre, a man with even a minor role may upset the plot by noncooperation, or by thrusting himself forward against the wishes of the director. In life, similarly, the divine plan is hampered when the actors do not intelligently play the parts assigned to them.

❖ *Finding one's God-given role in life* ❖

When a man tries to find out by meditation what activities he should perform according to the divine plan, he also discovers, to his discomfiture, that he has to work out many other activities of karmic debt engendered by egotistical desires and actions of former incarnations. If, for example, a man has been a material businessman in a former incarnation, and later (through disillusionment with worldly life) attains birth in a spiritual environment, he will nevertheless find that recurrent material desires will crop up in his mind unless he has concurrently cultivated a firm desire for God. He should eliminate the past-life material desires by discrimination, saying within himself: "In this life I will perform only the divine duty of knowing God; I will have no other ambition."

If his mind still does not find satisfaction, he may engage himself in some material activity, thinking: "Since I am impelled by a desire of a former incarnation to carry on a business, I will fulfil the desire this time by working not for the gratification of my egotistical self, but only to please God."

Strong prenatal evil tendencies must not be catered to, but rather severed by the sword of wisdom. If one finds the task beyond him ("the spirit is willing but the flesh is weak"), he should daily implore the unfailing aid of God.

Anyone who tries sincerely and unceasingly to work out the tendencies of his past incarnations, not for egotistical satisfaction but for spiritual freedom, finally becomes liberated through not having succumbed to karmic compulsions. The man who tries to work out his past karma with the thought of pleasing the Lord alone ultimately understands the fine distinctions between the duties instigated by his own past egotistical tendencies and the duties assigned by God.

Human existence is not predestined; every man is given free choice to accept the divine plan of existence or to follow the path of ignorance and misery. If people rightly understood this point, Utopia would dawn!

To summarize the precepts of this stanza: A man is on the right path when he concentrates on the performance of his duties only to please God. He succumbs neither to inactivity—the ego's escape into comfortable lethargy—nor to the performance of duty to satisfy egotistical desires, but does his part to fulfil the perfect cosmic plan.

Those who work for themselves as the beneficiaries of their actions are continuously led from one desire to another until they become so completely involved that they cannot liberate themselves from their entanglement in misery-making "personal fruits of action." The impersonal or non-karma-making fruits of action, on the other hand, follow those activities that are performed only to please God. When this is man's sole motive, he can eat, sleep, walk, exercise, look after his family, earn money, and do good in the world with no resultant karmic bondage. Remaining untouched by success and failure, he always enjoys the blessing of a peaceful conscience.

Principles of right action, interpreted esoterically

A DEEPER INTERPRETATION of this stanza can also be given. All beginners in the path of meditation are partially tied to the activity and distractions of the senses when they try to go deep in divine communion. This unsatisfactory state is called unspiritual activity or nonactivity. (Not idleness merely, but any activity that is not productive of spiritual progress is "nonactivity.")

The persevering yogi succeeds in rising above the sensations of the body and directs his consciousness between the lumbar and the medullary centres until he reaches the Christ-consciousness centre between the eyebrows. Sometimes the yogi, free from all sensory activities and feeling a state of great joy, experiences a sense of inactivity, a lack of desire for further progress.

Any yogi who is satisfied with this state of sattvic joy does not try to reach the cerebral region to perceive there the infinite bliss of final liberation. Therefore the Gita is advising the yogi to continue on the highway of meditation without being attached to the wayside joys and powers. The determined yogi does not become engrossed with any minor states of intuitive joyous perceptions but goes on developing until he reaches the Absolute Spirit.

Thus, even the highly developed yogi is reminded that he should meditate only to find God and to win His divine approval, and not to satisfy any latent egotistical desires for spiritual powers and phenomenal experiences.

When a person becomes interested in a particular phase of the ever-changing motion pictures of life, even those of a spiritual nature, he remains limited. But when he watches all motion pictures of life to learn the divine lesson in them in order to find the One behind them, he becomes supremely happy and free!

VERSE 48

योगस्थः कुरु कर्माणि सङ्गं त्यक्त्वा धनञ्जय।
सिद्ध्यसिद्ध्योः समो भूत्वा समत्वं योग उच्यते॥

O Dhananjaya (Arjuna), remaining immersed in yoga, perform all actions, forsaking attachment (to their fruits), being indifferent to success and failure. This mental evenness is termed yoga.

"O WINNER OF WEALTH!" intoxicated with the joy of divine union, perform dutifully all your actions without being attached to the outcome, whether of success or failure. Just as an invisible river beneath undulated tracts of sand glides smoothly and silently, so should mental equilibrium flow rippleless beneath all successful or unsuccessful activities. To remain ensconced in evenmindedness during all states of activities is yoga; he who can preserve in himself this mental balance in every kind of changeful circumstance is a yogi.

The word *yoga* signifies the perfect poise or mental evenness that is the result of communion of the mind with Spirit. Yoga indicates also the spiritual technique of meditation through which one attains union with Spirit. Yoga signifies, further, any act that leads to this divine union.

Performing one's actions while inwardly united with the joy of Spirit

Mental evenness is the native state of the soul. The ordinary man, by identifying himself with the world, divorces his consciousness from union with Spirit. The remedy for this all-too-often-disastrous disassociation lies in performing one's actions while inwardly united with the joy of Spirit. God's consciousness is perpetually in the state of yoga or everlasting evenness that remains unaffected by the incessant changes of creation. Man also, made in God's image, should learn to manifest that divine equilibrium by which he can live and act in this world without being victimized by its dualities.

The devotee who feels no attachment to the results of either meditative or mundane activities remains unconcerned as regards success or failure. To perform actions thus undisturbed by their results is to maintain the mental balance of yoga. This state of evenness becomes an altar for Spirit.

The worldly man engages in activity with his full concentration on the results thereof. Consequently, he is persistently affected by his interchanging triumphs and defeats. Working for himself and not for God, he is elated by gain and cast down by loss. A mind attached to the meagre fruits of actions springing from limited material or meditative activities cannot feel the omniscient tranquillity of the omnipresent Spirit.

The little mind of the little man attached to little things cannot possibly identify itself with the universal consciousness of God. Just as a wavy mirror cannot properly reflect the objects in front of it, so a mind whose calmness is distorted by the thoughts of success or failure is unable to reflect the unchangeable Spirit. Man's consciousness, when constantly identified with material changes or mental disturbances, cannot mirror the immutable Divine, whose image is present within him as his true Self, or soul.

The devotee should perform activities with the mind immersed in God. Anyone who carries out all actions in this way is in the state of liberation, even as the Heavenly Father works through all creation without being attached to or bound by its constant flux. The Lord's consciousness manifests in all states of creation, preservation, and destruction—yet remains unchanged. As God is omnipresent in the cosmos but is undisturbed by its variety, so man, who as a soul is individualized Spirit, must learn to participate in this cosmic drama with a perfectly poised and equilibrated mind.

Endowed with free choice, man has misused his independence and identified himself with a transient body and a cosmos of antithetical organized chaos. He should train his mind away from restlessness to the perception of changelessness. The ordinary individual, through restlessness, perceives only the tumultuous universe. The man following the art of yoga (inner calmness) perceives the immanent-transcendent ever tranquil Spirit.

The spiritual aspirant should counterbalance his restlessness-producing material activity by calmness-producing spiritual meditation. He should learn to perform material duties as well as meditation with a mental evenness that does not look for material or spiritual gain, and is not disturbed by material or spiritual failure.

No material or spiritual activities performed with attachment (mental unevenness) can produce lasting happiness. The *bhogi,* or the man of attachment, reaps unhappiness. A *yogi,* whether engaged or not in outer activities, feels the unending ever new joy of Spirit.

Man is a walking God. No human being should behave like an animal, identified with his lower nature. He should manifest his true divine Self. The Lord works in all creation with undifferentiated poise; the man who learns to perform all activities with inner balance, without attachment to anything and without restlessness, remembers his true Self and reclaims his oneness with God.

The only way one can permanently establish himself in the inner evenness of yoga is by meditation. So the words of Krishna to Arjuna are particularly significant to the meditating devotee. Any yogi practising meditation who is impatient or easily disturbed by the seemingly meagre and slow results of meditation is acting with a selfish motive focused on the fruits of his actions. He should meditate only with the thought of pleasing and loving God; then yoga, or divine union with the immutable Spirit, is sure to follow.

VERSE 49

दूरेण ह्यवरं कर्म बुद्धियोगाद्धनञ्जय।
बुद्धौ शरणमन्विच्छ कृपणाः फलहेतवः ॥

Ordinary action (performed with desire) is greatly inferior to action united to the guidance of wisdom; therefore, O Dhananjaya (Arjuna), seek shelter in the ever-directing wisdom. Miserable are those who perform actions only for their fruits.

ALL MEN GO ASTRAY in the dense shadowy forest of activity except those who are guided by their inner discrimination. Therefore, O devotee, seek protection from the darkness of error by keeping the lamp of divine remembrance ever burning to light the way! Miserably lost and disillusioned are those who wander in lightlessness, groping for ever elusive fancied treasures of lasting happiness.

Activities motivated by material desire are an inferior way of fulfilling life's duties; they entangle the doer in a tight net of ever-growing desires that must be worked out in subsequent lives. Actions guided by the soul's inner intuitive discrimination (*buddhi-yoga*) are instituted only to satisfy the cosmic plan and therefore leave no traces of misery-making karma.

The devotee should never act in a desultory way, driven by whims, moods, and habits, or by the customs and fashions of the environment, or by inherited or prenatal desires. He should place all his activities under the shelter of the God-directed wisdom that is felt in meditation. Any action done with the inspiration of God does not in any way bind the performer with the cords of results. When the devotee acts under the inspiration of God, it is the Lord who is responsible for those activities, just as the father is responsible for an obedient son.

Intelligence that is guided by egotistical motives is liable to error, but wisdom guided by God-consciousness can never make mistakes. The ordinary individual, ignorantly performing actions with the desire for earthly results, wanders through ages in the dark abyss of reincarnations. The yogi follows to freedom the path of action that is illumined by the inner light of true wisdom.

As a mule carrying a heavy bag of gold does not profit by it but only suffers under its weight, so does a rich miser suffer through the burden and responsibility of possessing wealth without having any benefit from it. As miserly people are only conscious of the weight of responsibility of possessing riches, so people who are prodded by their desires work incessantly with their minds weighted down by the desire for worldly results—wishing for more and more—without being able to know true joy.

The devotee is counselled to live and work in the world for God and thus remain aloof from reincarnation-making desires. All devotees who work under the guidance of wisdom are free; all ignorant people who work for gain are bound to know misery, because the results of actions are uncertain and transitory.

It is therefore foolish and an inferior mode of behaviour continuously to work for personal gain, gathering only troubles through ever-increasing desires. It is wisdom to live and work to please God and thus remain free and divinely content.

VERSE 50

बुद्धियुक्तो जहातीह उभे सुकृतदुष्कृते ।
तस्माद्योगाय युज्यस्व योगः कर्मसु कौशलम् ॥

One who is united to cosmic wisdom goes beyond the effects of both virtue and vice, even here in this life. Therefore, devote thyself to yoga, divine union. Yoga is the art of proper action.

THAT EXALTED ONE WHO by ecstatic meditation has united his consciousness with the Universal Omniscience remains no longer imprisoned by the judgements of karmic law. In this very life, the prison bars of karma and desires—the effects of ego-instigated good and evil actions—are removed. Therefore, O devotee, strive above all else to become merged in constant divine union; in oneness with the transcendent wisdom of God perform all your actions. To work united with God is the greatest art to be mastered in this world. To carry on all activities with God-consciousness is the supreme yoga (*nirvikalpa samadhi yoga*).

When a man is identified with material life, owing to a false consciousness of himself as the doer of actions, he is bound to reap the good and bad results of his prenatal and postnatal actions. But when he becomes one with omnipresent wisdom he possesses immunity to the limiting good and bad influences in the prison-house of earthly life. He feels not the ego but God working in all his actions.

To earn money in difficult times, to create anything unusual in this world, to invent new things, to attain great skill—these achievements are laudatory; but when a person's actions are performed solely with the consciousness of God, he has become a specialist in the greatest art of all. To carry on life's activities with God-consciousness is called the supreme art of proper action because it totally frees the soul from the earthly bondage of karmic effects of actions and ensures permanent freedom in Spirit.

A prisoner who serves his time rebelliously is not set at liberty until he has worked out his full term, but a prisoner who works to please the warden by right action and behaviour may find himself quickly paroled! Similarly, men who labour in this world guided by their rebellious desires find themselves long imprisoned in misery, while those who work only to please God find themselves quickly liberated.

The ordinary individual, in everything he does, is wholly identified with the body, its sensations, and the multiple desires patterned after its sensations. When such a man dies he takes with him from this world his unfinished longings and karmic debts. Just recompense being due, he has to come back again.

The supreme art of action, which totally frees the soul from karma

In the state of ecstasy the false consciousness of the ego as the doer is dissolved. Hence the vanished ego's prenatal seeds of good and evil actions, implanted in the brain, wither away, not finding any egotistical consciousness as soil on which to grow.

Yoga, or union with Spirit, is the only way to evade being swept along in the flood of the effects of good and evil past actions. Being otherwise unable to stem the karmic tide, the devotee should seek refuge by meditating on the oneness of the little self with the almighty Spirit. The expanded consciousness is thereby rendered invulnerable; the flood of action sweeps past without affecting it. The effects of past actions cannot impress themselves on a God-tuned ego. Yoga is thus spoken of as the art of preventing past karma from overwhelming the soul.

A soul united to God becomes God; that soul automatically disowns all the effects of its past actions of past lives. The status of the soul is changed from a body-identified, limited, and karma-bound entity to a state ever free, beyond the influence of karma. Therefore the yogi should always remain concentrated at the Christ-consciousness centre between the eyebrows, feeling the omnipresent joy of God even while attentively performing dutiful actions. When he is able to do that, he knows the greatest art of action and is a true yogi.

Bhagavan Krishna's instruction to the highly advanced disciple Arjuna concerning divine union expresses the ultimate state to be attained. Though unbroken continuity in God-consciousness while yet performing all of life's exacting duties (*nirvikalpa samadhi*) is not quickly attained by even the veteran devotee, yet every moment of deep meditation spent in seeking union with God, every effort to practice evenmindedness and renunciation of desire for the fruits of actions, brings its reward—removing sorrow and establishing peace and joy; and mitigating karma and lessening errors in decisive actions by greater attunement with God's guiding wisdom.

As advised by the Gita, in serious spiritual endeavour the blessing and guidance of the guru are essential. The true disciple follows with great devotion the *sadhana* (the path of spiritual discipline and yoga technique of meditation) given by the guru. Through this *sadhana,* his guru invisibly helps him to attain the successively higher steps in the art of divine union. The disciple who daily and deeply practices his spiritual exercises and advances in the path may find the guru appearing visibly on the astral plane to guide him onward. With the help of the guru, all the screens of ignorance in the true disciple are burnt away, revealing to him the indescribable glory of the inner world of soul and Spirit.

VERSE 51

**कर्मजं बुद्धियुक्ता हि फलं त्यक्त्वा मनीषिणः।
जन्मबन्धविनिर्मुक्ताः पदं गच्छन्त्यनामयम्॥**

Those who have mastered their minds become engrossed in infinite wisdom; they have no further interest in any fruits of actions. Freed thus from the chain of rebirth, they attain the state beyond sorrow.

THE REWARD OF PERFORMING all actions with a God-tuned mind—desireless and with discrimination unruffled by emotion—is freedom from the fetters of rebirths, liberation from all forms of misery-making evil.

The purpose of God's plan for man is not an endless series of rebirths. The divine scheme is to afford man countless opportunities to use his free choice and discrimination to distinguish between body and soul, to forsake the miserable life of the senses by reclaiming his true identity in Spirit.

As soon as man discovers the true purpose of existence, he has made the first step toward salvation. He understands that he is not compelled to reincarnate again and again. By performing, in this one life, all actions with the consciousness of God, he can win the final liberation.

God had planned to liberate the human soul after a short wisdom-experience on this earth. Through misuse of his free will, however, man became earthbound, involving himself needlessly in a prolonged series of reincarnations.*

Human misery is not part of God's plan. The unhappy man is simply the one who is out of touch with the Lord. God has gone to considerable trouble to produce this drama of life; it hurts Him when we miss the whole point and wear a long face!

VERSE 52

**यदा ते मोहकलिलं बुद्धिर्व्यतितरिष्यति।
तदा गन्तासि निर्वेदं श्रोतव्यस्य श्रुतस्य च॥**

---

* See also commentary on XV:1—explanation of story of Adam and Eve.

When thine intelligence penetrates beyond the darkness of delusion, then wilt thou attain indifference regarding matters that have been heard and matters yet to be heard.

A YOGI WHOSE DISCRIMINATIVE intelligence is fixed in the Infinite Wisdom becomes impervious to delusive feelings of the delusive senses—no longer influenced by their fallacious past counsel and promises, nor will he be susceptible to their wily lures in future. He acts in the dualistic dream drama without attachment, his wisdom untainted by emotion, free of haunting desires—past or future.

The deluded man, habitually compelled by the inner voice of the sense mind, sorrows about unaccomplished experiences of the past and is greedy for future satisfactions. In contrast, the advanced yogi, who has routed egoistic desires and inclinations from his mental castle and re-established the wisdom rule of the soul, is impervious to past fears and future hopes.

The ordinary person is bound like a prisoner in a dungeon; his life experiences are narrowly confined to the dismal realm of the senses. The advanced yogi, on the other hand, is so overwhelmed by having contacted the Surprise of all surprises—the ever new bliss of God—that he becomes indifferent to all thoughts of sense pleasures. His mind is no longer disturbed either by memories of past sense joys or by daydreams for the future. He is conscious only of glorious Omnipresence and Its everlasting joy.

The man who does not meditate is indifferent to the soul because he does not know any better, but the yogi is indifferent to the senses because he knows them too well! The devotee who has known both sense inclinations and the soul bliss possesses a standard of comparison that is nonexistent for the worldly man.

The separative and relative qualities inherent in the sense-identified consciousness compel it to behold, not the Unity of God, but the multiplicity of creation. The "Eternal Now" is split for man into inconstant states of past, present, future. In cosmic consciousness these delusions of relativity disappear; and with them, the illusory dreams of past sense pleasures and unfulfilled desires, and future will-o'-the-wisp hopes and promises. The yogi in blissful cosmic consciousness experiences the eternal undifferentiated Sole Reality.

The deeply meditating devotee ascends to this realization by several steps: First, by practice of a specific yoga technique of meditation on the Cosmic Vibration (the *Aum*, or Amen), he ceases to "hear" the voice of the senses as he rises above all physical sounds and distractions and concentrates within on the spiritual vibratory sounds emanating from the astral body. He must go beyond the astral "music" and listen to the Cosmic *Aum.* Within the Cosmic *Aum* he perceives the Spirit as Cosmic Light. He must penetrate the Light and contact Cosmic Consciousness. He then unites his soul with Cosmic Consciousness, becoming one with Spirit.

VERSE 53

श्रुतिविप्रतिपन्ना ते यदा स्थास्यति निश्चला।
समाधावचला बुद्धिस्तदा योगमवाप्स्यसि॥

When thine intelligence, bewildered by the variety of revealed truths, becomes securely anchored in the ecstasy of soul bliss, then wilt thou attain the final union (yoga).

AS A STORM-TOSSED SHIP finds safety once it reaches the calm harbour, and being well-anchored cannot drift out to sea; similarly, when the discriminating intellect, buffeted by theological opinions, enters the transcendent *samadhi* state of intuitive Self-realization and becomes immovably settled therein, the devotee attains the desirable consummation and destined goal of all souls—the ultimate yoga, final union with Spirit. From this union there is never again any separation.

The previous stanza stressed to the devotee the importance of becoming impervious to the voice of the senses by going beyond delusion to the ever new joy of God. This present stanza cites the prerequisite of *samadhi* meditation, not theological knowledge, as the means to reach that ultimate end. In the beginning, when the sense mind is rejected as not being a suitable guide to right action, the devotee turns to the authority of the saints or scriptures for counsel. But to his unenlightened mind, this presents a bewildering variety of ways and means—not always homogeneous, and not infrequently contradictory.

In their underlying unity, all true scriptures reveal the same truths about Spirit. The Vedas, the Old and the New Testament of the Christian Bible, and all other scriptures of divine authority have one refrain—the indissoluble unity of God and man. The seeming differences of revelations are on the surface merely, caused by the racial and environmental influences surrounding the prophets. Each one is singing his own hymn of the same one Infinite.

When a devotee tries to understand various revelations by the limited powers of reason and inference, which are rigidly conditioned by the testimony "heard" from the voice of the senses, he is misled and becomes lost in a theological wilderness. The unity of all true scriptures is perceived only through meditation-developed intuition, the all-knowing faculty of the soul.

The necessity for the guidance of a true guru, and for the loyalty of the disciple

Here again is highlighted the necessity for the guidance of a true guru, and for the loyalty of the disciple who will follow the guru's *sadhana* faithfully. With guru-given techniques of divine communion, the devotee's spiritual intelligence grows from sense-bound rationalism to the developed intuition of deep meditation. By following the steps summarized in the commentary of the previous stanza, the yogi attains unshakeable steadiness in the realization of his true Self in the state of *samadhi.* When he can remain unbrokenly in that soul bliss, then he is ready for the final union—of the beatific bliss of the soul with the Omnipresent Eternal Bliss of Spirit. This is the ultimate state of yoga. When the devotee attains this final union, he can never fall; he need never again be parted from God.

QUALITIES OF THE SELF-REALIZED

VERSE 54

अर्जुन उवाच
स्थितप्रज्ञस्य का भाषा समाधिस्थस्य केशव।
स्थितधीः किं प्रभाषेत किमासीत व्रजेत किम्॥

Arjuna said:

O Keshava (Krishna)! what are the characteristics of the sage who possesses ever calm wisdom and who is steeped in samadhi (ecstasy)? How does this man of steady wisdom speak and sit and walk?

"O KRISHNA, MY SPIRITUAL CURIOSITY is inflamed by thy words about the ultimate state of *samadhi*-yoga; what is that sage like who is settled in this final union? Does he behave like other men in his speech and actions?"

After attaining union with Spirit, a devotee's consciousness never descends. Once established in God-consciousness, the devotee remains in *samadhi*-union. His plane of activity changes; instead of working in the world while looking toward God, he feels himself in God while working in the world. His discrimination is merged with the Spirit, even when he sleeps, eats, or works. He realizes that God has become his nature, his little self, as well as all other selves. He beholds the entire material world as a God-saturated cosmos. Even in the wakeful state he enjoys *nirvikalpa samadhi* or the state in which the devotee perceives both Nature and God. To be in divine ecstasy and simultaneously to be actively wakeful is the *paramahansa* state; the "royal swan" of the soul floats in the cosmic ocean, beholding both its body and the ocean as manifestations of the same Spirit.

VERSE 55

श्रीभगवानुवाच
प्रजहाति यदा कामान्सर्वान्पार्थ मनोगतान्।
आत्मन्येवात्मना तुष्टः स्थितप्रज्ञस्तदोच्यते॥

The Blessed Lord replied:

O Partha (Arjuna)! when a man completely relinquishes all desires of the mind, and is entirely contented in the Self, by the Self, he is then considered to be one settled in wisdom.

WHEN BY THE MEDITATIVE and spiritualized actions of the outer or ego-self the yogi drinks unceasingly the pure nectar of bliss from the chalice of the inner or true Self, he is so wholly satisfied by that joy that he casts away all poisoned honey of human cravings—his ego-self is supremely happy in its true Self. This being is then said to be a perfect sage, a man of Self-realization encircled by the ever-protecting halo of steady wisdom.

In this stanza there is a play on the word *atman,* the Self or soul, to express its dual nature in the incarnate man: (1) the outer Self or ego, the pseudosoul, with its bodily instruments and faculties (the experiencer of the world of the sense mind without, and of the soul within); and (2) the inner or true Self (that which is to be experienced by the ego, and which in turn then experiences God). The outer nature of even the perfect sage retains at least some degree of egoity, or individualized consciousness, for without this the soul could not remain in the body, but would dissolve in Spirit. When *by* the action of the outer Self, or spiritualized ego, the divine man attains *samadhi* and is able to hold on to the effects of this blissful union even after meditation, then the ego-Self may be said to be ever content *in* the true Self alone.

Most people do not understand why the Gita advises man to do away with sense pleasures and to concentrate on the soul. There could be no pleasures of the flesh except through the delusive identification of the soul with the body—just as a mad lover, identified with his beloved, thinks his happiness dependent on her and her alone!

The ordinary person is like a king who goes out of his beautiful palace and becomes engrossed in sordid pastimes in the slums. He is bound to suffer from the effects of his indiscriminate actions. The wise man perceives that his inner Self contains within it all bliss. He who is satisfied only with that complete joy possesses the steady wisdom characteristic of that being who has attained the final union.

VERSE 56

दुःखेष्वनुद्विग्नमनाः सुखेषु विगतस्पृहः ।
वीतरागभयक्रोधः स्थितधीर्मुनिरुच्यते ॥

He whose consciousness is not shaken by anxiety under afflictions nor by attachment to happiness under favourable circumstances; he who is free from worldly loves, fears, and angers—he is called a muni of steady discrimination.

THE MEDITATION-PERCEIVED SPIRIT continues Its revelation to the introspective devotee concerning the behaviour or marks of a wise man:

He is a mastermind, a *muni* (one who can dissolve his mind in God), who remains in the calm depths of soul bliss beyond reach of common human emotions. Afflictions do not distract his steady wisdom; favourable circumstances do not rouse in him attachment to the pleasure of that condition nor desire for its tempting offerings.

The *muni* or man of wisdom has withdrawn his consciousness from the distorted testimony of the sense mind and has focused it on the soul. The searchlight of his wisdom is thrown steadily on the kingdom of an inner everlasting joy.

The divine man, finding the nature of the soul to be different from the nature of the body, does not become inwardly ruffled when trouble invades the body, nor unduly elated over impermanent worldly joys. The soul is not in any way identified with the transitory bodily experiences. Thus, when the ego-self is settled in the true Self, wisdom-paralyzing emotions cannot impinge upon the consciousness of that superman.

The "worldly loves" of the ego toward its prized possessions—its inordinate affection for the body, for sensory pleasures, for fickle human attachments—touch not the man of wisdom.

As fear is caused by a sense of impending misfortune, the wise man, identified with the soul, never has cause for alarm.

Anger results from the nonfulfillment of a bodily or mental desire; the *muni* harbours no such desires.

Having noted the difference in the sorrows and pleasures of the wakeful or conscious state of bodily identification, and the pure calm of sleep in the subconscious state, and the untrammelled joy of the superconscious state of soul awareness, the *muni* by discrimination sets his goal above the lesser states and through meditation permanently establishes his wisdom in the everlasting joy of the inner Self.

VERSE 57

यः सर्वत्रानभिस्नेहस्तत्तत्प्राप्य शुभाशुभम् ।
नाभिनन्दति न द्वेष्टि तस्य प्रज्ञा प्रतिष्ठिता ॥

He who is everywhere nonattached, neither joyously excited by encountering good nor disturbed by evil, has an established wisdom.

HE WHO CAN GLIDE like a swan in the waters of life without wetting the feathers of his faculties in a deep sea of attachment, who is not excited while riding on the sunny crests of the waves nor afraid while floating down the dark currents of evil happenings, has a wisdom ever poised, unwavering.

The previous two stanzas emphasized the "aboveness" of the sage of steady wisdom. He is desireless, content in his true Self, and free from emotions because he is united to the ever new joy of his inner soul nature. This present stanza elaborates that as a result of this identification with the soul, the Self-realized *muni* is "everywhere"—at all times and under all conditions—in a state of neutrality toward good and evil, the light-and-shadow pictures of creation that cause the ordinary man to react with pleasure or pain. The neutrality of the wise man is not a heartless indifference, but the conscious control and calming of the faculties of consciousness. In the man who is a puppet of Nature, the mind components of feeling, ego, senses, and discrimination (*chitta, ahamkara, manas,* and *buddhi*) are an excitable mix of delusion-influenced actions and reactions. Though a divine man of steady wisdom must live and move in a body, mind, and external environment like every other man, he has achieved what Patanjali describes in *Yoga Sutras* (I:2) as *"chitta vritti nirodha,"* cessation of the modifications of the mind-stuff.* His perceptions are not through the excitable distortions of Nature, but from the calm perspective of pure soul wisdom.

Just as the ordinary man remains indifferent to the pleasures and pains of a stranger, the divine man learns to ignore the pleasures and pains of that intimate stranger—his body. One should try to rid his body and mind of the causes of suffering, while at the same time realizing that these afflictions are not his own; they do not belong to the soul. The soul is ever at peace, while the sense-identified body and mind ceaselessly experience the phenomenal dualities—good and evil, pleasure and pain.

A person who can perceive the separateness between the blessedness of his soul and the excitable nature of the body and mind, and, further, can control the instruments of this excitability, is spoken of as one having a fixed discrimination, an established wisdom.

VERSE 58

यदा संहरते चायं कूर्मोऽङ्गानीव सर्वशः।
इन्द्रियाणीन्द्रियार्थेभ्यस्तस्य प्रज्ञा प्रतिष्ठिता॥

When the yogi, like a tortoise withdrawing its limbs, can fully retire his senses from the objects of perception, his wisdom manifests steadiness.

THE TORTOISE SWIFTLY WITHDRAWS its limbs within the armour of its shell to protect itself from harm. Similarly, when the five senses of a yogi are withdrawn in his subconscious mind during sleep, or dis-

* See commentary on I:4–6, page 70.

solved in his superconsciousness during deep concentration, or disconnected any time at will in the conscious state by Self-mastery or by *nirvikalpa samadhi,* that *muni* of steady wisdom is protected from the contact or tempting invasion of the sensory world.

Control of the senses is vitally linked to control of the *prana* or life energy in the body—an intelligent, electric-like medium whose instrumentality enlivens the whole human mechanism. In the sensory nerves, *prana* makes perceptions possible; all messages of the senses, all pleasurable and painful sensations from the periphery of the body, are reported to the brain through the medium of this life energy. In the motor nerves, *prana* makes movement possible. It is responsible for the activity of the involuntary organs; and thoughts and will require its help to express themselves in action.

Prana holds the key to the bodily dwelling and to its inner apartments of the brain and consciousness. It lets in or shuts out all welcome or unwelcome visitors of sensations and actions, according to the guidance it receives or the free rein it is allowed.

When the devotee's mind is identified with the *prana* or energy in the optical, auditory, olfactory, gustatory, and tactual nerves, he is tempted by beauty, music, fragrances, tastes, sex, and other attractive sensations. The holy Gita tells the yogi to learn to withdraw his mind and energy from the five sensory channels to attain Self-mastery.

If, for example, a man has determined not to eat sweets, he may not be successful with will power alone, but he can conquer temptation scientifically by the technique of withdrawing his mind and energy from the nerves of taste and thus temporarily banish the thought and sensation of sweetness. If a telephone is disconnected, its message is cut off instantly. The yogi must be an expert switchboard operator for his sense telephones, able at will to switch on and off his mind and life force flowing through the five message-carriers of sight, hearing, smell, taste, and touch.

If a rose is held before a sleeping man, he will not see it. Neither can he smell the rose nor hear any sound. One who is in the state of deep sleep will not taste food that may be put in his mouth, nor feel sensations of gentle touch. The yogi can consciously attain this freedom from sensory intrusion.

A devotee is not being advised by the Gita to banish all sensory temptations by a continuous escape into sleep or into the superconsciousness! Nevertheless, at the slightest command of will, the devotee should be able to withdraw the mind and energy from any of the five senses. Eventually, undesirable sense lures lose all power of attraction.

For example: During excitement of the sex impulse in the nerves it is almost impossible to control the mind and its desire. That is why people in general succumb to sex temptation. The impulse results from identification of the mind with the physiological sex nerves. The yogi knows the art of withdrawing the mind and energy from the procreative nerves so completely that no unwanted sexual arousal in the body nor any outside object of sexual temptation can overcome him. By this mastery of the mind and life force, he wholly releases himself from both physiological and mental temptation.

Controlling the senses and attaining self-mastery through Kriya Yoga

When the mind is identified with any sense sensation, it finds itself unable to understand the difference between its own happiness and the pleasures of the senses. When the yogi learns how to withdraw his mind and energy from the senses, his mind concentrates on its own real joy found in the soul contact and interiorization; the pleasures of the senses by comparison then seem foreign and repugnant.

If a hungry person feeds somebody else he can never thus appease his own hunger. Similarly, when a soul is hungry to find its own lost happiness, it cannot do so through the senses. All sense addicts find themselves disillusioned and dissatisfied because they are seeking happiness in foreign territory hostile to soul bliss.

The *Kriya Yoga* technique taught by Lahiri Mahasaya (my guru's guru) is a form of highest *pranayama*—the art of switching off the *prana* or life force from the five senses. Breath is the cord that ties the consciousness to the body and senses. Breath control is a sequel of control of the heart and the life force. Even to quiet the heart partially, at will, is to be able to switch off the life current from the five sense telephones. By control of the heart (the switchboard of the telephonic five senses) the yogi can disconnect his mind from the five forms of sensations. When the heart is controlled, breath control follows.

It is erroneous to think that the unscientific holding of breath in the lungs leads to the control of the heart. Those, too, who try to control the mind only by mental meditations find it takes a long time for the mind to control the heart effectively. Only the science of yoga—a technique such as *Kriya Yoga*—follows the quick or "airplane" route to God, since it advocates a psychophysical method by which the heart can be quieted in a natural way, causing it to withdraw the life force from the senses.

In order to control the heart one must control the body, lessen the carbon in the blood by following a non-toxin-creating diet (which includes a bounty of fresh fruits), and learn the yoga art of burning the carbon in the venous blood so that the heart will not have to pump dark blood into the lungs for purification. By deep stillness the heart is released from constant work and is then automatically free to withdraw the life force from the five senses. No sensations then reach the brain to harass the mind.

In the bodily house there are actually two sets of telephones—the motor nerves and the sensory receptors. Through the motor nerves man works his muscles and limbs and internal organs. Through his sensory telephones his brain receives sensations from the outside world of sight, smell, hearing, taste, and touch. A yogi at will can both still all voluntary and involuntary movements of his body, and also switch off his mind and life force from sensory perceptions.

The ordinary person can disconnect his mind from the senses, and partially from the body, only in the unconscious state of sleep. The yogi learns that the true way of happiness lies in the art of controlling mind and life force at will, consciously. The ordinary person cannot disengage his mind from the senses when they are tempted; but the yogi, like the tortoise, can securely withdraw his limbs of mind and life force from any sensory attack.

Bhagavan Krishna thus tells the yogi to follow the art of scientific control of the senses. An adept yogi can withdraw his mind from all sensations of the material world and can unite his mind and energy with the intoxicating joy of inner ecstasy or *samadhi.** In a high state of yoga perception and deep interiorization of the mind, the yogi feels retirement of the senses of smell, taste, sound, touch, and sight into the cosmic sound *Aum,* which ultimately melts into Cosmic Consciousness.† This experience is one that can be understood only by those who have gone into a deep state of meditation.

---

* Christ issued a similar commandment to his disciples: "But thou, when thou prayest, enter into thy closet (the silence within), and when thou hast shut thy door (withdrawn the mind from the senses), pray to thy Father which is in secret (in the inner transcendent divine consciousness); and thy Father which seeth in secret shall reward thee openly (shall bless you with the ever new Bliss of His Being)" (Matthew 6:6).

† Reference to the technique of withdrawing life and consciousness upward through the spinal centres, dissolving the grosser into the successively finer manifestations of the holy creative vibration of *Aum,* and *Aum* into Spirit. (See Gita commentary I:15–18 and II:39.)

VERSE 59

विषया विनिवर्तन्ते निराहारस्य देहिनः ।
रसवर्जं रसोऽप्यस्य परं दृष्ट्वा निवर्तते ॥

The man who physically fasts from sense objects finds that the sense objects fall away for a little while, leaving behind only the longing for them. But he who beholds the Supreme is freed even from longings.

AN ABSTINENT MAN UNGUIDED by wisdom is not delivered from the dark mental forest of lurking longings. He only outwardly shuts his eyes to the sense objects, while the spectres of sense longings continue to haunt him inwardly. But the wise man who opens his eyes of wisdom and sees the Supreme Light everywhere perceives no lingering shadows of sensory desires.

The greedy man by the penance of physical fasting may stay away for a time from food, but at the slightest thought or suggestion of food, his partially subdued longing for it is roused and quickly revives his sense of taste, weakened only temporarily by fasting. Similarly, by physical self-control without mental self-control, the sensual man may for a while distance himself from sense lures, but his mind, constantly dwelling on temptation, will sooner or later cause him to fall a victim to it.

Physical renunciation must be accompanied by mental renunciation and by constant discrimination between body and soul.

The royal road to safety, however, is experience of the supreme joy of Spirit. Once the yogi has tasted the unparalleled bliss of God he takes no interest in the insignificant offerings of sense pleasures.

Yoga: inner renunciation for monastics and householders

In this stanza the Gita may be said to be comparing the exterior method of renunciation as followed by monks and swamis to the interior method as followed by yogis. Many monastics believe that by living in a hermitage and by not marrying they will be free from attachment to worldly objects. The truth is that all swamis and other renunciants who do not, in addition, become yogis (those who practise a scientific method of God-union) are in grave danger of losing sight of their divine goal, as are householder yogis who do not practise inner nonattachment.

By physical renunciation alone the recalcitrant mind is not convinced fully that the pleasures of the senses must be forsaken. But the yogi, be he a monastic or a householder, who contacts the supreme joy of Spirit by deep meditation not only thinks but *knows* that a man is a fool not to renounce the lesser joy of the senses for the supreme joy of Spirit.

The ordinary renunciant, outwardly forsaking the objects of pleasure, has won only the first round with the senses. The inner longings have by no means acknowledged defeat! So the renunciant must learn not only the outer but the inner art of self-defense.

Water added to milk freely mixes with it and dilutes its natural character; milk that has become butter, however, can float in water without undergoing any adulteration. Similarly, the ordinary renunciant's mind has to stay away from the diluting potential of sensory temptations; yet the yogi who has churned the butter of realization finds himself impervious, inwardly and outwardly, to all attachment to sense objects even when he is surrounded by them.

Renunciation of the world without practising a definite yoga technique of meditation, which controls the life force in the senses, is not only unlikely to yield the desired spiritual benefits, but often places the monk in an awkward hypocritical position. Outwardly a renunciant, inwardly he is tormented by temptations.

Yoga says to fill the mind to the brim with the joy of God! In that overwhelming bliss can one still long for sense pleasures? Yoga is thus the true royal road to salvation.

VERSE 60

यततो ह्यपि कौन्तेय पुरुषस्य विपश्चितः ।
इन्द्रियाणि प्रमाथीनि हरन्ति प्रसभं मनः ॥

O son of Kunti (Arjuna), the eager excitable senses do forcibly seize the consciousness even of one who has a high degree of enlightenment, and is striving (for liberation).

THE POWERFUL SENSES EXTEND their psychological tentacles and occasionally get a dangerous octopus-grip on even advanced devotees who are close to escape from the dark waters of delusion.

A note of warning is given to the smug and self-satisfied devotee who may have attained some spiritual advancement and a degree of self-control over his life and thus considers himself immune to the subtle lures of the senses. No one is actually safe from the predatory senses—not even the nearly perfect wise man—until he has reached the final shelter of unbreakable union with Spirit.

A devotee may long separate himself from objects that excite temptation in the senses and thus rashly believe that their inner luring activity is gone. They are quite as likely to be merely dormant, hibernating within him, ready to spring into movement under a sudden contact of suitable circumstances.

No one is safe from the predatory senses until he has attained unbreakable union with Spirit

No germ of evil, however seemingly insignificant, should be allowed to remain lurking within, growing and undetected. As contact with germs may not appear harmful at first because one's immune qualities hold them in check, so also a slight measure of evil may apparently be untroublesome when one's spiritual health is good and strong; but if in any way the immune spiritual qualities become weakened, then the bacteria of evil are quickly aroused and invigorated, and quite overwhelm the vulnerable host.

Thus the wise man should introspect and find out whether his greed, sex temptation, love of physical beauty, desire for flattery, and so forth have been actually slain by wisdom or whether they are only feigning their demise.

Even without the outward contact of specific objects, the five senses of knowledge (sight, hearing, smell, taste, touch) and the five executive powers (speech, hand and foot movement, sexual and excretory activities) may internally be excited by mere thought. For instance, a wise man trying to overcome a particular temptation not only must stay away outwardly from all stimulating occupations and people akin to his weakness but also must control his senses internally so they do not feed his mind with associated images that arise from the subconscious mind owing to its picturizing power or to its memory of past sensual experiences.

No devotee should underestimate the formidable power of the subconsciousness, whose tentacles are more far-reaching than those of the conscious mind.

VERSE 61

तानि सर्वाणि संयम्य युक्त आसीत मत्परः ।
वशे हि यस्येन्द्रियाणि तस्य प्रज्ञा प्रतिष्ठिता ॥

He who unites his spirit to Me, having subjugated all his senses, remains concentrated on Me as the Supremely Desirable. The intuitive wisdom of that yogi becomes steadfast whose senses are under his sway.

SCORNING THE TINSEL LUMINOSITY of sense objects, the God-united devotee focuses his thoughts on the ever joyous Spirit. His senses soon forsake their rebellion and obey him as their rightful sovereign.

Two things are required of a wise man. First, he must withdraw his mind from the senses; secondly, he must keep the mind united with the Deity, yielding only to that Supreme Temptation!

This outer and inner control makes the wisdom of the devotee unwavering—that is, not hovering between divine and sensual pleasures. The advanced yogi finds his senses ever obedient, well trained in subservience to the better and finer joys of God-perception.

A man's intellect is not steady if he is the victim of self-indulgences. A sense slave's mind and judgement are persistently clouded; he passes from one error to another, from one wrong action to another, from one pitfall to another.

The sage of steady wisdom exercises good judgement in all decisions and actions, for his inner intuitive wisdom is ever united to the omniscience of Spirit.

VERSES 62–63

ध्यायतो विषयान्पुंसः सङ्गस्तेषूपजायते ।
सङ्गात्सञ्जायते कामः कामात्क्रोधोऽभिजायते ॥ *(62)*

क्रोधाद्भवति सम्मोहः सम्मोहात्स्मृतिविभ्रमः ।
स्मृतिभ्रंशाद् बुद्धिनाशो बुद्धिनाशात्प्रणश्यति ॥ *(63)*

Brooding on sense objects causes attachment to them. Attachment breeds craving; craving breeds anger. Anger breeds delusion; delusion breeds loss of memory (of the Self). Loss of right memory causes decay of the discriminating faculty. From decay of discrimination, annihilation (of spiritual life) follows.

VISUALIZING SENSORY HAPPINESS produces an increasing attachment to that feeling of attraction. Such attachment becomes crystallised into an active desire for acquirement, giving birth to crafty cravings, the pernicious foe of peace. Desires unfulfilled enmesh man in the travails of anger. Wrath creates a distorting cloud of delusion. From delusion flows the loss of memory and self-respect of one's own position and normal behaviour. From a mangled memory of one's proper self exudes the stench of decayed discrimination. When discrimination degenerates, the destruction of the spiritual life follows.

The Hindu sages were psychological experts.* They recognized the futility of merely laying down commandments and passing laws—neither of which can balk man's ingenuity for breaking constraints. By appealing to the rationality of the human mind, the sages instead presented compelling analyses of the "why" of right conduct.

In concise verse, these two Gita stanzas describe the fateful step-by-step descent of potentially noble man down the ladder of temptation into ruin. These stages of descent are the baneful results of brooding over sense lures, the psychological origin of desire and its offspring and their consequences. The sage views with detachment all external beauty, whether in the face of a woman or a jewel or a flower; he has no longings for possession. The sense slave craves possession; and, as beautiful women and costly treasures are numerous in this world, so are his desires! And when he is frustrated by nonpossession, he finds himself in a state of bitterness or anger.

❖

Step-by-step descent of noble man down the ladder of temptation into ruin

❖

Anger arises from nonfulfilment of desires, good or bad. Obstruction of good desires gives birth to a righteous anger; hindrance

---

* In *Autobiography of a Yogi,* Paramahansa Yogananda wrote: "Studies in consciousness by Western psychologists are largely confined to investigations of the subconscious mind and of mental diseases that are treated through psychiatry and psychoanalysis. There is little research into the origin and fundamental formation of normal mental states and their emotional and volitional expressions—a truly basic subject not neglected in Indian philosophy. Precise classifications are made, in the *Sankhya* and *Yoga* systems, of the various links in normal mental modifications and of the characteristic functions of *buddhi* (discriminative intellect), *ahamkara* (egoistic principle), and *manas* (mind or sense consciousness)."

"For every psychological term in English, there are four in Greek and forty in Sanskrit," Professor Huston Smith, renowned authority on world religions, quoted the great art historian A. K. Coomaraswamy as saying. "The West has no psychology of liberation as India does. The unconscious has been acknowledged in the West as something that can make us sick or make us do things we don't want to do. But in the East they know the unconscious can be in health and can feed intuition and insight into the conscious mind" (*The San Diego Union,* April 14, 1990). *(Publisher's Note)*

of evil desires rouses a destructive and unreasonable wrath.

Righteous indignation may inspire a man to extraordinary efforts to right some wrong. A righteous anger employs reasonable and constructive methods for the attainment of a good end. But egotistical anger blinds a man so that he becomes increasingly irrational in trying to fulfil his obstructed desires. Unrighteous anger causes a man to lose his inner balance. Through anger, many men have been unwillingly and suddenly turned into criminals and murderers, and doers of sundry ungodly actions. All unenlightened men are subject to the inner or outer wrath of nonfulfilment of desires. The Gita warns man, therefore, against the blind worship of sense objects.

Devotees should picture to themselves the way in which anger originates from frustrated desires, and how it leads to grave consequences.

The paroxysm of anger has physiological and psychological effects. Physiologically, the angry man's whole system undergoes a change. The heart action is accelerated. The heat of the blood rises, and the angry man feels a burning sensation all over his body. There is a rush of blood to the head, causing internal tension of the tissues of the brain. The electric circuits of the nerves become overloaded. Chemicals at toxic levels are secreted and circulated throughout the body. The functions of the digestive apparatus are arrested or adversely affected. Extreme, uncontrollable anger has been known to trigger heart attacks, strokes, and death. In persons who are susceptible to outbursts of anger, which they love to indulge rather than transmute, the heart and nervous system begin to weaken from the repeated emotional shocks. The beautiful face of man, wherein wonderful peace-giving emotions can be registered, undergoes ugly contortions in the angry man.

The psychological effect of anger is equally acute, and spiritually lethal. It stupefies the mind, anaesthetizing its functioning power. At this stage, strong motor impulses of anger are very apt to overrule the rational guidelines set by the normal psychological state. The motor area of the angry man will react more quickly than the anger-dulled psychological reason. The motor impulses of anger, eager for an outlet, gush forth in channels of irresponsible activities leading to gravest consequences. A man who in his sane moments could never dream of injuring anyone, may become abusive and violent under the motor paroxysm of anger. Before the person realizes the dangerous magnitude of his action, before his mind realizes the gravity of his heinous act, the motor impulse has done the deed.

Thus the Gita warns that anger gives birth to an enveloping delusion, a state of psychological blindness that spreads through all the reasonable faculties. It overclouds the mind and makes it grope aimlessly. In the normal state one knows what he ought to do. The light of reason is present to guide the man of normal consciousness. But as soon as the thunderbolt of anger extinguishes that light, the angry man is left in the darkness of delusion without a guide and doesn't remember what he is supposed to do. Thus it is said that loss of memory follows delusion.

Under the hypnotic influence of delusion produced by anger, a man loses his memory of what he was and how he should behave according to what is becoming to his inner real nature. The memory of his normal feelings and good sentiments fades. Under continued darkness, the angry man's memory of himself and his good qualities becomes chronically confused and utterly forgotten.

Reasonable thought finds no means of expression in an angry person. Reasonable words have no effect because they are directed not to the real man but to the angry self, who from confused memory has lost the consciousness of his true Self. Confused memory is utterly incompatible with discriminative reason.

With discrimination lost, the way of destruction is speedily paved.

An example: A man who is cheerfully driving a car on the way to a picnic ground is suddenly requested by his wife to change the destination and to go, instead, to the house of his mother-in-law. His joy changes to anger. (I choose this particular example in full confidence that it possesses a fairly wide applicability!)

In ordinary cases, the result is either that the husband refuses to change the destination or (more commonly) that he fumingly complies with his wife's demand. In either case, anger has disrupted the harmony of the day. Sometimes, however, in the case of a violent-tempered man, the initial anger leads to tragedy. His wrath affects his memory: he may have temporary mental blocks of his recall of safe driving habits, or he fails to exercise his customary caution about other vehicles on the road. Result: an accident, sometimes fatal.

Anger and its evolutes freeze the steering wheel of the car of life and stop it from reaching its material and spiritual destination.

The evolution from sense attraction to destruction may thus be summarized as follows: Sense attractions, if not sublimated in the beginning, are bound to grow into desires. Obstruction of desires agitates the calmness of the consciousness and rouses a blinding confusion in the normally working mind. When this obscuring fog arises in the average man he loses memory of his own human dignity. The loss of

ॐ

When war became inevitable, Arjuna for the Pandus and Duryodhana for the Kurus sought Krishna's aid in their cause. Duryodhana arrived first at Krishna's palace and seated himself boldly at the head of the couch upon which Krishna was resting, feigning sleep. Arjuna arrived and stood humbly with folded hands at Krishna's feet. When the avatar opened his eyes, it was, therefore, Arjuna whom he saw first. Both requested Krishna to side with them in the war. Krishna stated that one party could have his massive army, and the other side could have himself as a personal counselor—though he would not take up arms in the combat. Arjuna was given first choice. Without hesitation he wisely chose Krishna himself; the greedy Duryodhana rejoiced to be awarded the army.

———❖———

"Where Krishna is, there is victory."

"The Pandavas' chief counsellor and support is the Lord Himself, who, in the form of Krishna, represents variously the Spirit, the soul, or intuition…or as the guru instructing his disciple, the devotee Arjuna. Within the devotee, Lord Krishna is thus the guiding Divine Intelligence speaking to the lower self that has gone astray in the entanglements of sensory consciousness. This Higher Intelligence is the master and teacher, and the lower mental intellect is the disciple; the Higher Intelligence advises the lower vitiated self on how to uplift itself in accord with the eternal verities, and in fulfilment of its inherent God-given duty."

❖

"Any devotee who will emulate Arjuna—epitome of the ideal disciple—and perform his rightful duty with nonattachment, and perfect his practice of yoga meditation…will similarly draw the blessings and guidance of God and win the victory of Self-realization."

—Paramahansa Yogananda

memory confuses and blocks his discrimination, the motivating force of all right action. When the steering wheel of discrimination in the mental car of man's life is broken he ends up in a ditch of misery.

ALL THE FOREGOING, concerning the ordinary man and his material desires, is pertinent also to the yogi and his encounters with what are sometimes more subtle entrapments. Even he who has progressed far on the spiritual path may suddenly find some sense attraction catching hold of his consciousness. Immediate action by the discrimination and self-control applied toward stronger spiritual effort and deeper meditation will save him. But allowing the mind to dwell "harmlessly" on that attraction, or to feed it in any way, is to invite the ensuing consequences. Though it may manifest more subtly, the course it takes and the spiritually destructive result are the same: sense attraction degenerating into loss of remembrance of the true Self or soul and its divine contentment, along with the loss of the guidance of discrimination that attracts the consciousness toward Spirit.

Society as a whole is also subject to degradation through the same process as individuals

Society as a whole is also subject to degradation through the same process as individuals, who, after all, are the constituents of communities and nations. All the miseries and ghastly terrors of civilization have their roots in indiscrimination, which is the gradual ripening of the evil that sprouts unwittingly in the mind of man through the stages of attraction and attachment, longing and desire, anger and passion, delusion and recklessness, and impropriety from loss of memory of man's true divine Self. Thus does yoga adjure man to maintain an iron grip on the thought system of his mind. Self-control must not be lost even at the greatest provocation. When evil exists within, then what appears without is its double. He who conquers the mind, conquers the world.

VERSE 64

रागद्वेषवियुक्तैस्तु विषयानिन्द्रियैश्चरन्।
आत्मवश्यैर्विधेयात्मा प्रसादमधिगच्छति॥

The man of self-control, roaming among material objects with subjugated senses, and devoid of attraction and repulsion, attains an unshakeable inner calmness.

WHEN THE SPIRITUAL WARRIOR, armoured with self-control, passes over the dangerous territory of tempting objects with a band of disciplined, obedient sense soldiers, guiding them around the snares of attraction or aversion by strong commands of discrimination, he is secure in an inner joyousness that is confident of victory.

The man of self-control who finds his senses under the full control of the soul's discrimination abandons attraction and aversion—the root cause of entanglement in material objects—using his obedient, unprejudiced, unentangled senses to perform duties rightfully and joyously.

Just as a rich man who succumbs to flattery and temptation loses his money and health, so any man, inherently rich in his soul, when lured by sense inclinations loses his wealth of peace and his health of spirit.

The ordinary, untrained, unguarded individual who wanders into the territories of temptation falls captive to sense attraction or aversion; being thus waylaid, he fails to reach the kingdom of happiness.

Attraction to certain sensations of taste, touch, sound, sight, and smell carries with it an invariable companion: aversion. Sudden attachments and aversions—likes and dislikes—to sense objects prejudice the mind's power of free judgement and make human beings slaves to moods and habits. Millions of men, solely through habit and lack of inner reflection, engage in "pleasures" that have long lost any real savour.

Just as a man who becomes attached to a practice of the speeding of a high-powered automobile and runs it over tempting but dangerous mountain roads may swerve off the path and meet injury or death, so a man who becomes enamoured of the charming sense power of the bodily machine and speeds heedlessly on the difficult roads of sense pleasures is sure to leave the straight and narrow path of the soul's tranquillity.

The pathway of life that every incarnate soul must travel to the Ultimate Goal leads through the territory of sensations and sense traps. Only the man of self-control knows how to behave in the material surroundings through which he must perforce roam and work. The man of self-control puts on an armour of wisdom and nonattachment while he performs his duties in the tricky sense world.

VERSE 65

प्रसादे सर्वदुःखानां हानिरस्योपजायते ।
प्रसन्नचेतसो ह्याशु बुद्धिः पर्यवतिष्ठते ॥

In soul bliss* all grief is annihilated. Indeed, the discrimination of the blissful man soon becomes firmly established (in the Self).

All dark shadows of sorrow are banished from the consciousness of him who enters the state of the soul's perfect inner tranquillity and remains concentrated on the clear guiding light of his true ever joyous Self. Verily, the magnetic needle of his mind soon becomes immovably fixed, ever facing the North Star of soul bliss.

The man of self-control enjoying the immutable bliss of the soul has passed beyond the grief-bestowing phenomenal world. Man's wavering reason, becoming fixed on the soul, changes into an unswerving discrimination. When the light of soul happiness comes, the accumulated darkness of incarnations is dispelled in a trice.

The sense-entangled often find their reason jumping from one sense pleasure to another, seeking the permanent happiness that is promised but never granted by the deceitful senses.

The wise man, enjoying the pure unchanging bliss of the soul in constant meditation, finds that his reason no longer tempts him to fly from one material object to another; he is guided and guarded solely by a stable discrimination. Human reason can always find the pros and cons for good and for bad actions alike; it is inherently disloyal. Discrimination acknowledges only one polestar criterion: the soul.

Verse 66

नास्ति बुद्धिरयुक्तस्य न चायुक्तस्य भावना।
न चाभावयतः शान्तिरशान्तस्य कुतः सुखम्॥

To the disunited (one not established in the Self) does not belong wisdom, nor has he meditation. To the unmeditative there is no tranquillity. To the peaceless how comes happiness?

He who does not remain concentrated on his true Self, intent on the qualities of his pure soul-nature, is wanting in the divine discrimination inherent in the soul. Without this wisdom, his mind is diffused and distracted, scattered by the whims of the senses, leaving him bereft of the

* "In soul bliss," *prasāde:* "In the all-satisfying state of inner calmness (i.e., that perfect tranquillity of the Self that is permeated with the soul's pure nature, ever new bliss)."

faculty of deep meditation with its bestowal of ineffable peace. The unmeditative man, peaceless, finds lasting happiness ever eluding him.

The individual who is attached to the senses is, as a logical consequence, disunited from the soul, utterly uncognizant of its superb qualities. If one is not in light he is in darkness; similarly, he who is not aware of the luminous beauties of the soul is identified with the dark delusions of the senses. Identification of the human mind with the senses produces a state of "disunion" characterized by restlessness, inharmony, and scattered faculties. It thus follows that the man who has separated his mind from the soul cannot manifest a true discrimination.

The intellect can be cultured by education, but discrimination flows from intuition and is obtained only through soul force, through contact with the soul. Both reason and discrimination consist of a process of passing through a series of judgements in order to reach a conclusion. Reason, however, is guided by the imperfect intellect, which is full of the limitations of emotions, desires, habits; therefore, even the highest flights of thought, the most mathematical and calculating reason, are uncertain and liable to errors. Discrimination born of intuition through soul contact insures right judgement in any given situation. The soul, through the agency of intuition, drops divine guidance into the consciousness of the devotee; the intuitive guidance manifests as wisdom through the discriminative faculty to guide the intellect or reason to the right determination. Theoretical philosophers limit themselves to the development of error-prone discursive reasoning; yogis devote themselves to acquiring unerring intuition through soul contact in meditation.

Peace, also, is a quality of the soul; he who is not in tune with the soul has no peace. The peaceless person has no happiness, because peace means absence of sorrow, a prerequisite to happiness.

Sadness is usually followed by mental indifference—the negative state of peace. When peace in its negative state of absence-of-sorrow has been immediately preceded by deep grief, then through contrast a mental tranquillity is experienced, which the ignorant man calls "peace." His peace is conditional on sadness. For him, "I have long been peaceful" signifies "I have long been without excitement of troubles." Negative peace, unmarred by the contrast of pain, in time becomes insipid or meaningless—a state of sheer boredom.

Positive peace, however, emanates from the soul and is the sacred inner environment in which true happiness unfolds. This positive state of peace may be said to be the precursor of divine bliss.

Happiness is positive and tangible. In order to be really happy, however, one must first win the state of unbroken peace. One who is in tune with the soul possesses all its qualities, including peace, divine bliss, and unerring wisdom.

VERSE 67

इन्द्रियाणां हि चरतां यन्मनोऽनुविधीयते।
तदस्य हरति प्रज्ञां वायुर्नावमिवाम्भसि॥

As a boat on the waters is carried off course by a gale, so an individual's discrimination is driven from its intended path when the mind succumbs to the wandering senses.

A BOAT PLYING ON PEACEFUL WATERS is tossed willy-nilly and thrown off course when suddenly struck by a furious wind; similarly, man's discrimination, sailing its destined chartered course of right action toward Spirit, is helplessly set adrift when the mind yields its steerage to the helter-skelter storm of the senses.

On calm seas during good weather, a boat has smooth sailing and reaches its destination without difficulty. But a boat venturing out during stormy weather will certainly be buffeted and possibly sunk. Similarly, the devotee who sails the sea of life in the good weather of spiritual habits is bound to reach easily the shores of Infinite Bliss. But the man of spiritual aspirations who navigates his life through the stormy waters of an ungoverned mind will surely be diverted from his course of good intentions, and may even lose sight completely of the Divine Polestar.

This does not mean that a man who encounters tempests of sensuality should not try to navigate toward divine shores in spite of the gusts of his bad habits and temptations. The lines of this verse merely remind us that he who would sail *smoothly* toward Spirit must calm the storms of the senses.

Even a yogi who is rapidly nearing his Goal may find himself amidst storms of sense addictiveness through error or through past life or postnatal subconscious bad habits; then, by the Christ-power of his soul's strong will he should command the sensory gales to subside.

VERSE 68

तस्माद्यस्य महाबाहो निगृहीतानि सर्वशः ।
इन्द्रियाणीन्द्रियार्थेभ्यस्तस्य प्रज्ञा प्रतिष्ठिता ॥

O Mighty-armed (Arjuna), his wisdom is well-established whose sense faculties are wholly subjugated in regard to sense objects.

"O SCION OF SELF-CONTROL," a person whose consistent wisdom is the charioteer of the stallions of the senses prevents them from racing wildly over the precarious terrain of sense objects; he guides them with a sure and steady rein over the straight pathway to blessed liberation.

A man without discriminating self-control is powerless to hold the steeds of his senses on the straight and narrow path of virtue. A man who is ruled by his senses is confused. His calm inner soul judgement is displaced by the restless, purposeless habits of a whim-governed, dissatisfied, sense-enslaved mind. Such a person can never have peace. The aspiring yogi must keep the stallions of the senses under his full control.

The driver of life's chariot is not counselled to tie up his sense stallions and consign them to inactivity out of a fear that they might run wild. That would be unwise. All that is necessary is so to train his steeds that they remain obedient and allow him to make all decisions.

"Wherefore if thy hand or thy foot offend thee, cut them off, and cast them from thee: it is better for thee to enter into life halt or maimed, rather than having two hands or two feet to be cast into everlasting fire."*

When Jesus urged, "If thy hand offend thee" (prevent thee from entering into God's kingdom) "cut it off," he was not advising literal dismemberment, but rather the severance of the impulse that had actuated it to do evil.

Removal of a man's eyes does not destroy his desire for sensuous beauty. Cutting off the hands does not affect one's power of desire to hurt or to steal. What is needed is to control the misery-making *desires* that guide man's instruments of perception and action.

I was once told about an obsessive woman thief, who in a moment of repentance followed the Biblical advice literally and cut off both her hands. But so compulsive was her habit that she started to steal articles with her toes and mouth!

---

* Matthew 18:8.

The senses are mere instruments of the mind; they cannot act by themselves. It is the mind and discrimination that must be freed from enslavement. A wise man keeps his wisdom free and steady, directing his life on the Godward path.

VERSE 69

या निशा सर्वभूतानां तस्यां जागर्ति संयमी।
यस्यां जाग्रति भूतानि सा निशा पश्यतो मुनेः॥

That which is night (of slumber) to all creatures is (luminous) wakefulness to the man of self-mastery. And what is wakefulness to ordinary men, that is night (a time for slumber) to the divinely perceptive sage.

WHILE CREATURES SLUMBER in delusion's gloom, the X-ray eyes of the seer are open to wisdom's light. The power of *maya* that keeps all beings engrossed in the wakefulness of attachment to material objects induces in saints only the slumber of nonattachment.

This stanza uses as an analogy the habit of those Hindu yogis who devote their nights to meditation, when people of the world are asleep. These yogis sleep for a few hours in the daytime, when most men are awake and busy with material pursuits.

The metaphysical correlation is that while most people are spiritually somnolent, immersed in the delusive dreams of life, the man of realization is spiritually awake, his alert divine vision ever intent on the luminous Reality behind the dark "night" of *maya*. People who are engrossed in matter use all wakeful hours to pursue their goals. Realizing the wasteful, foolish lives of such men, the yogi remains in a slumber of indifference toward worldly concerns. The yogi whose whole attention is fixed on God withdraws himself from the world, undergoing a state of spiritual "somnambulism." He is in the world but not of the world. Seeing, the yogi sees not (cares not). Though physically awake in the world, the yogi is spiritually asleep in the oblivion of nonattachment.

Thus it can be said that the worldly man is alive or awake in material pursuits, and asleep in spiritual matters. The yogi, in contrast, is spiritually awake and materially asleep. The worldly man is asleep in ignorance and the yogi is awake in wisdom. The wise man is slumbering in indifference while the average man is awake in pursuing matter.

The sense-hypnotized man sees nothing but the world and is unable to perceive God. The wise man wakefully enjoys the presence of God in all things.

The Gita does not literally mean that all yogis should sleep during the day and remain awake at night, nor that all worldly people should labour at night and join the yogi in daily slumber! A fine topsy-turvy "Alice-Through-the-Looking-Glass" world we should have then!

A yogi does not achieve his goal just by remaining awake at night! He must practise meditation and lead a life of self-discipline, service, and active kindness to all.

A worldly man, busy during the day with reasonable material duties, should slumber at night but should use some part of the quiet hours to meditate and to devote himself to spiritual duties. Little sleep suffices when the habit of meditation is well established.

True yogis, perceiving the indestructible Omnipresence, the true Reality, automatically remain indifferent to the delusive appearances of material unreality.

People should not remain engrossed in impermanent material pleasures, oblivious of the everlasting blessedness hidden in the soul. Nor should the yogi, indifferent to material desires, neglect to perform his worldly duties. The yogi who loves God can never forget Him just because of outward activities. An unselfish man pursuing material duties with the constant remembrance and perception of God is not asleep in ignorance but is ever awake in Him.

Nonactivity is far from God-consciousness. The lazy man, bound to flesh, is not free; he is not a yogi. The materially active man, ever fixed in the inward peace, is not a worldly man but one united to God; he is a true yogi.

The sincere devotee loves God deeply whether he is nonactive and silently meditating on God, or in the midst of a whirl of outer activities. He is awake in God during all hours and in all walks of life. He does not become so deeply engrossed in material duties as to be oblivious to the inner state of divine bliss.

To ignore the cultivation of God-consciousness through being overwhelmed with material duties is man's common error. To be inactive, on the other hand, with the pretense of being "spiritual," is dangerous self-deceit.

The worldly man should lessen his material activities sufficiently to give him time for meditation. He should remember he could not perform his material duties if God suddenly said: "Well, I am so busy with cosmic creation that I cannot throb in your heart!"

Nor should the yogi, just because he meditates upon God, refuse to fulfil his necessary material responsibilities. When a devotee becomes really engrossed in God, during both the state of nonactivity and intense activity, the compassionate Lord arranges for his pension, his liberation from earthly duties. But the yogi should abide by God's will in everything and not depend complacently on this promise!

VERSE 70

आपूर्यमाणमचलप्रतिष्ठंसमुद्रमापः प्रविशन्ति यद्वत्।
तद्वत्कामा यं प्रविशन्ति सर्वे स शान्तिमाप्नोति न कामकामी॥

He is full with contentment who absorbs all desires within, as the brimful ocean remains unmoved (unchanged) by waters entering into it—not he who lusts after desires.

AS RIVERS FLOWING INTO THE SEA keep it ever full but do not disturb its changeless vastness, so the streams of desires, transmuted and absorbed within the changeless oceanic Self, have no ripple effect in the *muni,* but keep him overflowing with energy, contentment, and a peace that never oscillates.

The ordinary man has no peace. His shallow mental reservoir is constantly roiled by the inrush of sensory stimulation. Restlessly he bores holes of desires in the dam of consciousness, draining away his inner powers and contentment.

This stanza was a favourite with my great master, Swami Sri Yukteswarji, and was oft quoted by him. He would experience some new manifestation arising from his vast inner ocean of peace (an infinite sea informed and fed by absorbing, transmuting, the inflowing rivers of all material desires); then he would express in a sonorous voice the realizations he was feeling within. His very face shone with a great inward light. At such times, those around him who were spiritually sensitive could feel my Master's overflowing perception of peace being transferred to them. I often inwardly hear him reciting this Gita verse in Sanskrit, just as I used to in years gone by.

When the waters of the reservoir of inner peace trickle out through many tapholes of little desires, those streamlets are greedily absorbed by the desert soil of material perceptions. Soon the reservoir and the desert alike are dry!

The sea, unlike a small reservoir, is vast, ever newly supplied by the rivers that flow into it. The sea is deep, too; its mighty heart seems quiet, motionless.

But such a tide as moving seems asleep,
*Too full for sound and foam....**

In the man of peace, his soul is a sea of contentment in which his whole consciousness is immersed. Instead of losing that peace through the avenues of small yearnings, he absorbs within himself all the rivers of desires, thereby keeping his quiescent sea filled to the brim!

On the contrary, a man who possesses a small reservoir of peace and, instead of enlarging it by self-control and meditation, lets the waters run out through a thousand channels of harmful desires, soon loses all his contentment.

Thus the advice of the Gita: Do not drain dry your reservoir of peace by diverting its waters into channels of small but ever-growing desires. The true devotee desires less and less and finds more and more in his soul a sea of contentment.

This counsel does not mean that one should abandon good aspirations, such as helping others to know God. By noble desires the devotee does not lose his peace, which gathers reinforcement by distribution! This paradox is similar to Jesus' words: "For unto every one that hath shall be given, and he shall have abundance; but from him that hath not shall be taken away even that which he hath."† In spiritual life, giving is receiving.

A desire to give joy to others and the outgoing activity of giving peace to others bring back to the devotee a greater peace and joy. But the satisfaction of any selfish desire leaves the devotee a poorer man.

Letting the soul peace run out through the channels of harmful desires is wrong, but reinforcing the soul with spiritual ambitions that yield joy is right.

Everyone should try to become an ocean of peace by bringing within himself the rivers of joy from the ecstasy with God and from association with good men, study of the scriptures, selfless serviceful activities, and nurturing spiritual desires and ambitions. The inner bed

---

* Alfred, Lord Tennyson, "Crossing the Bar."

† Matthew 25:29.

of one's consciousness should be dug deeper and deeper with the dredging machine of profound meditation, that the incoming joys of others and their powers of virtue, and the rivers of all other sources of goodness, may find ample accommodation.

The man of God is constant and changeless in his joys, like to a vast deep ocean. His mental reservoir has become expanded into the sea of the divine Self. He attracts the rivers of goodness in other souls to flow into his being, all finally commingling in the Eternal Sea of God.

VERSE 71

विहाय कामान्यः सर्वान्पुमांश्चरति निःस्पृहः।
निर्ममो निरहङ्कारः स शान्तिमधिगच्छति॥

That person realizes peace who, relinquishing all desires, exists without craving and is unidentified with the mortal ego and its sense of "mine-ness."

HE WHO ROAMS ON EARTH, having freed himself from the compulsions of past desires, and who keeps himself impervious to the invasion of new cravings, and is no slave to the ego's mean consciousness of "I" and "mine," is wholly free from bondage. With the magic flute of his soul he enchants the peace within him to follow faithfully wherever he goes.

The formula of peace given in this stanza of the Bhagavad Gita is much quoted by complete renunciants and monks whose ascetic lives are free from worldly duties. A recluse seeks peace by minimizing bodily cares and renouncing worldly possession, and by keeping the field of his mind ablaze with wisdom thoughts so that no seeds of material desires may ever again take root. By perfect renunciation he severs all links with the personal or human ego with its desires for temporal possessions.

Peace is the first product of freedom from all desires. To the recluse of the *Jnana Yoga* school, the rationale of asceticism is that even desires for health and ordinary creature comforts, considered good by most people, are to be looked upon as producers of evil. All desires born of the bodily contact cause endless roamings in the corridors of earthly incarnations, since one desire leads to another—like being lost in a maddening labyrinth!

When a person dies without having cast off all desires, he remains tied to rebirth on earth. Hence the renunciant not only forsakes evil desires that deeply entangle the soul in the insatiable weavings of lust for sense objects, but also does away with all personal good desires, as these may also enmesh one in earthly longings. (Noble inclinations and spiritual ambitions that are free of ego and selfish interest, and are motivated solely by a wish to please God, are desireless desires and carry no binding effects.)

In relinquishing past desires, lest they spread like cancer roots and ultimately strangle his peace, the renunciant also prevents by proper thoughts, actions, and environment all possible growths of new desires. He observes an eternal vigil, keeping ever burning the sacred flame of wisdom. He learns also to separate his soul from his ego, the only absolute means of immunity to delusion. He who can disconnect his mind at will from the body realizes the difference between the pure soul made in the image of God and the soul in bondage to the body—the ego.

A king slept on a bed of gold in a stately castle and dreamed he was a beggar. He cried: "Please give me a penny—give me a penny—I am a hungry beggar." When the queen awakened him, he sat up, free from his dream delusions, amused by their absurdity.

The kingly soul, a perfect image of the omnipresent all-powerful Spirit, is similarly sleeping in ignorance, dreaming that it is a poor mortal with afflictions and limitations. When by meditation this false body consciousness or ego consciousness disappears, the soul realizes its own status as the prince-son of the King of the Universe.

The renunciant and the wise man therefore train themselves not to identify the transcendent Self with the mortal ego and its reincarnation-making desires. Free from the ego and its afflictions and attachments to earthbound existence, man inherits the everlasting peace that is his birthright.

The philosophy in this stanza, as noted, is particularly applicable to the life of the renunciant, the man of wisdom who has burnt up nearly all roots of desires of this life and of past lives, and naturally inclines to a casting-off of ordinary worldly pursuits and possessions.

But to the modern householder who wants to perform worldly duties as well as find God, the Bhagavad Gita gives other counsel in Chapter III on *Karma Yoga*, wherein Krishna teaches that he who renounces actions is not a renunciant, nor a yogi united to God; by merely forsaking action, no one reaches perfection and the actionless state. To this end my Guru had said to me, shortly before I became a monk of the Swami Order, "He who rejects the usual worldly duties can justify himself only by assuming some kind of responsibility for a much larger family." Both the renunciant and the householder must learn to be wholly active, but without desiring the fruits of actions.

Any man who renounces the fruits of action and acts only for God is a man of renunciation as well as a yogi. He is a man of renunciation because he relinquishes the desire to be the beneficiary of his actions; he is also a yogi, united to God, because he works only to please Him.

A devotee can attend to his health, his family, his business, and still be a renunciant within. He says to himself: "I did not create this body or this world. So why should I have attachments to them? I perform my material duties to family and others, because God gave those tasks to me. I will meditate deeply and play this temporary role just to please Him." Such a man of inner renunciation is also a yogi, for he is ever moving toward union with God through both meditation and right action.

By this way of being in the world but not of the world one can obtain peace. It is difficult, but it can be accomplished by an iron will. The path of outward renunciation, complete escape from the earthly scenes of material trouble, relinquishing longings by constant discrimination and withdrawal from objects of temptation, is suited to the nature of a choice few devotees.

The yogi-householder, who moves among sense objects, must free himself from internal desires that cause bondage more real than the temptations of the outer world. The man of renunciation must remove himself from the entanglements of the outer jungle of material objects as well as free himself from inner longings for the objects he has relinquished. Then and then only—whether in the world or in a woodland seclusion, whether a householder or a renunciant—one can attain peace.

Working in the world or sitting silently in a forest, the one objective of the yogi should be to recover the lost peace of the soul, and the soul's lost identity with Spirit. He who is wholly desireless and ego-free has realized this objective.

VERSE 72

एषा ब्राह्मी स्थितिः पार्थ नैनां प्राप्य विमुह्यति।
स्थित्वास्यामन्तकालेऽपि ब्रह्मनिर्वाणमृच्छति॥

O Partha (Arjuna)! this is the "established in Brahman" state. Anyone entering this state is never (again) deluded. Even at the very moment of transition (from the physical to the astral), if one becomes anchored therein, he attains the final, irrevocable, state of Spirit-communion.

ENTHRONEMENT IN THE OMNIPRESENT consciousness of Spirit is spoken of as *Brahmasthiti,* the state of reigning in the Royal Spirit. The Spirit-reigning yogi, freed while living, is never again deluded, nor does he come down to a lesser state. He lives in the consciousness of God. His soul expands into the Spirit, yet he retains his individuality, immersed everlastingly in Spirit-communion. When the yogi is established in the Ethereal Infinitude, even if attained only at the moment when the soul slips from the physical tenement into the astral, that soul enters *Brahmanirvana,* expansion in Spirit through the extinguishment of ego and all desires that compel a soul to reincarnate. An omnipresent being cannot be caged behind the bars of finite incarnations. He can of his own free will retain a physical or an astral body, but it cannot imprison his overarching spirit.

Thus Krishna tells his disciple Arjuna: "He who forsakes desires for sense enjoyments, is unattached to sense objects, and is devoid of the consciousness of the limited ego, relinquishing its afflictions of 'me and mine,' receives the lasting joy of God-peace—that permanent blessedness of Spirit-communion spoken of as *Brahmasthiti* or 'anchored-in-the-Infinite state.'"

Anyone who tastes this ultimate state of Spirit-union finds all his desires immediately and completely satisfied for all time. He cannot possibly stoop to lesser pleasures, even as a person having access to a store of orange-blossom honey could not crave rancid molasses.

Through his counsel to Arjuna, Krishna tells God-seekers of all eras: "It is worthwhile, this struggle! Attain the final goal! Drink the nectar of Bliss, never flat, never stale, always fresh and new!"

Krishna further says encouragingly that it does not matter when and how man attains this state of finality; that if a devotee is successful, even at the very moment preceding death, in acquiring the all-blessed state (through his past, continuous, ever-increasing meditative efforts), he will certainly never again be parted from that Spirit-Blessedness.

Unsatisfied desires at the time of death are the cause of reincarnation. The man who still roams in the wilderness of matter, seeking the temporary blossoms of pleasures, works out his mortal desires by reincarnation; desireless, he finally enters the perfection of Spirit. Krishna advises the devotee to keep on working for this state of emancipation, even up to the moment before death. "Him that overcometh will I make a pillar in the temple of my God, and he shall go no more out (will reincarnate no more)," Jesus assures man.* A soul must attain freedom from earthly desires and egoity before death in order to escape from the merry-go-round wheel of births and deaths. If this freedom is not attained before physical death one has to incarnate again on earth. For man to tarry in ignorance is stupid and unwholesome, fraught with untold miseries; one can never tell into what abysmal troubles his ego and unsatisfied mundane desires may lead him.

Strive ceaselessly; never be impatient. Once the finality is achieved, incarnations of troubles will be over in a second, just as when light is admitted within a room that has been locked for decades, the darkness vanishes instantly.

ॐ तत्सदिति श्रीमद्भगवद्गीतासूपनिषत्सु
ब्रह्मविद्यायां योगशास्त्रे श्रीकृष्णार्जुनसंवादे
साङ्ख्ययोगो नाम द्वितीयोऽध्यायः ॥

Aum, Tat, Sat.
In the Upanishad of the holy Bhagavad Gita—the discourse of Lord Krishna to Arjuna, which is the scripture of yoga and the science of God-realization—this is the second chapter, called "Sankhya-Yoga."

---

* Revelation 3:12.

CHAPTER III

KARMA YOGA: THE PATH OF SPIRITUAL ACTION

❖

Why Is Activity a Necessary Part of the Path to Liberation?

❖

The Nature of Right Action:
Performing All Works as Oblations (Yajna)

❖

Righteous Duty, Performed With Nonattachment, Is Godly

❖

How Egoless Action Frees the Yogi From Nature's Dualities and the Bondage of Karma

❖

Right Attitude Toward One's Spiritual Guide and Sadhana

❖

Conquering the Two-sided Passion, Desire and Anger

"From the vibrationless region, through a cosmic rhythm of ordered activity, the Spirit brought into being all vibratory creation. Man is a part of that vibratory cosmic activity. As an integral entity in the cosmic plan that all creation, projected out of Spirit, must evolve back into Spirit, man also must ascend through activity in harmony with the divine schema."

KARMA YOGA: THE PATH OF SPIRITUAL ACTION

WHY IS ACTIVITY A NECESSARY PART OF THE PATH TO LIBERATION?

VERSE 1

अर्जुन उवाच
ज्यायसी चेत्कर्मणस्ते मता बुद्धिर्जनार्दन।
तत्किं कर्मणि घोरे मां नियोजयसि केशव॥

Arjuna said:

O Janardana (Krishna)! if thou dost consider understanding to be superior to action, why then, O Keshava (Krishna), dost thou enjoin on me this awful activity?

"YOUR DISCOURSE, O DIVINE DELIVERER, holds that it is better to behold through aloof eyes of wisdom the dramatic events of life as a dream issuing from Spirit, rather than be emotionally caught up in the histrionics of this world of delusion. Why then, O Lord, dost Thou harness me to dreadful, boisterous activity, like a stallion yoked to a chariot of war?"

When Arjuna here addresses Krishna as Janardana, the epithet signifies the ideal guru who shows the devotee the way to eradicate the causes of rebirth and thereby achieve salvation. *Keshava* signifies the ultimate state of Spirit-oneness—beyond vibratory conditions of creation, preservation, and dissolution—attained by destroying the demon of evil, delusion, which disunites the soul from Spirit. Allegorically, the devotee, in his contact with God through intuitive experience, addresses the inner Divine Consciousness as the guiding Guru who is pointing the way to liberation, and also as the Supreme Absolute beyond all modifications of delusion. This stanza depicts the mental conflict of a devotee who occasionally contacts God through fitful intuition; and who often wonders why the Inner Voice, while extolling the primacy of intuitive wisdom, nevertheless insists that the devotee engage in tremendous mind-engrossing activities!

ULTIMATE WISDOM IS ETERNAL Infinite Intelligence, the Ocean of Bliss devoid of nature's changeable waves (passing sorrows or momentary pleasures or any form of actions that belong to the world of temporal vibrations). The unchangeable sea of Spirit is superior to Its manifesting waves of changeable vibratory creation—as an ocean is superior to its waves because it is the foundation and substance of the waves, and because the ocean can exist without the waves whereas the waves cannot exist without the ocean.

Employing action to attain inaction

Spirit is the supreme cause—changeless, self-sufficient Intelligence. All vibratory activities coming out of the Absolute are conditioned, and hence inferior. Similarly, ultimate wisdom is found in man's deepest interior consciousness, his soul; the waves of vibrating activities coming out of that intelligence are found in his exterior body. Hence, though bodily activities are indeed inferior to soul wisdom, nevertheless, wisdom cannot be achieved by man without some sort of mental and bodily participation. The vibrationless state of all-supreme wisdom cannot be attained by man in the beginning, as he is born to a "natural" body consciousness. Until the body delusion is conquered, man is totally unable to manifest wisdom.

To destroy his false identity with the body, man has to engage in the "inferior," yet necessary, liberating outer activities. Employing action to attain inaction is illustrated in the Hindu scriptures as "using a thorn to remove another thorn," just as a man may use a sharp thorn to eject from his finger a painful thorn embedded there. Once the devotee has rid himself of the delusions of body consciousness, he is automatically freed from the necessity for action (karmic duties). He now "throws away both thorns" (that is, neither the body nor its activities have any further value; they have already served the purpose for which they were created), and the yogi is ripe for the manifestation of wisdom—the ultimate state transcending all activities.

THE DEEPER ESOTERIC IMPLICATION of Arjuna's query in this stanza, developed in the following several verses, is in reference to Sri Krishna's repeated exhortation that the devotee must engage in the wisdom-procuring action of conquering sensual body consciousness by yoga meditation. The coccygeal, sacral, lumbar, dorsal, cervical, and medullary plexuses should become centres of man's conscious spiritual activities. The devotee, by the processes of proper breathing methods and various deep meditative activities (as in *Kriya Yoga*), should constantly centralize his consciousness in the spinal centres. Thus he becomes eligible to remain in the vibrationless, nonactive state within the cerebral thousand-rayed lotus light of Spirit.

Necessity for meditation techniques

Some devotees, temporarily attaining the vision of the centralized light of Spirit in the brain, give up their definite yoga exercises, considering them to be inferior meditation. This is a mistake. All spiritual activities, special meditations, and proper *pranayama* techniques (*Kriya Yoga*) must be continuously followed in order to have not only the vision of the thousand-rayed light of Spirit in the brain, but to be permanently anchored there. Meditative activities are inferior to wisdom after it is attained, but they inexorably precede that final realization.

VERSE 2

व्यामिश्रेणेव वाक्येन बुद्धिं मोहयसीव मे।
तदेकं वद निश्चित्य येन श्रेयोऽहमाप्नुयाम्॥

[Arjuna continues:]

With these apparently conflicting speeches thou art, as it were, confusing my intelligence. Please let me know for certain that one thing by which I will achieve the highest good.

"YOUR COUNSEL, THOUGH ELOQUENT and assuredly wise, is yet seemingly contradictory. My grasping power is bewildered by Your subtly conflicting words. Can you not simply point out to me that one portal which leads directly into the palace of perfection?"

This typifies the psychological state of the devotee whose understanding is not yet finely tuned to intuition. He is often confused by apparently contradictory advice from the scriptures or his guru.

For example, when a master once told his disciple, "You must eat and you mustn't eat," the disciple replied, "Master, I do not understand; your commands are contradictory!"

The master replied, "True—you do not understand! My advice is perfectly harmonious. What I mean is that you must eat when you are truly hungry, only to give proper nutrition to your body for maintaining the temple of your soul. But you must not eat when you are tempted by the deep-seated wicked appetite of greed, under the guidance of which you will overeat and destroy your health."

Similarly, whenever Krishna advises, in essence, "Live in this world but do not live in it," he meant that man should live and fulfil his duties in this world since God put him here, but he should not live in attachment to its wiles and ways.

Spiritual advice is often paradoxical. Far from being contradictory, it rather reflects the inadequacy of corporeal expression to convey that which is above the familiar "this or that" duality of Nature. Among Christian saints, how given to paradoxes is Saint John of the Cross in his mystical poesy: "The music without sound," "With fire that can consume and yet do no harm," "Eternal life you render / And change my death to life, even while killing!" Jesus said: "For whosoever will save his life shall lose it: but whosoever will lose his life for my sake, the same shall save it."*

God is the Great Paradox: the sole Life, the only Being—yet invisible, intangible! The Formless and the Every Form!

In spiritual life worldly standards are reversed. "Sell all thou hast and give to the poor...." "Take ye no thought for the morrow...."†
These uncompromising reversals of "common sense" are dismissed by the average man as bewildering or "paradoxical."

Arjuna is thus confused at the advice of his guru, Krishna, who extols wisdom as superior to action and at the same time advises him to act.

VERSE 3

श्रीभगवानुवाच
लोकेऽस्मिन्द्विविधा निष्ठा पुरा प्रोक्ता मयानघ।
ज्ञानयोगेन साङ्ख्यानां कर्मयोगेन योगिनाम्॥

The Cosmic Lord said:

O Sinless One, at the onset of creation, a twofold way of salvation was given by Me to this world: for the wise, divine union through wisdom; for the yogis, divine union through active meditation.

---

* Luke 9:24.

† Matthew 19:21 and Matthew 6:34 respectively.

"When I sent man out in creation, I gave him two paths by which he could retrace his steps to Me—discrimination (Sankhya, or *Jnana Yoga*) and right action (*Karma Yoga,* the highest activity of which is the scientific meditation of the yogis). Both take man on the right course toward salvation. But when the devotee is nearing ultimate freedom, then wisdom and meditative action merge into one inner highway to Self-realization, the culmination of which is union of the soul with Spirit."

Commonly interpreted, *Jnana Yoga* is the way of knowledge and discrimination (Sankhya); *Karma Yoga,* the way of right action—spiritual and meditative. The way of discrimination is for the rare, keen-eyed wise man; for all others, the path of activity and meditation combined.

In this stanza, however, Krishna refers specifically, in both cases, to divine union (*yoga*)—the liberation of the soul in Spirit. In this higher context, the paths of discrimination and spiritual action are really one "twofold" highway of Self-realization (wisdom) produced by following a definite technique of active meditation. (Meditative activity, and not just ordinary activity, is implicit in Krishna's reference to *Karma Yoga* as the path *for the "yogis."*) Ultimate knowledge of God is the goal of human freedom, but this final all-satisfying lore cannot be attained without first having practised the methods of meditation.

Jnana Yoga and Karma Yoga are two stages of one path

As an apple blossom and the apple are inseparably linked, so are meditation and wisdom. No blossom, no apple—no meditation, no wisdom. Wisdom is the house, meditation is the foundation.

The Gita emphasizes both wisdom and meditation because many devotees falsely imagine that a theoretical knowledge of scriptures without meditation will lead to ultimate freedom. But mere theoretical study of scriptures is detrimental to real attainment of wisdom if it produces egotism and the false conviction that one knows when one does not know. Scriptural knowledge is gainful only when it produces the desire to demonstrate in one's own life the validity of the spiritual precepts.

Thus, after all, there is only one way to God-wisdom. Even the *jnana yogi* who achieves God-union through the sole path of Vedanta or constant mental discrimination ("God alone is real; all else is unreal") has been, in past lives, a yogi or successful follower of a meditation technique of interiorization for God-communion. Such an advanced being has been born in his present life with an already established wisdom acquired from past-life meditative efforts. He is one of the "wise" referred to in this Gita verse—one who is already far along on the path of wisdom, or God-realization. With the stimulus of divine ardour and wisdom thoughts, he rouses the wisdom *samskaras* (karmic propensities) already within him, and attains God-union without further application of a formal technique of meditation. For the final union, his consciousness, as that of all ascending beings, follows the inner meditative route of ascension through the cerebrospinal yogic centres to Spirit.

Even the yogi, however, does not attain perfection if he meditates without concentrating on the final goal of wisdom, like a man who becomes so fond of walking on a path that he saunters aimlessly without reaching a predetermined destination. Many devotees love meditation and the joy of it (or they become enamoured with seeking powers or phenomena), forgetting that meditation is only a means to an end—the goal is God.

Because God-wisdom is unattainable except by following the path of deep meditation, the Gita here speaks of wisdom and meditation as the two ways—or the twofold way—to the Infinite. In this stanza nothing is mentioned of devotion, or of spiritual activities for redeeming others, or of the discriminative study of scriptures, or of prayer—they are all byways; that is, insufficient in themselves.*

Meditation is the ultimate liberating action

God-wisdom is not attained by such religious activities as trying to save others' souls without having first achieved one's own salvation. Nor does man find God through ordinary distracted prayers or chants or spiritual singing—a superficial devotion during which the mind runs in sundry directions.

Spiritual activities are necessary bypaths that one should follow in order to reach the highway of meditation. After one has finished travelling over the highway of meditation he attains the all-coveted God-wisdom.

No devotee of any religion should be satisfied with untested beliefs and dogmas, but should engage himself in practical efforts to attain God-realization. Union with Spirit is possible only when the devotee, casting aside the superficial method of ceremonial worship or of the ineffective "going into the silence," begins to practise a scientific technique of God-realization. One cannot reach this goal just by mental meditation. Only deep concentration that disconnects the mind from breath, life force, and senses, and that unites the ego to the soul is successful in producing the God-wisdom of Self-realization. All other methods are preliminary or supportive bypaths.

---

* See XII:3, page 841.

Withdrawing mind and life force from the sensory and motor nerves, the yogi leads them through the spine into the brain into eternal light. Here the mind and life become united with the eternal wisdom of Spirit manifested in the cerebrum.

The centre of consciousness for the average individual is his body and the outer world. The yogi changes his centre of consciousness by nonattachment to the body and to worldly hopes and fears. By a technique—such as *Kriya Yoga*—of consciously controlling the life processes that tie the consciousness to the body (stilling the heart and breath), the yogi becomes established in the eternal wisdom-perception of Spirit that manifests in the spiritual centre of cosmic consciousness in the brain. The yogi who can change his centre of consciousness from the sentient body to the cerebral throne of Spirit ultimately centralizes his consciousness on omnipresence. He attains the Eternal Wisdom.

VERSE 4

न कर्मणामनारम्भान्नैष्कर्म्यं पुरुषोऽश्नुते।
न च सन्न्यसनादेव सिद्धिं समधिगच्छति॥

Actionlessness is not attained simply by avoiding actions. By forsaking work no one reaches perfection.

NONE REACH DIVINE ACTIONLESSNESS without having worked for the pension of that blissful state. By rash renunciation of responsibilities one finds no true felicity.

The Unmanifested Absolute, by projecting a portion of His consciousness as a cosmic creative force, descended from His nonactive or vibrationless state into the active or vibratory state that upholds the universe. From the vibrationless region, through a cosmic rhythm of ordered activity, the Spirit thus brought into being all vibratory creation. Man is a part of that vibratory cosmic activity. As an integral entity in the cosmic plan that all creation, projected out of Spirit, must evolve back into Spirit, man also must ascend through activity in harmony with the divine schema.

All activity is intelligent vibration. Evil actions are wrong disordered vibrations, repulsive forces, that take man away from Spirit and involve him, by his indulgence in them, with the gross world of matter. Good actions are attractive vibrations that direct the devotee toward the Spirit.

Through the vibratory state of proper activity of the world in which he has been born, man ascends into the high vibrationless state of the transcendent Spirit. By ordered activities of body and mind and by self-discipline, the devotee withdraws from different vibratory spheres, from gross matter to the finer realms of consciousness, into the region of the vibrationless Spirit that is beyond the activity of all creation.

Worklessness in the mystical sense is the goal of life. It can be attained not through idleness, nor through material or evil activities—nor, as commonly assumed, by merely leading a normally "good" life—but only through intense liberating activities.

A lazy man cannot be one with Spirit. If he does not go forward he is bound to drift backward. Many seekers erroneously think that to forsake all worldly activities and to remain in idle seclusion is the way to the highest or inactive state of Spirit! But the ordinary man—whose mind is identified with the senses and bodily environments, and who equates himself with the breath and body—is imprisoned in a material world. Even if he tries to "leave the world" and lives in the seclusion of a jungle, he will find that without proper meditation his mind will still be attached to his senses. Simple renunciation alone is not a net ample enough to capture the omnipresent Spirit!

❖
The real workless state not attained by forsaking action
❖

The renunciant should not be satisfied with living idly as a recluse. He should learn to practise breathlessness and heart control by which he can switch off the life force from the five sense-telephones of sight, hearing, smell, taste, and touch. By such intense spiritual activity, devoid of laziness, the devotee learns to disengage his mind from the invasion of thought-creating sensations. When the mind is disconnected from the senses in deep sleep, it is free from the disturbances of sensations and thoughts. In deep meditation the mind is *consciously* liberated from all sensations and their train of multifarious, disruptive cognitions.

As the mind in deep dreamless sleep reaches a passive inactive state, so in deep meditation the mind reaches a conscious inactive state. But as idleness produces insomnia or lack of that refreshing sleep which is readily bestowed after hard physical or mental work, so spiritual inertia gives no beneficial results that are readily available if one is engaged in proper activities. The real workless state is therefore attained by the intense good activities of meditation and service, never by forsaking action and becoming paralysed with idleness.

IN INDIA MANY RENUNCIANTS who leave the world, doing no work socially or meditatively, and living on charity, become lazy and worthless, never attaining God-consciousness. But those who sincerely perform good actions and who are active inwardly in meditation receive the spiritual pension of remaining forever in the free inactive state of the Spirit.

The rightly guided devotee is intensely active in a divine way

The rightly guided devotee is intensely active in a divine way, disengaging his mind from restlessness and desires. By following moral principles, bodily disciplines, practice of life-force control, meditation, spiritual service by interesting others in the divine path, interiorization of the mind, and *samadhi* (ecstasy), the true student lifts himself from the eddies and whirlpools of wrong activities and rides the crest of the rhythmic waves of good activities toward the vibrationless inactive state of Spirit.

By ordered activities the devotee gradually arrives at the inactive state of divine union (the highest or *paramahansa* state). Even as God the Father is free from all vibratory creation, so any of His sons who returns home becomes free; he is under no karmic compulsion to work.

A master is one who, by intense humanitarian and spiritual meditative activities, has attained God-union. Free from all worldly desires, he can be active or inactive, ever one with the vibrationless Spirit beyond all creation. No mortal or conscription of nature has control over a master; he is a pensioner only of God!

The aspiring devotee should heed the warning of the Bhagavad Gita: Though wisdom is superior to activity, still ultimate knowledge cannot be attained without activity. Social, moral, religious, and meditative actions are all spiritual activities. They are different rungs on the ladder of salvation that every devotee must first climb in order to reach the illimitable sky of wisdom. When one has attained the finality, he is then not bound to any activity, though he may continue, at will, to perform actions.

To set a good example to their followers, fully emancipated masters such as Jesus, Babaji, Lahiri Mahasaya, and my own guru Sri Yukteswar engaged themselves in various spiritual activities.

The meaning in this stanza of the Gita can be illustrated in the following way:

A businessman by intense activity becomes rich and then takes life easy; he is one of the "deserving" idle. But if a poor man is ambitionless and lazy, and remains inactive, he is one of the "undeserving" idle. His lot is misery. When man makes idleness his goal it is very harmful to him. The rich idler is a far better man (other things being equal) than the poor idler. Similarly, the workless man who is a master has attained his state after earning a pension in the office of good activities. But the idle spiritual beginner has no right to a workless state.

The ordinary idle man is body-bound; the motionless meditative man, though apparently idle, is free from the body, working and resting in the omnipresent Spirit. The idle man is a slave to the body, afraid to work, while the calm meditative man is a master of the body, never hesitating to engage it in intense activity.

A DEVOTEE MUST CONTINUE to travel on the path of spirituality until he reaches his goal. One day, lo! he is there! He will not have to continue his walk in order to get there again!

The flower comes before the fruit. When the fruit is ready to appear, the flower falls off. The flower has been indispensable for the production of the fruit, but the fruit is a tree's highest achievement.

Attainment of wisdom brings everlasting pension of peace

The flower of liberating action is necessary to attain the fruit of wisdom. When wisdom is achieved it is complete and whole, making action unnecessary. It is not all work and effort throughout eternity! When God's wisdom is attained the devotee has earned the everlasting pension of peace.

In *Autobiography of a Yogi** I quoted the Persian mystic Abu Said, with the following commentary: "'To buy and sell, yet never to forget God!' The ideal is that hand and heart work harmoniously together. Certain Western writers claim that the Hindu goal is one of timid 'escape,' of inactivity and antisocial withdrawal. The fourfold Vedic plan for a man's life, however, is a well-balanced one for the masses, allotting half the span to study and householder duties; the second half to contemplation and meditational practices.

"Solitude (time for meditation and thoughts of God) is necessary to become established in the Self, but masters then return to the world to serve it. Even saints who engage in no outward work bestow, through their thoughts and holy vibrations, more precious benefits on the world than can be given by the most strenuous humanitarian activities of unenlightened men. The great ones, each in his own way and often against bitter opposition, strive selflessly to inspire and up-

* Chapter 5: "A 'Perfume Saint' Displays His Wonders."

lift their fellows....The Bhagavad Gita (III:4–8) points out that activity is inherent in man's very nature. Sloth is simply 'wrong activity.'"

VERSE 5

न हि कश्चित्क्षणमपि जातु तिष्ठत्यकर्मकृत्।
कार्यते ह्यवशः कर्म सर्वः प्रकृतिजैर्गुणैः ॥

Verily, no one can stay for even a moment without working; all are indeed compelled to perform actions willy-nilly, prodded by the qualities (gunas) born of Nature (Prakriti).

NO BEING UNDER THE SWAY of Nature can remain action-free even for a trice, for all perforce must abide by the laws that govern a universe whose every part owes its existence and character to the constant flux and silent influence of three inherent *gunas,* or qualities.*

The *gunas* of Nature—her qualities or modes of expression—are *sattva* (positive or elevating); *rajas* (neutral, activating); and *tamas* (negative, obstructing). *Sattva* produces Godward-leading qualities; *rajas,* materially progressive qualities; and *tamas,* evil- and ignorance-producing qualities.

The entire cosmos is created and guided by the action and interaction of these three *gunas* on the twenty-four attributes of Nature. The human body, a product of Cosmic Nature, is inexorably ruled by the three motion-producing qualities. Man cannot stand still—he will be compelled to perform actions of good, bad, or mixed qualities.

Tamasic or evil activities make one abnormal and unhappy. Rajasic or energizing activities make one normal and able in disciplining the body and mind. Sattvic or good activities awaken God-consciousness and guide man to the region of Spirit.

The soul is beyond the creative vibratory attributes of Nature, but when it becomes identified with the mind, life force, and body, it puts on their restless active nature. As ego it cannot remain without some sort of organized mental, vital, and bodily actions. This stanza elucidates the preceding verse that worklessness cannot be achieved without having followed some kind of interiorizing activity. No beginner in the spiritual path must dream of resting on the roof of work-

---

* See I:1 (page 12) and VIII:6–7.

lessness without having first made the active effort of climbing the stairway!

He who is still a stranger to his soul, which is beyond all active states, must choose to move inward by good activities or he will be forced by Nature to move outward by material activities or by God-eclipsing evil actions.

Every man is thrown, as it were, into a boisterous river of the activities of Nature. If he does not swim, if he tries to remain neutral, he will disappear from a world whose keynote is "Struggle!" The universal flux does not accommodate a stationary man. He who does not move forward with wisdom and determination, will surely drift backward—just another bit of flotsam caught in the current of delusion. But if he ceaselessly swims, he will reach land, safe from the raging river!

Idleness or so-called nonactivity acts like a petrifying agent on the mental and bodily processes, preventing one from making a free-will choice to go either backward or forward. But the Gita says that even the idle person cannot remain wholly without activity. His undisciplined mind will be active in delusion, even as his body is inactive in sloth. His organic processes of life will be working, moved by the laws of nature. He may lie down and forsake all bodily movements; even so, without the technique of yoga, he is unable to stop his heart action, breath, circulation, and the activity of his internal organs, not to mention the activities of his thoughts and memory! For him nonactivity is impossible.

The hardworking honest worldly man, devoted to duty, is extolled in the Gita as better than the self-deceiving recluse who leads an idle nonmeditative existence. The man who meditates, however—be he householder or renunciant—is actively moving Godward and is better than the worthy worldly man who moves very slowly toward perfection through the purifying influence of good activities only.

Wisdom-guided activity: meditation, introspection, right behaviour, moral discipline

Activity of mind and body guided by the soul's discrimination or by the guidance of a guru is called wisdom-guided or sattvic activity. It consists in control of the senses, meditation, introspection, right behaviour, moral discipline, and spiritual culture. This wisdom-guided activity should be substituted for wrong activities in which the senses govern the mind by a lure of temporary pleasure. Wisdom-guided activity leads to eternal ever new bliss and should therefore govern the devotee's entire life.

When the yogi advances and can disengage his soul from the body by controlling the heart and by switching off the life current and the pulsation of the life force and mind in the body, he has reached the refuge of the eternal nonactive calmness. The yogi who rests on the Self becomes established in the vibrationless calm joy of the Infinite. After uniting with the Spirit that dwells beyond all vibrations, then alone can one be free from the compulsory influence of all active vibrations of the cosmos.

The idle, slothful man is helpless; his soul is ruled by body and mind. The ordinary man cannot help being active, voluntarily or involuntarily; but he is restlessly active and actively restless. The calm yogi can whirl his body and mind into intense action without being identified with them, and can then instantly return to his inner action-free state of meditative communion with Spirit. He is ever calmly active and actively calm.

VERSE 6

कर्मेन्द्रियाणि संयम्य य आस्ते मनसा स्मरन्।
इन्द्रियार्थान्विमूढात्मा मिथ्याचारः स उच्यते॥

The individual who forcibly controls the organs of action, but whose mind rotates around thoughts of sense objects, is said to be a hypocrite, deluding himself.

HE WHO SUBDUES HIS SENSES outwardly and not inwardly, as might a recluse who renounces worldly pleasures but continually broods over objects of his deprivation, is self-deluded and living a lie. A false sense of assurance and self-sufficiency will allow temptation to catch him off guard.

At whatever level of activity one begins his spiritual ascent—dutiful or serviceful actions, altruism, religious worship, meditation—the spiritualizing of that activity must begin in the mind and not in outward behaviour only.

Many people refrain from certain acts, but not from thoughts about them! A man may inwardly covet the beautiful wife of another, but restrain himself from getting involved for fear of trouble. His inner inclination, reinforced by constant brooding, however, is likely to lead him to succumb to temptation.

Destroy evil in thought as well as in deed. Persons who do not harmonize their thoughts with their actions cannot trust themselves;

their inner temptations daily become stronger by being fed with continuous supportive thoughts. These thoughts of temptation are the real cause of trouble. If the inner temptation increases to floodlike proportions, the little embankment of outward self-control is swept away. It is thus unsafe to forsake outwardly an evil action and inwardly to keep on nurturing it. When the evil thought becomes strong enough, it will destroy all the obstructions of outward self-control.

Of course, it is better to exercise even an outward control than loosely to succumb to temptations. A man who flouts moral laws just because he feels tempted is evil and disgraces himself and others. Even a hypocrite, if he has enough mental power to control his sensual activities, although he cannot restrain himself from lustful thoughts, is a better and stronger man than the boasting libertine.

In the long run, however, it is inadequate to control the organs of action from outward evil without also controlling the mind—the real instigator of all actions. Those who remain in a castle with all gates closed against intruders cannot long be safe if enemies are hidden within the castle itself.

Control of actions begins with control of the mind

If one wants to conquer a temptation and to be free from the physical, social, mental, and spiritual troubles that it brings, he must exterminate within himself the seed of evil that may otherwise grow into a huge tree, bearing the fruits of misery. Like a cancer, the inside roots of evil must be taken out lest they suddenly spread and destroy the spiritual life.

Oversexuality, greed for food or money—the "many foolish and hurtful lusts, which drown men in destruction and perdition"*—in the end unfailingly bring unhappiness, after having overcome the tempted one with the chloroform of a temporary joy. The delusive pleasure-coating of evil eclipses the right judgement of people, making them choose pleasure-coated poisonous evil and forsake good. Good is the sweet pill of lasting happiness, coated over with a momentarily bitter difficulty of discipline. Each person must judge for himself and make the wiser choice.

In overcoming a temptation or bad habit, man should first seek to convince his mind, giving the reasons for abandoning the evil. Then he should reject the thoughts of temptation as they appear, as well as relinquish the habitual actions. Repetition of evil acts produces and reinforces evil thoughts; evil thoughts lead to and reinforce evil actions. Both must be restrained!

---

* I Timothy 6:9.

Whatever a superior being does, inferior persons imitate. His actions set a standard for people of the world.

O Son of Pritha (Arjuna), no compelling duty have I to perform; there is naught that I have not acquired; nothing in the three worlds remains for Me to gain! Yet I am consciously present in the performance of all actions.

—Bhagavad Gita III:21–22

❖

"We hear of saintly ascetics, or prophets in the woods or secluded haunts, who were men of renunciation only; but Sri Krishna was one of the greatest exemplars of divinity, because he lived and manifested himself as a Christ and at the same time performed the duties of a noble king. His life demonstrates the ideal not of renunciation of action—which is a conflicting doctrine for man circumscribed by a world whose life breath is activity—but rather the renunciation of earth-binding desires for the fruits of action....

"Sri Krishna's message in the Bhagavad Gita is the perfect answer for the modern age, and any age: Yoga of dutiful action, of nonattachment, and of meditation for God-realization. To work without the inner peace of God is Hades; and to work with His joy ever bubbling through the soul is to carry a portable paradise within, wherever one goes."

—Paramahansa Yogananda

Hypocrisy is an assumed physical pose or conduct that does not sincerely represent the corresponding mental state.

The Gita warns one against such mental inconsistencies as hypocrisy; but it does not say that because of a lack of inner self-control, outer restraint should be given up. Outer self-control should ideally be preceded and accompanied by inner discipline; nevertheless a merely outward self-control is better than no control at all!

To renounce worldly pleasures without forsaking them inwardly, just to impress others or to escape into a less taxing reclusive sanctuary—that is hypocritical. But to renounce the world to seek God in a positive way even though there is still a struggle with inner desires, that is not hypocrisy, but spiritual heroism. To sit like a calm yogi in lotus posture, inwardly engaging in earthly thoughts like a worldly man, is hypocrisy if the intent is to win the praise and adulation of others rather than to secure the bliss of God. But it is not hypocrisy to practise scientific meditation sincerely in a self-controlled quiet bodily posture, even if the mind is restless, when the goal is God. Eventually, this highest form of action will harmonize the restless mental state with the calm physical pose. When the mind and body are both quieted by yoga, the devotee quickly advances toward the joyous state of Spirit.

VERSE 7

यस्त्विन्द्रियाणि मनसा नियम्यारभतेऽर्जुन।
कर्मेन्द्रियैः कर्मयोगमसक्तः स विशिष्यते॥

But that man succeeds supremely, O Arjuna, who, disciplining the senses by the mind, unattached, keeps his organs of activity steadfast on the path of God-uniting actions.

HE WHO WITH NONATTACHMENT to sensory pleasures governs the stallions of his senses, by holding tight the reins of the mind, keeps them on the wisdom-directed, *Karma Yoga*–prescribed path of proper action; a royal expert, he rides the bodily chariot to the supreme Goal.

The man of worldly responsibilities who keeps his senses under mental control, who works only for God and thus remains unattached to his own desires or ambitions, ultimately by right action will reach the divine goal. The ordinary worldly man erroneously thinks he is in the world to chalk out his own selfish career. The spiritual man engaged in material duties realizes he is in the world not to satisfy his own desires and sense appetites but to fulfil a divine mission—that of attaining God-realization and liberation in Him by performing those serviceful actions most pleasing to God.

The moral man who governs his senses by his mind and remains unattached to the body, looking after it only as a divinely given charge, and who, with such controlled senses and wisdom, directs his organs of activity (brain, hands, mouth, feet, sex, speech) to the path of right action in everything, specializes in activity that leads to the supreme goal of life—the attainment of God and His ever new joy.

The spiritual devotee masters the activities of the senses by controlling the mind in meditation and turning it Godward, constraining the senses to follow.* He is unattached to the fruits of his meditation; he meditates, not solely for the enjoyment of supreme bliss, but to please God by returning home from the tour of incarnations to be reunited with the Divine One after whose image he is made. His motive is therefore not selfish joy, but a desire not to desecrate that perfect image. The spiritual man so loves God that he becomes spiritual only to please Him. The true devotee finds his happiness only in what is pleasing to God.

The words *Karma Yoga* (the path of works or activity) have been used in this stanza to signify those proper activities (*karma*) that unite the soul with Spirit *(yoga)*. Whenever the good worldly man, or the moral man, or the meditative spiritual man keeps his senses under control, and harnesses his wisdom-guided desires to the organs of actions, he moves in the proper path of activity. All God-leading activity is *Karma Yoga*.

The worldly way of good action provides a lengthy path to God. A life of moral discipline is a quicker way to God. The meditative life is the fastest way to God.

Meditation may seem to be a withdrawal from activity because it demands from the beginner an absence of bodily movement. But deep meditation is intense mental activity—the highest form of action. Through the divine science of *Kriya Yoga,* the advanced yogi is able to

* "If the mind is fixed on God and continues so, the senses will obey it. It is like hanging a needle on a magnet and then another needle onto that, and so on.... As long as the first needle clings to the magnet, the rest will hang on to it; but if the first drops off, it will lose the rest. And so, as long as the mind is firmly fixed on God, the senses will obey it; but when the mind drops away from God, the senses drop off from the mind and are unruly."—*Meister Eckhart (a fourteenth-century Dominican monk, and renowned German mystic)*

withdraw his mind from the physical senses and direct their subtle astral powers to the inner activities of soul-freeing work. Such a spiritual specialist performs the true God-uniting activity (*Karma Yoga*).

This is the highest path of karma or action. It leads directly to God, as differentiated from outer activities of religion, such as ceremonies and missionary work in which the mind is on precepts rather than absorbed in the actual inner experience of God. Many preach the kingdom of God; yogis find it within.

VERSE 8

नियतं कुरु कर्म त्वं कर्म ज्यायो ह्यकर्मणः ।
शरीरयात्रापि च ते न प्रसिद्ध्येदकर्मणः ॥

Perform thou those actions that are obligatory, for action is better than inactivity; even simple maintenance of thy body would be impossible through inaction.

NO ACCOMPLISHMENT IS POSSIBLE in a state of inertia; complete inactivity precludes even bare bodily existence. Having understood that dynamic activity is superior to devitalizing idleness, one should embrace those requisite duties to which one is bound by the laws of nature, and those divine duties that foster soul culture.

Activity of life none can completely forsake and live—even the idle man has to maintain his body. However, it is not merely action itself that is purifying and uplifting, but dutiful actions. These attract the devotee to the path of Spirit. Evil actions—on the contrary—repulse the soul vibrations. Inaction is inhibitory, stultifying.

When idleness hypnotizes the ego into inactivity, it may bring no apparent trouble, whereas evil actions may swiftly result in dire miseries. Yet it takes a long time for lazy people to get back to God—pushed along by the slow evolutionary process operable in even apparently inert matter—whereas an enterprising, somewhat unscrupulous businessman, for example, might (after abandoning evil!) progress swiftly in his search for God simply because he had already cultivated progressive activity, resourcefulness, and initiative! The habitually idle man and the unscrupulous businessman, however, have one obstacle in common—both find it very difficult to change their respective habits, and so remain enslaved.

As wrong business exploitation is a social crime, idleness is a spiritual crime that debases the human being. Hence the Gita adjures man to be spiritually active and keep moving onward through dutiful actions rather than remain a prisoner of the flesh through indolence.

In His Absolute Nature as Spirit, God transcends all the activity of creation, yet He works in every atomic cell of His vast body of the physical cosmos. God expects man, created in His image, to perform similarly the duties connected with his daily life and the maintenance of the body, and, at the same time, to remain aloof inwardly, enthroned in his soul perception.

Mind in conjunction with the senses has to work. Mind drawn into God becomes inactive and transcendental like the Spirit. Anyone who can gradually transmute the work of the life current in the body, by switching off the life force from the nerve-telephones and disconnecting the mind from the senses, attains the true inactive state of the Spirit. When the yogi by this method has reached *savikalpa samadhi* he can keep his body indefinitely entranced in God, if he wishes to do so—remaining above all activities.

In the highest state, *nirvikalpa samadhi,* the yogi is consciously united with God without the necessity of suspending the activities of the body. Being one with the Supreme, and having no personal desires, he performs all of his actions only to please God; hence, they are termed *inactive actions* (*nishkama karma,* desire-free actions that produce no binding effects). When one acts only to please God, he has achieved the real or spiritual inactive state that is free from both obligatory duties and from karmic bondage resulting from actions.

The highest dutiful activity, therefore, consists in practising those methods of meditation through which the devotee is ultimately freed from worldly karmas.

Admonition to monastics who leave the world

To become a renunciant and forsake meditative activities as well as worldly activities will not free one from identification with the body and its other prenatal karmic tendencies. A renunciant who is satisfied by merely withdrawing from the world and who makes no definite effort to reach God through meditation does not attain the ultimate goal. But whether a yogi is living in the world as a family man or away from the world as a renunciant, if he learns the right technique of meditation from a true guru and diligently practises it and lives rightly, in time he will burn away all the stored-up evil tendencies of past lives and become free to unite with God.

In stressing dutiful actions, this stanza of the Gita is an admonition addressed especially to monks and all renunciants who leave the world in order to live in an endowed hermitage and there pass the time in eating, sleeping, reading, and chatting, doing very little uplifting work for themselves or others. Such monastics are bound to be idlers; they live on the earnings of the hardworking worldly man without fulfilling their duty to give, in return, spiritual or material service.

The inactive man does not do his duty to his Creator or to the society that maintains him. The recluse who devotes his entire life to sincere effort in meditation fulfils part of his duty by trying to find and love God, and thus spiritualize his own life. To improve one's self is to help society by the example of virtue and by making at least one of its members good!

But the yogi (monastic or householder) who does his duty to God, and also to the world through some form of uplifting service, is the most highly evolved type of being. He becomes a master (a *siddha*) when by such dutiful action he attains the supreme inactive state (*nirvikalpa* God-union), which is free from karmic effects of actions and is filled with the bliss of Spirit.

THE NATURE OF RIGHT ACTION: PERFORMING ALL WORKS AS OBLATIONS (YAJNA)

VERSE 9

यज्ञार्थात्कर्मणोऽन्यत्र लोकोऽयं कर्मबन्धनः ।
तदर्थं कर्म कौन्तेय मुक्तसङ्गः समाचर ॥

Worldly people are karmically bound by activities that differ from those performed as yajna (religious rites); O Son of Kunti (Arjuna), labour thou, nonattached, in the spirit of yajna, offering actions as oblations.

WORLDLY PEOPLE PERFORM ACTIONS with selfish motives and the desire to gain material profit and happiness. Owing to that inclination, they are karmically tied to the earth throughout successive incarnations. The yogi, however, strives to perform good actions in a spirit of self-lessness and nonattachment; he thereby quickens his evolution toward soul freedom. All such liberating divine duties may be termed *yajna.*

The word *yajna* has many meanings. It refers not only to the act of ritualistic worship, but to the sacrifice or oblation offered into the sacred fire; it is also the fire itself, and the Deity (Vishnu)* to whom the offering is made. *Yajna* is any selfless act or sacrifice offered solely to God. It is the religious rite in which the soul offers itself as an oblation in the Fire of Spirit.

A number of Fire Offerings are described in the Hindu scriptures as follows:

(1) *Pitri Yajna*—Offering oblations to ancestors, i.e., the past, essence of whose wisdom illumines man today.

(2) *Nri Yajna*—Offering food to the hungry, i.e., the present responsibilities of man, his duties to contemporaries.

(3) *Bhuta Yajna*—Offering food to the animal kingdom, i.e., man's obligations to less evolved forms of creation, instinctively tied to body identification (a delusion that affects man also), but lacking in that quality of liberating reason which is peculiar to humanity. Thus the ceremony of Bhuta Yajna symbolizes man's readiness to succour the weak, as man in turn is comforted by countless solicitudes of higher unseen beings. Humanity is also under bond for rejuvenating gifts of Nature herself, prodigal in earth, sea, and sky. The evolutionary barrier of incommunicability among Nature, animals, man, and astral angels is thus overcome by offices of silent love.

(4) *Deva Yajna*—Offering life current from the senses, as sacrifices to soul sight. This "Rite to the Gods" is performed by advanced yogis, as a preliminary step to the fifth rite.

(5) *Brahma Yajna*—Offering the soul on the altar of the all-pervading Spirit. This finality is attainable only after faithful performance of the preceding four ceremonies, which inwardly as well as outwardly acknowledge man's debt to (1) past, (2) present, (3) worlds of lower beings, and (4) worlds of higher beings. Thus proving his fidelity to creation, man is fit to touch the hem of the Creator's robe.

* The Vedic scriptures declare, "*Yajna* verily is Vishnu's own Self" (*Taittiriya-Samhita* 1:7.4). Actions performed as *yajna,* therefore, are solely for God. As oblations to Him they must be absolutely pure: desire-free and devoid of self and selfish motive.

MOST PEOPLE THINK of religious rites as the performance of ordinary ceremonies. Formal worship is better than worldly actions, but, in itself, is not a bestower of wisdom. When the outward rite is observed with the proper chanting and concentration, it produces some result of peace even in worldly people because it diverts their minds from material concerns to the spiritual calmness within. But when such rites are habitually performed with absentmindedness, they yield neither peace, nor wisdom, nor significant benefit of any kind.

Esoteric meaning of fire rite understood through yoga

The formal rite in India of pouring into a fire clarified butter (ghee)—a form of fire-purified matter—is symbolical of uniting life energy with cosmic energy.

The initiate in guru-given yoga meditation performs the *esoteric* real fire rite enjoined by the Hindu scriptures. He withdraws his life force from the sensory and motor nerves and pours that energy into the sacred fires of life gathered in the seven occult cerebrospinal centres. When the yogi switches off the life current from the nerves, he finds his mind disconnected from the senses. This act of withdrawing life from the body and uniting that energy with the light of God is the highest *yajna,* the real fire rite—casting the little flame of life into the Great Divine Fire, burning all human desire in the divine desire for God. Then the yogi takes his sense-withdrawn mind and casts it into the fire of Cosmic Consciousness; realizing, finally, his own soul as something entirely different from the body, he casts that Self into the fire of Eternal Spirit.

The true *exoteric* fire rite of life—by which the bodily life is united with the Cosmic Life, and the human mind and soul are united with the Cosmic Mind and Spirit—consists in offering right actions to God, without desire or attachment. These followers of right actions performed as *yajna* do not remain tied to the earth, but are liberated.

Exoteric meaning: desireless action offered to God

The blessed state of the *jivanmukta* (one who has overcome delusion and recovered his divine Identity, becoming freed while still incarnate) cannot be won by neglecting or running away from the duties of this life; by such unworthy conduct a man ignores God in His aspect of Lord of the World. The true *jivanmukta* therefore makes a "sacrifice" of his bodily powers in God's service, and thus works in sinlessness, his actions creating no new seeds of earth-binding karma.

Ordinary people who work in the factory of life with only their desires as tools, and without any spiritual training, receive mostly sorrow; just as an untrained mechanic who tries to handle an intricate piece of machinery gets hurt. The Gita therefore advises all men to perform the soul-redeeming activities of meditation, devotion, morality, service, and divine love as their observance of a purifying spiritual fire rite in which all mortal blemishes are burnt.

Work actuated by selfish desires militates against the divine plan. The worldly man is inclined to perform wrong actions in obedience to the entangling shortsighted ego. To fulfil his self-created, ever-increasing desires, the worldly man has to reincarnate again and again until he is free. But the yogi who works to please God alone is already free. Fulfilling his divine mission on earth, he becomes liberated. Even the spiritual fire rite of casting human ignorance in the flames of wisdom must be performed solely with the desire to please God, and not because of spiritual ambition. The divine man performs right actions for God only. His every act is *yajna.*

VERSE 10

सहयज्ञाः प्रजाः सृष्ट्वा पुरोवाच प्रजापतिः ।
अनेन प्रसविष्यध्वमेष वोऽस्त्विष्टकामधुक् ॥

Prajapati (Brahma as the Creator of praja or human beings), having made mankind in the beginning, along with Yajna, said: "By this shalt thou propagate; this will be the milch cow of thy longings.... [See continuation, verse 11.]

FROM THE BEGINNING there was *Yajna,* the Cosmic Fire or Light imbued with God's Cosmic Intelligence from which the Lord's Creative Consciousness brought forth all human beings—souls made of Cosmic Intelligence informed or individualized by God's creative light. The Creator-Lord commanded, "Thou shalt multiply thyself after the wisdom-image in which thou art made. The divine wisdom within thee shalt be the all-fulfilling milch cow* offering the milk of happiness to all thy desires."

---

* In Hindu mythology, a chief possession of Indra, Lord of all the gods, was Kamadhuk, a milch cow able to fulfil all desires.

Of primordial creation it is written in Genesis: "In the beginning...God said, Let there be light: and there was light."* Inherent in this light is God's Cosmic Intelligence, *Kutastha Chaitanya,* the Krishna or Christ Consciousness, God's reflection in all creation.† This Intelligence is the upholder of creation, the first expression of God made manifest. (In this sense, it is sometimes personified as Vishnu, the Preserver.) The Creator formed all human creatures after the image of His luminous preservative force (Light and Intelligence), souls shining with the light of perfect wisdom.

Expressing through the conscience in man, God commands, "Ye shall develop and nourish thyself through the soul-born discrimination within thee." As the motherless child is nourished by the milk of the cow, so the devotee, orphaned without the contact of God, may feed all his mental powers with the milk of wisdom, drawn from his soul by discrimination. Man has the potential to direct himself always through inner guidance, in every phase of his material, mental, and spiritual life. This is the blessed truth! "To err is human," is a comfortable, if invalid, excuse for nonuse of man's God-given faculty of discrimination.

For the yogi, the milch cow of inner wisdom fulfils all his spiritual longings. During meditation, he beholds the "*yajna* fire" of astral light and receives wondrous spiritual perceptions and powers that fill him with inner joy. But the true aspirant does not remain content with these initial gifts of Spirit. From divine wisdom, poured out through intuition, he begets those soul qualities and realizations of higher and higher states of consciousness, and receives finally the ultimate boon of emancipation in Spirit, which quenches forever all accumulated desires of incarnations.

VERSE 11

देवान्भावयतानेन ते देवा भावयन्तु वः ।
परस्परं भावयन्तः श्रेयः परमवाप्स्यथ ॥

* Genesis 1:1–3. (See Gita III:14–15 for elaboration in this same context.)

† See III:15. "Brahma is inherently and inseparably present in *Yajna*": Creative Consciousness as *Kutastha Chaitanya* or Christ Intelligence is indivisibly inherent in the cosmic light (*yajna*), which is the essence of all components of vibratory creation.

[Prajapati continues:] "With this yajna, meditate on the devas, and may those devas think of thee; thus communing with one another, thou shalt receive the Supreme Good.... [See continuation, verse 12.]

"WITH THE TRUE INNER FIRE RITE performed in yoga meditation, become attuned to the *devas* (literally, 'shining ones')—the astral forces, angels, divine souls who as God's cosmic agents are instrumental in the governing of the worlds; to those in harmony with the exacting laws of Nature, the *devas* respond favourably. Thus, continuing in this manner of attunement, thou wilt become eligible to unite with the Formless Spirit, Creator of the astral deities who supervise the workings of this ordered universe."

Among the customs of all ancient peoples were nature rites whose purpose was to acknowledge man's dependence on the natural forces and bounty of his environment. Instinctively, they recognized the debt and reverence owed to a Higher Intelligence working within the circumambient wonders. It is no coincidence that the godlessness prevalent in the modern age has spawned a civilization out of touch with the beneficence of Nature. The God-given role of guardianship of the earth did not confer on man absolute sovereignty. His wanton domination is destructive of the very conditions necessary for his existence.

The universal structure and man's infinitesimal place in it are made possible only by the working together in precise harmony of an awesome combination of intelligent cosmic forces guided by a Supreme Creator. Man would do well to put himself in attunement with these. For modern man to hold that the mathematical perfection of the universe could come about by chance is nothing but an expression of man's egotism—a loathing to concede that there could be Something greater than he from which he only borrows his powers and intelligence, and to which he owes his humble allegiance and worship.

The Hindu masters of ancient times knew the art of worshipping with special fire ceremonies and vibratory chants by which they could invoke the manifestation of the angels of God. Correspondingly, a literal interpretation of this stanza is that, through fire oblations and chants, properly performed, one should invoke and pay honour to the astral deities, superior to man in the order of evolution, who through the divine laws of Nature carry on the cosmic functions. Thus, man will create good karma that will free his life from the hazards of sudden fruition of effects from unseen evil causes set in motion by him in the past.

Materially minded people live their days by the "sweat of their brows," like a mule that carries a huge bag of gold; this treasure is not only of no use to the mule, through the animal's ignorance, but is the cause of its active suffering from the burden of the weight. Worldly men, like the dumb animal, carry a heavy burden of material duties, suffering and fearing but reaping little benefit from onerous labours. They only eat, sleep, earn, and procreate, giving not a single truly reflective thought to God or to His spiritual government. When misfortune visits such men, they call it ill luck or fate. When good fortune smiles on them, they say it is good luck or chance. Few realize that their lives are governed by the effects of past actions (karma), and that they are subject to universal laws administered by higher forces.

The Gita therefore points out that, instead of leading an ignorant life, the average man should perform certain spiritual ceremonies, religious observances outlined by saints, to place one's self in harmony with high astral deities and the unseen laws they govern, thus bringing about a conscious control of life's developments.

❖

SPIRITUAL UNDERSTANDING OF ASTROLOGY

ALL PLANETS AND STARS, for example, are in the charge of divine astral beings. The influence on man from the heavenly bodies is the result of a universal symbiosis, governed by laws upheld by these higher beings. Planets and stars of themselves have no conscious power to guide or determine the destiny of man. But as the whole universe consists of and is held in existence by Nature's creative vibratory power, each individual unit radiates a characteristic electromagnetic vibration that links it with other units in the cosmos. Depending on the interaction, these vibrations are productive of good or ill.

❖ *Relation of astrological forces to spinal chakras* ❖

Man is a miniature of the universe in which he lives. His basic composition—of which his physical body is merely a gross manifestation—is his astral body formed from the thoughts of God and structured around and from the creative forces and consciousness in the spiritual eye and the subtle cerebrospinal centres. The spiritual eye has a correspondence with the cosmic sun; and the six—twelve by polarity—spinal centres (medullary, cervical, dorsal, lumbar, sacral, and coccygeal plexuses) correspond to planetary influences represented by the twelve zodiacal signs of astrology.

The astrological stars of a person are nothing but an environment that he himself has chosen by the karmic pattern he has fashioned by his past-life actions. According to this karmic pattern he is attracted to be reborn on earth at a given time that is favourable to the fulfilment of that pattern. In that sense, astrology is only a very poor way of finding out what one's past karma is. It is at best an unsure art when practised by those who lack divine intuitive perception. I wrote at length about this in *Autobiography of a Yogi,* "Outwitting the Stars."

As commonly calculated today, an astrological chart is drawn for a person according to the time and place of birth; even a slight inaccuracy in this data affects the accuracy of the chart. Further, one is actually "born" at the moment of conception, when the soul enters the first cell of its new body. One's karmic pattern has already begun to unfold at that instant. The intuition of wise men, such as my guru Sri Yukteswarji, who was masterful in astrology as the divine science it was intended to be, knows how to factor this "birth at conception" into calculating a horoscope.

In any case, it is not the stars themselves that control the happenings in man's life, but rather his individual karma that, when ripe for fruition, is affected beneficially or adversely by the electromagnetic vibrations of the heavenly bodies. The relation of the stars to the human body and mind is very subtle. The astral forces radiating to the earth from the heavens interreact with those in the spinal centres that sustain man's body. Ignorant man does not realize how body and mind are changed through his good and bad actions, and how his actions affect—positively or negatively—the centres of the spine. Persons whose bodies and minds and material environment are out of order, the result of transgressions of spiritual law, have inharmony between the energies in the spinal centres and those radiating from the twelve signs of the zodiac.

The true science of astrology, therefore, is mathematics of one's own actions, not the mathematics of the brainless stars. Karma governs the stars and one's destiny, but karma is governed by one's will power. What is to be does not necessarily have to be. Man's free will and divine determination can change the course of events in his life, or at the least mitigate adverse aspects. One whose body and mind are very strong is impervious to adverse astrological influences; there may be no outwardly observable reaction at all, even when evil vibrations may be radiating from negative configuration of the stars. But if body and mind have been weakened by wrong eating, wrong thinking, bad character, and bad company, then the stellar rays have the power to activate latent harmful effects of past karma.

On a cosmic scale, the combined karma of groups of individuals—social or racial groups, or nations, for example—or of the world at large, constitute the mass karma of the earth or portions thereof. This mass karma responds to the electromagnetic vibrations of the earth's cosmic neighbours according to the same laws that affect each individual, thereby inducing beneficial or malevolent changes in the course of world and natural events. A store of good mass karma from living in harmony with divine laws and forces blesses man's earthly environment with peace, health, prosperity. Accumulated bad mass karma precipitates wars, diseases, poverty, devastating earthquakes, and other such calamities. During times of prevalent negative vibratory influences, the individual must thus contend not only with his personal karma, but also with the mass karma affecting the planet on which he lives.

Therefore, it is beneficial to follow certain astrological injunctions, based on the mathematical or orderly nature of the unified cosmos—if such advice is received from Self-realized sages, and not from the superficial professional caster of horoscopes.

Horoscopes tend to influence and paralyse the free choice of man's inherent divine-will-to-conquer. Further, intuition is needed to read correctly the messages of the heavens and to interpret their significance in relation to one's individual karma. For guidance and support it is far better to appeal to God and His angelic agents. Why look to the mute stars? From them man can receive neither sympathetic response to his plight, nor personal succour in the form of divine grace.

When one is following God's path, to give too much thought to such lesser sciences as astrology is a hindrance. The highest way to create the right influences in one's life, the yogi's way, is to commune with God. All stars bow down before the presence of God.

By meditation the yogi reinforces the positive spiritual power in the cerebrospinal centres that are acted upon by the planetary influences. In this way, the yogi harmonizes body and mind with the universal laws and God's divine cosmic agents who govern them.

❖

CONTACT WITH THE DEVAS, OR ANGELIC FORCES

CONTACT WITH THE *DEVAS* by attuning the consciousness to these higher forces in meditation elevates man, who may thus avoid the fructification of evil karma; misfortune can be greatly lessened, while the liberating effects of good actions are enhanced. Man and his astral preceptors in higher realms, by mutual communion, can find great good and control destiny.* Eventually, by constant contact with spiritual forces, the devotee comes into harmony with the Supreme Creator, Organizer of all higher and all lower beings.

Scriptures of all religions bear testimony to the intercession of divine beings between God and man. References to angels are common in the Biblical narrative of the life of Jesus: His birth was foretold to Mary by an angel of God;† angels heralded his nativity;‡ he was protected from the death decree of King Herod by an angel's warning to Joseph.§ When Jesus fasted forty days in the wilderness, the "angels came and ministered unto him."¤ When he prayed in the Garden of Gethsemane, before his arrest and crucifixion: "Father, if thou be willing, remove this cup from me....there appeared an angel unto him from heaven, strengthening him."** And when he was taken into custody by soldiers sent to arrest him, he declared: "Thinkest thou that I cannot now pray to my Father, and he shall presently give me more than twelve legions of angels? But how then shall the scriptures be fulfilled, that thus it must be?"†† When Christ's disciples were imprisoned, "The angel of the Lord by night opened the prison door, and brought them forth."‡‡

In the Old Testament, also, are frequent references to God's aid to man through angels: When Abraham was commanded, as a test, to sacrifice his son, "The angel of the Lord called out unto him out of heaven. ...Lay not thine hand upon the lad...for now I know that thou fearest God, seeing thou hast not withheld thy son, thine only son from me."§§ Elijah in the wilderness, as was Jesus, was ministered to by an angel of the Lord: "...As he lay and slept under a juniper tree, behold, then an angel touched him, and said unto him, Arise and eat.... And he did eat and drink, and laid him down again."¤¤

---

* Saint Guthlac, a seventh-century monk and hermit, related on his deathbed his wondrous communication with a messenger of God, cited here as typical of the wisdom conveyed by the *devas* to advanced souls: "From the second year that I began to dwell in this hermitage the Lord has sent an angel to be my consolation and to speak with me every morning and evening. He has revealed mysteries to me which it is not lawful for man to tell. He has softened the harshness of my life with messages from heaven; and he has revealed distant things to me, putting them before me as though done in my presence." (Clinton Albertson, S.J., *Anglo-Saxon Saints and Heroes,* New York: Fordham University Press, 1967.) *(Publisher's Note)*

† Luke 1:28 ff.

‡ Ibid. 2:8 ff.

§ Matthew 2:13 ff.

¤ Ibid. 4:11.

** Luke 22:42–43.

†† Matthew 26:53–54.

‡‡ Acts 5:19.

§§ Genesis 22:11–12.

¤¤ I Kings 19:5–6.

As God personified Himself in the soul of every human being, so to fulfil His purpose in creation He personified in many divine forms His multifaceted personality as the Creator, through which to govern the universal structure. Joining the ranks of these God-manifested angels and deities are the souls of liberated human beings who when freed choose not to dissolve their natures in the Infinite, but to remain in the higher realms of creation to work for the upliftment of still-evolving souls.

Communion with these *devas* or "shining ones" is not to be misunderstood as the spirit communion of spiritualists.* Truly divine ones cannot be contacted by this means. Only by lifting one's own consciousness, through the right method of meditation, to the higher spiritual realms of the astral heaven—home of the divine forces that uphold the material world—can such attunement with the deities be realized. The worldly man, unable consciously to commune with astral deities, gains the same result by associating with earthly angels—true God-knowing saints—and by following their counsel.

Receiving blessings of the deities in the spinal chakras

A DEEPER INTERPRETATION of this stanza can be understood only by advanced yogis. It follows: Withdraw the life force from the muscles, efferent and afferent nerves, heart, and other bodily activities, and unite it with the subtler astral nerve currents in the spine—the subtle centres in the coccygeal, sacral, lumbar, dorsal, and cervical regions, where enthroned, respectively, are the five astral angels: Ganesh, god of success; Shakti, goddess of power; Surya-Creator, god of fire; Vishnu, god of preservation; Shiva, god of dissolution.

These deities, as differentiated forces of God's creative consciousness, sustain the human body and are naught else than diverse manifestations of the One Spirit. The yogi should let the life current automatically flow from the lower spinal centres to the higher ones by mental pushes of concentration; he should never be unduly attracted to the beauty of one centre, for thus his attention would remain locked there, unable to proceed to the medulla and the cranial or highest centre.

The five spinal deities are temporary manifestations of Spirit in man; in time they are dissolved in the higher centres of consciousness.

* See XVII:4 for expanded commentary on spiritualism.

After the yogi can direct his life force to the throne of light occupied by each of the five temporary deities, he learns to withdraw the current and unite it in the medullary centre and the *Kutastha* (Christ) centre, at the point between the two eyebrows—the single or spiritual eye where the Changeless Spirit dwells on the thousand-rayed throne in the cranium, the principal seat of the individualized Spirit, or soul.

In the astral withdrawal of life force, the yogi perceives his blue life current commingling with the variously coloured currents in the five spinal centres, and is also cognizant of the different states of consciousness resident in and characteristic of each centre. In the astral withdrawal, the yogi is principally concentrated on visible lights and other phenomena.

But during a higher or spiritual withdrawal of mind from the body through the centres, the yogi, after experiencing the outstanding states of consciousness present in the five regions, then unites the current with the Christ consciousness prevailing in the spiritual eye. (The medullary centre in the back of the head and the *Kutastha,* Christ-consciousness, centre in the forehead are two poles that act in conjunction, and are thus often referred to as one centre, the *ajna chakra*.)

The yogi who has reached his goal, the *Kutastha* centre, is then able to unite himself with Cosmic Consciousness, perceived in the brain as a starting point. He then feels his mind united simultaneously with *Kutastha* (Christ) Consciousness—present throughout all vibratory creation—and with Cosmic Consciousness, which exists beyond the limits of any vibratory phenomena.

In the superior spiritual withdrawal, even though the yogi may perceive lights and astral beings, he dissolves them in the different states of consciousness in the spine. He first unites his mind with semiconsciousness, subconsciousness, and superconsciousness, in the three lower spinal centres—coccygeal, sacral, lumbar—then lifts his mind to unite it with a higher state of superconsciousness present in the dorsal and cervical regions. Then he unites himself with *Kutastha* (Christ) Consciousness (the Omnipresent Mind *in* creation) and finally with Cosmic Consciousness (the Absolute Spirit in the vibrationless realms *beyond* creation).

The Lord Buddha's ascension to enlightenment, as his consciousness rose through the dark illusions and temptations of earth, then through the heavenly spheres of the *devas* (experienced as the yogi unlocks the mystery doors of ascension in the spine), is wondrously described by the masterful pen of Sir Edwin Arnold in *The Light of Asia*:

And in the middle watch
Our Lord attained Abhidjna—insight vast
Ranging beyond this sphere to spheres unnamed....
He saw those Lords of Light who hold their worlds
By bonds invisible, how they themselves
Circle obedient round mightier orbs
Which serve profounder splendours, star to star
Flashing the ceaseless radiance of life
From centres ever shifting unto cirques
Knowing no uttermost. These he beheld
With unsealed vision, and of all those worlds...
Measureless unto speech—whereby these wax
And wane; whereby each of this heavenly host
Fulfils its shining life and darkling dies.

****

But when the fourth watch came the secret came....
The outcome of him on the Universe,
Grows pure and sinless; either never more
Needing to find a body and a place,
Or so informing what fresh frame it takes
In new existence that the new toils prove
Lighter and lighter not to be at all,
Thus "finishing the Path."...
Blessed Nirvana—sinless, stirless rest—
That change which never changes!

This interpretation, then, is the higher meaning of this stanza: The yogi must first attain conscious attunement ("communion") with higher forms of consciousness in the various spinal centres and thus become eligible to unite with the Higher Good, the Spirit, *in* creation as *Kutastha Chaitanya* or Christ Consciousness, and *beyond* creation as *Brahman Chaitanya* or Cosmic Consciousness.

VERSE 12

इष्टान्भोगान्हि वो देवा दास्यन्ते यज्ञभाविताः ।
तैर्दत्तानप्रदायैभ्यो यो भुङ्क्ते स्तेन एव सः ॥

[Prajapati concludes:] "The devas communed with by yajna will grant thee the craved-for gifts of life." He who enjoys benefactions of the universal deities without due offerings to them is indeed a thief.

All life's processes are controlled by the inner or astral deities. With the divine fire rite of meditation, every man thus should seek attunement with these "shining ones." He should worship with the offering of respectful devotion these enriching influences or agents of God for bounties of life, health, knowledge, prosperity (received according to one's individual karma). Materially minded persons who thoughtlessly accept the gifts of life without conveying in some way their respects to the Giver are ingrates indeed, pilferers before a shrine.

As the Absolute Verity is abstract beyond the comprehension of ordinary men, these should reflect upon the cosmical angels, sleeplessly labouring for universal maintenance, whose conceptual formulations are within the scope even of unlettered peasants. The mythology and folklore of every land are rich in personifications of these potent intercessionary influences.

Reverence for cosmical agents on whom all life depends

Gross man seldom or never realizes that his body is a kingdom governed by Emperor Soul on the throne of the cranium, with subsidiary regents in the six spinal centres or spheres of consciousness. This theocracy extends over a throng of obedient subjects: trillions of cells (endowed with a sure if seemingly automatic intelligence by which they perform all duties of bodily growths, transformations, and dissolutions) and fifty million substratal thoughts, emotions, and variations of alternating phases in man's consciousness in a life span of sixty years.* Any apparent insurrection in the human body or mind against Emperor Soul, manifesting as disease or irrationality, is due not to disloyalty among the humble subjects, but stems from past or present misuse by man of his individuality or free will—given to him simultaneously with a soul, and revocable never.

Each man's intellectual reactions, feelings, moods, and habits are

* The number fifty million in reference to man's mental activities is postulated not on individual units of thoughts, feelings, reactions (i.e., so many words or impressions per second necessary to form an idea), but refers rather to the totality of an idea, emotional response, or change of consciousness that is meaningful in influencing or developing man's nature and behaviour.

circumscribed by effects of past actions, whether of this or a prior life. Lofty above all such influences, however, is his regal soul.

The human being seeking a more spiritual consciousness should not withhold a natural expression of gratitude for the possession and functioning powers of his bodily temple—for the forces that throb in his heart; circulate in his blood; speed his digestion; condition his telephonic nervous system to receive and transmit all communications among soul, body, and outward world; and direct the metabolic, crystallizing, assimilating, procreative, and eliminative functions of his body, the ramifications of thought and will in his brain, and the emotional responses of his heart.

Man, identifying himself with a shallow ego, takes for granted that it is he alone who thinks, wills, feels, digests meals, and keeps himself alive, never admitting through reflection (only a little would suffice) that in his ordinary life he is naught but a puppet of past actions (karma) and of Nature, directed and controlled by intelligent deities. Man is thus out of touch with universal harmonies, and is little better than a lawless pirate, rendering no homage to countless forces that mercifully provide for the whole of his allotted span.

Ancient scriptures, for this reason, extolled the value to man of some form of worship that would acknowledge his indebtedness to cosmical agents on whom depends the proper functioning of all life. By such reverence, man finds the untoward effects of already-performed evil actions much lessened, since ignorance of true causes is also lessened.

The Gita, in this stanza, tries to inspire man, that he "be not like dumb, driven cattle" on the road of life.* Universal perceptions arise when man strives to understand the powers that work in the silent humility of all Nature, and behind his body and his mind in conformance with the rulings of Emperor Soul. Each one should know he has been born, not solely owing to compulsions of past actions, but primarily because God created him as a soul, dowered with individuality, and therefore essential to the universal structure, whether in the temporary role of pillar or parasite.

Each one should understand that death comes not only as the cumulative effect of past actions, but also by the secret decree of deities in the subtle spinal centres. They work God's will to remove a man from earth for at least an invigorating space, his duties of that life being terminated normally by righteous fulfilment, or prematurely by

* Longfellow, "A Psalm of Life."

destructions caused by his evil tendencies, oft hidden from the casual sight.

Kriya Yoga: the real fire rite extolled by the Gita

A HIGHER OR MORE ESOTERIC interpretation of this Gita stanza is counsel to yogis that life force can be withdrawn from enslavement to body and senses, to be united with liberating subtle currents and forces in the seven cerebrospinal shrines. Lives of such yogis are influenced, not by effects of past actions, but solely by directions of the soul deities. These enable aspirants to avoid the slow, evolutionary monitors of egoistic actions, good and bad, of common life—cumbrous and snail-like to the eagle hearts.

The superior mode of soul living frees the yogi: emerging from his ego prison, he tastes the deep air of omnipresence. The thralldom of natural living is, in contrast, set in a pace humiliating. Conforming his life merely to the evolutionary order, a man can command no concessionary haste from Nature. Though he live without error against the laws that govern his body and mind, he still requires about a million years of masquerading incarnations to attain final emancipation.

The telescopic methods of a yogi, disengaging himself from physical and mental identifications in favour of soul-individuality, are therefore commended to those who eye with revolt a thousand thousand years. This numerical periphery is enlarged for the ordinary man, who lives in harmony not even with Nature, let alone his soul; pursuing instead unnatural complexities and offending in his thoughts and body the sweet sanities of Nature. For him, two times a million years can scarce suffice for liberation.

By practice of *Kriya Yoga,* deep meditation, and guidance of an enlightened guru, a determined soul can accomplish a million years of evolutionary unfoldment within a space of forty-eight or twenty-four or twelve or six or even three years, according to the adamance of his efforts and the quality of his past karma.

By *Kriya,* the outgoing life force is not wasted and abused in the senses, but is constrained to reunite with subtler currents in the astral spinal centres. By such reinforcement of life force, the yogi's body and brain cells are electrified with the spiritual elixir. Thus he removes himself from studied observance of natural laws, which can only guide him (by circuitous means as given by proper food, sunlight, and inoffensive habits) to a million-year Goal. It needs twelve years of normal healthful living to effect even slight refinements in brain structure; a million solar returns are exacted to purify the cerebral tenement sufficiently for manifestation of cosmic consciousness.

This, then, is the real *yajna* or fire rite mentioned in the Gita. The life current in the senses is withdrawn and united in the vaster flame of the light of Spirit present in the main brain region and in the subdynamos of the spinal centres.* This fire ceremony alone can give true knowledge to one who understands how to practise it, and differs much from the little-effective outward fire rites, where perception of truth is oft burnt, to chanted accompaniment, along with the incense!

The true yogi, withholding his mind, will, and feeling from false identifications with bodily desires, uniting them with the superconscious forces in the seven cerebrospinal shrines, thus lives in this world as God hath planned; he is impelled neither by impulses from the past nor by fresh motivations of human witlessness. Receiving fulfilment of his Supreme Desire, he is safe in the final haven of inexhaustibly blissful Spirit. This is indeed the true fire ceremony, in which all past and present desires are fuel consumed by love for God. The Ultimate Flame receives the sacrifice of all human madness, and man is pure of dross. His metaphorical bones stripped of all desirous flesh, his karmic skeleton bleached in the antiseptic sun of wisdom, inoffensive before man and Maker, he is clean at last.

O Man! Offer thy labyrinthine longings into a monotheistic bonfire consecrated to the unparalleled God. Burn desire for human affection in the fire of aspiration for God alone, a love solitary because omnipresent! Throw faggots of ignorance to incandesce the blaze of insight! Devour all sorrows in sorrow for God's absence! Consume all regrets in meditative bliss!†

Verse 13

यज्ञशिष्टाशिनः सन्तो मुच्यन्ते सर्वकिल्बिषैः ।
भुञ्जते ते त्वघं पापा ये पचन्त्यात्मकारणात् ॥

* "Is not light grander than fire? It is the same element in a state of purity."—*Thomas Carlyle*

† Paramahansa Yogananda's first draft of the commentary on this Gita verse was written during the same period in which he was working on *Autobiography of a Yogi.* Portions of the commentary were adapted and included by him in relative passages on *Kriya Yoga* in his *Autobiography. (Publisher's Note)*

Saints—those who eat the remnants of due fire offerings (yajna) —are freed from all sin; but sinners—those who make food just for themselves—feast on sin.

TO EAT AFTER OFFERING THE FOOD to the Giver is an act free from the binding effects of mortal karmic laws. Those who live, eat, and behave like mortals, oblivious to the spring of Infinitude within, remain under the compulsions of the law of karma, which causes sufferings and rebirth.

During a fire ceremony, as enjoined by the Hindu scriptures, a fire is built into which the worshipper pours ghee (clarified melted butter) and other symbolic items of nourishment while uttering certain awakening vibratory chants, offering these to God and to the various deities who govern the human body and the cosmos. Though neither God nor the angels eat mortal food, They receive the gift of the devotional attention and concentration of Their devotees.

When an offering is made of flowers or incense or flame from oil lamps or candles on the altar, they represent the devotion of man to God. The flowers symbolize the fragrant love of the devotee; the incense conveys reverence; the flame typifies the light of calmness in which is revealed the Divine Deity, residing on the altar of the heart.

The Gita thus points out that a true devotee eats food only after having performed the outer ritual of a fire ceremony, or having inwardly offered the food directly to the Creator. Worldly people who eat without thanks commit a sin of ignorance: forgetfulness of the Giver.

However, the real or inner fire ceremony to which this verse refers is the uniting of life with the greater Life, by practice of *pranayama* or *Kriya Yoga,* the technique of life control. And "food" refers to the divine cosmic energy imbibed from this inner rite. In sleep the bodily life retires into the fires of spinal centres. This is an unconscious performance of the fire ceremony, in which the sleeper is made to unite his life current with the superior currents in the spine; he thus unknowingly moves toward the cosmic energy that sustains all life.

❖
Kriya Yoga: astral way of feeding the body cells
❖

By life-control technique, the yogi consciously retires his life current from bodily muscles and from the heart into the spine. With the awakening of the spinal centres, he saturates and feeds all his bodily cells with undecaying light, and keeps them in a magnetized state. This practice makes the body healthful, filled with divine life, as the yogi realizes that the body, too, is a shadow of the Infinite Energy, and can be transmuted into it. This is the astral way of feeding the body cells, superseding the lower method of using physical food and oxygen. By the astral method the body can remain magnetized or in a suspended state, registering no decay.

Prana, the divine life-energy in the body, is the subjective intelligent worker in all the bodily cells. It is the "soul" of the cells. Outgoing life (which as pure *prana* is spiritual and subjective) becomes dependent on food and breath when it is identified with matter. But ever since this intelligent life energy was projected as a vibratory force from the soul into the body, it has been trying to spiritualize the bodily cells, while gross food and breath as secondary sources of life keep the cells matter-bound, in the domain of change and death. *Prana* subjectively preaches the soul's message to the cells and works to awaken in them divine consciousness of immortality.

When in the astral fire-rite the pranic current withdraws into the subtle centres of the spine and brain, then instead of wasting its energies in reforming matter-bound cells, the freed reinforced prana awakens those cells with divine life by baptizing them with the light of Spirit.

For the determined yogi, the time may come when through discipline of the cells by the practice of *pranayama* he will be able to live unconditioned by food or breath—when his soul will manifest life in the body in perfect freedom from the limited laws of nature. The soul will no longer have to obey or suit the conditions of the body, but can command the body as its servant to accept any condition it chooses to impose upon it.

Kriya frees man from bodily laws that govern mortal beings

The body of man, however healthy or observant of natural laws, has to die and decay—unless it becomes spiritualized, which immortalizes the body if the soul so wills. Certain yogis can thus keep their bodies indefinitely. My param param Gurudeva, Mahavatar Babaji, has a young body, preserved for many centuries through this system of astral feeding. To use food to replace decayed material in the body involves constant changes in the physical cells, which ultimately give up their limited power of absorbing food, deteriorate, and die. By the astral way, the yogi performs the astral fire-ceremony, feeding his cells with immortal fire. Such a yogi becomes free from the sins of the bodily laws of action (karma) that govern every mortal being. The yogi can register even immortality in his body, by transmuting its cells into energy. Certain yogis, like Elijah and Kabir, converted their bodies into astral currents and merged them in the Cosmic Light without having experienced the ordinary phenomena of death.*

Worldly people digest food in the mortal way and thus witness death—a result of the sinful habits of living in ignorance of God and His cosmic laws and creative forces. The divine yogi unites his soul with God by ecstatic meditation. He saturates his body cells and all his thoughts with the joy of God. Beginners who meditate feel great joy, but when they have concluded their meditation, they again become identified with their mortal bodily habits. Men who unite their minds with sense pleasures (eating the food of various sensations, to satisfy the human ego) become easily dissatisfied, and suffer from disillusionment—the inevitable outcome of all temporarily enjoyable pastimes. Such actions are karmically binding. But advanced saints, united with God, spread their joy over all the actions of daily life. Such yogis no longer live like human beings, but as God-men. By substituting divine joy for human happiness, they become completely free from the human law of karma and rebirth, forever nourished by God's bliss.

VERSES 14–15

अन्नाद्भवन्ति भूतानि पर्जन्यादन्नसम्भवः ।
यज्ञाद्भवति पर्जन्यो यज्ञः कर्मसमुद्भवः ॥ *(14)*

कर्म ब्रह्मोद्भवं विद्धि ब्रह्माक्षरसमुद्भवम् ।
तस्मात्सर्वगतं ब्रह्म नित्यं यज्ञे प्रतिष्ठितम् ॥ *(15)*

(14) From food, creatures spring forth; from rain, food is begotten. From Yajna (the sacrificial cosmic fire), rain issues forth; the cosmic fire (cosmic light) is born of karma (divine vibratory action).

(15) Know this divine vibratory activity to have come into being from Brahma (God's Creative Consciousness); and this Creative Consciousness to derive from the Imperishable (the Everlasting Spirit). Therefore, God's Creative Consciousness (Brahma), which is all-pervading, is inherently and inseparably present in Yajna (the cosmic fire or light, which in turn is the essence of all components of vibratory creation).

---

* "Behold, there appeared a chariot of fire, and horses of fire...and Elijah went up by a whirlwind into heaven....They sought three days, but found him not" (II Kings 2:11, 17).

See II:18, page 209, regarding Kabir.

"FOOD IS THE FOUNTAIN OF LIFE, and rain is the stream that brings forth body-sustaining food. Cosmic fire, cosmic light, the quintessence of matter, condenses into enlivening rain; and Cosmic Vibration, the creator of cosmic light, throbs out of the heart of Brahma,* the Creative Consciousness of God immanent in creation. The supreme cause from which evolve these successive links in the chain of creation is the Sole Imperishable, the Everlasting Spirit beyond creation. Spirit's reflection in vibratory creation as the divine Creative Consciousness is omnipresent, indivisibly inherent in every part and particle of the manifested universe."

These stanzas describe the entire law of creation: the outward evolution of creation from Spirit into Cosmic Vibration, and the condensation of vibration as light into man and the universe in causal, astral, and physical forms.

All living creatures evolved from matter (earth, "food"). As every form of material life and life-sustaining nourishment issued forth from the primordial ocean of gathered waters or liquids ("rains") that formed as the earth solidified from gaseous nebulae, so in turn the nebulae (and all inanimate and animate matter) were precipitated from the ocean of gathered rains of astral cosmic energy, which is the essence of atoms, electrons, and the other elemental particles of matter. The "rains" of astral cosmic energy stream out of the cosmic light (*Yajna*); and cosmic light, or "fire," results from the ordered vibration or will of God (cosmic karma or vibratory activity).†

---

* The Sanskrit rendering of *Brahma* in this verse, with a short *a* at the end (*Brahma*), denotes God's all-inclusive Creative Consciousness, not the circumscribed concept of the personal "Brahma-the-Creator" of the Brahma-Vishnu-Shiva triad (which is rendered with a long *ā* at the end, *Brahmā*. The Holy Triad is a personalization or part of the all-inclusive Creative Consciousness.) This Creative Consciousness is the container of Mula-Prakriti, uncreated or undifferentiated Nature, the germ or original source out of which all forms of matter evolve. (See XIV:3–4 in which the word Brahma is again used to connote the Great Prakriti as the Mother of creation.)

† In his acclaimed work *Cosmos* (New York: Random House, 1980), Dr. Carl Sagan, Professor of Astronomy and Space Sciences and Director of the Laboratory for Planetary Studies at Cornell University, provides a concise description of modern science's view of how the earth and its creatures were born, which has an interesting correspondence to this Gita verse:

"For unknown ages after the explosive outpouring of matter and energy of the Big Bang, the Cosmos was without form. There were no galaxies, no planets, no life. Deep, impenetrable darkness was everywhere, hydrogen atoms in the void. Here and there denser accumulations of gas were imperceptibly growing, globes of matter were condensing—hydrogen raindrops more massive than suns. Within these globes of gas

The Bible puts it thus: "In the beginning God created the heaven and the earth. And the earth was without form, and void (being of the finest expression of vibration, or God's thought); and darkness (*maya,* that divides the One into the many) was upon the face of the deep. And the Spirit of God moved (vibrated His active will) upon the face of the waters (creative elements). And God said, Let there be light: and there was light."*

From God's consciousness came Cosmic Light, and all creation

The cosmic vibration and laws of action (karma), which govern the universe, came from the Brahma or Christ Consciousness (Kutastha Chaitanya), God's Infinite Intelligence inherently present in all vibratory creation. This consciousness of God the Son (Tat) immanent in all vibratory creation sprang from the Immutable God the Father (Sat) existing beyond all vibratory creation. The Christ Consciousness or Creative Brahma, being a reflected consciousness and existing in relation to the cosmos, is therefore a temporary manifestation, dissolving in Spirit when at the time of cosmic dissolution

---

was first kindled the nuclear fire latent in matter. A first generation of stars was born, flooding the Cosmos with light. There were in those times not yet any planets to receive the light, no living creatures to admire the radiance of the heavens. Deep in the stellar furnaces the alchemy of nuclear fusion created heavy elements, the ashes of hydrogen burning, the atomic building materials of future planets and life-forms. Massive stars soon exhausted their stores of nuclear fuel. Rocked by colossal explosions, they returned most of their substance back into the thin gas from which they had once condensed. Here in the dark lush clouds between the stars, new raindrops made of many elements were forming, later generations of stars being born. Nearby, smaller raindrops grew, bodies far too little to ignite the nuclear fire, droplets in the interstellar mist on their way to form the planets. Among them was a small world of stone and iron, the early Earth.

"Congealing and warming, the Earth released the methane, ammonia, water, and hydrogen gases that had been trapped within, forming the primitive atmosphere and the first oceans. Starlight from the Sun bathed and warmed the primeval Earth, drove storms, generated lightning and thunder. Volcanos overflowed with lava. These processes disrupted molecules of the primitive atmosphere; the fragments fell back together again into more and more complex forms, which dissolved in the early oceans. After a time the seas achieved the consistency of a warm, dilute soup. Molecules were organized, and complex chemical reactions driven.... And the primitive oceanic broth gradually grew thin as it was consumed by and transformed into complex condensations of self-replicating organic molecules. Gradually, imperceptibly, life had begun." *(Publisher's Note)*

* Genesis 1:1–3. Light is Cosmic Vibration's first expression of creation (concurrent with the sound of *Aum* or Amen). It is the essence or building block of the trifold universe and man—ideational, the subtlest form of light as thought or idea; astral, the light of lifetronic energy; and material, the light of atoms, electrons, protons, that structure all matter.

all creation resolves back into the Absolute, the Sole Imperishable.

Within the Brahma Creative Consciousness is Mula-Prakriti, uncreated or undifferentiated Nature, which holds the seed of all creation. Through the outflowing vibratory activity (karma) of God's will in the form of intelligent creative Cosmic Vibration (*Aum* or Amen, or the Holy Ghost), the quiescent Mula-Prakriti is differentiated; and as various vibratory forces and energies, the now-active Prakriti brings into manifestation the multiform creation.

The intelligent Cosmic Vibration has two properties, cosmic light (*Yajna,* creative fire, or light—"Ethereal, first of things, quintessence, pure"*) and the cosmic sound of *Aum*. The *Aum* or Amen or Holy Ghost—all are significations of the Cosmic Vibration, all are the "witness"† or evidence of the Creator in His creation.

Man, the microcosm, also born of the Cosmic Light

Relative to the creation of man, this verse may be explained as follows: The cosmic energy of the creative Cosmic Vibration is the immediate source of all life and life-sustaining food. Thus man, who is a microcosm of the universe, is a product of cosmic energy, of astral life current that became the condensed vibratory current of earth or matter, referred to in this verse as "food." The gross outer sheath of the soul (and of all matter) is called *annamaya kosha,* literally, the "covering made from food," and refers to the physical body. This gross or solid vibration of earth or matter sprang from and is in turn nourished by the subtler or liquid-flowing vibration of astral energy, referred to in this verse as "rain." As rain nourishes the life of the earth, so astral life energy vitalizes all matter. The fluid vibrations of astral cosmic energy are condensations of the subtle cosmic fire, or cosmic light, which is the essence, the building block, of all things. And cosmic light is born from the intelligent creative Cosmic Vibration (*Aum* or Holy Ghost), the active vibratory will of God as the forces of Prakriti or Nature in man. This ordered vibration, expression of divine law, springs forth from the soul, the individualized Brahma Creative Consciousness in man. And the soul is the reflected consciousness of Spirit or Cosmic Consciousness. Thus, ultimately, man is made in the image of God, Eternal Consciousness.

---

* Milton.

† "These things saith the Amen, the faithful and true witness, the beginning of the creation of God" (Revelation 3:14).

God's Creative Consciousness may be described as a Dreamer who dreams the ideational, astral, and physical creation of man and the cosmos. The Creator dreamed, and the cosmos and man became dream realities in thought- or idea-form. From this ideational or causal dream, God made the astral energy-creation. From the energy-creation, God called forth the so-called solid universe and man with his illusory heavy body. The weight of the body, or a piece of clod, is a suggestion of God. The body as matter is in actuality an electromagnetic wave.

In a dream, one can think and work merely in thought or ideas, or work with dream electrical currents, or build dream houses out of dream bricks for dream people. In the dream state there appears to be differentiation among the dream thought, dream electricity, and dream brick houses for dream people. But on waking, the dreamer realizes that everything in his visionary world was nothing more than different vibrations and manifestations of his frozen mind-stuff. From the unity of his dream consciousness came all the illusory objects and events of his dream.

Man is thus the materialized mind of God. All creatures are informed or materialized from the "frozen mind" or ideas of God. All illusions of solid matter came from the liquid astral energy or fluid frozen mind of God. This frozen liquid-mind of God came from the cosmic energy as light or fiery frozen mind of God. The source of this light is the active vibratory frozen mind of God—intelligent Cosmic Vibration, Holy Ghost or Prakriti—which directs all laws of the entire illusory vibratory creation that is nothing but dreams of God.*

This active Cosmic Vibration of God came from the reflected consciousness of God, or Brahma Creative Consciousness, Lord of all illusive creation. His Creative Consciousness, which mentally vibrated the cosmic dream creation, came from the original unchangeable Cosmic Consciousness—the Uncreated—that exists beyond the vibratory or created realms.

---

* "The ultimate stuff of the universe is mind-stuff," stated British astronomer Sir Arthur Eddington. His contemporary, Sir James Jeans, put it this way: "The universe can be best pictured, though still very imperfectly and inadequately, as consisting of pure thought, the thought of what we must describe as a mathematical thinker....If the universe is a universe of thought, then its creation must have been an act of thought." And the great Albert Einstein declared: "I want to know how God created this world. I am not interested in this or that phenomenon. I want to know His thoughts; the rest are details." *(Publisher's Note)*

Verse 16

एवं प्रवर्तितं चक्रं नानुवर्तयतीह यः ।
अघायुरिन्द्रियारामो मोघं पार्थ स जीवति ॥

That man, O Son of Pritha (Arjuna), who in this world does not follow the wheel thus set rotating, living in iniquity and contented in the senses, lives in vain!

Cosmic creation and man's place within it is a great revolving wheel of activity, descending from Spirit and reascending to liberation. The benighted man—having descended and become intoxicated with the wine of sense pleasures, and failing to climb aboard the ascending cycle of the wheel with its lawful disciplinarian activities of life—remains in the pit of sinful misery, rendering useless the purpose of his God-given life.

He who does not heed the liberating laws laid down by his Creator misses the sole point of earthly existence. He who identifies himself with his senses is rooted in the soil of materialism. As a person who mounts a Ferris wheel can climb high and see a beautiful panorama, or can climb down again, so a person who, instead of remaining stationary on the ground of materialism, climbs on the wheel of uplifting action can reach the high points in evolution; he is free to go to any world, whether the lower plane of earth or the rarefied regions of the *devas.*

The man who performs higher and higher duties rises steadily in the scale of evolution. The sense-identified person walks dully on the lowly levels of material consciousness. His sorrow-producing error lies in not acquiring a standard of comparison, which can only be found by mounting the rotating wheel of right actions. Such men never know the purpose of life: the search for the Holy Grail, the chalice of supreme bliss!

A deeper interpretation of this Gita stanza is that of the human spine as the descending and ascending wheel of life. The consciousness of man has come down from its home in the cerebrum, descending through the six plexuses. After reaching the lowest or coccygeal centre, consciousness spreads out in the nervous system and becomes responsive to the outer world. The soul descending into the flesh thus becomes entangled, remaining a prisoner of the

The human spine as the descending and ascending wheel of life

momentary-pleasure-producing sensations. The man who allows his consciousness to become saturated with the delusive pleasures of sensations finds that his life is vain; it leads but to negation.

The purpose of life is to ascend the six spinal centres, reinforcing the human consciousness progressively with greater and greater lights, until it is able to unite with the all-pervading, thousand-rayed brilliance in the highest centre in the brain. This ascent of the consciousness through the spine may be achieved slowly through right actions and right thoughts. The yogi, however, chooses the quicker and more scientific method of meditation.

The soul in man has descended from Cosmic Consciousness to the immanent Christ Consciousness and thence to the vibratory creation. It continued to descend until it became encased in a physical body, which is characteristically permeated with sense consciousness. When a man becomes a yogi, his soul consciousness begins to follow the path of ascension. It first leaves the soil of material attachments and concentrates away not only from objects of bodily enjoyment but from the body itself. The yogi detaches himself first from the possessive consciousness and then from all sense identifications. Thus he removes his mind from the three lower centres that connect man with all bodily sensations and attachments.

The yogi then immerses his consciousness in the Divine Love radiating from the heart centre. He ascends further to enjoy the Cosmic Calmness of the cervical centre. Climbing on, the yogi rests in the Christ Consciousness in the medulla and the point between the eyebrows. Here he experiences the joy and wisdom of God inherent and omnipresent in all vibratory creation. He finally stabilizes himself in the cerebral centre of Cosmic Consciousness, the "uncaused" Infinite Bliss beyond the cause-effect reciprocity of vibratory creation.

The internal consciousness of ordinary people operates only from the lumbar, sacral, and coccygeal centres that direct all material sensory perceptions and enjoyments. The divine lovers and celestial poets work from the heart centre. The calm unshaken yogi operates from the cervical centre. He who can feel his presence in the entire vibratory creation has awakened the medullary and Christ centres. The illumined yogi functions in the cerebral centre of Cosmic Consciousness; he may be spoken of as an ascended yogi.

The sense-identified man who knows nothing of his higher, inner life is a "descended one," a mortal, conscious only of the lowest rung of human evolution.

VERSES 17–18

यस्त्वात्मरतिरेव स्यादात्मतृप्तश्च मानवः ।
आत्मन्येव च सन्तुष्टस्तस्य कार्यं न विद्यते ॥ (17)

नैव तस्य कृतेनार्थो नाकृतेनेह कश्चन ।
न चास्य सर्वभूतेषु कश्चिदर्थव्यपाश्रयः ॥ (18)

(17) But the individual who truly loves the soul and is fully satisfied with the soul and finds utter contentment in the soul alone, for him no duty exists.

(18) Such a person has no purpose of gain in this world by performing actions, nor does he lose anything by their nonperformance. He is not dependent on anyone for anything.

A MAN IDENTIFIED WITH HIS BODY becomes the ego. The ego views as reality the unreal world. When by yoga that man unites his ego with his soul, he beholds life as a dream of God in which the soul as individualized Spirit is a participant. When by further advancement he finds supreme contentment by uniting his soul with unending bliss of Spirit, he no longer has to perform any duties in the Lord's dream playhouse.

He who realizes and manifests his soul's oneness with God, and who can switch off his life current from the senses and unite his life with Eternal Life, feels neither profit nor loss by keeping his senses working or not working. Dependent wholly on God, he has no karmic involvement with creation.

The man possessing self-respect, remembering always that he is a child of God, protects and reflects that soul-image by performing right duties and by behaving properly toward others. He follows an inner guidance and, as though automatically, does what is right morally, religiously, socially, and in every other way. Such people do not need others' counsel. Those who know how to command from others a spontaneous respect by reflecting true soul qualities, and how to manifest toward others the respect due them as souls—for such illumined men no compulsion of karmic duties exists.

❖
Dependent wholly on God, the yogi has no karmic involvement with creation
❖

The yogi who has discovered the ever new joy in the soul by deep meditation is completely satisfied; he has found within a perfect happiness. He has achieved the purpose of life! fulfilled the duty for which he was born! In reuniting himself with God, he has automatically discharged all his obligations to creation.

A Biblical story illustrates this point. Mary was completely satisfied to serve Jesus, a natural outpouring of the pure intense devotion of her soul, transcending thought of other duties (to Martha's dismay!). Martha considered it necessary to put worldly duties first, hoping to please God through the path of outward good works. Christ, however, commended Mary for having chosen the better part,* one that released her from the observance of all lesser duties.

All mortals who live and work solely for pleasure and gain, remaining ignorant of the divine purpose of life, are inexorably bound by their actions—elevated by performance of proper actions and degraded by evil actions. But the yogi who has by Self-realization attained the supreme goal of life is neither required to perform actions nor, if he does, is he bound by any karmic results of such actions. Having fulfilled all his desires by attaining the all-satisfying supreme bliss of Spirit, he possesses no motive for worldly gain through actions.

Far above any selfish motivation, the accomplished yogi may engage in dutiful actions for the sole purpose of setting a good example to others. Some great yogis live and teach in the world just to demonstrate to mankind the way to freedom; while other illumined masters remain aloof, never mixing with the world.

I myself prefer the first kind of yogi—the one who shares with others his divine lore. Yet I can understand the yogi who wants only to be with God and not to mingle in the world—for he knows whether or not his ever present Lord wants him to work in ways other than meditation and silent intercession to uplift and save others. Many self-appointed religionists try to "save souls" without having saved themselves. God guides the enlightened yogi to action in the world or to complete withdrawal from it; and in either case, his spiritual attainment bestows its blessings on others.

* Luke 10:42.

RIGHTEOUS DUTY, PERFORMED WITH NONATTACHMENT, IS GODLY

VERSE 19

तस्मादसक्तः सततं कार्यं कर्म समाचर।
असक्तो ह्याचरन्कर्म परमाप्नोति पूरुषः ॥

Therefore, always conscientiously perform good material actions (karyam) and spiritual actions (karman) without attachment. By doing all actions without attachment, one attains the highest.*

THE YOGI WHO FORSAKES EVIL ACTIONS and performs noble material duties and meditative religious actions without selfish attachment is a worker for God, and attains thereby union with Him.

Worldly people work day and night to gain ephemeral material objects. The yogi becomes increasingly attached to spiritual actions and thereby displaces material desires by spiritual ones. Then, says the Gita, when attachment to divine actions has produced contact with God, one no longer has attachment even to spiritual actions.

That is the meaning of "performing all actions with nonattachment." All actions, as motions, are confined to the realm of vibration. Material actions performed with desire lead one away from God, while spiritual actions lead one to God. After the devotee is united to the Infinite, however, he has reached the vibrationless state beyond all action.

Material actions are performed by engaging the life current and mind with the senses; meditative actions are performed by withdrawing energy and mind from the senses. At first the devotee must cultivate attachment to spiritual actions in order to banish attachment to material actions. Reaching the Finality, however, the devotee is freed from all attachment (cause-effect involvements with creation).

---

* *Karma,* from the root *kṛi,* "to do," has the general meaning of "action." It can also mean, specifically, material action or dutiful action; religious rite or spiritual action—as also, the effects one reaps from his actions. The variants of the word *karma* have also interchangeable meanings, the intent determined by the context. Thus, in this verse, *karyam* refers to "dutiful material action" and *karman* denotes "religious rite, or spiritual action (i.e., meditative action)." *(Publisher's Note)*

VERSE 20

कर्मणैव हि संसिद्धिमास्थिता जनकादयः ।
लोकसङ्ग्रहमेवापि सम्पश्यन्कर्तुमर्हसि ॥

By the path of right action alone, Janaka and others like him reached perfection. Also, simply for the purpose of rightly guiding mortals, thou shouldst perform action.

JANAKA, A NOBLE KING and an enlightened yogi of antehistorical India, performed his proper worldly mission (good government of his subjects) and also accomplished the supreme duty enjoined on every incarnate soul, the attainment of God-realization. Already perfected beings such as Janaka, who are no longer required to perform actions for their own evolution, continue nevertheless to engage in constructive actions in order to set a high example to society, whose members can be liberated only by good actions and not by unearned presumptuous inaction.

The great saint Janaka was so strong-willed that he never permitted his intricate state duties to interfere with his supreme engagement with God. Ordinary devotees, on the other hand, incline to overemphasize the necessity for performance of their worldly duties as a condition to happiness. Engrossed in these pursuits they neglect meditation for the attainment of everlasting Divine Bliss.

Idlers, and error-stricken immature yogis, citing the actionless state some illumined yogis have attained, conveniently conclude that the Supreme Goal can be attained without action. The Gita therefore reminds them that King Janaka and similar saints attained perfection by right action (and neither by desire-influenced selfish actions nor by a premature assumption of actionlessness).

Great yogis can keep the life force switched off from the senses in ecstasy so that the body is inert, corpselike. They have attained complete control over the body by *pranayama* (life-control techniques). They may forgo that state part of the time, however, just to illustrate to young yogis the necessity for performing certain duties in the divinely planned cosmic drama before they can reach the inactive state.

Commenting upon stanzas 19 and 20, Swami Pranabananda*

* Swami Pranabananda was an exalted *Kriya Yoga* disciple of the great Yogavatar Lahiri Mahasaya. Through the diligent practice of *Kriya* meditation and the blessing of his Guru, Pranabananda became a fully illumined master. My meeting with the saint is told in *Autobiography of a Yogi,* "The Saint With Two Bodies."

says that in them the difference between material action and spiritual action has been shown: "Material actions are those that are performed in connection with the physical man, whereas spiritual actions are those that are performed in connection with the spiritual man." Physical actions are gross and tangible. Spiritual actions are real but subtle. The purpose of material actions is to acquire some material comfort in the world. The aim of spiritual actions is to find the soul.

"By material actions (cleanliness, right diet, and proper worldly behaviour), the devotee purifies his body and makes it more harmonious for spiritual culture. But spiritual actions (dispassion to sense objects, love of soul, intuition, meditation), although intangible, are imperatively required to find the hidden power of the soul."

It may appear to a devotee that the Gita's emphasis on nonattachment means even nonattachment to the soul. That interpretation is not valid, because the misery-producing thorn of attachment to sensations can only be plucked out by the use of the sharp thorn of attachment to the divine love in the soul.

Lahiri Mahasaya often quoted the great *rishi* Ashtavakra's teaching: "If you want freedom from reincarnation, abhor sense pleasures as you would sugarcoated poison; and be as devotedly attached to acts of forgiveness, pity, contentment, love of truth, and God, as to drinking nectar!"

VERSE 21

यद्यदाचरति श्रेष्ठस्तत्तदेवेतरो जनः ।
स यत्प्रमाणं कुरुते लोकस्तदनुवर्तते ॥

Whatever a superior being does, inferior persons imitate. His actions set a standard for people of the world.

KNOWING THAT EXAMPLE SPEAKS louder than words, many masters, even after they have attained the Ultimate and thereby transcended the circumscriptions of cosmic imperatives, nevertheless continue to observe the rules of right conduct and constructive action as a proper criterion for well-intentioned but unadvanced worldly people.

By his mere presence one who has reformed himself is able to reform thousands, though he may not utter a single word. Like a rose, he diffuses his fragrance to all.

A man who has attained God could smoke or drink or eat meat, could marry and have children—all without losing his divine status. For the sake of setting an example, however, he would probably do none of these actions but would continue his ascetic conduct because asceticism is imperative for yogi-beginners. Persons of ordinary consciousness may reason: "Jesus drank wine and ate fish; therefore I will imitate those actions. I shall imitate his spiritual actions later!"

One who has reformed himself is able to reform thousands

How readily people imitate any worldly habit of a master, but must inevitably omit following his highest virtues if these are hidden in his soul and are not outwardly illustrated.

Untrained disciples may reason: "Master does this or that with no ill effects. He doesn't meditate regularly; therefore I needn't do so."

The disciple does not understand the spiritual state of a master: once a master is one with God he has attained the object of meditation and thus no longer requires that *sadhana*. The aspiring disciple enjoys no such exemption.

A devotee may say to himself, albeit perhaps unconsciously, "Why shouldn't I follow Master's actions rather than his words?" The Gita therefore reminds the "superior individual" to be careful for the sake of others, since his meditations and practice of good habits are really a series of demonstrations for those who follow him, or even for those who watch him from a distance or otherwise hear of him. Worldly people are as quick to misunderstand the outward actions of a master as they are slow to grasp his divine message!

Even though great masters sometimes ignore the rules established for novices, they can always prove to a true disciple that they are not attached to nor affected by any material habit. I often cite the story of the meat-eating saint who with equal ease consumed and digested molten nails to chasten his nonunderstanding vegetarian disciple.*

THE WORDS OF THIS STANZA of the Gita can also be interpreted as referring to powers rather than to persons. When the life force is withdrawn from the senses and transferred toward the brain, a sense of superior power ensues in which the inferior bodily sensations are dissolved. A yogi has learned that he must not keep the life force attached continually to the senses, or it will remain dictatorially habituated to

* See I:1, page 42.

the enjoyment of sensations. By ecstatic meditation he withdraws his life force to the superior path of spine and brain, automatically causing all the inferior senses to follow, that is, to be absorbed in the cerebral light. This experience occurs even in deep sleep, when all sensory perceptions are absorbed in the semiconscious enjoyment of the soul. In the very deep state of dreamless sleep, the life force is switched off completely from any subconscious cognition of the outer world. Tuned in with supreme Bliss, man's senses are revitalized, causing him to say upon awakening: "I had a wonderful sleep!"

Similarly, one can think of the mind as the superior force in the body. Whatever the mind sees and stresses will be blindly followed by the inclinations, moods, desires, and habits. They automatically put on the dominant habits and actions of the mind and reflect its salient traits. The supreme force of the mind must outwardly be kept busy in a routine of constructive actions even while it is inwardly united to the supreme Bliss. If the mind indulges in moods or anger, the senses will exhibit gloom or wrath; but if the mind is blissful, the senses too will register bliss.*

---

* "The mind, being the brain, feeling, and perception of all living cells, can keep the human body alert or depressed," Paramahansa Yogananda said. "The mind is the king, and all its cellular subjects behave exactly according to the mood of their royal master. Just as we concern ourselves with the nutritive value of our daily food menus, so should we consider the nutritive potency of the psychological menus that we daily serve the mind."

Norman Cousins, the noted editor of *Saturday Review* who taught at the UCLA Medical School, wrote: "What we put into our minds can be as important as what we put into our bodies. Attitudes have a great deal to do with health. Negative emotions, persisting over a long period of time, can impair the immune system, thus lowering the body's defenses against disease."

More than 1,300 scientific articles showing the influence of the mind on the immune system were published between 1976 and 1982, according to a bibliography compiled by Steven Locke, M.D., and Mady Horning-Rohan.

Bernard Siegel, M.D., Professor, Yale University School of Medicine, wrote in *Love, Medicine and Miracles* (New York: Harper and Row, 1986): "Other doctors' scientific research and my own day-to-day clinical experience have convinced me that the state of the mind changes the state of the body by working through the central nervous system, the endocrine system, and the immune system. Peace of mind sends the body a 'live' message, while depression, fear, and unresolved conflict give it a 'die' message."

"If one accepts that mind and body are inextricably linked, it comes as no surprise that optimists have the edge on health," Marian Sandmaier wrote in an article published in *Self-Realization* magazine. "Psychologist Martin Seligman reports that optimists catch fewer infectious diseases than pessimists do and are less susceptible to serious health problems in middle and old age. Perhaps the most impressive—and scariest—evidence comes from an ongoing fifty-year study of the health of two hundred Harvard men. Working with noted psychoanalyst George Vaillant and others, Seligman discovered that optimism at age twenty-five strongly predicted health at age sixty. Beginning

VERSE 22

न मे पार्थास्ति कर्तव्यं त्रिषु लोकेषु किञ्चन।
नानवाप्तमवाप्तव्यं वर्त एव च कर्मणि॥

O Son of Pritha (Arjuna), no compelling duty have I to perform; there is naught that I have not acquired; nothing in the three worlds remains for Me to gain! Yet I am consciously present in the performance of all actions.

"I AM THE COSMIC BEAM that creates the various dream pictures of life, not from any necessity, but from a desireless desire to express Myself as many dream forms. I am the Ultimate; nothing remains for Me to attain in My dream dramas, for nothing is outside of Myself. I continue, however, to produce My dream shows and to keep an active part in them, that My children, the individualized multiforms of My One Being, may similarly act in them as divine beings, and then return to Me in My dreamless home of eternal blessedness."

The Infinite is the Supreme Cause behind all causation, all cause-evolved objects. Krishna therefore says to the perplexed disciple Arjuna: "When you attain My consciousness you will discover that the Originating Spirit has no obligatory duty to perform. The threefold creation evolved from My mind as an intricately organized pleasure ground (*lila,* play of the Lord)."

God, popularly conceived as the omnific Creator and Ruler of the universe, appears thus to most men to be in eternal motion, or activity, only because they perceive creation through the delusory powers of the senses. The man of cosmic consciousness perceives God not only

---

around age forty-five, the pessimists begin to develop more diseases of middle age, and to suffer more severe symptoms, than did their more upbeat counterparts....

"The immune system simply can't withstand chronic gloom. In a large study of older Americans, his research team analyzed blood samples to find that pessimists actually had weaker immune activity than did optimists—regardless of their general state of health."

"The physical benefits of meditation have recently been well documented by Western medical researchers," states Dr. Siegel. "It tends to lower or normalize blood pressure, pulse rate, and the levels of stress hormones in the blood. It produces changes in brain-wave patterns, showing less excitability. These physical changes reflect changes in attitude, which show up on psychological tests as a reduction in the overcompetitive Type A behaviour that increases the risk of heart attack. Meditation also raises the pain threshold and reduces one's biological age....In short, it reduces wear and tear on both body and mind, helping people live longer and better." *(Publisher's Note)*

as a whirlpool of eternal motion but as the vibrationless infinitude of eternal joy.

The Infinite is divided into two: The vibrationless sphere of the Absolute—quiescent, unborn, self-contained, eternal; and the vibratory cosmos wherein Spirit dreams Itself into the many. As the universe is naught but God's dreaming consciousness, He is omnipresent therein, impartially witnessing and indirectly directing the ordered activity of creation as the Cosmic Intelligence (*Kutastha Chaitanya*), and actively giving birth to all forms through His Creative Consciousness (Nature or Prakriti). Similarly, all human beings made in the image of God have a vibrationless, blissful soul within; and also the soul's guiding intelligence, and its pseudonature as the ego active in the mind, vital forces, and bodily activities. Every human being ought to behave like the Spirit-image he is: transcendentally calm and locked in ecstatic bliss in his soul, and simultaneously active in the body without entanglement in delusive desires and their resultant karmic complications.

Learning to be transcendentally calm and simultaneously active

"The three worlds" refers to the triple cosmos: causal (mental), astral (energy), physical (matter). God created all matter mentally; then He manifested the causal ideas as an astral or energy universe; finally He precipitated the astral lifetrons into the forms of the visible universe. The *essential* nature of matter is thus the mind-stuff of God. By the law of relativity He differentiated mind, energy, and matter so that they seem divergent, different. They all are as real and as unreal as the substance of a dream. Through cosmic delusion God makes us aware of seeming differences among the three forms of vibration: consciousness, astral energy, and physical substance.

God knows the world as a creation of His mind; He has no hopes or fears about it. But He continues to act in and through it that by reminders of His innate Presence His deluded children, too, may realize that this universe is an ever to-be-continued cosmic cinema serial, not to be taken seriously as a reality, but to be viewed as an entertaining and educational spectacle.

Krishna encourages Arjuna to manifest his oneness with Spirit instead of indefinitely remaining a beggar, frustrated by unfulfilment, dissatisfied with paltry crumbs of pleasure and insults of pain. By divine unity the devotee understands that all things which belong to his Father belong also to him. He has regained the lost inward paradise.

"But," the Lord emphasizes, "even as I am nonattached to the cosmos and yet am present in every action, so each of My divine offspring must do some work to help My deluded creation and its mortals to come back home to Me." *All must work since the Lord of the cosmos has chosen to work.*

Because it is the Almighty's desireless will to work in everything as the Cosmic Intelligence, He realizes well that man and the vibratory life in all created atoms do not remember their oneness with Spirit. What misery! Human beings and all particles of nature are therefore being helped by God and by each liberated saint to regain their lost memory. In this intercession, we find God's sublime assurance that all souls who went forth from Him *will* return to Him. That is why, as the Divine Intelligence, He continues to work through man's conscience, and through the prophets, who rouse man to his heritage by such beautiful wisdom as Jesus expressed in: "Seek ye first the kingdom of God, and his righteousness; and all these things shall be added unto you."*

By using His unlimited soul force, God could act like a Cosmic Dictator and forcibly retire creation into Himself. But since He has given all men free choice to accept Him or to reject Him, He works secretly, and through His saints, sweetly to persuade alienated mortals to come back to Him.

VERSE 23

यदि ह्यहं न वर्तेयं जातु कर्मण्यतन्द्रितः ।
मम वर्त्मानुवर्तन्ते मनुष्याः पार्थ सर्वशः ॥

O Partha (Arjuna), if at any time I did not continue to perform actions, without pause, men would wholly imitate My way.

"I, THE CREATOR OF ALL THINGS in the vibratory cosmos, am ceaselessly working—bringing worlds into being; keeping them balanced by the laws of attraction and repulsion; throbbing in human intelligence, heart, and activity. Through My colossal example, and by My having given man compelling responsibility for a soul, mind, body, family, country, world—I am unmistakably telling him that there is no salvation without proper activity on earth.

* Matthew 6:33.

"All My human children—made in My image, and for whom I have built this ever-changing cosmic home—must perforce act, even as I do. In atoms, stars, and all creation I work ceaselessly, through My immanent intelligence, that all mortals be silently inspired and empowered to act intelligently and spiritually according to My cosmic plan. This plan has been revealed in scriptures by My illumined children who, attaining Me, know My wishes. If I upheld the universal structure, yet ceased to work in creation as the intelligent silent influence of goodness and righteousness, man, too, would cease to act rightly. Falling into degenerative sloth, he would neither progress himself nor help to promote the betterment of the world he lives in. He would be unable to come back to Me, because of a lack of active involuntary motion, through which I work to push him and all nature upward in progressive evolution, aided (when not hampered) by the choices of his free will.

"But if I, the Creator, ceaselessly work to serve creation with My intelligence and influence of goodness, then My reflections—human beings—will perforce continue to help My creation to its goal of perfection."

VERSE 24

उत्सीदेयुरिमे लोका न कुर्यां कर्म चेदहम्।
सङ्करस्य च कर्ता स्यामुपहन्यामिमाः प्रजाः ॥

If I did not perform actions (in a balanced way), these universes would be annihilated. I would be the cause of dire confusion ("the improper admixture of duties"). I would thus be the instrument of men's ruination.

GOD, AS THE CREATOR OF UNIVERSES, works immanently as the Universal Intelligence in matter and in human consciousness for the purpose of maintaining order while working out His cosmic plan. He says, "If I, the Father of all, did not act in creation, all universes would explode and vanish. My cosmic consciousness keeps the floating islands of planets swimming rhythmically in the cosmic sea. It is My intelligence as *Kutastha Chaitanya* that consciously holds all atoms together and keeps them working in coordination.*

"If I did not work through the lives of saints, balancing material duties with spiritual obligations, humanity, without the presence of exemplary lives, would lead unbalanced lives, be confused about their duties, and perish."

If God removed His cohesive Intelligence, all universes and beings would disappear from objectivity, just as the scenes and actors vanish from a screen when the light running through a film is shut off.

Without the Lord's secret but active intelligent guidance, utter confusion would arise among men; admixture of duties would be the result, causing ruination.

Many nonunderstanding people interpret the reference to "admixture" in this stanza of the Gita as a proscription against the mixing of castes or races. This interpretation reinforces blind orthodoxy and prejudice, and fosters division and strife. This verse does not support the caste system; nor does it refer to the admixture of ethnological races, on the basis of colour or on any other basis.

All human races and skin colours have come from one spiritual Father, God, and from the first created human parents. It is right, therefore, that spiritual siblings should acknowledge their divine kinship. God has created a charming diversity of humanity in the olive-coloured,

---

* A corresponding view of God's manifestation as an immanent omnipresent Intelligence in creation (the Hindu's concept of *Kutastha Chaitanya*—the Krishna or Christ Consciousness) is discussed in relation to the Bible by biophysicist Donald MacKay in *Science and Christian Faith Today* (London: CPAS Publishers, 1960):

"The Bible as a whole represents God in far too intimate and active relationship to daily events to be represented in mechanical terms. He does not come in only at the beginning of time to 'wind up the works'; He continually 'upholds all things by the word of His power' (Hebrews 1:3). 'In him (i.e., Christ) all things hold together' (Colossians 1:17)....It is not only the physically inexplicable happenings (if any), but the whole going concern, that the Bible associates with the constant activity of God....

"An imaginative artist brings into being a world of his own invention. He does it normally by laying down patches of paint on canvas, in a certain spatial order (or disorder!). The order which he gives the paint determines the form of the world he invents. Imagine now an artist able to bring his world into being, not by laying down paint on canvas, but by producing an extremely rapid succession of sparks of light on the screen of a television tube. (This is in fact the way in which a normal television picture is held into being.) The world he invents is now not static but dynamic, able to change and evolve at his will....The scene is steady and unchanging just for as long as he wills it so; but if he were to cease his activity, his invented world would not become chaotic; it would simply cease to be. The God in whom the Bible invites belief is...the Cosmic Artist, the creative Upholder, without whose continual activity there would be not even chaos, but just nothing." *(Publisher's Note)*

dark, yellow, red, and white races in order that man may solve the riddle of the apparent differences and please Him by forming a United States of the World.

Concerning castes, it may rightly be said that every nation has four castes or types. The four divisions are dependent on quality and have nothing to do with race or caste as these are understood today. As the Gita says elsewhere (IV:13): "According to the differentiation of attributes and actions (in man), I have created the four castes."

All human beings confined to a physical body inherit at birth the body-identified (*kayastha*) caste of Sudra. The two physical eyes reveal to man nothing but an outer world of duality. After spiritual initiation by a guru, a devotee learns to open his spiritual eye, and by cultivating wisdom he enters the caste of a Vaishya; and then by fighting the senses he rises to the higher caste of a Kshatriya. Eventually, attaining God-realization, he becomes a Brahmin (one with Brahman, Spirit).

❖
Four steps on the ladder of Self-realization, each characterized by ennobling duties
❖

In a material sense all nations recognize the natural divisions of castes, according to ability: viz., the labourers, the businessmen, the soldiers and rulers, the teachers and clergymen. A labourer can become a businessman or a soldier or a clergyman; therefore these four groups are interchangeable on the material plane.

The vested priesthood (not the sages) in India have fixed the four castes as noninterchangeable, in defiance of early Vedic teachings about natural and progressively interchangeable castes. Even today, however, a Hindu who adopts the religious path is considered "beyond caste": He receives from his guru a spiritual initiation in which he casts off his old self with all of its egoistic identifications of family, name, possessions, and desires, and receives a new "birth" and a new name that betrays no caste identification.

This stanza alludes to the "duties" or four states required in human evolution—four necessary steps on the ladder of Self-realization, each characterized by ennobling duties.

If Divine Intelligence ceased to work through the conscience of man, all human beings would remain engrossed in matter, confused and forgetful of the duties inherent in the four graded steps—material, wisdom-cultivating, sense-fighting, and Spirit-attaining—required for final emancipation.

The goal of all men should be to leave behind the painful material state and to reach successively the other three higher states of human consciousness. When wisdom arises in the soul, all human creative impulses retire into Spirit—there is no admixture of human nature with divine Nature!

VERSES 25–26

सक्ताः कर्मण्यविद्वांसो यथा कुर्वन्ति भारत।
कुर्याद्विद्वांस्तथासक्तश्चिकीर्षुर्लोकसङ्ग्रहम्॥ *(25)*

न बुद्धिभेदं जनयेदज्ञानां कर्मसङ्गिनाम्।
जोषयेत्सर्वकर्माणि विद्वान्युक्तः समाचरन्॥ *(26)*

(25) O Descendant of Bharata (Arjuna), as the ignorant perform actions with attachment and hope of reward, so the wise should act with dispassionate nonattachment, to serve gladly as a guide for the multitudes.

(26) Under no circumstances should the wise disturb the understanding of ignorant persons who are attached to actions. Instead, the illumined being, by conscientiously performing activities, should inspire in the ignorant a desire for all dutiful actions.

UNDEVELOPED MEN ARE HIGHLY motivated to act by their matter-inclined impulses and longing for name, fame, prosperity, and sensory happiness. The wise, on the other hand, have detached themselves from worldly pleasures; their incentive is the joy they find in working for God. Incidentally and yet purposefully, the inspiring examples of such men bring others to the path of lasting happiness. They set a right standard for all who are lower on the ladder of Self-realization.

An illumined being, above all law, has the preference of acting or of remaining inactive. Since God acts in creation even though it is unnecessary for Him to do so, He exhorts His devotees also to act, and to increase the desire for earnest action even in those whose work is still guided by innate material instincts. By activity, all beings are helping (mostly indirectly and unknowingly) to work out the divine cosmic plan.

If all the people of the world chose to renounce worldly life and to enter jungles to find God, cities would have to be built there too, and industries founded, or people would die of starvation, exposure, and epidemics. Final freedom must be found not in the avoidance of life's problems but by activity in the world with the sole purpose of working for God.

The Lord creates on a vast scale by forming universes; and in a detailed way in knitting atoms together and in creating a little ant's body, as delicately and carefully planned as a human form. But even though God is so mightily and tinily active in creation, He never loses an iota of His divine bliss. This constancy is possible solely because of nonattachment (lack of hopes and fears). The wise man, remembering that he is made in the image of God, does not act miserably, like the ignorant materialist, but acts in happy detachment.

Acts of creation are not necessary for the perfection of an already perfect God. Creation, therefore, is a "hobby" of God. He is blissful with it or without it. All His children must learn to work in the world with that same divine attitude of nonchalant interest. As a boy builds a playhouse and then tears it down, just to be busy playing, so man should keep busy in the world but be indifferent to all material changes—even to the destruction of his work by divine ordinance.

Man must learn to work in the world with a divine attitude of nonchalant interest

This does not mean that a poor man should not try to be prosperous nor that a restless man should not try to be calm, nor that a sick man should not try to be healthy. But man should look after his body and seek prosperity and mental health without any consequent violent agitation within. Jesus advised his followers to take no heed for their bodies, not to trouble about what they should eat or wear. He knew that they must feed and clothe themselves, even as he himself did, but he wanted them to understand that the way to supreme happiness lies in doing necessary material duties without attachment.

Only fools take life so seriously that they are constantly hurt. The wise look upon childhood, youth, old age, life, and death as passing dramas; hence everything entertains them. When one becomes momentarily identified with a tragic picture, he feels miserable; but when he realizes that it is only a part of an entertaining variety show, he feels happy. God wants man to behold the changing pictures of personal and worldly life as a sort of variety entertainment. Often at the end of a plotful melodrama the audience feels: "That was a good picture!"

The devotee should realize that God and His human children are the audience for ever-changing presentations in this Cosmic Cinema House, maintained for instruction and entertainment. As a man enjoys himself while he is beholding an engrossing picture and is especially interested if he learns something new, returning home happily when the show is over, so man should cheerfully perform both his simple and his difficult duties while on earth, leaving it with a smile when the drama of life is over. God happily creates and watches His ever-changing shows in different cosmic cycles, and, when complete dissolution comes, rests happily within Himself. He expects His sons to behave as He does.

The Gita repeatedly warns man against egoistic attachment to the changing scenes of life, since attachment is the root cause of all human suffering. Working because of an attachment becomes a necessity; and when that necessity is not fulfilled, man experiences misery.

Yet, the question in the ordinary man's mind is: "What is the sense in working without desire or attachment? It must be insipid to work without an incentive!"

The answer lies in a consideration of the things we do for pleasure, without thought of gain or fame. It is so much more enjoyable when one makes a garden of flowers and takes infinite pains just to satisfy a hobby than when he is compelled to tend that garden in order to eke out a living. Anyone can name many activities that are pursued for their own sakes rather than for gainful results. All duties performed under the compelling whip of material desire and attachment produce misery, but when they are worked out as a sort of hobby, without fear of, or craving for, specific results, the incentive endures, yielding pure pleasure.

The material man takes life seriously and *makes* it full of worries, sorrow, and tragedy. The divine man makes life an enjoyable game. The desire-infested man is full of mental ups and downs and mind-corroding moods, while the desireless yogi is evenly happy although he is variously active. There is no excuse for any man to live miserably, oblivious of his divine nature. If man could only work as happily as God does in the ever-changing creation, he would understand all of its anomalies as comparable to the complex variety of a motion picture designed only for entertainment free from monotony. Performing all actions with God-consciousness neutralises all inner and outer calamities.

Worldly man's life is full of worries; divine man makes life an enjoyable game

Therefore, as the materialist works untiringly for sense pleasures, which produce constant affliction, so the yogi works hard and unceasingly at meditation, which brings ultimate happiness. When the yogi, by working with subtler laws instead of sense attachments, attains oneness with Spirit, the Lord then exhorts him to continue to render proper service in the world, free of desire and attachment, to set an exemplary pattern for the inspiration and encouragement of others.

HOW EGOLESS ACTION FREES THE YOGI FROM NATURE'S DUALITIES AND THE BONDAGE OF KARMA

VERSE 27

प्रकृतेः क्रियमाणानि गुणैः कर्माणि सर्वशः ।
अहङ्कारविमूढात्मा कर्ताहमिति मन्यते ॥

All action is universally engendered by the attributes (gunas) of primordial Nature (Prakriti). A man whose Self is deluded by egoity thinks, "I am the doer."

A GOOD MONK DREAMING HIMSELF to be a businessman or a villain does not in reality become so. Similarly, man, a son of God, playing different parts in the divine dream drama, should not identify himself with any of the activities that are a part of his temporary mortal existence.

The delusion-drunk egotist deems himself the author and doer of his actions, knowing not that those activities are instigated by the attributes of Nature. Primordial Prakriti is the cause of man's individualized existence, and governs by the operation of cosmic laws his ability to act in and respond to his material environment.

God created Nature. It manifests the attributes of the Creator, but under a camouflage of delusion. Man is the product of invisible God and visible Nature; therefore he is dual—pure Spirit hidden in a physical body and brain whose functions are governed by the attributes of Nature (the three modes of Prakriti—*sattva, rajas,* and *tamas*—whose activating power works on the twenty-four creative principles of Nature).

The four kingdoms of creation—man, animals, plants, and the inorganic substances—possess fixed and characteristic actions and reactions that differentiate them. All alike are guided by the *gunas* (attributes) of Nature.

An average person lives from sixty to eighty years; his physical and mental habits are different from those, for instance, of a dog, which barks and wags its tail and lives only one or two decades; or of a redwood tree, which is rooted to the ground but which may live as long as four thousand years.

Man dwells on the apparent differences between himself and the rest of creation, ignorant of the truth that his activity and that of all other manifestations spring from a common source. The individualized Spirit, residing in every form and working through Nature's attributes, is the real Doer.

By disengaging his mind from the senses, man can identify himself with his soul and know that it, rather than the ego, is the conscious life in the body that activates and sustains the creative attributes. An intrinsic quality of the soul is free will; the fully illumined yogi is a man of free will. The brutish man is bound, almost like an animal, to his instincts or unthinking material habits bequeathed by Nature. The higher an individual rises in the scale of evolution, the more he exercises his soul prerogative of free will.

An awakened devotee realizes that all his human qualities are created by God, initiated in his individualized body by his soul, and governed by the confining attributes of Nature; he therefore refuses to let his body-engrossed ego deem itself the doer of actions.

Man, however, by the exercise of his free will, wrongly or rightly creates specific personal karma that modifies the influence on him of the universal or general environmental karma ordained by Nature. By his good karma, actions in consonance with Nature (natural living), and meditation on the perfect God, man ascends toward perfection; by evil actions, the body-bound egotist, devoid of true wisdom, descends and becomes trapped in the meshes of material desires.

Each devotee should analyze himself and find out whether he is living according to the upward evolutional influence of Nature, or by the even higher soul impulses, or only by his human nature, distorted by prenatal and postnatal effects of evil actions that manifest through habits, moods, and inclinations. When the sunshine of wisdom breaks upon the dark mind of the egotist, he realizes that the soul (the sole Life) is the performer of all actions, and not his unpredictable "individuality." The soul, or Spirit, is the only activator of the attributes.

The human machine has many parts. The cerebrum, cerebellum, and spinal plexuses are instigators of different forms of activity. The nose, eyes, ears, and other organs of sense and action are external instruments; the brain is the vehicle of thoughts and inner faculties. Mind (*manas*) has a hundred expressions; intelligence (*buddhi*) has five.

The mental clan (the Kurus, or offspring of Dhritarashtra, the blind sense mind) includes jealousy, fear, hate, greed, anger, attraction, repulsion, egotism, delusion, pain, pleasure, shame, envy, pride, repentance, worry, complacency, hope, desire, etc. Calmness, control of life energy, self-control, power to refrain from evil impulses, and power to act according to good inclinations are attributes of intelligence (the Pandus, offspring of Pandu or pure discriminative intelligence).

When man is influenced by the attributes of the sense mind, he is susceptible to pleasure and pain, heat and cold, and all other dualities. But when guided by intelligence to the soul regions, he finds himself swirling no more in the eddies of psychological relativities but safe on the shore of eternal bliss.

The egotist, conceiving himself as the doer of actions, makes a tragedy out of the melodrama of life. But by deep meditation he awakens and realizes that he has been assigned, by the Cosmic Director, a specific part on the stage of contemporary life. He is then happy to enact his role, whether joyous or doleful, large or small.

Soul, mind, body, brain, senses, the world, the cosmos—all are creations of Spirit. The wise man, not conceiving himself as the architect of anything (not even his own destiny), does not laugh or cry or disturb himself with the ups and downs of dualities. An egotist is never satisfied, be he rich, poor, a clerk, or king of the world. A divine man is happy, whether in a palace, a poor hut, or a monk's cell.

The wise do not laugh or cry over the ups and downs of dualities

The helpless kitten, dependent on the mother cat, is quite contented to be transferred from a king's palace to a coal bin. Similarly, a yogi whose being is surrendered to God does not mind whether his given role is that of a prince or pauper.

When Lord Krishna was among his devotees in Brindaban, he lived near the river Yamuna. The *gopis* (devotee milkmaids) often brought him his favourite food—fresh curds. Once, when the banks of the river were flooded, the devotees, laden with curd offerings for Krishna, could not get to their Master on the other side of the river. They noticed the great sage Vyasa sitting near the riverbank, his eyes gleaming with Krishna-intoxication. Knowing his divine power, the *gopis* requested his help.

"You want to give all that cheese to Krishna?" he inquired. "What about poor me?" So they set the offering before Vyasa, who ate and ate. The devotees began to worry; there seemed scarcely enough left for Krishna.

Vyasa rose to his feet and addressed the torrential river: "Yamuna, if I did not eat anything, divide and part!" To the *gopis'* ears the request sounded facetious. The Yamuna, however (as did the Jordan for the Israelites*), immediately separated itself into two walls of water, with a miraculous floor of dry land between. The astonished *gopis* entered the narrow path and safely reached the other shore.

But they did not find Krishna coming to greet them as usual; he was soundly sleeping. They wakened him; he looked at the cheese without interest.

"Master, what is the matter?" they asked. "Do you not crave curds today?"

Krishna smiled sleepily. "Oh," he replied, "that fellow Vyasa, on the other side of the river, has already fed me an overabundance of cheese!"

The *gopis* thus understood that Vyasa, while eating the curd, had been conscious only of his unity with the all-pervading Lord Krishna.

If men could feel God in their every action even as did Vyasa, they would be free from universal and individual karma; they would perform activities guided by divine wisdom and not by Nature-controlled egoism. To understand this stanza of the Bhagavad Gita one must live it in everyday life by thinking of God during the commencement, performance, and end of all actions.

VERSE 28

तत्त्ववित्तु महाबाहो गुणकर्मविभागयोः ।
गुणा गुणेषु वर्तन्त इति मत्वा न सज्जते ॥

O Mighty-armed (Arjuna)! the knower of truth about the divisions of the gunas (attributes of Nature) and their actions—realizing it is the gunas as sense attributes that are attached to the gunas as sense objects—keeps (his Self) unattached to them.

AS GOD IS BEYOND THE ATTRIBUTES of Nature and its multifarious activities, so the God-reflected individualized Self is above the senses and the objects perceived and coveted by them.

When a man in the process of dreaming becomes conscious that

* Joshua 3:14 ff.

he is dreaming, he is no longer identified with the phenomena; he is not affected exultantly or dolefully. God consciously dreams His cosmic play and is unaffected by its dualities. A yogi who perceives his real Self as separate from his active senses and their objects never becomes attached to anything. He is aware of the dream nature of the universe and watches it without being entangled in its complex but ephemeral nature.

The Bhagavad Gita in this stanza reiterates the fact that the knower of the Self (the devotee who has attained Self-realization) is Godlike in his attitude toward life. In his own small sphere he emulates the Lord, who created and lives in His active universe without being attached to its countless changes, and is thus free from all effects of cosmic actions or of cosmic objects. The furiously exploding atomic bomb of a sunlike star or the cold or heat in space cannot affect God. A body-engrossed man suffers from the depressed or inflated moods of his senses, from the extremes of cold and heat, and from the effects of earthly catastrophes. But he who knows his soul to be a true image of indestructible Spirit, and his body and the surrounding world to be clusters of organized atomic or lifetronic energy, is not affected in his spiritual nature any more than was Christ, who said: "Destroy this temple, and in three days I will raise it up."*

The illumined know themselves to be above the reach of the twenty-four Nature-attributes; they realize that the bodily senses must act according to the nature of the objects of sense perception that surround them. Since the senses and their objects all spring from the attributes of primordial Nature (Prakriti), a man of Self-realization does not deem himself the doer of any action, and therefore cannot be attached to any ensuing effect.

VERSE 29

प्रकृतेर्गुणसम्मूढाः सज्जन्ते गुणकर्मसु।
तानकृत्स्नविदो मन्दान्कृत्स्नविन्न विचालयेत्॥

The yogi of perfect wisdom should not bewilder the minds of men who have imperfect understanding. Deluded by the attributes of primordial Nature, the ignorant must cling to the activities engendered by those gunas.

---

* John 2:19.

PEOPLE OF DULL INTELLIGENCE, those who lack keen understanding, are inherently compelled by Nature to be engrossed in the performance of material duties. Illumined beings should not disturb the enactment of material duties by such persons, whose redemption lies through this evolutionary stage. Baldly told to embrace the principle of nonattachment to the world, unspiritual people would neglect their material duties. They would fall into sloth, offering their vacant minds as workshops of the devil.

This injunction of the Gita does not mean that a saint should not awaken people at all; they should be gradually roused, and instructed in higher principles only when they are receptive—when they begin to wonder about the mysteries of life, either as a result of introspective thinking or of worldly misfortune and material disillusionment.

After being told that the world is "false and meaningless," many staunch votaries of material duties become understandably discouraged, and often degenerate into a state of mental inertia (the dark *tamas* quality). A materialist who follows the active path is at least developing the second activating *rajas* attribute, and thus should not fall back to the lower strata of dark *tamas* qualities.

The wise, therefore, should not unsettle the imperfect understanding of the dull-witted, lest they cease their activities—the only means of their slow salvation—and remain undecided between heaven and earth, following neither the spiritual nor the progressive material path.

The materialist, after carrying the load of material duties—without a compensation of true happiness—begins of his own accord to think of cultivating divine qualities such as equanimity and calmness, and thereby starts a spontaneous introspection. It is at this juncture that wise men should strive to lift him to the higher strata of the good *sattva* attributes—discernment, meditation, and performance of actions without attachment.*

VERSE 30

मयि सर्वाणि कर्माणि सन्न्यस्याध्यात्मचेतसा।
निराशीर्निर्ममो भूत्वा युध्यस्व विगतज्वरः ॥

* "By three roads we can reach wisdom: the road of experience, and this is the most difficult; the road of action, and this is the easiest; the road of reflection, and this is the noblest."—*Confucius*

Relinquish all activities unto Me! Devoid of egotism and expectation, with your attention concentrated on the soul, free from feverish worry, be engaged in the battle (of activity).

SINCERE GOD-SEEKERS DO NOT RENOUNCE true duties or the proper activities necessary to perform them. They overcome egotism, which makes one responsible as the doer and as the receiver of good and bad karma. True devotees feel that since God created them, He alone is responsible for all their activities. They work for God without worrying, knowing it is He who is working through their soul faculties, as sensed in the depths of calm meditation.

Materialists who feel deserving of the fruits of actions, egotistically believing in their own leadership, create karmic bonds that entangle them in meshes of good and evil. Yogis, acting in attunement with God's will and ascribing to Him all actions and their fruits, make God responsible. In the performance of both worldly and divine duties, yogis thus remain unattached and free.

The actions of selfish men spring from desires born of ego hopes. The divine man works neither at the dictates of egotism nor at those of selfish desires; he is devoid of "I-ness," the idea of "I am the doer." Since he is working for God, he has no individual desires, nor does he hope to attain any material goal.

The Gita stresses the renouncement, repeated so often! of ego consciousness, material hopes, and desires, because these renew the roots of cancerous longings that devour the soul's peace. The roots of unfulfilled desires and frustrated expectations sprout into worries and misery-making reincarnations.

The enlightened man performs actions to please God, known to him as the sole Creator and Genesis of all activities, and tunes in with the wishes of God, who guides him to his proper activities. He does not try to frustrate the divine plan by selfish will, nor to impede its fulfilment by nonaction.

Vanquish the driving ego-inspired desires; enjoy the calm blissful Self

The true devotee says: "Lord, steer my boat of activity and meditation to the shore of Thy presence." Just as men nightly forsake all physical and mental activities to enjoy the pleasure of sleep, so the yogi relinquishes all desire for the fruits of his daily activities to enjoy the ecstasy of attunement with God. Without vanquishing the driving ego-inspired expectations and desires, the devotee cannot enjoy the consciousness of the calm blissful Self, as is felt in *Kriya Yoga* meditation, in which all material consciousness is automatically dissolved in the union of soul and Spirit. The material man is an ego, plus worries; the divine man is a calm soul, plus the eternal joy of Spirit.

The yogi not only relinquishes egotism during the all-surrendering union (yoga) of mind with Bliss in meditation, but during ordinary wakeful activity as well. In the highest state of ecstasy the yogi can remain united to Spirit even while working with mind and body to carry out the divine plan. By engaging with divine consciousness in all of his activities, the devotee is free of egoistic limitations during wakefulness, as is the ordinary man during sleep.

The Lord does not ask man to be without divine ambition, divine desires, or divine activities that lead to liberation, but rather to stop working under the influence of the manipulative ego, which casts the soul again and again, endlessly, into pits of reincarnations.

The Lord's macrocosmic cosmic consciousness guides all creation and its activities; one should not interfere with that liberating divine rhythm by following the dark counsels of egotism. Forsaking all selfish motives, expectations, and aims, the devotee should realize his unity with God, performing all activities as dictated by his intuitive perception of Divinity.

RIGHT ATTITUDE TOWARD ONE'S SPIRITUAL GUIDE AND SADHANA

VERSE 31

ये मे मतमिदं नित्यमनुतिष्ठन्ति मानवाः ।
श्रद्धावन्तोऽनसूयन्तो मुच्यन्ते तेऽपि कर्मभिः ॥

Men, devotion-filled, who ceaselessly practise My precepts, without fault-finding, they too become free from all karma.

HAVING GIVEN LOFTY COUNSEL on the requisites of nonbinding action for the attainment of salvation, the Lord now assures the devotee that even if his actions do not at once reach that standard, he will nevertheless make his way to freedom if he follows a prescribed *sadhana* with the right attitude—the firstborn quality of spiritual progress. God counts generously the merits of the devotee's heart and strivings!

Nominal followers, lacking in devotion, tend to justify their non-understanding by criticizing the wisdom-dictated disciplinary measures prescribed by a true guru. They miss their goal. Full devotion helps to instil greater effort into a student; it quickens his spiritual pace and clarifies his vision of the spiritual summit. Instead of finding fault with the guru or the path, a devotee's analytical power should be used in finding out his own hidden psychological blemishes.

Judge not others, judge yourself. Condemning others makes a man oblivious of his own faults, which therefore flourish unrebuked. Many individuals hide their own serious flaws behind a critical spirit; they may criticize others' tempers and quite overlook their own violent wrath! They cannot stand the painful operation of being themselves corrected.

Such persons expend their energy and intelligence on superficialities and so have neither time nor vitality left to concentrate on essentials. A critical person, for example, may point out the repetitions in the lectures or writings of a guru, or in a scriptural treatise, and concentrate on these with such zeal that he never realizes or profits by the colossal truths expressed in those repetitions. How else than by repetition can truth infiltrate the fixed notions of the human intellect! The Gita itself is a paradigm of repetition, but redundant never!

Could a Canadian, for instance, reach New York if he forever tarries, criticizing all the modes, vehicles, and pathways leading to that city, and never placing faith in any method of travel? To get to God the devotee should listen to a true guru who is able to supply a time-proven technique, such as *Kriya Yoga,* and with full devotion and uncritical spirit should follow him and practise the method.

When the devotee adopts the right course and follows it with the right attitude, the entanglements of good and bad karma will be gradually destroyed and final freedom achieved. Avoid or cast out such doubts and criticisms as: "This method is difficult"; or "Maybe it is incorrect"; or "It may be detrimental." If you are a student of Self-Realization, then with full devotion practise *Kriya Yoga,* and the increased life force coursing toward your brain will "cauterize" the seeds of all reincarnation-making good and bad karma grooved in the cerebrum and subconscious mind.

Faith in one's spiritual guide and loyalty to the *sadhana* he prescribes is not an implied license for the blind to lead the blind. Cult figures, themselves blind to truth, put out the eyes of reason in their adherents; leader and acolyte end up tumbling into the same ditch of ignorance.

I have often told the following story to illustrate this point: A charlatan pretending to be a master trained his followers to be implicitly obedient to him. One day, he seated himself pompously before his intent disciples. Raising his hand in blessing, he said, "I will show you the way to God provided you heed my instruction without question." (His teachings could scarce survive intelligent scrutiny!) The teacher demanded, "Do you promise, from this moment on, to follow me exactly?" Ready assent arose in a united chorus from his audience.

So the teacher began his instruction: "Sit upright." Two hundred followers immediately echoed: "Sit upright." At this unexpected answer the teacher looked around and frowned; the disciples, following their teacher exactly, also looked around and frowned. The disgusted teacher began to pray, but his every word came back to him from his obedient followers. Even a cough to clear his throat caused an epidemic of coughing among the audience. Now the teacher was angry. "Quiet, you fools! Don't cough, and don't imitate me." But his well-trained disciples happily shouted back: "Quiet, you fools! Don't cough, and don't imitate me."

No matter what the exasperated teacher said or did, his matchless disciples did likewise. Quite forgetting his position, he commanded, "This lunacy must stop!" He forcefully swung his palm with a resounding slap on the cheek of one of his thoughtless group. Unquestioningly, two hundred disciples followed suit, dealing stinging slaps to one another and to their master.

The teacher, now frantic to escape the idiot-automatons of his own creation, ran from their midst. In his unheeding haste, he jumped into a well to hide. His mindless disciples, obedient to the end, jumped into the well on top of him. They all, indeed, "went to heaven" together.

Misguided intelligence is a dangerous power; oblivious of truth it can lead to disaster. Intelligence wedded to intuition—the divine wisdom of the soul—can be compared to a kite flying high in the skies with its cord held skillfully by its owner. Intelligence divorced from intuition is like the haphazard flight of a kite whose guiding cord has been snapped. The true master teaches the disciple to open his inner eye of all-knowing soul intuition. The devotee who gives to that master and his teaching the devotion and uncavilling loyalty referred to in this Gita verse is thereby assured salvation.

VERSE 32

ये त्वेतदभ्यसूयन्तो नानुतिष्ठन्ति मे मतम्।
सर्वज्ञानविमूढांस्तान्विद्धि नष्टानचेतसः ॥

But those who denounce this teaching of Mine and do not live according to it, wholly deluded in regard to true wisdom, know them, devoid of understanding, to be doomed.

THOSE WHO DECRY THE WISDOM emanating from Spirit (as declared by the scriptures, by saints, and by soul intuition in divine communion), and who live disorderly lives, find all avenues of divine wisdom closed to them. Without understanding, the ignorant pursue the path to spiritual ruin.

Men who do not live according to the inner dictates of the meditation-born peace of the soul find themselves entangled with the sensory perceptions and objects of smell, sight, sound, taste, and touch. Thus confused, they lose the true sense of direction toward the Godward goal of life.

Numerous people, ridiculing the possibility of a final standard of truth, shut their minds to every spiritual pathway of escape; they slowly starve for lack of spiritual nourishment, and thus perish in a self-created prison of ignorance. Thinking the path of Self-knowledge painful or difficult, those who never travel on it lose all understanding and peace.

Intelligence is a complex, ever progressive force of consciousness by which objects and experiences of the phenomenal world are analyzed and explained. Intelligence was not given to man just for its own sake, as an instrument of cognizance, but for the purpose of discriminative thought and action for the nurture of soul wisdom. The powerful force of intelligence is wondrously good, provided it is not misused.

Right guidance of intelligence, reason, and logic

In tracing the evolution of intelligence in man, we find it has been generally developed for its own sake, to satisfy the pride and sense of accomplishment of the ego. Only the wise few have discovered and consciously nurtured the wisdom-producing intuition that lies hidden in the expression of intelligence. Reason carries with it the power of conviction derived from the instinctive intuition latent in it. If intuition is not awakened and fully operative, the conclusions of the reasoning intelligence may be erroneous. Thus it is that at first sight mathematically calculated syllogistic reasoning produces in man a sense of conviction. But unless there is a means of comparing it to truth, its possible fallacy may not be detected. The syllogism itself may be perfect in its adherence to the rules of logic, but by the standard of truth, it may be useless. Syllogisms that not only correctly conform to the laws of logic but also inculcate the doctrines of truth are intrinsically valuable to mankind.

Truth endures, false intelligence disappears. Wonderfully reasoned-out books that are inimical to the laws of truth may for a period in cosmic time attract public support, but in the end they cannot stand the test of time. The works of mighty intellects can be dazzling to the eye of mankind's imagination, but if not founded in truth they are like fireworks that amaze the beholder but fade quickly.

Intellectual giants, masters of many languages, veritable walking libraries of knowledge and deductive philosophy, but who are devoid of the help of clear-eyed intuition, have a deluded intelligence—functional on the plane of relativity, but obstructive to divine wisdom. Hence, the development of intelligence should not be left without the guide of intuition. The more the intelligence is made complex, diluted and broadened by the rationalizations of delusion, the less its depth and focusing power in discovering the true nature of things and of one's Self. But when by meditation and devotional practice of divine teachings the soul's intuition begins to guide the development of intelligence, it is then that delusion instead of wisdom is doomed to destruction.

VERSES 33–34

सदृशं चेष्टते स्वस्याः प्रकृतेर्ज्ञानवानपि।
प्रकृतिं यान्ति भूतानि निग्रहः किं करिष्यति॥ *(33)*

इन्द्रियस्येन्द्रियस्यार्थे रागद्वेषौ व्यवस्थितौ।
तयोर्न वशमागच्छेत्तौ ह्यस्य परिपन्थिनौ॥ *(34)*

(33) Even the wise man acts according to the tendencies of his own nature. All living creatures go according to Nature; what can (superficial) suppression avail?

(34) Attachment and repulsion of the senses for their specific objects are Nature-ordained. Beware the influence of this duality. Verily, these two (psychological qualities) are one's enemies!

EVEN A WISE MAN—not to speak of ordinary individuals—finds his senses governed by his general nature, or inherent tendencies. That is, the senses, in accordance with habits formed through previous prenatal and postnatal actions, feel compelling attraction to certain things and are repulsed from others. The basic behaviour and character of all living things are determined by the laws of Nature, most specifically by mass karma, or the universal cause-effect principle. But each man is additionally subject to his previous *individual* karma, which determines his own characteristic moods, inclinations, and habits that govern his thoughts and actions. A superficial suppression, or mere restraint on external effects, will not suffice to alter the course of Nature's laws.

Since attachment and repulsion to objects of the senses are the result of man's self-created karmic inclinations, and are the cause of his bondage, these dual obstructions in the path of liberation must be removed. Man should be governed by wisdom, and not by prejudiced moods and habits ruled by the dictators of attraction and repulsion. Torturing the senses—as in protracted fasting to control greed, or in lying on a bed of nails to remove the desire for a comfortable mattress, or extreme suppression of strong inclinations—will not bring liberation from the underlying desires, which are fed by obstinate previously acquired impulses.

This whole universe is governed by the laws of karma; no one can escape them by crude force. Only by gradually taming the senses through wisdom-guided sense experience and by self-control can man be free from identifying himself with attachments and repulsions.

A lover of truth under no circumstance should imitate the bond-slave of the senses, who is unwilling even to fight for freedom. The sincere devotee must never slacken in his efforts to overcome all impulses of sensory attachment or aversion.

Understanding how likes and dislikes colour one's perception

The soul, as a perfect image of Spirit, is ever contented. The pseudosoul or ego of the body-identified individual is never satisfied. Enslaved by the attachments and aversions of the senses, the diversified mentality of the ego fails to perceive the eclipsed unconditioned bliss of the soul. To avoid this calamity, the natural, or habit-created, dual inclinations of the senses are to be shunned, thus preventing a blackout of the inner divine bliss.

The ego gazes through the Nature-created reddish-dark spectacles of attraction or repulsion, so everything appears as red and gloomy (the "colours" of *rajas* and *tamas*). By turning away the vision from the senses and their natural limitations, the wise devotee perceives within his soul the constant luminescent happiness.

Those who practise spiritual exercises regularly but not deeply will encounter both satisfactory and unsatisfactory experiences. While meditating on the Cosmic Sound, they may hear it clearly and feel its vibratory power and peace; or they may experience little or no manifestation at all. They may see the spiritual eye clearly, or only dimly. According to their experiences of the moment, they alternate between attachment and aversion to meditation. This attitude leads to spasmodic efforts—to deep meditation after glorious results, and to relaxation of attention when good results are not forthcoming.

The earnest devotee must not indulge in these retarding longings for and aversions to meditation. Ardent consistency in spiritual effort is necessary. Otherwise, the senses will all too often impose the "second nature" of the dual psychological sensory conflicts that prevent Self-realization.

"Natural" inclinations in man—that is, inclinations born of his material nature—are fundamentally unnatural for soul perception. For this reason Jesus pointed out that while it is "natural" for men to seek bread and earthly goals, the wise *first* seek the truly native kingdom of spiritual happiness. "And seek not ye what ye shall eat, or what ye shall drink, neither be ye of doubtful mind. For all these things do the nations of the world seek after: and your Father knoweth that ye have need of these things. But rather seek ye the kingdom of God; and all these things shall be added unto you."*

VERSE 35

श्रेयान्स्वधर्मो विगुणः परधर्मात्स्वनुष्ठितात्।
स्वधर्मे निधनं श्रेयः परधर्मो भयावहः ॥

One's own duty (svadharma), though deficient in quality, is superior to duty other than one's own (paradharma), though well accomplished. Better it is to die in svadharma; paradharma is fraught with fear and danger.

---

* Luke 12:29–31.

MAN'S FIRST AND HIGHEST obligation is to follow those righteous principles and actions pertinent to the unfoldment of the Self (*Sva*). Even if one is presently devoid of adequate qualifications for perfect performance of divine duties, it is far better to die with the good karma of spiritual effort that moves him nearer to his goal than to spend life in egoistic bondage to opposite (*para*) duties that are imposed on man by Nature, and which thus cater to sensory satisfactions. No matter how well accomplished, material goals, unlike spiritual attainments, are fraught with inevitable disappointments and sorrow—all the fears and dangers inherent in a life lived in ignorance of the true Self.

An obvious, practical interpretation of this verse is that one should analyze his continuous inner urge, or consult a divine guru, to diagnose his past karmic impulses, to find out the life to which he is most suited. That path will bring him more lasting satisfaction than will his performance of perhaps nobler duties for which he is unsuited, even if accompanied by momentary success.

Comparison of one's own simpler duties with another's colossal duties is not wise, for one may be tempted to forsake his own self-evolving duties and try unsuccessfully to adopt difficult duties of others for which he is ill-fitted, and thus lose out in every way.

Of course, one should try to better his karmic condition (the accumulated effects of past actions) rather than surrender passively to an ill "fate." But one should not run from those karmically imposed duties that place before him lessons that are essential to his self-evolvement. Shirkers merely delay and multiply the inevitable consequences of delusive behaviour, which can be neutralised only by dutiful action, wisdom, and God-contact.

On the basis of this general interpretation, this verse is often quoted in support of the duties assigned to man according to his caste. It is valid insofar as "caste" is understood as man's natural self-evolving propensities (as discussed in II:31 and III:24), not as the circumscriptions of his class heritage at birth.

Deeper meaning of svadharma—one's natural duty

The deeper meaning of this verse, however, is that *svadharma* ("soul's duty") signifies the spiritual duty necessary for the realization of the Self (*Sva*). *Para,* in *paradharma,* means "opposite; another (different from one's self); enemy or adversary." That which is opposite of and inimical to the true Self or soul is the sense-identified ego. The Lord adjures the devotee that it is better to die trying to develop spiritually, even if results are not immediate or spectacular, than to follow the momentarily joyous life of the senses (greed, avarice, attachment, egotistic desire for name and fame—the revolting enemies of man's true happiness).

He is a superior being, though he remain unheeded and unknown, who follows the simple virtues of life and the path of calm meditation that slowly but steadily unveil the soul, compared to one who pursues well-performed spectacular worldly duties catering to the senses, or who performs superficial ceremonious religious duties. It is better to lead a quiet life that is brightened by daily meditation than to pursue the sensual worldly life that seems attractive and engaging for a time, but in the end proves fatal to soul realization.

The consciousness of soul, the true substance of the Self, is individualized ever-existing, ever-conscious, ever-new Bliss. The pseudosoul, ego or *ahamkara,* is identified with twenty-four ever changeable attributes of Nature. The nature of the Self, perceiving Spirit, is bliss; the nature of the ego and the senses, manifesting Nature's attributes, is ever-changing excitement. Man should concentrate on the immutable divine bliss of the soul and not on the mutating ignorant perceptions of the inimical senses.

The neutralization in *Kriya Yoga* meditation of the good, bad, and activating qualities of Nature harmonizes the natural attributes in man. He then manifests the true Self, beyond the entanglements of the threefold qualities and their twenty-four attributes.

Owing to the mind's running in all directions, meditation is difficult for the beginner. Yet to strive labouriously to attain bliss is far superior to obtaining promptly and easily the pleasures of the senses. When the difficult way is persistently followed, the devotee will eventually succeed. By ecstatic meditation he can then rise above all bodily limitations to infinite bliss—a far better outcome for man than is an indefinitely prolonged ride on the dangerous Ferris wheel of births and deaths.

CONQUERING THE TWO-SIDED PASSION, DESIRE AND ANGER

VERSE 36

अर्जुन उवाच
अथ केन प्रयुक्तोऽयं पापं चरति पूरुषः ।
अनिच्छन्नपि वार्ष्णेय बलादिव नियोजितः ॥

Arjuna said:
O Varshneya* (Krishna), by what is man impelled, even against his will, to perform evil—compelled, it seems, by force?

EVERY MAN SOMETIMES EXPERIENCES a peculiar state: even as he strives toward virtuous action, he seems to be dragged into temptation, almost by force.

The businessman trying to carry on an honest business, and finding dishonest tradesmen more prosperous than himself, is often so strongly tempted to follow their example that he says he is "forced" to do so.

Many a moralist trying to control the strongest mental and physical impulse created by Nature—the sex impulse—finds his mind driven, seemingly automatically, to sex thoughts and sex desires, and consequent illicit sex acts.

Attraction to pleasant tastes and odours, or even to beauty, art, and music, may harmfully lure the strict ascetic who wants to rise above them and concentrate on self-control.

During meditation and practice of *Kriya Yoga,* the devotee finds his mind concentrated in the spiritual eye and in the joy of the Self, beyond the entanglements of sensations and thoughts, with no other longing than to remain locked within that peace. Suddenly, without warning, he discovers he has been dragged down, as it were, by some mysterious force—thrown into a mire of restlessness and the dark consciousness of corporeal sensations. Instead of remaining in the motionless perception of the blessed soul, he seems impelled to forsake

---

* An epithet of Krishna, referring to a descendant of the Vrishni dynasty of the Yadava race.

that state and indulge in sensory-motor activities that aggravate bodily consciousness.

The businessman, the moralist, the ascetic, and the devotee therefore ask the common question, introspectively: "Why is it that I am compelled, as though by force, and against my resisting wish, to commit error in thought and deed?"

Repeated performance of good or bad actions forms good or bad habits. Habits are psychological automatic machines that enable man to perform actions without conscious effort. To be able to perform good actions under the compelling influence of habit is beneficial, because good habits make easy the performance of good actions. The psychological machine of a good habit can create good activities by mass production. Without the automatic power of a worthy habit, a fresh difficult effort has to be made each time one strives to perform a good action.

It follows, then, that the devotee should never form any evil habit, lest it enslave his will. To use the mechanical power of a habit in doing undesirable acts is misusing this God-given law of mind: "Ease comes with repetition." This law should be used only to ease the performance of good works. Bad habits are destructive to health, morality, and inner peace. Overeating, for instance, or overindulgence of any sense under the spell of the habit of greed, causes physical disease or mental satiety or inner unhappiness.

According to its training, a parrot will repeat a holy name or a vile epithet, anytime, anywhere. So the bird should be taught to utter only good words, otherwise there will be embarrassing moments before select company! A bad habit, like an evilly taught parrot, repeats evil against one's will any moment, anywhere—and brings humiliation and misery.

Regarding Arjuna's query to Krishna, it can be said that people misuse the coercive power of habit to perform evil, while they should use that force only to perform good. Ignorance, lack of watchfulness, want of discretion in selecting right actions, and carelessness in choosing proper friends often entrap a person in a quicksand of bad habits that draws him down against his will. The influence of constant association is usually stronger than that of judgement or will power. Good or bad company is more potent than one's inner resistance. The devotee who has noticed this fact might be moved to ask: "Why is it, Lord, that saints so easily act nobly, while wicked persons seem to be forced to act malevolently?"

Lord Krishna travelled to the Kurus' capital city to attempt a peaceful reconciliation one last time before war began. He offered the solution that an equable compromise would be to restore half the kingdom to the Pandavas. The avaricious Duryodhana rebuffed this suggestion—despite the entreaties of his parents King Dhritarashtra and Queen Gandhari (centre), his teachers Drona (seated to the left of the throne, with his son Ashvatthaman standing behind) and Kripa (standing, far left), and his grandsire Bhishma (standing, left foreground). Encouraged by Duhshasana and his other evil Kuru brothers (right), Duryodhana shouted: "I will not give back one village; I will not give back one inch of the kingdom; I will not give back so much land as will fit on the point of a needle!"

❖

"Duryodhana represents Material Desire...which wields power over all the other sense inclinations of the bodily kingdom.... Material desire is extremely powerful, for it is the king and leader of all worldly enjoyments, and is the cause and perpetrator of the battle against the soul's rightful claim to the bodily kingdom."

❖

"Coercive materialistic desire is the instigator of man's wrong thoughts and actions. Interacting with the other forces that obstruct man's divine nature—influencing as well as being influenced by them—lustful desire is the consummate enemy. The perfect exemplar is Duryodhana, whose unwillingness to part with even an inch of sensory territory or pleasure was the cause of the war of Kurukshetra. Only little by little, with fierce determination in battle, could the Pandavas win back their kingdom."

—Paramahansa Yogananda

A person is free to choose between good and bad actions before his inclinations solidify into habits. Once he becomes used to good or evil, he is no longer free.

"The diminutive chains of habit are seldom heavy enough to be felt until they are too strong to be broken."* Some people form habits more easily than others. A person who is despondently ill or weak-willed or mentally deficient will fall readily into bad habits. In the subconscious mind of a moron, for instance, one act of smoking may form the seed of a habit. Even a devotee who is not easily influenced must guard against the unconscious creation of bad habits. If he has already been poisoned by a bad habit he should cure himself by continuously using the antidote of good actions, good habits, and good company. Strange it is! often a person—even while loathing his own actions—finds himself indulging in anger, lust, prevarication, dishonesty, overeating, sloth, disorderly life, and so on, owing to his careless creation of bad habits.

Bad habits of past lives appear as strong moods and octopus-like inclinations whose tentacles are strengthened by evil company and thoughtless actions. Wrong tendencies should be curtailed by man's seeking good company and practising self-control; and he should wholly consume those evils with the fire of discrimination and meditation.

Verse 37

श्रीभगवानुवाच
काम एष क्रोध एष रजोगुणसमुद्भवः ।
महाशनो महापाप्मा विद्ध्येनमिह वैरिणम् ॥

The Blessed Lord said:

Born of the activating attribute of Nature (rajo-guna), it is desire, it is anger, (that is the impelling force)—full of unappeasable craving and great evil: know this (two-sided passion) to be the foulest enemy here on earth.

While habit is the automatic force that impels man to act even against his will (see III:36), the root cause of compulsive action is the Nature-instigated delusive duo of desire and its corollary of anger, or

* Samuel Johnson.

frustrated desire. Desires are silken threads of material pleasures which the spider of habit continuously spins around the soul to form the shrouding cocoon of ignorance. The soul must manage to cut through this stifling cocoon of ignorance to reemerge as the butterfly of omnipresence. Voracious desire and frustration spring from Nature's activating quality, which spawns illimitable variety and enticement, exciting man into indiscriminate, habit-forming actions. Since this pair binds man to a world of illusions and quite destroys his ability to recollect his true omnipresent nature of all-satisfying divine bliss, there can be no fouler foe than this.

The soul of man, identified with conditioned physical existence, forgets its divine heritage of unconditional, all-fulfilling bliss, and as ego it starts walking toward an ever-receding mutable mirage of desires. Soon man is burning with the thirst of unfulfilment. Obstructed desire then turns for support to its ugly brother-companion we call anger.* The longer one travels with unfulfilled desire through the desert of delusion (*maya*), the more acute his thirst for new oases of fulfilment. Unhappy, disillusioned, angry, unappeased, he is scorched with a heat of unending lusts.

❖
How desire and anger bind man to world of illusions
❖

Beset by delusive desires, man wanders ever farther from the blissful heaven within. He tries to cross the endless ever-burning sands of dissatisfaction, seeking waters of happiness in the wastelands of droughty longings instead of in the well of peace that can be uncovered by meditation.

Both material desires and anger are created by man while he is incarnate on earth, working under the activating influence of the *rajas* quality of nature. This activating quality produces in man the desire for pulsating change. The soul, having descended into the senses from the sphere of unvaried calmness, becomes feverishly active with desire, anger, and habits arising from actions, and thereby finds itself identified with the body, the fluctuating mind, material environment, moods, and inclinations inherited from the past or recently acquired.

The soul itself is motionless unfluctuating bliss. But once man has wilfully wandered into the activating attributes (*rajo-guna*) he becomes the ego, and goes unwillingly whirling, swirling, blindly struggling in a whirlwind of ever-revolving desires. The wise devotee will not leave his inner oasis of spiritual poise for the swirl of destructive change.

Matter is imperfect at best, being but the shadow of Spirit. Constantly mutating material vibrations can never reflect the unchanging

---

* See I:9: Allegory of Duryodhana (desire) and his brother Duhshasana (anger).

bliss of Spirit. It is only by looking beyond the alternating pale light of good and the darkness of evil that one beholds the Divine Sun.

Desire and anger can never be appeased by fulfilment, not even by control over all matter. Every material desire leads man farther away from bliss, delaying his task of finding the way back to his native state of absolute peace. The unfulfilled longing of desire and the obstructed longing of anger, therefore, are disastrously inimical to the recovery of bliss. Lord Krishna warns that this duo-force is man's great enemy.

VERSE 38

धूमेनाव्रियते वह्निर्यथादर्शो मलेन च।
यथोल्बेनावृतो गर्भस्तथा तेनेदमावृतम्॥

As fire is obscured by smoke, as a looking glass by dust, as an embryo is enveloped by the womb, so it (wisdom) is covered by this (desire).

THE BLISSFUL WISDOM-NATURE of the soul is enveloped and obscured by the impelling and often wrathful force of desire in one whose consciousness is identified with the attributes of Nature. By the commanding influence of the three qualities (*triguna*) of Nature through which desire expresses itself, the concealment of the blissful soul wisdom is of varying degrees, comparable to the progressively grosser coverings produced by smoke, dust, and the density of the womb.

The soul is bedimmed by any relativity, whether of the good, active, or evil modes of Nature. Influenced by environmental attributes, the soul succumbs to desire and adopts the guises of Nature. When the soul's pure nature is hidden behind sattvic (good) attributes—as a fire is covered by smoke—the smoke screen is easily dispersed by a strong breeze of discrimination. Even through this screen the soul's dazzling bliss can be slightly perceived, though in a distorted way. The devotee looks beyond good attributes, distinguishing their paleness from the brilliance of the soul. Goodness gives a semipermanent mental happiness, but soul realization imparts unending, changeless bliss.

When the rajasic (activating) qualities dim the soul's splendour—as dust obscures a mirror—one needs the cloth of continuous right effort to wipe off the ever cumulative covering of selfish, desire-producing activities. In other words, it is more difficult to remove the thick rajasic layer of restless, active, selfish desires from the soul than it is to disperse the smoke of sattvic qualities.

When the tamasic (evil) attributes are paramount, the soul is as hampered and darkened and hidden as an embryo in the womb. It is very difficult to release it from the desires of the tamasic qualities of ignorance and sloth.

VERSE 39

आवृतं ज्ञानमेतेन ज्ञानिनो नित्यवैरिणा।
कामरूपेण कौन्तेय दुष्पूरेणानलेन च॥

O Son of Kunti (Arjuna)! the constant enemy of wise men is the unslakable flame of desire, by which wisdom is concealed.

WOOD SUSTAINS FIRE; the flame vanishes with the exhaustion of the fuel. Similarly, sense pleasures sustain the fire of material desires that hide any view of the soul. When a sense pleasure is exhausted, the fire of longing ceases for a moment. But, owing to a lack of knowledge as to the nature of inflammable desires, the foolish man soon adds more fuel of sense indulgence; the raging fire continues to obscure wisdom. While such stupidity continues, a man never finds the peace of lasting satisfaction; he momentarily wakes up to this fact only when his longings are thwarted. He doesn't realize the consuming power of desires because his sense of discrimination is paralysed. Thus desire is the hail-fellow-well-met companion of the foolish man; the wise man knows desire to be a relentless foe.

There are two types of wise men. Rare on earth is the fully liberated man; realizing that all is Spirit, he becomes one with the Infinite. Such a being manifests this divine oneness by complete self-mastery. He can at will withdraw his life force and consciousness from matter, senses, sensory and motor nerves, muscles, heart, spine, and the seven subtle cerebrospinal centres into Spirit. While remaining immutably established in this divine union, he can return life and consciousness to the body so that he walks, works, and meditates from that plane of wisdom, yet is untouched inwardly by any circumscription or illusion of Nature.

The second type is one who, after realizing his oneness with Spirit, then centres his consciousness in the spiritual eye. He works through the third-eye plane in which he is still partially identified with the psychological and sensory phenomena of his body. Wise men of this class are occasionally subject to the wisdom-hampering flames of inimical desires, but never fail to recognize and thwart them, owing to the constant vigilance of inner introspection.

The liberated man transcends bodily consciousness and works from Spirit. The partially uplifted wise man works through his discrimination and the intuitive guidance received from concentration on his spiritual eye. But the worldly man's mind and life activities are centred in the lumbar, sacral, and coccygeal centres, which are identified with the gross senses and material desires. So the devotee should ever strive to keep his mind concentrated not on centres of taste, touch, sight, smell, or hearing, but in the forehead—the seat of the spiritual eye and of discrimination that empowers self-control.

The materialist is identified with the body surface and is goaded to action by sense temptations. The wise man watches and governs his mind processes with discrimination and self-control. The sensual man does not realize the destructive power of desires; he embraces them and is consumed by them, like an insect that is burned by its attraction to a flame. The thinking, watchful devotee is conscious whenever even a slight spark of malevolent desire starts to spread in the huge timbers of inner wisdom; he puts out the fire of desire at its first tantalizing flicker.

VERSE 40

इन्द्रियाणि मनो बुद्धिरस्याधिष्ठानमुच्यते ।
एतैर्विमोहयत्येष ज्ञानमावृत्य देहिनम् ॥

The senses, mind, and intellect are said to be desire's formidable stronghold; through these, desire deludes the embodied soul by eclipsing its wisdom.

THE BLISSFUL SOUL IS PERFECT WISDOM, knowing all things by intuition —direct perception without any instrumental intermediary. In its embodied consciousness, however, the soul works through the instruments of senses, mind, and intellect. These provide the medium of exchange between the perceiving soul and its bodily encasement and the objects of its external environment. Contact of the senses with the objects of the senses is made possible by the operation of the mind, which receives incoming impressions and relays outgoing impulses. These are cognized and interpreted and guided by the action of the intellect. The result of this communication between the soul and matter is an enjoyment and attachment that rouses a responsive feeling—desire. The excitation of desire causes the consciousness to become increasingly dependent on and identified with the gross instruments of perception and expression. In this way, desire deludes the external consciousness of the soul by obscuring its expression of wisdom, deriving from direct perception of truth, with mere inferential conceptions born of the interacting forces of Nature. With the support of the deluded consciousness (the pseudosoul or ego), desire becomes firmly ensconced in the senses, mind, and intellect. It finds in these instruments a perfect citadel wherein it can reign and wield its power in totalitarian authority throughout the bodily kingdom and its activities.

Intellect, mind, and senses —a triune receptacle for desire

The five instruments of action (speech, hands and feet, rectal and genital muscles) and the five instruments of knowledge (sight, hearing, smell, taste, and touch) are manipulated by the subtle powers of the senses. Psychological acts of perception, cognition, meditation, determination, self-control, and so on, are performed by the mind and intellect. Intellect, mind, and senses, being instruments of Nature, are a triune receptacle for desire, the outcome of the enjoyment of Nature. Wisdom, in greater or lesser degree according to how densely it is veiled by Nature's forces, also manifests through these three. Desire and wisdom thus constantly battle within this castle. Material desires should be driven from the inner fortress of the senses, mind, and intellect, and wisdom established there.

Meditational experience reveals that desire cannot exert its influence beyond the spiritual eye of concentration centred in the forehead, because thoughts dissolve in its powerful light; divine wisdom, however, whose source is in the soul, soars beyond the inner eye and through the cerebral centres into infinitude, circumventing all bodily limitations.

When the devotee concentrates on the sunlike rays of wisdom, the resultant power unfolds the omniscient, omnipresent lotus petals of the soul. Desire, on the other hand, befogs the inner vision with a dark veil of ignorance. In the all-pervading inner light, the yogi beholds with equal clarity the boundless territory of Cosmic Consciousness and the confinements of cosmic delusion. When the mind, intellect, and senses are wet with the waters of material desires, then, like water-soaked matchsticks, they fail to produce the spark of wisdom when called upon for light. The soul is then obscured beneath the darkness of desires, and sheds no outward illumination.

In the initial state, during meditation and afterward in the performance of activities, the yogi is still engrossed in the consciousness of body and matter, and does not perceive the cosmic beam from which they emanate. With open eyes the neophyte yogi perceives material vibrations, and with closed eyes he beholds darkness (absence of material vibrations); hence, in both these states he is under the spell of delusion.

But when the advanced yogi meditates deeply with closed eyes and dissolves his sense perceptions and thoughts in pure intuitive experience, he is able to behold the auric sun rising out of the surrounding gloom. With this meditational flame of wisdom, the devotee can stave off new desires and "cauterize" his pristine prenatal and habitual postnatal desires. When the veil of delusion is removed by this deep meditation, he beholds himself not as a body but as an omnipresent being. In ecstatic awakening, the dark body-dream of the soul disappears as the soul realizes its oneness with omnipresent Spirit. The awakened soul, finding the absolute completeness of Spirit within itself, laughs at its ridiculous desires of incarnations in which so many times the Self, a prince of infinity, had impersonated a mortal beggar.

VERSE 41

तस्मात्त्वमिन्द्रियाण्यादौ नियम्य भरतर्षभ ।
पाप्मानं प्रजहि ह्येनं ज्ञानविज्ञाननाशनम् ॥

Therefore, O Best of the Bharata Dynasty (Arjuna)!* first discipline the senses, then destroy desire, the sinful annihilator of wisdom and Self-realization.

SENSE ACTS CREATE SENSE HABITS. Sense habits create sense desires. Sense desires create sense acts. This vicious circle is to be avoided. So the temporarily charming catering-to-the-senses acts must be stopped, first by discriminating and staying away from the objects of temptation, then by using the fire of wisdom to destroy the inner tendencies toward temptation.

---

* *Bharata-rishabha:* lit., "Bull of the Bharatas," meaning the highest or best, or prince, of the descendants of Bharata.

The self-disciplined devotee who does not enslave himself to the inordinate demands of, for instance, his gustatory servant, the appetite, finds that his desire for food remains normal, obedient to his wisdom. But if he indulges in a constant desire to eat, an unnatural state is created in which the evil desire is repeatedly fed by fresh acts of greedily swallowing food.

The greater one's sense indulgence, the more urgent and increasing the desire to cater to the senses. As the sense desires increase, like tenacious weeds they choke the growth of the healing herbs of discrimination and meditation-born Self-realization. Matter exists without; Spirit within—the former exists opposite the latter. As the sensuous desire to look without increases, the discriminating desire to look within decreases. The concentration on sense temptation automatically destroys the vision of Spirit, simply because they exist in diverse spheres; the paths to matter and Spirit lie in opposite directions.

To find freedom from the enslaving power of the senses, the greedy, angry, sensual individual first must avoid the material environment that easily excites his specific psychophysical weakness, and then must kill the inner desires that will otherwise accompany him wherever he goes. The devotee who exercises outward self-restraint and thereby feels secure against temptation should introspectively remind himself: "Perhaps you can easily run away from outer temptations, but can you escape from the inner living photograph of hypnotic eyes of desires that you have created and preserved within yourself? Let not their subtle manipulative power catch you in a moment of vulnerability!" These inimical desires must be brought out from their subconscious hiding places and slain by the counteracting agents of spiritual perception developed by meditation. The more awareness of lasting inner bliss one attains, the less he is entrapped by desire.

VERSE 42

इन्द्रियाणि पराण्याहुरिन्द्रियेभ्यः परं मनः ।
मनसस्तु परा बुद्धिर्यो बुद्धेः परतस्तु सः ॥

The senses are said to be superior (to the physical body); the mind is superior to the sense faculties; the intelligence is superior to the mind; but he (the Self) is superior to the intelligence.

WITHOUT THE ENLIVENING ten sensory powers, the body is inert matter. The effects produced by the sensory powers are relative to their perception by the mind (*manas*). Perception is meaningful only in subservience to the cognition and determination of the intelligence (*buddhi*). Intelligence borrows its power from intuition, the pure wisdom of the all-supreme blissful soul.

In the sacred scriptures of India, a carriage drawn by ten horses and guided by a driver who holds the reins is compared to the soul riding in a body-chariot drawn by ten sensory-motor stallions reined in by the mind and charioteered by the intelligence. The owner is most important, for the carriage is his responsibility. Next to him in importance is the driver, then the reins which are necessary for control. Then come the horses, and lastly, the vehicle itself.

Similarly, the soul, the creator of the bodily carriage, is most important. Next to the soul comes the directing intelligence; then the mind or instrument of control; then the sense stallions; then the body.

The bodily vehicle cannot move without the senses; that is, a sleeping or dead body cannot manifest intelligent activity. The senses cannot work harmoniously without the mind to coordinate them. The absentminded man has slackened the rein on his senses and cannot act intelligently until he gathers up the reins of the mind. The mentally ill person is one whose directing driver has dropped the reins, so that the contact between intelligence and the senses is temporarily or permanently broken.

Body, mind, and soul: analogy of the chariot and horses

The driver of the chariot is sometimes referred to as the mind when *mind* is used in the common collective sense for all the faculties of intelligence, not just specifically *manas* or the sense mind. Then, the reins are referred to as the brain (the instrument used by the mind). Again, the driver may be referred to as the ego. When Krishna and Arjuna, however, are shown in the chariot, the symbol is that of the Supreme Soul (Krishna as the Lord or Krishna Consciousness—the Infinite Intelligence, Supreme Wisdom—or as the individualized soul) as the charioteer, guiding the spiritually inclined ego of the devotee concerning the proper way to use discriminative intelligence (*buddhi*) and sense mind (*manas*) to govern the senses and to carry the body-chariot along the road of life.

A man should have a sturdy carriage, well-kept horses, strong reins, an alert well-trained driver, and a wisely chosen path to travel over to reach his destination. A devotee moving toward Self-realization should have a healthy body, well-behaved senses trained by self-control, strong mental reins to hold them, and a keen discriminative intelligence to guide them. Then the body-chariot can traverse the straight and narrow path of right action to its destination.

A reckless man depending on a rickety carriage drawn by uncontrolled horses, guided by loose reins held by a careless driver, while travelling a zigzag stony path, may easily careen into a ditch.

Similar analogies may be drawn as follows:

A worldly man in a vulnerable body, who has poor discrimination and weak mental faculties, and who thus allows his strong impulses to roam at will, uncontrolled, over the rough road of life, will surely meet with a disastrous fate of wrecked health and material failures.

The intellectual or emotional man who moves over dogmatic pathways of knowledge and beliefs, and whose mental sense impressions are guided by nondiscriminative habits of bigotry and blind emotion, is certain to become mired in the muddy ruts of ignorance.

The devotee is aware that the most important objective in life is to attain the goal of Self-realization: to know through meditation his true soul nature and its oneness with ever blissful Spirit. That he may not be waylaid by tumbling into ditches of physical, mental, and spiritual suffering, he learns also to develop discriminative intelligence, clear harmonious mental faculties of perception, self-controlled senses, and a body imbued with health and vitality—that they may all serve the soul, for whom and for which purpose alone these instruments were brought together. Indeed, without the consciousness and intuitive wisdom of the soul behind them, they would not even exist.

In other words, the devotee realizes the proper priorities in self-development—first and always in his soul consciousness, then in his intelligence, mind, senses, and body. The man in delusion caters first to the appetites of his body, in utter disregard of the development of its superiors—senses, mind, intellect, and soul.

VERSE 43

एवं बुद्धेः परं बुद्ध्वा संस्तभ्यात्मानमात्मना ।
जहि शत्रुं महाबाहो कामरूपं दुरासदम् ॥

O Mighty-armed (Arjuna)! thus cognizing the Self as superior to the intelligence, and disciplining the self (ego) by the Self (soul), annihilate the foe! hard-to-conquer, wearing the form of desire.

WITH A STRONG-WILLED EGO, meditate on the blessedness of the soul; becoming imbued with its superior joy, the ego will lose desire for lesser sense pleasures—a desire hard to conquer without attaining this standard of comparison.

Golden butter does not change its colour when floating on water in a black or green vessel. But the water looks black or green according to the specific colour of its container. Similarly, the soul's golden bliss always remains unchanged, even while floating on the dark waters of the sense-identified, deluded intelligence.

The soul, being immutable and transcendental, is thus superior to the easily influenced human intellect. By meditation the incorruptible blessed nature of the soul is discovered. Soul perception is so delightful and insightful that it restrains the errant desires of the prodigal ego. After disciplining the sense desires by spiritual means, the devotee is ultimately able to destroy the almost unconquerable lust of material desire that is such a powerful enemy of Self-realization.

Man should depend on soul wisdom, not fickle intellect

By inner calmness born of self-control, discrimination, and meditation, the devotee should try to remain on the plane of intuitive soul perception, which is always stable, and not depend too heavily on the fickle intellect, which like a sharp dagger can be misused to slay the soul's wisdom instead of the desire-filled enemy senses.

Those who meditate deeply seldom fall, whereas an exceptionally clever individual who depends only on his superior intellect often finds himself cut off from true happiness through using rationalization to countenance sense indulgence and desires.

The only reliable disciplinarian and guide for the ego-self is the true Self, or omniscient soul. "Wisdom never lies."* Soul wisdom is revealed to man through the agency of intuition, direct perception of truth, not by amassing knowledge through the intellect. The seeker after wisdom should understand the difference between intuition and man's limited faculty of intelligence.

Human beings have perception and intelligence to understand the world of objects; the soul is endowed with the power of intuition to understand not only the world of objects, but also all inner psychical phenomena and their intrinsic spiritual nature. Intelligence interprets phenomena, the outward appearance of things; intuition reveals the

* Homer: *Odyssey,* III.

underlying noumena. Through the sense windows man looks at the objects of sense; but in deep inner perception, where the senses and intellect cannot reach, intuition prevails.

Man's intelligence is dependent on data supplied by the world of objective senses. All his knowledge is about the different objects of sense, inferred from their activities and their phenomena of colour (form), sound, smell, taste, and touch. This acquisition of knowledge by inference is called *parokshajnana*. By the vibratory exchange between the senses and their objects, man's inferential intelligence remains engrossed in the thought of matter. His intelligence is like a very aggressive businessman: As all the brain energy of the high-powered businessman is engaged in making money, so the intellect is single-pointed on the world of the senses; it interprets everything according to the "facts and figures" of its big account book of the mind.

As long as there is inferential thought going on within a person's mind, he does not have direct realization of underlying realities pertinent to that subject. One who thinks deeply and clearly, however—as in calm concentration and meditation—goes beyond the reasoning process of thought to a keen perception manifesting in his conscious thoughts, arising from within rather than from data accumulated from without. This knowing of truth by direct perception is called *aparokshajnana*. Some people say this is mystical. It is not mystical; it is most practical, and a natural faculty of man's true Self.

❖ *Intuition is practical, and a natural faculty of man's true Self* ❖

Science should try to understand intuition, even as it has systematically researched intelligence. If one tries to tell a savage, who has had no contact with world progress, of the wonders of modern science, he will not understand. With the growth of civilization, there have been progressive stages of intellectual advancement; but in the understanding and development of intuition, man's state is still relatively primal.

Understanding and intuition are interrelated. Intuition does not go against Nature's laws of understanding, but it goes beyond them. To illustrate: The electric current flowing into a light bulb manifests in a tangible way in the form of light, the brilliance of which is determined by the wattage of the bulb; but it is the electricity itself, travelling invisibly through the wires to the bulb, that is the cause of the light. Similarly, man's intelligence is the light of cognition in the body, and intuition is the current flowing through the wires of mind and intellect to produce that light.

According to the capacity or limitations of an individual's discriminating intelligence, the expression of intuitional power through that instrumentality varies at different times, as evidenced by the accuracy of understanding, or the lack of it, manifested in one's thoughts. By this it is seen that intuition can be developed or decreased. But though intuition acts in a limited way through intellect and mind, it is independent of them. The light shining in the bulb cannot exist without the electric current to sustain it, but the current exists whether or not it shines forth through the bulb. So also, intelligence cannot work without the power of intuition behind it, but intuition remains even without the instruments of rational thought.

The mind unites and coordinates the senses; intelligence is the cognizer; intuition is the rein of power behind all of man's mental phenomena—thought, attention, will, sensation, perception, memory, apperception, feelings, impulses. The mental powers could not act in cooperation and harmony if there were no invisible master of intuition to guide them, secretly touching the thoughts, feelings, and process of cognition, directing them to act in cooperation for fulfilling the wishes of the soul. When an individual's intelligence is deluded by the twenty-four attributes and three activating qualities of Nature, it often acts in error, against intuition. Thus the devotee must be careful not to mistake his vague imaginings or obstinate inclinations for the pure guidance of soul intuition.

But intelligence guided by intuition, cultivated by contacting the soul in meditation, rightly disciplines and leads the error-prone ego. And by its revelations of truth, intuition inspires the ego to forsake delusive desires in favour of the obviously superior everlasting bliss of the soul.

Rid of the parasites of ego and finite desires, the exquisitely perfect soul spreads its multiblossomed branches of divine qualities in the infinite sunlight of Spirit.

ॐ तत्सदिति श्रीमद्भगवद्गीतासूपनिषत्सु
ब्रह्मविद्यायां योगशास्त्रे श्रीकृष्णार्जुनसंवादे
कर्मयोगो नाम तृतीयोऽध्यायः ॥

Aum, Tat, Sat.
In the Upanishad of the holy Bhagavad Gita—the discourse of Lord Krishna to Arjuna, which is the scripture of yoga and the science of God-realization—this is the third chapter, called "Karma Yoga."

CHAPTER IV

THE SUPREME SCIENCE OF KNOWING GOD

❖

The Historical Basis and Esoteric Essence of Yoga

❖

The Incarnations of the Divine

❖

Paths of Liberation From the Rounds of Rebirth

❖

The Lord's Modes of Action Within His Creation

❖

Freedom From Karma: The Nature of Right Action, Wrong Action, and Inaction

❖

Yajna, the Spiritual Fire Rite That Consumes All Karma

❖

The All-sanctifying Wisdom, Imparted by a True Guru

"Even though almost completely buried during the Material Age, the science of yoga can never be annihilated, for it is linked to the Reality within man. Whenever he questions the phenomena of life and awakens spiritually, through God's grace he encounters a true guru who acquaints him with the art of divine union."

THE SUPREME SCIENCE OF KNOWING GOD

THE HISTORICAL BASIS AND ESOTERIC ESSENCE OF YOGA

VERSES 1–2

श्रीभगवानुवाच
इमं विवस्वते योगं प्रोक्तवानहमव्ययम्।
विवस्वान्मनवे प्राह मनुरिक्ष्वाकवेऽब्रवीत्॥ *(1)*

एवं परम्पराप्राप्तमिमं राजर्षयो विदुः।
स कालेनेह महता योगो नष्टः परन्तप॥ *(2)*

The exalted Lord said to Arjuna:

I gave this imperishable Yoga to Vivasvat (the sun-god); Vivasvat passed on the knowledge to Manu (the Hindu law-giver); Manu told it to Ikshvaku (founder of the solar dynasty of the Kshatriyas). Handed down in this way in orderly succession, the Rajarishis (royal rishis) knew it. But, O Scorcher of Foes (Arjuna)! by the long passage of time, this Yoga was lost sight of on earth.

SPIRIT (COSMIC CONSCIOUSNESS, here symbolized as Krishna) gave the indestructible *Raja Yoga* science—the technique of uniting soul and Spirit—to the ancient illuminato, Vivasvat, the "Deity of the Sun" (symbolic of God's omnipresent Light or creative Cosmic Energy, which is manifested also in man as the microcosmic sun or light of the spiritual eye, epitome of all life and consciousness in the incarnate being). Vivasvat imparted this sacred Yoga to the great exponent of *dharma,* Manu (symbolizing *manas,* the mind, the instrument from which sentient human consciousness derives). Manu bestowed it on the founder of the solar dynasty of Kshatriyas, Ikshvaku (symbolic of the intuitive astral eye of life and consciousness in man). In this orderly succession, this Yoga was then bequeathed to the royal sages (symbolizing the descent of the life and consciousness into the senses, giving man sensory perception of and interaction with the material world). Thereafter, when the cycles of the world entered the Dark Ages, knowledge of this divine science deteriorated and was lost (symbolically, throughout many incarnations the senses are engrossed in and identified with matter, and man thus loses the knowledge and ability of reuniting his soul with Spirit).

These two verses thus proclaim the historical antiquity of *Raja* ("royal") *Yoga,* the eternal, immutable science of uniting soul and Spirit. At the same time, understood esoterically, they give a concise description of that science—the steps by which the soul descends from Cosmic Consciousness to the mortal state of identification with the human body, and the route it must take to reascend to its Source, the all-blissful Eternal Spirit.

In the beginning of creation and the advent of man, the Infinite impregnated His intelligent creative Cosmic Energy (Maha-Prakriti or Holy Ghost) with not only the power of repulsion—the individualizing of Cosmic Consciousness into souls and a universe of matter—but also with the power of recalling souls from their prodigal wanderings in matter back to unity with Spirit. All things come from, are made of and sustained by, and ultimately resolve into this intelligent Cosmic Energy, and thence into Spirit. Ascension follows in reverse the exact course of descension. In man, that course is the inner highway to the Infinite, the only route to divine union for followers of all religions in all ages. By whatever bypath of beliefs or practices a being reaches that singular highway, the final ascension from body consciousness to Spirit is the same for everyone: the withdrawal of life and consciousness from the senses upward through the gates of light in the subtle cerebrospinal centres, dissolving the consciousness of matter into life force, life force into mind, mind into soul, and soul into Spirit. The method of ascension is *Raja Yoga,* the eternal science that has been integral in creation from its inception.

❖

The Revival of Yoga for the Present Age

The literal or historic interpretation of these verses is as follows: Through vision, or intuitional guidance, God first revealed to the illumined sage Vivasvat (now known as the presiding deity of the sun) the royal science of Spirit. Vivasvat taught the sacred yoga to Manu, a divinely inspired *rishi* and legislator of India's antehistorical period, whose law codes are, to this day, the guiding principles of Hindu society. Manu, in turn, was the preceptor of Ikshvaku, the great solar dynasty Kshatriya king. Handed down from Ikshvaku, the imperishable science of yoga was practised by a long line of royal *rishis* and sages, including the renowned King Janaka. With the advent of Kali Yuga (the Dark or Material Age), the science of yoga was almost forgotten.*

The world has gone through numerous equinoctial cycles of upward and downward evolution: one full upward and downward cycle occupies 24,000 years (the Ascending Arc of the Material Age [1,200], Atomic Age [2,400], Mental Age [3,600], Spiritual Age [4,800]; then the Descending Arc, of the same length, beginning with 4,800 years of the descending Spiritual Age). Thus it may be said that a full cycle of civilization is 24,000 years—climbing upward for 12,000 years and slowly descending for 12,000 years. This ascent and decline of the ages is not a circular evolution that ends as low as it began; it is spiral. But the evolution of the beings therein is linear. The material man—one who lives a "normal" average life—after prodigally wandering through innumerable reincarnations, finds the Spiritual Age of any 24,000-year cycle to be the most propitious for Self-realization. During the descent of man from a Spiritual Age to a Material Age, the knowledge of the science of yoga declines and is forgotten. Nevertheless, as Spirit is eternal, so yoga—the art of reuniting the outgoing differentiated soul-ray with the omnipresent Spiritual Sun—also is imperishable.

---

* My guru Sri Yukteswar discovered the mathematical application of a 24,000-year equinoctial cycle to the solar system of which earth is a part. As planets revolve around their sun, so the sun has for its dual a distant star around which it rotates in about 24,000 earth-years. According to Hindu cosmology, the rotating sun, additionally, moves in a far vaster cycle around a magnetic nucleus of Spirit (Vishnunabhi), the "Grand Centre," seat of the creative power of Brahma. The 24,000-year cycle is divided into an Ascending Arc and a Descending Arc, each of 12,000 years. Within each Arc fall four *yugas* or Ages, called Kali, Dwapara, Treta, and Satya, corresponding to the Greek ideas of Iron, Bronze, Silver, and Golden Ages. To identify the predominant characteristic of each Age, I have referred to them, respectively, as the Material Age, the Electric or Atomic Age, the Mental Age, and the Spiritual Age. During the Ascending Arc of each cycle, when the solar system in an inward evolution begins to move closer to the "Grand Centre" of Spirit, there is a gradual unfoldment of intellectual and spiritual qualities, reaching a zenith of enlightenment in Satya Yuga, or the Spiritual Age. The shadow of delusion then slowly begins to eclipse the light of knowledge during the Descending Arc to the Kali Yuga or Material Age farthest from Spirit. These cycles are expounded more fully in the first part of Sri Yukteswar's book, *The Holy Science* (published by Yogoda Satsanga Society of India). See also IV:7–8.

Western astronomers have postulated an equinoctial cycle of our solar system as consisting of 25,920 years, based on a cosmic phenomenon known to astronomers as

Even though almost completely buried during the Material Age, the science of yoga can never be annihilated, for it is linked to the Reality within man. Whenever he questions the phenomena of life and awakens spiritually, through God's grace he encounters a true guru who acquaints him with the art of divine union—no matter in what cycle the devotee has been incarnated. While it is true that each Age is distinguished by the predominance of material, atomic, mental, or spiritual development, the Age is never devoted to that aspect alone; it always contains traces of the attributes of other Ages. Thus, spiritual development continues in some degree even in a Kali Yuga or Material Age.

The year A.D. 1951 has already left the Material Age behind (by over 250 years).* In this once-more-ascending Atomic Age, the indestructible science of *Raja Yoga* is being revived as *Kriya Yoga* through the grace of Mahavatar Babaji, Shyama Charan Lahiri Mahasaya, Swami Sri Yukteswar, and their disciples. (Eminent among the great *Kriya Yogis* initiated by Lahiri Mahasaya were Swami Pranabananda, Swami Kebalananda, Swami Keshabananda, Panchanon Bhattacharya, Ram Gopal Muzumdar, and Bhupendra Nath Sanyal, about whom I have written in *Autobiography of a Yogi*.) Foremost among Lahiri Mahasaya's *Kriya Yoga* disciples was my guru, Sri Yukteswarji, for he was chosen by Babaji to continue the lineage through which the sacred science would be disseminated in all lands.

As a matter of special divine dispensation, through Krishna, Christ, Mahavatar Babaji, Lahiri Mahasaya, and Swami Sri Yukteswar I was selected to spread the *Kriya Yoga* science worldwide through the united original Yoga of Krishna and original Christianity of Christ as represented in the teachings of Yogoda Satsanga Society of India/Self-Realization Fellowship.†

"Precession of the Equinox," determined by the present rate of motion. According to the Hindus, however, that rate varies at different stages of the cycle.

* The Material Age last began in the Descending Arc of the equinoctial cycle about 700 B.C. and ended in the Ascending Arc about A.D. 1700.

"The Hindu scriptures place the present world-age as occurring within the Kali Yuga of a much longer universal cycle than the simple 24,000-year equinoctial cycle with which Sri Yukteswar was concerned....The start of the materialistic ages, according to Hindu scriptural reckoning, was 3102 B.C. That year was the beginning of the last Descending Dwapara Yuga of the equinoctial cycle, and also the start of the Kali Yuga of the Universal Cycle. Most anthropologists, believing that 10,000 years ago humanity was living in a barbarous Stone Age, summarily dismiss as 'myths' the widespread traditions of very ancient civilizations in Lemuria, Atlantis, India, China, Japan, Egypt, Mexico, and many other lands" (*Autobiography of a Yogi*). See also VIII:17–19, page 732.

† It is through the instance and blessings of Mahavatar Babaji (whom I ever perceive as one with Krishna in Spirit) and of Christ and my Guru and Paramguru that I was sent

Krishna is the divine exemplar of yoga in the East; Christ was chosen by God as the exemplar of God-union for the West. That Jesus knew and taught to his disciples the *Raja Yoga* technique of uniting soul with Spirit is evidenced in the deeply symbolic Biblical chapter "The Revelation of Jesus Christ to Saint John."*

In *Autobiography of a Yogi* I have written: "Babaji is ever in communion with Christ; together they send out vibrations of redemption and have planned the spiritual technique of salvation for this age. ...Babaji is well aware of the trend of modern times, especially of the influence and complexities of Western civilization, and realizes the necessity of spreading the self-liberations of yoga equally in the West and in the East."

The Soul's Descent Into Human Consciousness

Esoterically interpreted, these two stanzas of the Gita explain the genesis of yoga. The first manifestation of Spirit is Cosmic Light. God vibrated His cosmic consciousness as intelligent creative Cosmic Energy, or Cosmic Light, referred to in these verses as Vivasvat, "one who shines forth or diffuses light" (the illumined *rishi* of ancient times who came to be known as the sun god). This omnipresent Cosmic Energy or Light exists in man as the microcosmic sun of the spiritual eye, which becomes visible during meditation when the devotee's consciousness and the dual current of the two physical eyes is concentrated at the point between the eyebrows. "The light of the body is the eye: if therefore thine eye be sin-

---

to the West and undertook the task of founding Self-Realization Fellowship to serve as the instrumentality for the preservation and dissemination worldwide of the *Kriya Yoga* science. In bestowing his blessings on me before I came to America in 1920, Mahavatar Babaji told me that I had been chosen for this sacred mission: "You are the one I have chosen to spread the message of *Kriya Yoga* in the West. Long ago I met your guru Yukteswar at a Kumbha Mela; I told him then I would send you to him for training." Babaji then predicted: "*Kriya Yoga*, the scientific technique of God-realization, will ultimately spread in all lands, and aid in harmonizing the nations through man's personal, transcendental perception of the Infinite Father."

The salvation of souls through *Kriya Yoga* is my singular aim. I take no credit; it belongs to God and to the Great Ones who sent me. But my soul rejoices, for the channel is blessed by what flows through it.

* John speaks of the "mystery of the seven stars" and the "seven churches" (Revelation 1:20); these symbols refer to the seven astral centres of light in the spine. The recondite imagery throughout this nonunderstood chapter of the Bible is an allegorical representation of the revelations that come with the opening of these centres of life and consciousness, the "book sealed with seven seals" (Revelation 5:1).

gle, thy whole body shall be full of light"* is not an idle promise, but refers to this resplendent manifestation. All the intelligent creative power of omnipresent Cosmic Energy is present microcosmically in the spiritual eye. It is through the spiritual eye—the various states experienced therein, correlating to the activities of the cerebrospinal centres of life and consciousness in the physical, astral, and causal bodies†—that the soul descends into embodiment and ultimately reascends to Spirit.

Every soul emerges from Cosmic Consciousness. It experiences a slightly lower vibratory state of Cosmic Light, or, symbolically, Vivasvat.

Esoteric significance of "Vivasvat"

After that, the soul loses the awareness of being Spirit clothed in Cosmic Light; it becomes individualized consciousness or spiritual ego, a causal being of pure consciousness encased in an astral body. This encasement comes about as follows:

The outward projecting creative power of God that is imposed upon the soul creates feeling (*chitta*), that consciousness by which the soul knows or experiences its existence. The activities of feeling excite the "thinking" or cognitive processes. When this God-sent feeling becomes distorted by delusion, the ego (*ahamkara*) evolves. Ego's consciousness is, "I am the experiencer." Along with the ego evolves its guiding intelligence (*buddhi*). Intelligence manifests its nature in thinking, egoity, and discrimination. When afflicted by delusion, the intelligence gives rise to the blind mind (*manas*). The mind is a coordinating instrument, the outward-inclined mediary between the sensory world and the ego with its discerning intelligence.

There are four phases of the nature of the mind: (1) sensory impressions, (2) assertive discrimination (the activation of the organs of action by the will at the command of intelligence), (3) wish (excitement or desire arising from contact with objects of the senses), and (4) imagination (the delusion of believing that phenomena are reality). Through these quadruple channels, the dual (attractive and repulsive) desires of the heart (feeling or *chitta*) and of the ego are consummated. These activities of the mind are the cause of human consciousness.

When the descending soul comes under the influence of mind, it becomes limited by identification with human consciousness in general. This is termed the Manu state of the descending soul.

The omnipresent Cosmic Energy (Vivasvat) becomes manifest as life force in man through the influence of mind, referred to here as passing

* Matthew 6:22. † See I:4–6.

the knowledge (the power of yoga) to Manu. *Manu* means man, the possessor of the thinking principle, from the Sanskrit *manas,* mind. Vyasa, the writer of the Gita, has therefore used the name of Manu to indicate the part played by the mind in the descension of consciousness and life into embodiment. Manu's name is additionally significant in that this illumined *rishi* of old—epitome of the highest in human beings, a representative father of the human race—possessed full knowledge about the mind (*manas*) and its role in creating the human consciousness.

Omnipresent Cosmic Energy (Vivasvat) is the source of the life force that becomes manifest in the astral body of man through the instrumentality of the mind (Manu). Thus life force and mind are intimately associated, for in the body of man one cannot exist without the other. When they descend from Cosmic Consciousness and Cosmic Energy, their pristine manifestation is through the eye of intuition (causal phase of the spiritual eye relating to the causal "spinal" channel of consciousness) and thence into the astral eye (the astral phase of the spiritual eye, corresponding to the three spinal channels of the astral body). (See I:4–6.) The astral eye, through which life and consciousness come into astral embodiment, is symbolically referred to in these verses as Ikshvaku (son of Manu and first king of a great solar dynasty of Kshatriyas). Vyasa thus uses the name Ikshvaku to signify the birth of the astral eye—astral life force and consciousness—through the instrumentality of the mind, or Manu. *Ikshvaku* is derived from *īksh,* "to discern" or "to see."*

Through mind ("Manu"), Cosmic Energy becomes manifest as life force in the body

* The noun form of the Sanskrit root *īksh,* i.e., *īkshanam* (discerning, seeing, visualizing) means, additionally, and significantly in the context of this Gita verse: eye.

Ikshvaku is a Vedic name, appearing in both the Rig Veda and the Atharva Veda; and though it is rendered with a short *i,* there is a recognized Vedic license whereby a long *ī* can change into a short *i,* as in the case of Ikshvaku.

In the Upanishads, the grammatical derivatives of *īksh* imply a state of seeing or knowing as a creative omniscient consciousness. This is developed by Adi Shankaracharya in his commentary on the *Brahma Sutra* (which is regarded as the ultimate authority on Vedanta) in which he cites, for example: "That (Brahman) *saw,* May I become many...." (*Chandogya Upanishad* VI:2:3); "In the beginning, the Self, verily, was one, only one...He *saw,* Let me create the worlds" (*Aitareya Upanishad* I:i.1). The "seeing" is thus esoterically akin to the Biblical "said" in Genesis: "God *said,* Let there be light...."; "God *said,* Let us make man...."—reference to the intelligent vibratory force sent forth by God, which gave birth to creation.

Īksh, in its meaning as a root element of Ikshvaku, is therefore not ordinary seeing, but the omniscient creative consciousness of the Supreme Being, capable of forming the

Thus, from the Manu state, the soul flows down into a specific channel of the intuitive sense (the causal intuitive eye), and thence into the astral channels of life force and consciousness (the astral eye).

Through the astral eye ("Ikshvaku"), soul enters the astral body

In this Ikshvaku state, the soul is identified with the intuitive state of ego perception; that is, it experiences its individualized existence as limited by confinement in the astral body in which the astral ego's power of knowing and perception comes not from sensory experience but through the sixth sense, intuition. The astral ego perceives the forces at work in the astral body as the true components of matter.

From the intuitive astral Ikshvaku state, the soul then further descends to the various powerful sense-perceptive states, manifesting first as the more subtle astral sensory powers (*jnanendriyas*) and then flowing into the gross physical manifestation of the senses. This is spoken of as the Rajarishi, or sense-identified, state. When the dual currents of mind and life force flow into the nervous system and into the optical, auditory, olfactory, gustatory, and tactual nerves of the five instruments of knowledge (the senses of sight, hearing, smell, taste, and touch), five sense specializations occur. By contrast, the astral powers, being pure life force or *prana,* are not so circumscribed; the intellection being intuitive, the astral being can experience any or all sensations through any singular sensory instrument.*

---

various stages of creation. This intelligent divine consciousness and energy is manifested in the microcosm of man as the pure intuitive discernment and intelligent vibratory force of the astral eye, which is able to bring form into manifestation, i.e., to create and empower man's physical body. *(Publisher's Note)*

* "During the 1960s researchers in the United States and USSR explored the curious ability of some people to detect colour, light, and occasionally even pattern through the skin....individuals who could 'see' without their eyes....The investigators began training volunteers to perceive colour through their fingertips....Reportedly, some measure of fingertip vision could be trained in all blind children in whom the visual cortex was intact. The optic nerve does not seem to be necessary for this perception, but damage to the brain's visual centre precludes it....

"Eyeless sight is usually not experienced as normal vision but rather as a tactile sensation or a sensation of light. Even when the skin is several inches from the test stimulus, the trained subject feels what he usually describes as stickiness, roughness, smoothness, coolness, heat, all characteristic of different colours. This response is somehow refined into genuine visual sensation in some subjects who, over a period of time, begin to describe subtle shades of colour and detail of pictures, and who can read printed material via the new sense."—*The Brain Revolution* by Marilyn Ferguson (New York: Bantam, 1973). *(Publisher's Note)*

The five instruments of intellection are described as "royal sages" (Rajarishis) because all wisdom from outside sources (scriptures or saints) has to reach the mind and intelligence through the sense channels. These are "royal" or glorious instruments for perceiving and enjoying the Lord's entertaining phenomenal universe when they are well-educated and guided by the discriminative intelligence of the soul's wisdom. But when soul meditation is forgotten, the senses of knowledge become dulled and unreceptive to spiritual teachings because of constant identification with material desires and sense objects. Man's consciousness, having thereby descended to the plane of materialistic attachments, loses the memory of its union with Spirit; during the long dark period of material consciousness, man's knowledge of yoga or divine union thus declines and is forgotten.

❖ *Descending into the senses ("Rajarishis"), soul consciousness is forgotten* ❖

In summary, yoga signifies union of Spirit and soul. The Spirit, as Cosmic Consciousness, is united to omnipresent Cosmic Energy, which is linked to the microcosmic spiritual eye of life and consciousness in man. Life and consciousness are linked to the mind. The mind is linked to the astral eye and the intuitive mind of the astral body. And astral life and mind are linked with the five sensory instruments of knowledge.

Man, descending from Cosmic Consciousness into the body, becomes immersed in many incarnations of material living and forgets yoga (the points of union of his senses [Rajarishis] with life force [Ikshvaku], of his life with mind [Manu], of his mind with Cosmic Energy [Vivasvat], and of Cosmic Energy with Cosmic Consciousness [Krishna]). Nevertheless, the laws by which man can recall the forgotten links (of his ego with the senses, life force, mind, soul, and Spirit) exist eternally within him, ready to be used and demonstrated.

These two instructive stanzas give eternal hope to man. In spite of his long forgetfulness, he must some day realize that the links of union (yoga) with Spirit are indestructibly present within him. Man does not remember how the Spirit vibrated into different states; the soul is forgotten after having descended into the senses. However, any time he wishes, by practising *Kriya Yoga* man can remember the eternal links between soul and Spirit. This yoga or divine science is revived again whenever a devotee detaches his true Self from the senses by practising *Kriya Yoga*, and thus reunites the soul with Spirit.

VERSE 3

स एवायं मया तेऽद्य योगः प्रोक्तः पुरातनः।
भक्तोऽसि मे सखा चेति रहस्यं ह्येतदुत्तमम्॥

I have this day informed thee about that same ancient yoga, for thou art My devotee and friend. This sacred mystery (of yoga) is, indeed, the producer of supreme benefit (to mankind).

"O ARJUNA, THROUGH YOUR ECSTATIC meditational experiences during these moments of spiritual perception, I, Cosmic Consciousness (Krishna), have reminded you of the same ancient yoga science and technique of union of soul with Spirit learned by you in a previous incarnation. Because you partially united your soul with My spirit before, I am reminding you of that supreme inner highway by which you will become irrevocably united with Spirit. The blessing of this sacred mystery is again revealed to you because you are devoted to Me in the reverential distance of awe observed by a devotee in the initial stage of divine communion; and because you are also My friend, no longer reserved, but one with Me in the higher state of ecstasy. Knowledge of this supreme secret science, hidden from the body-identified, is humanity's highest boon."

Just as Krishna explained to Arjuna the important truths mentioned in previous stanzas, so when a high state of development is reached the Heavenly Spirit lovingly imparts to the devotee, through his intuition and ecstatic experiences, the meaning of the different states of spiritual development that ultimately lead, by the selfsame ancient spinal highway through which all devotees must travel, to final liberation.

In the early stages of divine communion, the devotee feels an awesome mental distance between himself and God, a worshipful reverence and timidity before the eminence of Omnipresence. But as the devotee experiences successively higher states of ecstasy, mental barriers are broken and he joyously recalls his long-lost familiar friendly state of oneness with God. Then he rejoices to hear the voice of God call him devotee and friend, and confide to him all the mysteries of the universe. He thanks the Lord for granting him the supreme blessing of divine union—incomparable, nonpareil bliss.

VERSE 4

अर्जुन उवाच
अपरं भवतो जन्म परं जन्म विवस्वतः ।
कथमेतद्विजानीयां त्वमादौ प्रोक्तवानिति ॥

Arjuna said:

Vivasvat was born first, and thy birth occurred later. How then can I comprehend thy words that thou didst communicate this yoga in the beginning (before thy birth)?

KRISHNA, BEING AN INCARNATION of the One Limitless God, as well as the personal guru of Arjuna, knew in his omnipresent timeless consciousness all events that had occurred, even in the beginning of creation. He it was—the Self and Spirit being indivisibly one—who had evolved the conscious Cosmic Vibratory Light (Vivasvat) out of which all souls are created, and in which, after many births, all souls are dissolved.

In the Bible, Jesus says: "Before Abraham was, I am."* Even though Abraham was born prior to Jesus, the statement was true because Jesus was filled with the Supreme Spirit that is conscious of only the eternal present, which includes the so-called past and future. At one with Cosmic Consciousness the Creator, Jesus could well say that He existed before Abraham or any other created being.

Similarly, Krishna knew that He existed as the Spirit before Its manifestation as the conscious Cosmic Vibratory Energy (Vivasvat), the divine instrument of all created beings. Krishna's body had been born after and out of the creation of the Conscious Cosmic Light, but His Eternal Spirit is ever prior to, and the cause of, creation.

IN RELATION TO THE DEVOTEE'S experience of yoga, the following interpretation of this verse applies:

Cosmic Consciousness manifests in the devotee after the perception of Light. Thus in the yogi's ascending consciousness, Light (Vivasvat) is born before Cosmic Consciousness (Krishna).

The yogi wonderingly introspects, "O Spirit, I first found the Cosmic Light (Vivasvat) as the spiritual astral eye (Ikshvaku) born within me—after that, Thy Cosmic Consciousness became manifest. How then

---

* John 8:58.

could Spirit have already become enthroned within me before the appearance of Spiritual Light?"

The soul descends from Cosmic Consciousness to the plane of light, and down to the region of flesh. The pure soul, the *atman,* is called the *jiva* when it is identified with its mortal coverings—body, mind, senses, and other principles of Nature. Even so, the true essence of the soul remains untainted Spirit—the Divinity in every being. It is only owing to the outer identification with the physical paraphernalia that the inner light and divine consciousness become screened behind delusion. Meditation clears the cosmic mist as the descended consciousness of the soul starts ascending to its lost higher planes of existence.

The upwardly climbing yogi experiences the inner light first, then cosmic perception. When he is looking inward toward Spirit, it seems that the Spiritual Noumenon evolves from the astral phenomena. But when the yogi is one with Spirit, looking outward toward Nature, then Spirit is seen as the supreme first cause of all astral and physical emanations.

THE INCARNATIONS OF THE DIVINE

VERSE 5

श्रीभगवानुवाच
बहूनि मे व्यतीतानि जन्मानि तव चार्जुन।
तान्यहं वेद सर्वाणि न त्वं वेत्थ परन्तप॥

The Blessed Lord said:

O Arjuna, many births have been experienced by Me and by thee. I am acquainted with them all, whereas thou rememberest them not, O Scorcher of Foes.

"O ARJUNA, YOU WHO ARE THE DESTROYER of the limitations of delusion with the fire of your self-control, know that my liberated consciousness, being one with Spirit, has not suffered from the delusion of oblivion of past lives during my voluntary incarnations on earth at various times in various forms. With the omnipresent memory of Spirit, I see one unbroken chain of conscious existence consisting of all my previous births on earth, including the long-ago incarnation when I imparted the sacred science of yoga to Vivasvat. The same all-knowing Spirit that is my Self is your soul as well, Arjuna, which also took many forms in many lives. Though your yet-to-be-fully-liberated memory recalls them not, I know all the lifetimes shared with you, my ideal disciple before me now in your present form as Arjuna."

Omnipresent memory is not possessed by devotees who are still travelling the razor-edge path to Self-realization. Not even an Arjuna, but only a fully liberated soul, a manifestation of God such as Krishna, can remember all births, deaths, and their interim periods.

Whenever consciousness, like a shining sword, enters the various scabbards of Nature's twenty-four principles, its appearance differs according to the specific covering. This encasement of consciousness—in intelligence, mind, ego, feeling, senses (five instruments of knowledge and five of action), and the five elements of the body—is called birth. The time between death and rebirth is spent in the astral sphere. The ego cannot remember its experiences in the prenatal or embryonic state or even in the postnatal state of infancy; similarly, unenlightened men do not recall their existences (after physical death) in the astral worlds; nor do they remember former lives on this earth.

Why God causes man to forget experiences of past incarnations

It is God's mercy that a benighted soul, ailing from various material discrepancies, becomes forgetful of these from one incarnation to the next. This oblivion to the miseries and shortcomings of previous existence is one of the most gracious of mental anaesthetics given by God to each human being, that he be not burdened by memories of all the physical and mental sorrows of past lives. He is spared from carrying with him the evil and discouragements of one life into another, and is thus given a fresh start on the straight and narrow path leading to his highest goal. It is enough that proddings of his innate good or evil tendencies—the effects of good and bad karma of previous lives—remain with him as reminders of lessons yet to be learned and victories already won.

Those evil or good experiences of past lives manifest as evil or good moods or habits from one's very birth in his present life. This fact accounts for persons who are born evildoers, and others who are born saints. As evil is the harbinger of misery, those who are born evil should strive to work free from their prenatal evil traits by cultivating good company and meditation. Those who are born good should not be satisfied with their goodness, but should try to be even better, until they have reached the complete safety of the Cosmic Spirit and are free from the wheel of birth and rebirth.

God (or His incarnations) never forgets anything; as soon as a devotee is fully liberated, he too can remember all the various forms he had displayed in birth and lost in death—forms enshrouded in their virtuous achievements as well as their careless lapses into the ignorance of evils. When the liberated being is awake in God and understands the mystery of this dream of life, only then is he ready for this awesome review.

ESOTERICALLY INTERPRETED, the questions and answers between Krishna and Arjuna are the intuitional exchanges of wisdom between the Spirit (which is born again and again with the rebirths of every soul) and the ecstasy-attuned soul of the ideal devotee. The Original Spirit that manifested yogic unity with an advanced devotee as the Vivasvat Cosmic Light had also been present with Arjuna during his various rebirths. When a devotee can consciously commune with the Divinity (in the highest *nirvikalpa* ecstatic state), he inwardly asks all sorts of questions of the Spirit.

All past incarnations are revealed by light of Cosmic Consciousness

The all-seeing light of Cosmic Consciousness gradually illumines and reveals to the yogi the heretofore dark gulfs linking incarnations. In the advanced state, the yogi sees the Cosmic Light, or manifested Spirit ("Me"), and the soul ("thee") as having existed together through many incarnations. He realizes that his forgetful body-identified pseudosoul, intoxicated with the delusion of mortal consciousness, was utterly oblivious of that divine togetherness.

Spirit is the immanent sole sustainer of all souls throughout their numerous incarnations. Hence, the Spirit remembers all the lifetimes that have been necessary for a soul to attain liberation—after which, the soul becomes Spirit. Then that liberated soul addresses its lower self: "I realize I have been Spirit in my higher Self as an ever conscious witness of my unbroken existence in many lifetimes; and simultaneously, I have been the body-bound ego, oblivious of all but one self-centred life at a time. As Spirit, I know all the bodily garments put on by you, my lower self, even though you remembered them not. O my deluded lower self, I the omnipresent Spirit, thy Creator, have invisibly and transcendentally nurtured thee in schools of many lives. I, the higher Self, can recount all the shiftings from one body to another which you, my lower self, carried on in the somnambulistic state of utter oblivion to all the befores and afters of your deluded dreaming existence."

Every human being is assured that someday, after his liberation, he will know all about his rebirths as individualized manifestations of Spirit, whether on this earth or in other planes of existence. The liberated yogi transfers his consciousness from one soul wave to the Spiritual Ocean with all Its many waves of incarnated beings. The fully freed devotee realizes that it is the Spirit which has taken the various forms of all his rebirths. Then he does not say: "I took so many forms," but, "The Spirit appeared in all the forms that encased my soul until final liberation."

VERSE 6

अजोऽपि सन्नव्ययात्मा भूतानामीश्वरोऽपि सन्।
प्रकृतिं स्वामधिष्ठाय सम्भवाम्यात्ममायया॥

Unborn though I am, of changeless Essence! yet becoming Lord of all creation, abiding in My own Cosmic Nature (Prakriti), I embody Myself by Self-evolved maya-delusion.

"ALTHOUGH I AM CAUSELESS and unborn, and of immutable mien, yet, upon entering Nature, I Myself—the Lord of all beings and their cosmic domain—don the cosmic garment of My Self-created own *maya* (delusion), but its illusory power does not change Me."

This verse speaks of the immanent-transcendent nature of the omnipresent Creator-Lord—both as Ruler of the cosmos through the manifestations of Prakriti, and as incarnate in human form as an avatar.*

A clerk in a store is compelled to work ("no work, no pay!"); the owner, however, who may willingly assume the active duties of a clerk, is not compelled to do so, nor is he limited to the clerical role. Similarly, ordinary beings are forced to be born by Cosmic Delusion and its law of cause and effect (karma). God, the Creator of delusion (*maya*) and the law of action (karma), is not subject to them; yet He follows these laws when He descends as an avatar (a divinely incarnated being). Inwardly, however, he remains unaffected by the compulsions of *maya* and karma.

---

* The Sanskrit word *avatara* means "descent"; from *ava,* "down," and *tri,* "to pass." In the Hindu scriptures, *avatara* signifies the descent of Divinity into flesh.

Ordinary individuals, entering into their nature-made bodies, are tossed about on the waves of sensory pleasures, ignorant of the vast ocean of Spirit existing beneath them. But the yogi, reaching the final state of emancipation, beholds the ever-existing changeless (hence unborn) invisible Ocean of God, existing unaffected in Its ever-mutating visible cosmic waves of vibratory Nature, stirred by Its Self-made storm of delusion.

The consciousness of man under the influence of Cosmic Delusion is bounded by attachment to material possessions and mental faculties. The yogi of Self-realization, on the other hand, finds that he can possess a physical body and work through it without bondage to material desires and their karmic effects, just as the Lord remains unattached and free from karma even while His intelligence silently acts throughout the cosmic vibratory body of creation, ruled by His delusory law of relativity.

During the highest (the wakeful) state of ecstasy, the liberated yogi feels: "The realm of my consciousness extends beyond the limits of my mortal frame to the boundaries of eternity—whence I, the Cosmic Sea, watch the little ego floating in me. No sparrow falls, no grain of sand is blown away, without my sight. All space floats like an iceberg in my mental sea. I am the colossal container of all things made." He simultaneously perceives the Spirit as a waveless ocean of Eternal Calm, and the Spirit manifesting Itself in the restless waves of creation that dance on Its infinite bosom.

This stanza affords great encouragement to man. By avoiding the misuse of the gift of free choice, and by practising *Kriya Yoga*, he can shine forth as an image of God—an image hitherto delusion-eclipsed. Remembering himself as the image of Spirit, the wisdom-lit yogi learns that he, even as God, can work in the world unfettered by bodily environment, or by karma, or by Cosmic Nature's ever-changing attributes (*gunas*).

God has spun this eventful cosmic play on the stage of time to entertain us, but we take the shadows as serious realities! There is only one Serious Reality—God!

V.V. Sapar

Hear about the wisdom of Yoga, equipped with which, O Partha (Arjuna), thou shalt shatter the bonds of karma.... Even a tiny bit of this real religion protects one from great fear (the colossal sufferings inherent in the repeated cycles of birth and death).

In soul bliss all grief is annihilated. Indeed, the discrimination of the blissful man soon becomes firmly established (in the Self).

—Bhagavad Gita II:39–40, 65

❖

"The Pandavas...represent the principles necessary for the yogi to attain realization or oneness with God; the Kauravas...are metaphorically representative of specific principles that oppose spiritual progress."

❖

"The yogi, after each practice of concentrated meditation, asks his power of introspection: 'Assembled in the region of consciousness in the cerebrospinal axis and on the field of the body's sensory activity, eager for battle, the mental sense-faculties that try to pull the consciousness outward, and the children of the soul's discriminative tendencies that seek to reclaim the inner kingdom—what did they? who won this day?'"

❖

"Krishna says: 'By the practice of yoga meditation withdraw your mind, intelligence, life force, and heart from the clutches of the ego, from the physical sensations of sight, hearing, smell, taste, and touch, and from the objects of sense pleasures! Forsake all duties toward them! Be a yogi by uniting yourself to My blessed presence in your soul....'

"The ordinary man's mind is usually identified with external possessions and sense pleasures connected with the surface of the body....The yogi reverses the searchlights of intelligence, mind, and life force inward through a secret astral passage... to reveal finally the soul's presence in the highest centre (sahasrara) in the brain. ...He experiences in the sahasrara the ineffable bliss of his soul."

—Paramahansa Yogananda

VERSES 7–8

यदा यदा हि धर्मस्य ग्लानिर्भवति भारत।
अभ्युत्थानमधर्मस्य तदात्मानं सृजाम्यहम्॥ *(7)*

परित्राणाय साधूनां विनाशाय च दुष्कृताम्।
धर्मसंस्थापनार्थाय सम्भवामि युगे युगे॥ *(8)*

O Bharata (Arjuna)! whenever virtue (dharma) declines and vice (adharma) predominates, I incarnate as an Avatar. In visible form I appear from age to age to protect the virtuous and to destroy evildoing in order to reestablish righteousness.

THIS EARTH IS A STAGE whereon a divine drama is being evolved. Whenever the majority of human actors misuse their God-given freedom, and by the creation of evil bring suffering and upset the divine plans concerning their fellow beings and their own destiny (plans intended to be carried out by man's proper use of free choice), then God, the Cosmic Director, appears on the stage in a human form (an avatar) to instruct the amateur thespians in the proper art of living. God thus teaches man, made in His image, how to evolve by using free will, manifesting the divine nature inherent in the human nature.

THE NATURE OF AN AVATAR

THE QUESTION IS: Can God Himself ever incarnate as a human being? To say that God can *not* do a certain thing is to limit Him. But there are so many things that God can do, yet does not do—at least not as human beings expect of Him. God has never been known to have taken a human form called "God" and dwelt in it among men. ("Why callest thou me good? There is none good but one, that is, God," Jesus said,* to distinguish himself, an avatar, from God the Father, the Absolute, the Formless.) The Lord has condescended many times, however, to manifest Himself through the incarnation of a fully liberated being who, once an ordinary human being, has become a true reflection or "son of God." God, who is almighty and can do anything, thus operates His Omniscience through the human body of an avatar. Just as the ocean of Cosmic Consciousness is aware of a soul wave manifesting

* Matthew 19:17.

on its surface, so the soul wave of an avatar is aware of the ocean of Cosmic Consciousness manifesting through its form.

Great prophets and minor saints differ only in degree—the former manifest God fully through wide-open windows of their consciousness; the latter manifest God through small crevices of certain divine realizations. It can be said that the full manifestation of divinity in an avatar is greater than is the partial manifestation in a saint who has not yet attained absolute liberation.

All human beings are potential gods; the wise man and the ignorant one both are true image-incarnations of God. The Divine Omnipresence fills each soul-image even as the mighty ocean is present in each wave. However, unless a wave dissolves itself and becomes one with the ocean, it remains inordinately limited. Until a devotee is fully liberated, he cannot truly assert: "I and my Father are one."

There is no "special" avatar or a "unique" incarnation of God (except as regards form, time, and place); any liberated soul may descend to earth or to other spheres as a full avatar or saviour.

From the study of earthly chronology it is evident that, like a person, every nation undergoes the necessary evolutionary stages of development. For the earth, these four successive stages are the material, atomic, mental, and spiritual cycles, termed such according to the predominance of physical, electrical, psychical, or spiritual qualities in the majority of people. However, in every age tenacious wickedness is more or less active, even when virtue is prevalent. So whenever ignorance, selfishness, war, and misery are prominent, the Supreme Lord manifests through masters who, through many incarnations, have had earthly experiences as partially or fully liberated beings. They may appear on earth as minor saints or as great masters according to their degree of realization, to serve as living examples of virtue and to inspire spiritual aspirants to destroy their inward and outward evils. In this way Spirit appears through many liberated and partially liberated souls, shining more or less through the various degrees of unbefogged—clear and partially clear—mentalities of yoga-purified beings. Divine ones who are not fully liberated, or who come to earth to aid in the redemption of souls but have no obvious world mission, are called *khanda avatars* (partial incarnations).

❖
Partial and full manifestations of God's consciousness in saints and avatars
❖

But whenever the spectre of vice stalks unexorcised on the earth, in every such age God incarnates as a saviour (in the form of a fully liberated being) to resurrect fading virtue, protect the spiritual, help in the removal of evil currents, and destroy the evil propensities of the wicked. Such manifestations are called *purna avatars* (full incarnations).

As every wave, if it were conscious, could feel the ocean beneath it, so every liberated being feels the entire Sea of Spirit behind his perception. As the ocean appears in part, then in greater and greater vastness as a person views it first from the shore and then from an airplane, so saints of various intuitional powers have lesser or greater realizations of Spirit. But fully liberated souls such as Krishna, Jesus Christ, Babaji, Lahiri Mahasaya, Sri Yukteswarji, and many others, are themselves full manifestations of God. That is what is meant by the Bible statement: "But as many as received him (that is, fully manifested God through the purity of their intuition), to them (all liberated beings of all ages before and after Jesus Christ was born) gave he power to become the sons of God (the power to appear as full manifestations of God)."* A veritable "son of God" is a true image of omnipresent Spirit.

AS VERSE IV:8 IS OFTEN TRANSLATED to refer to "the destruction of *evildoers,*" and as many legendary stories in the *Puranas* also cite the annihilation of the wicked by holy beings, certain theologians claim that a Hindu incarnation of God comes to protect the virtuous by destroying evildoers, in contradistinction to Jesus Christ who came on earth to liberate not only virtuous men but malefactors! However, the truth is that virtue always causes the destruction of evil.

Divine virtue manifested by an avatar destroys evil

We read in the Bible that even Elisha, Elijah, and Peter were instrumental in the destruction of evildoers who had resisted the powerful vibrations of virtue. Swami Shankara and various saints of India have had similar experiences. An insulated wire carrying a million volts of current is harmless when touched, but an exposed live wire is deadly. When a person, in spite of warning, deliberately ventures to contact that powerful live wire without its cover, he is electrocuted. Similarly, God's potent energy, present everywhere, is insulated from man by a cover of delusive ignorance. Thus an ignorant man blaspheming God is not immediately punished; but a wicked man who is a contemporary and acquaintance of an avatar or a great master is inviting instant retribution if, after warning, he continues to defy the Spirit flaming through the pure vehicle of the Great One. For instance, Peter was able to perceive God without any insulation of delusion. The Holy

* John 1:12.

Spirit was fully manifest in him, and when the married couple*—in spite of Peter's warning—lied before the live Spirit, they were destroyed. Their wilful evil collided with the omnipotent harmony of the Divine.

God or His saints seldom deliberately hurt anyone, and then only to mitigate the effects of that person's bad karma, or to give a direct lesson to hasten redemption. Neither God nor His avatars ever turn Their omnipotence against any evildoers out of wrath or vengeance. People hurt themselves by manifesting unnatural evils. The knuckles of a person are broken when he performs the stupid or unnatural act of striking them hard against a stone wall. The stone wall is innocent of all evil intention, just as virtue is innocent when vice foolishly hurls itself against it.

The same principle is at work empowering the divine man, with or without a conscious act on his part, to bestow blessings on those who are receptive. Devotees who approach Divinity with the harmony of a pure heart and mind, attract instant blessings from the sight or touch of a holy person (*darshan*). For example, in the press of a great crowd, Jesus suddenly said, "Somebody hath touched me: for I perceive that virtue is gone out of me." A woman had been healed instantly when with faith she came up behind Jesus and touched the border of his garment.†

Avatars such as Krishna and Christ have such power of the Almighty within them that they could open their spiritual eye and annihilate the wicked, even as God could destroy the universe in a second. Little does frail man realize the Power he pits himself against when he chooses to oppose Divinity! Yet he needn't fear the wrath of a tyrannical God. Neither He nor His saints and avatars stoop to obvious human methods of either chastisement or compensation. God coaxes His children back to Him only by the attracting power of His love, incarnate in every atom of creation and in every soul. Similarly, His saints and avatars almost always use the mild method of spiritual persuasion to inspire the wicked to reform.

Man, made in the image of God with free will like His Creator, rewards or punishes himself by the results of his merits or demerits; he himself operates the exacting law of karma. Divine intervention, when on occasion it is warranted, expresses neither vengefulness nor favouritism, but is meted out for man's highest good by a just and loving God, or through his equally compassionate incarnations.

---

* Acts 5:1–10. † Luke 8:43–48.

MANY THINKERS POSIT GOD AS INFINITE and impersonal, and that He cannot be finite and personal. This conception limits the almightiness of God. Just as invisible hydrogen-oxygen gas can be condensed into vapour, or water, or frozen into a solid as ice, so God the impersonal Spirit and invisible Cosmic Consciousness can and does materialize Itself into a Great Light, into an Intelligible Voice of any language, into any desired form, and into a finite personal body.

Though fully manifest in an avatar, God is not limited to one form

God, who has created all human beings and is secretly present in them, can be perceptibly manifest in saints, or can materialize a new human body that can be seen or touched or heard by an advanced devotee or by any number of persons. One can say with truth that the entire Absolute God is vibrating and manifesting in that newly materialized body, but it would be a metaphysical blunder to say that God is limited to that body. The Infinite God can and does manifest in a three-dimensional form. He has appeared to many liberated souls in this way, in whatever concept they longed to see. But God is not confined to that form, nor has He adopted any such form as His sole personal image. The Infinite is infinite in His expressions; that is why God has never had a permanent definite form.

God prefers to employ His own Self-created law of limitation, the law of relativity, when He appears as a human being. He chooses to incarnate in the bodies of liberated masters. In this way, He appears in various costumes of flesh to suit the desires and needs of His devotees through the ages. For example, as Rama or Krishna or Jesus or Babaji, and so on, He has been born in different forms to help the growth of virtue and the dissolution of vice in the world. God, being Infinite, can rematerialize any form, and does so at times. But He never allows a divinely manifested form such as Krishna or Jesus to be visibly present for a long period before the staring gaze of ignorant people. Therefore, the deathless Babaji, who has a human form at the present time, remains in utmost secrecy in the northern Himalayas near Badrinarayan. However, any liberated being can instantaneously materialize himself before an advanced saint or even (for special purposes) before a group of ordinary men, as did Jesus and Babaji.

Why does God prefer to manifest Himself through partially liberated and fully liberated beings whom He sends to reincarnate on earth (by "immaculate" or by ordinary sexual creation) to quicken the evolution of virtuous people and to dissolve the wickedness of vicious beings? Because such advanced souls were once ordinary human beings subject to all the temptations and delusions of Cosmic Nature. Such divine agents have sympathy, humour, and understanding; they can tell their fellow beings: "Behold, we were once bound by the flesh, just as you are now! By dint of self-control, discrimination, meditation, and spiritual labour, we have reaped the plenteous harvest of omnipresent Spirit. If we have done that, you too can overcome the weak, difficult flesh by a continuous expansion of consciousness and strengthening of the Spirit that is also within you!"

God could produce Jesus Christs and Babajis by the thousands by direct materialization or via the ordinary embryonic creation, and could have them act out their sacred lives as divine puppets. But could such beings, lacking past personal experience of the intricate compulsions of sense temptations, serve realistically as exemplars to teach human beings the art of conquering flesh allurements by natural human methods of self-control? Devotees admire Christ because he came among men as one of them. He was humanly tempted, and he suffered at the hands of persecutors; but he overcame all human ordeals by will, effort, and love for God! A sacred puppet, acting out a divine drama of temptation and victory, would be only a spurious actor on the stage of life. But a human being who becomes a master is a spiritual artist who can show other fellow beings how to destroy evil and become divine.

The soul of an ignorant being and of a master are the same in essence, and are perfect, even as the one moon's reflections appearing distorted in pots of agitated and muddy water, or undistorted in calm and clear water, are reflections of the same object—the moon.

When the water in the pot is muddy and agitated by a breeze, the moon reflected there appears distorted even though it is not so in reality; muddy minds agitated with the restlessness caused by the attributes of Nature similarly cause a seeming distortion of the soul. When, by yoga meditation, the muddied mind of ignorance settles, restlessness disappears; the clear soul is manifest.

As the moon's reflection may be distorted beyond recognition in swirling water, so is the soul's reflection grossly distorted in a materialistic man. As the moon is recognizably reflected in slightly agitated clear water, or perfectly reflected in completely calm clear water, so enlightened souls are either partial or full manifestations of God. As calm clear water in various pots reflects perfectly the same shining moon, so all liberated souls manifest the same pure soul essence. When the pots are broken and the water released, the reflected images that had appeared to be confined in various pots become one with the moon whose light is spread all over the sky; similarly, all fully liberated masters who can separate their reflected souls from their bodies at will and yet live in bodily forms are perfect and equal soul-images of God. There is a delusive difference in the appearance, but when they dematerialize their bodily confinements they are the same One Omnipresent Spirit.

❖
Belief that one liberated master is greater than another is dogmatic ignorance
❖

Dogmatic disciples with their little minds strive to represent their own particular master as greater than other masters. Who may say with authority: "My master is a fully liberated incarnation of God"? Only he who has true intuition and is himself perfected in the wisdom of God-attunement.

Anyone who says, "My master is the greatest incarnation of God, or the only liberated master," is unquestionably ignorant. The yardstick of judging fully liberated masters is possessed only by fully liberated disciples. A liberated disciple is completely loyal to his master, the guru who had shown him the way to liberation, but he always respects other avatars and masters. Masters and disciples who have achieved Self-realization after wandering through various bypaths of beliefs love all saints as one in God. Ignorant disciples, trying to glorify a certain avatar as supreme over other avatars, instead belittle that master through their bigotry, intolerance, hate, inquisitions, crusades, and religious wars.

In Omnipresence there is no labour foreman, no president, nor servant; no great, greater, and greatest. All are equal and one with the Spirit—a joyous conclave of Divine Amity.

❖

HOW SPIRIT INCARNATES IN THE SUCCESSIVE STRATA OF CREATION

THESE STANZAS of the Gita may also be interpreted as a reference to the history of creation. "Whenever there is a distortion of My Spirit (the protecting shelter or *dharma* of the universe) through the action of My delusory *maya*, then My Infinite Oneness is divided into finite waves of creation, colliding with one another in the evil of pain and disharmony. In order to bring back the harmonious goodness of My One United Being and to destroy the ominous evils of seeming relativities, My Spirit (limited when displayed as warring matter, minerals, plants, animals, and human beings) continuously incarnates Itself in repeated evolutionary influxes until, by dissolving the unsalutary clashing dualities, all recover the eternal blissful state of oneness."

The above brings out two points:

(1) Spirit, by eclipsing Itself in cosmic delusion, appears as myriad ever-changing material phenomena. It is by this process, this malevolent delusive medium, that Spirit re-creates Itself from the macrocosmic Infinitude to infinitesimal, microcosmic, almost unendingly divisible ions of energy. "I beheld Satan as lightning fall from heaven."* Cosmic energy flowing down from Spirit manifests the troublesome material nature (Apara-Prakriti; Maya, Satan).

(2) After outwardly projecting Itself as energy into atomic matter, the utmost density of delusion, Spirit sees the constant roil of the atomic forces of finite creation—colliding, uniting, warring, dividing according to laws of attraction and repulsion—as etheric, gaseous, fiery, liquid, solid forms emerging, dissolving, ever changing. Spirit, disappointed that delusive *maya* does not reflect Its perfection in creation, halts this outward repulsion and begins the process of reunification by incarnating Itself in progressively higher forms of life and expression. Asleep in the inert minerals of matter, Spirit begins to dream in the vegetative life of trees and flowers. Then Spirit partially awakens in the sentient mobility of the tiny amoeba and the mighty beast. Fully awake in man, Spirit's discriminative intelligence reaches out as a conqueror of the delusive mysteries of life. And in the illumined man, Spirit's incarnation is complete!†

AT WHATEVER PERIOD of eternity Spirit first created Itself into various forms of creation, including the first human beings, all Its manifested objects easily reflected Its spiritual quality during a Spiritual Age of 4,800 years. The original purity of creation evidenced its emergence from causal manifestation into astral and then material form.

Descent of humanity from original Golden Age

Adam and Eve, symbolic of the first human beings specially created by God, were fully conscious of their divinity until through the temptation of Nature they indulged in sex creation, causing their godly consciousness to descend from the higher cerebrospinal centres of spiritual perception to the lower channels of life identified with sensual mortal consciousness.‡

---

* Luke 10:18.

† See explanation of the unfolding of the five *koshas* of delusion by which higher forms of life come into being (I:4, page 63).

‡ See I:1, page 28 and XV:1, page 930; also Sri Yukteswar's insightful discourse on the Adam and Eve allegory, recorded in *Autobiography of a Yogi,* Chapter 16, "Outwitting the Stars." Though the creation of life-forms through the process of evolution is a fact, the

After the Spiritual Age, reincarnating earthly beings and their cosmic environment, under the influence of the outgoing separative desire of Spirit to create (manifesting as *maya* or the Cosmic Delusive Force), began to descend to the Mental Age of 3,600 years, the Atomic Age of 2,400 years, and the Material Age of 1,200 years.

After the general populace on earth and the entire solar universe had manifested the vibrations of the Material Age, then Spirit—to stop Its creation from further devolution—created a magnetic upward pull so that the Material Age began to evolve into the Atomic, Mental, and Spiritual Ages again, covering 12,000 more years.

The yugas, or evolutionary cycles of history

THESE DOWNWARD AND UPWARD evolutionary cycles, each complete equinoctial cycle taking 24,000 years, have been gone through about 83,000 times during the two billion years that scientists estimate the earth has already existed.* Whenever this earthly school has fulfilled its temporary purpose in God's scheme according to cyclic timing, or whenever all the inhabitants have been fully educated in manifesting complete divinity, then, through a cosmic deluge, Spirit will not only release human beings but also the karma-tortured active atoms of the earth. In partial dissolutions, only certain areas of the earth are "dissolved," such as the continent of Atlantis and the Land of Mu (Lemuria) in the Pacific. Plato recounts the legends of one such partial dissolution when (about 9000 B.C.) the land vibrated and trembled and great fissures appeared; Atlantis disappeared into the surrounding water with its multitudinous inhabitants.†

Lord's highest creature, original man, was a special creation, materialized by the force of God's will. The Creator endowed the new human species with unique cerebrospinal centres of life and consciousness, potentially capable of expressing Divinity. Into these first prototype human bodies the Lord placed enlightened souls from the causal and astral realms, and also transferred souls that had evolved upward through lower evolutional forms. The human body provided these souls with an instrumental medium through which they could reclaim and fully manifest the Divine Image in which they were made.

* As of 1995, scientific evidence has dated the earth at closer to five billion years.

† In addition to the *yugas,* the Hindu scriptures mention cosmic cycles called Days and Nights of Brahma, and Ages of Brahma (see VIII:17–19). According to the *Surya Siddhanta,* all creatures are destroyed at the end of Brahma's Day, though the substance of the universe is not. At the end of the Age of Brahma, however, matter itself is resolved back into Spirit. Other sources state that the Day of Brahma is the lifespan of a solar system, while the Age of Brahma constitutes the lifespan of the entire universe.

In X:6, reference is made to another cycle, the patriarchate or *manvantara* (literally "another Manu" or "the interval of a Manu"), of which the scriptures say there are four-

History could hardly record complete cosmic or earthly dissolutions! At such times a planet, for example, and all things on it are converted into diaphanous energy. Only liberated masters, through visions, have seen such cosmic dissolutions; and no one except God has kept a record of how many times the earthly school-building and its pupils have been entirely dematerialized into astral or causal form, or into mere seed-ideas in the mind of the Creator, and then brought forth again throughout the many "Days of Creation"—periods of manifestation, which are then followed by "Nights of Dissolution."

With each reemergence of the cosmic schoolhouse, God begins anew to train its pupils—some who are newly arrived, and others who are repeaters (as Krishna explains in VIII:19). Advancing through the different grades of incarnations, they must ultimately pass the final examination of liberation. As the lifespan for a whole universe, according to ancient seers, is over 300 trillion years—an Age of Brahma—no doubt God (garbed as Krishna) declares: "Arjuna, I have attained all, I have nothing to attain, yet I go on working" (III:22).

The Infinite Spirit has been in ecstasy in vibrationless space, and active in vibratory space, for countless aeons of eternity. The Spirit thus divides Itself in creation by the declining-power of delusion, and then brings back to Itself all prodigal outgoing forms through upward evolution. At the end of the universal lifespan, the wandering organic and inorganic forces are transmuted as fluid energy into His Cosmic Consciousness. The storm of delusion is recalled; all waves of animate and inanimate creation become again the sea of Spirit. But that is not the end! After a time, the seeds of creation, carefully preserved in Spirit, are cast forth again to begin their productive cycle anew.

The Downward and Upward Evolution of the Soul

LASTLY, THESE TWO STANZAS of the Gita relate also to the evolution of the individualized soul. During an incarnation, whenever a devotee finds himself in delusion owing to sense identification, the Spirit manifests Itself in him by trying to foster his longing for soul bliss.

Man's desire to seek salvation often arises out of the torturing power of affliction. However, many mortals suffer through a long pe-

---

teen in each Day of Brahma. The *Surya Siddhanta* and the *Vishnu Purana* state that in each patriarchate there arises a new Manu, who becomes for his own period the progenitor of mankind. At the end of each *manvantara* is a deluge, followed by a new race of humans. *(Publisher's Note)*

riod of incarnations without experiencing any awakening. A deluded man is finally roused through the indwelling divine aid that urges him continuously to attempt to regain the image of Spirit; he discovers Its presence recreated within him by each new effort.

Thus, as often as man's body-identified or depraved nature (*adharma*) manifests, owing to the effects of the misuse of free choice, so often does the soul's real nature (*dharma*) emerge through spiritual self-effort, stimulated by the inward manifestations of the ever awake, ever kind Spirit:

"I manifest Myself in the soul of man to rally his good qualities (the springs of good actions) to conquer his human demerits (the springs of evil activities). I infuse My power in the devotee who inspirits his noble qualities of discrimination and calm intuitive conscience, dispassion, life-force control, self-control, self-discipline to avoid unrighteous actions, and spiritual patience in adherence to meditation, renunciation, and austerity. With the advent of My Spirit and Its reinforcement, the stimulated virtuous qualities cause the dissolution of the human vicious demerits—desire, anger, greed, attachment, egoity, jealousy, hate, illusion and delusion."

The final victory of the evolution of the soul—of "virtue" over "vice"—is the inner realization or experience of ascension into Spirit. The first two verses of this Gita chapter described the spiritual symbolical aspect of the various stages (Vivasvat, Manu, Ikshvaku, and the Rajarishis) through which the soul of the devotee has descended from the Infinite to the finite.

Emerging from Cosmic Consciousness, the soul enters the vibratory state of Cosmic Light, or Vivasvat. When it comes under the influence of the mind (*manas*) it becomes individualized, limited by identification with human consciousness in general, termed the Manu state of the descending soul. Thence it flows down into astral life and consciousness, or the Ikshvaku state. The soul then further descends into the Rajarishis, or sense-identified state.

During a long lapse of time, the soul remains identified with the body and forgets its union with the Spirit. The soul thus leaves the higher cosmic spatial palace of Omnipresence to descend the darkening stairway of limitations, and begins to wander on the low plains of materialism; "vice" (*adharma*) prevails.

It follows that every prodigal son, seeking to ascend by retracing his footsteps upward to Spirit, must attune himself to the inner urgings of Spirit—incarnate in his soul—and through proper yoga meditation leave behind him the identification with material habits and sense enjoyments

(Rajarishis), intuitive perception of astral life and consciousness (Ikshvaku), the sum total of individualized human consciousness (Manu), and Cosmic Light (Vivasvat). Reaching the Spirit, the soul "breathes" a long sigh of joyous relief! Perfect "virtue" (*dharma*) is re-established.

PATHS OF LIBERATION FROM THE ROUNDS OF REBIRTH

VERSE 9

जन्म कर्म च मे दिव्यमेवं यो वेत्ति तत्त्वतः।
त्यक्त्वा देहं पुनर्जन्म नैति मामेति सोऽर्जुन॥

He who thus intuits, in their reality of orderly principles, My divine manifestations and vibratory actions, is not reborn after death; he obtains Me, O Arjuna!

WHENEVER SPIRIT DESCENDS into vibratory matter, taking rebirth therein by the action of *maya*, delusion, It passes through several stages, the effects of the orderly creative principles (*tattvas*) of Nature: cosmic consciousness, energy, gases, liquids, solids, macrocosmic matter (the universe), microcosmic matter (man, with soul, consciousness, life force, and body). The soul thus descends with Spirit and becomes body-locked.

The Spirit remains free even though reborn or manifested as matter; but man, as individualized Spirit or a soul, becomes identified with his little universe—body, senses, and possessions.

By renunciation of outer and inner attachment, a yogi begins to ascend from the planes of objective possessions; he disentangles himself from the senses, sensory and motor mechanism, influences of his subconscious mind and of his karma of many lives, and begins to climb to the superconscious state. He ceases his wandering in matter and realizes himself a perfect image of Spirit, dwelling in the body but unattached to it.

When the yogi has united his soul with Spirit by higher ecstasies, he sees how the Cosmic Light of Spirit has transformed Itself through the principles of Nature into various forms of matter on the canvas of ether, just as a clear beam of light proceeding from a booth in a motion picture house and passing through a film changes into pictures of mountain scenery, trees, lakes, oceans, human beings, and so on, thus producing the illusion of solids, liquids, gases, organic and inorganic matter, interacting on the screen.

Krishna says that he who can actually perceive the true nature of the rebirth of Spirit as matter becomes liberated. An enlightened yogi realizes by intuitive experience how omnipresent Spirit is born in the body of cosmic matter and resides therein without entanglement. Such a yogi, being one with Spirit, is liberated even though he wears a fleshly garment.

VERSE 10

वीतरागभयक्रोधा मन्मया मामुपाश्रिताः ।
बहवो ज्ञानतपसा पूता मद्भावमागताः ॥

Sanctified by the asceticism of wisdom, disengaged from attachment, fear, and ire, engrossed and sheltered in Me, many beings have attained My nature.

AS A PERSON EXCITEDLY ENGROSSED in a motion picture can dismiss his emotional involvement and behold with calmness the beam of light overhead that is producing the pictures, even so an advanced yogi by neutralizing his emotions can see the dream pictures of life issuing out of the Omnipresent Beam of Spirit. Engrossed in the Infinite Reality, that being becomes liberated.

The Hindu scriptures compare the following of the spiritual path to walking on a razor's edge. This refers not only to the necessity of following a virtuous God-centred life, but specifically to the erect, straight spine of meditation, the sole path through which one ascends to the realization of God and union with Him.* Throughout the ages many devotees—sanctified by the proper moral and physical discipline, by meditation, and by such a technique as *Kriya Yoga*—have kindled the purifying fire of Self-realization and have seen in that lambent light the

---

* Jesus similarly spoke of the "narrow way," esoterically referring to the ascent in meditation of the life force and consciousness through the gateway at the base of the spine (*muladhara chakra*) and the narrow passageway of the *sushumna:* "Enter ye in at the strait gate: for wide is the gate, and broad is the way, that leadeth to destruction, and many there be which go in thereat: Because strait is the gate, and narrow is the way, which leadeth unto life, and few there be that find it" (Matthew 7:13–14).

Omnipresent Spirit. Uniting their body-confined souls with all-pervading Spirit, the devotee loses attachment to the fear-and-anger-exciting physical miasma and becomes immersed and secure in Omnipresent Spirit.

Materialists are so attached to the enjoyment of sense objects that they live their lives full of fear, fear lest they lose the gross pleasures of health or physical comforts; and they are consumed by anger when it does happen. But the wise, recognizing the body as a brittle basket of pleasure, do not put into it all the eggs of their happiness, knowing the consequence will be a scrambled pile of humpty-dumpties.

VERSE 11

ये यथा मां प्रपद्यन्ते तांस्तथैव भजाम्यहम्।
मम वर्त्मानुवर्तन्ते मनुष्याः पार्थ सर्वशः॥

O Partha (Arjuna)! in whatever way people are devoted to Me, in that measure I manifest Myself to them. All men, in every manner (of seeking Me), pursue a path to Me.

"AS MEN OF VARIOUS NATURES offer their devotion to Me in different ways, so do I variously respond, according to their heart's desire, their degree of understanding, and their manner of worship. All beings, regardless of their mode of seeking, wend their way to Me."

Throughout the ages, the strong motivating force of human love has been expressed in diverse ways—filial, conjugal, friendly, family, serviceful, humanitarian. All human love is borrowed from Divine Love, but by comparison is a meagre expression. Dissatisfied with the imperfections of human love, man finally turns toward the perfect love of God. As the love of His children is the one thing the Lord is seeking, it is that devotion, freely given—in whatever form of expression, endeavour, or worship—that brings His divine response. He makes Himself known to a seeker in a measure commensurate with that person's mentality and capacity to receive.

Devotees worship the Lord variously—as the Infinite or Heavenly Father or Divine Mother, or as Divine Friend (like the relationship between Krishna and Arjuna), or as Divine Lover, Divine Beloved, Divine Master, Divine Child. God responds to the devotee in whatever aspect he holds dear. To the true monist He reveals Himself as the Infinite; to the sincere dualist He appears in the desired finite form.

Water may manifest as small or big waves on the ocean; or as surf foam or bubbles; or as raindrops or icebergs—but in these various forms it is water just the same. By the power of *maya* or delusion, the Spirit similarly assumes many forms, manifesting Itself as numerous human beings endowed with free choice, working their way through various evolutionary stages—good or evil, bound or free, attached or nonattached, desireful or desireless. It is only because of restless delusion that men feel themselves apart from Spirit, and do not perceive His immanence within themselves and all Nature. The yogi quiets this movement of duality by the meditation-born consciousness of Unity, realizing thus how all dual manifestations of Nature arise from and dissolve into the oneness of Spirit.

Spirit became the twenty-four attributes of Nature, and through the action of delusion manifests as the infinite variety of combinations of these attributes. No matter how variegated the objects and people of this earth appear, they all come from the one spiritual Source. The conceptions held by human beings concerning this Source, however, are biased by each person's self-created screen of delusion (his personal interactions with Nature's attributes) through which all of his perceptions and thoughts are filtered. Thus arises from the customized needs of different mentalities a man-made necessity for a variety of religions (for various expressions of the one Truth), to which the Lord gives assent and blessing. But there are obstructions that separate religion from God—these are dogmatic fanaticism, bigotry, and intolerance. In the Lord's eyes, the real infidel is he who dishonours Him in any of his ennobling manifestations. All true paths—whether theological, serviceful, discriminative, devotional, or scientific (*Raja Yoga*)—can in greater or lesser degree bestow on the sincere follower a corresponding insight or illumination.*

---

* "By religion, I do not mean formal religion, or customary religion, but that religion which underlies all religions, which brings us face to face with our Maker.

"Indeed religion should pervade every one of our actions. Here religion does not mean sectarianism. It means a belief in ordered moral government of the universe. It is not less real because it is unseen. This religion transcends Hinduism, Islam, Christianity, etc. It does not supersede them. It harmonizes them and gives them reality.

"My Hinduism is not sectarian. It includes all the best that I know to be the best in Islam, Christianity, Buddhism and Zoroastrianism.

"Religions are different roads converging to the same point. What does it matter that we take different roads, so long as we reach the same goal?

"The need of the moment is not one religion, but mutual respect and tolerance of the devotees of the different religions. We want to reach not the dead level, but unity in diversity. The soul of religions is one, but it is encased in a multitude of forms. The latter will persist to the end of time."—*Mahatma Gandhi (Publisher's Note)*

Some seekers follow the path of pure renunciation (realization of the sensory world as transitory and God as the only true Life), while others pursue the difficult path of wisdom-guided worldly life, and still others travel the circuitous deluding path of sense pleasures. Whether seeking contentment by renunciation, or by activity combined with spiritual discrimination, or by pleasure in sensuality, mankind is in pursuit of true happiness. Everyone, therefore, sooner or later will have to turn to the Source, and thereby will find the divine bliss of Spirit. The wise reach the goal quickly, through meditation; worldly people more slowly, by comparison of good and evil; while those who are now "wicked" will seek true spiritual bliss only after many disillusionments prove the folly of their misdirected course.

VERSE 12

काङ्क्षन्तः कर्मणां सिद्धिं यजन्त इह देवताः ।
क्षिप्रं हि मानुषे लोके सिद्धिर्भवति कर्मजा ॥

Desiring success of their actions here on earth, men adore the gods (various ideals), because achievement accruing from activity is readily attained in the world of men.

THE MATERIALIST KNOWS that proper action will bring success to his endeavours; his thoughts and prayers propitiate the "gods" of those forces and factors necessary to accomplish his material goals.

The yogi knows that here and now, even while he is still incarnate on earth, he can be successful in attaining Self-realization by proper actions of yoga practice; through these he becomes attuned to the divine creative forces that have made him a limited human being and that can retransform him into an illumined liberated soul.

Success in obtaining material goals and pleasures is relatively easy in a world fashioned for this purpose. Thus man pursues the obvious immediate gains, the "tangibles," all of which are treacherously evanescent.

Lasting success consists in freeing the soul from the threefold sorrow (physical, mental, and spiritual) inevitable in the limited human being, and in attaining the bliss of final liberation.

In order to attain scientifically that true success, *Kriya Yogis* learn to withdraw life force and mind by *pranayama,* leading them upward from the sensory-motor nerves to the cosmic consciousness of the thousand-rayed current in the cerebrum. By this mode of scientific "worship," the yogi communicates with the various deities (becomes attuned with the powers) at the six centres in the cerebrospinal axis. By this *Kriya Yoga* ascension, the miraculous powers (*siddhis*) over mind and matter mentioned by Patanjali are in time attained.* The yogi then discards those inferior powers for the supreme Miracle—God. Finding Him, the devotee has achieved true success.

Pranayama meditation brings ultimate spiritual success

The mind (*manas*) moving outward into the sensory-motor nerves is the originator of all actions that lead to various forms of earthly accomplishments. When this mind is withdrawn from the muscles, senses, involuntary organs, and spine into the brain, the mind-identified ego becomes the perfect soul. The soul then becomes united with the Spirit shining in the thousand-rayed lotus of light.

By the proper and intense practice of Spirit-and-soul-uniting technique, the yogi attains mastery and ultimate liberation in a relatively short time. Compare this effort and its lasting success to the continual material activity and small results obtainable in this mundane world—gains that slip away or must be left behind at death. Yogi "industrialists"—accomplished yogis who continue to live and serve in the world—by their increased mind-power, achieve quicker "business success" than can the ordinary shrewd but not deep-visioned worldly man.

THE LORD'S MODES OF ACTION WITHIN HIS CREATION

VERSE 13

चातुर्वर्ण्यं मया सृष्टं गुणकर्मविभागशः ।
तस्य कर्तारमपि मां विद्ध्यकर्तारमव्ययम् ॥

According to the differentiation of attributes (gunas) and actions (karma), I have created the four castes. Though thus the Doer, yet know Me to be the Nonperformer, beyond all change.

THE LORD, AS THE COSMIC CREATOR, has fashioned a world of beings patterned after the activities of His own nature: Cosmic Intelligence,

* See VIII:17–19, page 736 n.

Cosmic Energy, Cosmic Organization or Orderly Law, and Cosmic Motion. In man, these activities are expressed under the differentiating influence of the three *gunas* or qualities with which the Lord has imbued Nature: *sattva* (elevating), *rajas* (activating), and *tamas* (degrading). From the actions and the good, active, or evil qualities of man arise the four natural castes: spiritual (Intelligence, or Brahmins), ruling and protecting (Energy, or Kshatriyas), organizing or business-cultivating (Orderly Law, or Vaishyas), and labour (Motion, or Sudras). God's consciousness, pure and beyond all attributes, assumes an outward appearance of differentiation when expressed through the variety of human qualities and behaviour. As a pure white light remains unchanged and yet appears different when viewed through glasses of different colours, so the one Spirit expressing through the good, active, and evil qualities and characteristic activities of human beings looks different in each case, but is nevertheless the one Spirit.

❖

UNDERSTANDING THE CASTE SYSTEM

THE SUN, MOON, STARS, planets, creatures, man, are the result of God's intelligence, energy, and motion moving through space in an organized manner. Intelligence is God's "brain"; energy is His "life"; motion is His "body"; and organization or orderly law is His plan of the universe. These four activities were combined into the form of the human being. Intelligence became the head. Cosmic Energy provided the life and vitality in the body. Motion created the feet. And organization in the body came from orderly law, God's organizing power.

These four activities are the blueprint from which all races are made. (1) The intelligentsia, or wisdom-guided. They are the natural Brahmins who live close to God and reflect His Intelligence by discriminative thought and spiritual activity. (2) The energetic warriors and rulers. They are the natural Kshatriyas. The direct result of God's Energy, they like to be active, to fight for a cause, to defend their country, to protect the defenseless and the weak. In every society, there are those who become evil and have to be checked by the idealistic strong. (3) The organizers. These are the business leaders. They are the natural Vaishyas. As an outgrowth of God's orderly activity, they have an ability to organize the economic and labour structures of society. (4) The labouring class. They are the natural Sudras. They express the motion of God, without which the universal and social machinery would come to a halt.

❖
Organization of creation mirrored in organization of society
❖

The differences in these four natural castes of activity do not make one greater or less than the others. All are necessary to the Cosmic Plan. When in man's body the brain, or the feet, or the hands, or the orderly life functions refuse to cooperate, the whole body suffers as a consequence. If in a society the superior intellects, the rulers and soldiers, the business leaders, and the labourers all fight each other, they will all suffer and perish. The welfare of one group cannot be sacrificed for the aggrandizement of another group falsely considered more elite or important.

Scriptures and history show that among all peoples, savage and civilized alike, a fourfold division of men has been made for the proper government of a large clan, race, or nation.* Even from primeval times there seems to have been in all races a God-ordained natural classification of peoples into types—based not on heredity but on inherent characteristics.

In India certain powerful religious leaders among the Brahmins—not unlike the Pharisees in the time of Christ—arranged to base the caste system entirely on heredity to suit their own despotic purposes. For a long time the general masses fell prey to the theory that the vocation of priest or warrior or businessman or labourer should be determined according to heredity, and not according to innate tastes or abilities. The son of a Brahmin was automatically a Brahmin even if he knew nothing of religious or philosophical life, or even if he had tendencies to act like a businessman or a warrior or a sense slave. When the warriors in India lost out against foreign aggression, the businessmen, labourers, and priests stood by, inactive, saying, "Too bad the Kshatriyas (warriors) lost; it is, of course, against our hereditary custom for us from the other three castes to fight." This wrong attitude is one of the reasons why India lost her liberty when the land was invaded by enemies.

This accursed hereditary view of caste always has been condemned by wise swamis, yogis, and other enlightened men of India. Shankara, the founder of the Swami Order, wrote: "No birth, no death, no caste have I." He renounced the Brahmin caste in which he had been born. The followers of Mahatma Gandhi and of other modern leaders in India are doing much good in reforming the caste system.†

Of course, it can be rightfully assumed that through the influence

---

* See also references to "caste"—Brahmins, Kshatriyas, Vaishyas, and Sudras—in II:31, III:24, and XVIII:41–46.

† "Part of Gandhi's legacy is the protection the Indian constitution offers to untouchables," according to *The Economist,* June 8, 1991. Ratified in 1950, India's constitution abolishes caste "untouchability" and forbids any other restriction on public facilities arising out of caste membership. Former outcastes ("untouchables"—whom Gandhi lovingly renamed *harijans,* "children of God") "have reserved seats in the lower houses of

of heredity and environment, the offspring of priests, warriors, businessmen, and labourers are usually bound to show many "family" traits. It may be easier for a son of a priest to become a priest, and for a son of a warrior to become a soldier. But it is also true that the strongest instincts in offspring do not always reflect the qualities of the parents. The sons of ministers are proverbially known to choose other vocations; and so it is with the other "castes." The son of Napoleon was by no means a military genius! Two children whose natures are in direct opposition are often found in one family. A single cause of affinity, such as a love of harmony, is responsible for the rebirth of a materially inclined person in a spiritually harmonious family.

To classify a person's caste by heredity is pure ignorance

It is therefore pure ignorance to classify castes according to heredity, for we know that a labourer's child may be a musical genius, and that the son of a warrior may be a good businessman. In accordance with modern military draft laws, sons of clergymen, businessmen, and labourers—and not only the offspring of warriors—have been drawn into the vortex of war; all classes have shown equal reluctance—and equal bravery!

Each man, the reincarnation of an ego with various personal traits and instincts, born in a family whose characteristics may be quite foreign to him, should be allowed to pursue the work most congenial to him.

THIS VERSE OF THE GITA, mentioning the creation of the four castes, refers not only to the activities toward which man is naturally inclined, but also to the fact that, although souls have all been made in the same image of Spirit, yet, when introduced into various bodies, they are allowed free choice to be influenced by the three *gunas* of Nature. These *three* qualities produce the *four* natural qualitative castes. All men display an admixture of all the *gunas,* thus accounting for the bewildering variety of human nature in general, and also for the bewildering variety sometimes found in one person!

Man's caste determined by how he responds to the gunas

---

both the central and state legislatures, a quota of government jobs, and reserved places at schools and colleges," *The Economist* reported.

To remove the lingering evil roots of caste and race prejudice from the hearts of men and women in all nations of the world today, greater spiritual understanding is needed in addition to legislative efforts. "As soon as we learn in meditation to love God," Paramahansa Yogananda said, "we shall love all mankind as we love our own family. Those who have found God through their own Self-realization—those who have actually experienced God—they alone *can* love mankind; not impersonally, but as their blood brothers, children of the same one Father." *(Publisher's Note)*

Each man is marked with his natural caste by the predominance in himself of one of the following *gunas* or *guna*-mixtures: (1) *sattva* (good qualities), (2) *sattva-rajas* (mixture of good and active qualities), (3) *rajas-tamas* (mixture of active and materialistic qualities), (4) *tamas* (dark or evil qualities).

In accordance with personal karma, a man is born into (1) the natural Brahmin caste, "knowers of Brahma or Spirit," or (2) the natural Kshatriya caste, in which a mixture of good and activity-loving qualities predominates, or (3) the natural Vaishya caste, marked by a mixture of activity-loving and materialistic tendencies, or (4) the natural Sudra caste, characterized chiefly by love of bodily pleasures.

These four *guna*-states also influence meditation. In the attainment of yogic realization, the first state of meditation is surrounded by darkness. ("And the light shineth in darkness; and the darkness comprehended it not."*) The devotee is spoken of as being in the Sudra state when his mind is fully engrossed in the muscular and sensory restlessness of the body. When the yogi meditates deeper he beholds a reddish light on a dark background; he begins to cultivate the seeds of various spiritual perceptions on the soil of intuition, and has then risen to the next or Vaishya state.

The yogi develops further; with his divine-and-active attributes, he begins consciously to win the battle between sense distractions and soul intuitions. He becomes a veteran warrior, able to destroy successfully his invading sensations and subconscious thoughts by switching off his life force from the sensory-motor nerves. This is the sense-victorious Kshatriya state, in which the yogi sees a white light with a reddish glow—the light of the accumulated energy that has been withdrawn from the senses.

He learns how to withdraw this energy from the six spinal fortresses where the senses and the superior perceptions are ever locked in a battle between body consciousness and spiritual perceptions. In this fourth state, the yogi is successful in disconnecting his consciousness from earthly possessions, bodily sensations, subconscious thoughts, and life forces, and takes his ego (pseudosoul) through the sensory and motor nerves, the six spinal knots of flesh and mind to the frontal lobes of the brain in the fontanelle region,† and becomes united with the indescribable

* John 1:5.

† I.e., reference to the location of the thousand-petalled lotus in the astral body, which in the physical body corresponds to the area in the brain in the region where in the

white light of the Omnipresent Spirit (Brahman), manifestly expressed or seated on the subtly luminous throne of thousand-rayed spiritual perceptions. This is the supreme state of the natural Brahmin.

Verse 14

न मां कर्माणि लिम्पन्ति न मे कर्मफले स्पृहा।
इति मां योऽभिजानाति कर्मभिर्न स बध्यते ॥

Actions do not cause attachment in Me, nor have I longings for their fruits. He who is identified with Me, who knows My nature, is also free from the karmic fetters of works.

God, the Creator of all vibratory motion, manifested as cosmic energy and as atoms and island universes, remains free of any taint of attachment (*na limpanti**) to the repercussions of all motile energies. Neither has the Lord any special desire to attain a definite result from His harmonized forces of Nature. Those persons who cast off delusion and realize they are "made in the image of God" become, like the Lord, untrammelled by karmic bondage.

The Sanskrit phrase "*mam yas abhi-janati,*"† translated in this verse as "who is identified with Me, who knows My nature," is a reference to the devotee who in meditation turns his consciousness towards, or enters into, the inner perception of Spirit. He realizes thereby the identification of his true Self, the soul, with the Ever Perfect Lord.

Owing to the action of *maya* (delusion) operating through the active forces of Nature, man's mind flows outward through the senses, and the soul thereby becomes identified with the body and its possessions and environment. Thus begrimed with attachment, the pure nature of the soul is obscured; it becomes the pseudosoul or ego, with its individual delusion that develops likes and dislikes, the instigators of material entanglements. Only after many incarnations of suffering dis-

---

foetal stage and young infants there is a membranous-covered opening in the roof of the skull, called the frontal fontanelle, and commonly referred to as the "soft spot." (In the second year of life, the fontanelle transforms itself into bone, closing the skull opening.)

* From the Sanskrit root *lip,* "to be attached to; to smear, taint"; and *na,* "not."

† Literally: *abhi:* "into, towards"; *janati:* "remembers or recollects, knows"; *mam:* "Me"; *yas:* "who, whomever."

illusionments from expecting lasting happiness from an impermanent body and its pleasures does man gradually take steps to give up his egoistic nature and turn to a sincere search for fulfilment in inner calmness, introspection, and discriminative action. It is then that God sends a guru who acquaints the devotee with the art of reuniting the matter-bound ego with Spirit. By interiorization of the mind, the soul forsakes its egoistic body-bound nature and its attachments to the activities and desires of the body and the senses and begins to remember and express its true nature as a perfect reflection of Spirit.

No matter how long the obscuring mud of delusion has been imposed upon the golden image of the ever blessed soul, man has the free choice of solidifying and adding to the delusion by further acts of error, or of scraping off the mire with the instruments of discrimination and meditation.

The Lord plainly expresses His law in this Gita stanza: "Any of My children who want to attain My state of freedom and fulfilment must remember their identity with My Nature and avoid karmic entanglements by properly engaging in actions in this cosmic drama as I do—without desire for the fruits of actions, and without taint from delusive identifications and attachments arising therefrom." By following this rule, one can play the drama of pleasure or pain, prosperity or poverty, health or ill health, without mental upheavals and karmic consequences, even as actors play their comic or tragic parts without being affected inwardly.

God is Completeness; His acting in this universe in all its outer manifestations does not affect His inner being, His blissful transcendence. All His children can behave like Him, unaffected in the inner Self. They have freedom to become attached to actions and thus eclipse the soul-image in misery, or to act without attachment as does God, centring their consciousness on the inner perfect divine image. In any case, *all* human beings must act in some wise on this earth—even as God Himself has chosen the path of action. He is the Director, the actors, the plot, the stage, the scenery, and the audience—all factors connected with the cosmic drama. He acts in everything without seeking rewards or being delusively identified with any of His manifestations. But the fact remains that God does act; the "show does go on"! although the play is not necessary in order to fulfil any personal desire of His—even as a rich man, who has all the wealth he wants, may engage in some industry as a hobby, without any attachment to it or desire for financial gain.

I was once dining with a friend who enjoyed running a big farm of six hundred acres—at a loss! He was boasting about his expensive eggs. "They cost me ninety cents apiece!"

I laughed. "Then why do you operate the ranch at all?"

"I don't care whether it is successful or not," he replied. "I don't need the money, so I don't expect anything from it. I just run it to keep myself busy and to give jobs to others."

To God, this colossal cosmos is a hobby only. His true children must not take the earthly drama to heart; it is only a temporary activity! Being potential gods, all human beings—no matter how long bound to rebirths through the ever-winding chain of evil karma—will sometime have to make conscious efforts to achieve liberation. So although cosmic delusion holds the majority of human beings in its fetters of physical attachments, desires, misery, and death, now and then the few who try hard do escape!

VERSE 15

एवं ज्ञात्वा कृतं कर्म पूर्वैरपि मुमुक्षुभिः ।
कुरु कर्मैव तस्मात्त्वं पूर्वैः पूर्वतरं कृतम् ॥

Understanding this, wise men who have sought after salvation, since pristine times, have performed dutiful actions. Therefore, do thou also act dutifully, even as did the ancients of bygone ages.

FROM TIME IMMEMORIAL, seekers after spiritual freedom, remembering their identity with the true nature of God, who remains impersonal and unfettered midst all His creative activities, have thus behaved similarly—performing only rightful actions, free from egoistic entanglement. Every true devotee should learn to discriminate between God-sanctioned actions and material desire-instigated actions. He should then perform the God-inspired actions without any desire to be the beneficiary of the fruits thereof.

At first it seems drear and meaningless to act without desire for the result of material gain. But one eventually realizes that self-motivated actions interrupt and distort the drama of God, and that it is unwise and ungainful to act at cross-purposes with His divine plan. Therefore only dutiful actions should be performed, and those without attachment.

"God does not talk to me," the devotee may lament. "How then am I to know what actions to perform?" The answer is that God speaks to a devotee through his true guru-preceptor and the spiritual teachings given through that channel. When in doubt about actions, one can seek the aid of his guru, or of certain advanced disciples of the guru who are sanctioned to give such help. The technique of salvation given by the guru enables the disciple to attain divine attunement. By the disciple's practice of deep, guru-given meditation, God and one's guru—their power invisibly vibrating within the devotee—will guide him aright.

Never cease performing worthwhile actions! Krishna, Christ, Babaji, all worked, and still work, to save souls and to do their share to help God's drama of creation. Follow that example, that pattern of right action, set by the great ones throughout the ages.

The scriptures are full of instances warning that even advanced devotees fall from the heights if they do not work. *Outward* renunciation without right activity and meditation is dangerous; it concentrates the mind on its accustomed poisoned pleasures of the senses that are supposedly being relinquished. Without the joy of ecstasy or the actions of meditation and of service, the idle mind becomes an abode of evil thoughts and moods. Until final liberation is attained, nonactivity leads to mental sloth, sense attachment, and loss of God-consciousness. A good businessman is thus better than a slothful monk. But to renounce all for God, thinking of Him all the time during worthwhile spiritual activities, serving Him and His children without monetary gain, and meditating deeply on God at night and in the little daytime gaps of free time—that is the highest way.

The earnest devotee, renunciant and householder alike, meditates intensely at night when he is free from the interruptions of the world, and at daybreak before he begins his duties; and works throughout the day just to please God and His true servant, his guru, whose only wish is to help the disciple find God. One should feel the Divine Presence, and, inspired by It, work in obedience to the spiritual guidance (the *sadhana*) given by the guru; one thereby follows the surest way to live and work without misery. To do what one *wants* to do is not freedom; but to do what one *should* do, guided by the wisdom of a true guru, leads to complete emancipation.

FREEDOM FROM KARMA: THE NATURE OF RIGHT ACTION, WRONG ACTION, AND INACTION

VERSE 16

किं कर्म किमकर्मेति कवयोऽप्यत्र मोहिताः ।
तत्ते कर्म प्रवक्ष्यामि यज्ज्ञात्वा मोक्ष्यसेऽशुभात् ॥

Even the wise are confused about action and inaction. Therefore I will explain what constitutes true action—a knowledge that will free thee from evil.

EVEN SAGES WHO HAVE ATTAINED some communion with Spirit become identified with the senses again after their ecstatic state is gone, and thus remain bewildered as to what is right action. A saint who can retain his ecstatic state in the midst of activities is the doer of right actions (God-directed actions). Only actions performed with divine consciousness may be considered "right actions." Actions performed with ego consciousness are "wrong actions" (karma-involving actions).*

The yogi who does not persevere in meditation until he achieves the final unshakeable state of *nirvikalpa samadhi* is unable to retain God-communion in the midst of his material activities. The soul awakes in the ecstatic state but falls asleep (becomes the pseudosoul or ego) in the human wakeful state.

In the egoistic state even wise men become bewildered about the distinction between right action and wrong action. The yogi in the egoistic state begins to identify himself with the bodily conditions and impulses. Thus misled, he acts wrongly (in accordance with the dictates of the senses).

The difference between good action and ill action can be recognized if one keeps a constant vigil during the wakeful state. For example, a hungry yogi begins to eat a meal (nothing wrong here). But as he eats, his mind becomes concentrated on the taste ("dangerous curves ahead!"). Finally he overeats (incurs a karmic debt to Nature). Thus even a wise man may forget to distinguish the almost indivisible dividing line

* The meaning of "inaction," as being quite distinct from wrong action, is elaborated in succeeding stanzas.

between self-controlled eating and uncontrolled eating; and, in general, between soul-identified actions and body-identified actions.

All the evils and miseries of human existence begin when the soul forgets to use the body and the senses as its instruments and servants. When the soul becomes identified with the body, its consciousness is turned senseward, away from the inner intuitive perception of truth. After once attaining ecstasy and communion with God, all devotees must try their utmost to be conscious of the divine state even during the egoistic or human state. This steady centring of the consciousness will preclude all confusion between good and bad actions.

During the ecstatic state, and during introspection, the devotee wants to perform all actions guided only by wisdom and self-control. But as soon as he becomes identified with the senses, he submits to their dictates.

The Gita advises man to refrain from any form of sense indulgence that leads to physical, mental, or spiritual suffering. The yogi, therefore, must watch the senses with an unrelaxing vigilance, that the reins of control pass not from the soul to the ego.

VERSE 17

कर्मणो ह्यपि बोद्धव्यं बोद्धव्यं च विकर्मणः ।
अकर्मणश्च बोद्धव्यं गहना कर्मणो गतिः ॥

The nature of karma (action) is very difficult to know. Verily, in order to understand fully the nature of proper action, one has also to understand the nature of contrary (wrong) action and the nature of inaction.

GOD IS EXPRESSING HIMSELF through Nature in innumerable activities. To the casual observer, to students of history, the earth is full of contradictions. This is because it is a world whose very existence depends on relativities—all activities interacting with one another to produce varying results. What might be right in one set of circumstances may be wrong in another; or an action performed with one motive might be good, but that action instigated by another motive could be evil. Also, man's perspective and thus his cognition is shortsighted, looking to immediate results; but only by a long purview of history or of subsequent incarnations of an individual, or through the shortcut of farsighted wisdom, can the ultimate outcome of most actions, for good or evil, be truly known.

THE THREE CATEGORIES OF HUMAN ACTION

ONE MAY THUS STUDY and compare all forms of human activities without receiving any absolute guidance about what actions should be followed for man's ultimate highest good. Lord Krishna, therefore, divides all human action into three categories: right or proper action, contrary or evil action, and inaction.

Right Action: When the action performed tends to arouse soul consciousness it may be called proper action. All activities that lead the mind of the doer away from sense enslavement to soul enjoyment are proper actions. All actions that bring about the union of the ego with the soul and of the soul with God are proper actions. Under this category comes a wide range of activities that contribute to liberation from the bondage of the senses, the "normal" body-identified state of the mortal being.

Right actions are those that arouse soul consciousness

For example, the wise man eats just enough food to satisfy his nutritional requirements. He performs that physical duty in the realization that it is a God-given task to maintain the body-temple of the soul. Similarly orienting all of his activities toward the soul, he performs only right actions.

Actions in themselves have no meaning; the discriminative intention and self-control behind them determines whether they lead to liberation or to karmic slavery. Therefore the spiritual man must not be blamed for the similarity between, for instance, his act of eating and that of the greedy man. The man of self-control eats and strengthens his body while performing right action; but the greedy man overeats and follows an improper diet pleasing to his sense of taste, and thereby acts wrongly and harms his body.

Similarly, if harmonious music and sweet words can be converted into soul awakening, they are contributing to the cause of one's liberation; but he who becomes a slave to music or sweet words of flattery unbalances his life and entangles himself in egotism. By using the sense of hearing wrongly, he is failing to heed the law of right action. If a piece of music has no high or holy vibrations, it arouses frivolous, nervous, or even base emotions. Spiritual music, such as hymns and devotional chants, raises the listener's consciousness, dispelling coarser vibrations.*

* "Hindu music is a subjective, spiritual, and individualistic art, aiming not at symphonic brilliance but at personal harmony with the Over-Soul....The *sankirtans* or musical gatherings [for devotional chanting] are an effective form of yoga or spiritual discipline, necessitating intense concentration, absorption in the seed thought and sound. Because man

In the same way, the senses of sight and touch and smell can be converted into sources of soul awakening by right action; but careless indulgence gives rise to grave troubles. Thus, a love of beautiful faces, or the sense of touch, might lead to sexual promiscuity and consequent disease. The wise man sees all beauty as expressions of the Divine; he converts the sense of touch into the thrill of joy that permeates every cell of his body during ecstatic communion with God. He uses all of his senses only for divine enjoyment, harnessing these wild stallions to lead the car of his life to spiritual freedom.

Contrary action: harmful to body, mind, or soul

Contrary Action: Any action harmful to body, mind, or soul is contrary or wrong action, and is to be avoided. The sensual man overindulges in using the senses of sight, hearing, smell, taste, and touch until he finds that all these mediums of happiness give him nothing but satiety and discomfort. The indulgent alcoholic is an example. He drinks himself into insensibility and suddenly realizes he has destroyed his health and all hope of happiness. Other types of men are so enslaved

---

himself is an expression of the Creative Word, sound exercises on him a potent and immediate effect. Great religious music of East and West bestows joy on man because it causes a temporary vibratory awakening of one of his occult spinal centres. In those blissful moments a dim memory comes to him of his divine origin" (*Autobiography of a Yogi*).

In addition to the spiritual potency of music, its therapeutic value as a force for physical and mental healing has been known since antiquity—used in ancient India, China, Tibet, and other cultures. Pythagoras in the sixth century B.C. used special melodies to cure specific disharmonies such as worry, sorrow, fear, and anger. He considered the physical body to be an instrument, immediately able to respond to the vibratory effects of sound.

More recently, doctors in North America, Europe, and Japan have begun applying the healing power of music. *Science Digest* reported in January 1982 that in one experiment at a hospital in Montreal, classical music worked so well as a painkiller that many terminally ill cancer patients could be taken off analgesic drugs completely. Around the world, medical facilities are combining this new "medicine" with conventional forms of treatment, finding that music is very effective for decreasing chronic pain, easing childbirth, inducing relaxation to reduce stress, reducing risks of high-blood pressure, and accelerating learning.

Dorothy Retallack, in her book *The Sound of Music and Plants* (Marina del Rey, California: DeVorss & Co., 1976), reported her work using galvanic skin response monitors and charting growth records of plants under differing sound environments. Her plants grew toward the speakers and thrived when exposed to certain types of music, and shrivelled away from other types. Her plants appeared to respond positively to classical music, especially that of India, but recoiled strongly or died when heavy rock music was played to them.

Studies have shown that slow, peaceful instrumental music, such as the largo or adagio movements of baroque and classical sonatas and symphonies, has the effect of lowering the heart rate and blood pressure, and reducing muscle tension. In addition, such music has been clinically proven to induce the alpha brainwaves characteristic of deep mental relaxation. *(Publisher's Note)*

to beauty, taste, touch, smell, and hearing that they make their lives a living hades. Where is the "enjoyment" in actions that destroy all the charm of life? When the stallions of the senses lead the car of life headlong into the ditch of satiety, misery, and ill health, the blame cannot be shifted to any other agency than the careless driver.

Just as the wrong action of tasting poisoned honey is senseless, even though for a moment the taste is delightful, so the tasting of evil is equally senseless, though pleasant—at first! For his own interests, for the sake of his own true happiness, every man—whether he is worldly or religious—should use his sensory instruments with discrimination and self-control. The spiritual commandments were not given to torture human beings, nor to deprive them of happiness, but to guide them away from poisoned pleasures that result in dire karmic consequences.

To use again the example of the greedy man who eats only to please the senses, he offends both the laws of the soul and the laws of nature. He ultimately dies of some greed-caused disease. Even if that result is not immediately apparent, when he is reborn, he still carries with him both greed and a tendency toward disease. His harmful body-identified activities are thus termed "wrong actions."

The lifestyle of many wealthy people is another example. Because rich people have no financial embarrassments, they may generally overindulge their sensory appetites and bad habits until ill health or premature death overtakes them. Wealth in itself is not evil; it simply should not be used selfishly or for self-destruction, but for satisfying the soul impulses of generosity to others less fortunate—to alleviate their physical, mental, and spiritual needs.

As for sex, it should be used, rarely, to bring children into a family. The greater the victory over sex, the more buoyant the health, the more abundant the happiness. By keeping the mind on lofty thoughts, and by strenuous exercise, continuous action for God, and meditation, one can transmute the sacred and powerful creative force into physical strength and health, mental creativity, and divine ecstasy in God-communion.

Unnecessary indulgences such as smoking, drinking, and remaining in bad company are gateways to physical and mental discomforts. One should seek pleasure in good company that helps to shape one's will and judgement to pursue true happiness. It is through evil company that man, who is naturally imitative, learns to perform misery-making actions. If one wants to find liberation and to understand what right actions are, he needs to seek the society of those who love God and meditate on Him.

Inaction: True inaction occurs when the devotee has freed himself from all karma-producing actions, evil or good. He is then through with all compulsory forms of action; he has reached the state of inaction (that is, complete freedom from the necessity of and desire for action) that is characteristic of God the Father. The liberated yogi bubbles with ceaseless inner merriment whether he is sitting still or actively busy. Performing actions with only the desire to please God is thus considered "inaction," or nonbinding action. After attaining this state of inaction the way is open to the devotee's liberation.

Complete freedom from the necessity of and desire for action

Mahavatar Babaji, Lahiri Mahasaya, Sri Yukteswarji, and all great masters are intensely busy in actions that are spiritually helpful to humanity, even though the masters themselves have reached the state of inaction or liberation.

Lahiri Mahasaya held a government post as accountant for thirty-five years of his life, rising meanwhile to full expression of his inner state of spiritual emancipation. In the latter part of his life, he seldom slept, but gave all his daytime hours to teaching disciples who came to him from all over India; his nights were spent with advanced monks who preferred to seek him out in the quiet hours. All were transformed by his peerless exposition of the Gita and its application to the sacred science of *Kriya Yoga.*

Lord Krishna, in his oneness with Spirit, said: "Even though I have attained all things, still I work on, without desire."

Jesus, too, worked mightily in the world—preached to the multitudes, healed thousands of their physical, mental, and spiritual suffering, and laid the groundwork for the worldwide spread of his divine message. He did not seek the seclusion of a cave nor stop his liberating work even though he knew that by retirement from public life he could escape the horrifying drama of his wrongful execution.

Like God, Jesus worked on without the praise of men. Thus he could say, just before crucifixion: "Father...I have glorified Thee on the earth: I have finished the work which Thou gavest me to do."*

VERSE 18

कर्मण्यकर्म यः पश्येदकर्मणि च कर्म यः।
स बुद्धिमान्मनुष्येषु स युक्तः कृत्स्नकर्मकृत्॥

* John 17:4.

He is a yogi, discriminative among men, who beholds inactivity in action and action in inaction. He has attained the goal of all actions (and is free).

THE YOGI DISINTERESTEDLY plays in the dream drama of life just to please God—hence he is really inactive in action. Yet because the yogi works enthusiastically and ambitiously for God, he is spoken of as truly active. A person who performs all actions for God only, not for the ego, satisfies the divine plan. A man is in touch with Truth when he realizes that not he, but the Lord through the forces of Nature, is the doer of all actions.

All human activities lead either outwardly to sensory world consciousness or inwardly to soul consciousness. The worldly man employs all his activities toward the increase of his physical, mental, domestic, and social welfare. The yogi employs his time (man's only wealth) in meditation, introspection, and spiritual service to others. He reaps calmness and true soul happiness, as distinguished from the materially minded man who by outward activities reaps a little temporary pleasure mixed with much restlessness and discomfort.

"Inaction in action" emphasizes inward soul aloofness from the body's activities. "Action in inaction" signifies that while the spiritual man is aloof, acting for God, he is not working mechanically like a robot, but is carefully proceeding with the business at hand even while he inwardly disowns the fruits of his acts. He is never afraid of work, but has a healthful fear of karmic involvements!

He who can thus act for God with subjective aloofness, and yet retain objective enthusiasm in activity for the sake of pleasing God and not for satisfying his own desires, is a true yogi. Knowing that the purpose of all human activities is to get back to God, the yogi looks for His guiding hand in everything, knowing too well the ego's propensity for "putting its foot" in the wrong places! Thus the yogi plays in this drama of life without resorting to individual egotistical desires and without succumbing to a dejected aloofness (laziness or indifference); in this way he fulfils his spiritual duty to please the Cosmic Dramatist, God.

An actor who is shot with a mock pistol would be considered a fool if he died of fright. The worldly man, similarly, is a bad actor when he takes his God-assigned tragic parts seriously and thus courts disaster. Then again, if a human player acts out his part with a lackadaisical mental attitude, he too fails to please the Cosmic Dramatist, and has to do a retake, in another or many other lives, until he gets it right!

Acting for self is the root cause of all human miseries. Every man should ponder the fact that he was not created by his own will but by divine decree. As an employee cannot reasonably hope to gain anything by thwarting his employer's wishes, so man must realize that his own happiness lies, not in pleasing men (all humble employees) but God, the earth's sole President and Owner!

VERSE 19

यस्य सर्वे समारम्भाः कामसङ्कल्पवर्जिताः ।
ज्ञानाग्निदग्धकर्माणं तमाहुः पण्डितं बुधाः ॥

The sages call that man wise whose pursuits are all without selfish plan or longings for results, and whose activities are purified (cauterized of karmic outgrowths) by the fire of wisdom.

ONE SHOULD NOT INTERPRET this stanza to mean that yogis and saints act without discretion, or without striving for proper results. The worldly man plans with success for himself in view; his gods are ego and self-interest. The yogi enthusiastically plans his divinely inspired activities in order to achieve the best result for God; his selfless motivation is to accomplish God's will—whatever it may be. In fact, true devotees in India perform their hermitage duties more attentively to please God than they ever would to satisfy their personal desires. The sages call such yogis wise because they know better than to work for the misery-bestowing ego.

A worldly man grieves when he does not reap the desired fruits of his selfish activities. The spiritual man, if not successful at first in his unselfish activities, keeps on trying again and again. To succeed for God is the most enthralling incentive. And when God is present in the devotee's undertaking, Nature's automatic karmic outgrowths of action are thoroughly cauterized in the flame of the inherent Divine Wisdom.

VERSE 20

त्यक्त्वा कर्मफलासङ्गं नित्यतृप्तो निराश्रयः ।
कर्मण्यभिप्रवृत्तोऽपि नैव किञ्चित्करोति सः ॥

Relinquishing attachment to the fruits of work, always contented, independent (of material rewards), the wise do not perform any (binding) action even in the midst of activities.

A YOGI WHO APPARENTLY "works" for God to please Him, does not really act at all, esoterically speaking, for his actions have no connection with the interests of his own ego.

The problem of "action" and "inaction" becomes simple when one understands that, just as a man is not responsible for the actions of others, so a yogi is not karmically bound by the actions of that stranger, his body. He politely assists the body to achieve its welfare, without personal attachment or identification with the fate that befalls it. It is impossible for a devotee who has merged himself in the vastness of Spirit to consider himself confined to any human personality. What activities a yogi engages in are in the nature of an impersonal "carrying out of orders."

A yogi who undertakes complex divine works, such as maintaining a hermitage for his disciples or an organization to serve the spiritual needs of mankind, or performing educational or charitable activities, is not thereby entangled in any personal karma, provided he has joyfully resigned his will to God's.

His state of freedom in action is in marked contrast to that of a karma-accruing worldly man who may engage in philanthropic activities for the satisfaction of his ego, or for gaining praise from others, or for escaping income taxes!

VERSE 21

निराशीर्यतचित्तात्मा त्यक्तसर्वपरिग्रहः ।
शारीरं केवलं कर्म कुर्वन्नाप्नोति किल्बिषम् ॥

He incurs no evil performing mere bodily actions who has renounced all sense of possession, who is free from (delusive human) hopes, and whose heart (the power of feeling) is controlled by the soul.*

---

* *Yata-citta-ātmā:* Lit., "his soul having controlled his heart (*chitta*)." *Chitta* is a comprehensive term for the aggregate of mind-stuff that produces intelligent consciousness, the power of feeling.

Karmic bondage is caused not by the actions of the bodily instrument itself, but by the consciousness that manipulates those activities. When the ego, with its delusion-enforced desires and attachments, is in control, the body and mind are subject to the cause-effect laws of Nature. But when the true Self or soul, the image of God in man, is in command, the body and mind work just the same, but the would-be enslaving effects of those actions remain neutralised, owing to the absence of the catalytic agent of delusion.

Man's "possessions" consist not only of the material objects he gathers about himself, but also the sum total of all the illusions of Nature with which he is identified as an ego—his body, mind, feelings, senses, habits, desires. Unless by Self-realization he becomes established in soul consciousness and thereby renounces attachments to these inner as well as outer possessions, he will be enslaved by the karmic effects arising from the activities they engender.

Wherever a person goes, whatever be his pursuits, his egoistic karma goes with him, even as the shadow follows the form. But a man of God has no karma; the ego in him is "not at home." It has sought safety in flight!

Those who by ecstatic meditation attain this state of inner non-attachment are the true renunciants. It does not matter whether such devotees are in the world or in the forest, or whether they have few, or many, or no material possessions. Acting for God with a disciplined mind, the true renunciant is free from the results of all present actions and from the moods and propensities manifesting from his past karma.

Performing good actions, even with an egotistical motive, is better than performing evil actions. Both types of actions, however, keep the soul confined by the law of karma. An action performed only to please God produces no karma, whether "good" or "ill"; it is thus superior to any action, however good, that is referred to the ego and thus calls into play the law of karma. The man of good karma is still subject to cause-and-effect fetters of the phenomenal world, while the man of no karma is divinely free!

Verse 22

यदृच्छालाभसन्तुष्टो द्वन्द्वातीतो विमत्सरः ।
समः सिद्धावसिद्धौ च कृत्वापि न निबध्यते ॥

That man of action is free from karma who receives with contentment whate'er befalls him, who is poised above the dualities, who is devoid of jealousy or envy or enmity, and who looks equally on gain and loss.

THE WISE MAN SEES the Spirit everywhere. Devoid of longings for self and of any will to gratify selfish desires, he is content to receive whatever comes naturally for fulfilling the needs of his body, mind, and soul. He rises above all dualities, the manifestations of which are either good or evil; both cause bondage. Having found the Unity, he has no consciousness of "me and mine." He entertains no inimical thoughts toward anyone, beholding in all the one Spirit. Attaining the Ultimate, he is indifferent to worldly success and failure. In performing dutiful actions for God, he is ever nonattached and unbound.

By "contentment" a yogi displays his faith in the Lord's power to direct all happenings to a Final Good. Free of selfish desires, happy and fulfilled within himself, he automatically relinquishes the excess material baggage of unnecessary "necessities" and egotistical strivings in favour of God-ordained dutiful actions imposed upon him by his body and his obligations to family, society, and the world.

To attain spiritual freedom, the aspirant must also learn to free his mind from extreme sensitivity to cold or heat, pain or pleasure. In Indian hermitages, the true guru teaches the students not to be affected by externals, that the mind may become an altar for the changelessness of Spirit. By catering to the demands of contrary sensations, worldly people are unnecessarily restless—one of Nature's most cunning ploys to keep the consciousness ensnared. The advice in this stanza, however, does not mean that the devotee should deliberately expose himself to extreme cold and catch pneumonia, or burn himself crisp under the midday sun. He should practice *titiksha* (dispassionate endurance), even while adopting reasonable measures to remove external discomfort. In the practise of *titiksha,* evenmindedness is cultivated by will and imagination (powerful suggestions to the mind); neutrality is attained scientifically by yoga meditation wherein the yogi learns to disconnect the ego from the sensations received through the mind. (See II:14.)

A devotee who cannot remain calm under difficulties is still a slave of the phenomenal world and its calamitous pairs of opposites. Worldly people are constantly catering to the effects of cold and heat and other extremes, thereby increasing the bondage of the soul to the body.

The aspiring devotee must keep the soul uncontaminated from the dual consciousness natural to the body. This practice is difficult because the soul, empathizing with the finicky, sensitive bodily friend, puts on its good and bad characteristics. In order to free the soul from identification with the variable states of the body, the devotee is urged to noncooperate mentally with the misery-making dual consciousness of the body and the mind. The worldly man becomes jubilant at the advent of pleasure and depressed during the reign of pain, but the successful devotee is always inwardly calm, unaffected by the various upheavals that constitute the "normal" state of life.

During sorrow or pain, the yogi remains concentrated on his soul's bliss; unlike the worldly man, he is clever enough to retain his equanimity and joy under all favourable or unfavourable physical or psychological circumstances. He is able to sympathize with sufferers without being overwhelmed by their misery; thus, by his inward joy, he is frequently able to remove the sorrows of others. By the example of his calmness he teaches worldly people not to engage in emotional reactions.

The yogi who is not envious, who bears no enmity toward anyone but accepts friends and foes alike, does not fall into the pits of dangerous anger and jealousy. Worldly people who indulge in these scarring emotions lose not only their happiness but sometimes their bodies too, by committing murder and suffering capital punishment, or alas! by resorting to suicide.

Whether a yogi meets gain or loss in the course of performing dutiful actions, he remains evenminded. Both success and failure are bound to come at various times in response to the inherent duality in the structure of the body, mind, and world; the devotee who constantly reminds himself of his soul has little temptation to identify himself with the physical and mental phantasmagoria.

YAJNA, THE SPIRITUAL FIRE RITE THAT CONSUMES ALL KARMA

VERSE 23

गतसङ्गस्य मुक्तस्य ज्ञानावस्थितचेतसः ।
यज्ञायाचरतः कर्म समग्रं प्रविलीयते ॥

All karma, or effects of actions, completely melts away from the liberated being who, free from attachments, with his mind enveloped in wisdom, performs the true spiritual fire rite (yajna).*

WHEN THE YOGI'S MIND is negatively free from attachments (sensory entanglements and distractions), it becomes positively concentrated on cosmic wisdom. At this stage he withdraws his mind and life force from the physical sensory and motor nerves, and thence from the astral sensory powers, and gives them as oblations unto the seven fires of the spine.† Through this *yajna* of purification, the yogi ultimately attains the final state of unity with Divinity, the omnipresent Cosmic Fire. When the life force that is withdrawn from the senses is concentrated in the thousand-petalled lotus in the brain, that powerful effulgence burns out all *samskaras* (habits, impulses, and all other effects of past actions) lodged in the subconsciousness and superconsciousness of the brain, bestowing on the devotee freedom from all past karmic fetters.

The yogi who withdraws his mind and desires from sense lures offers them as fuel to the fire of Cosmic Consciousness; his mortal desires are burnt like faggots in the Sacred Flame. When the yogi is able to commingle his life force and consciousness with Eternal Life and Cosmic Consciousness, his status is no longer that of a mortal. His limited egoistic consciousness and body identification are gone; the dissolution of the ego permits the full view of soul consciousness. Knowing the soul as a perfect image of Spirit, and unentangled by ego, the yogi becomes free from all good and bad karma, which belongs only to the realm of duality and relativity. It is thus by uniting pure life with Cosmic Life and pure consciousness with Cosmic Consciousness that the yogi finds liberation.

---

* Lit., *yajñāya,* "for the purpose of sacrificial worship"; *ācaratas,* "casting into the fire."

† Reference to the seven principal *vayus,* vital currents, in the spine. (See page 1120.)

As an external religious rite mentioned in the Hindu scriptures, one form of *yajna* is a ceremony in which ghee (clarified butter) and other oblations such as incense and flowers are offered into a sacred fire to the accompaniment of specific chants and prayers. The performance of such fire ceremonies without understanding their symbolism is of little value. Can the mind be purified of evil desires by outer rites?

Knowledge of the symbolical significance of *yajna,* while performing the rite with devotion, produces some sanctity of mind. Offering clarified butter in the fire symbolizes the uniting of man's purified mind with the Cosmic Consciousness of God; flower offerings signify the purified life force—not that life force which is contaminated by constantly indulging in sensory pleasures, but life force that has been withdrawn from the senses by concentration and thrown into the seven sacred spinal fires and then into the omnipresent Cosmic Flame. The offering of flowers during a *yajna* fire ceremony also symbolizes the casting of all flowering qualities of the mind into Cosmic Consciousness.

Another interpretation of *yajna* or ceremonial rite is that the articles used in traditional worship represent the five senses that must be purified by trials (fire) and then given back to God. For example, flowers with their beautiful colours and textures represent sight and touch. Fruit and ghee represent taste; incense is a symbol of the sense of smell; the conch shell symbolizes sound.

VERSE 24

ब्रह्मार्पणं ब्रह्म हविर्ब्रह्माग्नौ ब्रह्मणा हुतम्।
ब्रह्मैव तेन गन्तव्यं ब्रह्मकर्मसमाधिना॥

The process of offering and the oblation itself—both are Spirit. The fire and he who makes oblation into it are other forms of Spirit. By realizing this, being absorbed in Brahman (Spirit) during all activities, verily such a one goes to Spirit alone.

ALL MANIFESTATION IS a variegated ritual of the one Cosmic Consciousness of God. The personal soul (*atman*) is not different from the Universal Soul or God (Paramatman); thus, it is He who is the Giver and the Acceptor of all sacrifices (activities). It is also He who is the oblation—the objects involved in the rite. The yogi, by realizing this, enters *samadhi* or oneness with God.

Anyone who performs an outer ritual should understand its symbolic value. In the *yajna* of pouring ghee into a consecrated altar fire, if one's mind is unshakeably concentrated on the inner significance of the act so that he performs the inner as well as the outer rite, he will enter a state of ecstasy or God-oneness, in which he perceives that the flame of human life and Cosmic Fire, the physical process of oblation in pouring the clarified butter into the fire, and the intuitive process of casting his consciousness into the Cosmic Flame are all unsubstantial nothings in themselves, deriving their significance from their nature as mere reflections of Cosmic Light and Cosmic Consciousness, played upon by the law of relativity.

The mind of a person in a theatre, engrossed in a complex drama shown on a motion-picture screen, may be disturbed by various emotions—pleasure, pain, excitement, expectancy. But if a companion, seated by his side, tells him to withdraw his mind from the vivid drama (the effect) and concentrate on the relativity of shadows and light (the cause), he is soon able to observe dispassionately that each scene—be it that of mountain, river, trees, earth, ocean, human beings, gun play, fire, electricity, storms, lightning, or priests performing fire oblations—is in reality composed merely of light from the beam interspersed with shadows, issuing from the projection booth.

By offering actions and life force to God, the yogi lives in ecstasy

Similarly, when the spiritual aspirant is awakened by divine ecstasy, he beholds the world, not as a drama of sorrow and joy, but as a pictorial manifestation of the Cosmic Beam of light and shadows of delusory substance, proceeding from the booth of Infinity in the cinema house of the cosmic sphere.

Even as the colourless, shadowless beam has to pass through a coloured film in order to produce "technicoloured" pictures, so the pure colourless omnipresent Cosmic Beam has to pass through the coloured film of delusive relativity in order to produce on the screen of space the variegated cosmic "movie."

The state of the mortal man is full of relativities—experiences of dualities, hazards, reversals. The yogi who has realized the whole cosmic motion picture to be an outcome of the Cosmic Light passes his life as one perpetual Cosmic Fire Ceremony. In yoga meditation, he withdraws his life force from the senses and unites it with the Cosmic Flame. By this *yajna,* he finds his erstwhile separated life to be a part of the Cosmic Life, Brahman, and he offers his life and all of its actions to the Cosmic Life, as a part of the eternal activity in

Spirit. Like ghee poured into a sacrificial fire, he sees his own life as Spirit going into the Cosmic Fire of Brahman.

In this way the yogi, his mind drawn away from the cosmic drama and his personal mortal significance in the world, remains consciously in ecstasy, beholding the one light of Spirit in every process of life. After this realization is attained, he in time enters the state of absolute unity with Spirit. In other words, there is first an intermediate state of consciousness, a borderline state. A man absorbed in a dream is certain of its reality; but if he happens suddenly to be partially aroused from the dream, and realizes that he is dreaming, he discovers that all the emotions felt and all the substances perceived in the dream were nothing more than materializations of his own mind. Similarly, when the yogi is partially engrossed in this cosmic dream, yet also partially in ecstasy with God, he sees with astonishment that this mundane dream with all its dualities is no more than materializations of the consciousness of God, influenced by the phenomenal law of delusive relativity.

When a person fully wakes from a dream, he realizes that its seeming physical and psychological manifestations were mere textures of dream-stuff. Similarly, when a yogi fully wakes from the cosmic dream by becoming one with God, he realizes that all the subjects, objects, and activities in the cosmos are results of one Cosmic Consciousness. Seeing the cosmos as a dream motion picture of God, he beholds the offering of his life itself as Brahman, and also the fire of Cosmic Life in which his life is given as an offering, as Brahman. He finds the Lord of this Cosmic Fire Ceremony and of all activities that are connected with it (the externalized expressions of Cosmic Consciousness) to be Brahman.

By the inner illumination of divine awakening, the yogi ceases to be a mortal being with gross perceptions of the universe; he realizes that the whole cosmos is a cosmic motion picture. His body is only "a dream walking."

Verse 25

दैवमेवापरे यज्ञं योगिनः पर्युपासते ।
ब्रह्माग्नावपरे यज्ञं यज्ञेनैवोपजुह्वति ॥

In truth, there are those yogis who sacrifice to devas; others offer the self, as a sacrifice made by the self, in the fire of Spirit alone.

In stanzas 25 to 29 we find reference to different types of fire ceremonies performed by spiritual aspirants according to their various inner propensities.

The Deity-Powers That Govern the Cosmos

"Sacrifice to devas" refers to certain ceremonies for invoking the presence of liberated saints, or of astral gods or other aspects of the Godhead who govern various functions of the universe.

In Revelation of the Christian Bible, we read that God has "seven angels" before His throne.* The Hindu scriptures also mention these supreme deities (power aspects of God), and identify them as follows:

The macrocosmic ideational (causal) universe is created and governed by Ishvara, "Lord of Creation," the omniscient reflection of Spirit as Creator. The law of causation begins with Ishvara, the First Cause of all matter.† The macrocosmic astral universe is maintained by Hiranyagarbha, who forms the "blueprints" of the causal ideas. The macrocosmic physical universe (the materialization of the causal ideas and the astral blueprints) is controlled by Virata. The microcosmic ideational form of man and of all objects is governed by Prajna. The microcosmic astral form of man and of all objects is controlled by Taijas. The physical form of man and of all material things is maintained by Vishva.

These six deities governing the six states of the cosmos are in turn transcendentally guided by the creative intelligence and manifesting principles of the seventh "angel," Maha-Prakriti—the Great Mother Nature, or the Holy Ghost, the *active* expression of *Kutastha Chaitanya* or Christ Consciousness, which is the reflection of Cosmic Consciousness.

These are the seven angels before the throne of God.‡

God differentiated Himself into these seven deities, imposing a different personality on each so that they could carry on the various

---

* Revelation 8:2.

† The Absolute united to Its Creative Intelligence, Maha-Prakriti, becomes Ishvara, the Cosmic Ruler, God the Father of Creation, the Causal Universal Dreamer by whose divine will universes evolve and dissolve in orderly cycles. Ishvara is thus both transcendent and immanent—beyond vibratory manifestation and active through Maha-Prakriti in bringing forth the primordial causal forms of all becomings.

‡ Hindu scripture refers to *Kutastha Chaitanya* as an eighth deity while the Christian scripture, referring to seven, equates Christ Consciousness with God or Cosmic Consciousness—the undifferentiated Spirit within creation and beyond creation being essentially one and the same.

functions of the universe—even as the same sunbeam is reflected differently when it falls on the blue sapphire, red ruby, yellow topaz, green emerald, multicoloured opal, purple amethyst, and white diamond.

It is possible for man to reach God directly, as the Supreme Deity over the seven deities, just as a man may personally contact any important personage. However, just as it is sometimes difficult to get to the head of a corporation without first seeing the responsible secretary, so it is taught by advocates of *deva* worship that it is easier first to contact God through one of His seven regents.

Prayers to the One Spirit manifesting as many deities

A devotee in need of healing may pray to the god Vishva: "Manifest in me as health!" Those seeking a stronger life force may say: "Good Taijas, recharge my energies!" Those wanting insight and wisdom may pray to God as Prajna: "Reinforce my wisdom and guide its determinations to its goal." Devotees who want a perception of the whole physical universe may pray to God as Virata: "Make me feel Thy presence in all the cosmos." Those who would know God as the Cosmic Life Force may pray: "O Cosmic Astral Engineer, Hiranyagarbha! manifest Thyself to me as Cosmic Light." Seekers of the supernal wisdom of the First Cause of all being may pray: "O God as Ishvara! implant in me the omniscience of Cosmic Intelligence." Those who want release from *maya*, cosmic delusion, may direct their prayer to Maha-Prakriti, the Holy Ghost, the active divine conjurer of all illusory manifestations: "O Cosmic Mother, show me the One Reality behind all Thy veils of delusion."

Devotees who desire union with the Universal Intelligence of God omnipresent in the seven-aspected phenomenal world should pray to the immanent *Kutastha Chaitanya:* "O Christ Consciousness—O Krishna Consciousness—be Thou manifest in the ecstasy-expanded cup of my consciousness!" Those, finally, who want God, the Absolute beyond creation, should pray: "O Cosmic Consciousness, reveal Thyself! Reveal Thyself!"

In all these prayers, the devotee should realize that he must continuously throw the "clarified butter" of devotion into the flame of Spirit within these seven deities, or into the Cosmic Fire of God.

There are many, many other deities in the universe. The *Tantra Shastra,* a scripture dealing with chants and fire ceremonies, describes in detail the specific vibratory chants and root sounds that should be properly intoned during a fire ceremony to invoke the presence of lesser or greater deities for the acquisition of power and boons. Such worship of the *devas* includes the practice of certain physical postures (*asanas*) and spiritual techniques that awaken various nerve forces, which, in turn, stimulate the tissues, glands, and muscular vigour of the body.*

The Bhagavad Gita elsewhere (IX:25) says, however, that those who worship the lesser gods go on to them after this mortal coil is cast away; and that those who are devotees of Spirit become one with Spirit. Satisfaction with anything less than the Supreme Lord Himself continues to tie one to the limited realm of *maya*.

The inner yajna performed by the yogi

PERFORMANCE OF FIRE CEREMONIES to please the *devas* has another, deeper and more liberating significance. Real yogis who practice *Kriya Yoga* withdraw the life force from the body cells and sensory-motor nerves and offer it—as ghee is offered into a sacrificial fire—to the seven deities or divine powers that reside in the seven astral fires in the spine, beginning from the coccyx and rising to the cerebrum.†

The second half of stanza 25 refers to followers of the path of wisdom who use the soul's devotion to offer the self as a sacrificial offering into the fire of Spirit. (This "rite" is different from the supreme fire ceremony mentioned in stanza 24, wherein is described the highest state of the yogi, that in which he sees his action of offering as Spirit in motion, and offers his soul, which he sees also as Spirit, into the fire of Spirit.)

The devotee (of stanza 25) has not yet attained the realization in which all his perceptions are but various aspects of the Infinite. He has first to realize his inner self intuitively, then, to unite his soul perception with cosmic perception of the illimitable Brahman. The offering of the self (the ego self) by that self therefore denotes a narrower

---

* Responding to a journalist's question about tantric practices, Paramahansaji said in 1951:

"They all originally had some good in them, when correctly understood in their pure scriptural form; but as practised today they are mostly bad, because they advocate fantastic methods that are not suitable to the common man. Some *tantrikas* who know the spiritual seed-words, vibratory mantras, by which they can attune their consciousness to see visions of deities (personifications of God's divine powers), and thence ultimately commune with God, are very good; but *tantrikas* who indulge in sex, wine, and evil practices are not good....

"Yogis usually condemn this path, for most seekers merely find in it an excuse to indulge their baser instincts and lusts rather than to attain self-control. The path of inner renunciation and scientific meditation for contact of God as Bliss advocated by the Bhagavad Gita is the supreme path."

† See commentary on III:11–12.

form of consciousness—only the limited form of intuition required to offer the self into the cosmic fire of infinite perception for the purpose of uniting it with the soul, and thence with Spirit. By this does the *jnana yogi* unite his wisdom with Cosmic Wisdom.

BY CONCENTRATION ON WISDOM one can invoke great souls such as that of Swami Shankara who lived the life of a true sage, or of Sri Yukteswar who found liberation through wisdom. Similarly, in order to find Christ, one must use faith, for Jesus was liberated by absolute faith in oneness with God.

Many saints in India have prayed to God to manifest as the Divine Mother or in the forms of various deities, and have had those prayers answered. When an advanced devotee's devotion is strong enough to persuade God to materialize Himself in some specific aspect, as imagined by the devotee, the form assumed by that deity remains in the ether as a permanent "blueprint" and personality.

❖
Conceiving of God in a personal form, such as the Divine Mother
❖

When any other devotee calls with sufficient devotion on a deity who has been thus visualized and seen by a God-communing saint, that same deity, in the same form, appears before the new devotee. The deities are all permanently present as symbols in the ether and can be invoked by any seeker in deep meditation.

For example, Mother Kali and Durga represent two aspects of Cosmic Nature, the active creative energy of Spirit. Kali is shown as a four-armed woman, standing on the breast of Lord Shiva. Her four hands hold symbols of prosperity, protection, discipline, and bestowal of wisdom. Shiva represents the Infinite that is the foundation of Cosmic Nature.

Goddess Durga is usually depicted with ten hands, representing the ten human senses (five sensory instruments and five instruments of action). She, too, is associated with the Infinite Shiva, and is often shown destroying a beast or demon that symbolizes Ignorance. She is surrounded by the deities Sarasvati (wisdom), Lakshmi (prosperity), Ganesh (success), and Kartik (power).

When the senses are controlled and the demon of ignorance conquered, man realizes that Cosmic Nature with all her paradoxes is only an emanation from the Pure Infinite. Humanity is destined to find, by conquering human nature and consequently Cosmic Nature, the Infinite hidden behind them—even as the villain in a movie is designed to concentrate attention, through contrast, on the hero. The darkness of evil is a means of God to show us the beauty of the opposition—the light of goodness.

Many devotees are not satisfied with the thought of a vast Infinite, but need to conceive God through some tangible form. In His infinite mercy, the invisible God materializes before the true devotee in the desired visible form. As invisible water vapour is transformed by the chill of frost into ice, so by the transmuting power of devotion, the invisible God and His Cosmic Light can be "frozen" into the objectivity that satisfies the yearning seeker. Nevertheless, Spirit is only One; His multifaceted divine aspects, informed as *devas,* are merely temporary personifications of His attributes and powers.

VERSE 26

श्रोत्रादीनीन्द्रियाण्यन्ये संयमाग्निषु जुह्वति।
शब्दादीन्विषयानन्य इन्द्रियाग्निषु जुह्वति॥

Certain devotees offer, as oblations in the fire of inner control, their powers of hearing and other senses. Others offer as sacrifice, in the fire of the senses, sound and other sense objects.

THE FIRST RITE REFERRED to in this stanza describes the symbolical fire ceremony practised by all *brahmacharis* (self-disciplinarians). By *pratyahara* (interiorization) the man of discipline withdraws his consciousness and life force from the auditory, optical, olfactory, gustatory, and tactual nerve centres, casting sensory perceptions into the flame of controlled inner awareness of peace. By deep meditation (*samyama,* self-mastery through *dharana, dhyana,* and *samadhi*), the yogi of inner self-control succeeds in freeing his mind from the tug-of-war with the five senses, and is able to dissolve all perceptions of the five senses into the one indivisible perception—that of the bliss of the Self. This is the state of the devotees who win the true victory in the battle between the senses and the God-aspiring mind. In the earlier stages of meditation the five senses attempt to distract the attention of the inwardly moving devotee; imaginary, invisible perceptions are presented while the devotee, with closed eyes and ears, is seeking perfect at-one-ness with the Self.

The oblation of the senses is a "sacrifice" that may easily and naturally be made by anyone, even by a worldly man who is willing to pursue methodically a definite scientific technique of God-realization.

The rite described in the latter half of this stanza refers to the symbolic fire ceremony practised by the methodical worldly man, he who seeks progress toward liberation through constructive right action. There is a difference between a mechanical worldly individual and a self-controlled, discriminative material person. The mechanical man is sensory reflexive. Responding unthinkingly to sense objects, he casts his energy in the fire of automatic material efforts and gains very little therefrom. The well-ordered worldly man oblates his energy in the fire of intelligent efforts and gains success and some happiness. His goals and acquisitions are kept in proper perspective; the objects of senses do not rule him, but rather are offered into the fire of his sensory powers, which are controlled by discrimination.*

THE FOUR ASHRAMAS: DIVINE PLAN FOR THE CONDUCT OF LIFE

A DISCUSSION IS NEEDED here to clarify the Gita's conception of a "worldly man," i.e., one not completely dedicated in his heart to God alone.

We see around us human beings in all stages of mental and spiritual evolution, just as the earth gives us the spectacle of evolution in "inanimate" and animate life (the scientists are hard put to it these days to find anything "inanimate!"). At one end of the human scale, we find brutelike individuals, those just evolved from animal bodies; at the other, and glorious, end of the evolutionary chain, the great masters and Godlike sages appear. The mass of humanity lies sandwiched between these two extremes; the lives of these billions are not especially wicked or particularly good. Deficient in wisdom, or knowledge of God's laws, most human beings are fairly content to live narrow, uninspired lives—eating, procreating, working at some petty task, and then dying, like oxen fed on a little grass and soon led dumbly to the slaughter.

Worldly people have no clear realization that all possessions, including the human body, have no permanency; they ignore the soul,

* Yoga makes a distinction between sensory powers and sensory objects. The sensory powers are seeing, hearing, smelling, tasting, and touching. The corresponding sensory objects are form and colour (*rupa*), sound (*shabda*), odour (*gandha*), flavour (*rasa*), and tangibility or the feeling of touching (*sparsha*). The aim of the disciplined individual is to neutralise the enslaving capacity of the senses by offering the objects of sense into the self-controlled use of the powers of sense.

which, alone, really belongs to them eternally. For this reason, worldly people are considered by yogis to be living in an "unsheltered state." The yogis, seekers of liberation, are spoken of in the scriptures as members of a true *ashram,* "home" or "hermitage." In Vedic India the majority of men led a righteous material life, using the senses but keeping them under full control, until by self-controlled enjoyment they rose above all desire for sense experience—which, because of its ephemeral nature, is by turns tantalizing and satiating.

In the early days, therefore, the ordinary family life was called a life of the hermitage (*ashram* or discipline). The family man knew that there were four ashrams or shelters through which we must pass: *brahmacharya* (celibate student life); *garhasthya* (married householder life); *vanaprastha* (retirement and contemplation); and *sannyas* (monastic life). Life then was not an endless struggle after money until all ended in disease and disillusionment.

In ancient times every child, at the age of seven, entered a *brahmacharya ashram* or hermitage of discipline that was in the charge of a wise guru-preceptor; the child was thus freed from the more limiting environment of parents and family and social traditions. The students were given spiritual initiation (*diksha*) and received from the guru a sacred symbol (the sacred thread) as an insignia of purity of life. The children were not permitted to mix with the opposite sex or with materially minded people.

Up to the tenth year the "*brahmachari*" was taught the scriptures and meditational practices. In his eleventh year he learned the duties of a soldier for the protection of others; the following year he was taught business methods and the art of proper dealings in worldly affairs. The young man remained in his guru's hermitage until in his twenties. The second stage of his life then started; he returned to his family, took up a householder's duties, and begot children. At the age of fifty the man went back again to the forest hermitage, seeking fuller communion with God and spiritual training from the guru. This constituted the third or "forest-hermitage" state of life.

In this way the individual first pursued spiritual and secular knowledge and practised self-discipline; then, with character formed, he entered family life. Later, giving half of his worldly possessions to his children and the other half to his guru's hermitage, the man (often with his wife) retired to the guru's place in the forest.

The fourth or final *ashram* or disciplinary state of life consisted in complete renunciation of all worldly ties; the man and his wife became homeless ascetics, wandering over India, receiving the veneration of all householders and bestowing on all receptive hearts the blessings of wisdom.

SUCH WAS THE FOURFOLD PATH of life pursued by the ordinary person of Vedic India. But extraordinary individuals, then as now, do not require the usual life-purificatory processes of the various *ashrams* or methodical stages of soul progress. In ancient and modern times, such great souls would remain at the guru's hermitage from the beginning to the end of life, freeing their own souls and helping others toward liberation. Such evolved souls did not need to appease their sense desires before seeking God wholly; they pursued a straight and immediate path to Him through a lifetime of *brahmacharya* and *sannyas,* ignoring the formalities of the family or householder's life, the forest life, and that of a wandering ascetic.

Value of monastic hermitage life

Jesus, Babaji, and many great prophets of all ages adopted only the direct, undeviating path; for them it was unnecessary to enter the whirlpool of ordinary material life. Great souls have long since assimilated (in previous lives) the childish or kindergarten lessons afforded by worldly experiences.

In modern life, a young person who prefers to have a family first, thinking he will seek God afterward, is in serious error. Owing to the lack of early training in a hermitage of discipline, the man of today finds his senses and desires uncontrolled. When he enters the householder's state in the natural course of events, he becomes so overburdened with duties—maintaining a family by running after the dollar—that he usually forgets to say even a tiny prayer to God, let alone engage in a wholehearted search for Him.

This hoary scriptural simile should be remembered: Milk cannot float on water, but the butter that is churned out of it *can* float on water. Similarly, a man whose childhood has been spent in churning the butter of Self-realization from the milky waters of his mind is able to remain in the world, active for God, without getting mixed up with worldly desires and attachments.

Therefore, any man or woman of modern times who finds within himself or herself a craving for God should run after God first. No delay! That is why Jesus advised us: "And seek not ye what ye shall eat, or what ye shall drink, neither be ye of doubtful mind. For all these things do the nations of the world seek after: and your Father knoweth that ye have need of these things. But rather seek ye the kingdom of God; and all these things shall be added unto you."*

There is much difference, as we have seen, between a self-controlled family life preceded by a life of discipline, and the worldly life of modern times. Today a domestic demon is usually present—want, disharmony, worries, fears. There are exceptions, of course; in a very few homes God reigns in harmony, self-control, peace, and joy.

There is no reason for anyone to continue in a state of misery. A worldly life without God leads to misery; life with God, whether in the world or in the forest, is sheer heaven.

All family members should understand that they will forfeit peace by not controlling their senses. Husbands and wives who think that the "holy bonds of matrimony" permit them to indulge in oversexuality, greed, anger, or displays of "temperament" are ignorant of the true laws of life. The inharmonious families and the rising number of divorces found everywhere today are glaring warnings that marriage does not mean license to indulge the desires, lusts, moods, and emotions of the senses.

Persons of sense control referred to in this 26th stanza are those who, pursuing the householder's disciplinary stage of life, use their senses rightly—employing their sight, smell, taste, touch, and hearing without being enslaved by them—seeking merely to gain experience of the essentially transitory sensory world. Once all desires subconsciously present in one's mind are satisfied, he finds peace and freedom from all lusts; he is ready for the third *ashram* of life, withdrawal from worldly pursuits. Through increased spiritual endeavour, he then offers, as a true and acceptable "sacrifice" to the Lord, even the self-controlled use of his senses. Mastering the sensory powers in meditation, that yogi (the perfect renunciant or "*sannyasi*") becomes liberated.

The advice in this stanza is especially fitting for people who are already married and entangled in the world, and who cannot seem to escape from their confinement of material harassments and thus find peace. Any human being, in whatever circumstance of life, is empowered to make this "sensory sacrifice" to the Lord. The grandest purpose of life (contrary to the implications of novelists) is not to know human love or to produce children or to win men's fickle acclaim; man's sole worthwhile aim is to find the everlasting bliss of God.†

---

* Luke 12:29–31.

† The Gita does not counsel that every married person who is seeking God should immediately become celibate. As Paramahansa Yogananda explains in his commentary

The best way of life, even today, is to live in a hermitage under the discipline of a true guru or man of God, pursuing active duties for the good of all, never egotistically desiring the "fruits of action." Those who have not founded a family, and who feel the renunciant's single-hearted inner call, should by all means seek God at once, not risking involvement in the maze of family life and material pursuits.

Anyone who has not achieved full God-realization is on dangerous ground when he attempts to deal with the senses even in a self-controlled way. There is always the risk of sense enslavement, for the mind usually gets mixed up with whatever is in proximity with it. The mind ordinarily follows the rule of "first come, first served"; so if sense enjoyments are placed before it, the mind gets used to indulging in transitory human pleasures, forgetting any effort to experience the permanently blissful nature of the true Self. But once a devotee has fully experienced the bliss that flows from God, that joy becomes the most tempting, and the senses forever lose all hold. They can offer no competition.

There is no reason, however, why those who are already married should remain entangled in worldly consciousness, feeling spiritually bereft, with no hope of finding God. Human love, desire for praise, fame, money, food, material possessions, mental acquisitions, and so forth are all tests of God for the true devotee. God has everything. He wants to prove the devotee's heart—does he prefer God? or does he prefer God's gifts? When a devotee satisfies God that he is not shaken by any temptation, nor willing to accept as a final good anything less than God Himself—then, and then alone, no matter what the devotee's outer circumstance, the Lord reveals His face in all its endless glory.

VERSE 27

सर्वाणीन्द्रियकर्माणि प्राणकर्माणि चापरे ।
आत्मसंयमयोगाग्नौ जुह्वति ज्ञानदीपिते ॥

on XVIII:60: "The art of taming one's natural tendencies is not in the application of futile brute force but in gradual psychophysical steps." Paramahansa Yogananda's advice on this and the other aspects of ideal married life are presented in the *Yogoda Satsanga Lessons. (Publisher's Note)*

Again, others (followers of the path of Jnana Yoga) offer all their sense activities and the functions of the life force as oblations in the wisdom-kindled yoga flame of inner control in Self.

YOGIS WHO FOLLOW the path of discrimination (*Jnana Yoga*) firmly picture, in their consciousness within, the supreme truth: the indivisible relation of soul and Spirit. The *jnana yogi* focuses his attention at the point between the eyebrows, and concentrates his mind solely on the inner presence of the Self. By wholeheartedly following this difficult path of realization, the true *jnana yogi* is eventually able to kindle the fire of inner perceptive wisdom. With this consummation, all the sense activities and the life forces from the afferent and efferent nerves, attracted by the irresistible magnetic flame of inner wisdom, plunge headlong into that sacred flame.

This stanza refers to the method of God-union enjoined by the Vedanta philosophy of India. The method consists in listening to the scriptural wisdom and continuously meditating on it, thereby becoming one with it—provided the mind is not pulled toward the senses by the life force and by restless subconscious thoughts.

There is a difference between "self-control," and "the fire of control in Self" referred to in this stanza. Self-control often signifies the limited power of will used in subjugating a certain sense; or it may signify the power of self-control possessed by an average man. But "the fire of control in Self" refers to the supreme and unlimited power of mastery that the Self possesses as a true reflection of the Spirit.

The follower of the path of discrimination, by continuous use of will, tries to unite his ego with the unlimited power of the Self. If he succeeds, he can then unite that Self with Spirit. He then finds his ten senses (the five instruments of action and the five instruments of knowledge) and the five life forces to be automatically withdrawn into the Cosmic Fire, destroying all sensory and bodily restlessness.

Difficulty of controlling senses by mental discrimination

BUT *JNANA YOGA* IS NOT so easy as it seems. Its greatest drawback is that it ignores the scientific method: spinal-ascent yoga techniques that disconnect the mind from the senses by withdrawing from the nervous system all life forces. The follower of the path of discrimination (*jnana*) is usually subjected to violent resistances from the senses and from the life forces whose natural flow is toward the nerve endings and their connections with the outer world.

The difficulty of the *Jnana Yoga* path is illustrated in the following story. A man was determined to reach a certain destination (God) in a chariot (the body) pulled by ten wild horses (the senses). Several friends (the consensus of the sages) suggested that the man should first tame the steeds, and in the meantime he would be more likely to reach his destination if he ignored the unruly horses and proceeded peacefully on foot (proceeded by the step-by-step methods of scientific yoga). The man, however, stubbornly resisted this advice; he and his horses must arrive together!

Final outcome to this sad tale: After dire struggles with the animals, the hapless man lay badly wounded by the roadside, still far removed from his intended journey's end.

God cannot be reached through the sole path of mental discrimination except by a man so differently constituted from his fellows that he may justly be called a superman. Only such an individual can attain his goal "along with his horses"! The exclusive path of *Jnana Yoga,* therefore, cannot be recommended for the average man—only for a Sandow of discrimination!*

The follower of the path of discrimination, attempting meditation on the Supreme Spirit, is subject to the "drag" of the ten horses of the senses behind him, plus the pull of the life current flowing through the sensory and motor nerves and also the pull of subconscious thoughts—he is facing in one direction and his "horses" and "chariot" are headed the opposite way. It is true that a *jnana yogi* of dauntless determination may succeed, even by the unscientific "hit-or-miss" method of inner concentration, in fully concentrating his mind on Brahman or God (thus "offering his senses and life as oblations to the fire of the Infinite"). But the path of *Jnana Yoga* is not only precarious but lengthy. By *Kriya Yoga,* on the other hand, an ardent practitioner may speedily attain liberation.

THE DIFFERENCE BETWEEN this fire ceremony of *jnana* or wisdom and the scientific fire ceremony of *Kriya Yoga* can be best illustrated in the following way:

Two men were meditating in different rooms, each of which contained a telephone. The telephone rang in each room. One man said to himself, in a mood of intellectual bullheadedness: "I will concentrate so deeply that I will not be able to hear the rings of the telephone!" It is true that, in spite of external noise, he *may* succeed in concentrating

* Eugene Sandow (1867–1925), known as "the world's strongest man."

within; but he has needlessly complicated his task. This man may be compared to a *jnana yogi* who tries to meditate on God, ignoring the unceasing telephonic messages of sight, sound, smell, taste, and touch, as well as the outward pulls of the life force.

❖ *Scientific self-control through Kriya Yoga* ❖

The second man in our illustration had no illusions about his power to ignore the rude clamour of the telephone. He prudently withdrew the electrical plug and disconnected the instrument. He may be compared to the *Kriya Yogi* who prevents any sensory distractions during meditation by disconnecting the life force from the senses; he then reverses its flow, toward higher centres.

By controlling the life force, as is accomplished in the performance of the *Kriya Yoga* technique, the yogi can assuredly gain a state of deep divine ecstasy. By the perfect performance of *Kriya* 1,728 times in one posture (that is, at one time), and by practising a total of 20,736 *Kriya*s, a devotee can reach the state of *samadhi* (God-union). But *Kriya* cannot be practised so many times by a beginner. When the body and mind of the *Kriya Yogi* are adequately prepared to accommodate the high voltage of so much *Kriya Yoga* practice, his guru will advise him that he is ready for the experience of *samadhi.* When my mind and body were ready, my Guru gave me *samadhi.* Before that, when I was not yet spiritually prepared for that state, my request for *samadhi* was rightly denied by the great yogi, Ram Gopal Muzumdar.* Through a thin wire only a certain amount of current can be passed, but many amperes of current can be discharged through a thick wire. Similarly, the body of an ordinary individual in the initial state of *Kriya* practice is like a thin weak wire that can only absorb with benefit the gradually increased amount of current generated by the twice daily practice of *Kriya Yoga* from 14 to 24 times, and thereafter increased in increments of 12, up to 108 (as advised by the guru).

---

* A great disciple of Lahiri Mahasaya, Ram Gopal Muzumdar was known as the "sleepless saint"—one who was ever awake in ecstatic consciousness. Giving only token maintenance and sustenance to his body, he spent his secluded life in unbroken meditation for eighteen to twenty hours daily. Paramahansa Yogananda's meeting with the saint occurred when Paramahansaji was a young boy not long out of high school, intent on his quest for God. When he petitioned the ecstatic saint to grant him the *samadhi* experience of the Divine, Ram Gopal replied, "Dear one, I would be glad to convey the divine contact, but it is not my place to do so. Your master [Swami Sri Yukteswar] will bestow that experience on you shortly. Your body is not tuned just yet." It was only days later that Sri Yukteswar gave his young chela the blessing of *samadhi.* The story is fully recounted in *Autobiography of a Yogi,* "The Sleepless Saint." *(Publisher's Note)*

By *Kriya Yoga* one scientifically marches toward God, quickening his evolution by step-by-step methods and by a greater or lesser number of correct practices of the *Kriya Yoga* technique.

When the yogi by years of practice of *Kriya Yoga* makes his body and nerves adaptable, he can manifest within his body—ecstatically, easily—all the current generated by the practice of 20,736 *Kriya*s, and much more. The adept *Kriya Yogi* concentrates the ecstasy-producing power not in the numbers of *Kriya,* but in *each Kriya*. After years of intense practise, and through the blessing of my Guru and Paramgurus, now when I do only one to three *Kriya*s my consciousness enters the blissful *samadhi* state. My Beloved Lord is never more than a *Kriya* away.

In *Kriya Yoga* ecstasy, the body is perceived not as flesh but as electro-lifetronic energy. The body thus realized as life force becomes one with Cosmic Energy. The ego consciousness is transmuted into the inconceivable bliss of the soul. The soul and its bliss commingle with the cosmic blessedness of Spirit. In the state of ecstasy the yogi knows the body to be a motion picture of divine energy, which in turn is a dream of God's consciousness; and he, the Self, is an eternal part of that dreaming Consciousness.

VERSE 28

द्रव्ययज्ञास्तपोयज्ञा योगयज्ञास्तथापरे।
स्वाध्यायज्ञानयज्ञाश्च यतयः संशितव्रताः॥

Other devotees offer as oblations wealth, self-discipline, and the methods of Yoga; while other individuals, self-controlled and keeping strict vows, offer as sacrifices the study of self and the acquirement of scriptural wisdom.

THIS STANZA CONTINUES the enumeration of various types of devotees whose particular disciplines constitute "spiritual fire ceremonies."

Some devotees properly use their wealth or other material resources to help others as an "offering" to the Spirit. Ascetics possessing self-control and deep resolve consider their austerities as "oblations." Some rigidly observe spiritual vows and the various "do's" and "don'ts" of self-disciplinarians. Certain types of *sadhus* (anchorites) sit from morning till sundown under the sun; others, while chanting, immerse their bodies to the neck in cold water for several hours, or practise meditation in extreme cold or heat. Some devotees try to control the sense of greed by mixing together cold, hot, sweet, and sour foods, eating this conglomeration while practising mental aloofness from the sense of taste. "Since all foods become one in the stomach," they say, "why not mix them together before they reach the stomach? Thus one may nourish the body without catering to the sensation of greed." In spite of this reasonable counsel, one hardly expects this particular austerity to become common!

Self-disciplinarians practise truth-speaking, calmness, and sweetness to all even under provocation. They do not steal or indulge in any wrongdoing that is expressly forbidden by the scriptures. Such persons are the high moralists found in all religions. Their minds sometimes become more enwrapped in "righteousness" than in God! They derive such sanctimonious satisfaction from travel on the spiritual path that they lose sight of God-realization as their destination.

However, those who persistently and intelligently practise austerities, motivated by great devotion for God, find that the "oblations" of their self-discipline ultimately help them to unite with the Cosmic Fire of Spirit.

God-union through eightfold path of yoga

OTHER DEVOTEES FOLLOW THE EIGHTFOLD path of yoga, neutralizing the scintillations of the feeling (*chitta*) so that in its clear waters they can see the undistorted reflection of the moon of the soul. Such yogis observe the "do's" and "don'ts" of self-discipline *(yama-niyama)*, but they go further. They practise body control by postures (*asana*) in order to make the body amenable to their will, able to sit quietly during long hours of meditation and protracted ecstasy. The yogi then assumes any correct posture and practises life-force control (*pranayama*) by a technique such as *Kriya Yoga*. With this technique he disconnects his mind from body consciousness by switching off the life current from the senses, and unites mind and life force with superconsciousness in the spine and brain. He thus reaches the state of true interiorization, or withdrawal of the mind and the life force from the senses (*pratyahara*).

After the yogi becomes strong in body and mind by self-discipline, posture, life-force control, and interiorization of consciousness, he devotes his newly mastered body and mind to concentration on the Infinite (*samyama: dharana, dhyana,* and *samadhi*), conceiving Spirit as the cosmic *Aum* vibration. Not satisfied with listening to the *Aum* vibration, he begins to expand with it—feeling the vibration not only in his own body but in the vast cosmos. The yogi is then able to attain the ecstasy of oneness with God—vibrating in the universe as Cosmic Sound or Cosmic Light—the Holy Ghost vibration. Inherent in this Vibration he finds the Krishna (*Kutastha*) or Christ consciousness, and through that he merges with the Lord as Cosmic Consciousness.

By following the "do's" and "don'ts" of the moral code, and by posture, life-force control, interiorization of the mind, meditation (concentration of the attention), cosmic conception of God, and ecstasy, the self of man can be united to the Spirit. Practice of the eightfold yoga dissolves the waves of likes and dislikes, the desires that infest the intuitive feeling of *chitta* (heart). When the waters of *chitta* are free from waves of sensations, thoughts, likes, and dislikes, the clear waters of intuition reflect the soul as a perfect *image* of the Spirit-Moon. Then the yogi unites his soul reflected in the calm heart with the actual Source, the Moon of omnipresent Spirit.

Benefits and pitfalls of scriptural study

ANOTHER TYPE OF DEVOTEE, seeking an understanding of himself and his relationship to God and the universe, reads scriptural wisdom, meditates on it with self-controlled absorbed mind, and strictly applies the scriptural injunctions in his daily life. Thus he gradually learns to offer the "oblation" of his self-study and intuitive scriptural knowledge into the fire of Spirit. It is not the intellectual "walking scriptural dictionary" who knows the wisdom of the prophets; it is rather the man of meditation and application whose scriptural knowledge shines forth every day in his face and his actions.

Knowledge of the scriptures is beneficial only when it stimulates a desire for practical realization; otherwise, theoretical knowledge gives one a false conviction of wisdom. Unrealized knowledge of scriptures may thus become a detriment to the practical realization of spiritual truths. But when theoretical scriptural knowledge is continuously converted into inner perceptions of wisdom, that knowledge is a source of redemption. Many pundits and learned professors—for all their mental acumen—daily demonstrate by their uncontrolled lives their failure to put philosophy to any practical use.

A man without scriptural knowledge or inner realization is sadly ignorant. A person with a theoretical knowledge of scriptures but without Self-realization is like a man who eats much food but cannot digest it. The man with divine realization, even if lacking scriptural knowledge, has attained God and is a worthy example to society. A man possessing both scriptural knowledge and Self-realization has not only attained God but is an admirable teacher for imparting God-consciousness to others.

My Guru never permitted his disciples to read the stanzas of the Bhagavad Gita or Patanjali with a merely theoretical interest. "Meditate on the scriptural truths until you become one with them," he would say. After I had mastered a few scriptural stanzas in the deeply perceptive way under his tutelage, he refused to teach me further. "You will see," he said, "that you now possess a true key to the scriptures, a key of inward intuitive perception rather than of mere reason and conjecture. All scriptures will open their secrets to you."

Reading Patanjali or the Gita or the Bible with no more than intellectual insight may enable a man to pass examinations on them brilliantly but will not provide an infallible access to true meaning. The kernels of truth in the scriptural sayings are covered by the hard shell of language and ambiguity. Through the help of a guru one learns how to use the nutcracker of intuitive perception to open the verbal shells and obtain the divine meat within.

VERSE 29

अपाने जुह्वति प्राणं प्राणेऽपानं तथापरे।
प्राणापानगती रुद्ध्वा प्राणायामपरायणाः ॥

Other devotees offer as sacrifice the incoming breath of prana in the outgoing breath of apana, and the outgoing breath of apana in the incoming breath of prana, thus arresting the cause of inhalation and exhalation (rendering breath unnecessary) by intent practice of pranayama (the life-control technique of Kriya Yoga).

BY THE CONCENTRATED PRACTICE of *Kriya Yoga pranayama*—offering the inhaling breath into the exhaling breath (*prana* into *apana*) and offering the exhaling breath into the inhaling breath (*apana* into *prana*)—the yogi neutralises these two life currents and their resulting mutations of decay and growth, the causative agents of breath and heart action and concomitant body consciousness. By recharging the blood and cells with life energy that has been distilled from breath and reinforced with the pure spiritualized life force in the spine and brain, the *Kriya Yogi* stops bodily decay, thereby quieting the breath and heart by rendering their purifying actions unnecessary. The yogi thus attains conscious life-force control.

The Bhagavad Gita clearly mentions in this stanza the theory of *Kriya Yoga*, the technique of God-communion that Lahiri Mahasaya gave to the world in the nineteenth century. *Kriya Yoga pranayama* or life control teaches man to untie the cord of breath that binds the soul to the body, thus scientifically empowering the soul to fly from the bodily cage into the skies of omnipresent Spirit, and come back, at will, into its little cage. No flight of fancy, this is rather the singular experience of Reality: the knowing of one's true nature and the recognition of its source in the bliss of Spirit. By *Kriya Yoga pranayama* or life control as described in this 29th stanza, the soul can be released from identification with the body and united to Spirit.

THE KRIYA YOGA SCIENCE OF LIFE-FORCE CONTROL

PRANAYAMA IS DERIVED from two Sanskrit words—*prana* (life) and *āyāma* (control). *Pranayama* is therefore life control and not "breath control." The broadest meaning of the word *prana* is force or energy. In this sense, the universe is filled with *prana;* all creation is a manifestation of force, a play of force. Everything that was, is, or shall be, is nothing but the different modes of expression of that universal force. The universal *prana* is thus the Para-Prakriti (pure Nature), the immanent energy or force which is derived from the Infinite Spirit, and which permeates and sustains the universe.

In the strictest sense, on the other hand, *prana* means what is ordinarily called life or vitality of an organism on earth—the *prana* of a plant, an animal, or a man means the life force or vital force enlivening that form.

Mechanical principles are operative in every part of the body—in the heart, arteries, limbs, joints, bowels, muscles. Chemical principles are also operative—in the lungs, stomach, liver, kidneys. But to all of these activities do we not have to add something that is not mechanical or chemical in order to create and sustain life in an organism? That "something" is the vital force or energy, superior to other agents of life support. The vital energy utilizes mechanical force to pump blood, to move food along the digestive tract, to flex muscles. It uses chemical forces to digest food, to purify blood, to prepare bile. There is a wonderful connection and cooperation among the cells in all parts of the body. This is organization; and *prana* is the ruler of this organization. It is the superintending, organizing, coordinating, building, repairing power of the body.

Prana is an intelligent force, but has no consciousness in the empirical, nor transcendental, sense. It is the basis of the empirical consciousness, but soul is the conscious unit. Soul through ego dictates, and *prana,* its servant, obeys. *Prana,* neither grossly material nor purely spiritual, borrows from the soul its power of activating the body. It is the power lodged between soul and matter for the purpose of expressing the former and moving the latter. The soul can exist without *prana,* but the *prana* in the body cannot exist without a soul as its substratum.

Universal prana: energy that pervades all creation

Universal *prana* came into being in the following way: At the beginning, One Great Spirit wished to create. Being One, He wished to be many. This desire of His, being omnipotent, had a creative force to go outward, to project the universe. It split the One into many, Unity into diversity. But the One did not want to lose His wholeness into many. So simultaneously He wished to draw the many back into Singularity. A kind of tug-of-war thus broke out between the wish to be many from One, and the wish to draw many into One—between projective force and indrawing force, between attraction and repulsion, between centripetal force and centrifugal force. The result of the pull between the two almighty opposing forces is universal vibration, the evident sign of the first disturbance of spiritual equilibrium before creation. In this vibration is blended the creative wish of the Spirit to be many, and the attracting wish of the Spirit to be One from many. Spirit, instead of becoming absolutely Many, or absolutely One, became One in many.

The universal *prana* underlying all combinations in creation is the basis of unity that has prevented the One Spirit from being irrevocably split into many. It pervades all atoms of the universe and every place in the cosmos. It is the primal, direct, subtle link between matter and Spirit—less spiritual than the Great Spirit, but more spiritual than the material atoms. This universal *prana* is the father of all so-called forces, which Spirit (in Its immanent form) utilizes to create and sustain the universe.

When different atoms coordinate into an organism—a tree, an animal, a human being—then the universal *prana* embedded in each atom becomes coordinated in a particular way, and we then call it specific *prana,* vital force or life. Though each cell—nay, each atom—

of a man's body has a unit of *prana* in it, still, all the units of all the atoms and cells are ruled over by one coordinating *prana,* which is called specific *prana,* or life force.

SPECIFIC *PRANA* ENTERS THE BODY with the soul (in the soul's astral encasement) at the time of conception. At the soul's command, the specific *prana* gradually builds from a primal single cell the body of the infant—according to that individual's astral karmic pattern—and continues to sustain that form throughout its lifetime. This bodily *prana* is continuously reinforced not only by gross sources such as food and oxygen, but primarily by the universal *prana,* the cosmic energy, which enters the body through the medulla ("the mouth of God") and is stored in the reservoir of life in the cerebrum, and in the centres of the spine, whence it is distributed by the functions of the specific *prana.*

Specific prana: life principle in the body

Specific *prana* pervades the whole body and differs in its functions in different parts. It can be classified into five different *pranas* according to these functions: (1) *prana* (by preeminence), or the crystallizing power that brings all other functions into manifestation; (2) *apana,* or the power of excretion, the scavenger energy of the body by which bodily waste products are thrown out; (3) *vyana,* or the power of circulation; (4) *samana,* or assimilation, digestion, by which various foods are processed and assimilated for the nourishment of the body and for building new cells; and (5) *udana,* or the power by which cells are differentiated in their functions (some growing hair, or skin, or muscle, and so on) by infinite disintegrations and integrations among themselves.

These five *pranas,* though separate, are interrelated and act in harmony and interdependence. In truth, they are but the one *prana* acting in five different but indissolubly connected ways. (More on the five *pranas* is given in the text of the next *sloka.*)

The basis, or primary seat, of bodily *prana* is the nervous system and cells of the cerebrospinal axis and sympathetic system; but it is also in their infinite ramifications in the forms of cells, fibres, nerves, ganglia in even the remotest corner of the body. Thus *prana* works primarily in the sympathetic or involuntary system; but in addition, voluntary activities are possible only because *prana,* in its five constituent forces, pervades and works throughout the body.

THIS PRESENT GITA VERSE DEALS with two specific functions of life force in its differentiations as *prana* and *apana.* As there is a "tug-of-war" on the macrocosmic scale reflecting Spirit's projecting wish to create and His opposing attracting wish to bring the many back into the One (see page 12), so does this same contest in duality take place on a microcosmic scale in man's body. One expression of this positive-negative duality involves the interaction between *prana* and *apana.*

Prana and apana: two main currents in the body

There are two main currents in the body. One, the *apana* current, flows from the point between the eyebrows to the coccyx. This downwardly flowing current distributes itself through the coccyx centre to the sensory and motor nerves and keeps the consciousness of man delusively tied to the body. The *apana* current is restless and engrosses man in sensory experiences.

The other main current is that of *prana,* which flows from the coccyx to the point between the eyebrows. The nature of this life current is calm; it withdraws inwardly the devotee's attention during sleep and in the wakeful state, and in meditation unites the soul with Spirit in the *Kutastha* Centre in the brain.

There is thus an opposite pull exercised by the downwardly flowing current (*apana*) and the upwardly flowing current (*prana*). Human consciousness is pulled downward or upward by the tug-of-war between these two currents to bind or release the soul.

The vital current flowing outward from the brain and spine to the cells, tissues, and nerves becomes attached to and clogged up in matter. It is used up, like electricity, through bodily motor movements (voluntary and involuntary) and mental activity. As the life in the cells, tissues, and nerves begins to be exhausted by this motor and sense-perceptive activity—especially through excessive, inharmonious, nonequilibrated actions—*prana* works to recharge them and keep them vitalized. In the process of consuming life energy, however, they give off waste products, "decay." One such product is carbon dioxide excreted by the cells into the blood stream; the immediate purifying action of *prana* becomes necessary to remove the accumulation of this "decay" or death would soon occur. The physiology of this exchange is breath.

FROM THE OPPOSITE PULLS of the *prana* and *apana* currents in the spine, the inhalations and exhalations of breath are born. When the *prana* current goes upward, it pulls the vital breath laden with oxygen into the lungs. There *prana* quickly distils a quantity of necessary life force from the electronic and lifetronic composition of the oxygen atoms. (It takes a longer time for *prana* to distil life force from the grosser liquid and solid foods present in the stomach.) That refined energy is sent by the *prana* current to all bodily cells. Without such replenishment of pure life force, the cells would be powerless to carry on their many physiological functions; they would die. The life energy distilled from the oxygen also helps to reinforce the life-force centres in the spine and at the point between the eyebrows, and the main reservoir of life energy in the cerebrum. The surplus oxygen from the inhaled breath is carried by the blood throughout the body, where it is utilized by the five vital *pranas* in various physiological processes.

Breath: cord that ties soul to the body

As noted, bodily activity produces decay and the consequent waste product of carbon dioxide. This waste is excreted from the cells by the *apana,* or eliminating, current, and is carried by the blood to the lungs. Then the downwardly flowing *apana* current in the spine causes exhalation and pushes out the impurities of the lungs through the exhaling breath.

Respiration, activated by the dual currents of *prana* and *apana,* is accomplished physiologically through a series of complex nervous reflexes—chemical and mechanical—involving primarily the medulla oblongata and the sympathetic, or involuntary, nervous system. The intricate sympathetic system, in turn, is empowered by the *prana* and *apana* currents working through the vital branches of astral life currents that correspond to the physical sympathetic nervous system—the main branches of which are called *ida* and *pingala.* (See page 61.) To study the physiology of breath without an appreciable understanding of the subtle life principles behind it is like studying Shakespeare's *Hamlet* while leaving out the parts portrayed by the character Hamlet.

Inspiration and expiration go on largely involuntarily throughout one's life. So long as the life current (*prana*) pulls the inhaling breath into the lungs, man lives; whenever the downwardly flowing current (*apana*) in the exhalation becomes more powerful, man dies. The *apana* current then pulls the astral body out of the physical body. When the final breath leaves the body through the action of the outgoing current, *apana,* the astral body follows it to an astral world.

It is thus said that the human breath knots the soul to the body. It is the process of exhalation and inhalation resulting from the two opposite spinal currents that gives man perception of the external world. The dual breath is the storm that creates form-waves (sensations) in the lake of the mind. These sensations also produce body consciousness and duality and thus obliterate the unified soul consciousness.

God dreamed the soul and encased it in a dream body heaving with dream breath. The mystery of the breath holds the solution to the secret of human existence. There is even a direct connection between respiration and physical longevity. The dog, for instance, breathes fast and has a short life. The crocodile breathes very slowly and may live to over one hundred years. Stout persons breathe heavily and die prematurely. When through disease, old age, or any other physical cause the dream breath vanishes, the death of the dream body follows. Yogis therefore reasoned that if the body did not decay and toxins did not collect in the cells, breathing would not be required; that scientific mastery of breath by preventing decay in the body would make the flow of breath unnecessary and provide control over life and death. From this intuitive perception of the ancient *rishis* came the science and art of *pranayama,* life-control.

Pranayama is suggested by the Bhagavad Gita as a universally suitable method for man to use to release his soul from the bondage of breath.

Kriya Yoga: controlling the currents of prana and apana

THE GITA STATES: "The yogi is greater than body-disciplining ascetics, greater even than the followers of the path of wisdom or of the path of action; be thou a yogi!" (VI:46). That it is *Kriya Yoga pranayama* that is referred to is evidenced not only in this verse IV:29, but also in V:27–28: "That meditation expert (*muni*) becomes eternally free who, seeking the Supreme Goal, is able to withdraw from external phenomena by fixing his gaze within the midspot of the eyebrows and by neutralizing the even currents of *prana* and *apana* [that flow] within the nostrils and lungs...."* The ancient sage Patanjali, foremost exponent of yoga, also extols *Kriya Yoga pranayama:* "Liberation can be attained by that *pranayama* which is accomplished by disjoining the course of inspiration and expiration" (*Yoga Sutras* II:49).

Breath, lungs, heart slow down in sleep but are not completely stilled. But by *Kriya Yoga* the breath is gradually quieted and the movements in the lungs and the body stilled. When motion leaves the entire body, owing to lack of agitation and to complete physical and mental stillness, venous blood ceases to accumulate. Venous blood is ordinarily pumped by the heart into the lungs for purification. Freed

* A paraphrase translation; see V:27–28 for literal translation.

All karma, or effects of actions, completely melts away from the liberated being who, free from attachments, with his mind enveloped in wisdom, performs the true spiritual fire rite (yajna).

—Bhagavad Gita IV:23

❖

"The formal rite in India of pouring into a fire clarified butter (ghee)—a form of fire-purified matter—is symbolical of uniting life energy with cosmic energy.

"The initiate in guru-given yoga meditation performs the esoteric real fire rite enjoined by the Hindu scriptures. He withdraws his life force from the sensory and motor nerves and pours that energy into the sacred fires of life gathered in the seven occult cerebrospinal centres. When the yogi switches off the life current from the nerves, he finds his mind disconnected from the senses. This act of withdrawing life from the body and uniting that energy with the light of God is the highest yajna, the real fire rite—casting the little flame of life into the Great Divine Fire, burning all human desire in the divine desire for God. Then the yogi takes his sense-withdrawn mind and casts it into the fire of Cosmic Consciousness; realizing, finally, his own soul as something entirely different from the body, he casts that Self into the fire of Eternal Spirit."

❖

"When the life force that is withdrawn from the senses is concentrated in the thousand-petalled lotus in the brain, that powerful effulgence burns out all samskaras (habits, impulses, and all other effects of past actions) lodged in the subconsciousness and superconsciousness of the brain, bestowing on the devotee freedom from all past karmic fetters."

—Paramahansa Yogananda

from this constant work of blood purification, the heart and the lungs are quieted. Breath ceases to go in and out of the lungs by the mechanical action of the diaphragm.

Kriya Yoga pranayama stops the bodily decay associated with *apana,* manifest in the exhaling breath, by fresh oblations of life force or *prana,* distilled from the inhaling breath. This practice enables the devotee to dispel the illusion of growth and decay of the body as flesh; he then realizes it as made of lifetrons.

The body of the *Kriya Yogi* is recharged with extra energy distilled from breath and reinforced by the tremendous dynamo of energy generated in the spine; the decay of bodily tissues decreases. This lessens and ultimately makes unnecessary the blood-cleansing function of the heart. When the pulsating life of the heart pump becomes quiet, owing to nonpumping of venous blood, exhalation and inhalation are no longer needed. The life force, which was dissipated in cellular, nervous, respiratory, and heart action, withdraws from the external senses and organs and unites with the current in the spine. The *Kriya Yogi* then learns how to commingle the upwardly flowing life current (*prana*) into the downwardly flowing current (*apana*) and commingle the downwardly flowing current (*apana*) into the upwardly flowing current (*prana*). He thus neutralises the dual movement, and by will power withdraws both currents into one revealing sphere of spiritual light at the point between the eyebrows. This light of pure life energy scintillates from the cerebrospinal centres directly to all the bodily cells, magnetizing them, arresting decay and growth, and making them vitally self-sustained, independent of breath or any external source of life.

So long as this light is flowing up and down as the two battling currents of *prana* and *apana*—the breaths of inhalation and exhalation—they lend their life and light to the sensory perceptions, and to the mortal processes of growth and decay. But when the yogi can neutralise the downward and upward pull of the spinal currents, and can withdraw all life force from the senses and sensory motor nerves, and can keep the life force still at the point between the eyebrows, the cerebral light gives the yogi life control or power over *prana* (*Kriya Yoga pranayama*). Life force withdrawn from the senses becomes concentrated into a steady inner light in which Spirit and Its Cosmic Light are revealed.

Kriya Yoga pranayama, the scientific method of neutralization of breath, has nothing in common with the foolish practice of trying to control life current by forcible retention of breath in the lungs—an unscientific, unnatural, and harmful practice. Anyone holding the breath for a few minutes in the lungs feels pain, suffocation, and heart strain. This adverse bodily effect should be sufficient proof that yogis would not recommend such unnatural practices. Certain teachers do advise unscientific, not to say impossible, long retention of breath in the lungs—a practice completely tabooed by God-enlightened yogis.

Kriya Yoga is not breath control, but life-force control

Many writers in the West condemn the science of yoga on the false grounds that it is unsuited to Westerners. Science knows no East or West. In the past, many orthodox Hindus condemned disinfected water conveyed by pipes (introduced by the English) as "sinful, heathen" water; electricity was branded "evil and destructive energy"! But all Hindus now like "heathen" water better than their polluted malarious well-waters; they also prefer "evil" electricity to their old dim oil-lamps, in which the flame was constantly blown out by even light winds. The unreasonable objections of the Hindus to Western science were no more discreditable than the ignorant condemnations uttered by certain Westerners about the time-honoured science of yoga.

Yoga, the highest knowledge of mankind, is not a cult nor a dogmatic belief, but rather commends itself to the greatest scientists of the East and the West.

True *kumbhaka,* or the retention of the breath mentioned in enlightened yoga treatises, refers not to the forcible holding of the breath in the lungs, but to the natural breathlessness brought about by scientific *pranayama,* which renders breathing unnecessary.

Kriya Yoga is referred to obliquely in several scriptures and yoga treatises as *Kevali Pranayama* or *Kevala Kumbhaka*—true *pranayama* or life control that has transcended the need for inhalation (*puraka*) and exhalation (*rechaka*); breath is transmuted into inner life-force currents under the complete control of the mind.* Of the various stages of *pranayama* breathlessness (*kumbhaka*), *Kevali* is extolled by adept yogis as the best or highest. Though in principle it may be equated with *Kriya*

* "When the breath stops effortlessly, without either *rechaka* (exhalation) or *puraka* (inhalation), that is called *Kevala Kumbhaka.*"—*Hatha-Yoga Pradipika* II:73.

"The aspirant who can perform *Kevali Kumbhaka,* he only is the true knower of Yoga."—*Gheranda Samhita* V:95.

"One who is adept in *Kevala Kumbhaka,* which has no *rechaka* and *puraka,* he has nothing unattainable in the three worlds."—*Siva Samhita* III:46–47.

Yoga, Kevali Pranayama is not as explicit as the specific *Kriya Yoga* science and technique revived and clarified for this age by Mahavatar Babaji and given to the world through Lahiri Mahasaya.

WHEN BY *KRIYA YOGA* the mortal breath disappears scientifically from the lungs, the yogi consciously experiences, without dying, the death process by which energy is switched off from the senses (causing the disappearance of the body consciousness and the simultaneous appearance of the soul consciousness). Unlike the ordinary man, the yogi realizes that his life is not conditioned by exhalation and inhalation, but that the steady life force in the brain is continuously reinforced through the medulla from the omnipresent cosmic current. Even mortal man during the nightly state of sleep rises psychologically above the consciousness of breath; his life force then partially becomes still and reveals a glimpse of the soul as the deep joy of sleep. The breathless yogi, however, realizes the state of conscious "death" as a far deeper and more blessed state than that bestowed by the deepest blissful semi-superconscious sleep. When breath ceases in the *Kriya Yogi*, he is suffused with an incomparable bliss. He realizes then that it is the storm of human breath that is responsible for the creation of the dream wave of the human body and its sensations; it is breath that causes body consciousness.

How Kriya produces conscious ecstasy and body transcendence

St. Paul said, "I protest by our rejoicing which I have in Christ Jesus our Lord, I die daily"* (live daily without breath). St. Paul was able by life-force control—through *Kriya* or a similar technique—to dissolve the consciousness of his dream body into the everlasting rejoicing of the Christ Consciousness.

When with cessation of breath and the quieting of the heart the life force is switched off from the senses, the mind becomes detached and interiorized, able at last to perceive consciously the inner astral worlds and supernal spheres of divine consciousness.

In the first stages of ecstasy by *Kriya Yoga,* the yogi perceives the soul blessedness. By higher ecstasies that come as a result of complete mastery of the breathless state, he realizes the physical body to be made of lifetrons that are surrounded by a halo of grosser electroatomic cells. The yogi perceives the illusion of the body dream dematerialize into the reality of God. By experiencing the reality of the body as *prana*

* I Corinthians 15:31.

or lifetrons, controlled by the thought of God, the yogi becomes one with Him. With that divine consciousness the yogi is able to create, preserve, or dematerialize the dream atoms of his body or of any other object in creation. Attaining this power, the yogi has the option of leaving his physical dream body on earth to gradually disintegrate into cosmic atoms; or he can keep his dream body on earth indefinitely like Babaji; or, like Elijah, he can dematerialize its dream atoms into the Divine Fire. Elisha witnessed the body of Elijah become etheric, ascending in a chariot of fiery atoms and lifetrons commingled with the cosmic light of God. His luminous physical and astral dream bodies and his causal body and soul merged into Cosmic Consciousness.*

A *Kriya Yogi* should have exact understanding of the rationale of the yogic science that is recommended in this stanza of the Bhagavad Gita. An explanation of the dream state will be helpful. A man sees himself in a dream; the power of his mind creates the consciousness of a real physical body. Similarly, by materializing His thought, the Lord has made dream men walking about a dream creation in dream bodies of flesh. The body is nothing but a materialized dream of God.

The Lord surrounded man's soul first with an idea body. Then He encased the idea body with a very fine or subtle light (the astral body). The third or final encasement was the electroatomic dream body, the illusion of a fleshly form.† The reason, therefore, that the Gita advises devotees to practise the *pranayama* life-control technique is to enable them to realize that the body is made not of flesh, but of life force condensed from the thought of God.

When by the proper *pranayama* technique of meditation the concentrated *Kriya Yogi* distils life force from breath and reinforces the *prana* already present in the body cells and cerebrospinal centres, then even the yogi-beginner occasionally sees his spiritual eye of light. By deeper practice of *Kriya Yoga* or breathlessness, he perceives his astral body. Finally he is able to see his physical body as an electroatomic structure, an emanation in grosser form (by denser vibratory force) of the fine rays of the astral body.

By further advancement the yogi realizes the astral body with its texture of light to be an "idea" or materialized thought of God. When

* "And it came to pass, as they [Elijah and Elisha] still went on, and talked, that, behold, there appeared a chariot of fire, and horses of fire, and parted them both asunder; and Elijah went up by a whirlwind into heaven....and he saw him no more" (II Kings 2:11,12).

† See page 366.

he has fully understood the ideational body, he is able to withdraw his consciousness from the three bodily prisons and unite himself as soul with the dreamless blessedness of God.

This, then, is the reason the practice of *Kriya Yoga pranayama* or life-control technique is imperative if man would transcend the delusion of the body as an exasperating mass of flesh and bones.

VERSE 30

अपरे नियताहाराः प्राणान्प्राणेषु जुह्वति।
सर्वेऽप्येते यज्ञविदो यज्ञक्षपितकल्मषाः ॥

Other devotees, by a scheme of proper diet, offer all the different kinds of prana and their functions as oblations in the fire of the one common prana.

All such devotees (adepts in all the foregoing yajnas) are knowers of the true fire ceremony (of wisdom) that consumes their karmic sins.

THE FIRST PART OF THIS *SLOKA* is sometimes coupled with verse 29, appropriately so when understood in its deepest sense relative to *Kriya Yoga pranayama.* The regulated "diet" of the advanced yogi is the vitalizing sustenance of pure life force distilled from the breath and charged with cosmic energy by neutralizing the actions of growth (*prana*) and decay (*apana*) in the body. When the yogi thus controls the life force, he is spoken of as one who has "eaten up" the two currents (*prana* and *apana*)* of inhalation and exhalation: one who nourishes his soul by absorbing the two currents into the one light of Spirit reflected in the brain. The *pranayama* of *Kriya Yoga* is therefore the true "spiritual fire ceremony" in which oblations of exhalation and inhalation are offered into the flame of inner light and perceptions of the Spirit.

❖

YOGA TEACHINGS ON PROPER DIET

THE MORE LITERAL interpretation of this Gita verse is as follows:

Other devotees employ fasting and strictly regulated diet to harmonize and control the five differentiations of *prana* (the five life forces or vital airs) and their

* See reference to "food eaten in four ways," XV:14, page 947.

functions throughout the body, thus spiritualizing the body with health and vital energy. By this method, the yogi trains the body to be less and less dependent on gross food and other material sources for life and vitality. Correspondingly, the fivefold *prana* and its functions become more and more reliant on cosmic energy for sustenance (i.e., the different kinds of *prana* and their functions are oblated in the fire of the one common *prana* of cosmic energy). By this lengthy and arduous process, when cosmic energy ultimately becomes the sole support of life —the *prana* and *apana* spinal currents and their ramifications in the fivefold *prana* having been neutralised—growth and decay in the body are arrested. The yogi thereby attains life control and the realization that the body is made of lifetrons.

Various forms of diet were advanced by the ancient yogis. On one such regimen, disciples were taught to eat once a day; to eat rice or other cooked natural whole cereals; and generally to avoid oily or greasy food. Also advised was the daily use of milk mixed with water. But it is neither necessary nor advisable for active yogis of modern times to confine themselves to such a meagre diet. Those, however, who are meditating day and night in the last stages of *Kriya Yoga* need little food.

It is important, as Sri Yukteswarji often pointed out, for everyone to follow a course of regulated diet, otherwise wrong eating habits lead to disease and to difficulty in concentrating the mind during spiritual exercises.

Some yogis teach their students to consider the stomach as though it were divided into four parts. Rice or other solid food may fill two parts, and one part may receive liquids such as lentil soup or milk. The remaining one-fourth part should always be kept empty for the free passage of the digestive juices, and to afford scope for vital airs to circulate freely if the yogi practises *pranayama* soon after eating. In other words, one should always leave the table not fully satisfied, slightly hungry. Any oil used should be pure, fresh, and sweet. Gas-producing foods should be eschewed. Meals should be eaten at regular hours and in a contented frame of mind. Some texts say: "*Stokam stokam annakhada*"—"Little by little eat many times, but never eat much at one time." Various forms of diet may be followed with benefit, according to the counsel of a guru.

Proper diet and occasional fasting* help destroy unnatural cravings for sex experience, and bestow the blessing of a healthy body.

---

* The theory and practice of fasting is explained in detail by Paramahansa Yogananda in the *Yogoda Satsanga Lessons,* and in *Man's Eternal Quest* (see page 1128). Persons in

Most people not only fail to find the supreme bliss of Brahman hidden within themselves but are not able even to enjoy the possession of a diseaseless body.

THE STUDENT OF YOGA can learn much from the discoveries of modern science. A deficient or incorrect diet causes sickness, brings premature old age, and hastens the advent of death. A balanced vegetarian diet is needed—sufficient proteins, carbohydrates, vitamins and minerals, and limited fats.

Beef and pork, though rich in protein, release toxins that remain lodged in the tissues, promoting various diseases.* The immune system cannot destroy all the quantities of meat toxins that remain in the tissues. Therefore, other foods are preferable as sources of protein and other essential nutrients found in meat, such as fresh curd from milk, cottage cheese, carrot juice, almonds, pecans, and pignolia nuts, whole grains, and beans and lentils (well cooked!). An abundance of fresh fruits and vegetables supplies the vitamin and mineral needs of the body; carbohydrates are found in beans, natural sugars such as honey and dates, and the whole kernels of cereals. The best fats are derived from vegetable protein foods, including nut butters such as almond butter and peanut butter.

---

good health should experience no difficulty in fasting for three days; longer fasts should be undertaken only under experienced supervision. Anyone suffering from a chronic ailment or an organic defect should apply the dietary and health recommendations offered here only upon the advice of a physician. *(Publisher's Note)*

* Evidence of the link between consumption of red meat and cancer in humans was presented by Dr. Alan Boobis of the Royal Postgraduate Medical School in London on April 6, 1995. He told a meeting of Britain's Biochemical Society that red meat contains compounds that could be toxic to humans.

"We know from epidemiological studies that consumption of cooked red meat is associated with the development of bowel cancer," Boobis said. "The reasons for this association are not known, but it has been found that during the cooking process, the action of heat on natural components of the meat results in the formation of a group of compounds known as HAs (heterocyclic amines) which can cause cell mutation."

HA compounds, research has shown, are toxic to DNA—the molecular building block of life forms—and have been shown to cause cancer in animals, according to Dr. Boobis.

A 12-year study, reported in the *British Medical Journal* (June 1994), compared 6,000 vegetarians to 5,000 meat-eaters, and found that those with a meatless diet had a 40 percent lower risk of dying from cancer. These results could not be explained by differences in smoking habits, body weight, or other risk factors. In 1992 the (U. S.) National Cancer Institute published a review of 156 specific studies on how various foods influence disease. Of these studies, 82 percent showed that "the evidence between fruit and vegetable consumption and cancer prevention is exceptionally strong and consistent." *(Publisher's Note)*

Garbanzo beans are one of the richest vegetable sources of protein. They should be eaten raw (after soaking them overnight in water and peeling off the skins) and thoroughly chewed. Starting with a teaspoonful one may gradually increase the amount to half a cup at one meal (if one can digest them). Persons doing hard manual labour can use a cupful at a meal; they are very strengthening. Raw garbanzos are more digestible than soy beans or any other beans. Cooked garbanzos are heavy and gas-producing.

Important factors for health of the body

Whole rice is often preferable to whole wheat. People suffering from high blood pressure or heart disease or arthritis or any allergy will do better to eat whole rice rather than whole wheat.

Everyone should suit his diet to the special needs of his body. The yogi should distil life force and energy and not sickness from his diet.

He should also derive energy from the cosmic *prana* present in sunshine and fresh air—by exposing his body to the sun for short periods of time; and by practising deep inhalation and exhalation in the fresh air to absorb pure *prana*-laden oxygen, which is carbon- and toxin-destroying. The following breathing exercise is excellent. Face the oncoming air currents outdoors, or stand in front of an open window. Quickly throw out the breath with a double exhalation through the mouth, with the aspirated sound of *huh-huhhh*. Then inhale quickly through the nose, in a double inhalation. Repeat several times with full concentration. Start and end with exhalation.

Healthful exercise and the right mental attitude are, additionally, essential nourishers of one's life energy.

IN THESE WAYS—proper diet and other health measures—the yogi stimulates the correct functioning of the five life forces, or *pranas,* which are empowered to perform the five essential functions of the body.

Lack of proper functioning of the crystallizing current (*prana*) produces diseases of decay. Without sufficient *prana* current, food cannot be transmuted into new tissues. If the circulating current (*vyana*) works irregularly, inharmonious conditions such as anaemia or high or low blood pressure may result. Lack of the assimilating current (*samana*) produces diseases of faulty digestion. Lack of metabolizing current (*udana*) prevents the specialized formation and growth of the body's various organs, bones, muscles, and other specific tissues, which are built from the same one protoplasm. The impaired function-

Correct functioning of the five pranas is essential factor in health

ing of the eliminating current (*apana*) creates poisons, gas, tumours, cancers, and all diseases that result from the nonelimination of toxins.

The yogi, converting the five life forces into the one undifferentiated life force, unites them with the Cosmic Life. This is the fire of oblation in which energy derived from material sources stimulates the life force, all then being given as oblations in the Cosmic Fire.

Under the competent guidance of a guru, a student can learn to regulate his breath and life current by certain yoga methods that include a special diet alternated with fasting. By eating less and less, and by confining the diet to small amounts of extremely nourishing foods (known to the guru), the life force and breath can be quieted and the soul kept free from body consciousness. "Man doth not live by bread only" but by superior foods like oxygen, sunlight, and the millions of volts of life energy hidden in the brain, which in turn is constantly reinforced from the cosmic energy entering the body through the medulla.

Quickening one's evolution through yogic diet is a difficult and circuitous path. Through it, however, rare yogis succeed in freeing themselves from dependence first on gross food and then even on finer foods like breath, oxygen, sunshine, and inner life energy. When such a yogi succeeds in living on pure infinite cosmic energy directly sustaining every atom of his being, he has contacted the vibrating cosmic consciousness of God. He knows all life to be naught but a transmutation of consciousness.

Health faddists seem unable to discuss intelligently any subject on earth except the body and food. A wise man discovers a simple diet suited to his constitution, follows it religiously—and forgets it! Endless preoccupation with diet ties the health faddist to intense body consciousness. Advanced yogis learn to keep the body alive, free from disease, and free from the bondage of reincarnation, solely through development of God-consciousness.

All devotees who become adept in any of the foregoing *yajnas* (enumerated in verses 25–30) are knowers of the true fire ceremony. In the ensuing flame of inner wisdom (Self-realization) all of their karmic bonds of mortal consciousness are sacrificed and consumed.

VERSE 31

यज्ञशिष्टामृतभुजो यान्ति ब्रह्म सनातनम्।
नायं लोकोऽस्त्ययज्ञस्य कुतोऽन्यः कुरुसत्तम॥

By partaking of the nectar-remnant of any of these spiritual fire ceremonies, they (the yogis) go to the Infinite Spirit (Brahman). But this realization of Spirit belongs not to ordinary men of this world who are nonperformers of the true spiritual rites. Without real sacrifice, O Flower of the Kurus (Arjuna), whence comes any better world (any better existence or elevated state of consciousness)?

THE GITA HERE CONTRASTS the right-living yogis who effectively perform any or all of the soul-and-Spirit-uniting "fire ceremonies" (as mentioned in stanzas 25–30) with superficial persons who perform mere mechanical rites—or none at all—and know nothing of self-discipline. Without the inner transformation of Self-realization, men remain identified with the misery-making experiences of the body, losing not only the Infinite Bliss within but also the joys of a balanced normal life even in this world.

Between two stools, the poor worldly man falls to the ground! Pursuing the shadow, he not only fails to capture it, but loses, as well, the eternal shadow-casting Substance.

In justice to his dignified status, every human being must work and think, eschewing an aimless existence. He should not be like a football kicked about by the hobnailed boots of circumstance.

VERSE 32

एवं बहुविधा यज्ञा वितता ब्रह्मणो मुखे।
कर्मजान्विद्धि तान्सर्वानेवं ज्ञात्वा विमोक्ष्यसे ॥

Various spiritual ceremonies (yajnas performed with wisdom or with material objects) are thus found in the wisdom-temple of the Vedas ("mouth of Brahman"). Know them all to be the offsprings of action; and understanding this (and by the performance of those actions), thou shalt find salvation.

STUDYING VARIOUS FORMS of liberating actions described in the Vedas, or learned from yogis, or realized by intuition, the devotee adopts the particular method of spiritual ceremony most suitable for himself and pursues it wholeheartedly to the goal of liberation.

The yogi who performs the inner rite of spinal awakening—through which ascension to Spirit is attained—finds the first altar of Spirit in the coccygeal centre (*muladhara chakra*), the subtle centre of life and consciousness at the base of the spine. This centre is called the earth *chakra,* the seat of creation of the earthly body and its activities and perceptions. It is described in yoga scriptures as a four-petalled lotus—the "petals" being symbolic of four specific rays of conscious creative vibration, the medium of the centre's activities. The scriptures further detail within the *chakra* a four-pointed diagram that contains a three-pointed symbol, a triangle, the centre of creative force.* In the middle of this triangle is the starting point of the astral spine (*sushumna*) that runs from the coccyx centre through the spinal cord to the astral brain. The opening of this astral tube in the coccygeal *chakra* is referred to in this verse as the "mouth of Brahman," leading the yogi's consciousness inwardly to Spirit ensconced in the highest centre of cosmic consciousness in the brain, or communicating outwardly through the coccygeal centre to direct the creative activities of the body. This earth centre is thus said to be the abode of Brahma the Creator (the active manifestation of the Absolute) in the microcosm of man's body.

Vedic saints who had concentrated on the *muladhara chakra* wrote down the truths they learned from their perceptions of this centre, their realizations thus gleaned from the lips of Brahma. A highly advanced yogi, concentrating on the coccygeal centre, can behold the truths and creative forces in this centre personified as the Creator Brahma—a Being with four arms or aspects, seated on a four-petalled lotus of light. The ardent devotee can behold this Being by following the instruction from the lips of his guru about the esoteric lore that is found in the Vedas, the highest Hindu scriptures (themselves being symbolically referred to as the "mouth of Brahman"). By concentrating at this centre, the devotee can feel the vibrations of truth and wisdom perceived by the *rishis;* or like these sages of old, can even put questions to and receive answers from the inwardly perceived image of Brahma.

By perceiving this centre and communing with the divine Creative Consciousness of God enthroned therein, the yogi realizes that all actions of the body, mind, and speech involved in connection with any form of soul-and-Spirit-uniting "fire ceremonies" can be particularly initiated through this centre. He realizes that all spiritual fire ceremonies are born of spiritual activities. Their true symbolical significance

* As modern-day physicists depict universal principles and structures in mathematical equations, the ancient *rishis* used diagrams and symbols to represent concisely the complexities of Nature's macrocosmic and microcosmic activities.

can be realized only by concentrating on the wisdom underlying the performance of any rite, sacrifice, or activity. The ultimate purpose of any *yajna* is liberation. The true devotee knows that spiritual activity alone can bestow salvation. Therefore he performs spiritual actions; he receives the resultant inner perception; he becomes liberated.

VERSE 33

श्रेयान्द्रव्यमयाद्यज्ञाज्ज्ञानयज्ञः परन्तप।
सर्वं कर्माखिलं पार्थ ज्ञाने परिसमाप्यते॥

The spiritual fire ceremony of wisdom, O Scorcher of Foes (Arjuna)! is superior to any material ritual. All action in its entirety (the act, the cause, the karmic effect) is consummated in wisdom.

THE INNER SPIRITUAL fire ceremony of wisdom is here extolled in contradistinction to the mere outward or material aspects of the various fire rites referred to in the foregoing stanzas (self-discipline, asceticism, regulation of diet, and so forth). But whether one practises outward bodily discipline and other oblatory activities or inner self-mastery by wisdom, all such spiritual actions are effective, gradually or in enhanced degree, in dissolving the soul-binding karmic effects of present and past actions, good and evil alike.

When the devotee concentrates on many outwardly diverting methods of physical control ("fire ceremonies with material objects"), he finds it more difficult to attain inner poise. In the performance of material or outward "sacrifices," the devotee, thinking carefully about external routine, body posture, physical discipline, may easily forget the ultimate goal of attaining Cosmic Consciousness.

By interiorization of the mind the devotee performs the highest rite of casting the senses into the inner fire of wisdom; he has taken the quickest path to the Infinite.

THE ALL-SANCTIFYING WISDOM, IMPARTED BY A TRUE GURU

VERSE 34

तद्विद्धि प्रणिपातेन परिप्रश्नेन सेवया।
उपदेक्ष्यन्ति ते ज्ञानं ज्ञानिनस्तत्त्वदर्शिनः ॥

Understand this! By surrendering thyself (to the guru), by questioning (the guru and thine inner perception), and by service (to the guru), the sages who have realized truth will impart that wisdom to thee.

CHRIST SAID, "NO MAN can come to me, except the Father which hath sent me draw him: and I will raise him up at the last day."* When a devotee's prayers touch the Supreme Being, He sends him a guru through whose agency He draws the seeker to Himself. It is God who speaks through the guru's voice and guides the devotee through his spiritual perceptions.

There are three ways of tuning in with the guru: by self-surrender, by intelligent questions, and by service. A disciple (*chela*) who is in tune with the guru learns through unalterable devotion to perceive Spirit behind the egoless transparency of the guru's personality. The exalted guru who knows Spirit is one with Spirit Itself. A true guru who adores God only and perceives Him constantly in the temple of his body and mind accepts the devotion of a disciple only to transmit it to the Lord. Unconditioned devotion to the guru enables him to pour peacefully the ocean of his wisdom into the expanding being of his *chela*. Without deep devotion the debris of doubt clogs the mental channel of the disciple's perception; he cannot faithfully receive the guru's subtle inflowing rivulets of enlightenment.

Another right approach that the *chela* may adopt is that of reverent questions to the guru. The charcoal-black ignorance of *maya* within the worldly mind can best be dispelled by permitting the guru to bestow the sunshine of truthful teachings.

A third approach: service to a Self-realized guru. The devotee

* John 6:44.

learns to serve the Lord in the guru-preceptor, for God is fully manifest in any of His true sons.

A sincere *chela* humbly asks his guru: What is wisdom? what is knowledge? what is ego? Eagerly serving the guru—especially by dedication to exemplifying and promoting his ideals and principles—the disciple's intuition develops; he automatically receives the wisdom-vibrations of his master.

Receiving the guru's blessing and guidance after he has left the body

A disciple residing far away from the guru may practise a spiritual method of communion. The guru, one with God, is present everywhere including the wisdom-centre (the point between the eyebrows) of all men. At the end of meditation each day the disciple should concentrate at the point between the eyebrows and visualize his guru. Thinking of him with love and devotion, the disciple should ask the questions he wants answered. If visualization of and concentration on the guru are deep, the *chela* will invariably receive silent answers to his questions in the form of accruing inner perceptions. In this way the advanced disciple can contact the guru even after the master has left the mortal flesh for invisible Omnipresence.

When the *Kriya Yogi*, by the above methods of attunement with the guidance and blessings of the guru, withdraws his life force and mind from the body and senses and surrenders them with devotion at the wisdom and life-energy centre at the point between the eyebrows, he then, through "introduction" by the guru, meets the Infinite or Cosmic Guru.

VERSE 35

यज्ज्ञात्वा न पुनर्मोहमेवं यास्यसि पाण्डव।
येन भूतान्यशेषेण द्रक्ष्यस्यात्मन्यथो मयि॥

Comprehending that wisdom from a guru, thou, O Pandava (Arjuna)! wilt not again fall into delusion; for by that wisdom thou shalt behold the entire creation in thyself, and then in Me (Spirit).

"A TRUE SEEKER LIKE YOU, O Arjuna! receiving the cosmic wisdom taught by a true guru, will never again be deluded by *maya*."

Blessed by the advent of his guru's spiritual perception impinging its revelatory light on the inner darkness of delusory ignorance, a sincere devotee beholds the entire cosmic dream of God as a projection on the screen of his own consciousness. It is said: "The knower of Brahma becomes Brahma." The disciple liberated by realizing the guru's cosmic perception finds his soul one with God. He then perceives all waves of phenomena as floating in the ocean of Divinity.

VERSE 36

अपि चेदसि पापेभ्यः सर्वेभ्यः पापकृत्तमः ।
सर्वं ज्ञानप्लवेनैव वृजिनं सन्तरिष्यसि ॥

Even if thou art the chief sinner among all sinners, yet by the sole raft of wisdom thou shalt safely cross the sea of sin.

HE WHO IS LURED by the temporary charm of evil to perform wrong actions is spoken of as a "sinner." Sin and error are spiritually synonymous. Error is ignorance, delusion, a distortion of reality disposing man to consequent responses contrary to universal laws and principles of righteousness, or truth.

As it is an error of judgement, ignorance, to seek pleasurable taste from poisoned honey and suffer death, so it is wrong judgement, ignorance, that makes one indulge in the momentary charm of evil actions that ultimately lead to pain and death.

When one breaks a law of his country, that is a crime. There is perhaps in that act no sin against God. Some crimes are sins, but not all sins are crimes. Thus man, comfortably situated in the standards of his environment, rationalizes that he is "home free" if his wrong actions go undetected or if "there is no law against it."* But the Lord's universal laws are relentlessly exacting; their blind justice moves sometimes slowly but ever surely. Every action produces a karmic reaction, manifesting sooner or later for good or ill. Every action also leaves a trace in the subconscious mind, and tends to repeat itself until it becomes a formidable, automatically performing habit. People who are held in the octopus-grip of evil habits, and who must constantly do battle with the spectres of bad karma, find salvation impossible.

"Rid yourself of sin by wisdom!" By these words the Bhagavad Gita gives hope to the hopeless. This wonderful consolation, voiced

* "Truth is a gem that is found at a great depth; whilst on the surface of this world, all things are weighed by the false scale of custom."—*Byron*

by those who know the nature of the soul, is based on a psychological and spiritual truth. The soul is perfect, being the reflection of God; consequently it can never be defiled. The ego, which rules in place of the soul in the body-identified man, is the apparent doer and perceiver in the sphere of Nature's forces. Sin and virtue, and their consequences and rewards, are relevant only to the ego. The ego could not know what darkness is if there were no contrast of light—and such is the dual nature of sin and virtue. The ego, perceiving its existence through the ignorance of delusion, accepts *maya's* laws of relativity and is precipitantly bound by them. But the soul has no part in this duality. When one rises to soul consciousness, he is above the cause-effect interplay of sin and virtue; he is virtue itself. Thus Self-realization, wisdom—direct perception of truth in soul consciousness—is the sole rescuer of man from the sea of sin.

Even if one is the greediest of the greedy, the most sexual of the licentious, the most violent-tempered among the wrathful, the most wealth-loving among the materialists—still, by lovingly following the prescriptions of a real spiritual doctor, a God-knowing guru, that "sinner" will be able to banish even the memory of evil habits. Undiscouraged by the vast extent of one's evil habits, the aspirant should go on little by little tasting the joys of good habits. Ultimately he will free himself not only from the grip of all sensual habits but from attachment to any habit, even a good one.*

The liberated man is free from the aftereffects of past evil actions as well as the aftereffects of present good actions. Finding oneness with Spirit and Its eternal bliss, the yogi rises above all bondage to karma, which, with its ceaseless alternates of good and evil, operates as an inexorable law only in the phenomenal world.

---

* The great horticultural scientist Luther Burbank, a devoted student and beloved friend of Paramahansa Yogananda's, once commented that his successful improvements of traits in numerous plant species "have made me see the practicality and the worthwhileness of helping men to change harmful habits into good ones. Some plant improvements, commenced two dozen years ago, are still incomplete. We should be as patient in our efforts to improve ourselves.

"If we instil a new, useful habit...we should not conclude that our work is wasted because it is overcome by a deeply established evil tendency. We do not give up if a plant reverts to a lower stage. Habits, even strong hereditary tendencies, can be broken—this is known to every plant breeder. When I change a plant in some important respect, I must break forces which have led it along a certain line for thousands of years.... Human habits are weak things compared with those of plants. Knowing that tremendous transformations can be wrought in plants, how can a man weakly say that he cannot conquer a pernicious habit which has held him just a few years?" *(Publisher's Note)*

The consciousness of mortal man is seen by spiritual masters to be identified with the three lower centres of the spine (coccygeal, sacral, and lumbar), which operate under karmic law. The liberated man rises above these three lower centres and penetrates to the dorsal, cervical, and Christ-consciousness centres. When the yogi's consciousness reaches the Christ centre of wisdom, the seat of *Kutastha* or universal Intelligence, he beholds his soul as a true reflection of the perfect Spirit, beyond all reach of ignorance and its companionate law of karma.

VERSE 37

यथैधांसि समिद्धोऽग्निर्भस्मसात्कुरुतेऽर्जुन।
ज्ञानाग्निः सर्वकर्माणि भस्मसात्कुरुते तथा॥

O Arjuna, as enkindled flame converts firewood into ashes, so does the fire of wisdom consume to ashes all karma.

DARKNESS REMAINED WITHIN King "Tut's" tomb for millenniums; yet, when it was opened, sunlight dispersed darkness in a second. Bring the light in, and darkness is no more! Similarly, with the advent of ecstatic wisdom all the darkness of karmic slavery is instantaneously banished. The light of God dispels forever the darkness of human delusion.

According to the scriptures there are four kinds of actions and the effects thereof.

(1) *Purushakara*—present actions initiated by the power of free will, uninfluenced by compulsions of past karma.

(2) *Prarabdha*—actions or results arising from the influence of past actions. These influences are antagonistic to man's free will; they serve in large measure to shape his physical and mental development and to determine his environmental opportunities (family, nationality, success ratio). There are two kinds of *prarabdha* karma: (a) fruits of past actions that are now operative in one's life, e.g., the present body (result of past karma), (b) accruing fruits of actions, seeds not sprouting at present in the individual, but ready to sprout at any moment in the present lifetime under the encouragement of suitable circumstances. It is this type of *prarabdha* karma that is operative when a man suddenly finds some unexpected change in his life—from good to evil, or from evil to good, or some surprising enhancement of either good or evil—

according to the nature of the past karma that has just found some available channel for outward expression.

(3) *Pararabdha*—unsprouted seeds of past karma that are reserved for outward manifestation in some future embodiment; also, those actions yet unaccomplished but already subtly set in motion by the *samskaras* (impressions) of past habits, and which will come to growth either in one's present life or in a future incarnation. In constant succession, every action begets a new action, legacy of its offspring impression. Oft repeated, these *samskaras* form habits that automatically impel the thinking and behaviour of their captive.*

Thus are the past and future intertwined and inescapable as woven by the above three forms of action and their karmic effects. The man under *maya* knows neither what he has been in the past (great or little) nor what he will be in the future (good or bad). It is for these lawful "uncertainties" that karma is called "slavery"; the wise man has the liveliest desire to rid himself of all connection with it!

(4) *Prahadara*—actions accomplished after the yogi has ignited the fire of wisdom, thus destroying the seeds of past karma and roasting any potential seeds of present and future actions, causing them to fall away in ashes. This destruction of the bonds of karma is the special significance of the reference to "Arjuna" in this verse, rather than the use of one of his many epithets. The name Arjuna is linked metaphorically to the Sanskrit *a-rajju,* "having no cord or binding." As roasted seeds do not germinate, so a burnt rope may appear to bind, but falls away in ashes.

The liberated man becomes free from the effects of all four forms of action. He acts only by the guidance of his intuition-tuned free will, finding that the stored-up seeds of all good and bad past karma are consumed (made null and void) in the fire of wisdom. The results of past actions do not touch him, even as dewdrops slide off the lotus leaf. In other words, the yogi does not perform his present actions through the influence of stored-up fruits of past actions as does the deluded man. The yogi resigns his life into God's hands with full trust that He will make a better job of it than he himself has ever been able to do! Thus he becomes free from the results of all actions connected with the past, present, or future.

The yogi realizes his body to be a result of sprouting *prarabdha* (the results of past actions); he is determined to rise above the necessity for

---

* See influence of *samskaras,* I:2, 7–8.

future predetermined embodiments. He beholds his own body as nothing more than a motion picture cast on the screen of his consciousness by the Cosmic Beam. Discovering this secret, well-hidden truth about the body, the yogi laughs at the discomfited magician, Maya. He has seen through her "laws" of karma—nothing but brazen-faced tricks!

Verse 38

न हि ज्ञानेन सदृशं पवित्रमिह विद्यते।
तत्स्वयं योगसंसिद्धः कालेनात्मनि विन्दति॥

Verily, nothing else in this world is as sanctifying as wisdom. In due course of time, the devotee who is successful in yoga will spontaneously realize this within his Self.

Any insufficiency or disturbance in a devotee's attunement with cosmic wisdom causes Nature's twenty-four elements of sensory perception to spring forth as dilutions of his consciousness of Oneness, God. The deluded man sees not his Source, the Spirit, but only the body, which is a mere conglomeration of the twenty-four inner elements of *maya*—twenty-four veils that shroud the Spirit.* The scriptures call man "fallen" or "evil" when his consciousness is identified with "original sin"—the twenty-four-armed Mother Nature whose sole function is to divert man from Spirit to matter.

Of all qualities the purest is wisdom. Its unpollutable flame of light is the only effective adversary of darkness, ignorance. In due course of time, when the yogi reaches the ultimate success of freeing his consciousness from the gross perception of the body and the cosmic elements, he realizes, within himself—in the Self or soul—his lost-and-found wisdom as the sole liberator.

The mention of "time" in this stanza is significant. Man's mind, operating as a part of Nature's twenty-four elements, is engrossed in the material manifestations wrought by the five elements of earth, water, fire, air, and ether, which are subject to the law of relativity and time—the divisions of the timeless, eternal now into the progression of past, present, and future. To escape the flux of time, the devotee must rise to the Spirit beyond Nature's compartments of rel-

* See page 267.

ativity. The Absoluteness of Cosmic Consciousness is the only cure for the relativity of mortal consciousness.

The world and the mini-sphere of the body is the realm of delusion or darkness. Those who travel in this darkness are bound by its laws. If in a dark room, for example, one runs about indiscriminately, he is sure to suffer injury from collision with other objects. But if he obeys the laws of caution applicable to movement in darkness, he can navigate safely. If, on the other hand, the room is suddenly flooded with light, those laws are spontaneously invalidated. Similarly, spiritual methods, and the gradual progression they ensure, are the laws that serve as safe guides in *maya's* land of darkness. But when by these methods the light of wisdom is at last made manifest, the laws of relativity are transcended with the instant banishment of darkness.

The Gita therefore says that "in due course of time," through step-by-step ascension, the successful yogi will attain Self-realization; and in that spontaneous enlightenment of union of the soul with Spirit, he will manifest the Infinite.

VERSE 39

श्रद्धावाँल्लभते ज्ञानं तत्परः संयतेन्द्रियः ।
ज्ञानं लब्ध्वा परां शान्तिमचिरेणाधिगच्छति ॥

The man of devotion who is engrossed in the Infinite, who has controlled the senses, achieves wisdom. Having obtained wisdom, he immediately attains supreme peace.

GOD DOES NOT TALK to the average devotee, a beginner in the spiritual path. His only chance to know the will of God is by serving a true guru and devotionally tuning in with his guidance. By following the instructions for liberation, the yogi becomes ripe in wisdom. His mind is not chained to the three lower centres of consciousness, but has risen to union with the higher centres; he is therefore said to have "controlled his senses." The devotee through his guru learns to perceive God and become devoted unto Him.

Devotion in this *sloka* is referred to as *shraddha,* the natural inclination of the heart quality to turn toward its Source in faith and surrender.*

* See I:4, page 70.

There are two stages of divine devotion. The initial stage is imperfect and spasmodic and conditional, consisting in external forms of worship, in bowing down to God within one's heart, in questioning Him within, and in serving mankind.

The second stage is unshakeable and unconditional devotion to the Lord; it becomes manifest through devotion to the guru, through regard for the words of the scriptures, through control over the senses, and through the right technique of meditation.

This latter stage of devotion is greater, because it includes a scientific method for realizing God as He has tangibly manifested Himself through an exemplary guru, scriptural truth, self-mastery of the divinely subjugated senses, and through the bliss of ecstasy in meditation. Man's abandonment of spurious pleasures for divine ecstasy pleases God. That devotee is wise who uses his divine power of free choice to prefer the Giver to His gifts.

One of the most decisive reasons why men succumb to the lesser pleasure of temptations is because that is their first taste of enjoyment. If they had attained the superior joy of ecstasy first, they would find all sense pleasures insipid and flat. After tasting the best cheese, no one likes to eat rotten cheese. He who experiences the ever new, unending bliss of ecstasy becomes indifferent to sense lures.

True devotion to the Spirit—the fixity of consciousness in divine communion that is necessary to ignite the inner flame of wisdom—starts when the devotee in meditation is no longer conscious of his breath and when his mind achieves an ecstatic union with Spirit. He becomes completely devoted to Spirit and thinks of nothing else. His mind rises above sensory distractions and material attachment. His Self becomes the Cosmic Spirit; the scintillations of his feelings merge into a changeless perception of Bliss. This is the state of complete establishment in Brahman that bestows the "peace of God, which passeth all understanding."*

VERSE 40

अज्ञश्चाश्रद्दधानश्च संशयात्मा विनश्यति ।
नायं लोकोऽस्ति न परो न सुखं संशयात्मनः ॥

* Phillipians 4:7.

The ignorant, the man lacking in devotion, the doubt-filled man, ultimately perishes. The unsettled individual has neither this world (earthly happiness), nor the next (astral happiness), nor the supreme happiness of God.

THOSE WHO ARE IGNORANT (*ajnaś*) and refuse to strive for knowledge; those who are without any devotion (*shraddha*) to spiritual things, the guru, and God; and, in particular, those who remain in an unsettled mental state (*samshaya*) about the value of the soul—all gradually decay in spiritual evolution. The ignorant man suffers dumbly, hardly aware of his ignorance. Those without devotion to high ideals have dried-up hearts; they cannot enjoy the real beauty in life. The doubt-afflicted are captives of their own imaginative responses to delusion. The ignorant, the nondevotional, and the doubtful hamper their orderly natural evolution toward God, both here and in the hereafter.

Even the worldly man who yet has a desire for knowledge, and who is devoted and active in acquiring it, automatically climbs the ladder of spiritual evolution. But soul decay sets in for the man who refuses to know, being satisfied with the senses—who does not want to acquire wisdom nor to bestir his mind, lest he learn something!

Soul decay sets in for sense-satisfied man who seeks no higher wisdom

The man of doubt or irresolution is even worse off than the man who is habitually ignorant and does not know any better; the latter is placidly content in his ignorance. The man with an unsettled mind, however, lacking commitment to anything, neither enjoys the innocent joys of earthly life nor is he eligible for the joys of the hereafter (because astral happiness is a reward for man's earnest endeavours in performing good deeds on earth). The man of doubt is restrained by inertia—paralysed into inaction, he remains stationary, a motionless object out of harmony with a world in constant flux.

It is better to work hard for material accomplishments than not to work at all; the man of action receives various benefits by exercising his mental and physical faculties. A man of spiritual action goes definitely forward. But the man with a doubting disposition depresses all his desires for activity.* By lack of motion he converts himself almost

* "Our doubts are traitors
And make us lose the good we oft might win,
By fearing to attempt."
—Shakespeare: *Measure for Measure,* I:4.

to a state of paralysis—hardly a man at all! A human being has been sent into a world of activity and motion; unless he pursues spiritual motion and action by relinquishing doubts, he cannot progress.

Doubts are the result of man's responses to the influences of delusion on his intelligence. When expressed through Nature's principles of mind, intellect, and senses, intelligence lacks the capacity and quality of direct cognition. It may be compared to the light of a lighthouse, appearing only intermittently in intervals of darkness—alternate states of the light of conviction and the darkness of doubt. If the light of intelligence were steady within man, he would, without effort or doubt, understand truth in all things. But since the rays of intelligence are oscillating with the darkness of delusion, the ordinary man remains most of the time in a state of doubt, causing irresolution and fierce loyalty to misconceptions.

The process of knowledge in man consists in a succession of changing thoughts. Each new thought carries a sort of conviction or sense of knowing, but gradually it grows old and is displaced by a new convincing thought. In this way, intelligence is either developed by receptivity to suggestions of truth, or decreased by the influence of delusion-born misconceptions and doubt.

Intelligence made restless by sensory bombardment loses its focussing power. By calmness, intelligence focuses objects and ideas to provide the clearest possible perception. Hence, by restlessness, or an undirected process of mental change, intelligence can be converted into false, meaningless thoughts and notions; or, by the centralization of its forces, intelligence can be converted into intuition.

The clear-thinking man should be distinguished from the man who thinks too much. The latter, fond of exercising his intellectual powers in a desultory way, is led in wrong directions and can hardly choose correctly from a number of seemingly true propositions. The fruitful utility of such complex intellectuality is insignificant, for its unguided exuberance of intellectual energy disrupts inner calmness, rendering intuition impotent. Intuition manifests only in calmness; in the undeveloped man, it only occasionally peeps in through the loopholes of leisure periods of the active mind and restless senses. The clear-thinking individual does not allow intellect to overrule intuition; by his patient calmness, he permits the full play of intuition in guiding him to right determinations.

Do not allow intellect to overrule intuition

Under the influence of delusion, man has an imaginative temperament that destroys his natural ability to perceive truth. A little suggestion might produce different images in different minds. Looking at a distant tree, one person might perceive on one of the branches a yellow leaf; someone else sees it as a lemon; another perceives it as a yellow bird. Each is sure he is right. The result, doubt—which conception is truth? Only by direct close observation of the object can its true nature be known. This is the function of intuition, that power of knowing which springs within and carries conviction through actual experience or realization. The product of intuition is true wisdom, the ultimate panacea for doubt, or not-knowing. Because man does not develop this intuitive power inherent within him, he remains in the domain of delusion-afflicted intelligence, plagued by misconception and doubt.

MANY INDIVIDUALS IN THIS WORLD manifest nothing but doubts; they develop a peculiar complex about the absolute value of doubts! Association with such people, whose malady is highly contagious, fills the vulnerable person with a sort of resentful uncertainty by which he may lose present happiness as well as desires to work for future happiness.

The disconcerting man of doubts invariably considers himself "broad-minded" and "acutely discerning." To him all saints—those who perceive the Unity behind diversity—are "simpletons."

Man's best remedy for doubts is to mix with "simpletons" of positive and sanguine dispositions. Doubters, however, like to mix only with their own kind. They often become extremely negative individuals, graphically called, in America, "sourpusses." Full of bitterness and distrust they can neither enjoy the pleasures that come in their path nor look forward to any happiness in the future. Doubters seem to enjoy masochistically the state of inner oscillation and unhappy turmoil. They find, too, sadistic pleasure in unsettling the minds of others who are imbued with faith and happiness.

The habit of doubt must be obliterated within and without. As both doubt and joy are contagious, all yogi beginners should associate only with those who are full of divine joy, or enthusiastic seekers of it.

The doubting individual must rouse himself to extraordinary efforts in order to be free from his paralyzing habit. As soon as doubts arise in the mind, he must nip them in the bud. He should take a vow not to hurt the faith of others with the corroding acid of his own doubts. He should not transmit his scepticism to others by argumentative discussions and conjectures. His mind, wasting away from the disease of doubt, will be rejuvenated by the culture of wisdom and association with those "simple" men who possess the One Certainty—God.

VERSE 41

योगसन्न्यस्तकर्माणं ज्ञानसञ्छिन्नसंशयम्।
आत्मवन्तं न कर्माणि निबध्नन्ति धनञ्जय॥

O Winner of Wealth (Arjuna), he who has relinquished work by yoga, and who has torn apart his doubts by wisdom, becomes poised in the Self; actions do not entangle him.

THIS STANZA REFERS to the two main paths: (1) union of the soul with God through *Raja Yoga*; (2) perceiving the Infinite by wisdom.

(1) Those who perform the gradated actions of yogic meditations become united to God. Through these and other divine actions in daily life (*sadhana*) they rise above all attachment and desires, and become true renunciants.

(2) Devotees find spiritual fulfilment by concentrating their minds with devotion and faith on scriptural and guru-bestowed wisdom. Dispelling doubts by reason and ultimate inner intuitive conviction, their whole concentration becomes poised in the Self.

Taken together as one path, as advised in the all-inclusive *Raja Yoga*, or followed separately as singular paths, both the yogi and the sage find that even though they work with the body, they are no longer bound by fruits of action; God dwells within them as the true Performer of works. Unidentified with the ego, egotistic actions, and the body, these devotees become free.

The relinquishing of actions by yoga signifies that the yogi performs actions only for God. The Gita again and again points out that literal "renunciation of actions," relished by "spiritual" idlers, is not the true renunciation. Acting for God and renouncing the *fruits* of action—not actionlessness—mark the true man of renunciation. Such a devotee is a yogi and a man of renunciation because he is united to God and has renounced the fruits of action. This is the meaning of "relinquishing work by yoga." By renunciation of love for all worldly objects—no longer desiring those fruits of actions—a devotee escapes from the phenomenal world into the noumenal world of truth. He tears asunder the ego's illusory doubts about what is Reality and what is unreality, and becomes poised in his true Self, transcendentally free of the binding effects of the karmic strings that knit the ego to the world.

VERSE 42

तस्मादज्ञानसम्भूतं हृत्स्थं ज्ञानासिनात्मनः ।
छित्त्वैनं संशयं योगमातिष्ठोत्तिष्ठ भारत ॥

Therefore, O Descendant of Bharata (Arjuna), arise! Take shelter in yoga, slashing with the sword of wisdom this ignorance-born doubt existing in thy heart about the Self!

"O DEVOTEE, THOU WHO ART a descendant of Cosmic Consciousness! now you know how you can acquire wisdom. By self-effort in following the wisdom dictates of the scriptures and the guru, and by yoga meditation, you can easily forsake the doubt about the Self as made in the image of Spirit. Your confusion has been caused by your response to cosmic delusion and ignorance. Owing to this doubt you have not united yourself with this Supreme Spirit by a practice of yoga. O devotee, rouse yourself from the hypnosis of doubt! With the wisdom of guru-given discrimination, distinguish between the Substance and the delusive appearances. Instead of tenaciously clinging to the delusion-caused doubt, it is far easier to cling tenaciously to the yoga-discovered Divine Certainty!"

Instead of indulging in doubts about the true purposes of life and about the possibility of finding God, man should cut away his mental imperfections with the sword of wisdom from a guru; and by practice of yoga techniques, enjoy the doubt-dispelling, ever-blessed communion with God.

ॐ तत्सदिति श्रीमद्भगवद्गीतासूपनिषत्सु
ब्रह्मविद्यायां योगशास्त्रे श्रीकृष्णार्जुनसंवादे
ज्ञानकर्मसन्न्यासयोगो नाम चतुर्थोऽध्यायः ॥

Aum, Tat, Sat.
In the Upanishad of the holy Bhagavad Gita—the discourse of Lord Krishna to Arjuna, which is the scripture of yoga and the science of God-realization—this is the fourth chapter, called "Jnana Yoga" ("Union Through Knowledge of the Divine").

CHAPTER V

Freedom Through Inner Renunciation

❖

Which Is Better—Serving in the World or Seeking Wisdom in Seclusion?

❖

The Gita's Way of Freedom: Meditation on God Plus Desireless Activity

❖

The Self as Transcendental Witness: Ensconced in Bliss, Unaffected by the World

❖

Good and Evil and Their Relation to the Soul

❖

The Knower of Spirit Abides in the Supreme Being

❖

Transcending the Sensory World, Attaining the Bliss Indestructible

"Unattracted to the sensory world, the yogi experiences the ever new joy inherent in the Self. Engaged in divine union of the soul with Spirit, he attains bliss indestructible.... Renunciants who are desireless and wrathless, mind-controlled, and Self-realized, are completely free both in this world and in the beyond."

FREEDOM THROUGH INNER RENUNCIATION

WHICH IS BETTER: SERVING IN THE WORLD OR SEEKING WISDOM IN SECLUSION?

VERSE 1

अर्जुन उवाच
सन्न्यासं कर्मणां कृष्ण पुनर्योगं च शंससि।
यच्छ्रेय एतयोरेकं तन्मे ब्रूहि सुनिश्चितम्॥

Arjuna said:
O Krishna, you speak of renunciation of actions; at the same time, you advise their performance. Of these two, which is the better path? Please tell me for certain.

ARJUNA, LIKE MANY ANOTHER true devotee, is not yet free from perplexities. When a yogi begins to meditate deeply, he is so happy with his new world of inner perceptions that he wonders: "Should I ever return to activity in the world? Should I not rather confine myself wholly to secluded meditation?" These two paths have been the cause of many controversies.

The initial romance with the Infinite in the path of meditation is likely to make the devotee one-sided; he inclines to forsake the path of action. The cosmic law, however, compels man to activity, regardless of what mental determination he may entertain regarding his conduct in life. He who is part of creation has obligations toward creation; he is forced even against his conscious will to play his equitable part. Just as a man cannot successfully decide with his mind that he will stop breathing, so he cannot effectively decide with his mind that he will stop acting.

There are exceptional cases: A yogi who has destroyed the roots of all past actions with their resultant longings may be filled with the consciousness of God to such an extent that his only activity consists in divine meditation. For such rare yogis there is no necessity for outer actions—or, if actions are performed, no karma accrues.

Even great yogis, however, who do not engage in outward activities, nevertheless perform a certain minimum of actions; inwardly they are very active in sending forth divine vibrations by which they help in others' liberation. No devotee comes on earth only to meditate on the Lord and to do nothing else. Had that been his goal, he would have found many other worlds in God's vast creation far better suited to his purpose!

The Lord Himself declares: "Arjuna, I have attained everything; there is nothing more for which I can wish, and yet I work on! Those who emulate Me are those who in yoga meditation attain oneness with Me as the quiescent Absolute, and who also perform dutiful activities—even as do I Myself."*

Man should thus practise yoga techniques in order to realize his oneness with the Lord; at the same time he must perform his worldly duties as a "sacrifice" before the altar of the Prodigious Worker—God.

VERSE 2

श्रीभगवानुवाच
सन्न्यासः कर्मयोगश्च निःश्रेयसकरावुभौ।
तयोस्तु कर्मसन्न्यासात्कर्मयोगो विशिष्यते॥

The Blessed Lord answered:

Salvation is found by both renunciation and performance of action. But of these two, the Yoga of works is better than renunciation of works.

THE LORD'S ANSWER IS UNEQUIVOCAL here: "It is better to perform one's spiritual and material duties; the devotee who renounces all activities and seeks out a sequestered cave for solitary meditation on God has chosen the inferior (because one-sided) path."

Salvation has a twofold foundation: Man as a true image of God must renounce all his mortal desires instigated by cosmic delusion; at

* See III:22.

the same time man must contact the Supreme Being, his Cosmic Counterpart. The devotee intuitively receives the answer from the Lord during ecstatic union: "The path of performance of right actions without desire for their fruit, plus meditation on Me by yoga technique, is superior to the life of meditation without outer activity."

The path of performance of dutiful actions without desire for their fruits, together with meditation on God, is the better way because it gives the devotee a chance to work out his karma by employing his material desires in the service of God. In this way the devotee's mind is engaged in pure activities, unlike the vacant mind of the worldly idler.

The monk in the cell, on the other hand, may easily abandon contact with worldly objects and yet be unable to cast off his innate material desires from past incarnations. It is very difficult to exorcise the demons of longings, passions, greed, and sex propensities ever present within the undisciplined mind. A monk may renounce the world without being able to flee from inner psychological enemies that exasperatingly follow him to his cave. In that case, it is the better path to live in the world but not belong to the world. Then a devotee's mind does not feel frustrated longings for the world as a monk might feel for it in his solitude. Anyone will find solitude tormenting if his mind dwells on what he has renounced and not on the all-absorbing Divine Presence.

The superior way of acting for the Lord and meditating upon Him

Yogis completely immersed in God are not required to perform worldly duties because they have extirpated all egoistic desires of this life and of past incarnations. In the superior way of acting for the Lord and also of meditating upon Him, the yogi takes no chances of losing Him; whereas the restless monk in his cell, employing no scientific steps to quell his passions, may remain indefinitely without divine communion.

It is far better, however, for the God-seeker not to get mixed up in a worldly environment, but to live in a hermitage under the guidance of a true guru, working only for God through serviceful activities, practising renunciation of the fruits of actions, and cultivating ecstasy with God by meditating ceaselessly on the Lord. That life is infinitely superior to a well-intentioned but ineffectual complete outward renunciation of activities and consequent shirking of all human duties. Even the outward donning of the swami's robe or the monk's habit is not proper (lest worldly people lose respect for the religious orders) until one is a monk *at heart,* has renounced all worldly desires, and is immersed in God. There is no meaning in monasticism without the inward joy of God.

Aspiring worldly people are benefited by occasionally seeking solitude, or, better still, by visiting a hermitage where they can see and absorb the true and proper ways of divine living.

The value of occasional solitude is not to be underestimated, for it affords man an undisturbed opportunity to think of God and nothing else. Then the refreshed devotee can return to the world or to the hermitage to assume his usual duties. But if one considers the night to be his "forest of solitude and cell of silence," it will be unnecessary for him to make expensive or difficult trips to find solitude. Above all, the seeker must learn so to love God that wherever he is, as soon as he closes his eyes he is surrounded by a cell of silence, the Cosmic Deity throbbing in his heart as ever new Joy. The blissful Light shines behind the darkness; in deep silence, with closed eyes, any devotee may behold It. "Be still, and know that I am God."*

VERSE 3

ज्ञेयः स नित्यसन्न्यासी यो न द्वेष्टि न काङ्क्षति।
निर्द्वन्द्वो हि महाबाहो सुखं बन्धात्प्रमुच्यते॥

O Mighty-armed (Arjuna), he is to be known as a constant sannyasi (renunciant), easily liberated from all entanglements, who has neither likes nor dislikes because he is unbound by the dualities (Nature's pairs of opposites).

THE TRUE RENUNCIANT, whatever be his place or duty in life, is the God-centred devotee. With divine nonchalance he experiences the world as a play on ideas coursing through his mind and made pleasurable or painful by their warring contrasts.

To think on the causes of pain or to be afraid of pain (pain being anything that rouses displeasure or dislike) is to be bound by the body. To dwell mentally on the causes of pleasure (pleasure being that which causes attraction and liking) also means body identification. The devo-

* Psalms 46:10. "You need not go to heaven to see God; nor need you speak loud, as if God were far away; nor need you cry for wings like a dove to fly to Him. Only be in silence, and you will come upon God within yourself."—*Saint Teresa of Avila*

The Pandavas and Draupadi Retire to the Himalayas, Entering the Heaven of Divine Union

The ultimate outcome of the Battle of Kurukshetra was complete victory for the Pandavas. "The five brothers reigned nobly under the kingship of the eldest, Yudhisthira, until at the end of their lives they retired to the Himalayas, and there entered the heavenly realm." The Mahabharata story recounts that along the way, first Draupadi expires, then each of the five brothers, in reverse order of their birth—except Yudhisthira, the eldest, who consciously enters heaven to search for his beloved kin. Ultimately they are all reunited in the highest heavenly realm.

This final Mahabharata episode may also be understood in light of the Gita's spiritual allegory, in which the Pandavas metaphorically represent the spiritual powers in the five spinal chakras, and Draupadi represents the Kundalini force in the spine, which is "wedded" to these powers. In the spiritually awakening devotee, the Kundalini force, which fed the body's external senses of perception and action, withdraws ("dies") and flows up through each of the spinal centres, until it reaches the highest centre—the thousand petalled lotus of divine consciousness in the brain. In this process, the outer activity or expression of each chakra "dies," that is, becomes spiritually transmuted into progressively higher states of consciousness. Symbolically, each of the Pandava brothers—representing, respectively, the spiritual powers in the coccyx, sacral, lumbar, dorsal, and cervical chakras—"dies" (or retires inward) as the life force and consciousness ascend to union with the divine soul or Spirit consciousness, symbolically represented by Sri Krishna.

———❖———

"The final ascension from body consciousness to Spirit is the same for everyone: the withdrawal of life and consciousness from the senses upward through the gates of light in the subtle cerebrospinal centres, dissolving the consciousness of matter into life force, life force into mind, mind into soul, and soul into Spirit. The method of ascension is Raja Yoga, the eternal science that has been integral in creation from its inception....

"Even though almost completely buried during the Material Age, the science of yoga can never be annihilated, for it is linked to the Reality within man. Whenever he questions the phenomena of life and awakens spiritually, through God's grace he encounters a true guru who acquaints him with the art of divine union."

—Paramahansa Yogananda

tee who wants to regain the lost paradise of unconditional happiness learns to be indifferent to pain and pleasure of the body, receiving neutrally all external sensations.

This teaching of the Gita is not a philosophy of negativeness or of negligence. Man has his proper duty to the body. The devotee should practise *titiksha*—imperturbability. This discipline allows for the removing, without inner impatience, of pain or causes of pain. The physical temple should be protected until final salvation is reached; the body should be sensibly guarded as long as God wants to work through it.

The man of self-discipline never allows himself to be attached to or mentally identified with the physical body, but sensibly maintains it as a matter of divine duty. The yogi tries to keep the body well because it is easier to hold the mind on God without the distraction of pain. Nevertheless, his endeavours to feel the Divine Presence are not deterred even when aches invade the body and even when he is trying to remove them. When the yogi can retain his inner calm and happiness during the experience of physical pleasure or of physical pain, he becomes one with his ever blessed Self.

Negligence of the body, therefore, does not necessarily denote a man of renunciation (as some people think). The yogi is a man of God-realization; he has found the happiness of his soul. He is also a man of renunciation, uninfluenced by the ever-changing conditions of the world. Such divine beings who remain above the entangling reach of the senses even while they engage in action are the true *sannyasis* (renunciants).

VERSES 4–5

साङ्ख्ययोगौ पृथग्बालाः प्रवदन्ति न पण्डिताः।
एकमप्यास्थितःसम्यगुभयोर्विन्दते फलम्॥ *(4)*

यत्साङ्ख्यैः प्राप्यते स्थानं तद्योगैरपि गम्यते।
एकं साङ्ख्यं च योगं च यः पश्यति स पश्यति॥ *(5)*

(4) Not sages but children speak of differences between the path of wisdom (Sankhya) and the path of spiritual activity (Yoga). He who is truly established in either one receives the fruits of both.

(5) The state attained by the wise (the jnana yogis who successfully follow the wisdom path of discrimination—Sankhya) is also attained by the doers (the karma yogis who succeed through the performance of the scientific methods of yoga). He has truth who beholds as one both wisdom and right action.

THE COMPARISON HERE IS BETWEEN THE successful performance of scientific methods of liberating actions—dutiful and meditative—by *karma yogis,* and the nonperformance of such actions by *jnana yogis* who instead succeed in the purely mental or wisdom approach to realization.*

Even intellectually learned men are like uninstructed children if they see differences between the path of wisdom and the path of right action. The wise engage in activities; the doer of right actions is wise. Those who study the scriptures only intellectually make a distinction between the path of wisdom and the path of action. The true yogi sees no division between wisdom and right action. He who truly follows one path receives the benefits of both paths.

The ecstatic union with inner wisdom or the performance of divine and meditative actions leads to the same plane—the perception of cosmic consciousness and cosmic bliss. The yogi who is immersed in wisdom and the yogi who performs action see two modes of salvation as one; they alone are the perceivers of truth.

The Vedantic way of acquiring wisdom consists of listening to scriptural wisdom, explained by a Self-realized guru, and meditating on it, perceiving its essence by becoming one with it. The far different theoretical method of learning scriptures does not produce real wisdom—merely imaginary ideas about it.

God is Wisdom and Bliss. When wisdom is gained by the Vedantic way of meditation, it produces God-realization. Similarly, when bliss is gained through the scientific methods and meditation techniques of Yoga, it produces God-realization.

Thus the sage first attains the Wisdom-aspect of God, while the yogi first attains His Bliss-aspect. The wise man realizes God as the Sea of Perceptions; the yogi feels God as the Ocean of Eternal Bliss. By a slow, circuitous, difficult path, the sage reaches the same divine goal that the yogi attains by the "airplane route" of scientific Self-realization.

---

* See also III:3 defining the path of wisdom (discriminative *Sankhya,* or *Jnana Yoga*) and the path of spiritual and meditative action (*Karma Yoga*), and how the two unite as one.

The wisdom path (*Jnana Yoga*) is long, dry, and hard. The Yoga way is short, easy, and strewn with perceptions of ever new bliss. Wisdom is not as impelling a force as divine bliss!

THE GITA'S WAY OF FREEDOM: MEDITATION ON GOD PLUS DESIRELESS ACTIVITY

VERSES 6–7

सन्न्यासस्तु महाबाहो दुःखमाप्तुमयोगतः ।
योगयुक्तो मुनिर्ब्रह्म नचिरेणाधिगच्छति ॥ *(6)*

योगयुक्तो विशुद्धात्मा विजितात्मा जितेन्द्रियः ।
सर्वभूतात्मभूतात्मा कुर्वन्नपि न लिप्यते ॥ *(7)*

(6) But renunciation, O Mighty-armed (Arjuna)! is difficult to achieve without God-uniting actions (yoga). By the practice of yoga, the muni ("he whose mind is absorbed in God") quickly attains the Infinite.

(7) No taint (karmic involvement) touches the sanctified man of action who is engaged in divine communion (yoga), who has conquered ego consciousness (by attaining soul perception), who is victorious over his senses, and who feels his self as the Self existing in all beings.

THE TRUE STATE OF RENUNCIATION (transcendental freedom from sense attractions and repulsions) is difficult to obtain without the accompaniment of meditational activities. The Gita is again pointing out that renunciation is more naturally and easily attained through the inward discipline of yoga.

When the yogi, after ecstatic union with God, comes down to the perception of his body and engages in activities for Him, he finds his soul purified from all traces of past good and bad karma, which are now utterly destroyed by the fire of wisdom. Victorious over his senses, he rises above bodily consciousness and retains soul perception. Even though he satisfies the bare needs of his body, and performs all other necessary duties, he is not entangled in any karmic results. He performs actions not as a mortal man but as the Self permeating all beings.

VERSES 8–9

नैव किञ्चित्करोमीति युक्तो मन्येत तत्त्ववित्।
पश्यञ्शृण्वन्स्पृशञ्जिघ्रन्नश्नन्गच्छन्स्वपञ्श्वसन्॥ *(8)*

प्रलपन्विसृजन्गृह्णन्नुन्मिषन्निमिषन्नपि।
इन्द्रियाणीन्द्रियार्थेषु वर्तन्त इति धारयन्॥ *(9)*

The cognizer of truth, united to God, automatically perceives, "I myself do nothing"—even though he sees, hears, touches, smells, eats, moves, sleeps, breathes, speaks, rejects, holds, opens or closes his eyes—realizing that it is the senses (activated by Nature) that work amid sense objects.

THE YOGI WHO CAN RETAIN ecstatic union with God in his wakeful state realizes that when he works with the five instruments of knowledge (the senses of seeing, hearing, touching, smelling, and tasting), it is God (in the aspect of Mother Nature) who is employing those five instruments. Working with the five instruments of action (the anus, genitals, hands, feet, and organs of speech), the yogi similarly feels the Cosmic Deity to be the operator of those organs.

Perceiving his five life forces (those involved in inhalation and exhalation, in cleansing of poisons, in bodily metabolism, in circulation, and in assimilation); concentrating on the senses, or withdrawing his attention from them (work performed by the mind); or utilizing the instrument of discrimination (employed in dreaming, and in perceiving inner and outer wisdom), the yogi realizes that he is not doing anything, that all bodily activities are being carried on not by any personal physical power but by the nineteen elements of the astral body, which in turn is guided by the ideational sheath, which in turn is the sheer thought of God.

The body-identified man imagines his ego to be the doer of all actions. During all activities performed by the senses, mind, and intelligent life force, the egotist thinks: "I am the doer." He is engrossed in the "I am" feelings—"I am seeing," "I am walking," "I am living," "I am discriminating," and so on.

But when man achieves ecstatic union with God he loses all egotism and finds the true Self, the perfect image of God, which, instead of his ego, is the true Doer of all actions. The beginner yogi delusively perceives his body and mind as independent forces, but as he becomes more and more able to retain consciousness of God, he understands clearly that it is the astral body of nineteen elements guided by the true Self that is the sole Doer.

Thus the yogi who is one with Spirit may sleep or not sleep, eat or not eat, see or not see, work or not work, walk or not walk. Whether he performs any worldly actions or not, he realizes his body to be activated solely by Cosmic Consciousness. Such a yogi is free from all fears and hopes, all mental ups and downs. His feelings are untainted with emotional likes and dislikes. Through the transparency of his heart (*chitta*), the yogi perceives the Spirit and not the ego as the Activator. "Where 'I' remain, Thou art not; when Thou comest, I am naught!"*

The undisciplined man and the self-controlled sage both perform bodily actions. The sensualist is bound by desires; and if he dies without conquering them, he is born again to satisfy his unfulfilled human longings. But the yogi who performs his duties as enjoined by God, without personal motives, remains free from any karma resulting from working in any way with the body. He is not required to be reborn because of personal desires connected with his body or mind.

The Gita's counsel: perceive God, not ego, as the Doer of all actions

The Bhagavad Gita here reveals one of the most effective ways by which man can free himself from the shackles of good and bad karma. When a novice in the spiritual path eats, for instance, he should enjoy eating only as a pleasurable duty for preserving the temple of God. When he sleeps he should think the body is being quieted that he may subconsciously enjoy the restful presence of God. When he meditates he should feel God manifesting through him as Joy. When he perceives the workings of life energy within his body he should consider the Cosmic Dynamo to be lighting up the lamp of his flesh. When he is thinking he should feel that the Cosmic Wisdom is working through his discrimination. Whether he is thinking, willing, or feeling he should consider that God is employing his faculties. When he is working with the five instruments of sensory knowledge and the five instruments of bodily execution he should consider God to be working through those ten instruments of cognition and activity.

* Ravidas, mystical poet of fifteenth-century India.

By living in this consciousness the yogi dutifully acts out the part assigned to him by God on the stage of life; no matter what he does, he is free (i.e., he is acting in his own nature, the soul, which is free).

"The senses work amid sense objects" means that the yogi beholds his senses of sight, hearing, smelling, tasting, and touching, and of moving and working in the objective world, as guided by the cosmic plan of God and not by the whims of his ego. When the yogi beholds his senses as divinely guided, he lives in this world as God has planned. The yogi is disinterested in working for himself but is proud to be associated with the fascinating works of God.

VERSE 10

ब्रह्मण्याधाय कर्माणि सङ्गं त्यक्त्वा करोति यः ।
लिप्यते न स पापेन पद्मपत्रमिवाम्भसा ॥

Like unto the lotus leaf that remains unsullied by water, the yogi who performs actions, forswearing attachment and surrendering his actions to the Infinite, remains unbound by entanglement in the senses.

THOUGH FLOATING IN MUDDY WATER, the lotus leaf remains impermeable, unsoiled by its environment. So also lives the emancipated yogi in this muddied sensory world of *maya*.

An excitable man becomes emotionally stirred up by viewing a melodramatic motion picture; a calm man remains unaffected. Similarly, worldly people are full of turmoil while beholding the good and evil dream pictures of life. Yogis, on the other hand, are undisturbed. Milk cannot float on water; butter can. Minds liquefied with troubles and compelling sensory impulses become mixed with and defiled by the waters of poisonous evil environments. Devotees who precipitate the butter of Self-realization can easily float, untainted, on the venomous waters of *maya*.

THERE IS A DEEPER MEANING to this stanza that will be understood by advanced yogis. I will explain it as simply as possible. When perused with insight, the Gita discourse becomes a wonderful exposition of the science of yoga.

When the yogi in ecstatic meditation withdraws his life force from the body's trillions of cells and from the nerves, he beholds the life-force currents like little streams trickling back from the shores of the flesh through innumerable small channels into the large channel of the spinal cord. All the currents of the body thus withdrawn into the spine then pass, successively, into and through the three luminous *nadis* (subtle tubes or channels of life force) of the astral spine (the *sushumna,* the *vajra,* and the *chitra*) and become one current as it passes through the innermost channel, the *brahmanadi,* the "spine" of the causal body.* The *brahmanadi* is so called because it is the primal channel through which Brahma—the Spirit as soul, life, and consciousness—descended into the body and through which the yogi attains ascension into Spirit.

In descension, the Spirit or Brahma present in the soul of man came down through the *brahmanadi* and later entered the three astral tubes, passing finally through their openings into the grosser channels of nerves and cells of the entire physical body. An advanced yogi who experiences the retirement, or ascension, into the *brahmanadi* of all the activities of the life force and of the processes of consciousness is spoken of as one who has "surrendered his actions to the Infinite," the Spirit or Cosmic Consciousness present in the *brahmanadi.*

True surrender to the Infinite: retiring life force through the brahmanadi

When the yogi retires his life force and processes of consciousness through the *brahmanadi,* he sees, from that point of divine origin, wondrous astral phenomena. He is warned not to be attached to them (as any form of attachment forces the yogi to come down again to the sensory surface of the body). He should bypass the miraculous phenomena until he reaches the Universal Essence.

The advanced yogi takes his ego, life force, and processes of consciousness up through the *brahmanadi* causal "spine" to its opening (*Brahmarandhra*) at the top of the head, in order to enable his transformed ego (the soul), life energy, and mind to pass beyond bodily confinement and attachment and be united with the Omnipresent Blessedness.

When the yogi is thus able to unite his soul with the Infinite, this union destroys all his past karma, and he is known as one who has ascended from the flesh. Burning all his past karma in the fire of ecstasy

* The astral tubes are composed of the finest or most subtle form of life energy, "lifetrons"—electrons and protons made of *prana.* The causal *brahmanadi* is a still finer channel of "thoughtrons," vibratory consciousness—the tenacious fabric on which the patterns of the universe and man's being are imprinted. (See pages 59–62.)

(*savikalpa samadhi*), he perceives God without creation. He then learns by the highest ecstasy (*nirvikalpa samadhi*) to manifest his God-consciousness in the flesh and to perform all actions without being entangled by their good and evil effects. In this highest state the yogi perceives God, creation, and his bodily perceptions to be existing and working together in harmony (as described in V:8–9). The yogi then performs all activities of body and mind without attachment, beholding them equally as waves of Cosmic Consciousness.

A person being tossed on a wave in the ocean cannot very well perceive the whole ocean; but as he comes out of that wave and stands on the shore, he can see the vast ocean without concentrating on any individual wave. A yogi similarly withdraws himself from the motion of the wave of his specific life and watches from the shore of divine blessedness the ocean of Cosmic Consciousness without the waves of creation (*savikalpa samadhi*). Just as a man on a beach can view the immense ocean as a single mass of water, then can notice the individual waves as well as the ocean as a whole, so a yogi, after perceiving the sea of Cosmic Consciousness without the waves of creation, can increase the depth of his intuition to perceive simultaneously the ocean of Cosmic Consciousness and also the waves of all creation (*nirvikalpa* or highest *samadhi*).

VERSE 11

कायेन मनसा बुद्ध्या केवलैरिन्द्रियैरपि।
योगिनः कर्म कुर्वन्ति सङ्गं त्यक्त्वात्मशुद्धये॥

For sanctification of the ego, yogis perform actions solely with (the instruments of action) the body, the mind, discrimination, or even the senses, forsaking attachment (disallowing ego involvement, with its attachments and desires).

THE ART OF PROPER ACTION leads to purification of the ego. This means the performance of good actions that counteract or undo the effects of past wrong actions and that contribute to the transformation of the ego into its pristine state as the soul.

The ego is always identified with and engrossed in material things. Its effect on actions results in self-perpetuating attachments and desires. Desire is produced by the contact of the instruments of action with matter when those instruments are under the influence of the ego.

The yogi uses his God-given instruments of action, but restrains participation of their usual boon companion, the ego, and thus acts without attachment and desire.

Attachment is the offspring of desire; attachment then gives birth to further desire. Attachment is not possible without desire, but desiring can be initiated without an obvious prior prompting of attachment. This is because of the underlying ego's intrinsic attachment to things material.

Every time the egoistic man entertains a desire, he puts a condition on himself that he will have to fulfil. Every desire is a burden that he will have to work out at some future time. Even a forgotten desire continues to lurk behind the screen of his subconsciousness, ready at an opportune moment to ensnare its host and exact its dues. With every desire, man travels further from the natural peace of his soul, because desire's indiscriminate temperament makes him forget the purpose of his existence. He is led by attachment, born of desire, to cling to those things that are incompatible with his soul's nature; he prays for things that are even dangerous to its peace.

The soul thus enmeshed in desires becomes the limited, superficial, material ego, with its tunnel-vision attachment that shuts out the perception of superior soul bliss. The clear-sighted yogi, however, knows that activity with attachment and desire is the harbinger of trouble and suffering, whereas activity without these disturbing elements reveals one's true duties, which in turn purify the self and restore the permanent peace and bliss of the soul, as noted in the next Gita verse.

Therefore, yogis should not perform any action instigated by egoism with its attachments and desires arising from likes and dislikes of the heart; they should perform dutiful actions as inspired by God and the guru, merely using in a nonattached way the instruments of body, senses, mind, and intellect. One who cannot distinguish between divine inspiration and selfish desires should seek the guidance of his guru.

When a devotee discovers his life's duties, he should perform them with intense interest to please God and the guru, without being attached to the fruits of action. A true lover of the Lord is happy to succeed in any of his divine adventures. But when he is thwarted or opposed, he does not weep and lose enthusiasm; he tries with deeper interest and stronger effort to achieve what he had previously failed to accomplish for God, unless his guru directs him to do otherwise.

For the advanced student a few hints are given in the following lines about "sanctification of the self."

The nerves are the main pathways of life force in the body. They correspond to the subtler and more intricate *nadis* of the astral body. Many nerve passages are "clogged up" or impaired in the ordinary man's body, owing to bodily toxins and unnatural living; also, the life force in nerves engaged in enjoying sense objects becomes matter-bent. The flow of the life force is from the brain to the senses, a descent that attracts the consciousness to material objects. These outward-bent nerve impulses and energies and their gross state of sense entanglement are contrary to soul perception. Yogis therefore advise proper diet, postures, and *Kriya Yoga* to purify the nerves so that they become Spirit-bent channels, leading the consciousness away from the senses. By *asanas, mudras,** control of life force, chanting, prayers, penetrating the mind and life energy through the seven cerebrospinal centres, concentration on the Infinite, and deep devotion, one can purify the body, mind, and heart to serve as receptacles of the Infinite.

VERSE 12

युक्तः कर्मफलं त्यक्त्वा शान्तिमाप्नोति नैष्ठिकीम् ।
अयुक्तः कामकारेण फले सक्तो निबध्यते ॥

The God-united yogi, abandoning attachment to fruits of actions, attains the peace unshakeable (peace born of self-discipline). The man who is not united to God is ruled by desires; through such attachment he remains in bondage.

THE YOGI WHO WORKS WITHOUT DESIRE for the fruits of his actions, through lack of needless distraction becomes united to God and finds divine peace.

Self-discipline or control of body and mind through the steadfast practice of the right methods of meditation and body purification (as cited in V:11) gives the devotee victory over the senses. When he is lord of the senses, he becomes one with God and manifests the Infinite Peace.

Those who lead unbalanced lives, devoid of spiritual discipline, perform actions for their egotistical interest. They confusedly roam

---

* *Asanas* are postures designed to unloosen pinched nerves, purify and strengthen the life force, and make the body supple and hardy to withstand long meditations.

Mudras used in yoga are postures combined with breath control to stimulate the life current to flow back from the senses to the brain.

in the labyrinth of endless longings. By performing actions to satisfy the unquenchable desires of the ego they forfeit all peace.

The emancipated yogi, one with the blessed God, works for Him only. He knows the earth to be a dream drama of divine activities.

The Self as Transcendental Witness: Ensconced in Bliss, Unaffected by the World

Verse 13

सर्वकर्माणि मनसा सन्न्यस्यास्ते सुखं वशी।
नवद्वारे पुरे देही नैव कुर्वन्न कारयन्॥

The embodied soul, controller of the senses, having mentally relinquished all activities, remains blissfully in the bodily city of nine gates—neither performing actions himself nor making others (the senses) perform actions.

The yogi who sees the omnipresent Cosmic Beam operating in his own body and in the bodies of all creatures and in all objects of the cosmic dream suddenly realizes he never was the doer of any action nor the cause of any material effect.

When the devotee, by self-discipline and concentration, rises above all attachment to the body, he becomes the king-victor of the senses, happily enthroned in a bodily palace. In the state of inner ecstasy he remains an aloof witness of the activities of his body and consciousness that perform all works solely by the silent power of the Divine. He refers none of his actions to his own powers, nor does he compel the senses to work according to the desires of the ego. In this state of highest ecstasy the yogi is conscious of Spirit within and of his environment without, yet is not entangled in any fruits of action.

The "city of nine gates" refers to the nine openings of the body; two eyes, two ears, two nostrils, two organs of excretion and procreation, and the mouth. The yogi, like a retired king, beholds his subjects (the bodily cells, senses, thoughts, and emotions) as guided by the inner presence of God and not by the ego. In this way the yogi, one with his transcendental soul, sees and feels himself to be inactive.

All actions connected with the body no longer concern the yogi; he beholds himself as the nonperformer of any action. Even as a man may observe unconcernedly the activities of a nearby individual, so the yogi established in God beholds his body to be performing all actions without affecting him.

It is very difficult for an ordinary man to picture the state of the yogi as described in this stanza of the Gita. Therefore it is well again to emphasize the point that a yogi united to God does not act like a puppet or an automaton. A man who is identified with his body suffers from any untoward results of his actions. But the devotee, seeing the Lord as the sole Doer, remains detached from all fruits of actions, good and bad, that have been performed by the body and mind. In this way the yogi is not only free from the fruits of present actions but also from the unpredictable future effects of past actions. As the victorious king of a city may delegate its regency to a virtuous successor, and himself live there in peaceful retirement, so the clever yogi conquers the bodily city of the unruly senses and then turns over its government to his beloved Lord; he himself remains quietly within, ensconced in bliss. In this high state the yogi finds that God guides and empowers him in all necessary forms of actions without making him responsible in any way for the fruits thereof.

The ordinary mortal may be said to be a bad actor, disrupting the dream drama of God. The yogi creates no dreams of his own; he unites his consciousness with the Lord and learns to dream with Him. He enjoys the cosmic dream as God blissfully dreams it, without egotistically introducing into it any disrupting nightmares of his own. Man may look around at the modern chaotic world and fervently declare that the ego has no regard for the dramatic unities!

VERSE 14

न कर्तृत्वं न कर्माणि लोकस्य सृजति प्रभुः ।
न कर्मफलसंयोगं स्वभावस्तु प्रवर्तते ॥

The Lord God does not create in men the consciousness of being doers of actions, nor does He cause actions by them, nor does He entangle them with the fruits of actions. Delusive Cosmic Nature is the originator of all these.

GOD IS THE CREATOR OF ALL, even of cosmic delusion; but it is man's response to *maya* through the misuse of the divine gift of free choice that creates in him the sense of egoism and the desire to act according to its dictates and to enjoy the fruits of actions.

When man exercises discrimination and does not respond to cosmic delusion, he uses his free will rightly to choose only the influence of the inner divine wisdom. Thus he escapes the punishment that results from the false conviction of being an independent doer of actions.

Ordinary individuals are guided by natural (Nature-born) tendencies that in fact are unnatural to the divinity of the soul, the perfect image of God. When the consciousness of man is one with God, he finds his own consciousness to be free from the influence of cosmic delusion and of "human" nature. But when man succumbs to the influence of cosmic delusion in human nature, he finds *maya* to be guiding and controlling his consciousness, creating physical and psychological hazards.

Nature is the consort and servitor of God. One who merges himself in the Lord finds Nature his servitor.

Even though the Lord is responsible for creating man and for placing him in cosmic delusion as present in Nature, yet He has given His sons the power of free choice—either to yield to the harmful misery-making temptations of his physical impulses and environment, or to follow the inner guidance of wisdom flowing from God. The ordinary man takes the so-called easy path of catering to his impulses, a choice that ultimately leads to the destruction of all his happiness. But the yogi uses his God-given free will to follow the inner guidance of conscience and intuitive wisdom and turns over the government of his bodily city to God; thus he regains his lost paradise.

The man identified with his body finds by self-analysis that the consciousness of egoism and the egotistical performance of all actions with the desire to enjoy their fruits originated in his error in responding to the influence of cosmic delusion in Nature. Not blaming the immaculate Lord as the Originator of his troubles, the wise man sees that all evils result from misuse of free choice, by which he has responded to Nature rather than to God.

Even though Nature or *maya* is responsible for the sufferings emanating from man's egotistical performance of actions, nevertheless, by the use of discrimination and will power, he can turn away from Nature to Spirit, ultimately making Nature his own slave even as it is the slave of God.

The devotee can always appeal to the Lord in deepest prayer and say: "Heavenly Father, I did not wish to be created, nor did I wish to be placed in proximity to alluring evil temptations. Please, O God, since You created me and put me to the test of life, without consulting me, bless me that I use my power of free choice to strengthen my will and to follow the path of freedom and not the path of delusion."

The divine omnipresent consciousness of the Lord is aware of all men's prayers. "He that planted the ear, shall He not hear? He that formed the eye, shall He not see?...He that teacheth man knowledge, shall not He know?"* God did not create man to suffer, but to overcome all bodily and material limitations by the unconquerable power of the soul.

GOOD AND EVIL AND THEIR RELATION TO THE SOUL

VERSE 15

नादत्ते कस्यचित्पापं न चैव सुकृतं विभुः ।
अज्ञानेनावृतं ज्ञानं तेन मुह्यन्ति जन्तवः ॥

The All-Pervading takes no account of anyone's virtue or sin. Wisdom is eclipsed by cosmic delusion; mankind is thereby bewildered.

THE OMNIPRESENT COSMIC BEAM creates, for entertainment, the dream pictures of men, their virtuous and sinful activities on this dream earthly stage. God is not a meticulous accountant of human merits and demerits. The Cosmic Beam, Its wisdom and ever new joy, are hidden behind the shadows of relativity and ignorance. Mortals, not perceiving the causative Light, stumble in the darkness of delusion.

As fog hides the right road to a destination and causes the driver of a car to go astray, so the mists of delusion obscure the wisdom path toward God, and man veers into ditches of mortal desires and ignorance.

The Spirit or *Sat-chit-ananda* (ever-existing, ever-conscious, ever-

---

* Psalms 94:9–10.

new Bliss) is uncontaminated by the darkness of delusion (Nature), even as a serpent, the possessor of poison, itself remains unaffected by its own venom. Though the poison is produced within the snake, the creature is not affected by it; similarly, even though the delusive dualities of Nature derive from God, He is uninfluenced by them.

When a serpent bites anyone, the victim is affected by the poison; similarly, man as a mortal is afflicted by cosmic delusion. Nevertheless, though *maya* is imposed on man, he can overcome it by refusing to yield to its temptations. The devotee should understand that the purpose of God in creating the world and Delusion is to develop perfect beings. This pastime is God's hobby!

To encourage perfection, the Lord gave men free will—and a challenge! He subjected them to the inner wholesome temptations of His goodness and to the outer unwholesome temptations of Nature. Human life is a vast and complicated puzzle that each man must solve at last.

When man skilfully uses his divine gift of free choice and discrimination to respond to the temptations of virtue and not of evil, he attains the necessary victory. He is "out" in the game of life; he returns to the blessed Home with his heavy winnings!

This, then, is the truth about the mystery of human life on earth. This is the reason why man should not yield (as many psychologists wrongly advise) to the "natural" impulses, but should be guided by the spiritual inclinations that are truly natural to his being, the soul.

Understanding the "rules of the game," and the justice of God

THOUGH GOD IS GOOD, and has originated Cosmic Evil only to test man and thereby afford him opportunity to return by free will to the kingdom of his Father, still the whole "plot" of God has caused man a lot of trouble! We must accept the fact philosophically, and realize that the more the human body is put under discipline, the more man will find joy in the soul. These are the rules of the game, and we can do nothing about it! Nor would we wish to change the rules if and when we understand the wisdom of their Divine Framer.

Even as God, surrounded by cosmic delusion, is not affected by it, so man, intrinsically an image of God, has within him all the divine powers. He too can remain in close proximity with the delusive senses without being subject to them. God has deliberately created each man with an eternal stamp of His own perfection. By succumbing to evil for a while or for long periods, man can eclipse the inner perfection of his soul, but he can never destroy it. As soon as he removes the enveloping delusion that persists through his own ignorance, he finds that he has always been perfect, even as God is, and never was otherwise.

The doubting heart should remember wherein lies the great justice of God: that He has not thrown us into evil permanently by destroying our inner divine nature and by making us mortal beings in actuality. He has instead made us essentially in His image, that we never obliterate His true nature during any test of environmental cosmic delusion. It would have been very difficult, if not impossible, for man to become divine if man were really only human. But it is undeniable truth: Man was first made in the image of God; then, and not till then, was he placed under the influence of cosmic delusion, and equipped with the power of free will—the power to choose between Nature (creation) and God (the Creator). Man, early or late, learns to make the right choice. Otherwise no one would be reading this book!

It is the great mercy of God that He did not create us in a mortal image, for that would have precluded our attainment of a divine nature, except by God's special grace. God sees every soul as made in His image, that no matter how heavily sunk in delusion man may be, even a sinner of sinners can wash away the mud of ignorance and discover the hidden purity of the soul. We are eternally divine; only temporarily are we slaves of delusion. "For we are His workmanship, created in (the perfect consciousness of) Christ Jesus unto good works, which God hath before ordained that we should walk in them."*

That is why all men should understand that sense enjoyment is not the goal of life; only a return to perfection can satisfy the human heart and the divine plan.

A MAN WITH EXTREMELY BAD KARMA may be immersed in delusion for many incarnations, but not forever, because he is eternally God's. A man who forgets his real Self for numerous lives becomes so riddled by suffering that he cannot stand himself or his own habits. As soon as he tries earnestly to improve, he discovers the path to divine joy.

Eternal perdition, or final immersion in delusion, is impossible. A piece of gold, though hidden under debris as large as the Himalayas, will remain always gold. When the dirt is removed, the gold in its

* Ephesians 2:10.

true nature shines forth. Similarly, a mountain of sin covering the soul cannot change its intrinsic nature as an image of Perfection.

This thought makes divine sense: that man has been made in the divine image and can therefore never be eternally consigned to a limbo of delusion. It is impossible for a soul to become eternally evil because *it is eternally good.*

No soul can be consigned everlastingly to hell

Bible students do injustice to its teachings when they believe a soul can be consigned everlastingly to hell. A worldly judge metes out sentence to a man only according to the measure of his sin; God, more just than any human judge, could never punish a man for one incarnation or for many incarnations of evil life with a disproportionate "eternal" sentence of banishment in the hellfire of delusion. Finite causes cannot produce infinite effects.

This oft-quoted stanza of the Bhagavad Gita says with wonderful truth that God does not take into account the sin or virtue of man. Man himself by his actions reaps the results of his good and bad karma owing to the proper use or misuse of his free will.

In this sense God does not remain in this universe as a watcher of human beings, constantly rewarding or punishing them according to their virtues or sins. But He has made laws, which do mete out invariable justice. "Be not deceived; God is not mocked: for whatsoever a man soweth, that shall he also reap. For he that soweth to his flesh shall of the flesh reap corruption; but he that soweth to the Spirit shall of the Spirit reap life everlasting. And let us not be weary in well doing: for in due season we shall reap, if we faint not."*

The Lord never punishes anyone for evil actions. Man himself is the sower and reaper of his own sufferings. Foolishly going against the divine laws and the nature of his own Being, he is the sole cause of his own hurt.

In India the most popular quotation from the Bhagavad Gita about the origin of evil is this part of stanza 15: "Wisdom is covered by ignorance; that is why people are deluded."

This point can be illustrated in the following way: If a man in a brightly lighted and beautifully furnished room closes his eyes and jumps about wildly, he would behold darkness, stumble, and hurt his limbs. Recovering his sanity, he would realize that the darkness and the hazards to life and limb had been caused by his self-imposed stupidities.

Similarly, the wise man who keeps his inner eye open, constantly

* Galatians 6:7–9.

viewing the light of God that permeates all matter, is never hurt but is suffused with joy. The man of ignorance closes his eye of wisdom and sees nothing on earth but darkness, delusion, and suffering. When with the help of a wise guru the blind devotee regains his true sight, he perceives that his own sorrows and those of all his fellow beings are caused by man's wilfully kept inner darkness; the wisdom-light of God is eclipsed. The permanent, ever-present inner joy of the soul is hidden by the lustful human ego and by the impermanent joys of the senses.

When man forsakes delusion he regains the inner paradise. The Gita therefore says that people suffer just because they do not open the eye of spiritual perception; they are immersed in the ever-changing outer world.

CERTAIN DOGMAS TRY TO "EXPLAIN AWAY" evil by saying that God is perfect and cannot know evil; yet Jesus prayed to God: "Lead us not into temptation, but deliver us from evil,"* i.e., "Do not allow us to succumb to the influence and test of the evil created by Thee."

The Omnipresent Lord knows that He is the creator of evil as a test to encourage human beings to shun sin and thus recover their inner divine nature. By creating a film of light-and-shadow images and passing it through a movie projector, a director manipulates the one beam that projects the pictures of both the villain and the hero on the screen; the villain was included to make people disgusted with his ways and, by use of discrimination, applaud the great hero. For the same reason, evil exists to turn people's attention to the better ways of virtue.

After learning the lesson of admiring the hero in preference to the villain, one realizes that both good and evil men are creations of the One Beam; as shadows, they have no intrinsic difference. Thus analyzing good and evil, one should try to rise above both, realizing that sin and virtue cannot affect the nondual changeless soul that is made in the image of God.

Why evil is a necessary and inherent part of God's creation

Good and evil must ever be complements on this earth. Everything created must bear some guise of imperfection. How else could God, the Sole Perfection, fragment His one consciousness into forms of creation distinguishable from Himself? There can be no images of light without

* Matthew 6:13.

contrasting shadows. Unless evil had been created, man would not know the opposite, good. Night brings out the bright contrast of day; sorrow teaches us the desirability of joy. Though evil must come, woe to him by whom it comes. He who is enticed by delusion to play the villain's part must suffer the villain's sad karmic fate, while the hero receives the hallowed reward of his virtue. Knowing this truth, we must shun evil; becoming good, we ultimately rise to God's high estate—beyond both evil and good.

One who looks from the cinema booth through the beam sees the villain and the hero both as pictures. When one is united with God, then and then only he sees no difference between good and evil. It is therefore dangerous in the mortal state to say there is neither good nor evil. People in the audience who are affected by a gripping picture feel a distinct difference between the villain and the hero! But a discriminating viewer realizes that the role of the villain was created to enhance the nobility of the hero by presenting a contrast of good and evil. When the picture is over, he is through with it; he is no longer affected by any involvement of his feeling with either the villain or the hero. He has risen above his temporary interest in the picture, and he knows that the villain and the hero have no intrinsic meaning; they were only different pictures issuing out of the beam bearing no true relation to himself.

In the highest divine state one similarly beholds the Cosmic Beam as the creator of good and evil on this earth. Conquering evil by good and then rising above both, man realizes that this world is only a divine motion picture, vastly entertaining.

VERSE 16

ज्ञानेन तु तदज्ञानं येषां नाशितमात्मनः ।
तेषामादित्यवज्ज्ञानं प्रकाशयति तत्परम् ॥

But in those who have banished ignorance by Self-knowledge, their wisdom, like the illuminating sun, makes manifest the Supreme Self.

WHEN THE DARKNESS OF DELUSIVE IGNORANCE has been driven away from the yogi's consciousness by the light of Self-realization, then in that inner illumination the Supreme Self, the Eternal Being, stands revealed as the ultimate and sole Reality. The devotee feels his little Self, the soul, merge as one with the Supreme Self, Spirit. Of such enlightened beings it may be said: "The Self shines forth like a sun in those who have banished ignorance by wisdom."

When the deeply meditating yogi—as in the practice of *Kriya Yoga*—withdraws his consciousness from all externals and concentrates within, he beholds the inner light of Spirit that is the creative substance of all manifestations. As the sun's first appearance in the sky destroys the shadows of night, so the first manifestation of the cosmic light in the devotee banishes the pictures of delusive relativity that are present on the screen-medium of the senses and the sky of space.

In the primary or *savikalpa* ecstasy the devotee perceives only the cosmic beam, without any panorama of creation. Later he sees the cosmic beam manifested as the checkered lights and shadows of the cinema drama of the cosmos.

It requires the higher state of *nirvikalpa* ecstasy to perceive the partner-dance of the cosmic light and shadows of creation; even as a man who withdraws his consciousness from the plot of a motion picture can observe, by peering closely, the causative commingling of light and shadows. In *nirvikalpa* the devotee perceives the cosmic light, his own body, and all the scenes of creation to be moving within himself as a series of motion pictures. In this state the present, past, and future are revealed as one; all variety is merged in the unity of the Eternal Presence.

THE KNOWER OF SPIRIT ABIDES IN THE SUPREME BEING

VERSE 17

तद्बुद्धयस्तदात्मानस्तन्निष्ठास्तत्परायणाः ।
गच्छन्त्यपुनरावृत्तिं ज्ञाननिर्धूतकल्मषाः ॥

Their thoughts immersed in That (Spirit), their souls one with Spirit, their sole allegiance and devotion given to Spirit, their beings purified from poisonous delusion by the antidote of wisdom—such men reach the state of nonreturn.

"THE STATE OF NONRETURN" is referred to in the Bible: "Him that overcometh will I make a pillar in the temple of my God, and he shall go no more out (shall reincarnate no more)."*

Devotees who use their power of discrimination to free themselves from identification with the drama of creation and behold in it only the play of the cosmic light and the shadows of delusion; who concentrate on the cosmic beam and not on the shadows; who perceive their souls as rays of the Cosmic Sun; who are continuously absorbed in It; who have destroyed delusion by wisdom—those sages attain liberation.

So long as a person has obsessive desires for the excitement of viewing motion pictures, so long he will seek no higher pastime. Similarly, so long as a man is interested in and attached to the drama of his present incarnation, at death he will depart with unfinished desires and be compelled to return to earth to experience other motion picture sequences, until all his fascinations have been fulfilled.

By nonattachment, by beholding the scenes of life as a divine panorama, and by meditation and ecstasy, man gradually realizes that God is the sole Director of the cosmic cinema. The wisdom so acquired brings about the reunion of the individualized soul with Spirit, thus ending—at last and forever—the long separation.

INHERENT IN THIS VERSE IS ANOTHER interpretation intended for guidance in the *sadhana* (spiritual practices) of the meditating devotee, according to the following rendering:

> *Thinking on That, merged in That, established in That, solely devoted to That, they go whence there is no return, their sins dispelled by wisdom.*

Thinking on That: Holding the attention on the object of meditation; for example, keeping the mind concentrated on the inner sound of the great *Aum* (Amen),† the universal cosmic vibration that is the manifested creative consciousness and power of God. The thinking state implies duality of experience: two poles, one upward toward Spirit and one downward toward matter.

---

* Revelation 3:12.

† See references to meditation on *Aum,* page 614.

Merged in That: Filled with the universal *Aum* vibration, excluding the intrusion of all thoughts born of the sentient mind. This second stage of concentration transcends the "thinking state"; it is oneness with the object of meditation experienced through the pure intuition of the soul. The merged state of concentration brings the devotee in direct touch and friendship with the Spirit through *Aum*. It is a blissful state filling the devotee to overflowing with confidence and faith in God. But the merged state in the beginning is not stable and abiding. Unless it is oft repeated and the habit correspondingly formed, it is liable to disappear and be lost whenever the devotee is beset by the bad habit of mental restlessness in meditation, or when he resumes his material activities after his meditations. Hence, this state is transitory because bad habits reappear as soon as new good habits and experiences complete their debut and make their exit. Devotees whose bad habits are strong easily become discouraged when confronted with the apparent unstability of spiritual experiences. Doubts arise, and the faithless may relegate spiritual experiences to the realm of impractical mysticism. The fault lies in the practitioners' lack of perseverance to make permanent their spiritual gains, the attainment of the third or established state of divine communion.

Established in That: Permanently and continuously abiding in the state of divine oneness, regardless of one's external activities (the *nirvikalpa* state).

Having mastered these three stages of concentration, thus changing the focus of the consciousness from matter to Spirit, the devotee no longer harbours any desire save devotion to God and to live for Him alone. In such devotees, all sins (past and present karma) are dispelled by the wisdom-light of God-realization, even as the accumulated darkness of night vanishes with the coming of the dawn. These devotees are released thereby from the dizzying whirl of the wheel of birth-death-rebirth. They "go no more out" from the presence of God.

VERSE 18

विद्याविनयसम्पन्ने ब्राह्मणे गवि हस्तिनि।
शुनि चैव श्वपाके च पण्डिताः समदर्शिनः ॥

Self-realized sages behold with an equal eye a learned and humble Brahmin, a cow, an elephant, a dog, and an outcaste.

UNDISCRIMINATINGLY ENGROSSED in a motion-picture drama in which appear mountains, oceans, skies, priests, merchants, beggars, cows, dogs, elephants, a spectator accepts the illusion that all the objects are "different." Yet the differences are in appearance only; essentially all the images are composed of relativities of light and shadows.

Objects in the phenomenal world are called relative because they exist only in relation to each other. Man's ordinary consciousness is relativity consciousness—i.e., he apprehends one thing only by interpreting it relative to something else. He cannot perceive the One, the Absolute, through that relative consciousness; it was given to him in order to appreciate the nature of the many. Ordinary waking consciousness, subconsciousness, super-subconsciousness—all forms of ego consciousness—share this characteristic: they are relative. The pure superconsciousness of the soul can apprehend Spirit, the Life and Substance underlying and pervading everything in the universe.*

---

* Decades after Paramahansa Yogananda wrote this commentary, more and more discoveries of modern physics are tending to confirm the literal truth of India's ancient cosmology of oneness. Michael Talbot writes in *The Holographic Universe* (New York: Harper Collins, 1991):

"There is evidence to suggest that our world and everything in it—from snowflakes to maple trees to falling stars and spinning electrons—are also only ghostly images, projections from a level of reality so beyond our own that it is literally beyond both space and time.

"[One of] the main architects of this idea [is] University of London physicist David Bohm, a protégé of Einstein's and one of the world's most respected quantum physicists.... One of Bohm's most startling assertions is that the tangible reality of our everyday lives is really a kind of illusion, like a holographic image. Underlying it is a deeper order of existence, a vast and more primary level of reality that gives birth to all the objects and appearances of our physical world in much the same way that a piece of holographic film gives birth to a hologram. Bohm calls this deeper level of reality the *implicate* (which means 'enfolded') order, and he refers to our own level of existence as the *explicate,* or unfolded, order....

"Most mind-boggling of all are Bohm's fully developed ideas about wholeness. Because everything in the cosmos is made out of the seamless holographic fabric of the implicate order, he believes it is as meaningless to view the universe as composed of 'parts,' as it is to view the different geysers in a fountain as separate from the water out of which they flow....

"This is a profound suggestion. In his general theory of relativity, Einstein astounded the world when he said that space and time are not separate entities, but are smoothly linked and part of a larger whole he called the space-time continuum. Bohm takes this idea a giant step further. He says that *everything* in the universe is part of a continuum. Despite the apparent separateness of things at the explicate level, everything is a seamless extension of everything else, and ultimately even the implicate and explicate orders blend into each other....One enormous 'something' [has] extended its uncountable arms and appendages into all the apparent objects, atoms, restless oceans, and twinkling stars in the cosmos.

"Bohm cautions that this does not mean the universe is a giant undifferentiated

The sage rejects a superficial acceptance of the seemingly objective reality of the world (a synchronized motion picture of sound, sight, smell, taste, and touch) and perceives all phenomena as manifestations of cosmic divine light and "technicoloured" shadows.

To the man of Self-realization, Spirit is perceived as reality and creation as the shadow of the Infinite. When the universe is called unreal—*Brahman satyam jagat mithya:* "Brahman is real, His manifestation is unreal"—it does not mean that the universe is nonexistent, but that God is the only reality and that the shadow of His manifestation in creation is not like Him. A shadow cannot be produced without an object; therefore the shadow is not nothing! The shadow appears to be like the object from which it is produced, yet it is not the object.

ANOTHER ILLUSTRATION WILL EXPLAIN how a true devotee actually sees equality in inanimate and animate objects. A sleeping man, beholding a dream drama, may cry out: "There's a low pariah! And there's my friend the priest! How noisy it is here—dogs barking, cows lowing, and elephants trumpeting!" Yet, on awakening, he realizes (if he remembers the dream) that the various "living" creatures possessed no inherent differences, all being unreal mind-spinnings.

All objects of mundane experience are ephemeral expressions of the divine dream-stuff

Similarly, the animate and inanimate objects of this world are nothing but the sheer dreams of God. The man who is awake in wisdom realizes all objects of mundane experience to be ephemeral expressions of the divine dream-stuff. When a devotee can view the earth with all its vast variety and perceive the unity of its underlying God-structure, then and not until then does he rightly know this world to be a dream creation.

If a dreaming person becomes half-awakened, his consciousness embraces a dual comprehension: he partly believes his dream objects to be real, and partly realizes them as mind-spun or unreal.

Similarly, in a "half-awake" state of ecstasy, a devotee beholds the world as manifoldness and yet also as a unified divine apparition. He sees all the objects in it—whether a thief or a sage, a cow, a dog,

mass. Things can be part of an undivided whole and still possess their own unique qualities. To illustrate what he means he points to the little eddies and whirlpools that often form in a river. At a glance such eddies appear to be separate things and possess many individual characteristics such as size, rate, and direction of rotation, et cetera. But careful scrutiny reveals that it is impossible to determine where any given whirlpool ends and the river begins." *(Publisher's Note)*

an elephant; whether matter or mind—as dream expressions of the one consciousness of God. It is in this state that a man of realization looks with an equal eye on inanimate and animate creation.

The first stage of divine ecstasy (*savikalpa samadhi*) gives the yogi the experience of God-union in which no memory is present of the phenomenal universe. When he returns to mortal consciousness, he finds it hard to retain his divine realization. By further practice of *Kriya Yoga* the devotee is able to experience God-union even during the wakeful state of activities in the world. He has then achieved the "half-awake" ecstatic state in which with open eyes he consciously sees the world around him as the divine dream. If the yogi makes no effort for further progress, the "half-awake" state slips away; he begins to perceive the world as it appears to the ordinary individual.

By deeper development, however, the devotee is able to remain in continuous ecstasy with open or closed eyes (*nirvikalpa samadhi*); he learns to commingle his consciousness fully in the Lord and also to produce from that consciousness the dream of the cosmos. In this state he can choose to remain awake in God, without viewing the dream of creation, or can remain in the "half-awake" blissful state, realizing the cosmos as a varied dream. When *nirvikalpa samadhi* is attained, the yogi no longer perceives the "actuality" of the world as does the ordinary man.

Modern science has discovered that the various material elements are nothing more than differently vibrating atoms. The universe is a cosmic motion picture of dancing atoms, which in turn are energy-sparks—not matter at all but vibratory waves.

The vast steps by which a yogi becomes able to say, through Self-realization, that "this universe is a divine dream" are as follows:

In the initial state of ecstasy the yogi is flooded with a superconscious joy. He begins to perceive lights and glimpses of the astral world. As his *samadhi* waxes deeper, his vision embraces the entire astral world that contains the astral counterparts of all the island universes roaming in space. The yogi then dissolves his vision of the astral cosmos into sheer thought forms; he rests in the ever-existing, ever-conscious, ever-new Bliss, feeling It as all-pervading and infinite.

The yogi later comes down to the astral sphere again and then back to body consciousness. He opens his eyes and looks steadfastly at the world before him; he sees himself surrounded by his spiritual eye of astral light. When at will he can vastly expand the sphere of his astral eye, he at once sees within it all the floating island universes.

Many suns and moons are there! vapours of nebulae, endless universes, tier upon tier, zone after zone, all revolving within him and finally resting in the centre of that infinitely expanded astral eye.

It is in this state that the yogi is able to perceive the physical cosmos and the astral cosmos to be no more than differently vibrated thoughts of God. Unless and until the yogi with closed or open eyes can feel everywhere the bliss of cosmic consciousness, and can behold at will the entire astral cosmos within his astral eye, and can see the astral island universes floating within him, he should not say that he has realized creation to be a dream.

A guru does not encourage a beginner yogi to say "the world is only a dream," lest he develop apathy to the performance of his rightful duties.

A man of God-consciousness learns to dream at will, perceiving then his dream world as reality. He learns, too, to dissolve his dream at will, realizing then that his dream creation was a mere mental phenomenon. All illusory nightmares gone, he merges his consciousness with the Divine Dreamer, ever witnessing the colourful premieres of "super-colossal" spectacle plays.

VERSE 19

इहैव तैर्जितः सर्गो येषां साम्ये स्थितं मनः ।
निर्दोषं हि समं ब्रह्म तस्माद्ब्रह्मणि ते स्थिताः ॥

The relativities of existence (birth and death, pleasure and pain) have been overcome, even here in this world, by those of fixed equal-mindedness. Thereby are they enthroned in Spirit—verily, the taintless, the perfectly balanced Spirit.

EQUAL-MINDEDNESS CAN BE ATTAINED by a technique such as *Kriya Yoga,* which not only disconnects the mind, but completely withdraws it from the senses. By interiorization of the mind, the yogi experiences a state of even, unchanging joy. When he can bring that inner ecstasy to all his perceptions in the state of wakefulness, he becomes blameless and faultless, one with the taintless Spirit.

Sages speak of the ordinary person as full of taint or flaw because he perceives (and accordingly reacts to) the dualities and relativities of existence: pain and pleasure, cold and heat, life and death.

Only he who can disconnect his consciousness at will from the perception of worldly objects is free from the disturbing dualities of the senses and thus rests in the tranquil Spirit. Those yogis who evenly perceive divine bliss in the subconscious, conscious, and superconscious states are pure and perfect like the Spirit.

The undisciplined man, embroiled in the relativities of this world, rides the uneven waves of joy or sorrow or despondency or wrath or apathy in the sea of his consciousness; he beholds only the ever-changing uncertainties of existence. When the undulating waves of consciousness are stilled by yoga, the sage beholds in the inner calm the omnipresent Eternal Tranquillity.

The world is full of excitable people who run the gamut of the emotions while participating in the unpredictabilities of daily life. In a life span of sixty years, man beholds 21,900 diurnal and nocturnal motion pictures, and is tossed on ceaseless waves of feeling. Buffeted and bewildered, he learns very little from the instructive panorama of life. Such men have to reincarnate until they are able to watch the worldly spectacle like calm, blissful gods.

The yogi views this world as entertainment. If he experiences in his own life a "tragedy" such as illness, poverty, persecution, or bereavement, he is able to say sincerely: "Ah, this dramatic spectacle is only a passing scene; it is not the ultimate reality!"—even as an ordinary man, viewing a motion picture of horror or tragedy, may say: "What an interesting drama!" If this cosmic show, morning, noon, and night, had only angels and smiles and no pain and tears, it would get boresome and monotonous.

Without suffering, mortals would not make the effort to know that they are immortals who cannot suffer. The spiritual aspirant is thus advised to conquer his emotional reactions to the inevitable dualities of the phenomenal universe, and to remain, like his Creator, in an even, ecstatic state. How easily body-identified man is moved by the dualities; but at death his beloved body cannot be emotionally stirred. The yogi accepts the hint given by Death; and so while occupying the body, he treats it kindly but impersonally like a total stranger.

VERSE 20

न प्रहृष्येत्प्रियं प्राप्य नोद्विजेत्प्राप्य चाप्रियम्।
स्थिरबुद्धिरसम्मूढो ब्रह्मविद् ब्रह्मणि स्थितः॥

The knower of Spirit, abiding in the Supreme Being, with unswerving discrimination, free from delusion, is thus neither jubilant at pleasant experiences nor downcast by unpleasant experiences.

THE ORDINARY MAN NEVER ANALYZES the lessons inherent in the cinema of daily life; he remains identified with those pictures, grieving or rejoicing as the case may be.

The yogi who roasts in a fire of wisdom all seeds of new desires becomes free from the thralldom of reincarnation. Nevertheless, not having finished the effects of all past actions, he encounters in his present life good and evil happenings, health or disease, flowing from his past karma. Possessing inner tranquillity and the joy of Spirit, he is not excited at the advent of good fortune; neither is he depressed by calamities. He watches with a calm indifferent attitude the joyous and sorrowful scenes of his life. What have they to do with him?

TRANSCENDING THE SENSORY WORLD, ATTAINING THE BLISS INDESTRUCTIBLE

VERSE 21

बाह्यस्पर्शेष्वसक्तात्मा विन्दत्यात्मनि यत्सुखम्।
स ब्रह्मयोगयुक्तात्मा सुखमक्षयमश्नुते ॥

Unattracted to the sensory world, the yogi experiences the ever new joy inherent in the Self. Engaged in divine union of the soul with Spirit, he attains bliss indestructible.

THE YOGI LEARNS TO CONTROL his *chitta* (primordial feeling), overcoming all likes and dislikes relative to external objects. Detaching his attention from the outer world into his true inner Self, he perceives the ever-existing, ever-conscious, ever-new joy of the soul. When the Self is fully established in union with Spirit, his ever new joy becomes immutable.

VERSE 22

ये हि संस्पर्शजा भोगा दुःखयोनय एव ते।
आद्यन्तवन्तः कौन्तेय न तेषु रमते बुधः ॥

O Son of Kunti (Arjuna)! because sense pleasures spring from outward contacts, and have beginning and end (are ephemeral), they are begetters only of misery. No sage seeks happiness from them.

THE TRUTH IN THESE WORDS from the Gita has been echoed down the centuries by many lacerated hearts. "O Lord! Give the support of Thy hand to me, the blind man who has been looted of his wealth of wisdom by the violent bandits called senses and who has been flung by them into the deep, desolate well of delusion."*

Pleasures obtained through the senses are limited and transitory. Overtaxed, the senses give unhappiness. Eating to excess or listening to music continually produces discomfort instead of joy. A saint therefore speaks of all pleasures that arise from sense contacts as generators of grief; they often create unhappiness in the beginning and in the end. Even the desire for sense enjoyments and the process of indulging in them involve some form of suffering; if not in conscience or body, then in the thought that they must end.

The person, for instance, who wishes to accumulate money by hook or crook goes through unending worries; perhaps, when he is successful and is receiving a little material happiness, other people try to relieve him of his wealth, which fills him with forebodings. Old and diseased, he finds his money cannot buy him youth or health. Death delivers the final painful disillusionment to the poor fellow; "he can't take it with him."

Knowing that the transitory pleasures of the material world always end in sorrow, saints do not concentrate on deriving happiness from the impure source of the senses.

When a man's mind gets used to exciting pictures, it loses the ability to appreciate the serener forms of joy. Similarly, finding ephemeral pleasure from the tumultuous scenes of life and from a constant search for recreation, one loses the power to concentrate within and to find the happiness of meditation. As a little boy accustomed to mischievous

---

* Swami Shankara, in *Lakshminrisimha Stotra.*

activity sees no joy in quietude, so an adult who adapts himself to a restless way of living finds no attraction in deep contemplation. When the mind like a gourmand insatiably pursues coarse sense pleasures, it is unable to form a taste for the finer fare of the soul.

Yogis know the superior quality of divine joy as compared with sense joy. The ordinary man is tempted by the lesser charm of the senses because he has not tasted the higher joy of the soul. Only by weighing material pleasures against meditational bliss can man be inspired to escape sense domination.

It is a wise man who can say: "O Supreme Blessedness, I have weighed Thee and sense lures in the balance of my experience, and have found Thee weightier, far more tempting than any other temptation!"

Man belies his unique status in creation when he remains satisfied with sense pleasures. "The human body, though transient, is capable of serving the supreme object of life," the *Srimad Bhagavata* points out. "It is only at the end of a long chain of evolution in lower forms that the ego passes into incarnation within a human body. Before that physical form falls a prey to death, the wise man should endeavour to obtain through it the highest good. Animals and even lower forms of life can pursue the objects of the senses—human existence should not be wasted on them."

Many human beings refuse to undergo the restraint of giving up sense pleasure for an unknown soul pleasure. Their reasoning is a travesty of human judgement. Sense indulgence forms bad habits and destroys the desire for superior pleasures. Most people follow their misery-making sense longings because they cannot picture the nature of divine bliss. Their bad habits blind them completely and destroy the power of envisioning any better joys. If young people, before getting entangled in worldly life, experience the bliss of meditation, they are little likely to fall victims to the ubiquitous sense delusions.

VERSE 23

शक्नोतीहैव यः सोढुं प्राक्शरीरविमोक्षणात्।
कामक्रोधोद्भवं वेगं स युक्तः स सुखी नरः॥

He is truly a yogi who, on this earth and up to the very time of death, is able to master every impulse of desire and wrath. He is a happy man!

EVEN AN ADVANCED YOGI MAY occasionally feel in his active life the impulses of lust and anger (owing to karmic impulses of the past). If he steadfastly perseveres in his yogic path, resisting up to the end of life the occasional "surprise visits" of undesirable emotions, he will attain the final union with Spirit.

The Gita instructs the devotee to die fighting his evil impulses rather than to succumb to them and again be enmeshed in the miseries of incarnation. The yogi is advised not only to remain concentrated on the divine bliss during meditation but to feel it during activity, in order successfully to combat the promptings of past harmful impulses buried in the subconscious mind. A person who fails to carry over the bliss of meditation into the activities of his daily life is liable to be overwhelmed by sudden remembrances of past evil worldly experiences. The yogi who always feels the inner joy of the soul is able to subdue any erratic emotional urges.

The desire to indulge in sensory temptations is called *kama*. When this desire is obstructed it gives rise to anger, *krodha*. These two impulses attack the devotee within and without—giving him thoughts of ephemeral external pleasures on the one hand, and, on the other, trying to make him forget the superior pleasures of the Spirit. During meditation and the practice of *Kriya Yoga,* when the devotee goes beyond the state of physical perceptions, he may feel a secret invasion of desires and wrath, arising from past karmic involvements. But if he continues his concentration, at the point between his eyebrows, on the state of divine bliss, and does not fulfil the evil impulses by outward expression, he will find victory and happiness both in meditation and in worldly activity.

VERSE 24

योऽन्तःसुखोऽन्तरारामस्तथान्तर्ज्योतिरेव यः।
स योगी ब्रह्मनिर्वाणं ब्रह्मभूतोऽधिगच्छति॥

Only that yogi who possesses the inner Bliss, who rests on the inner Foundation, who is one with the inner Light, becomes one with Spirit (after attaining freedom from karma connected with the physical, astral, and ideational bodies). He attains complete liberation in Spirit (even while living in the body).

TO BECOME FREE FOREVER the devotee must destroy all karma connected with each of his three bodies. Ordinarily, this is accomplished during the slow evolutionary process of countless incarnations (alternations of births and deaths first between the physical and astral worlds, and then between the astral and causal realms). However, one who has attained significant spiritual progress in previous lives and who is adept in *Kriya Yoga* can hasten his evolution by the inner method and attain liberation while still incarnate in the physical form, as cited in this Gita verse.

It is not enough to persist in fighting the sense impulses and thus strengthen the mind; to become one with Spirit the yogi must enter the deeper states of blissful *samadhi,* and keep his consciousness ever identified with the soul. Not only must he withdraw his attention from the sensory world, but by becoming immersed in the inner astral and wisdom (causal) light emanating from the soul, he must betake himself through the interpenetrating physical, astral, and ideational bodies into the infinite ocean of Spirit. (See page 213.)

So long as a man has any material desires, he has to work out his karma in a physical body. When he is able to extricate himself, by nonattachment and the practice of *Kriya Yoga,* from all fleshly delusions and bondage, he then finds himself confined in the astral body and entangled in his astral karma. By deeper immersion in ecstasy, the devotee escapes from the astral body and becomes lodged in the causal or ideational body, vibrating with the original subtle seeds of all past karmic impulses. When God thought out the complicated labyrinth of man's life, He really put His mind to it!

Jesus said that after the destruction of his body, he would rebuild it in three days.* By this statement he was implying that he would rise

* John 2:19.

above all past impulses (connected with the experiences of the physical, astral, and causal bodies) in three periods (days) of ecstatic upliftment or emergence. A yogi experiences attachment to different effects of past actions as he consciously ascends through his three bodies. Conquering all karma (physical, astral, and ideational), he is indeed free in Spirit.

VERSE 25

लभन्ते ब्रह्मनिर्वाणमृषयः क्षीणकल्मषाः ।
छिन्नद्वैधा यतात्मानः सर्वभूतहिते रताः ॥

With sins obliterated, doubts removed, senses subjugated, the rishis (sages), contributing to the welfare of mankind, attain emancipation in Spirit.

RISHIS (LITERALLY, "SEERS") ARE LIBERATED sages who by divine permission are reborn on earth, free from all karmic sins and the delusive confusion of mortal doubts, to serve as ideal human models for the inspiration of mankind.

In common parlance, however, the word *rishi* has been applied in reference to three types of advanced souls: (1) the true *rishi,* as noted in the preceding paragraph (*devarishis*); (2) the sage who is a knower of God, but who may not yet be fully liberated (*brahmarishis*); (3) the saint or the ascetic of divine temperament and spiritual accomplishment who is earnestly engaged in those spiritual practices through which he is rapidly acquiring *rishi*-like qualities and advancing toward liberation (*rajarishis,* "royal" *rishis*).

This Gita verse therefore speaks of the qualities that are eminently manifested in true *rishis* as being the qualities through which advanced souls will attain their liberation in Spirit.

A *yogi* is one who practises a technique for God-realization. A *swami* is one who has taken a formal vow of celibacy and personal non-possession; he is a member of the monastic Order of Swamis established in its present form by Adi Shankara over 1,000 years ago. Through divine ardour and the mergence of their lives in God, yogis, renunciants, and yogi-renunciants advance toward liberation. But a true *rishi,* a liberated soul who reincarnates with a God-ordained mission, is the rarest and highest type of human being, having come to earth to bring illumination to all. He is a man of God-realization as well as an active man of works. The external circumstances of his life have, for him, no meaning. Some *rishis,* such as Lahiri Mahasaya, were married men who assumed that difficult status in order to encourage worldly people to seek the divine path regardless of their outward entanglements. He who hungers for God will not allow any obstacle to stand in his way; conversely, those who are not in earnest about the spiritual life will permit the slightest difficulty to deter them.

VERSE 26

कामक्रोधवियुक्तानां यतीनां यतचेतसाम्।
अभितो ब्रह्मनिर्वाणं वर्तते विदितात्मनाम्॥

Renunciants who are desireless and wrathless, mind-controlled, and Self-realized, are completely free both in this world and in the beyond.

THE SPIRITUALLY ARDENT who have found their soul and its connection with Spirit achieve complete emancipation in this life, carrying with them the same realization into eternity.

The word *jivanmukta* (literally, "freed while living") in a strict sense applies to a yogi who, by refraining from new desires, has destroyed the very root-cause of reincarnation. A *jivanmukta,* however, may still possess subtle hidden seeds of past actions that have not been totally roasted by the fires of wisdom. Some *jivanmuktas* destroy these remnants of past material karma after death by certain work in the astral cosmos. Completing their lessons in the astral spheres, they remove any cause for having to return to this world. Other *jivanmuktas* are able, while still on earth, to materialize past karmic actions in visions and thus exhaust their reincarnation-making power.

A concrete illustration of destroying past karmic tendencies by materialization may be given here. A yogi might free himself from greed in eating, yet still retain the *samskaras* (impressions of past desires) for indulging in favourite foods; or he might have completely detached himself from worldly possessions, yet harbour seeds of a past unfulfilled longing for some particular material object or experience. He is thus not fully free; under tempting circumstances, those hidden seed-tendencies might again sprout into activity. By entering the superconscious state of conscious visions, or by interjecting superconscious dreams into the passive subconscious state of sleep, the yogi can materialize the substance of his past desires. With inner aloofness and complete detachment, he then renders powerless those desire-seeds by roasting them in the fires of awakened wisdom.

One who on earth has destroyed all desires and all karma—past as well as present—is truly "freed while living." That *jivanmukta* is then known as a *siddha*, "a perfected being." Such souls are the "renunciants" referred to in this verse—those who have abandoned forever all inner and outer causes of bondage.

VERSES 27–28

स्पर्शान्कृत्वा बहिर्बाह्यांश्चक्षुश्चैवान्तरे भ्रुवोः ।
प्राणापानौ समौ कृत्वा नासाभ्यन्तरचारिणौ ॥ *(27)*

यतेन्द्रियमनोबुद्धिर्मुनिर्मोक्षपरायणः ।
विगतेच्छाभयक्रोधो यः सदा मुक्त एव सः ॥ *(28)*

A muni—he who holds liberation as the sole object of life and therefore frees himself from longings, fears, and wrath—controls his senses, mind, and intelligence and removes their external contacts by (a technique of) making even, or neutralizing, the currents of prana and apana that manifest as inhalation and exhalation in the nostrils. He fixes his gaze at the middle of the two eyebrows (thus converting the dual current of the physical vision into the single current of the omniscient astral eye). Such a muni wins complete emancipation.

IN THESE TWO STANZAS, and in IV:29, the Gita leaves behind all abstractions and generalizations, and mentions the specific technique of salvation—*Kriya Yoga*.

A *muni* (literally, "united with the One") is a yogi who can withdraw his consciousness at will from external sense objects and from mental attractions toward them. The epithet *muni* is here applied to an accomplished yogi who by the technique of *Kriya Yoga* has succeeded in dissolving his mind in the Infinite Bliss. A *muni's* only goal is to ascend to the Cosmic Spirit from which the soul has descended. By discrimination the *muni* watches the soul (identified with the human ego by sense slavery) undergoing innumerable physical and mental miseries. His goal is to convert the ego into the pure soul by scientifically disengaging the mind and intellect from the senses.

❖

HOW KRIYA YOGA IMPARTS SOUL-REALIZATION

BY THE SPECIAL TECHNIQUE of *Kriya Yoga,* the ingoing breath of *prana* and the outgoing breath of *apana* are converted into cool and warm currents. In the beginning of the practice of *Kriya Yoga,* the devotee feels the cool *prana* current going up the spine and the warm *apana* current going down the spine, in accompaniment with the ingoing and outgoing breath. The advanced *Kriya Yogi* finds that the inhaling breath of *prana* and the exhaling breath of *apana* have been "evened"—neutralised or extinguished; he feels only the cool current of *prana* going up through the spine and the warm current of *apana* going down through the spine.

These subtle specialized currents of *prana* and *apana* are born of the ubiquitous *prana* or intelligent life force that creates and sustains the body. (See IV: 29–30.) The *prana* or crystallizing current is connected with the ingoing breath; it is the specific medium by which the oxygen in the ingoing breath is converted into life force. The *apana* or eliminating current (which removes the impurities of the body) manifests as the outgoing breath that rids the body of poisonous carbon dioxide gas.

Man's body of gross matter consists of tissues, constructed of molecules. Molecules are made of atoms; atoms are formed by electrons and protons. Electrons and protons consist of intelligent life force—*prana* or "lifetrons." Lifetrons can be further resolved into their source, the "thoughtrons" of God.

"In the beginning was the Word (cosmic vibration, the creative life energy or vibratory thoughts of God), and the Word was with God, and the Word was God.... All things were made by him (the Word); and without him was not any thing made that was made."*

"And God said, Let there be light: and there was light."† That is, God's thought vibrated into the light of cosmic life or cosmic *prana;* and cosmic *prana* was further materialized into electrons, protons, atoms, molecules, cells, and matter. Even as in a motion picture the illusions of solid earth, or water, or sunlight, or electricity, or gas, or atomic explosions, or manifestations of life and thought in men are all vibrations of light and shadows, so this earth with its solids, liq-

* John 1:1,3. † Genesis 1:3.

uids, gases, energy, life, and thoughts in human beings are all vibrations and relativities of God's thoughts and His cosmic light and the shadows of His delusive *maya*.*

The cosmic thought of God thus first materialized as the cosmic *prana* or life force of light, and finally as all matter of the macrocosm. The body of man is a microcosm of the Lord's creation. The microcosmic human body is a composite of the individual soul and life force.

---

* "Among the trillion mysteries of the cosmos, the most phenomenal is light," Paramahansaji wrote in *Autobiography of a Yogi*. Albert Einstein commented in 1951: "All the fifty years of conscious brooding have brought me no closer to the answer to the question, What are light quanta? Of course today every rascal thinks he knows the answer, but he is deluding himself." Half a century later, physicist Arthur Zajonc, Ph.D., of Amherst College acknowledged that science still lacked a complete understanding. He wrote in *Catching the Light: The Entwined History of Light and Mind* (New York: Bantam Books, 1993): "Quantum theory has framed a new theory of light that every great modern physicist from Albert Einstein to Richard Feynmann has struggled to understand—unsuccessfully, as they realized themselves.... For all the power, precision, and beauty of quantum optics, we still do not know what light is."

At the forefront of quantum theory, however, some scientists are beginning to describe light (electromagnetic waves moving through space governed by the laws of quantum physics) as the phenomenon that mediates consciousness (information) into matter (form).

"Does light give structure to matter?" inquired an article in *Brain/Mind Bulletin*, July 11, 1983. "Recently Dr. David Bohm, professor of physics at the University of London, spoke of matter as 'frozen light.' Mass is a phenomenon of connecting light rays that go back and forth, freezing themselves into a pattern. So matter is condensed light, moving at average speeds slower than the speed of light. Dr. Bohm said: 'In its generalized sense, light is the means by which the entire universe unfolds into itself. It is energy, information, content, form and structure. It is the potential of everything.'"

"If our universe is only a pale shadow of a deeper order, what else lies hidden, enfolded in the warp and weft of our reality?" asks Michael Talbot in *The Holographic Universe* (New York: Harper Collins, 1991). "[Physicist David] Bohm has a suggestion. According to our current understanding of physics, every region of space is awash with different kinds of fields composed of waves of varying lengths. Each wave always has at least some energy. When physicists calculate the minimum amount of energy a wave can possess, they find that every cubic centimetre of empty space contains more energy than the total energy of all the matter in the universe.

"Some physicists refuse to take this calculation seriously and believe it must somehow be in error. Bohm thinks this infinite ocean of energy does exist and tells us at least a little about the vast and hidden nature of the implicate order. He feels most physicists ignore the existence of this enormous ocean of energy because, like fish who are unaware of the water in which they swim, they have been taught to focus primarily on objects embedded in the ocean, on matter."

"One of the features of quantum electrodynamics was a new understanding of the vacuum, of emptiness," writes Arthur Zajonc. "Where before the vacuum had been understood as pure emptiness—no matter, no light, no heat—now there was a residual hidden energy.... After one has removed all matter and all light from space, an infinite energy remains." *(Publisher's Note)*

Consciousness, life, and flesh; cosmic consciousness, cosmic life, and cosmic matter are nothing but three different vibrations of God-thought.

WHEN THE *KRIYA YOGI* LEARNS to dissolve the ingoing and outgoing breath into a perception of the cool and warm currents going up and down the spine, he then feels his body as sustained by these inner currents of life force and not by their by-product of breath. He also realizes that the currents are sustained by the Word, the divine vibratory cosmic light of *prana,* that enters the body through the medulla. This life force becomes concentrated in and operative through the cerebral, medullary, cervical, dorsal, lumbar, sacral, and coccygeal centres that energize the body to its minutest cells.

Jesus testified that man shall not live by bread alone, but by every word that proceedeth out of the mouth of God.* This memorable passage signifies that man's body does not depend only on external sources of life force—distillations from breath, oxygen, sunshine, solids, and liquids—but also on a direct inner source of cosmic life that enters the body through the medulla, flowing then to the subtle centres in the brain and spine. In man, the medulla is spoken of as "the mouth of God" because it is the chief opening for the divine influx of cosmic vibratory life force, the "word" that then flows "out of the mouth of God" (the medulla) to the reservoir of life energy in the brain and the distributing centres in the spine.

Kriya process of converting breath into life force, realizing body as light

In successful meditation, the *Kriya Yogi* converts the two distinct impulses of inhalation and exhalation into two life currents, the cool *prana* and the warm *apana,* felt in the spine. He then realizes the truth of Jesus' saying—that man is not required to depend on external breath (or on "bread" or any other outward sustenance) as a condition of bodily existence. The yogi perceives the cool and warm currents in the spine to be constantly and magnetically pulling an extra voltage of current from the omnipresent cosmic life force ever flowing through the medulla. He gradually finds that these two spinal currents become converted into one life force, magnetically drawing reinforcements of *prana* from all the bodily cells and nerves. This strengthened life current flows upward to the point between the eyebrows and is seen as the tricoloured spherical astral eye: a luminous sun, in the centre of which is a blue sphere encircling a bright scintillating star.

---

* Matthew 4:4.

Jesus referred to this "single" eye in the centre of the forehead, and to the truth that the body is essentially formed of light, in the following words: "If therefore thine eye be single, thy whole body shall be full of light."*

When the yogi is able to penetrate his mind into the spiritual eye, he perceives his body as made not of flesh but of minute light-cells of protons and electrons and lifetrons. The physical body is formed from two layers of currents: atomic currents appearing as flesh, and a more subtle layer of electrons and protons. The electroprotonic body in turn emanates from the pranic light-currents of the superfine astral body.

The whole astral body of man consists of various densities of light, even as a physical body is built up of the different tissues of the skin, flesh, bones, and internal organs. Through his spherical eye the *Kriya Yogi* sees his astral body as made of lifetrons—the pranic astral cells. He perceives that the Cosmic Sunlight of Life reflects Its rays through the astral spiritual eye into the astral brain and astral plexuses and astral nerve-tubes (*nadis*) to sustain the astral body cells. He sees also that his physical body is nothing but a coarser light of electrons, protons, and atoms emanating from his finer astral body. By further advancement the yogi perceives both his physical and astral bodies to be emanating from his causal or ideational body, which is composed of the coordinated thoughtrons of God. (See pages 59 ff.)

❖
Experiencing body, life force, and mind as vibrations of the Word of God
❖

THIS KNOWLEDGE IS NECESSARY to understand that the body and life force and mind which form the encasement of the soul are in reality nothing more than differently vibrating thoughts of God. By the practice of *Kriya,* the yogi scientifically detaches his mind from gross sensory perceptions and realizes that consciousness and life force (*prana* or cosmic light) are the basis of all matter. The *Kriya Yogi* adopts a scientific method to divert his mind and reason from the perception of physical flesh; he perceives the body as light and consciousness by rising above the gross perception of breath.

All inner experiences like that of subconscious sleep can only take place when the consciousness of breath disappears. The *Kriya Yogi* has no need or desire to withhold breath forcibly in the lungs; he becomes mentally so calm that he feels himself to be aloof from breath. By the practice of *Kriya Yoga* he can consciously and at will

* Matthew 6:22.

attain the breathless state and sustain life in his body solely by the cool and warm currents flowing through the spine and trickling down from the spiritual eye.

If a wet battery, which is sustained by electricity and dependent on replenishment of its water supply,* could somehow be converted into a dry battery, it could do away with dependence on water and be sustained by its own reservoir of energy recharged solely by electricity. *Kriya Yoga* similarly helps the body-battery (which depends on cosmic life force flowing through the medulla, and on oxygen, sunshine, liquids, and solids) to become converted so that it can sustain itself solely on the life force flowing into the body from the cosmic source and stored in the regenerative reservoir of life energy in the brain and spinal centres.

The use of *Kriya Yoga* conclusively proves the truth in the Bible—that man's body-battery can live by the Word or vibratory current coming from God. The life in the body is directly sustained by the cosmic *prana* flowing through the medulla. Through the operation of *maya* or delusion, however, man believes that he cannot live without food and other outward aids. He becomes erroneously dependent on the gross sources of energy reinforcement through oxygen, sunshine, solids, and liquids. Man has formed a bad mortal habit in feeling that he cannot exist without a supply of energy from these material substances. That is why, if oxygen, sunshine, solids, and liquids are denied to the body, man's frightened consciousness permits the life force to depart.

❖
Neutralizing the currents of prana and apana: the breathless state of ecstasy
❖

WHEN THE DEVOTEE IS CONVINCED by *Kriya Yoga* that he can live solely by the inner source of cosmic energy, he realizes that the body is a wave of the all-sufficing cosmic ocean of life. By the special technique of *Kriya Yoga,* the devotee—through perfect calmness, through a greater supply of energy distilled from oxygen in the *Kriya* breath, and through an enhanced flow of cosmic energy coming into the body through the medulla—is less and less subject to the necessity for breathing. By deeper *Kriya Yoga* the bodily life, ordinarily dependent on reinforcement by life force distilled from

* When Paramahansa Yogananda put forth this hypothetical metaphor, it was necessary to regularly add water to wet batteries to replace that which was lost in evaporation. The more recently developed sealed batteries, common to most users today, require no such water replacement. *(Publisher's Note)*

gross outer sources, begins to be sustained by the cosmic life only; then breathing (inhalation and exhalation) ceases. All the trillions of bodily cells become like regenerating dry batteries needing nothing but the inner "electricity" recharged from the cosmic source of life.

In this way the bodily cells remain in a suspended state—that is, they neither grow nor decay. They are sustained and vitalized directly from the life-energy dynamos in the brain and spine. When the cells cease to grow, they are not required to depend on the life current distilled from oxygen; when decay ceases in the body, the cells no longer excrete impurities into the blood necessitating exhalation of the breath to expel carbon dioxide. Being no longer required to pump carbon dioxide–laden and oxygen-filled blood to and from the lungs, the heart becomes totally calmed.

Breath and breathing are acquired mortal habits of the life force. *Kriya Yoga* retrains the life force to remember that it lives only by the cosmic source. *Pranayama,* or *Kriya Yoga,* signifies one thing—controlling the life force in the body by conscious will so that it does not depend on oxygen, sunshine, solids, and liquids but on the inner source of cosmic life. *Kriya Yoga pranayama* withdraws life force from the activities of the heart and the body cells—by rendering those activities unnecessary—and unites that bodily *prana* with the cosmic life force; man's slavish dependence on breath is thus realized to be delusory. When the yogi-expert in *pranayama* can thus disengage at will the life force from its bondage to oxygen and so on, he can immortalize it by uniting it with the Cosmic Life.

This stanza of the Gita highlights the necessity of neutralizing or "making even" the currents of *prana* and *apana.* This effect is made possible by the practice of *Kriya Yoga,* which recharges the body cells by the inner cosmic life so that inhalation and exhalation become even—that is, still and unnecessary.

The life, mind, and intellect are active in the body and its senses when the life current flows outwardly through the afferent and efferent nerves as a result of the downflowing *apana* current. This outflowing current is "uneven," restless and erratic from the bombardment of impulses to and from the nerve centres—stimuli that constantly vary during the states of wakefulness and sleep. But when the life current is withdrawn into the spine and brain, this interiorization frees the life force from the excitants of the senses and their objects. The *prana* and *apana* currents flowing in the spine become calm and even, generating a tremendous magnetic power and joy.

AS THE MEDITATION DEEPENS, the downward-flowing *apana* current and the upward-flowing *prana* current become neutralised into one ascending current, seeking its source in the cerebrum. Breath is still, life is still, sensations and thoughts are dissolved. The divine light of life and consciousness perceived by the devotee in the cerebrospinal centres becomes one with the Cosmic Light and Cosmic Consciousness.

Uniting one's life and consciousness with Cosmic Light and Consciousness

Acquisition of the power of this realization enables the yogi to consciously detach his soul from identification with the body. He becomes free from the distressing bondage of desires (the body's attachment and longing for sensory gratification), fears (the thought of possible nonfulfilment of desires), and anger (the emotional response to obstacles that thwart fulfilment of desires). These three impelling forces in man are the greatest enemies of soul bliss; they must be destroyed by that devotee who aspires to reach God.

Life force is the connecting—and disconnecting—link between matter and Spirit, between body consciousness and soul consciousness. The ordinary man does not know how to get at the bodily *prana* directly. Therefore, this life force works automatically to enliven the body and senses and by the medium of breath ties man's attention solely to his physical existence. But by the use of *Kriya Yoga* the devotee learns how to distil life force out of breath, and how to control *prana.* With this control, the life force can be switched off at will from the five sense channels and turned inward, thus diverting the soul's attention from the perception of material phenomena to the perception of Spirit.

By this scientific step-by-step method, the yogi ascends from the senses in actuality and not by a mere ineffectual mental diversion from them. He completely disconnects mind and reason and attention from the body, by switching off the life force from the five senses. He learns scientifically to divert to the spine and brain the currents from his five sense channels and thus to unite his consciousness with the joy of higher spiritual perceptions in the seven centres. When he is able to remain immersed in divine bliss even in his active state, he does not become further involved in desires to enjoy external objects. Radiating the calmness of divine realizations, he is not disturbed by the springing up of fear and anger from nonfulfilments of material desires. He finds his soul no longer tied to matter but forever united to the cosmic bliss of Spirit.

Such a *Kriya Yogi,* who scientifically withdraws his mind and intellect from the senses and with unwinking gaze beholds the Spirit through the astral eye, is a true *muni*. The ordinary man watches the motion picture of matter in a limited portion of space, but the *muni* or accomplished yogi can behold, through his all-seeing spherical astral eye, the entire light of creation that sustains all the cosmic motion pictures of the physical, astral, and causal universes.

METHODS OF SPIRITUAL FREEDOM are various, but the actual attainment of liberation by ascent through the spine is universal. Whether through the intense devotion and prayer of the *bhakta,* or the pure discrimination of the *jnani,* or the nonattached selfless actions of the *karma yogi,* the consciousness purified and concentrated thereby still makes its final ascent to God through the subtle spinal channels through which it descended into flesh.

Universal path of liberation: ascent through the spine

The principles of *Kriya Yoga,* therefore, are not the formula of a sectarian rite, but a science through the application of which the individual may realize how his soul descended into the body and became identified with the senses, and how that soul may be withdrawn from the senses and reunited with Spirit by a scientific method of meditation. This route of descent and ascension is the one universal path that every soul must travel.

Kriya Yoga teaches first to withdraw the mind from sensory objects by self-control, and then scientifically to disconnect the mind and intelligence (*manas* and *buddhi*) from the senses by switching off the life force from the five sense channels, and then to take the ego, mind, and intellect through the five astral centres in the spine, through the sixth centre (the medulla, which is magnetically connected with the spiritual eye in the middle of the forehead), and finally into the seventh centre of omniscience in the middle of the cerebrum. The *Kriya Yogi* there attains perception of his self as soul, and finds his ego, intellect, and mind to be dissolved in soul ecstasy. He then learns how to take his soul from the prisons of the physical, astral, and causal bodies, and to reunite the soul with Spirit.

As the physical eyes, through frontal vision, reveal a portion of matter, so the omnipresent spiritual eye, through its boundless spherical vision, reveals the entire astral and ideational cosmoses. In the beginning, when the yogi is able to penetrate his mind through the astral eye, he first sees his astral body; by further advancement he sees the entire astral cosmos of which his body is but a part.

Without entering the spiritual (astral) eye, no one can know how to take his life force and consciousness through the astral plexuses in the spine. After entering the spiritual eye he passes, in a step-by-step way, through the perception of the physical body; the perception of the astral eye; the perception of the astral body; the perception of the astral cerebrospinal tunnel with the seven astral plexuses or trapdoors; and through the causal body into final freedom.

It requires intricate scientific explanation to interpret *Kriya Yoga,* but the art itself is very simple.* *Kriya Yoga,* practised deeply, will dissolve breath into mind, mind into intuition, intuition into the joyous perception of soul, and soul into the cosmic bliss of Spirit. The yogi then understands how his soul descended into matter and how his prodigal soul has been led from matter back to the mansion of omnipresence, there to enjoy the "fatted calf" of wisdom.

A man who has attained the Spirit by the universal way of *Kriya Yoga* is spoken of as an accomplished *Kriya Yogi* or a *muni.* After attaining this high *muni*-state the yogi can work in the world as a *rishi.* A *muni* is he who has ecstatically dissolved himself in God by the science of yoga. And a *rishi* is he who, after finding liberation as a *muni,* goes on to live in the world as an example to others of the effectiveness of yoga as the supreme science of liberation.

The science of *Kriya Yoga* has been preserved for mankind in this the highest Hindu Bible, the Bhagavad Gita. It is this *Kriya Yoga* that God gave to Manu, the original Adam, and through him to Janaka and other royal sages. The science became lost in the materialistic ages. *Kriya Yoga* was revived again in the nineteenth century by Mahavatar Babaji, guru of Lahiri Mahasaya. The ancient science of salvation is now spreading to all corners of the globe. (See IV:1–2.) In contradistinction to other teachings, *Kriya Yoga* not only points out a universal highway of ascending the soul to the Spirit, but gives mankind a daily usable technique through whose practise the devotee, with the help of a guru, may re-enter the kingdom of God. One theoretical teaching leads only to another, but any true practitioner of *Kriya Yoga* finds it to be the shortest way and quickest conveyance to the kingdom of Spirit.

---

* Detailed instruction in the actual techniques of *Kriya Yoga* is given to students of the Yogoda Satsanga *Lessons* who fulfil the requirements of certain preliminary spiritual disciplines. See page 1131. *(Publisher's Note)*

VERSE 29

भोक्तारं यज्ञतपसां सर्वलोकमहेश्वरम्।
सुहृदं सर्वभूतानां ज्ञात्वा मां शान्तिमृच्छति॥

He finds peace who knows Me as the Enjoyer of the holy rites (yajnas) and of the austerities (offered by devotees), as the Infinite Lord of Creation, and as the Good Friend of all creatures.

HE ATTAINS BLESSEDNESS WHO REALIZES the Lord to be the Creator of all dream creatures; the Receiver and Perceiver of all offerings and sacrifices; and the sustaining, unconditionally loving, always-ready-to-redeem, everlasting Friend of man.

Who can bring enough flowers of devotion to the altar of the God who speaks thus of His friendship for man? And what is devotion? "As its own seeds reach back the ankola tree, as a needle is drawn to a magnet, as a chaste wife remains with her spouse, as a creeper clings to a tree, and as the river merges in the ocean—if thought thus reaches the lotus feet of the Lord and remains there for all time, that is said to be devotion."*

ॐ तत्सदिति श्रीमद्भगवद्गीतासूपनिषत्सु
ब्रह्मविद्यायां योगशास्त्रे श्रीकृष्णार्जुनसंवादे
कर्मसन्न्यासयोगो नाम पञ्चमोऽध्यायः॥

Aum, Tat, Sat.
In the Upanishad of the holy Bhagavad Gita—the discourse of Lord Krishna to Arjuna, which is the scripture of yoga and the science of God-realization—this is the fifth chapter, called "Union Through Renunciation of the Fruits of Action."

---

* Swami Shankara, *Sivananda Lahari* 9:59–61.

APPENDIX

❖

TRANSLITERATION OF THE SLOKAS

❖

Chapters I - V

Chapter I

Verse 1

dhṛtarāṣṭra uvāca
dharmakṣetre kurukṣetre samavetā yuyutsavaḥ
māmakāḥ pāṇḍavāś caiva kim akurvata saṁjaya

Verse 2

saṁjaya uvāca
dṛṣṭvā tu pāṇḍavānīkaṁ vyūḍhaṁ duryodhanas tadā
ācāryam upasaṁgamya rājā vacanam abravīt

Verse 3

paśyaitāṁ pāṇḍuputrāṇām ācārya mahatīṁ camūm
vyūḍhāṁ drupadaputreṇa tava śiṣyeṇa dhīmatā

Verses 4–6

atra śūrā maheṣvāsā bhīmārjunasamā yudhi
yuyudhāno virāṭaś ca drupadaś ca mahārathaḥ (4)

dhṛṣṭaketuś cekitānaḥ kāśirājaś ca vīryavān
purujit kuntibhojaś ca śaibyaś ca narapuṁgavaḥ (5)

yudhāmanyuś ca vikrānta uttamaujāś ca vīryavān
saubhadro draupadeyāś ca sarva eva mahārathāḥ (6)

Verse 7

asmākaṁ tu viśiṣṭā ye tān nibodha dvijottama
nāyakā mama sainyasya saṁjñārthaṁ tān bravīmi te

Verse 8

bhavān bhīṣmaś ca karṇaś ca kṛpaś ca samitiṁjayaḥ
aśvatthāmā vikarṇaś ca saumadattirjayadrathaḥ

Verse 9

anye ca bahavaḥ śūrā madarthe tyaktajīvitāḥ
nānāśastrapraharaṇāḥ sarve yuddhaviśāradāḥ

VERSE 10

aparyāptaṁ tad asmākaṁ balaṁ bhīṣmābhirakṣitam
paryāptaṁ tvidam eteṣāṁ balaṁ bhīmābhirakṣitam

VERSE 11

ayaneṣu ca sarveṣu yathābhāgam avasthitāḥ
bhīṣmam evābhirakṣantu bhavantaḥ sarva eva hi

VERSE 12

tasya saṁjanayan harṣaṁ kuruvṛddhaḥ pitāmahaḥ
siṁhanādaṁ vinadyoccaiḥ śaṅkhaṁ dadhmau pratāpavān

VERSE 13

tataḥ ṣaṅkhāś ca bheryaś ca paṇavānakagomukhāḥ
sahasaivābhyahanyanta sa śabdas tumulo 'bhavat

VERSE 14

tataḥ śvetair hayair yukte mahati syandane sthitau
mādhavaḥ pāṇḍavaś caiva divyau śaṅkhau pradadhmatuḥ

VERSES 15–18

pāñcajanyaṁ hṛṣīkeśo devadattaṁ dhanaṁjayaḥ
pauṇḍraṁ dadhmau mahāśaṅkhaṁ bhīmakarmā vṛkodaraḥ (15)

anantavijayaṁ rājā kuntīputro yudhiṣṭhiraḥ
nakulaḥ sahadevaś ca sughoṣamaṇipuṣpakau (16)

kāśyaś ca parameṣvāsaḥ śikhaṇḍī ca mahārathaḥ
dhṛṣṭadyumno virāṭaś ca sātyakiś cāparājitaḥ (17)

drupado draupadeyāś ca sarvaśaḥ pṛthivīpate
saubhadraś ca mahābāhuḥ śaṅkhān dadhmuḥ pṛthakpṛthak (18)

VERSE 19

sa ghoṣo dhārtarāṣṭrāṇāṁ hṛdayāni vyadārayat
nabhaś ca pṛthivīṁ caiva tumulo vyanunādayan

VERSES 20–23

atha vyavasthitān dṛṣṭvā dhārtarāṣṭrān kapidhvajaḥ
pravṛtte śastrasaṁpāte dhanur udyamya pāṇḍavaḥ (20)

hṛṣīkeśaṁ tadā vākyam idam āha mahīpate
senayor ubhayor madhye rathaṁ sthāpaya me 'cyuta (21)

yāvad etān nirīkṣe 'haṁ yoddhukāmān avasthitān
kair mayā saha yoddhavyam asmin raṇasamudyame (22)

yotsyamānān avekṣe 'haṁ ya ete 'tra samāgatāḥ
dhārtarāṣṭrasya durbuddher yuddhe priyacikīrṣavaḥ (23)

VERSES 24–25

sanjaya uvaca
evam ukto hṛṣīkeśo guḍākeśena bhārata
senayor ubhayor madhye sthāpayitvā rathottamam (24)

bhīṣmadroṇapramukhataḥ sarveṣāṁ ca mahīkṣitām
uvāca pārtha paśyaitān samavetān kurūn iti (25)

VERSE 26

tatrāpaśyat sthitān pārthaḥ pitṛīn atha pitāmahān
ācāryān mātulān bhrātṛīn putrān pautrān sakhīṁs tathā (26)

śvaśurān suhṛdaś caiva senayor ubhayor api (27)

VERSE 27

tān samīkṣya sa kaunteyaḥ sarvān bandhūn avasthitān (27)

kṛpayā parayāviṣṭo viṣīdann idam abravīt (28)

VERSES 28–30

dṛṣṭvemaṁ svajanaṁ kṛṣṇa yuyutsuṁ samupasthitam (28)

sīdanti mama gātrāṇi mukhaṁ ca pariśuṣyati
vepathuś ca śarīre me romaharṣaś ca jāyate (29)

gāṇḍīvaṁ sraṁsate hastāt tvak caiva paridahyate
na ca śaknomy avasthātuṁ bhramatīva ca me manaḥ (30)

nimittāni ca paśyāmi viparītāni keśava (31)

Verse 31

na ca śreyo 'nupaśyāmi hatvā svajanam āhave (31)

na kāṅkṣe vijayaṁ kṛṣṇa na ca rājyaṁ sukhāni ca (32)

Verses 32–34

kiṁ no rājyena govinda kiṁ bhogair jīvitena vā (32)

yeṣām arthe kāṅkṣitaṁ no rājyaṁ bhogāḥ sukhāni ca
ta ime 'vasthitā yuddhe prāṇāṁs tyaktvā dhanāni ca (33)

ācāryāḥ pitaraḥ putrās tathaiva ca pitāmahāḥ
mātulāḥ śvaśurāḥ pautrāḥ śyālāḥ saṁbandhinas tathā (34)

Verse 35

etān na hantum icchāmi ghnato 'pi madhusūdana
api trailokyarājyasya hetoḥ kiṁ nu mahīkṛte

Verse 36

nihatya dhārtarāṣṭrān naḥ kā prītiḥ syāj janārdana
pāpam evāśrayed asmān hatvaitān ātatāyinaḥ

Verse 37

tasmān nārhā vayaṁ hantuṁ dhārtarāṣṭrān svabāndhavān
svajanaṁ hi kathaṁ hatvā sukhinaḥ syāma mādhava

Verses 38–39

yady apy ete na paśyanti lobhopahatacetasaḥ
kulakṣayakṛtaṁ doṣaṁ mitradrohe ca pātakam (38)

kathaṁ na jñeyam asmābhiḥ pāpād asmān nivartitum
kulakṣayakṛtaṁ doṣaṁ prapaśyadbhir janārdana (39)

VERSES 40–41

kulakṣaye praṇaśyanti kuladharmāḥ sanātanāḥ
dharme naṣṭe kulaṁ kṛtsnam adharmo 'bhibhavaty uta (40)

adharmābhibhavāt kṛṣṇa praduṣyanti kulastriyaḥ
strīṣu duṣṭāsu vārṣṇeya jāyate varṇasaṁkaraḥ (41)

VERSES 42–43

saṁkaro narakāyaiva kulaghnānāṁ kulasya ca
patanti pitaro hy eṣāṁ luptapiṇḍodakakriyāḥ (42)

doṣair etaiḥ kulaghnānāṁ varṇasaṁkarakārakaiḥ
utsādyante jātidharmāḥ kuladharmāś ca śāśvatāḥ (43)

VERSES 44–46

utsannakuladharmāṇāṁ manuṣyāṇāṁ janārdana
narake 'niyataṁ vāso bhavatīty anuśuśruma (44)

aho bata mahat pāpaṁ kartuṁ vyavasitā vayam
yadrājyasukhalobhena hantuṁ svajanam udyatāḥ (45)

yadi mām apratīkāram aśastraṁ śastrapāṇayaḥ
dhārtarāṣṭrā raṇe hanyus tan me kṣemataraṁ bhavet (46)

VERSE 47

saṁjaya uvāca
evam uktvārjunaḥ saṁkhye rathopastha upāviśat
visṛjya saśaraṁ cāpaṁ śokasaṁvignamānasaḥ

om tat sat iti śrīmadbhagavadgītāsu upaniṣatsu
brahmavidyāyām yogaśāstre śrīkṛṣṇārjunasaṁvāde
arjunaviṣādayogonāma prathamaḥ adhyāyaḥ

CHAPTER II

VERSE 1

saṁjaya uvāca
taṁ tathā kṛpayāviṣṭam aśrupūrṇākulekṣaṇam
viṣīdantam idaṁ vākyam uvāca madhusūdanaḥ

VERSE 2

śrībhagavān uvāca
kutastvā kaśmalam idaṁ viṣame samupasthitam
anāryajuṣṭam asvargyam akīrtikaram arjuna

VERSE 3

klaibyaṁ mā sma gamaḥ pārtha naitat tvayy upapadyate
kṣudraṁ hṛdayadaurbalyaṁ tyaktvottiṣṭha paraṁtapa

VERSE 4

arjuna uvāca
kathaṁ bhīṣmam ahaṁ saṁkhye droṇaṁ ca madhusūdana
iṣubhiḥ pratiyotsyāmi pūjārhāvarisūdana

VERSE 5

gurūn ahatvā hi mahānubhāvān śreyo bhoktuṁ bhaikṣyam
apīha loke
hatvārthakāmāṁs tu gurūn ihaiva bhuñjīya bhogān
rudhirapradigdhān

VERSE 6

na caitad vidmaḥ kataran no garīyo yad vā jayema yadi vā no
jayeyuḥ yān eva hatvā na jijīviṣāmas te 'vasthitāḥ pramukhe
dhārtarāṣṭrāḥ

VERSE 7

kārpaṇyadoṣopahatasvabhāvaḥ pṛcchāmi tvāṁ
dharmasaṁmūḍhacetāḥ
yacchreyaḥ syān niścitaṁ brūhi tan me śiṣyas te 'haṁ śādhi māṁ
tvāṁ prapannam

Verse 8

na hi prapaśyāmi mamāpanudyād yac chokam ucchoṣaṇam indriyāṇām
avāpya bhūmāvasapatnam ṛddhaṁ rājyaṁ surāṇām api cādhipatyam

Verse 9

saṁjaya uvāca
evam uktvā hṛṣīkeśaṁ guḍākeśaḥ paraṁtapaḥ
na yotsya iti govindam uktvā tūṣṇīṁ babhūva ha

Verse 10

tam uvāca hṛṣīkeśaḥ prahasann iva bhārata
senayor ubhayor madhye viṣīdantam idaṁ vacaḥ

Verse 11

śrībhagavān uvāca
aśocyān anvaśocas tvaṁ prajñāvādāṁś ca bhāṣase
gatāsūn agatāsūṁś ca nānuśocanti paṇḍitāḥ

Verse 12

na tvevāhaṁ jātu nāsaṁ na tvaṁ neme janādhipāḥ
na caiva na bhaviṣyāmaḥ sarve vayam ataḥ param

Verse 13

dehino 'smin yathā dehe kaumāraṁ yauvanaṁ jarā
tathā dehāntaraprāptir dhīras tatra na muhyati

Verse 14

mātrāsparśās tu kaunteya śītoṣṇasukhaduḥkhadāḥ
āgamāpāyino 'nityās tāṁs titikṣasva bhārata

Verse 15

yaṁ hi na vyathayantyete puruṣaṁ puruṣarṣabha
samaduḥkhasukhaṁ dhīraṁ so 'mṛtatvāya kalpate

Verse 16

nāsato vidyate bhāvo nābhāvo vidyate sataḥ
ubhayor api dṛṣṭo 'ntas tvanayos tattvadarśibhiḥ

Verse 17

avināśi tu tad viddhi yena sarvam idaṁ tatam
vināśam avyayasyāsya na kaścit kartum arhati

Verse 18

antavanta ime dehā nityasyoktāḥ śarīriṇaḥ
anāśino 'prameyasya tasmād yudhyasva bhārata

Verse 19

ya enaṁ vetti hantāraṁ yaścainaṁ manyate hatam
ubhau tau na vijānīto nāyaṁ hanti na hanyate

Verse 20

na jāyate mriyate vā kadācin nāyaṁ bhūtvā bhavitā vā na bhūyaḥ
ajo nityaḥ śāśvato 'yaṁ purāṇo na hanyate hanyamāne śarīre

Verse 21

vedāvināśinaṁ nityaṁ ya enam ajam avyayam
kathaṁ saḥ puruṣaḥ pārtha kaṁ ghātayati hanti kam

Verse 22

vāsāṁsi jīrṇāni yathā vihāya navāni gṛhṇāti naro 'parāṇi
tathā śarīrāṇi vihāya jīrṇāny anyāni saṁyāti navāni dehī

Verse 23

nainaṁ chindanti śastrāṇi nainaṁ dahati pāvakaḥ
na cainaṁ kledayantyāpo na śoṣayati mārutaḥ

Verse 24

acchedyo 'yam adāhyo 'yam akledyo 'śoṣya eva ca
nityaḥ sarvagataḥ sthāṇur acalo 'yaṁ sanātanaḥ

Verse 25

avyakto 'yam acintyo 'yam avikāryo 'yam ucyate
tasmād evaṁ viditvainaṁ nānuśocitum arhasi

Verses 26–27

atha cainaṁ nityajātaṁ nityaṁ vā manyase mṛtam
tathāpi tvaṁ mahābāho nainaṁ śocitum arhasi (26)

jātasya hi dhruvo mṛtyur dhruvaṁ janma mṛtasya ca
tasmād aparihārye 'rthe na tvaṁ śocitum arhasi (27)

Verse 28

avyaktādīni bhūtāni vyaktamadhyāni bhārata
avyaktanidhanānyeva tatra kā paridevanā

Verse 29

āścaryavat paśyati kaścid enam āścaryavad vadati tathaiva cānyaḥ
āścaryavaccainam anyaḥ śṛṇoti śrutvāpyenaṁ veda na caiva kaścit

Verse 30

dehī nityam avadhyo 'yaṁ dehe sarvasya bhārata
tasmāt sarvāṇi bhūtāni na tvaṁ śocitum arhasi

Verse 31

svadharmam api cāvekṣya na vikampitum arhasi
dharmyād dhi yuddhācchreyo 'nyat kṣatriyasya na vidyate

Verse 32

yadṛcchayā copapannaṁ svargadvāram apāvṛtam
sukhinaḥ kṣatriyāḥ pārtha labhante yuddham īdṛśam

Verse 33

atha cet tvam imaṁ dharmyaṁ saṁgrāmaṁ na kariṣyasi
tataḥ svadharmaṁ kīrtiṁ ca hitvā pāpam avāpsyasi

VERSE 34

akīrtiṁ cāpi bhūtāni kathayiṣyanti te 'vyayām
saṁbhāvitasya cākīrtir maraṇād atiricyate

VERSE 35

bhayād raṇād uparataṁ maṁsyante tvāṁ mahārathāḥ
yeṣāṁ ca tvaṁ bahumato bhūtvā yāsyasi lāghavam

VERSE 36

avācyavādāṁś ca bahūn vadiṣyanti tavā hitāḥ
nindantas tava sāmarthyaṁ tato duḥkhataraṁ nu kim

VERSE 37

hato vā prāpsyasi svargaṁ jitvā vā bhokṣyase mahīm
tasmād uttiṣṭha kaunteya yuddhāya kṛtaniścayaḥ

VERSE 38

sukhaduḥkhe same kṛtvā lābhālābhau jayājayau
tato yuddhāya yujyasva naivaṁ pāpam avāpsyasi

VERSE 39

eṣā te 'bhihitā sāṁkhye buddhir yoge tvimāṁ śṛṇu
buddhyā yukto yayā pārtha karmabandhaṁ prahāsyasi

VERSE 40

nehābhikramanāśo 'sti pratyavāyo na vidyate
svalpam apy asya dharmasya trāyate mahato bhayāt

VERSE 41

vyavasāyātmikā buddhir ekeha kurunandana
bahuśākhā hy anantāś ca buddhayo 'vyavasāyinām

VERSES 42–44

yām imāṁ puṣpitāṁ vācaṁ pravadanty avipaścitaḥ
vedavādaratāḥ pārtha nānyad astīti vādinaḥ (42)

kāmātmānaḥ svargaparā janmakarmaphalapradām
kriyāviśeṣabahulāṁ bhogaiśvaryagatiṁ prati (43)

bhogaiśvaryaprasaktānāṁ tayāpahṛtacetasām
vyavasāyātmikā buddhiḥ samādhau na vidhīyate (44)

VERSE 45

traiguṇyaviṣayā vedā nistraiguṇyo bhavārjuna
nirdvandvo nityasattvastho niryogakṣema ātmavān

VERSE 46

yāvān artha udapāne sarvataḥ saṁplutodake
tāvān sarveṣu vedeṣu brāhmaṇasya vijānataḥ

VERSE 47

karmaṇy evādhikāras te mā phaleṣu kadācana
mā karmaphalahetur bhūr mā te saṅgo 'stv akarmaṇi

VERSE 48

yogasthaḥ kuru karmāṇi saṅgaṁ tyaktvā dhanaṁjaya
siddhyasiddhyoḥ samo bhūtvā samatvaṁ yoga ucyate

VERSE 49

dūreṇa hy avaraṁ karma buddhiyogād dhanaṁjaya
buddhau śaraṇam anviccha kṛpaṇāḥ phalahetavaḥ

VERSE 50

buddhiyukto jahātīha ubhe sukṛtaduṣkṛte
tasmād yogāya yujyasva yogaḥ karmasu kauśalam

VERSE 51

karmajaṁ buddhiyuktā hi phalaṁ tyaktvā manīṣiṇaḥ
janmabandhavinirmuktāḥ padaṁ gacchanty anāmayam

Verse 52

yadā te mohakalilaṁ buddhir vyatitariṣyati
tadā gantāsi nirvedaṁ śrotavyasya śrutasya ca

Verse 53

śrutivipratipannā te yadā sthāsyati niścalā
samādhāv acalā buddhis tadā yogam avāpsyasi

Verse 54

arjuna uvāca
sthitaprajñasya kā bhāṣā samādhisthasya keśava
sthitadhīḥ kiṁ prabhāṣeta kim āsīta vrajeta kim

Verse 55

śrībhagavān uvāca
prajahāti yadā kāmān sarvān pārtha manogatān
ātmany evātmanā tuṣṭaḥ sthitaprajñas tadocyate

Verse 56

duḥkheṣv anudvignamanāḥ sukheṣu vigataspṛhaḥ
vītarāgabhayakrodhaḥ sthitadhīr munir ucyate

Verse 57

yaḥ sarvatrānabhisnehas tat-tat prāpya śubhāśubham
nābhinandati na dveṣṭi tasya prajñā pratiṣṭhitā

Verse 58

yadā saṁharate cāyaṁ kūrmo 'ṅgānīva sarvaśaḥ
indriyāṇīndriyārthebhyas tasya prajñā pratiṣṭhitā

Verse 59

viṣayā vinivartante nirāhārasya dehinaḥ
rasavarjaṁ raso 'py asya paraṁ dṛṣṭvā nivartate

Verse 60

yatato hy api kaunteya puruṣasya vipaścitaḥ
indriyāṇi pramāthīni haranti prasabhaṁ manaḥ

Verse 61

tāni sarvāṇi saṁyamya yukta āsīta matparaḥ
vaśe hi yasyendriyāṇi tasya prajñā pratiṣṭhitā

Verses 62–63

dhyāyato viṣayān puṁsaḥ saṅgas teṣūpajāyate
saṅgāt saṁjāyate kāmaḥ kāmāt krodho 'bhijāyate (62)

krodhād bhavati saṁmohaḥ saṁmohāt smṛtivibhramaḥ
smṛtibhraṁśād buddhināśo buddhināśāt praṇaśyati (63)

Verse 64

rāgadveṣaviyuktais tu viṣayān indriyaiś caran
ātmavaśyair vidheyātmā prasādam adhigacchati

Verse 65

prasāde sarvaduḥkhānāṁ hānir asyopajāyate
prasannacetaso hy āśu buddhiḥ paryavatiṣṭhate

Verse 66

nāsti buddhir ayuktasya na cāyuktasya bhāvanā
na cābhāvayataḥ śāntir aśāntasya kutaḥ sukham

Verse 67

indriyāṇāṁ hi caratāṁ yan mano 'nuvidhīyate
tad asya harati prajñāṁ vāyur nāvam ivāmbhasi

Verse 68

tasmād yasya mahābāho nigṛhītāni sarvaśaḥ
indriyāṇīndriyārthebhyas tasya prajñā pratiṣṭhitā

Verse 69

yā niśā sarvabhūtānāṁ tasyāṁ jāgarti saṁyamī
yasyāṁ jāgrati bhūtāni sā niśā paśyato muneḥ

Verse 70

āpūryamāṇam acalapratiṣṭhaṁ samudram āpaḥ praviśanti yadvat
tadvat kāmā yaṁ praviśanti sarve sa śāntim āpnoti na kāmakāmī

Verse 71

vihāya kāmān yaḥ sarvān pumāṁś carati niḥspṛhaḥ
nirmamo nirahaṁkāraḥ sa śāntim adhigacchati

Verse 72

eṣā brāhmī sthitiḥ pārtha naināṁ prāpya vimuhyati
sthitvāsyām antakāle 'pi brahmanirvāṇam ṛcchati

om tat sat iti śrīmadbhagavadgītāsu upaniṣatsu
brahmavidyāyām yogaśāstre śrīkṛṣṇārjunasaṁvāde
sāṁkhyayogonāma dvitīyaḥ adhyāyaḥ

Chapter III

Verse 1

arjuna uvāca
jyāyasī cet karmaṇas te matā buddhir janārdana
tat kiṁ karmaṇi ghore māṁ niyojayasi keśava

Verse 2

vyāmiśreṇeva vākyena buddhiṁ mohayasīva me
tad ekaṁ vada niścitya yena śreyo 'ham āpnuyām

Verse 3

śrībhagavān uvāca
loke 'smin dvividhā niṣṭhā purā proktā mayānagha
jñānayogena sāṁkhyānāṁ karmayogena yoginām

Verse 4

na karmaṇām anārambhān naiṣkarmyaṁ puruṣo 'śnute
na ca saṁnyasanād eva siddhiṁ samadhigacchati

Verse 5

na hi kaścit kṣaṇam api jātu tiṣṭhaty akarmakṛt
kāryate hy avaśaḥ karma sarvaḥ prakṛtijair guṇaiḥ

Verse 6

karmendriyāṇi saṁyamya ya āste manasā smaran
indriyārthān vimūḍhātmā mithyācāraḥ sa ucyate

Verse 7

yas tvindriyāṇi manasā niyamyārabhate 'rjuna
karmendriyaiḥ karmayogam asaktaḥ sa viśiṣyate

Verse 8

niyataṁ kuru karma tvaṁ karma jyāyo hy akarmaṇaḥ
śarīrayātrāpi ca te na prasidhyed akarmaṇaḥ

VERSE 9

yajñārthāt karmaṇo 'nyatra loko 'yam karmabandhanaḥ
tadarthaṁ karma kaunteya muktasaṅgaḥ samācara

VERSE 10

sahayajñāḥ prajāḥ sṛṣṭvā purovāca prajāpatiḥ
anena prasaviṣyadhvam eṣa vo 'stviṣṭakāmadhuk

VERSE 11

devān bhāvayatānena te devā bhāvayantu vaḥ
parasparaṁ bhāvayantaḥ śreyaḥ param avāpsyatha

VERSE 12

iṣṭān bhogān hi vo devā dāsyante yajñabhāvitāḥ
tair dattān apradāyaibhyo yo bhuṅkte stena eva saḥ

VERSE 13

yajñaśiṣṭāśinaḥ santo mucyante sarvakilbiṣaiḥ
bhuñjate te tvaghaṁ pāpā ye pacantyātmakāraṇāt

VERSES 14–15

annād bhavanti bhūtāni parjanyād annasaṁbhavaḥ
yajñād bhavati parjanyo yajñaḥ karmasamudbhavaḥ (14)

karma brahmodbhavaṁ viddhi brahmākṣarasamudbhavam
tasmāt sarvagataṁ brahma nityaṁ yajñe pratiṣṭhitam (15)

VERSE 16

evaṁ pravartitaṁ cakraṁ nānuvartayatīha yaḥ
aghāyurindriyārāmo moghaṁ pārtha sa jīvati

VERSES 17–18

yas tvātmaratir eva syād ātmatṛptaś ca mānavaḥ
ātmanyeva ca saṁtuṣṭas tasya kāryaṁ na vidyate (17)

naiva tasya kṛtenārtho nākṛteneha kaścana
na cāsya sarvabhūteṣu kaścid arthavyapāśrayaḥ (18)

VERSE 19

tasmād asaktaḥ satataṁ kāryaṁ karma samācara
asakto hyācaran karma param āpnoti pūruṣaḥ

VERSE 20

karmaṇaiva hi saṁsiddhim āsthitā janakādayaḥ
lokasaṁgraham evāpi saṁpaśyan kartum arhasi

VERSE 21

yadyad ācarati śreṣṭhas tattad evetaro janaḥ
sa yat pramāṇaṁ kurute lokas tad anuvartate

VERSE 22

na me pārthāsti kartavyaṁ triṣu lokeṣu kiṁcana
nānavāptam avāptavyaṁ varta eva ca karmaṇi

VERSE 23

yadi hyahaṁ na varteyaṁ jātu karmaṇyatandritaḥ
mama vartmānuvartante manuṣyāḥ pārtha sarvaśaḥ

VERSE 24

utsīdeyur ime lokā na kuryāṁ karma ced aham
saṁkarasya ca kartā syām upahanyām imāḥ prajāḥ

VERSES 25–26

saktāḥ karmaṇyavidvāṁso yathā kurvanti bhārata
kuryād vidvāṁs tathāsaktaś cikīrṣur lokasaṁgraham (25)

na buddhibhedaṁ janayed ajñānāṁ karmasaṅginām
joṣayet sarvakarmāṇi vidvān yuktaḥ samācaran (26)

VERSE 27

prakṛteḥ kriyamāṇāni guṇaiḥ karmāṇi sarvaśaḥ
ahaṁkāravimūḍhātmā kartāham iti manyate

Verse 28

tattvavit tu mahābāho guṇakarmavibhāgayoḥ
guṇā guṇeṣu vartanta iti matvā na sajjate

Verse 29

prakṛter guṇasaṁmūḍhāḥ sajjante guṇakarmasu
tān akṛtsnavido mandān kṛtsnavin na vicālayet

Verse 30

mayi sarvāṇi karmāṇi saṁnyasyādhyātmacetasā
nirāśīr nirmamo bhūtvā yudhyasva vigatajvaraḥ

Verse 31

ye me matam idaṁ nityam anutiṣṭhanti mānavāḥ
śraddhāvanto 'nasūyanto mucyante te 'pi karmabhiḥ

Verse 32

ye tvetad abhyasūyanto nānutiṣṭhanti me matam
sarvajñānavimūḍhāṁs tān viddhi naṣṭān acetasaḥ

Verses 33–34

sadṛśaṁ ceṣṭate svasyāḥ prakṛter jñānavān api
prakṛtiṁ yānti bhūtāni nigrahaḥ kiṁ kariṣyati (33)

indriyasyendriyasyārthe rāgadveṣau vyavasthitau
tayor na vaśam āgacchet tau hyasya paripanthinau (34)

Verse 35

śreyān svadharmo viguṇaḥ paradharmāt svanuṣṭhitāt
svadharme nidhanaṁ śreyaḥ paradharmo bhayāvahaḥ

Verse 36

arjuna uvāca
atha kena prayukto 'yaṁ pāpaṁ carati pūruṣaḥ
anicchannapi vārṣṇeya balādiva niyojitaḥ

Verse 37

śrībhagavān uvāca
kāma eṣa krodha eṣa rajoguṇasamudbhavaḥ
mahāśano mahāpāpmā viddhyenam iha vairiṇam

Verse 38

dhūmenāvriyate vahnir yathādarśo malena ca
yatholbenāvṛto garbhas tathā tenedam āvṛtam

Verse 39

āvṛtaṁ jñānam etena jñānino nityavairiṇā
kāmarūpeṇa kaunteya duṣpūreṇānalena ca

Verse 40

indriyāṇi mano buddhir asyādhiṣṭhānam ucyate
etair vimohayatyeṣa jñānam āvṛtya dehinam

Verse 41

tasmāt tvam indriyāṇyādau niyamya bharatarṣabha
pāpmānaṁ prajahi hyenaṁ jñānavijñānanāśanam

Verse 42

indriyāṇi parāṇyāhur indriyebhyaḥ paraṁ manaḥ
manasas tu parā buddhir yo buddheḥ paratas tu saḥ

Verse 43

evaṁ buddheḥ paraṁ buddhvā saṁstabhyātmānam ātmanā
jahi śatruṁ mahābāho kāmarūpaṁ durāsadam

om tat sat iti śrīmadbhagavadgītāsu upaniṣatsu
brahmavidyāyām yogaśāstre śrīkṛṣṇārjunasaṁvāde
karmayogonāma tṛtīyaḥ adhyāyaḥ

Chapter IV

Verses 1–2

śrībhagavān uvāca
imaṁ vivasvate yogaṁ proktavān aham avyayam
vivasvān manave prāha manur ikṣvākave 'bravīt (1)

evaṁ paramparāprāptam imaṁ rājarṣayo viduḥ
sa kāleneha mahatā yogo naṣṭaḥ paraṁtapa (2)

Verse 3

sa evāyaṁ mayā te 'dya yogaḥ proktaḥ purātanaḥ
bhakto 'si me sakhā ceti rahasyaṁ hyetad uttamam

Verse 4

arjuna uvāca
aparaṁ bhavato janma paraṁ janma vivasvataḥ
katham etad vijānīyāṁ tvam ādau proktavān iti

Verse 5

śrībhagavān uvāca
bahūni me vyatītāni janmāni tava cārjuna
tānyahaṁ veda sarvāṇi na tvaṁ vettha paraṁtapa

Verse 6

ajo 'pi sannavyayātmā bhūtānām īśvaro 'pi san
prakṛtiṁ svām adhiṣṭhāya saṁbhavāmyātmamāyayā

Verses 7–8

yadāyadā hi dharmasya glānir bhavati bhārata
abhyutthānam adharmasya tadātmānaṁ sṛjāmyaham (7)

paritrāṇāya sādhūnāṁ vināśāya ca duṣkṛtām
dharmasaṁsthāpanārthāya saṁbhavāmi yuge yuge (8)

Verse 9

janma karma ca me divyam evaṁ yo vetti tattvataḥ
tyaktvā dehaṁ punarjanma naiti mām eti so 'rjuna

Verse 10

vītarāgabhayakrodhā manmayā mām upāśritāḥ
bahavo jñānatapasā pūtā madbhāvam āgatāḥ

Verse 11

ye yathā māṁ prapadyante tāṁs tathaiva bhajāmyaham
mama vartmānuvartante manuṣyāḥ pārtha sarvaśaḥ

Verse 12

kāṅkṣantaḥ karmaṇāṁ siddhiṁ yajanta iha devatāḥ
kṣipraṁ hi mānuṣe loke siddhir bhavati karmajā

Verse 13

cāturvarṇyaṁ mayā sṛṣṭaṁ guṇakarmavibhāgaśaḥ
tasya kartāram api māṁ viddhyakartāram avyayam

Verse 14

na māṁ karmāṇi limpanti na me karmaphale spṛhā
iti māṁ yo 'bhijānāti karmabhir na sa badhyate

Verse 15

evaṁ jñātvā kṛtaṁ karma pūrvair api mumukṣubhiḥ
kuru karmaiva tasmāt tvaṁ pūrvaiḥ purvataraṁ kṛtam

Verse 16

kiṁ karma kim akarmeti kavayo 'py atra mohitāḥ
tat te karma pravakṣyāmi yaj jñātvā mokṣyase 'śubhāt

Verse 17

karmaṇo hyapi boddhavyaṁ boddhavyaṁ ca vikarmaṇaḥ
akarmaṇaśca boddhavyaṁ gahanā karmaṇo gatiḥ

Verse 18

karmaṇyakarma yaḥ paśyed akarmaṇi ca karma yaḥ
sa buddhimān manuṣyeṣu sa yuktaḥ kṛtsnakarmakṛt

Verse 19

yasya sarve samārambhāḥ kāmasaṁkalpavarjitāḥ
jñānāgnidagdhakarmāṇaṁ tam āhuḥ paṇḍitaṁ budhāḥ

Verse 20

tyaktvā karmaphalāsaṅgaṁ nityatṛpto nirāśrayaḥ
karmaṇy abhipravṛtto 'pi naiva kiṁcit karoti saḥ

Verse 21

nirāśīr yatacittātmā tyaktasarvaparigrahaḥ
śārīraṁ kevalaṁ karma kurvan nāpnoti kilbiṣam

Verse 22

yadṛcchālābhasaṁtuṣṭo dvandvātīto vimatsaraḥ
samaḥ siddhāv asiddhau ca kṛtvāpi na nibadhyate

Verse 23

gatasaṅgasya muktasya jñānāvasthitacetasaḥ
yajñāyācarataḥ karma samagraṁ pravilīyate

Verse 24

brahmārpaṇaṁ brahma havir brahmāgnau brahmaṇā hutam
brahmaiva tena gantavyaṁ brahmakarmasamādhinā

Verse 25

daivam evāpare yajñaṁ yoginaḥ paryupāsate
brahmāgnāv apare yajñaṁ yajñenaivopajuhvati

Verse 26

śrotrādīnīndriyāṇy anye saṁyamāgniśu juhvati
śabdādīn viśayān anya indriyāgniṣu juhvati

VERSE 27

sarvāṇīndriyakarmāṇi prāṇakarmāṇi cāpare
ātmasaṁyamayogāgnau juhvati jñānadīpite

VERSE 28

dravyayajñās tapoyajñā yogayajñās tathāpare
svādhyāyajñānayajñāśca yatayaḥ saṁśitavratāḥ

VERSE 29

apāne juhvati prāṇaṁ prāṇe 'pānaṁ tathāpare
prāṇāpānagatī ruddhvā prāṇāyāmaparāyaṇāḥ

VERSE 30

apare niyatāhārāḥ prāṇān prāṇeṣu juhvati
sarve 'pyete yajñavido yajñakṣapitakalmaṣāḥ

VERSE 31

yajñaśiṣṭāmṛtabhujo yānti brahma sanātanam
nāyaṁ loko 'sty ayajñasya kuto 'nyaḥ kurusattama

VERSE 32

evaṁ bahuvidhā yajñā vitatā brahmaṇo mukhe
karmajān viddhi tān sarvān evaṁ jñātvā vimokṣyase

VERSE 33

śreyān dravyamayād yajñāj jñānayajñaḥ paraṁtapa
sarvaṁ karmākhilaṁ pārtha jñāne parisamāpyate

VERSE 34

tad viddhi praṇipātena paripraśnena sevayā
upadekṣyanti te jñānaṁ jñāninas tattvadarśinaḥ

VERSE 35

yaj jñātvā na punar moham evaṁ yāsyasi pāṇḍava
yena bhūtāny aśeṣeṇa drakṣyasy ātmany atho mayi

Verse 36

api ced asi pāpebhyaḥ sarvebhyaḥ pāpakṛttamaḥ
sarvaṁ jñānaplavenaiva vṛjinaṁ saṁtariṣyasi

Verse 37

yathaidhāṁsi samiddho 'gnir bhasmasāt kurute 'rjuna
jñānāgniḥ sarvakarmāṇi bhasmasāt kurute tathā

Verse 38

na hi jñānena sadṛśaṁ pavitram iha vidyate
tat svayaṁ yogasaṁsiddhaḥ kālenātmani vindati

Verse 39

śraddhāvāṁl labhate jñānaṁ tatparaḥ saṁyatendriyaḥ
jñānaṁ labdhvā parāṁ śāntim acireṇādhigacchati

Verse 40

ajñaścāśraddadhānaśca saṁśayātmā vinaśyati
nāyaṁ loko 'sti na paro na sukhaṁ saṁśayātmanaḥ

Verse 41

yogasaṁnyastakarmāṇaṁ jñānasaṁchinnasaṁśayam
ātmavantaṁ na karmāṇi nibadhnanti dhanaṁjaya

Verse 42

tasmād ajñānasaṁbhūtaṁ hṛtsthaṁ jñānāsinātmanaḥ
chittvainaṁ saṁśayaṁ yogam ātiṣṭhottiṣṭha bhārata

oṁ tat sat iti śrīmadbhagavadgītāsu upaniṣatsu
brahmavidyāyām yogaśāstre śrīkṛṣṇārjunasaṁvāde
jñānayogonāma caturtho 'dhyāyaḥ

Chapter V

Verse 1

arjuna uvāca
saṁnyāsaṁ karmaṇāṁ kṛṣṇa punar yogaṁ ca śaṁsasi
yacchreya etayor ekaṁ tan me brūhi suniścitam

Verse 2

śrībhagavān uvāca
saṁnyāsaḥ karmayogaśca niḥśreyasakarāv ubhau
tayos tu karmasaṁnyāsāt karmayogo viśiṣyate

Verse 3

jñeyaḥ sa nityasaṁnyāsī yo na dveṣṭi na kāṅkṣati
nirdvandvo hi mahābāho sukhaṁ bandhāt pramucyate

Verses 4–5

śāṁkhyayogau pṛthagbālāḥ pravadanti na paṇḍitāḥ
ekam apy āsthitaḥ samyag ubhayor vindate phalaṁ (4)

yat sāṁkhyaiḥ prāpyate sthānaṁ tad yogair api gamyate
ekaṁ sāṁkhyaṁ ca yogaṁ ca yaḥ paśyati sa paśyati (5)

Verses 6–7

saṁnyāsas tu mahābāho duḥkham āptum ayogataḥ
yogayukto munir brahma nacireṇādhigacchati (6)

yogayukto viśuddhātmā vijitātmā jitendriyaḥ
sarvabhūtātmabhūtātmā kurvann api na lipyate (7)

Verses 8–9

naiva kiṁcit karomīti yukto manyeta tattvavit
paśyañ śṛṇvan spṛśañ jighrann aśnan gacchan svapañ śvasan (8)

pralapan visṛjan gṛhṇann unmiṣan nimiṣann api
indriyāṇīndriyārtheṣu vartanta iti dhārayan (9)

Verse 10

brahmaṇy ādhāya karmāṇi saṅgaṁ tyaktvā karoti yaḥ
lipyate na sa pāpena padmapatram ivāmbhasā

Verse 11

kāyena manasā buddhyā kevalair indriyair api
yoginaḥ karma kurvanti saṅgaṁ tyaktvātmaśuddhaye

Verse 12

yuktaḥ karmaphalaṁ tyaktvā śāntim āpnoti naiṣṭhikīm
ayuktaḥ kāmakāreṇa phale sakto nibadhyate

Verse 13

sarvakarmāṇi manasā saṁnyasyāste sukhaṁ vaśī
navadvāre pure dehī naiva kurvan na kārayan

Verse 14

na kartṛtvaṁ na karmāṇi lokasya sṛjati prabhuḥ
na karmaphalasaṁyogaṁ svabhāvas tu pravartate

Verse 15

nādatte kasyacit pāpaṁ na caiva sukṛtaṁ vibhuḥ
ajñānenāvṛtaṁ jñānaṁ tena muhyanti jantavaḥ

Verse 16

jñānena tu tad ajñānaṁ yeṣāṁ nāśitam ātmanaḥ
teṣām ādityavaj jñānaṁ prakāśayati tat param

Verse 17

tadbuddhayas tadātmānas tanniṣṭhās tatparāyaṇāḥ
gacchantyapunarāvṛttiṁ jñānanirdhūtakalmaṣāḥ

Verse 18

vidyāvinayasaṁpanne brāhmaṇe gavi hastini
śuni caiva śvapāke ca paṇḍitāḥ samadarśinaḥ

Verse 19

ihaiva tair jitaḥ sargo yeṣāṁ sāmye sthitaṁ manaḥ
nirdoṣaṁ hi samaṁ brahma tasmād brahmaṇi te sthitāḥ

Verse 20

na prahṛṣyet priyaṁ prāpya nodvijet prāpya cāpriyam
sthirabuddhir asaṁmūḍho brahmavid brahmaṇi sthitaḥ

Verse 21

bāhyasparśeṣvasaktātmā vindatyātmani yat sukham
sa brahmayogayuktātmā sukham akṣayam aśnute

Verse 22

ye hi saṁsparśajā bhogā duḥkhayonaya eva te
ādyantavantaḥ kaunteya na teṣu ramate budhaḥ

Verse 23

śaknotīhaiva yaḥ soḍhuṁ prāk śarīravimokṣaṇāt
kāmakrodhodbhavaṁ vegaṁ sa yuktaḥ sa sukhī naraḥ

Verse 24

yo 'ntaḥsukho 'ntarārāmas tathāntarjyotir eva yaḥ
sa yogī brahmanirvāṇaṁ brahmabhūto 'dhigacchati

Verse 25

labhante brahmanirvāṇaṁ ṛṣayaḥ kṣīṇakalmaṣāḥ
chinnadvaidhā yatātmānaḥ sarvabhūtahite ratāḥ

Verse 26

kāmakrodhaviyuktānāṁ yatīnāṁ yatacetasām
abhito brahmanirvāṇaṁ vartate viditātmanām

Verses 27–28

sparśān kṛtvā bahir bāhyāṁś cakṣuś caivāntare bhruvoḥ
prāṇāpānau samau kṛtvā nāsābhyantaracāriṇau (27)

yatendriyamanobuddhir munir mokṣaparāyaṇaḥ
vigatecchābhayakrodho yaḥ sadā mukta eva saḥ (28)

Verse 29

bhoktāraṁ yajñatapasāṁ sarvalokamaheśvaram
suhṛdaṁ sarvabhūtānāṁ jñātvā māṁ śāntim ṛcchati

om tat sat iti śrīmadbhagavadgītāsu upaniṣatsu
brahmavidyāyām yogaśāstre śrīkṛṣṇārjunasaṁvāde
karmasaṁnyāsayogo nāma pañcamo 'dhyāyaḥ

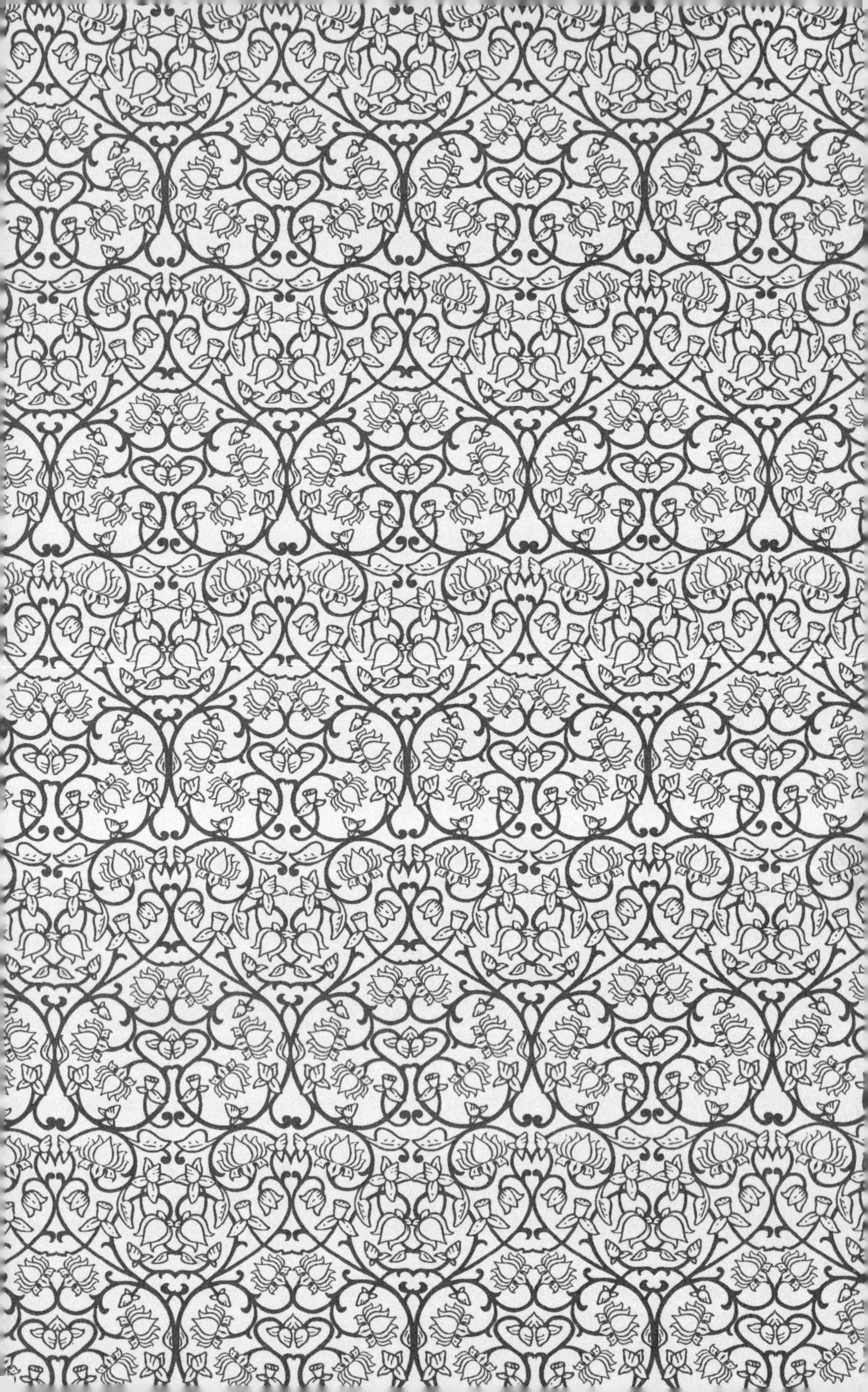